THE NEW INTERNATIONAL COMMENTARY
ON THE NEW TESTAMENT

GORDON D. FEE
General Editor

The Epistle to the

HEBREWS

Revised Edition

F. F. BRUCE

WILLIAM B. EERDMANS PUBLISHING COMPANY
GRAND RAPIDS, MICHIGAN / CAMBRIDGE, U.K.

Published 1990 by
Wm. B. Eerdmans Publishing Company
2140 Oak Industrial Drive N.E., Grand Rapids, Michigan 49505 /
P.O. Box 163 Cambridge CB3 9PU U.K.

12 11 10 09 08 07   18 17 16 15 14 13 12

Library of Congress Cataloging-in-Publication Data

Bruce, F. F. (Frederick Fyvie), 1910-
The Epistle to the Hebrews / by F. F. Bruce.—Rev. ed.
p.   cm.   —
(The New international commentary on the New Testament)
ISBN 978-0-8028-2514-8
1. Bible. N.T. Hebrews—Commentaries.   I. Title.   II. Series.
BS2775.3.B7   1990
227′.8707—dc20   90-32826
                                                  CIP

www.eerdmans.com

To the Memory
of
NED BERNARD STONEHOUSE

CONTENTS

PREFACE TO THE FIRST EDITION

On June 25, 1954, I received an invitation from Dr. N. B. Stonehouse, our first General Editor, to undertake the volume on the Epistle to the Hebrews for the New International Commentary on the New Testament. Since then I have spent a good part of my time with this epistle, and have learned to appreciate increasingly the viewpoint and purpose of its unknown author—still as much unknown by name to me as when I embarked on the serious study of his work, but not, I think, completely unknown in other respects.

For many readers the Epistle to the Hebrews is among the more difficult books of the New Testament. Its magnificent style, to which King James's revisers (following in William Tyndale's footsteps) did full justice, can be more easily appreciated than the details of its argument, which call for a greater familiarity with its Old Testament background and a better understanding of certain phases of first-century biblical exegesis than most readers possess. Sir Edmund Gosse in *Father and Son* tells of the difficulty which he found in his boyhood in following his father's reading and exposition of the epistle. "The melodious language, the divine forensic audacities, the magnificent ebb and flow of argument which make the 'Epistle to the Hebrews' such a miracle, were far and away beyond my reach, and they only bewildered me."

To many people, it is said, the Epistle to the Hebrews is just "the book about Melchizedek"—although Melchizedek occupies only some twenty out of the epistle's more than three hundred verses. Others find themselves out of their depth when they come across references to "the blood of bulls and of goats and the ashes of a heifer sprinkling the unclean," and wonder what all this has to do with true religion. The writer to the Hebrews, in fact, is concerned to argue that all this has nothing to do with true religion; but he is dealing with people who had been brought up to think that it had much to do with it. But what has his argument to say to readers today who are not at all disposed to think that animal sacrifices play any part in the worship of God? It has this to say: that true religion or the worship of God is not tied to externalities of any kind. Our author is insisting on the inwardness of true religion, on the necessity of a purified conscience as the one indispensable condition for offering God acceptable worship in that true sanctuary which no human hands have built.

Moreover, this is the book which establishes the finality of the gospel by asserting the supremacy of Christ—his supremacy as God's perfect word to man and man's perfect representative with God. More than any other New Testament book it deals with the ministry which our Lord is accomplishing on his people's behalf now. In a day of shaking foundations it speaks of the kingdom which cannot be shaken. It reminds Christians that it is no part of their calling to settle down and be content with things as they are, but to press forward continually in God's advancing purpose, along the trail already blazed by the Pioneer of Faith. And when they are tempted to be discouraged and give up the onward march, it revives their drooping spirits and supplies many incentives to press on to that eternal commonwealth which is the true homeland of loyal souls. A book which does all this, no matter what imagery it uses, is a book which speaks to the condition of the church throughout the world in the second half of the twentieth century.

My debt to others in the following pages is enormous, and can be acknowledged only very inadequately. Among previous expositors Calvin and Westcott, James Moffatt and Geerhardus Vos have been of great help. C. Spicq's encyclopaedic commentary has always been within arm's reach. For drawing out and applying to the conscience the practical lessons of the epistle G. H. Lang has few rivals. And I am not the only writer on the epistle in recent years for whom William Manson has provided it with a more convincing life-setting than anyone else has done. But this list is not exhaustive. Others who have helped me clamor for admittance: A. B. Davidson, E. Riggenbach, and H. Windisch—but the author's preface is not the place for a bibliography.

I must add a word of thanks to the Very Reverend D. E. W. Harrison, Dean of Bristol. In the winter of 1955-56, when he was Archdeacon of Sheffield and I lived in the same city, he and I jointly conducted a study class on the Epistle to the Hebrews for the Extramural Department of Sheffield University. My understanding of the epistle was very considerably deepened as a result of this happy collaboration with him.

To Dr. Stonehouse my debt of gratitude is great indeed, for the invitation to write this commentary and for many other tokens of friendship and fellowship. In acknowledgment, but by no means in repayment, of this debt the finished work is dedicated to his memory.

August 1963   F. F. B.

PREFACE TO THE REVISED EDITION

The policy of keeping the commentaries in this series up to date has dictated the revision, after a quarter of a century, of this volume on Hebrews.

In these twenty-five years my general understanding of this epistle has not changed in any material respect, but I have profited from my own further study of it and still more from the publications of a number of colleagues which have appeared since the first edition was issued. If one of these colleagues may be singled out for special mention, I have been greatly indebted to the work of Père Albert Vanhoye, S.J., of the Pontifical Biblical Institute. To his name I must add those of four former research students of mine from whom I have learned more about Hebrews than they ever learned from me— Bruce A. Demarest, Pauline Giles, David G. Peterson, and Norman H. Young. A teacher can have no greater satisfaction than to greet the output of students such as these.

As for all the original volumes of the New International Commentary on the New Testament, the American Standard Version of 1901 served as the basic text for the first edition of this. It has now been replaced by an *ad hoc* translation of my own.

January 1990   F. F. BRUCE

ABBREVIATIONS

AB	Anchor Bible
ad loc.	*ad locum* (at the place mentioned)
AJT	*American Journal of Theology*
ALGHJ	Arbeiten zur Literatur und Geschichte des hellenistischen Judentums (Leiden)
AnBib	Analecta Biblica (Rome)
ANRW	*Aufstieg und Niedergang der römischen Welt* (Berlin/New York)
Ant.	*Antiquities* (Josephus)
ARV	American Revised Version (American Standard Version), 1901
ATD	Das Alte Testament Deutsch (Göttingen)
AV	Authorized Version, 1611 (see KJV)
BA	*The Biblical Archaeologist*
BAGD	W. Bauer–W. F. Arndt–F. W. Gingrich–F. W. Danker, *Greek-English Lexicon of the New Testament and Early Christian Literature* (Chicago, 1957, ²1979)
BASOR	*Bulletin of the American Schools of Oriental Research*
BBB	Bonner Biblische Beiträge
BDF	F. Blass–A. Debrunner–R. W. Funk, *Greek Grammar of the New Testament and Other Early Christian Literature* (Chicago, 1961)
BGBE	Beiträge zur Geschichte der biblischen Exegese (Tübingen)
BJRL	*Bulletin of the John Rylands (University) Library* (Manchester)
BNTC	Black's New Testament Commentaries (= HNTC)
BU	Biblische Untersuchungen
BZAW	Beihefte zur Zeitschrift für die alttestamentliche Wissenschaft
BZNW	Beihefte zur Zeitschrift für die neutestamentliche Wissenschaft
CBQ	*Catholic Biblical Quarterly*
CBQM	Catholic Biblical Quarterly Monographs
CBSC	Cambridge Bible for Schools and Colleges
CD	Book of the Covenant of Damascus
CentB	Century Bible
CGT	Cambridge Greek Testament
CIA	*Corpus Inscriptionum Atticarum*
CIG	*Corpus Inscriptionum Graecarum*
1 Clem.	Epistle of Clement of Rome to the Corinthians
Clem. Hom.	*Clementine Homilies*

Clem. Recog.	*Clementine Recognitions*
CMRDM	*Corpus Monumentorum Religionis Dei Menis,* I-IV (Leiden, 1971-78)
DBSup	*Dictionnaire de la Bible: Supplément*
DJD	*Discoveries in the Judaean Desert,* I- (Oxford, 1955-)
DOTT	*Documents from Old Testament Times,* ed. D. W. Thomas (London/New York, 1958)
ÉB	Études Bibliques
ed.	edited by
EGT	*Expositor's Greek Testament*
Ep(p).	*Epistle(s)*
Ep. Barn.	*Epistle of Barnabas*
EQ	*Evangelical Quarterly*
ERV	English (British) Revised Version, 1881-85
E.T.	English translation
EV(V)	English version(s)
EvTh.	*Evangelische Theologie*
Exp.	*Expositor*
ExpB.	Expositor's Bible
ExT	*Expository Times*
FRLANT	Forschungen zur Religion und Literatur des Alten und Neuen Testaments (Göttingen)
FS	*Festschrift*
Gk.	Greek
GNBC	Good News Bible Commentary
GNT³	*Greek New Testament of United Bible Societies* (London/New York, ³1975)
HAT	Handbuch zum Alten Testament (Tübingen)
HCNT	*Handcommentar zum Neuen Testament,* ed. H. J. Holtzmann (Freiburg im Breisgau)
HDB	*Dictionary of the Bible,* ed. J. Hastings (Edinburgh)
HE/Hist. Eccl.	*Ecclesiastical History* (Eusebius, Socrates)
HNT	Handbuch zum Neuen Testament (Tübingen)
HNTC	Harper's New Testament Commentaries (= BNTC)
HTR	*Harvard Theological Review*
HUCA	*Hebrew Union College Annual*
IB	*Interpreter's Bible,* I-XII (New York/Nashville, 1952-57)
ibid.	*ibidem,* "in the same place (as that just mentioned)"
ICC	International Critical Commentary (Edinburgh)
IEJ	*Israel Exploration Journal*
IG	*Inscriptiones Graecae,* 1873-
INT	*Introduction to the New Testament*
JBL	*Journal of Biblical Literature*
JE	*Jewish Encyclopaedia* (New York)
JJS	*Journal of Jewish Studies*

JNES	*Journal of Near Eastern Studies*
JRS	*Journal of Roman Studies*
JSJ	*Journal for the Study of Judaism*
JSNT	*Journal for the Study of the New Testament*
JSS	*Journal of Semitic Studies*
JTC	*Journal for Theology and the Church*
JTS	*Journal of Theological Studies*
Jub.	Book of Jubilees
KHC	Kurzer Handcommentar zum Alten Testament (Tübingen)
Komm.	Kommentar
LBC	Layman's Bible Commentary
LD	Lectio Divina
Leg. Alleg.	*On the Allegorical Interpretation of the Laws* (Philo)
LSJ	*Greek-English Lexicon,* by H. G. Liddell and R. Scott, 9th edition revised by H. S. Jones (Oxford, 1940)
L.T.	Latin translation
LXX	Septuagint (Greek Old Testament)
mg.	margin
MHT	*Grammar of New Testament Greek,* by J. H. Moulton, W. F. Howard, and N. Turner, I-IV (Edinburgh, 1906-76)
MK	Meyer-Kommentar (Kritisch-exegetischer Kommentar über das Neue Testament, begrundet von H. A. W. Meyer)
MM	*The Vocabulary of the Greek Testament,* by J. H. Moulton and G. Milligan (London, 1930)
MNTC	Moffatt New Testament Commentary (London)
Mor.	*Moralia* (Plutarch)
MS(S)	manuscript(s)
MT	Masoretic text (of the Hebrew Bible)
NA[26]	E. and E. Nestle, K. Aland, etc., *Novum Testamentum Graece,* 26. neu bearbeitete Auflage (Stuttgart, 1979)
NBD[2]	*New Bible Dictionary,* ed. J. D. Douglas, N. Hillyer, etc., 2nd edition (Leicester, 1982)
NCBC	New Century Bible Commentary
NEB	New English Bible (1970)
New Docs.	*New Documents illustrating Early Christianity,* ed. G. H. R. Horsley, I- (Macquarie University, 1981-)
NF	Neue Folge
NICNT	New International Commentary on the New Testament (Grand Rapids)
NIDNTT	*New International Dictionary of New Testament Theology* (Exeter, 1975-78)
NIGTC	New International Greek Testament Commentary (Grand Rapids/ Exeter)
NIV	New International Version (Grand Rapids/London, 1978/84)
NovT	*Novum Testamentum*

NovTSup	Supplements to *Novum Testamentum*
n.s.	new series
NT	New Testament
NTC	New Testament Commentary, by W. Hendriksen and S. Kistemaker (Grand Rapids)
NTD	Das Neue Testament Deutsch (Göttingen)
NTS	*New Testament Studies*
OGIS	*Orientis Graeci Inscriptiones Selectae,* ed. W. Dittenberger
OT	Old Testament
OTL	Old Testament Library
OTS	*Oudtestamentische Studien* (Leiden)
p	*Papyrus (Papyri)*
P. Berl.	*Berlin Papyrus (Papyri)*
PEQ	*Palestine Exploration Quarterly*
P. Lond.	*London Papyrus (Papyri)*
P. Oxy.	*Oxyrhynchus Papyri*
Preliminary Studies	Philo's *On Mating with the Preliminary Studies (De Congressu Quaerendae Eruditionis Gratia)*
Ps. Sol.	Psalms of Solomon
PTR	*Princeton Theological Review*
Q	Qumran
1Q	(Manuscript from) Qumran Cave 1
1QH	*Hodayot* (Hymns of Thanksgiving) from Qumran Cave 1
1QM	*Milḥamah* (War Scroll) from Qumran Cave 1
1QpHab	*Pesher* (commentary) on Habakkuk from Qumran Cave 1
1QS	*Serekh* (Community Rule) from Qumran Cave 1
1QSa	*Serekh hāʿēdāh* (Rule of the Congregation) from Qumran Cave 1
4QDt^q	Fragment of Deuteronomy from Qumran Cave 4
4QpPs. 37	*Pesher* (commentary) on Ps. 37 from Qumran Cave 4
4Q*Florilegium*	Anthology of biblical texts from Qumran Cave 4
4Q*Testimonia*	Collection of "proof-texts" from Qumran Cave 4
RB	*Revue Biblique*
RBén	*Revue Bénédictine*
RÉJ	*Revue des Études juives*
RHPR	*Revue d'Histoire et de Philosophie Religieuses*
RNT	Regensburger Neues Testament
RQ	*Revue de Qumran*
RSR	*Revue des sciences religieuses* (Strasbourg)
RSV	Revised Standard Version (1952, ^{2}1971)
RTR	*Reformed Theological Review* (Australia)
SBLDS	Society for Biblical Literature Dissertation Series
SBLMS	Society for Biblical Literature Monograph Series
SBT	Studies in Biblical Theology
SE	*Studia Evangelica*
SJT	*Scottish Journal of Theology*

SN	Studia Neotestamentica
SNT	Studien zum Neuen Testament
SNTSM	Society of New Testament Studies Monograph(s)
SR	*Studies in Religion/Sciences religieuses*
s.v(v).	*sub vocabulo (-is)*, "under the word(s)"
TB	Babylonian Talmud
TC	Torch Commentaries
TDNT	*Theological Dictionary of the New Testament*, I-X, ed. G. Kittel and G. Friedrich (1933-76), E.T. by G. W. Bromiley (Grand Rapids, 1964-76)
TEH	Theologische Existenz Heute
Test.	*Testament* (e.g., *Test. Dan = Testament of Dan*)
TJ	Jerusalem (Palestinian) Talmud
TNTC	Tyndale New Testament Commentaries
TR	Received Text
TRE	*Theologische Realenzyklopädie*
TRu	*Theologische Rundschau*
TU	*Texte und Untersuchungen* (Berlin)
TynB	*Tyndale Bulletin*
TZ	*Theologische Zeitschrift*
Vg.	Vulgate (Latin Bible)
VH	*Vera Historia*, *"True History"* (Lucian)
VT	*Vetus Testamentum*
WA	Weimarer Ausgabe (Weimar edition of Luther's Works)
WC	Westminster Commentaries
WMANT	Wissenschaftliche Monographien zum Alten und Neuen Testament
WTJ	*Westminster Theological Journal* (Philadelphia)
WUNT	Wissenschaftliche Untersuchungen zum Neuen Testament (Tübingen)
ZAW	*Zeitschrift für die alttestamentliche Wissenschaft*
ZK	Zahn-Kommentar zum Neuen Testament
ZMR	*Zeitschrift für Missionskunde und Religionswissenschaft*
ZNW	*Zeitschrift für die neutestamentliche Wissenschaft*
ZTK	*Zeitschrift für Theologie und Kirche*

ARGUMENT OF THE EPISTLE TO THE HEBREWS

I

Heb. 1:1–2:18

God spoke in various ways to our fathers through the prophets, but now he has spoken his final word to us in his Son, his perfect representative. The Son of God is his agent not only in creation and revelation, but also—and preeminently—in the salvation of the human race. He is greater than any prophet; he is greater even than the angels, as the ancient scriptures abundantly testify. It was through angels that Moses' law was communicated, and its sanctions were severe enough; how much more perilous must it be to ignore the saving message brought by no angel, but by Jesus, the Son of God!

Jesus, the Son of God, is the one to whom the dominion of the world has been committed for all time to come. As the eighth psalm teaches us, God has put everything under the dominion of human beings, and it was the nature of humans—*our* nature—that the Son of God took upon himself in order to win back this dominion. To do this he had to conquer the devil who had usurped it, and rescue those whom he held in bondage; and he conquered the devil when in death he invaded the realm of death, which the devil had controlled until then. It is because Jesus is truly Man, moreover, that he is qualified to serve as high priest on his people's behalf; he knows all their trials from his own experiences and therefore can give them the timely help they need.

II

Heb. 3:1–4:14

But let us beware: those who rebelled against God in the days of the wilderness wanderings were excluded from his rest in the promised land. There is, however, a better rest than that which the Israelites found in Canaan; it is the rest which awaits the people of God. We must take care not to forfeit that rest by rebelling against God, when he speaks to us no longer through his servant Moses, as he did in those days, but through his Son, one greater than Moses.

III

Heb. 4:15–6:20

As has already been said, Jesus is our great high priest, able to sympathize with his people and help them. We may safely look for understanding and delivering grace to the one who endured the agony of Gethsemane. He has been called to his high-priestly office by God himself, as an inspired oracle makes clear: "The Lord has sworn and will not change his mind, 'You are a priest for ever, after the order of Melchizedek.'"

(I should like to enlarge on this subject, but really I do not know if I can; you are so spiritually immature. I must warn you solemnly that those who have once been baptized and tasted the blessings of the new age can never repeat the experience of repentance and conversion if they commit apostasy. Not that I think you actually mean to be apostates; I have better hopes of you than that. I want you rather to press on from the point you have reached, so as to attain full maturity, instead of sticking there, or slipping back.)

IV

Heb. 7:1-28

Jesus, then, is by divine appointment a high priest of Melchizedek's order. You remember the story of Melchizedek, priest of God Most High. He appears suddenly in the sacred record, without antecedents, and nothing is said of his subsequent career. Yet he was a very great man; our father Abraham paid him tithes and received his blessing. You might even say that Levi, ancestor of the priestly families of Israel, paid Melchizedek tithes in the person of his great-grandfather Abraham. This implies that Melchizedek is greater than Levi, and Melchizedek's priesthood better than Aaron's. And indeed that is obvious, for if perfect access to God had been attainable under the Aaronic priesthood, why should God have acclaimed the Messiah as priest of a different order?

In many ways Jesus' priesthood after Melchizedek's order is superior to Aaron's priesthood. Jesus, unlike Aaron and his successors, was confirmed in office by the oath of God. Jesus is immortal, whereas the priests of Aaron's line die one by one. Jesus is sinless, whereas the priests of Aaron's line have to present a sin offering for their own cleansing before they can present one for the people. *Their* sacrificial service must constantly be repeated because it is never truly effective; Jesus, by the single sacrifice of himself, put away his people's sin forever.

V

Heb. 8:1–10:18

The Aaronic priests minister under the old covenant instituted at Mount Sinai; Jesus is the Mediator of the new covenant—the covenant whose inauguration Jeremiah foretold. The introduction of a new covenant means that the former one is obsolete. The old covenant made provision for the removal of external pollution by means of animal sacrifices and similar rites, but these things could never remove *sin;* under the new covenant Jesus, by yielding up his life to God as an acceptable and efficacious sacrifice, cleanses the *conscience* from guilt and thus abolishes the barrier between his people and God. The Aaronic priests minister in an earthly sanctuary belonging to the old order, where access to the divine presence is barred by a curtain; Jesus exercises his high priesthood in the heavenly sanctuary, where there is no such barrier between the worshipers and God. And this heavenly sanctuary in which direct access to God is accorded through Jesus is that spiritual and eternal order of which the earthly sanctuary is only a temporary and inadequate copy. For the new order into which Christ brings his people is to the old Levitical order as substance to shadow.

IV

Heb. 10:19–12:29

Let us, then, abandon the old, obsolescent order and approach God along this new and living way which Jesus by his death has opened up for us. Let us maintain steadfast hope and faith in him. Thus we shall have a firm assurance of those eternal realities which are invisible to the outward eye; we shall be able to look forward with eager expectation to the sure advent of the Coming One. It was by such forward-looking faith that the saints of earlier days won the approval of God; they lived in the good of those promises whose fulfilment has come in our day. Let us follow their example; better still, let us follow the example of Jesus. He ran the race of faith from first to last, undeterred by the disgrace of the cross, and is now enthroned at God's right hand.

Let us not grow faint-hearted because of our trials: these trials are the proof that we are indeed the trueborn sons of God. And think of the glory which is our heritage in this age of fulfilment—something far surpassing what men and women of faith experienced in days gone by. How could we ever think of going back to the old ways?

VII

Heb. 13:1-25

So maintain your Christian confession in patience and hope; live as Christians should; and may God, who raised Jesus from the dead, help you to do his will in all things.[1]

---

1. The epistle is a carefully constructed literary work, revealing a concentric symmetry and an elaborate *inclusio*. Its structure has been studied most thoroughly by A. Vanhoye, *La structure littéraire de l'Épître aux Hébreux* (Paris/Bruges, 1976); he includes a critical discussion of earlier analyses. For criticisms of Vanhoye see J. Bligh, "The Structure of Hebrews," *Heythrop Journal* 5 (1964), pp. 170-77 (cf. his *Chiastic Structure of the Epistle to the Hebrews* [Oxford, 1968]), and J. Swetnam, "Form and Content in Hebrews 1–6," *Biblica* 53 (1972), pp. 368-85; "Form and Content in Hebrews 7–13," *Biblica* 55 (1974), pp. 333-48, with Vanhoye's reply, "Discussions sur la structure de l'Épître aux Hébreux," *Biblica* 55 (1974), pp. 349-80. See also B. Lindars, "The Rhetorical Structure of Hebrews," *NTS* 35 (1989), pp. 382-406.

The Epistle
to the
HEBREWS

INTRODUCTION

The Epistle to the Hebrews differs from most of the New Testament epistles in that, while it ends like a letter, it does not begin like one; it lacks the customary opening salutation containing the names of the writer and of the people addressed.[1] Yet, not only in the personal notes at the end[2] but throughout its length, it is clearly addressed to a particular community in which the writer takes a lively interest. Since, however, neither that community nor the writer is expressly identified in the text as it has been preserved to us, the document presents us at the outset with a number of critical problems to which no agreed solution has been found.

I. THE PEOPLE ADDRESSED

The document was known and quoted before the end of the first century,[3] but not under its traditional title "To (the) Hebrews." This title goes back to the last quarter of the second century,[4] if not earlier, and from that time on it is the regular designation for the work in New Testament manuscripts and Christian writers. How it originated is not known; it may very well be that when, in the course of the second century, the work was included in the Pau-

---

1. The one other exceptional document in this respect among the NT epistles is 1 John, which neither begins nor ends like a letter, but is from first to last, like the greater part of Hebrews, a "word of exhortation" (cf. pp. 25, 389).

2. Cf. 13:1 (pp. 367f. with nn. 2-4); 13:22ff. (pp. 390f. with nn. 126-28).

3. It was certainly known to Clement of Rome c. A.D. 96 (see p. 13 with n. 53), and almost as certainly to Hermas, also of Rome, not long afterward (cf. in the light of Heb. 3:12 his warnings against "apostasy from the living God" in *Shepherd*, Vision 2.3.2; 3.7.2; see also p. 100, n. 61; p. 144, n. 35; p. 148, n. 55; p. 149, n. 58; pp. 262f., nn. 142-46).

4. The earliest occurrence of Πρὸς ʽΕβραίους seems to be at the head of the copy of the epistle on folio 21r of 𝔭46, the oldest extant codex of the *corpus Paulinum*. Clement of Alexandria (c. A.D. 180), in the extract from his *Hypotyposes* quoted by Eusebius, does not use the precise phrase Πρὸς ʽΕβραίους, but evidently knew the epistle under this title, since he speaks of it as written "for Hebrews" (ʽΕβραίοις, Eusebius, *Hist. Eccl.* 6.14.3, 4). Tertullian, in his treatise *On Modesty* (20), written c. A.D. 220, knows it under the corresponding Latin title *ad Hebraeos* (cf. pp. 16, 148).

line corpus, the editor gave it this title by analogy with "To (the) Romans," etc.[5] But what precisely was understood by the term "Hebrews" we cannot say; the title may simply have reflected the editor's impression (shared, no doubt, with other readers) that the people addressed were Jews or, more probably, Jewish Christians.[6] There are a few places in the New Testament where the term "Hebrews" is used of a distinct class of Jews or Jewish Christians, as opposed to those who are called Hellenists;[7] but it is unlikely that this distinctive usage is reflected in the traditional title of our epistle.[8] Indeed, if we think in terms of the Hebrew-Hellenist division, we should naturally classify this epistle as a Hellenistic document.

If the title "To (the) Hebrews"[9] is an editorial label attached to the work for convenient reference, and not an original designation, we should not be greatly influenced by it in endeavoring to establish the identity of the

5. It is difficult to accept the suggestion of F. C. Synge that the title means "Against (the) Hebrews" (*Hebrews and the Scriptures* [London, 1959], p. 44).

6. For the general use of Ἑβραῖοι to designate Jewish Christians cf. M. Black, *The Scrolls and Christian Origins* (London, 1961), p. 78; it appears in this sense in the title of the *Gospel according to the Hebrews* and in the Paris magical papyrus 574, ll. 3018f., "I adjure you by Jesus the God of the Hebrews."

7. Cf. Acts 6:1; 2 Cor. 11:22; Phil. 3:5. See *Acts*, NICNT (Grand Rapids, ²1988), p. 120.

8. W. Manson, *The Epistle to the Hebrews* (London, 1951), p. 162, suggests that the epistle was intended for a minority of "Hebrews" in this distinctive sense, who formed "a section of the Jewish-Christian Church at Rome." On p. 44 he states that this minority, "in reaction from the larger freedom of the world-mission gospel were asserting principles and counterclaims akin to those of the original 'Hebrew' section in the Jerusalem Church." But we have only the scantiest means of knowing what principles and counterclaims were made by the "Hebrews" in the early Jerusalem church; and we do know that Stephen, who was presumably a Hellenist, and Paul, who was born and bred a "Hebrew," found equally bitter hostility among the non-Christian Hellenists of Jerusalem (Acts 6:9; 9:29). In general, however, I am in very great sympathy with W. Manson's thesis (see p. 14).

9. C. Spicq suggests that "To the Hebrews" means "To the pilgrims"—those "passing through" this world; he appeals to the probable kinship between Heb. *'ibrî* ("Hebrew") and *'ābar* ("pass through *or* over"); cf. the LXX translation of "Abram the Hebrew" (Gen. 14:13) as Ἀβρὰμ ὁ περάτης (see also p. 154 with n. 80, p. 292, n. 80; pp. 298f., nn. 114-23). Cf. E. Käsemann, *The Wandering People of God* (1938), E.T. (Minneapolis, 1984), p. 240, n. 182 (he cites to the same effect F. M. Schiele, "Harnack's 'Probabilia' concerning the Address and the Author of the Epistle to the Hebrews," *AJT* 9 (1905), pp. 290-308, and V. Monod, *De titulo epistulae vulgo ad Hebraeos inscriptae* (Montauban, 1910). Compare the title of R. Jewett's commentary on Hebrews: *Letter to the Pilgrims* (New York, 1981). Spicq points out how this sense of "Hebrew" is exploited by Philo (*L'Épître aux Hébreux*, I [Paris, 1952], pp. 243-46). In his later article, "L'Épître aux Hébreux: Apollos, Jean-Baptiste, les Hellénistes et Qumrân," *RQ* 1 (1958-59), pp. 365-90, he repeats this suggestion (quoting from Jerome, *On Jeremiah* 1.14: "Hebrew: that is περάτης, pilgrim and passer through"); he also points out that the designation μέτοχοι found in this epistle (e.g., in 3:1) may reflect the Hithpa'el of the verb *'ārab* (occurring in the sense "associate with" in the OT and the Qumran texts). This might suggest a play on the metathesis *'ābar*/*'ārab*, but μέτοχοι might also reflect Heb. *ḥăbērîm* ("associates" in a religious society or *ḥăbûrāh*); the thought of this as the word lying behind Ἑβραῖοι in the title of our epistle may commend itself to some (not to me).

addressees. This must be established, as far as possible, on the basis of internal evidence.

No doubt it was natural for second-century readers, like many others since their day, to think of the addressees as Jews or Jewish Christians. The whole argument is conducted against a background of Old Testament allusion; considerable familiarity with the Levitical ritual, and interest in it, are presupposed. Yet all this in itself does not require either the author or the people addressed to be Jewish; we have known Gentile Christians who were thoroughly familiar with the Old Testament, accepted it as sacred and authoritative Scripture, and manifested a lively interest in the details of the Mosaic tabernacle and the Levitical offerings, in which they found a remarkably full adumbration of the gospel. So, it has been pointed out, our author's knowledge of the Levitical ritual, like the knowledge which he presupposes in his readers, is a literary knowledge—that is to say, it is drawn from the Old Testament writings (with the aid, possibly, of some midrashic tradition)[10] and not from any firsthand acquaintance with procedure in the Jerusalem temple in the closing years of the Second Jewish Commonwealth. A number of scholars in the past generation or two, among whom the commentators Moffatt and Windisch are outstanding,[11] have maintained that the epistle was addressed to Gentile Christians, who were in danger of committing apostasy and thus renouncing true religion altogether—"deserting the living God," as our author puts it (3:12). If Jewish Christians relapsed into Judaism, it is implied, this would not involve a renunciation of "the living God"; relapsing into Judaism would at least mean that they continued to worship the God of Israel. And, further, is not a pagan past indicated in the repeated phrase "dead works"—when the readers are reminded of the "foundation of repentance from dead works" which, once laid, cannot be laid again (6:1), and of the efficacy of the blood of Christ to "cleanse our conscience from dead works so as to worship the living God" (9:14)?[12]

From our author's point of view deliberate disobedience to the living God was practical apostasy against him, whether those guilty of it were Jewish or Gentile by birth. When he warns his readers against falling away

10. Cf. p. 27, n. 115; p. 225, n. 137 (on 9:19).

11. Cf. J. Moffatt, *The Epistle to the Hebrews*, ICC (Edinburgh, 1924), p. xvi et passim; H. Windisch, *Der Hebräerbrief*, HNT (Tübingen, 1931), p. 31 (on 3:12) et passim; also A. C. McGiffert, *A History of Christianity in the Apostolic Age* (Edinburgh, 1897), pp. 463-82 (with bibliography on p. 468, n. 3); E. F. Scott, *The Epistle to the Hebrews* (Edinburgh, 1922); E. Käsemann, *The Wandering People of God;* G. Vos, *The Teaching of the Epistle to the Hebrews* (Grand Rapids, 1956); H. Koester, *Introduction to the New Testament*, II (Philadelphia, 1982), pp. 272-76.

12. The argument that προσεληλύθατε in 12:18, 22 implies that the readers were "proselytes" from paganism is not sufficiently strong to bear much weight; at most it identifies them as converts to Christianity (cf. p. 355 with nn. 142-44).

from the living God, he adduces the example of the Israelites in the wilderness under Moses who disobeyed God, rejected Moses' leadership, and failed to enter the promised land. What was possible for Israelites then was equally possible for Israelites now. And the "dead works" are things which call for repentance and cleansing, on the part of Jews and Gentiles without discrimination. More particularly, the whole "foundation" of 6:1f. implies the Jewish antecedents of the readers, as does the description of Christ's death in 9:15 as procuring "redemption of the transgressions committed under the first covenant."

Moreover, his insistence that the old covenant has been antiquated is expressed with a moral earnestness and driven home repeatedly in a manner which would be pointless if his readers were not especially disposed to live under that covenant, but which would be very much to the point if they were still trying to live under it, or imagined that, having passed beyond it, they could revert to it.[13]

Again, our author's appeals to the Old Testament scriptures reflect his confidence that his readers, even if their loyalty to the gospel is wearing thin, will recognize their authority. This they would indeed do if they were Jews; they had recognized the authority of those scriptures before they became Christians, and if they relapsed from Christianity into Judaism they would continue to recognize their authority. Converts to Christianity from paganism, on the other hand, adopted the Old Testament as their sacred book along with the Christian faith; if they were tempted to give up their Christian faith, the Old Testament would go with it. Not only so, but the very terms in which our author assumes on their part an acknowledgment of Old Testament authority imply that they accepted Jewish premises; for example, commenting on the announcement in Ps. 110:4 of a priesthood after the order of Melchizedek, he asks: "Now if perfection were attainable through the Levitical priesthood..., what further need would there be for another priest to arise after Melchizedek's order, instead of being called after Aaron's?" (7:11). This argument suggests that the people addressed took it for granted (rightly) that the Levitical priesthood was instituted by divine authority, and also might be inclined to take it for granted (wrongly) that it represented the final stage in this aspect of God's provision for them. Converts from paganism would not be so assured of the divine institution of the Levitical priesthood, and to the author's argument "if perfection were attainable through the Levitical priesthood..." their answer would naturally be: "We never thought

---

13. There is nothing in the argument to suggest that the readers were Gentile Christians exposed to judaizing propaganda like those to whom the Epistle to the Galatians was addressed. The nonmention of circumcision is not surprising in a letter to a Jewish-Christian community, where this would not be the issue it was among Gentile converts in the churches of Galatia or the Lycus valley.

it was!" And while, if we were compelled to regard the addressees as Gentiles, we might give some sort of meaning to the exhortation in 13:13 to go forth to Christ "outside the camp," such language is much more intelligible if addressed to Jews.

Some students of the epistle, concluding that the people addressed were Jews, have gone further and tried to identify them with a particular class of Jews. Karl Bornhäuser, for example, inferred from such a passage as 5:12 (where the readers are told that by this time they should have been able to teach others) that they were not rank-and-file Jewish Christians, but more probably converts from the Jewish priesthood—some of the "great number of the priests" who "were obedient to the faith" in the period before the expulsion of Hellenistic believers from Jerusalem (Acts 6:7).[14] Besides, priests would have a natural interest in the ritual details of our author's argument. Further points in support of this view are adduced by C. Spicq in his great commentary on the epistle.[15] Seven years after the publication of his commentary, Spicq elaborated this part of his thesis by arguing that these converted priests were "Esseno-Christians," including former members of the Qumran sect, whose "doctrinal and biblical formation, intellectual preoccupations and religious presuppositions" were well known to our author.[16]

Since the discovery of the Qumran documents in 1947 and the following years, repeated attempts have been made to bring their evidence into some kind of relation with the Epistle to the Hebrews. In 1955 F. M. Braun expressed the view that "of all the New Testament writings, the Epistle to the Hebrews is the one which gives the fullest answer to the basic tendencies of the [Qumran] sect."[17] Since then a number of other writers have elaborated this statement, none so fully as H. Kosmala in his work *Hebräer-Essener-Christen*, published in 1959, in which it is argued that the people addressed in the epistle were not Christians, but Jews who had come so far on the way to Christianity, but had stopped short of the goal—that they were, in fact, people holding views very similar to those of the Qumran sect and other Essenes. In his introduction to Hebrews in the "Layman's Bible Commentary"

14. K. Bornhäuser, *Empfänger und Verfasser des Briefes an die Hebräer* (Gütersloh, 1932), condensed by C. Sandegren, "The Addressees of the Epistle to the Hebrews," *EQ* 27 (1955), pp. 221-24.

15. *L'Épître aux Hébreux*, I (Paris, 1952), pp. 226-31.

16. *Revue de Qumran* 1 (1958-59), p. 390 (cf. p. 4, n. 9).

17. *RB* 62 (1955), p. 37 (in an article "L'arrière-fond judaïque du quatrième Évangile et la Communauté de l'Alliance," pp. 5-44). Cf. also Y. Yadin, "The Dead Sea Scrolls and the Epistle to the Hebrews," *Scripta Hierosolymitana* 4 (1958), pp. 36-55; D. Flusser, "The Dead Sea Sect and Pre-Pauline Christianity," *ibid.*, pp. 215-66; J. Daniélou, *The Dead Sea Scrolls and Primitive Christianity*, E.T. (Baltimore, 1958), pp. 111-14; H. Kosmala, *Hebräer-Essener-Christen* (Leiden, 1959).

J. W. Bowman maintains that the recipients of the epistle were members of the Hellenistic-Jewish Christian community of Palestine who had come under the influence of the Qumran sect. There were serious defects in their understanding of the gospel, and these the author set himself to correct. The particular group of Hellenists addressed is located by Bowman at Sychar, where John the Baptist and Jesus, and later Philip, had preached. But since Philip's evangelistic campaign in those parts, "the centre of Christian evangelistic effort had passed from Jerusalem to Syrian Antioch, bypassing Samaria and its Hellenistic-Jewish community on the way!"[18] In his volume on Hebrews in the Anchor Bible G. W. Buchanan envisages the recipients of the document as members of a monastic community who had come to the vicinity of "Mount Zion . . . , the city of the living God" (12:22) to await the signal for their entry into the heritage of the promised land. The time was at hand: it would be marked by the overthrow of the Romans and the enthronement of Jesus as Messiah over a liberated Israel, which would be tantamount to the establishment of "the heavenly Jerusalem."[19]

The most that can be said on this score, however, is that the recipients of the epistle were probably Jewish believers in Jesus whose background was not so much the normative Judaism represented by rabbinical tradition as the nonconformist Judaism of which the Essenes and the Qumran community are outstanding representatives, but not the only representatives.

One prominent feature of this nonconformist Judaism was its practice of ceremonial washings beyond those prescribed in the law.[20] Josephus, for example, tells us that the Essenes were distinguished from other Jews when they performed their sacrificial duties "by the superiority of the purifications which they habitually practised."[21] But the Essenes were not the only Jewish groups of which this could be said. There is evidence, indeed, that such "baptist" groups were found in the Diaspora as well as in Judaea. Philo does not speak of ceremonial washings when he describes the settlement of the Therapeutae near Lake Mareotis in Egypt[22]—he does not speak of them either in his descriptions of the Essenes—but the Therapeutae are certainly to be reckoned as an Egyptian offshoot of the Palestinian nonconformist tradition. As for the Jewish community in Rome, it appears to have preserved noncon-

---

18. J. W. Bowman, *Hebrews, James, I & II Peter*, LBC (London, 1962), pp. 13-16. For a critique of all such views see J. Coppens, *Les affinités qumrâniennes de l'Épître aux Hébreux* (Bruges-Paris/Louvain, 1962).

19. G. W. Buchanan, *To the Hebrews*, AB (Garden City, NY, 1972).

20. Cf. J. Thomas, *Le mouvement baptiste en Palestine et Syrie* (Gembloux, 1935); M. Black, *The Scrolls and Christian Origins*, pp. 91-101; J. A. T. Robinson, "The Baptism of John and the Qumran Community," *Twelve New Testament Studies* (London, 1962), pp. 11-27.

21. *Ant.* 18.19.

22. *The Contemplative Life* 21-39, 66-90.

formist features, especially in the matter of ceremonial washings, which in due course were taken over into Roman Christianity, as the *Apostclic Tradition* of Hippolytus testifies at the beginning of the third century A.D.[23] If the Epistle to the Hebrews was addressed to a group of Jewish Christians which retained such features, certain points which the author makes, such as his reference to "teaching about ablutions" in 6:2, could have had a more immediate relevance to their situation than might be readily apparent to twentieth-century readers.

The addressees appear, then, to have been a group of Jewish Christians who had never seen or heard Jesus in person, but learned of him (as the writer of the epistle also did) from some who had themselves listened to him.[24] Since their conversion they had been exposed to persecution—particularly at one stage shortly after the beginning of their Christian career[25]—but while they had had to endure public abuse, imprisonment, and the looting of their property, they had not yet been called upon to die for their faith.[26] They had given practical evidence of their faith by serving their fellow-Christians and especially by caring for those of their number who suffered most in the time of persecution.[27] Yet their Christian development had been arrested; instead of pressing ahead they were inclined to come to a full stop in their spiritual progress, if not indeed to slip back to a stage which they had left.[28] Very probably they were reluctant to sever their last ties with a religion which enjoyed the protection of Roman law and face the risks of irrevocable commitment to the Christian way. The writer, who has known them, or known about them, for a considerable time, and feels a pastoral concern for their welfare, warns them against falling back, for this may result in falling away from their Christian faith altogether; he encourages them with the assurance that they have everything to lose if they fall back, but everything to gain if they press on.[29]

We may infer from the epistle that they were Hellenists; they knew the Old Testament in the Greek version. It is implied, too, that their knowledge of the ancient sacrificial ritual of Israel was derived from the reading of the Old Testament and not from firsthand contact with the temple services in Jerusalem. Perhaps they formed a "house church" within the wider fellowship of a city church, and were tending to neglect the bonds of fellowship which bound them to other Christians outside their own inner circle.

23. See pp. 141f. with nn. 20-25 (on Heb. 6:2).
24. Cf. Heb. 2:3f.
25. 10:32.
26. 12:4 (cf. pp. 21, 267-70, 342).
27. 6:10; 10:34.
28. 5:11-14.
29. 2:1-4; 3:12–4:1; 6:4-8; 10:26-39; 12:15-29.

II. DESTINATION

Where did they live? We do not know. Opinions have ranged between Judaea in the east and Spain[30] in the west.

If their knowledge of the Jewish ritual was not derived from firsthand contact with the temple services, then Jerusalem seems to be excluded. They may, of course, have had an earlier association with the Jerusalem church; we recall the large exodus of Hellenistic believers from Jerusalem in the persecution which followed the death of Stephen. Those Hellenists scattered in many directions, carrying the gospel wherever they went;[31] one can easily think of the readers of this epistle as one of the communities of new believers founded at that time.

Even so, Jerusalem has not been without its advocates as the place to which the epistle was sent.[32] Sir William Ramsay, for example, hazarded the guess that it was written to the Jerusalem church from Caesarea during Paul's imprisonment in that city (A.D. 57-59) by one of his companions, Philip the evangelist perhaps.[33] C. H. Turner argued that it was sent to the Jerusalem church shortly before the outbreak of the war against Rome in A.D. 66, when they "had to face the issue squarely between the abandonment of their Christianity and the abandonment of their city. Criticism [he added] which shuts its eyes to such patent historical probabilities stands self-condemned."[34] Arnold Ehrhardt revived the theory of Franz Overbeck that the epistle was sent as "a message of consolation from the Church at Rome to Christians in the Holy Land after the fall of Jerusalem."[35]

But the religious situation in Jerusalem was dominated by the temple, to which no explicit reference is made by our author. When an earlier leader of his school, Stephen, addressed himself to the situation in Jerusalem, the temple occupied a prominent place in his polemic—the temple, moreover, in express distinction from the movable tabernacle of earlier days.[36] Our

---

30. So Nicolas of Lyra, d. 1349 (cf. C. Spicq, *L'Épître aux Hébreux*, I, p. 234, n. 4).

31. Cf. Acts 8:4; 11:19.

32. Cf. G. Salmon, *Introduction to the New Testament* (London, 1889), pp. 468-73; B. F. Westcott, *The Epistle to the Hebrews* (London, 1903), p. xl ("in Jerusalem, or in the neighbourhood of Jerusalem"); W. Leonard, *The Authorship of the Epistle to the Hebrews* (London, 1939); G. W. Buchanan, *To the Hebrews;* cf. P. E. Hughes, *A Commentary on the Epistle to the Hebrews* (Grand Rapids, 1977), pp. 18f. ("the probabilities increasingly favor a location somewhere in Palestine"). Spicq (*Hébreux*, I, p. 239, n. 1) lists many others who opt for a Jerusalem destination.

33. *Luke the Physician* (London, 1908), pp. 301-28.

34. *Catholic and Apostolic* (London, 1931), pp. 81f.

35. A. A. T. Ehrhardt, *The Framework of the New Testament Stories* (Manchester, 1964), p. 109; cf. F. Overbeck, *Zur Geschichte des Kanons: I. Die Tradition der Alten Kirche über den Hebräerbrief* (Chemnitz, 1880), pp. 3ff.

36. Acts 6:13f.; 7:44-50 (see *Acts*, NICNT, pp. 126ff., 130ff., 146ff.).

author has much to say about the tabernacle, but not about the temple. The priesthood and ritual associated with the tabernacle, of course, were in principle those associated with the temple too; but what we find in the epistle is literary allusion to the former and not, as might have been expected in an exhortation addressed to Jerusalem, contemporary allusion to the latter. Even at the latest reasonable date for the epistle, there would still have been a few members of the Jerusalem church who had seen and heard Jesus for themselves and did not have to depend on the testimony of others. And when the writer refers to his readers' long-standing and continued service "to his holy people" (6:10), we may reflect that throughout the apostolic age the Jerusalem church is more prominent as a recipient than as a giver of such ministry.

Other places in Palestine have been suggested: J. W. Bowman, as we have seen, thinks of Samaria (preferably Sychar); C. Spicq thinks of Caesarea, but regards Syrian Antioch as more probable.[37] T. W. Manson, leaving the beaten track, suggests Colossae or some neighboring place in the Lycus valley; he detects in the epistle references to the "Colossian heresy" at an earlier stage than that which it had reached by the time Paul wrote the Epistle to the Colossians.[38] W. F. Howard thinks of Ephesus; he envisages the people addressed as a group of wealthy and cultivated Jews who had been converted during Paul's Ephesian ministry, but whose faith waned after Paul's imprisonment and subsequent execution in Rome.[39] They had little sympathy with their fellow-Christians of Gentile birth, whom they despised as low-born and too much influenced by the lax morality of their pagan days. Cyprus has commended itself to Antony Snell;[40] this hangs together with his ascription of the authorship to Barnabas, whose close association with Cy-

---

37. *Hébreux*, I, pp. 247-52. The experiences of 10:32-34 could be placed in the context of the tension between the Jewish and Gentile populations of Caesarea in the decade preceding A.D. 66 (Josephus, *War* 2.266-70; *Ant.* 20.173-84). As for Antioch, see V. Burch, *The Epistle to the Hebrews* (London, 1936), p. 137, for the argument that the allusions to the Maccabaean martyr-cult in 11:35b-38 "are met by a Syrian notice of the cult which is markedly Antiochian in detail."

38. *Studies in the Gospels and Epistles* (Manchester, 1962), pp. 242-58 (article "The Problem of the Epistle to the Hebrews," reprinted from *BJRL* 32 [1949], pp. 3-19). The epistle was associated with the Lycus valley by some persons known to Filaster, bishop of Brescia, d. c. 397 (*Heresies* 89); they identified it with the Laodicean letter of Col. 4:16. According to Filaster, Hebrews was variously attributed to Paul, Barnabas, Clement of Rome, and Luke (J. B. Lightfoot, *Saint Paul's Epistles to the Colossians and to Philemon* [London, ²1879], p. 278). Cf. C. P. Anderson, "Hebrews among the Letters of Paul," *SR* 5 (1975), pp. 258-66.

39. "The Epistle to the Hebrews," *Interpretation* 5 (1951), pp. 80-91.

40. *New and Living Way* (London, 1959), p. 19. Cyprus had previously been suggested by E. Riggenbach, *Der Brief an die Hebräer*, ZK (Leipzig, 1913), pp. xlviff.—a work which Snell characterizes as "much the best commentary on the Epistle known to me" (*New and Living Way*, p. 22).

prus is well attested. H. Appel, F. lo Bue, and H. W. Montefiore have argued for a Corinthian destination.[41]

A number of scholars have thought of Alexandria in Egypt as the city where the readers lived.[42] Some Alexandrian association is evident throughout the epistle; the author is evidently acquainted with the literature of Alexandrian Judaism, like Wisdom and 4 Maccabees, and especially the writings of Philo. But this speaks more for his association with the city than for theirs. The Muratorian Canon, which makes no mention of Hebrews, does refer to an epistle "to the Alexandrines"; but as this is described as forged in Paul's name to support Marcion's heresy, it takes a powerful stretch of the imagination to identify it with our epistle. In the nineteenth century J. E. C. Schmidt,[43] A. Hilgenfeld,[44] and S. Davidson[45] argued for Alexandria; they were followed in the twentieth century by G. Hoennicke,[46] C. J. Cadoux,[47] and S. G. F. Brandon.[48] Alexandria indeed has much which could be urged in its favor;[49] but there is one great obstacle in the way of thinking that the epistle was sent there. That is that precisely in Alexandria the belief in its Pauline authorship first arose, and it is difficult to suppose that the Christians of the city to which the epistle was sent so quickly forgot who sent it to them and ascribed it to another. Clement of Alexandria refers to someone called "the blessed elder"—possibly his teacher Pantaenus—as saying that Paul, being the apostle of the Gentiles, wrote for the Hebrews anonymously since he recognized our Lord as Apostle to the Hebrews.[50] Thus, about a century after the epistle was written, it was being ascribed to Paul at Alexandria—perhaps because it was at Alexandria that the Epistle to the Hebrews was for the first time copied into a codex as part

---

41. H. Appel, *Der Hebräerbrief: ein Schreiben des Apollos an Judenchristen der korinthischen Gemeinde* (Leipzig, 1918); F. lo Bue, "The Historical Background of the Epistle to the Hebrews," *JBL* 75 (1958), pp. 52-57; H. W. Montefiore, *The Epistle to the Hebrews*, HNTC (New York, 1964), pp. 11-16.

42. Cf. Spicq, *Hébreux*, I, p. 237, n. 2, for a list.

43. *Einleitung in das Neue Testament*, I (Giessen, 1804), pp. 284, 293.

44. *Historisch-kritische Einleitung in das Neue Testament* (Leipzig, 1875), pp. 385ff.

45. *Introduction to the New Testament*, I (London, 1882), pp. 223ff.

46. *Das Judenchristentum im ersten und zweiten Jahrhundert* (Berlin, 1908), pp. 93ff.

47. "The Early Christian Church in Egypt," *ExT* 33 (1921-22), pp. 536-59.

48. *The Fall of Jerusalem and the Christian Church* (London, 1951), pp. 239f.

49. Not, however, the fact that the Jewish temple of Leontopolis was nearby. K. Wieseler argued that deviations in the description of the cultus in Hebrews from that prescribed in the OT and followed in Jerusalem (e.g., the daily ministration of the high priest, 7:27) reflected the practice at Leontopolis ("Die Leser des Hebräerbriefs und der Tempel zu Leontopolis," *Theologische Studien und Kritiken* 40 [1867], pp. 665-720). See p. 236, n. 11.

50. *Hypotyposes*, quoted by Eusebius, *Hist. Eccl.* 6.14.1-4. The identification of Clement's "elder" with Pantaenus was first suggested, it appears, by T. Zahn (*Introduction to the New Testament*, E.T., II [Edinburgh, 1909], p. 308, n. 5).

of the *corpus Paulinum*.[51] But could this ascription have been made so soon in a place where the true authorship was most likely to have been remembered?

The first place where, according to our extant literature, the Epistle to the Hebrews appears to have been known is Rome.[52] For Clement of Rome shows clear evidence of his acquaintance with it in the letter which he wrote on behalf of the Roman church to the Corinthian church *c.* A.D. 96.[53] Unfortunately he drops no hint about its authorship; he was writing for his contemporaries, not for us. But the Roman church, and the west in general, took a long time before they consented to regard it as one of the Pauline letters; their resistance to the belief in its Pauline authorship springs in all probability from an original positive knowledge that it was not written by Paul.

No certain inference in this regard can be drawn from the greetings which the writer sends his readers from "those from Italy" (13:24).[54] "Those from Italy" may have lived in Italy or outside Italy, so far as the language is concerned; and while the message is most easily construed in agreement with a Roman destination for the letter, it would not necessarily exclude Rome (or some other place in Italy) as the place where it was written.

What has been said above of the presence of "nonconformist" Jewish elements in the Christian community of Rome would chime in well with a Roman destination. There were many other places in the Diaspora as well as in Palestine where such elements were to be found, but it is at Rome that we have the best attestation of their survival for several generations in *Christian* practice.

One of the best-known statements of the case for the Roman destination of the epistle was an article by Adolf Harnack in the first issue of *Zeitschrift für die neutestamentliche Wissenschaft*, in which he related it to the early history of Christianity at Rome and envisaged it as sent to a "house

51. Cf. G. Zuntz, *The Text of the Epistles* (London, 1953), pp. 14-17, 276-79; also C. P. Anderson, "The Epistle to the Hebrews and the Pauline Letter Collection," *HTR* 59 (1966), pp. 429-38.

52. Some (e.g., E. Nestle, "On the Address of the Epistle to the Hebrews," *ExT* 10 [1898-99], p. 422; G. Milligan, *The Theology of the Epistle to the Hebrews* [Edinburgh, 1899], p. 50) have linked a Roman destination for the epistle with the presence in Rome of a "synagogue of the Hebrews" (συναγωγὴ Αἰβρέων, *CIG* 9909); this is a very doubtful link.

53. This is particularly evident in the précis of Heb. 1:3-7 interwoven into the language of 1 Clem. 36:1-5. See D. A. Hagner, *The Use of the Old and New Testaments in Clement of Rome*, NovTSup 34 (Leiden, 1973), pp. 179-84.

54. The "hypothesis that gives the most reasonable explanation for the largest amount of the data . . . is that which postulates that the epistle was written to a group or synagogue of Jewish Christians within the church of Rome in the late 60s" (J. A. T. Robinson, *Redating the New Testament* [London, 1976], p. 207). A Roman destination was first suggested by J. J. Wettstein (*Novum Testamentum Graece*, II [Amsterdam, 1752], p. 386). On Heb. 13:24 see p. 391 below with n. 132.

church" in that city by someone well acquainted with the addressees.[55] Later William Manson presented a persuasive case in the Baird Lecture delivered in New College, Edinburgh, in 1950.[56] The Roman church, he inferred from Rom. 11:13, 18, had a Jewish-Christian base. As a whole it had accepted the implications of the Gentile world-mission, but a small conservative enclave within it clung to the more conservative principles of traditional Judaism, and to this enclave in particular Hebrews is addressed. Professor Manson found a straight line running from the ministry of Stephen (the record of which in Acts forms the prelude to the rise of the Gentile world-mission) to the argument of the Epistle to the Hebrews. His thesis will be found to influence the present commentary at many points; but certainty on the destination of the epistle is unattainable in the present state of our knowledge, and fortunately its exegesis is for the most part independent of this question.

III. AUTHORSHIP

If we do not know for certain to whom the epistle was sent, neither do we know by whom it was sent. If Clement of Rome had any inkling of the author's identity, he gives us no indication of it. But we can be quite sure that he himself was not the author, although it has been suggested at various times that he was. In spite of Clement's familiarity with the epistle, he "turns his back on its central argument in order to buttress his own arguments about the Church's Ministry by an appeal to the ceremonial laws of the Old Testament."[57]

The Alexandrian belief that Paul was the author influenced the judgment of eastern Christianity,[58] and ultimately, from the middle of the fourth century, of western Christianity too. But even at Alexandria, the sense of literary criticism possessed by the leaders of the catechetical school made it

---

55. "Probabilia über die Adresse und den Verfasser des Hebräerbriefes," *ZNW* 1 (1900), pp. 16-41. A year earlier, T. Zahn had argued that the addressees were Jewish Christians in Rome, one group within the wider city church (*INT*, E.T., II, pp. 344-51; 358, nn. 5, 6; 359, n. 8). M. A. R. Tuker found support for the Roman association of the epistle in the Canon of the Roman Mass, in the reference to "thy supreme priest Melchizedek" *(summus sacerdos tuus Melchisedech):* in the Roman liturgy, he points out, "and in no other," are such words used. "Moreover, they are recorded in the oldest reference to the Roman Canon, and must take their place by the side of the 'Amen' of Justin as root-words of the Liturgy" (from "The Gospel according to Prisca," *Nineteenth Century*, January 1913, pp. 81f., quoted by A. Nairne, *The Epistle of Priesthood* [Edinburgh, 1913], p. 6, n. 1). See p. 158 below, n. 11.

56. *The Epistle to the Hebrews: An Historical and Theological Reconsideration.*

57. T. W. Manson, *The Church's Ministry* (London, 1948), pp. 13f.; he describes Clement's procedure in this regard as "a retrogression of the worst kind."

58. But even in the east, as late as the beginning of the fourth century, Methodius of Olympus treated Hebrews as anonymous (*Symposium* 4.1; 5.7).

plain that Pauline authorship could not be predicated *simpliciter* of this epistle as it could of Romans or Galatians. Attempts were therefore made to reconcile the Pauline ascription with the linguistic data. Clement of Alexandria in his *Hypotyposes*[59] said that it was written by Paul for Hebrews in the Hebrew language, but that Luke translated it and published it for the Greeks; thus he endeavored to account for the similarity in style between Hebrews and the Lukan writings. (As for the absence of the Pauline superscription, he accounted for that by saying that "in writing for Hebrews who had conceived a prejudice against him and suspected him, he very prudently did not put them off at the outset by setting down his name.")[60] Origen, a generation later, knowing as he did Hebrew in addition to Greek, probably realized that the Greek of the epistle bore no sign of having been translated from Hebrew.[61] His account of its authorship is as follows:

> The character of the diction of the epistle superscribed to the Hebrews lacks the apostle's rudeness of expression (a rudeness of expression or style which he himself acknowledged); the epistle is more idiomatically Greek in the composition of its diction. This will be acknowledged by anyone who is skilled to discern differences of style. But on the other hand the thoughts of the epistle are admirable and in no way inferior to those of the acknowledged writings of the apostle. The truth of this will be admitted by any one who pays attention to the reading of the apostle. . . .
>
> For my own part, if I may state my opinion, I should say that the thoughts are the apostle's, but that the style and composition are the work of someone who called to mind the apostle's teaching and wrote short notes, as it were, on what his master said. If any church, then, regards this epistle as Paul's, let it be commended on this score; for it was not for nothing that the men of old have handed it down to us as Paul's. But as to who actually wrote the epistle, God knows the truth of the matter. According to the account which has reached us, some say that the epistle was written by Clement, who became bishop of the Romans; others, that it was written by Luke, the writer of the Gospel and the Acts.[62]

---

59. Quoted by Eusebius, *Hist. Eccl.* 6.14.2.

60. Eusebius, *Hist. Eccl.* 6.14.3. Clement's account is followed in a fourth-century preface to the epistle included in most manuscripts of the Vulgate.

61. Against its being a translation from Hebrew (apart from the general consideration that it is not written in translation-Greek) certain specific points tell: thus, not only is the OT quoted in the LXX, but the author argues on the basis of a LXX deviation from the Hebrew text (cf. the use made of Ps. 40:6, "a body hast thou prepared me," in Heb. 10:5ff.); again, the argument of 9:15-20 depends on the double sense "covenant" and "testament" of Gk. διαθήκη and could not have been used with Heb. $b^erît$ (cf. Calvin, *ad loc.*).

62. Quoted by Eusebius, *Hist. Eccl.* 6.25.11-14.

Although the Pauline authorship was resisted in the west until late in the fourth century, the only positive ascription of authorship to come down to us from the west during that period is Tertullian's; he appeals to the epistle as having greater authority than the *Shepherd* of Hermas because of the eminence of its author, Barnabas, and he names Barnabas as the author of the epistle not as though he were expressing a private judgment of his own but as though this were a commonly agreed ascription in his circle.[63] The Muratorian Canon, Irenaeus,[64] Hippolytus,[65] and Gaius of Rome[66] did not regard the epistle as Pauline. Eusebius (*c.* A.D. 325) remarks that even in his day some among the Romans did not consider it to be the apostle's.[67] Half a century later the writer whom we call Ambrosiaster did not include Hebrews in the Pauline epistles on which he wrote commentaries; to him it is always an anonymous work, although he accepts it as canonical.[68]

63. *On Modesty* 20 (cf. p. 148 with n. 55). Whether this tradition was well founded or based, e.g., on a collocation of the λόγος παρακλήσεως of Heb. 13:22 with the υἱὸς παρακλήσεως of Acts 4:36 cannot be ascertained. It has been objected that a man who appears so early in Christian history as Barnabas could not have written in terms of Heb. 2:3b; but he may not have heard Jesus teach. Barnabas was regarded as the author in the later part of the fourth century by Gregory of Elvira (cf. Spicq, *Hébreux*, I, p. 199 with n. 7) and by a host of modern writers (cf. Spicq, *ibid.*, n. 8), including B. Weiss, MK (Göttingen, 1897), G. Salmon (*INT*, pp. 466-68), F. Blass (*Der Brief an die Hebräer* [Halle, 1903]), J. V. Bartlet ("Barnabas and his Genuine Epistle," *Exp.* VI.v [1902], pp. 409-27, vi [1902], pp. 28-30; "The Epistle to the Hebrews as the Work of Barnabas," *Exp.* VI.viii [1903], pp. 381-96; "More Words on the Epistle to the Hebrews," *Exp.* VI.xi [1905], pp. 381-96; he later gave up this view in favor of Apollos's authorship), C. R. Gregory (*Canon and Text of the New Testament* [Edinburgh, 1907], pp. 223f.), E. Riggenbach, ZK (Leipzig, 1913), C. J. Cadoux ("The Early Christian Church in Egypt," *ExT* 33 [1921-22], pp. 536-59; K. Bornhäuser (*Empfänger und Verfasser des Hebräerbriefs*, pp. 75ff.), H. Strathmann (*Der Brief an die Hebräer*, NTD [Göttingen, 1937], pp. 64f.), A. Snell (*New and Living Way*, pp. 17-20), P. E. Hughes (*Commentary on Hebrews*, pp. 24-29, tentatively). According to F. J. Badcock, "the voice is the voice of Barnabas the Levite, but the hand is the hand of Luke" (*The Pauline Epistles and the Epistle to the Hebrews in their Historical Setting* [London, 1937], p. 198); cf. p. 367, n. 3.

64. The epistle is not mentioned in the Muratorian Canon, which lists Paul's letters as addressed to seven named churches and three named individuals, thus clearly excluding Hebrews. Cf. also Cyprian (*Testimonies* 1.20; *To Fortunatus* 11); Victorinus of Pettau (d. 303), commenting on Rev. 1:11. On Irenaeus cf. C. H. Turner in *Novum Testamentum Sancti Irenaei*, ed. W. Sanday and C. H. Turner (Oxford, 1923), pp. 226f. Stephen Gobarus (quoted by Photius, *Bibliotheca* 232) says that Irenaeus denied the Pauline authorship of Hebrews.

65. According to Photius, *Bibliotheca* 121; cf. R. H. Connolly, "New Attributions to Hippolytus," *JTS* 46 (1945), pp. 199f.

66. According to Eusebius, *Hist. Eccl.* 6.20.3.

67. *Hist. Eccl.* 6.20.3.

68. A. Souter, *A Study of Ambrosiaster* (Cambridge, 1905), pp. 171f.; *The Earliest Latin Commentaries on the Epistles of St. Paul* (Oxford, 1927), pp. 53f. The commentary on Hebrews included in some manuscripts among Ambrosiaster's Pauline commentaries is actually by Alcuin of York (E. Riggenbach, *Die ältesten lateinischen Kommentare zum Hebräerbrief* [Leipzig, 1907], pp. 18-40). Pelagius regards Hebrews as Pauline, but perhaps not in the same sense as the thirteen epistles which bear Paul's name; he wrote commentaries on them, but not on Hebrews.

It was Jerome and Augustine who swayed opinion in the west toward accepting Hebrews as a Pauline epistle—not that they were convinced that it was so on grounds of literary criticism but rather because they were "moved" (to quote Augustine) "by the prestige of the eastern churches which include this epistle too among the canonical writings."[69] Even so, the earliest synodical promulgations of the canon in the west preserved for some time a distinction between this epistle and the others ascribed to Paul: both the Synod of Hippo in 393 and the Third Synod of Carthage in 397 enumerate "Of Paul the apostle, thirteen epistles; of the same to the Hebrews, one." But the Sixth Synod of Carthage (A.D. 419) assigns "fourteen epistles" in so many words to Paul, in terms which Athanasius of Alexandria had used in his Festal Letter of A.D. 367.[70] From then on the Pauline ascription became traditional in the west as in the east, although commentators of critical judgment continued to speak of Clement of Rome or Luke as translator or editor of the epistle. Thus Thomas Aquinas says that "Luke, who was an excellent advocate *(prolocutor),* translated it from Hebrew into that elegant Greek."[71]

But with the reopening of traditional questions in the age of the Reformation, fresh attention was directed to the authorship of Hebrews. Erasmus regarded the style of the epistle as excluding Pauline authorship, although he conceded that it was inspired by the mind of Paul.[72] Calvin[73] thought of Luke or Clement of Rome as the author, not merely translator or editor; while Luther[74] was apparently the first to make the brilliant guess that the author

---

69. *Forgiveness of Sins* 1.50. While he gives the number of Paul's letters as fourteen *(On Christian Learning* 2.13), Augustine does not foreclose the question of the authorship of Hebrews. "In his earliest writings (down to 406) he cites the Epistle as Paul's; in the middle period he wavers between Pauline authorship and anonymity; in his old age (409-30) he refers to it always as anonymous" (A. Souter, *The Text and Canon of the New Testament* [London, ²1954], p. 174). Jerome pays lip service to the Pauline authorship, following the Greek-speaking churches, but he knows that many of the Latins have doubts about this, and he distinguishes Hebrews from Paul's letters "to seven churches" *(Epistle* 53.9). In fact, he says, "it does not matter whose it is, since it is the work of a churchman *(ecclesiastici uiri)* and honored daily by being read in the churches" *(Epistle* 129.3).

70. See F. F. Bruce, *The Canon of Scripture* (Glasgow, 1988), pp. 208f.

71. *Preface to the Epistle to the Hebrews* (quoted by Spicq, *Hébreux,* I, p. 198, n. 1).

72. *Annotationes in Epistulam Pauli ad Hebraeos* ([1516] Paris, 1631), p. 707.

73. On Heb. 13:23.

74. Luther speaks as though others had suggested Apollos before him. In his *Lectures on Hebrews,* 1517-18 (WA LVIII.iii, p. 5) he still ascribes the epistle conventionally to Paul; but in his *Preface to Hebrews,* 1522 (WA, *Die deutsche Bibel,* VII, p. 344), he describes the author as "an excellent man of learning, who had been a disciple of the apostles and learned much from them, and who was very well versed in Scripture." In a sermon on 1 Cor. 3:4ff., in 1537 (WA, XLV, p. 389), he says that Hebrews was certainly the work of Apollos, and expresses the same view in his *Commentary on Genesis,* 1545 (WA, XLIV, p. 709). See H. Feld, *Martin Luthers und Wendelin Steinbachs Vorlesungen über den Hebräerbrief* (Wiesbaden, 1971), pp. 22-34.

was Apollos—a guess which has commended itself to many since his day, including H. Alford, E. Riehm, E. Reuss, A. Hilgenfeld, A. Klostermann, T. Zahn, H. Appel, J. V. Bartlet (in his later years), T. W. Manson, W. F. Howard, C. Spicq, and H. W. Montefiore.[75] The Alexandrian characteristics of the thought, style, and vocabulary of the epistle have been thought to speak in favor of Apollos's authorship; William Manson, however, while conceding that "Apollos would admirably suit the part in point of his Jewish-Alexandrian origin and training," finds it "difficult to think that the Alexandrian Church would not have preserved some knowledge of the fact in view of the distinguished rôle of this son of Alexandria in the world-mission, and that Clement would not have mentioned him in writing to the Corinthians in whose history Apollos had played a notable part." He adds that "other attempts to discover the writer's identity have no greater interest than a parlour-game."[76]

Among those other attempts, mention should certainly be made of Harnack's, who argued that the epistle was written by Priscilla and Aquila, with Priscilla as the dominant partner.[77] Their quality as teachers is attested by the

75. H. Alford, *The Greek Testament*, IV.1 (London, 1859), pp. 58-62; E. Riehm, *Der Lehrbegriff des Hebräerbriefs*, II (Basel, 1867), p. 894; E. Reuss, *Histoire de la théologie chrétienne au siècle apostolique*, II (Strasbourg, [3]1864), pp. 268f.; *L'Épître aux Hébreux* (Paris, 1878), pp. 22f.; A. Hilgenfeld, *Historisch-kritische Einleitung in das Neue Testament*, pp. 356, 386ff.; A. Klostermann, *Zur Theorie der biblischen Weissagung und zur Charakteristik des Hebräerbriefs* (Nördlingen, 1889), pp. 47ff.; T. Zahn, *INT*, II, p. 356; H. Appel, *Der Hebräerbrief: Ein Schreiben des Apollos an Judenchristen der korinthischen Gemeinde;* J. V. Bartlet, "The Riddle of the Epistle to the Hebrews," *Exp.* VIII.v (1913), pp. 548-51; "The Epistle to the Hebrews Once More," *ExT* 34 (1922-23), pp. 58-61; T. W. Manson, *Studies in the Gospels and Epistles*, pp. 254-58; W. F. Howard, "The Epistle to the Hebrews," *Interpretation* 5 (1951), pp. 80-91; C. Spicq, *Hébreux*, I, pp. 207-19; H. W. Montefiore, *Hebrews*, HNTC, pp. 9-15. See the fuller list in Spicq, *Hébreux*, I, p. 210, n. 2.

76. *The Epistle to the Hebrews*, pp. 171f. Cf. the suggested ascriptions to Peter (A. Welch, *The Authorship of the Epistle to the Hebrews* [Edinburgh, 1898]), Aristion (J. Chapman, "Aristion, Author of the Epistle to the Hebrews," *RBén* 17 [1905], pp. 50-62; R. Perdelwitz, "Das literarische Problem des Hebräerbriefs," *ZNW* 11 [1910], pp. 59-78, 105-23), Philip the evangelist (W. M. Ramsay, *Luke the Physician*, p. 304), Jude (A. M. Dubarle, "Rédacteur et destinataires de l'Épître aux Hébreux," *RB* 48 [1939], pp. 506-29), Silas/Silvanus (E. G. Selwyn, *The First Epistle of St. Peter* [London, 1946], pp. 464-66); T. Hewitt, *The Epistle to the Hebrews*, TNTC [London, 1960], pp. 26-31), Timothy (J. D. Legg, "Our brother Timothy," *EQ* 40 [1968], pp. 220-23; see below, p. 390, n. 127, on Heb. 13:23), Epaphras (C. P. Anderson, "Hebrews among the Letters of Paul," *SR* 5 [1975], pp. 258-66).

77. "Probabilia . . . ," *ZNW* 1 (1900), pp. 32-41 (cf. p. 14, n. 55). Cf. J. R. Harris, *Sidelights on New Testament Research* (London, 1908), pp. 148-76 (see below, p. 294, n. 92). The one place in the epistle where the requirements of Greek grammatical gender indicate the author's sex uses the masculine: in 11:32 the author says "the time will fail me telling (διηγούμενον). . . ." Harnack (*loc. cit.,* pp. 26f.) calls this "an indifferent phrase" (meaning, no doubt, that the masculine is purely formal); Harris (*Side-lights*, p. 175) treats it more seriously: "this masculine participle is the real rock in the track, if we want to refer the Epistle to the Hebrews (or even the eleventh chapter) to Priscilla. . . . And . . . it is only fair to say that the adverse evi-

instruction which they gave to Apollos;[78] they were closely associated with Timothy;[79] they were host and hostess to a house church in Rome[80] (if the salutations in Rom. 16:3-16 are intended for Rome); the transition back and forth between "we" and "I" would be suitable to a married couple;[81] the disappearance of the author's name from the memory of the church could be explained by the same antifeminist tendency as the Western text (more particularly Codex D) displays in toning down the relatively prominent part which Priscilla plays in Acts.[82]

A case can be made out for several of the suggested names because they have left no other writings by which we could judge whether Hebrews is written in their style or not.[83] Paul is in the opposite case; it is because we have other indubitable writings from his pen that we can say confidently with Calvin: "The manner of teaching and the style sufficiently show that Paul was not the author, and the writer himself confesses in the second chapter that he was one of the disciples of the apostles, which is wholly different from the way in which Paul spoke of himself."[84] What Paul and the author of Hebrews have in common is the basic apostolic teaching; but when we come to

---

dence at this point to the Priscilla hypothesis is very strong: and it would not be proper to cure the text of its difficulty by a conjectural emendation unless the case were already settled by other considerations." For Harris to resist the temptation to emend the text conjecturally argues uncommon self-restraint. See for a more recent presentation R. Hoppin, *Priscilla: Author of the Epistle to the Hebrews* (New York, 1969). A different feminine influence on the epistle has been discerned by J. M. Ford, "The Mother of Jesus and the Authorship of the Epistle to the Hebrews," *Bible Today* 82 (1976), pp. 683-94.

78. Acts 18:26.

79. Who, like them, was in Paul's company at Corinth and at Ephesus (Acts 18:5; 19:22; 1 Cor. 16:10, 19).

80. Rom. 16:5 (similarly they accommodated a church in their house at Ephesus during their stay there; cf. 1 Cor. 16:19).

81. "We" much more frequently than "I" (cf. Harnack, "Probabilia...," *ZNW* 1, p. 24). One may recall Sidney and Beatrice Webb; when they said, "Our thought is ...," those who knew them realized that it was Beatrice's thought that was being expressed.

82. For the Western text of Acts 18:26 see *Acts*, NICNT, p. 358, n. 67.

83. With the exception of Luke, to whom some part in the composition of the epistle has been ascribed since Clement of Alexandria. He has been regarded as author (not simply editor or translator) by Calvin (with Clement of Rome as an alternative), F. Delitzsch (*Commentary on the Epistle to the Hebrews*, E.T., II [Edinburgh, 1872], pp. 409-17), and others. Stylistically Hebrews is closer to the writings of Luke than to anything else in the NT; but this may be because our author and Luke approximate more closely than other NT writers to the models of literary Hellenistic—our author even more so than Luke. "Hebrews may be more typical of the cultured speech of the educated classes than any of the other documents in the New Testament" (M. E. Thrall, *Greek Particles in the New Testament* [Leiden, 1962], p. 9). Cf. C. P. M. Jones, "The Epistle to the Hebrews and the Lucan Writings," in *Studies in the Gospels*, ed. D. E. Nineham (Oxford, 1955), pp. 113-43.

84. *Calvin's Commentaries: The Epistle ... to the Hebrews and the First and Second Epistles of Peter*, trans. W. B. Johnston (Edinburgh, 1963), p. 1.

distinctive features we may say with certainty that the thought of the epistle is not Paul's, the language is not Paul's, and the technique of Old Testament quotation is not Paul's. In brief, "I can adduce no reason to show that Paul was its author."[85] So Calvin wisely sums up.[86]

The author was a second-generation Christian, well versed in the study of the Septuagint, which he interpreted according to a creative exegetical principle. He had a copious vocabulary and was the master of a fine rhetorical style, completely different from Paul's; we might well describe him as "a learned man, . . . mighty in the scriptures."[87] He was a Hellenist who inherited the outlook of those Hellenists described in Acts 6–8; 11:19ff., the associates of Stephen and Philip, pioneers in the Gentile mission.

"But as to who actually wrote the epistle, God knows the truth of the matter." Even today we have not got far beyond Origen's confession of ignorance. "It may be some compensation for our ignorance, however, to have it brought home to us that Early Christianity was even richer in creative minds and personalities than the exiguous surviving evidence of tradition gives us to understand."[88]

IV. DATE

When was it written? In the absence of any clear evidence for the identity of the recipients or the author, the date of the epistle is also uncertain. A first-

85. *Ibid.*

86. The latest substantial defense of Pauline authorship is by W. Leonard, *The Authorship of the Epistle to the Hebrews.* No weight can be attached to the argument that Hebrews is the Pauline letter referred to in 2 Pet. 3:15, written "to the same Hebrew Christians" (A. Saphir, *Expository Lectures on the Epistle to the Hebrews,* I [London, 1874], p. 2); 2 Peter was not written especially to "Hebrew Christians," and the reference in 2 Pet. 3:15 is surely to Rom. 2:4. (R. P. C. Hanson, *Tradition in the Early Church* [London, 1962], p. 189, hazards the guess that 2 Pet. 3:15f. is a reference to such passages as Heb. 5:11–6:10 and 12:4-13; he compares δυσνόητά τινα of 2 Pet. 3:16 with δυσερμήνευτος of Heb. 5:11. Unlike Saphir, he attaches no apostolic authority to 2 Peter.) As for the argument that Hebrews must be Pauline because then the number of Pauline epistles is a multiple of seven (cf. E. W. Bullinger, *Number in Scripture* [London, 1913], p. 26, also pp. 37ff.), that is a curiosity which has no place in serious Bible study. And to say, as another expositor does, that "the apostolic under-current is apparent to a spiritual mind" (J. N. Darby, *Collected Writings* [London, 1867-83], XXVII, p. 615), is simply to say that the expositor *feels* that an apostle was the author, and that anyone who feels otherwise is unspiritual. Contrast A. Vanhoye: "the author of Hebrews . . . in no way voices a claim to apostolic authority" (*TRE* 14 [Berlin, 1985], p. 495, *s.v.* "Hebräerbrief").

87. The description of Apollos in Acts 18:24, ERV. Whether λόγιος means "learned" (ERV, ARV mg., NEB mg.) or "eloquent" (AV/KJV, ARV, RSV, NEB) is uncertain; it may mean either, and Apollos may have been both.

88. W. Manson, *The Epistle to the Hebrews,* p. 172. Cf. B. F. Westcott, *The Epistle to the Hebrews,* p. lxxxix.

century date is required by the external evidence (the near-quotation of the epistle by Clement of Rome *c.* A.D. 96) and by the internal evidence, according to which the author and, probably, his readers came to know the gospel from people who themselves had listened to the teaching of Jesus (2:3). If Timothy, whose release is announced in 13:23, is (as seems likely) Paul's junior colleague of that name, a date within his active lifetime is indicated, but as we do not know when Timothy was born (he was considerably younger than Paul, and may not have been out of his teens when Paul co-opted him as a fellow-missionary in A.D. 49) or when he died, this does not help us to fix a more precise date.

If the words in 12:4, "you have not yet resisted to the point of shedding your blood," are to be taken literally (as is most probable), they would mean that the community addressed had not yet been called upon to suffer death for the faith, whatever lesser forms of persecution it had endured. This would seem to rule out the Jerusalem church; and if the epistle was sent to Rome, it would have to be dated before the Neronian persecution of A.D. 65 (the minor persecution of 10:32-34 could be placed in Rome about A.D. 49).[89] If, however, the language of 12:4 is figurative (in the sense that "unto blood" does not imply the actual shedding of their blood)[90]—and this seems a less natural way to take it—then the field is much more widely open. Zahn identified the addressees as Christians in Rome under the principate of Domitian (A.D. 81-96), and the events of 10:32-34 as those of A.D. 65.[91] The view tentatively adopted in this commentary is that the epistle was written before, but not long before, the outbreak of persecution in Rome in A.D. 65.

Another line of approach to its dating is to ask how it stands in relation to the destruction of the Jerusalem temple and the cessation of the cultus in A.D. 70. True, there is no overt reference to the temple; the ritual details which figure in the epistle are mostly taken from the Old Testament account of the tabernacle. Yet in principle the tabernacle and the temple were one; the ritual of the former was the ritual of the latter. And our author writes as if the ritual were still being enacted. "The priests go into the first tent continually in the discharge of their sacred offices; but into the second goes the high priest only, and that once a year, not without blood, which he offers for himself and for the people's sins of ignorance. In this way the Holy Spirit shows that, while the first tent still stands, the way into the holy place has not yet been opened up. This is a parable with a bearing on the present time: according to this order of worship gifts and sacrifices are offered which can never make the

89. See pp. 269f. with nn. 176-83.
90. See p. 342 with n. 64 for the sense of μέχρις αἵματος ("unto blood").
91. T. Zahn, *INT,* II, E.T., p. 347; to the contrary (and rightly) E. Riggenbach, ZK, pp. 332f.: "In Heb. 10:32-34 there is not the slightest hint of martyr deaths."

worshiper perfect as regards the conscience" (9:6-9). The recurring present tense in this passage would be more pointed if this state of affairs were still going on; but it could be explained as a literary present, setting forth rather vividly the state of affairs portrayed in the Old Testament record. Again, when our author quotes Jeremiah's prophecy of the new covenant,[92] he remarks that the very mention of a new covenant implies the supersession of the old one, and adds: "And that which is becoming old and aging will soon disappear" (8:13). This would be especially apt in the period immediately preceding A.D. 70; on the other hand, it could be said that he is simply stating a general truth and applying it to the situation in hand with the implication that Jeremiah's prophecy in itself involved the impending dissolution of the old covenant and all that went with it.

Later, in mentioning the endless repetition of the sacrifices offered under the law, he says that they could never bring the offerers to perfection (that is, to immediate and permanent access to God)—"otherwise they would have ceased to be offered" (10:1f.). This could mean that the Old Testament legislation made no provision for the end of the sacrificial order, but envisaged its indefinite continuation; but if in fact the sacrificial order had come to a full stop by the time our author wrote (as it did in the summer of A.D. 70),[93] the knowledge of this fact would probably have modified his wording here. In short, there are several passages which, while they do not demand a date before A.D. 70, would have special point if in fact the Jerusalem temple was still standing and the cultus still going on; while there is no passage which suggests that sanctuary and cultus were by now things of the past.

There is also the quotation in 3:7-11 of Ps. 95 (LXX 94):7b-11 with its emphasis on the forty years of probation and provocation in the wilderness. The period of forty years is not explicitly related to the contemporary situation; but here too the language would be the more pointed if in fact the fortieth year from the crucial events of A.D. 30 were approaching.[94]

V. CANONICITY

Canonicity and authorship are in principle quite distinct, but in the early Christian centuries, as a practical issue, the canonicity of New Testament books and their apostolic authorship were frequently involved with each other, and nowhere more so than in relation to this epistle. Augustine and

---

92. Jer. 31:31ff. (see pp. 195f.).

93. Josephus (*War* 6.94) records the cessation of the daily sacrifice on August 5, A.D. 70, with a solemnity which suggests that he saw in this the fulfilment of Dan. 9:27.

94. See p. 99 with n. 57.

Jerome, as we have seen, followed Alexandrian precedent in recognizing Hebrews as one of Paul's epistles not so much because they were convinced on internal evidence that it was by him (in point of fact they entertained private doubts on the matter), as because the ascription of apostolic authorship safeguarded its canonical status.[95]

Hebrews may be said to have first received some sort of canonical status when it was incorporated by a second-century editor (at Alexandria, in all probability) into a copy of the *corpus Paulinum*.[96] From that time forth its status was not questioned in Alexandria.[97] Origen did not doubt its scriptural merit, whatever reservations he might cherish about its authorship. He wrote homilies on it but, because he knew that some churches did not accept it, he classed it as a "disputed" book. Later, Eusebius of Caesarea included it among the "acknowledged" books, although he knew of the doubts about it in the west.[98] Athanasius of Alexandria, in his thirty-ninth festal letter (A.D. 367), reckoned it as a matter of course among the "fourteen epistles of the apostle Paul" when enumerating the books of the New Testament. Even before the time of Athanasius the example of Alexandria was followed in Syria: the Syriac fathers, from Ephrem (*c.* 300-373) onward, make it clear that its canonicity and apostolicity were undisputed in their part of the world. The Peshiṭta New Testament included it from the first.

It was otherwise in the west. Some histories of the New Testament canon have not made it sufficiently plain that for a book to be known and quoted is not tantamount to its being received as canonical. This distinction is well illustrated by the history of the Epistle to the Hebrews in the west. So far as extant records go, it was known and quoted in the west some decades before it was known in the east, but the west was slow in according it canonical status. Clement of Rome knows it so well that he weaves its language into his own,[99] but there is no suggestion in his letter that Hebrews is regarded as canonical or apostolic. Hermas almost certainly knows it.[100] Valentinus ap-

---

95. See p. 17 with n. 69.

96. See p. 13 with n. 51. It occupied various positions in relation to the Pauline epistles. In 𝔓[46] (the oldest manuscript of the *corpus Paulinum*) and originally in Syria it comes second, after Romans. It follows 2 Corinthians in the Sahidic Coptic; it follows Galatians in the archetype of B. In the great uncials and at Alexandria generally it comes between Paul's letters to churches and those to individuals. In the west and later in Syria it occupied the position with which we are most familiar, after the thirteen epistles which bear Paul's name; this position reflects the long western hesitation to reckon it as a Pauline epistle. See W. H. P. Hatch, "The Position of Hebrews in the Canon of the New Testament," *HTR* 29 (1936), pp. 133-51; B. M. Metzger, *A Textual Commentary on the Greek New Testament* (London/New York, 1971), pp. 661f.

97. Pantaenus, Clement, Origen, Dionysius, Theognostus, Peter Martyr, Alexander, and Athanasius of Alexandria all attest the unanimous tradition of their church.

98. *Hist. Eccl.* 3.3.5 ("the fourteen letters of Paul are obvious and plain").

99. See p. 13, n. 53.

100. See p. 100, n. 61; p. 262 with n. 142.

pears to know it and echoes its language;[101] there are possible, though not certain, allusions to it in Justin Martyr.[102] Gaius of Rome evidently did not treat it as apostolic or canonical; neither did Irenaeus or Hippolytus. Irenaeus's position is noteworthy in view of his Asian provenance.[103] Tertullian, as we have seen, personally thought highly of it and was disposed to accord it near-apostolic authority, although he accepted Barnabas as its author. Ultimately, however, the Alexandrian position on canonicity and authorship alike triumphed in the west, and we have seen that the epistle was included in the Canon by the Synod of Hippo (393) and by the Third (397) and Sixth (419) Synods of Carthage.

"*O felix culpa!*" says W. F. Howard, suggesting that we owe the presence of Hebrews in the New Testament to "the mistaken critical judgement of the ancient Church."[104] But one may wonder whether, in fact, the intrinsic merit of the epistle would not ultimately have won a place in the canon for it even had the name of Paul never been associated with it. At least, when the question was reopened at the Reformation, the uncertainty about its authorship did not affect its canonical recognition. Luther, indeed, gave it what might be called deuterocanonical status, but this was not on account of its non-Pauline authorship but rather because of his personal estimate of its quality, for he reckoned that some "wood, straw, or hay" might be found mingled with the "gold, silver, and precious stones" which were built into its fabric.[105] Calvin, on the other hand, while he was perfectly sure that Paul was

---

101. See p. 88, n. 86 (with reference there).

102. Justin's calling Christ ἀπόστολος (*First Apology* 12:9; 63:5, 10, 14; cf. Heb. 3:1) and ἀρχιερεύς (*Dialogue with Trypho* 116:1) might denote dependence on Hebrews, as might also his designation as ἀρχιερεύς by Ignatius (Philadelphians 9:1, "the high priest who has been entrusted with the holy of holies") and probably by Polycarp (*Epistle* 12:2, "the eternal high priest").

103. See p. 16, n. 64. Eusebius ascribed to Irenaeus "a little book of various discourses in which he makes mention of the Epistle to the Hebrews and the so-called Wisdom of Solomon, setting alongside each other certain quotations from them" (*Hist. Eccl.* 5.26). Marcion, who also came from Asia Minor, did not include Hebrews in his *Apostolikon;* quite apart from the question of authorship, the whole content of the epistle would have precluded his accepting it.

104. In *The Bible in its Ancient and English Versions,* ed. H. W. Robinson (Oxford, 1940), p. 68.

105. *Preface to Hebrews* (WA, VII, pp. 344f.). "One must not place it in all things on a level with the apostolic epistles," although it contains much good instruction which is to be received "with all honor." Indeed, in commenting on Gen. 14:18-20, he calls Heb. 7:1-4 "the most trustworthy testimony of the Holy Spirit" (WA, XLII, p. 545). In the list of books in his New Testament (1522) Luther numbers the first twenty-three, "the right certain capital books," in serial order, but separates the remaining four—Hebrews, James, Jude, and Revelation—from them by a space and gives no serial number to these. Tyndale's Cologne quarto (1525) does the same (and indeed this order was followed in successive editions of the English Bible until the Great Bible of 1539 reverted to the familiar order). But there is no particular reason to think that

in no sense its author, set a high value on its authority. "I class it without hesitation among the apostolical[106] writings," he said; "I do not doubt that it has been through the craft of Satan that any have been led to dispute its authority. There is, indeed, no book in Holy Scripture which speaks so clearly of the priesthood of Christ, which so highly exalts the virtue and dignity of that only true sacrifice which He offered by His death, which so abundantly deals with the use of ceremonies as well as their abrogation, and, in a word, so fully explains that Christ is the end of the Law. Let us therefore not allow the Church of God or ourselves to be deprived of so great a benefit, but firmly defend the possession of it."[107]

The canonical quality of the epistle, having thus been so clearly and properly distinguished from the question of authorship, continues, as is most justly due, to be acknowledged by the church.

VI. HEBREWS AND THE OLD TESTAMENT

Apart from the personal notes at the end the Epistle to the Hebrews is not an epistle or letter in the strict sense of the term. Its literary character is defined for us by the author himself: it is a "word of exhortation," as he puts it in 13:22.[108] A "word of exhortation" is a form of sermon or homily, as is made plain in Acts 13:15, where the rulers of the synagogue in Pisidian Antioch invite Paul and Barnabas to speak if they have "any word of exhortation for the people." The sermon by Paul, which is summarized in the following verses, is a good example of a "word of exhortation."[109] The main difference between such a sermon and the Epistle to the Hebrews is that the former was spoken, the latter written. "It is a midrash in rhetorical Greek prose—it is a homily."[110]

A synagogue homily would be based on one or more biblical texts,

---

Tyndale shared Luther's deuterocanonical evaluation of Hebrews and the other three books; indeed, in *his* preface to Hebrews he retains Luther's reference to the "gold, silver, and precious stones" but says nothing of "wood, straw, or hay."

106. "Apostolical" in authority, not in authorship (see p. 20).

107. E.T. by W. B. Johnston (cf. p. 20, n. 85), p. 1.

108. Gk. λόγος (τῆς) παρακλήσεως. See p. 389.

109. G. Vermes classes Hebrews and the Zadokite *Admonition* in the same literary genre (*The Dead Sea Scrolls in English* [Harmondsworth, ³1987], p. 82).

110. G. Zuntz, *The Text of the Epistles*, p. 286. As an outstanding reason for so describing it Zuntz mentions its repeated use of *synkrisis*—"a traditional device of encomiastic Greek and Latin rhetoric: the person or object to be praised is placed beside outstanding specimens of a comparable kind and his, or its, superiority (ὑπεροχή) urged. . . . And so does Hebrews, in contrasting Jesus, and his Church, with angels, Moses, Melchizedek, high-priests, the synagogue, the 'heroes of faith,' etc." This *a fortiori* argument is substantially that used by the rabbis under the designation *qal wā-ḥōmer* ("light and heavy"); cf. 1:4; 3:3; 12:4; also p. 45, n. 6; p. 68, n. 4; p. 344, n. 74.

drawn by preference from the lessons for the day. Professor Aileen Guilding points out that the early chapters of Hebrews appear to be based on the readings for Pentecost in the three successive years of the triennial lectionary— Gen. 14:18–15:21 (the Melchizedek story and the covenant with Abram), Ex. 19 (the arrival at Sinai), and Num. 18 (the account of Aaron's budding rod)[111]—and on Ps. 110, which was reached at Pentecost in the third year of the triennial reciting of the Psalter.[112] She further suggests that the season between Pentecost and New Year formed the background of a piece of Christian *didachē*, possibly called "The Way," and points out that the theme of the "new and living way" is prominent in Hebrews, while Pentecostal and New Year readings are telescoped in Heb. 12:18ff. (the enrolment in heaven and divine judgment being New Year themes).[113]

The form in which the Old Testament is quoted throughout the epistle is regularly that of the Septuagint version. Insofar as we can distinguish two Septuagint recensions, corresponding in the main to the texts exhibited by the Codices A (Alexandrinus) and B (Vaticanus), about twice as many of the quotations in Hebrews agree with the A-text as with the B-text. But it is unsatisfactory to categorize Septuagint quotations in a work of the first century A.D. on the basis of manuscripts of the fourth and fifth centuries. Our author used a type of text earlier than either the A-text or the B-text as we know these from extant witnesses, and one which occasionally deviates from both.[114] He may have selected his variants (where he knew more readings than one) for interpretational suitability. These variants were sometimes borrowed from other parts of the Greek Bible or from Philo, but appear for the most part to have been introduced on his own responsibility. It has been argued on the basis of his use of certain Old Testament quotations that he was familiar with the interpretations of Philo and used some quotations in such a way as to counter these interpretations.

---

111. "Some Obscured Rubrics and Lectionary Allusions in the Psalter," *JTS*, n.s. 3 (1952), p. 53; *The Fourth Gospel and Jewish Worship* (Oxford, 1960), p. 72. If we include the readings for the following sabbaths, we have the inauguration of the "old covenant" (Ex. 24) and the ritual of the red heifer (Num. 19); cf. Heb. 9:19 (pp. 224-26). This whole question has also been examined by C. H. Cave, *The Influences of the Lectionary of the Synagogue on the Formation of the Epistle to the Hebrews* (M.A. thesis, University of Nottingham, 1960).

112. *The Fourth Gospel and Jewish Worship*, p. 100. Cf. G. W. Buchanan, *To the Hebrews*, AB, p. 1: "The document entitled 'To the Hebrews' is a homiletical midrash based on Ps. 110."

113. *The Fourth Gospel and Jewish Worship*, p. 72.

114. This has been worked out in detail by K. J. Thomas, *The Use of the Septuagint in the Epistle to the Hebrews* (Ph.D. dissertation, University of Manchester, 1959), and "The Old Testament Citations in Hebrews," *NTS* 11 (1964-65), pp. 303-25, and by J. C. McCullough, *Hebrews and the Old Testament* (Ph.D. dissertation, Queen's University, Belfast, 1971), and "The Old Testament Quotations in Hebrews," *NTS* 26 (1979-80), pp. 363-79. See also G. Howard, "Hebrews and the Old Testament Quotations," *NovT* 10 (1968), pp. 208-16.

The variations which he introduced into the Septuagint text have to some extent influenced the form in which the Septuagint is quoted by early Christian writers, and even the text of some manuscripts of the Septuagint, but in extremely few instances (not more than two) do they appear to have influenced the A-text or B-text.

From time to time, especially in details of sacrificial ritual and sanctuary installations, the epistle gives some evidence of a strictly limited use of an oral midrash on the Pentateuch.[115]

To our author the Old Testament is a divine oracle from first to last; not only passages which in their original setting are the direct utterance of God (such as Ps. 110:4, "Thou art a priest for ever . . .") but others are treated as spoken by God—like the words of Moses in Deut. 32:43 (Heb. 1:6) and the words of psalmists concerning the messengers of God (Ps. 104:4, quoted in Heb. 1:7), addressed to a royal bridegroom (Ps. 45:6f., quoted in Heb. 1:8f.), or addressed to God (Ps. 102:25-27, quoted in Heb. 1:10-12). Heb. 3:7 introduces a quotation from Ps. 95:7-11 with the words "as the Holy Spirit says"—words which apply not only to the divine utterance quoted in Ps. 95:8ff., but to the psalmist's cry which precedes them: "If only you would listen to his voice today!" (Ps. 95:7b). In the details of the Old Testament sanctuary the Holy Spirit signifies spiritual truths for the present time (Heb. 9:8). The psalmist's words of consecration and obedience in Ps. 40:6-8 are spoken by the Messiah "at his coming into the world" (Heb. 10:5-7).[116] The narrative statement of Gen. 2:2 ("God . . . rested on the seventh day from all his works") is treated as a divine utterance in Heb. 4:4.

The Old Testament writings are treated by our author as a *mashal*, a parable or mystery which awaits its explanation,[117] and the explanation given in the pages of the epistle takes the form of messianic typology. "We never find

---

115. Cf. 7:5, on the receiving of tithes; 7:27, on the high priest's daily sacrificial duties; 9:4, on the position of the incense-altar and contents of the ark; 9:19, on the institution of the first covenant; 9:21, on the purifying of all the sanctuary vessels with blood; 12:21, on the Sinai theophany (with exposition and notes *ad loc.*).

116. Cf. B. F. Westcott, *The Epistle to the Hebrews*, pp. 471-97; J. van der Ploeg, "L'exégèse de l'Ancien Testament dans l'Épître aux Hébreux," *RB* 54 (1947), pp. 187-228; R. A. Stewart, *The Old Testament Usage in Philo, Rabbinic Writings and Hebrews* (M.Litt. diss., University of Cambridge, 1947); C. Spicq, *L'Épître aux Hébreux*, I, pp. 330-50; R. M. Grant, *The Letter and the Spirit* (London, 1957); F. C. Synge, *Hebrews and the Scriptures;* M. Barth, "The Old Testament in Hebrews," in *Current Issues in New Testament Interpretation*, ed. W. Klassen and G. F. Snyder (New York, 1962), pp. 53-78; A. T. Hanson, "Christ in the Old Testament according to Hebrews," *SE* 2 = *TU* 87 (Berlin, 1964), pp. 303-407; F. Schröger, *Der Verfasser des Hebräerbriefs als Schriftausleger* (Regensburg, 1968); G. Hughes, *Hebrews and Hermeneutics*, SNTSM 36 (Cambridge, 1979).

117. Cf. the *rāz-pesher* ("mystery-interpretation") pattern in biblical apocalyptic and in Qumran exegesis, as well as in Mark 4:11f. See F. F. Bruce, *Biblical Exegesis in the Qumran Texts* (London, 1960), pp. 7-11.

in our author the least trace of that allegorical exegesis which was to remain, alas, the specialty of the Alexandrian school"[118] and which is illustrated so abundantly in the works of Philo, a generation or so earlier than our epistle. This contrast is the more marked because of the affinities in thought and language which have otherwise been traced between our author and Philo.[119] But Philo treats the Old Testament characters and incidents as allegories setting forth eternal principles of ethics and metaphysics, while our author treats them as types of Christ and the gospel, temporary foreshadowings of the fulfilment which has now taken place once for all. By Philo, for example, Melchizedek is allegorized as Reason;[120] by our author he is interpreted as a type of Christ, "made like the Son of God" (7:3). There is much in common between the two writers' detailed exegetical procedures—both, for example, emphasize that Melchizedek, king of Salem, is "king of righteousness" and "king of peace"[121]—but their basic hermeneutical principles are quite distinct. The historical perspective of the Old Testament is well preserved in Hebrews because our author thinks of the age of anticipation as foreshadowing the age of fulfilment; he finds it necessary to look before and after. In chs. 3 and 4 he distinguishes between the wilderness period, when the Israelites looked forward to a "rest" which in fact they did not fully experience when they entered Canaan under Joshua; the age of David, "after such a long time" (4:7), when the same "rest" was still spoken of; and the present time, when there still remains "a sabbath rest for the people of God" (4:9). And in ch. 11 he shows a clear appreciation of the historical sequence of the Old Testament, as men and women of faith drew ever nearer to the time when God would fulfil the promises which they themselves greeted "from afar" (11:13).

The framework of much of our author's argument is supplied by quotations from the Psalter. Apart from the quotations from Pss. 2, 104, 45, 102, and 110 in ch. 1, we may think of the use made of Ps. 8:4-6 in ch. 2, of Ps. 95:7-11 in chs. 3 and 4, of Ps. 110:4 in 5:6-10; 6:20; 7:24, and of Ps. 40:6-8 in 10:5-10. First a section of the Psalter is quoted more or less verbatim, and then words and phrases from the quotation are incorporated into the following exposition, somewhat in the manner now familiar to us from the *pesher* texts at Qumran.[122] Again, more than once he starts a phase of his argument with a psalm quotation and then turns to other Old Testament passages deal-

118. C. Spicq, *Hébreux*, I, p. 61.

119. Spicq's discussion of the Philonism of Hebrews (*Hébreux*, I, pp. 39-91) must be corrected by reference to R. Williamson, *Philo and the Epistle to the Hebrews* (Leiden, 1970). See also S. G. Sowers, *The Hermeneutics of Philo and Hebrews* (Zürich, 1965). Cf. p. 33, n. 134.

120. *Leg. Alleg.* 3.82; see p. 158, n. 14.

121. Philo, *Leg. Alleg.* 3.79; Heb. 7:2.

122. Cf. S. Kistemaker, *The Psalm Citations in the Epistle to the Hebrews* (Amsterdam, 1961).

ing with the same theme for material to elaborate his argument.[123] Thus he elaborates his exegesis of Ps. 95:7-11 with references to the Pentateuchal narrative of the wilderness wanderings (Heb. 3:12ff.); and his exegesis of Ps. 110:4 by reference to the narrative of Melchizedek in Gen. 14 (Heb. 7:1ff.).

VII. HEBREWS AND THE GOSPEL

The purpose of our author's exegesis of Old Testament scripture, as of his general argument, is to establish the finality of the gospel by contrast with all that went before it (more particularly, by contrast with the Levitical cultus), as the way of perfection, the way which alone leads people to God without any barrier or interruption of access. He establishes the finality of Christianity by establishing the supremacy of Christ, in his person and in his work.[124]

As regards his person, Christ is greater than all the servants and spokesmen of God who have gone before—not only greater than other human servants and spokesmen (even Moses) but greater than angels. For he is the Son of God, his agent in creating and maintaining the universe, who yet became the Son of Man and submitted to humiliation and death. He is now exalted above all the heavens, enthroned at God's right hand, and he lives forever there as his people's representative.

The special aspect of the person and ministry of Christ which is emphasized in this epistle is his priesthood. This epistle, in fact, is the only New Testament document which expressly calls him a priest, although his priesthood is implied in others.[125] One source of our author's priestly Christology is the Old Testament: if the ruler addressed in Ps. 110 is the Davidic Messiah, as was believed by Jews and Christians alike, then it is the Messiah who is acclaimed in v. 4 of that psalm as "a priest for ever after the order of Melchizedek"—the perfect priest-king.[126] But the mere citation of an Old Testa-

123. Cf. R. Rendall, "The Method of the Writer to the Hebrews in Using Old Testament Quotations," *EQ* 27 (1955), pp. 214-20.

124. Cf. E. Riehm, *Der Lehrbegriff des Hebräerbriefs;* E. Ménégoz, *La Théologie de l'Épître aux Hébreux* (Paris, 1894); G. Milligan, *The Theology of the Epistle to the Hebrews* (Edinburgh, 1899); H. A. A. Kennedy, *The Theology of the Epistles* (London, 1919), pp. 182-221; R. V. G. Tasker, *The Gospel in the Epistle to the Hebrews* (London, 1950); G. Theissen, *Untersuchungen zum Hebräerbrief* (Gütersloh, 1969); H. Zimmermann, *Das Bekenntnis der Hoffnung,* BBB 47 (Cologne, 1977).

125. Especially in Revelation, where the garment reaching to the feet and the golden sash around his breast (1:13) are high-priestly vestments. See p. 30, n. 127.

126. Cf. A. J. B. Higgins, "Priest and Messiah," *VT* 3 (1953), pp. 321-36; "The Priestly Messiah," *NTS* 13 (1966-67), pp. 221-39; O. Cullmann, *The Christology of the New Testament,* E.T. (London, 1959), pp. 83-107. The inference from v. 1 to v. 4 of Ps. 110 is not made explicitly (and perhaps not even implied) in the Synoptic Gospels or anywhere else in the NT outside this epistle; our author may well have been the first Christian to make it.

ment text would have been pointless if the character and work of Christ had not had a recognizably priestly quality. And our author stresses repeatedly Jesus' qualifications to be his people's effective high priest—not only was he personally "holy, free from guile and defilement" (7:26) but having been tested "in all respects" as his people are, he can sympathize with them and supply the help they need in the hour of trial (4:15f.; 2:18).

This presentation of Jesus agrees with the testimony of the Gospels. In Luke 22:32 he prays for Peter, lest his faith should fail; in John 17 we hear him pray his prayer of consecration as he offers up his life to God on his followers' behalf, and his prayer of intercession for them that they may fulfil their witness in the world as he has fulfilled his.[127] Nor is this kind of activity confined to the earthly phase; we have his assurance in Luke 12:8: "Every one who acknowledges me before men, the Son of man will also acknowledge him before the angels of God."[128]

All this was appreciated in the early church. Stephen, condemned by the Sanhedrin, makes his confident appeal to the heavenly court, where he sees as his advocate "the Son of man standing at the right hand of God" (Acts 7:56).[129] To the same effect Paul challenges anyone to bring a charge against God's elect, since "it is Christ Jesus who died, yes, who was raised from the dead, who is at the right hand of God, who indeed intercedes for us" (Rom. 8:34).[130] And John, while he writes to his "little children" to guard against their sinning, reminds them that nevertheless, "if any one sins, we have an Advocate with the Father, Jesus Christ the righteous; and it is he who atones for our sins . . ." (1 John 2:1f.). Here the reference to atonement implies a priestly element in the advocacy and intercession of the risen Christ.[131] Our

127. C. Spicq finds a Johannine origin for the priestly portrayal of Christ elaborated in Hebrews; cf. his article "L'origine johannique de la conception du Christ-prêtre dans l'Épître aux Hébreux," in *Aux sources de la tradition chrétienne*, M. Goguel *FS* (Paris, 1950), pp. 258-69; in addition to the "high-priestly" prayer of John 17 he points to the seamless robe of John 19:23 as a high-priestly garment (cf. p. 29, n. 125). See also P. Giles, *Jesus, the High Priest* (Bognor Regis, 1984), with O. Cullmann, *Christology*, p. 105, for comments and further bibliography.

128. Cf. Matt. 10:32. In the Gospels the Son of Man acts both as παράκλητος ("advocate") and as κατήγορος ("prosecutor") in the heavenly court; for the latter rôle see Matt. 10:33; Mark 8:38; Luke 12:9. See on this general subject A. J. B. Higgins, "The OT and some aspects of NT Christology," in *Promise and Fulfilment*, S. H. Hooke *FS* (Edinburgh, 1963), pp. 128-41.

129. Cf. C. F. D. Moule, "From Defendant to Judge—and Deliverer," *Studiorum Novi Testamenti Societas* Bulletin 3 (Oxford, 1952), pp. 40-53, reprinted in *The Phenomenon of the New Testament*, SBT 2.1 (London, 1967), pp. 82-99.

130. Behind the last two clauses lies a unified exegesis of Ps. 110:1 and Isa. 53:12. The affirmations of faith are a reply to the challenge: "Who shall bring any charge against God's elect?" (Rom. 8:33)—the whole passage being an echo of the Servant of Yahweh's challenge in Isa. 50:7-9.

131. T. W. Manson (*Ministry and Priesthood* [London, 1958], p. 48, n. 16) expresses the view that in this respect the writer of Hebrews was anticipated by Paul in Rom. 3:21-26, and refers to his article *"ΙΛΑΣΤΗΡΙΟΝ,"* in *JTS* 46 (1945), pp. 1-10.

author then was not a complete innovator in presenting Christ as his people's high priest, but he elaborates the priesthood of Christ in quite a distinctive manner, and does so in order to establish that in Christ and the gospel God has spoken his final and perfect word to mankind.

Arguments of various kinds are adduced to show that the priesthood of Christ is not only superior to that of the Aaronic succession, but belongs to an entirely different order from theirs. It belongs to the new covenant foretold by Jeremiah—a new covenant marked by better promises and a better hope than the old covenant of Sinai, under which the Aaronic priests ministered. In particular, the priesthood of Christ is associated with a better sacrifice than any that went before, and is discharged in a better sanctuary than that prescribed in the Levitical cultus.

Priesthood and sacrifice are inseparable entities. The Aaronic priests offered up sacrifices repeatedly, and our author pays particular attention to the annual sin offering presented on the nation's behalf by the high priest on the Day of Atonement. But those animal sacrifices could not meet the real need of men and women. A sin-stained conscience is a barrier to communion with God, and the cleansing of the conscience could not be effected by such sacrifices as the Levitical cultus provided. But Christ exercises his priestly ministry on the basis of a real and efficacious sacrifice—"his own sacrifice" (Heb. 9:26). The nature of this sacrifice our author finds expressed in the language of Ps. 40:6-8, where someone who knows the uselessness of animal sacrifices dedicates his life to God for the obedient accomplishment of his will. This language is recognized as the language of Christ "at his coming into the world" (Heb. 10:5). In the body which God prepared for him he fulfilled the will of God, and at the end it was that consecrated body, that obedient life, which he offered up to God in death. Such a sacrifice must necessarily be acceptable to God, but it is not only acceptable to God in itself; it effectually cleanses in heart and conscience those who embrace Christ as their high priest with God. By the will of God, fulfilled in death as in life by Christ, his people "have been sanctified once for all through the offering of the body of Jesus Christ" (10:10) and have "freedom of access into the holy place by Jesus' blood" (10:19). It is his life, offered up to God, which is alternatively spoken of as his "body" or his "blood." And it is thanks to the efficacy of his sacrifice in the lives of his people that the new covenant comes into being, in which God undertakes to implant his law in their hearts (as it was implanted in the heart of Christ) and to remember their sins no more.[132]

---

132. T. F. Torrance ("Doctrinal Consensus on Holy Communion," *SJT* 15 [1962], pp. 4-21) distinguishes three aspects of the redemption or atonement wrought by Christ which he relates respectively to three Hebrew verbs—*pādāh*, the "dramatic" (i.e., the "Christus Victor") aspect; *kipper*, the "cultic-forensic" aspect; *gā'al*, the "incarnational" aspect. In different Prot-

This efficacy of the sacrifice of Christ on behalf of others could be readily inferred neither from Ps. 110 nor from Ps. 40. It was, of course, already a matter of vital experience for a whole generation of believers when our author wrote; they knew (however they expressed it) that through the Christ who died and rose again they had been inwardly purified from the defilement of sin and emancipated from its domination. Our author expresses this in terms of sacrifice and priesthood, but it was no new thing which he thus expressed.

He who offers up his life to God in unreserved consecration is both priest and sacrifice at once. This is true of the speaker in Ps. 40:6-8; it is even more explicitly true of the Isaianic Servant of the Lord, whose willing self-offering "to bear the sins of many" is interpreted of the work of Christ in Heb. 9:28. The Servant is introduced as a priest, destined to "sprinkle many nations" (Isa. 52:15), and he is equally a sacrifice, yielding himself up as "an offering for sin" (Isa. 53:10). His portrayal was fulfilled in history when "the Son of man also came not to be served, but to serve, and to give his life a ransom for many" (Mark 10:45). In this spirit Jesus accepted death, and the redemptive and cleansing efficacy of his death in the lives of his followers has been a matter of plain experience for over nineteen centuries. Our author is not airily theorizing when he speaks of priesthood and sacrifice, but expressing basic realities. Such a sacrifice as Christ's needs no repetition; its "once-for-all" character involves the finality of the gospel.

It is because of his concentration on the priestly aspect of Christ's work that our author has so much to say of his death and exaltation, but so little of his resurrection.[133] The two principal moments in the great sin offering of Old Testament times were the shedding of the victim's blood in the court of the sanctuary and the presentation of its blood inside the sanctuary. In the antitype these two moments were seen to correspond to the death of Christ on

---

estant traditions one or another of these aspects is emphasized to a point where insufficient justice is done to the rest. "A new and deeper biblical wholeness" could help to bring them together "through a more adequate doctrine of atonement. It has long been my conviction [he adds] that joint study of the *Epistle to the Hebrews* would have an immense part to play in such a rapprochement" (p. 9). A few items from the vast literature on priesthood and sacrifice with special relation to his epistle are J. Denney, *The Death of Christ* (London, [6]1907), pp. 204-40; A. Nairne, *The Epistle of Priesthood*; D. K. Burns, "The Epistle to the Hebrews," *ExT* 47 (1935-36), pp. 184-89; V. Taylor, *The Atonement in New Testament Teaching* (London, 1940), pp. 147-90; A. M. Stibbs, *The Meaning of the Word "Blood" in Scripture* (London, 1947), and *The Finished Work of Christ* (London, 1952); G. J. C. Marchant, "Sacrifice in the Epistle to the Hebrews," *EQ* 20 (1948), pp. 196-210; C. F. D. Moule, *The Sacrifice of Christ* (London, 1956); S. S. Smalley, "The Atonement in the Epistle to the Hebrews," *EQ* 33 (1961), pp. 34-43; L. L. Morris, *The Apostolic Preaching of the Cross* (Exeter, [3]1965), pp. 90-111, 121-28, 184-213; *The Cross in the New Testament* (Grand Rapids, 1965), pp. 270-308; A. Vanhoye, "L'oblation sacerdotale du Christ dans l'épître aux Hébreux," *Didaskalia* 14 (1984), pp. 11-29.

133. Cf. 13:20 (p. 388). But see pp. 86f. (on 2:15).

the cross and his appearance at the right hand of God. In this pattern the resurrection, as generally proclaimed in the apostolic preaching, finds no separate place.

The presence of God, the heavenly sanctuary, where Christ now ministers as his people's high priest, is naturally superior to any holy place on earth, and the priesthood which is exercised in the former is naturally superior to any priesthood which is exercised in one of the latter sanctuaries. The earthly sanctuary, where the Aaronic priests ministered, is but a material copy of "the true tent, pitched by the Lord, not by any human hand" (8:2). Here it is natural to recognize the influence of Platonic idealism in our author's thought and language, mediated through Philo and Alexandrian culture in general; and such influence need not be ruled out.[134] For Plato and his followers material and sensible objects are not the ultimate realities; they are but copies of archetypes or "ideas" laid up in heaven, which can be discerned only by the intellect.[135] But the idea of the earthly sanctuary as a copy of the heavenly dwelling-place of God goes back far beyond Plato's day. To Israel's neighbors in Old Testament times this idea was commonplace; and our author finds Old Testament authority for his view of the earthly sanctuary as a copy of the heavenly in the direction given to Moses to construct the tabernacle in all respects according to the model shown him by God on Mount Sinai.[136] This view of the relation of the earthly and heavenly sanctuaries finds frequent expression in apocalyptic literature, not least in the New Testament book of Revelation.

In the heavenly and eternal sanctuary where Christ ministers, his people inevitably enjoy more direct and permanent access to God through him than would be possible in any earthly and material shrine. But just how is this heavenly and eternal sanctuary envisaged? We must not think that because our author speaks of Jesus as having "passed through the heavens" and

---

134. It is going too far, however, to say with H. von Soden that "the Philonic logology is the armory for the Christology of the Epistle" (*Der Brief an die Hebräer*, HCNT, III [Freiburg, 1899], p. 6). He regards our author as the epoch-making man who brought Alexandrianism into the service of Christianity. Cf. J. B. Carpzov, *Sacrae exercitationes in epistolam ad Hebraeos ex Philone Alexandrino* (Amsterdam, 1750); E. Ménégoz, *Théologie*, pp. 197ff.; J. Cabantous, *Philon et l'Épître aux Hébreux* (Montauban, 1895); C. Spicq, *L'Épître aux Hébreux*, I, pp. 39-91; J. Héring, "Eschatologie biblique et idéalisme platonicien," in *The Background of the New Testament and its Eschatology* [C. H. Dodd *FS*], ed. W. D. Davies and D. Daube (Cambridge, 1956), pp. 444-63; S. G. Sowers, *The Hermeneutics of Philo and Hebrews;* R. Williamson, *Philo and the Epistle to the Hebrews;* L. K. K. Dey, *The Intermediary World and Patterns of Perfection in Philo and Hebrews*, SBLDS 25 (Missoula, MT, 1975).

135. With this is associated the Platonic theory of knowledge as remembrance (ἀνάμνησις); the soul remembers the perfect archetypes which it saw in its earlier existence in the supracelestial realm and recognizes things in this world as imperfect copies of these. Cf. p. 185 with nn. 33-35.

136. 8:5 (p. 184 with nn. 29, 30).

having "sat down at the right hand of the throne of God" he thought of the heavenly sanctuary as being, in reverse, a glorified replica of the sanctuary on earth, established in perpetuity on some higher plane. He uses pictorial language indeed, but uses it to denote realities of the spiritual order, where men and women, inwardly purified from a polluting conscience, draw near to God to worship him in spirit and in truth. This "perfection" is the inauguration of the eschatology which is soon to be consummated.[137] The sanctuary in which they worship God through Christ is the fellowship of the new covenant; it consists in the communion of saints. The house of God, over which Christ, as his Son, is Lord, comprises his people, "if we maintain our confidence and the hope in which we boast" (3:6). Our author in his own terms communicates the truth expressed by Paul when he speaks of Jewish and Gentile believers, made one in Christ, as having "access in one Spirit unto the Father . . . built together for a habitation of God in the Spirit" (Eph. 2:18, 22), or by Peter when he describes how those who have come to Christ "are built up a spiritual house, to be a holy priesthood, to offer up spiritual sacrifices, acceptable to God through Jesus Christ" (1 Pet. 2:5). It is the same truth which John sees consummated in the Apocalypse, when he describes the appearance of the glorified church on earth and hears a voice proclaiming that now the blessings of the new covenant are worldwide in their scope: "Behold, the tabernacle of God is with men, and he shall dwell with them, and they shall be his peoples, and God himself shall be with them, and be their God" (Rev. 21:3).

The Epistle to the Hebrews is no intruder into the New Testament, but makes its proper and indispensable contribution to the canonical literature of the Christian church.

VIII. SELECT BIBLIOGRAPHY

A. SURVEYS

Bruce, F. F. " 'To the Hebrews': A Document of Roman Christianity?" *ANRW* II.25.4 (Berlin/New York, 1987), pp. 3496-3521.

Buchanan, G. W. "The Present State of Scholarship on Hebrews," in *Christianity, Judaism and Other Greco-Jewish Cults: Studies for Morton Smith at Sixty*, ed. J. Neusner, I (Leiden, 1975), pp. 299-330.

---

137. Cf. 4:9; 9:27f.; 10:25, 36ff.; 12:26f.; 13:14. See C. K. Barrett, "The Eschatology of the Epistle to the Hebrews," in *The Background of the New Testament and its Eschatology*, ed. W. D. Davies and D. Daube, pp. 363-93; B. Klappert, *Die Eschatologie des Hebräerbriefs*, TEH 156 (Munich, 1969); also P. J. Du Plessis, *ΤΕΛΕΙΟΣ : The Idea of Perfection in the New Testament* (Kampen, 1959); D. G. Peterson, *Hebrews and Perfection*, SNTSM 47 (Cambridge, 1982).

Feld, H. *Der Hebräerbrief,* Erträge der Forschung 228 (Darmstadt, 1985).
Grässer, E. "Der Hebräerbrief, 1938-1963," *TRu* NF 30 (1964), pp. 138-236.
Spicq, C. *L'Épître aux Hébreux,* ÉB (Paris, ³1952), I, pp. 379-411 (*c.* 200-1950); "Paul, 5 (Épîtres attribuées à)," *DBSup,* VII (Paris, 1966), pp. 272-79 (1900-1961); *L'Épître aux Hébreux,* Sources Bibliques (Paris, 1977), pp. 44-54 (1961-77).
Vanhoye, A. "Hebräerbrief," *TRE,* XIV (Berlin/New York, 1985), pp. 494-505.

B. EDITIONS, COMMENTARIES, AND EXPOSITORY STUDIES*

*Alford, H. *The Greek Testament,* Vol. IV, Part I (Cambridge, 1870), pp. 1-87 (Prolegomena), 1-273 (Text and Commentary).
Anderson, R. *The Hebrews Epistle* (London, 1911).
Andrews, H. T. "Hebrews," in *The Abingdon Bible Commentary* (New York, 1929), pp. 1295-1326.
Andriessen, P., and Lenglet, A. *De Brief aan de Hebreeën,* Het Nieuwe Testament (Roermond, 1971).
*Attridge, H. W. *The Epistle to the Hebrews,* Hermeneia (Philadelphia, 1989).
Barclay, W. *The Letter to the Hebrews.* The Daily Study Bible (Edinburgh, ³1975).
*Bengel, J. A. *Gnomon Novi Testamenti* (Tübingen, 1734; repr. London, 1862); E.T. by A. R. Fausset, *Gnomon of the New Testament,* IV (Edinburgh, ²1877), pp. 333-502.
*Blass, F. *(Barnabas) Brief an die Hebräer: Text mit Angabe der Rhythmen* (Halle, 1903).
*Bleek, F. *Der Brief an die Hebräer,* I-III (Berlin, 1828, 1836, 1840).
Bonsirven, J. *Épître aux Hébreux.* Verbum Salutis (Paris, 1943).
Bowman, J. W. *Hebrews, James, I & II Peter.* Layman's Bible Commentary (London, 1962).
*Braun, H. *An die Hebräer,* HNT 14 (Tübingen, 1984).
Brown, J. *An Exposition of Hebrews* (Edinburgh, 1862; repr. London, 1961).
Brown, R. *Christ Above All: The Message of Hebrews* (Leicester, 1982).
Bruce, A. B. *The Epistle to the Hebrews: The First Apology for Christianity* (Edinburgh, 1899).
Buchanan, G. W. *To the Hebrews,* AB (Garden City, NY, 1972).
Calvin J. *Commentary on the Epistle to the Hebrews,* first edition, Latin

---

*Bibliographical entries marked with an asterisk are based on the Greek text.

(Geneva, 1549); E.T. by W. B. Johnston in *The Epistle of Paul the Apostle to the Hebrews and the First and Second Epistles of St. Peter* (Edinburgh, 1963), pp. ix-xiv, 1-216.

Darby, J. N. *Brief Analysis of the Epistle to the Hebrews. Collected Writings* (London, 1867-83), XV, pp. 308-66.

Darby, J. N. *Notes from Lectures on the Epistle to the Hebrews. Collected Writings,* XXVII, pp. 497-615.

Darby, J. N. *Notes on the Epistle to the Hebrews. Collected Writings,* XXVIII, pp. 1-51.

Davidson, A. B. *The Epistle to the Hebrews.* Handbooks for Bible Classes (Edinburgh, 1882).

Davies, J. H. *A Letter to Hebrews,* CBC (Cambridge, 1967).

*Delitzsch, F. *Commentary on the Epistle to the Hebrews,* E.T., 2 vols. (Edinburgh, 1872).

*Dods, M. "The Epistle to the Hebrews," *EGT,* IV (London, 1910), pp. 219-381.

Edwards, T. C. *The Epistle to the Hebrews,* ExpB (London, 1888).

Gayford, S. C. "The Epistle to the Hebrews," in *A New Commentary on Holy Scripture,* ed. C. Gore (London, 1928), NT, pp. 596-627.

Grant, F. C. *The Epistle to the Hebrews,* Harper's Annotated Bible Series (New York, 1956).

*Grosheide, F. W. *De Brief aan de Hebreeën,* in *De Brief aan de Hebreeën en de Brief van Jakobus.* Commentaar op het Nieuwe Testament (Kampen, 1955), pp. 5-322.

Guthrie, D. *The Letter to the Hebrews,* TNTC (Leicester, 1983).

Haering, T. *Der Brief an die Hebräer* (Stuttgart, 1925).

Hagner, D. A. *Hebrews,* GNC (San Francisco, 1983).

Haldane, J. A. *Notes on Exposition of Hebrews* (London, 1860).

Héring, J. *The Epistle to the Hebrews,* E.T. (London, 1970).

Hewitt, T. *The Epistle to the Hebrews,* TNTC (London, 1960).

Hofmann, J. C. K. von. *Der Brief an die Hebräer* (Nördlingen, 1873).

Holmes, W. H. G. *The Epistle to the Hebrews.* Indian Church Commentaries (London, 1919).

Hugedé, N. *Le sacerdoce du Fils. Commentaire de l'Épître aux Hébreux* (Paris, 1983).

Hughes, P. E. *A Commentary on the Epistle to the Hebrews* (Grand Rapids, 1977).

*Isaacs, W. H. *The Epistle to the Hebrews* (Oxford, 1933).

Javet, J. S. *Dieu nous parla. Commentaire sur l'Épître aux Hébreux* (Neuchâtel/Paris, 1945).

Jewett, R. *Letter to the Pilgrims. A Commentary on the Epistle to the Hebrews* (New York, 1981).

Kelly, W. *The Epistle to the Hebrews* (London, 1905).

Kistemaker, S. J. *Exposition of the Epistle to the Hebrews,* NTC (Grand Rapids/Welwyn, 1984).

Kuss, O. *Der Brief an die Hebräer,* RNT (Regensburg, 1953, ²1966).

Lang, G. H. *The Epistle to the Hebrews* (London, 1951).

Laubach, F. *Der Brief an die Hebräer,* Wuppertaler Studienbibel (Wuppertal, 1967, ⁷1977).

Lenski, R. C. H. *The Interpretation of the Epistle to the Hebrews and the Epistle of James* (Columbus, Ohio, 1937, ³1960).

Lincoln, W. *Lectures on the Epistle to the Hebrews* (London, 1873).

Lindsay, W. *Lectures on Hebrews,* 2 vols. (Edinburgh, 1867).

Lünemann, G. *Critical and Exegetical Handbook to the Epistle to the Hebrews,* E.T. (Edinburgh, 1883).

Luther, M. *Lectures on the Epistle to the Hebrews,* delivered in 1517-18 (WA, LVII, 1939, Part 3, pp. 1-238), E.T. by J. Atkinson in *Luther: Early Theological Works,* Library of Christian Classics, XVI (London, 1962), pp. 19-250.

McCaul, J. B. *The Epistle to the Hebrews: A Paraphrastic Commentary, with Illustrations from Philo, the Targums, the Mishna and Gemara,* etc. (London, 1871).

*Michel, O. *Der Brief an die Hebräer,* MK (Göttingen, 1949, ⁷1975).

*Moffatt, J. *The Epistle to the Hebrews,* ICC (Edinburgh, 1924).

Montefiore, H. W. *A Commentary on the Epistle to the Hebrews,* HNTC (New York/London, 1964).

Morgan, G. C. *God's Last Word to Man* (London, 1936).

Murray, A. *The Holiest of All: An Exposition of the Epistle to the Hebrews* (London, 1895; repr. 1924).

Nairne, A. *The Epistle of Priesthood* (Edinburgh, 1913).

Nairne, A. *The Alexandrine Gospel* (London, 1917).

*Nairne, A. *The Epistle to the Hebrews,* CGT (Cambridge, 1917).

Nairne, A. *The Epistle to the Hebrews,* CBSC (Cambridge, 1921).

Narborough, F. D. V. *The Epistle to the Hebrews,* Clarendon Bible (Oxford, 1930).

Neil, W. *The Epistle to the Hebrews.* Torch Commentaries (London, 1955).

*Olshausen, H., and Ebrard, J. H. A. *Biblical Commentary on the Epistle to the Hebrews,* E.T. (Edinburgh, 1853).

Owen, J. *Exposition of Hebrews,* 4 vols. (London, 1668-74), ed. W. H. Goold (Edinburgh, 1855; repr. Evansville, IN, 1960).

Peake, A. S. *The Epistle to the Hebrews,* CentB (Edinburgh, 1914).

Pink, A. W. *An Exposition of Hebrews* (Grand Rapids, 1954).

Purdy, A. C. "The Epistle to the Hebrews," in *IB*, XI (New York, 1955), pp. 575-763.

*Rendall, F. *The Epistle to the Hebrews* (London, 1883).

Reuss, E. *L'Épître aux Hébreux* (Paris, 1878).

*Riggenbach, E. *Der Brief an die Hebräer*, ZK (Leipzig, 1913, ²,³1922; repr. Wuppertal, 1987).

Robinson, T. H. *The Epistle to the Hebrews*, MNTC (London, 1933).

Saphir, A. *Expository Lectures on the Epistle to the Hebrews*, 2 vols. (London, 1874-75).

Schlatter, A. "Der Brief an die Hebräer," in *Erläuterungen zum Neuen Testament*, IX (Stuttgart, ⁵1950), pp. 220-436.

Schneider, J. *The Letter to the Hebrews*, E.T. (Grand Rapids, 1957).

Scott, E. F. *The Epistle to the Hebrews: Its Doctrine and Significance* (Edinburgh, 1922).

Snell, A. *New and Living Way* (London, 1959).

*Soden, H. von. "Der Brief an die Hebräer," in *HCNT*, ed. H. J. Holtzmann, III (Freiburg, 1899), pp. 1-114.

*Spicq, C. *L'Épître aux Hébreux*, ÉB, 2 vols. (Paris, 1952).[1]

Spicq, C. *L'Épître aux Hébreux*, Sources Bibliques (Paris, 1977).

Strack, H. L., and Billerbeck, P. *Kommentar zum Neuen Testament aus Talmud und Midrasch*, III (Munich, 1926), pp. 671-750.

Strathmann, H. *Der Brief an die Hebräer*. NTD 9 (Göttingen, 1935, ⁸1963).

Strobel, A. *Der Brief an die Hebräer*, NTD 9 (Göttingen, 1975).

Stuart, M. *A Commentary on the Epistle to the Hebrews* (London, 1937).

Thomas, W. H. G. *Let Us Go On* (London, 1923).

Vanhoye, A. *L'Épître aux Hébreux: Texte grec structuré* (Fano, 1966).

Vanhoye, A. *Situation du Christ: Épître aux Hébreux 1 et 2*, LD 58 (Paris, 1969).

*Vaughan, C. J. *The Epistle to the Hebrews* (London, 1890).

Vine, W. E. *The Epistle to the Hebrews* (London, 1952).

*Weiss, B. *Der Brief an die Hebräer*, MK (Göttingen, 1897).

*Westcott, B. F. *The Epistle to the Hebrews* (London, ²1892).

*Wettstein, J. J. *Hē Kainē Diathēkē*, II (Amsterdam, 1752), pp. 383-446.

Wickham, E. C. *The Epistle to the Hebrews*, WC (London, ²1922).

Wilson, G. B. *Hebrews: A Digest of Reformed Comment* (London, 1970).

Wilson, R. McL. *Hebrews*, NCBC (Grand Rapids/Basingstoke, 1987).

*Windisch, H. *Der Hebräerbrief*, HNT (Tübingen, 1931).

Wuest, K. S. *Hebrews in the Greek New Testament for the English Reader* (Grand Rapids, 1947).

---

1. This is the work cited as Spicq, *L'Épître aux Hébreux* (or simply *Hébreux*) throughout this commentary.

C. OTHER WORKS

Anderson, C. P. "The Epistle to the Hebrews and the Pauline Letter Collection," *HTR* 59 (1966), pp. 429-38.

Anderson, C. P. "Hebrews among the Letters of Paul," *SR* 5 (1975), pp. 258-66.

Appel, H. *Der Hebräerbrief: Ein Schreiben des Apollos an Judenchristen der korinthischen Gemeinde* (Leipzig, 1918).

Barclay, W. *Epistle to the Hebrews,* Bible Guides 20 (London/New York, 1965).

Barrett, C. K. "The Eschatology of the Epistle to the Hebrews," in *The Background of the New Testament and its Eschatology* (C. H. Dodd *FS*), ed. W. D. Davies and D. Daube (Cambridge, 1956), pp. 383-93.

Beare, F. W. "The Text of the Epistle to the Hebrews in $\mathfrak{p}^{46}$," *JBL* 63 (1944), pp. 379-96.

Bornhäuser, K. *Empfänger und Verfasser des Briefes an die Hebräer* (Gütersloh, 1932).

Braun, H. *Qumran und das Neue Testament* (Tübingen, 1966), I, pp. 241-78 ("Hebräer"), II, pp. 181-84 ("Fragen des Hebräerbriefes").

Büchsel, F. *Die Christologie des Hebräerbriefs* (Gütersloh, 1923).

Burch, V. *The Epistle to the Hebrews: Its Sources and Message* (London, 1936).

Cabantous, J. *Philon et l'Épître aux Hébreux* (Montauban, 1895).

Carlston, C. "The Vocabulary of Perfection in Philo and Hebrews," in *Unity and Diversity in New Testament Theology* (G. E. Ladd *FS*), ed. R. A. Guelich (Grand Rapids, 1978), pp. 133-60.

Carpzov, J. B. *Sacrae exercitationes in S. Pauli epistolam ad Hebraeos ex Philone Alexandrino* (Amsterdam, 1750).

Cody, A. *Heavenly Sanctuary and Liturgy in the Epistle to the Hebrews* (St. Meinrad, 1960).

Coppens, J. *Les affinités qumrâniennes de l'Épître aux Hébreux* (Bruges, Paris, and Louvain, 1962).

Dale, R. W. *The Jewish Temple and the Christian Church* (London, ²1870).

Demarest, B. A. *A History of Interpretation of Hebrews 7, 1-10 from the Reformation to the Present,* BGBE 19 (Tübingen, 1976).

Dey, L. K. K. *The Intermediary World and Patterns of Perfection in Philo and Hebrews,* SBLDS 25 (Missoula, MT, 1975).

Dickie, J. "The Literary Riddle of the Epistle to the Hebrews," *Exp.* VIII.v (1913), pp. 371-78.

Du Bose, W. P. *High Priesthood and Sacrifice* (New York, 1908).

Du Plessis, P. J. *TEΛEIOΣ : The Idea of Perfection in the New Testament* (Kampen, 1959), pp. 206-33.

Feld, H. *Martin Luthers und Wendelin Steinbachs Vorlesungen über den Hebräerbrief* (Wiesbaden, 1971).

Feld, H. "Der Hebräerbrief: Literarische Form, religionsgeschichtlicher Hintergrund, theologische Fragen," *ANRW* II.25.4 (Berlin/New York, 1987), pp. 3522-3601.

Gayford, S. C. *Sacrifice and Priesthood* (London, 1924).

Giles, P. *Jesus, the High Priest* (Bognor Regis, 1984).

Goppelt, L. *Typos: The Typological Interpretation of the Old Testament in the New,* E.T. (Grand Rapids, 1982), pp. 161-78.

Grässer, E. *Der Glaube im Hebräerbrief* (Marburg, 1963).

Greer, R. A. *The Captain of our Salvation: A Study in the Patristic Exegesis of Hebrews,* BGBE 15 (Tübingen, 1974).

Harnack, A. "Probabilia über die Adresse und den Verfasser des Hebräerbriefs," *ZNW* 1 (1900), pp. 16-41.

Harris, J. R. *Testimonies,* II (Cambridge, 1920), pp. 43-57.

Hatch, W. H. P. "The Position of Hebrews in the Canon of the New Testament," *HTR* 29 (1936), pp. 133-51.

Hicks, F. C. N. *The Fullness of Sacrifice* (London, 1930).

Hofius, O. *Katapausis: Die Vorstellung vom endzeitlichen Ruheort im Hebräerbrief,* WUNT 11 (Tübingen, 1970).

Hofius, O. *Der Vorhang vor dem Thron Gottes,* WUNT 14 (Tübingen, 1972).

Hoppin, R. *Priscilla, Author of the Epistle to the Hebrews and Other Essays* (New York, 1969).

Hughes, G. *Hebrews and Hermeneutics,* SNTSM 36 (Cambridge, 1979).

Johnsson, W. G. "The Cultus of Hebrews in Twentieth-Century Scholarship," *ExT* 89 (1977-78), pp. 104-08.

Kähler, M. *Der Hebräerbrief in genauer Wiedergabe seines Gedankenganges* (Halle, 1880, [2]1889).

Käsemann, E. *The Wandering People of God* (1938, [2]1957), E.T. (Minneapolis, 1984).

Kennedy, H. A. A. *The Theology of the Epistles* (London, 1919), pp. 182-221.

Kistemaker, S. *The Psalm Citations in the Epistle to the Hebrews* (Amsterdam, 1961).

Klappert, B. *Die Eschatologie des Hebräerbriefes,* TEH 156 (Munich, 1969).

Kögel, J. *Der Sohn und die Söhne: Eine exegetische Studie zu Hebr. 2, 5-18* (Gütersloh, 1904).

Kosmala, H. *Hebräer-Essener-Christen* (Leiden, 1959).

Laub, F. *Bekenntnis und Auslegung: Die paränetische Funktion der Christologie im Hebräerbrief,* BU 15 (Regensburg, 1980).

Lidgett, J. S. *Sonship and Salvation: A Study of the Epistle to the Hebrews* (London, 1921).

Loane, M. L. *Key-Texts in the Epistle to the Hebrews* (London, 1961).

Lo Bue, F. "The Historical Background of the Epistle to the Hebrews," *JBL* 85 (1956), pp. 52-57.

Longenecker, R. N. "The Melchizedek Argument of Hebrews: A Study in the Development and Circumstantial Expression of New Testament Thought," in *Unity and Diversity in New Testament Theology* (Ladd *FS*), ed. R. A. Guelich (Grand Rapids, 1978), pp. 161-85.

Manson, T. W. "The Problem of the Epistle to the Hebrews" (1949), reprinted in *Studies in the Gospels and Epistles* (Manchester, 1962), pp. 242-58.

Manson, W. *The Epistle to the Hebrews: An Historical and Theological Reconsideration* (London, 1951).

Maurice, F. D. *The Epistle to the Hebrews*. Warburton Lectures (London, 1846).

Ménégoz, E. *La Théologie de l'Épître aux Hébreux* (Paris, 1894).

Milligan, G. *The Theology of the Epistle to the Hebrews* (Edinburgh, 1899).

Milligan, G. "The Roman Destination of the Epistle to the Hebrews," *Exp.* VI.iv (1901), pp. 437-48.

Milligan, W. *The Ascension and Heavenly Priesthood of our Lord* (London, ^{2}1894).

Nash, R. H. "The Notion of Mediator in Alexandrian Judaism and the Epistle to the Hebrews," *WTJ* 40 (1977-78), pp. 89-115.

Nauck, W. "Zum Aufbau des Hebräerbriefes," in *Judentum, Urchristentum, Kirche (FS* für J. Jeremias), BZNW 26 (1960), pp. 199-206.

Peake, A. S. *The Heroes and Martyrs of Faith. Studies in the Eleventh Chapter of Hebrews* (London, 1910).

Peterson, D. *Hebrews and Perfection,* SNTSM 47 (Cambridge, 1982).

Ploeg, J. van der. "L'exégèse de l'Ancien Testament dans l'Épître aux Hébreux," *RB* 54 (1947), pp. 187-228.

Purdy, A. C. "The Epistle to the Hebrews in the Light of Recent Studies in Judaism," in *Amicitiae Corolla* (J. R. Harris *FS*), ed. H. G. Wood (London, 1933), pp. 253-64.

Quell, G., and Behm, J. Article διαθήκη in *TDNT,* II, pp. 106-34.

Ramsay, W. M. "The Date and Authorship of the Epistle to the Hebrews," in *Luke the Physician and Other Studies in the History of Religion* (London, 1908), pp. 299-328.

Riehm, E. *Der Lehrbegriff des Hebräerbriefs* (Basel, 1867).

Riggenbach, E. *Die ältesten lateinischen Kommentare zum Hebräerbrief.* Forschungen zur Geschichte des neutestamentlichen Kanons, ed. T. Zahn, VIII.1 (Leipzig, 1907).

Rissi, M. *Die Theologie des Hebräerbriefs: Ihre Verankerung in der Situation des Verfassers und seiner Leser,* WUNT 41 (Tübingen, 1987).

Sauer, E. *In the Arena of Faith* (Exposition of Hebrews 12), E.T. (London, 1955).

Schröger, F. *Der Verfasser des Hebräerbriefes als Schriftausleger,* BU 4 (Regensburg, 1968).

Scott, E. F. "The Epistle to the Hebrews and Roman Christianity," *HTR* 13 (1920), pp. 205-19.

Smith, J. *A Priest For Ever: A Study of Typology and Eschatology in Hebrews* (London/Sydney, 1969).

Sowers, S. G. *The Hermeneutics of Philo and Hebrews* (Zürich, 1965).

Spicq, C. "L'épître aux Hébreux: Apollos, Jean-Baptiste, les Hellénistes et Qumran," *RQ* 1 (1958-59), pp. 365-90.

Spicq, C. "L'épître aux Hébreux et Philon," *ANRW* II.25.4 (Berlin/New York, 1987), pp. 3602-18.

Synge, F. C. *Hebrews and the Scriptures* (London, 1959).

Tasker, R. V. G. *The Gospel in the Epistle to the Hebrews* (London, 1950).

Theissen, G. *Untersuchungen zum Hebräerbrief,* SNT 2 (Gütersloh, 1969).

Thompson, J. W. *The Beginnings of Christian Philosophy,* CBQM 13 (Washington, D.C., 1982).

Ungeheuer, J. *Der Grosse Priester über dem Hause Gottes: Die Christologie des Hebräerbriefes* (Würzburg, 1939).

Vaganay, L. "Le plan de l'Épître aux Hébreux," in *Memorial Lagrange* (Paris, 1940), pp. 269-77.

Vanhoye, A. *La structure littéraire de l'Épître aux Hébreux,* SN 1 (Paris/Bruges, 1963, ²1976).

Vanhoye, A. "Discussions sur la structure de l'Épître aux Hébreux," *Biblica* 55 (1974), pp. 349-80.

Vanhoye, A. *Old Testament Priests and the New Priest according to the New Testament,* E.T. (Leominster, 1986).

Vanhoye, A. "L'oblation sacerdotale du Christ dans l'épître aux Hébreux," *Didaskalia* 14 (1984), pp. 11-30.

Vos, G. "The Priesthood of Christ in the Epistle to the Hebrews," *PTR* 5 (1907), pp. 423-47, 579-604.

Vos, G. "Hebrews, the Epistle of the Diatheke," *PTR* 13 (1915), pp. 587-632, 14 (1916), pp. 1-61.

Vos, G. *The Teaching of the Epistle to the Hebrews* (Grand Rapids, 1956).

Weiss, B. *Der Hebräerbrief in zeitgeschichtlicher Beleuchtung* = *TU* 35, Heft 3 (Leipzig, 1910).

Williams, R. R. *Reading through Hebrews* (London, 1960).

Williamson, R. "Hebrews and Doctrine," *ExT* 81 (1969-70), pp. 371-76.

Williamson, R. *Philo and the Epistle to the Hebrews,* ALGHJ 4 (Leiden, 1970).

Williamson, R. "The Eucharist and the Epistle to the Hebrews," *NTS* 21 (1974-75), pp. 300-312.

Williamson, R. "The Epistle to the Hebrews: Its Background," *ExT* 87 (1975-76), pp. 232-37.

Wrede, W. *Das literarische Rätsel des Hebräerbriefs* (Göttingen, 1906).

Yadin, Y. "The Dead Sea Scrolls and the Epistle to the Hebrews," *Scripta Hierosolymitana* 4 (1958), pp. 36-55.

Young, N. H. "The Gospel according to Hebrews 9," *NTS* 27 (1980-81), pp. 198-210.

Zuntz, G. *The Text of the Epistles.* British Academy Schweich Lectures, 1946 (London, 1953).

Other relevant literature, especially articles in periodicals, will be found cited in the notes.

Text, Exposition, and Notes

HEBREWS 1

I. THE FINALITY OF CHRISTIANITY (1:1–2:18)

A. GOD'S FINAL REVELATION IN HIS SON (1:1-4)

1 *In earlier times God spoke to our fathers by the prophets at various days and in many ways,*[1]
2 *but in these last days he has spoken to us by one who is his Son,*[2] *the one whom he has appointed heir of all things, the one moreover through whom he made the universe.*
3 *This Son, the effulgence of God's glory and the very image of his being, who bears all things along*[3] *by his enabling word,*[4] *made puri-*

---

1. Gk. πολυμερῶς καὶ πολυτρόπως, lit. "in many parts and in many ways" (NEB "in fragmentary and varied fashion"). The alliteration with initial π is a familiar literary figure.

2. Gk. ἐν υἱῷ ("in [one who is] Son," "Son-wise").

3. Gk. φέρων, "upholding" or "carrying along"; for the latter rendering cf. A. H. McNeile, "The Spiritual Value of the Creation Story," *ExT* 16 (1904-5), p. 541. The first hand in B (cf. also the 4th-cent. Ps.-Serapion) has the scribal error φανερῶν ("manifesting"). A corrector deleted the superfluous letters αν, but a later reader (*c.* 13th cent.) replaced them and added a note rebuking the corrector: "Most ignorant and wicked man, leave the original (reading) alone; do not change it!"

4. Gk. τῷ ῥήματι τῆς δυνάμεως αὐτοῦ. In place of αὐτοῦ, "his" (the reading of ℵ A B D^b H* 6 33 etc.), 𝔭^46 and 1739 (with 0121b and 424**) have δι' αὐτοῦ or δι' ἑαυτοῦ, "through himself," which must be construed with the following clause. D* K L with the bulk of later manuscripts and the TR exhibit both readings, αὐτοῦ δι' ἑαυτοῦ (hence AV/KJV "upholding all things by the word of his power, when he had by himself purged our sins"). G. Zuntz (*The Text of the Epistles* [London, 1953], pp. 43-45) submits that δι' ἑαυτοῦ is the original reading, αὐτοῦ being an easy corruption and αὐτοῦ δι' ἑαυτοῦ the conflation of the other two; the text would then mean: "Jesus supports the universe by the word of power; through himself he has effected the purification of sins." He finds a further pointer to the original absence of the genitive αὐτοῦ after τῷ

44

fication for our sins and then sat down at the right hand of the Majesty on high.

4 *He has become so much superior to the angels[5] as[6] the name which he has inherited is superior to theirs.*

1-2a *"God has spoken."* This initial affirmation is basic to the whole argument of this epistle, as indeed it is basic to Christian faith. Had God remained silent, enshrouded in thick darkness, the plight of mankind would have been desperate indeed; but now he has spoken his revealing, redeeming, and life-giving word, and in his light we see light. Our author is not thinking of that general revelation of himself which God has given in creation, providence, and conscience—

"Lo, these are but the outskirts of his ways:
and how small a whisper do we hear of him!"[7]—

but of that special revelation which he has given in two stages: first, to the fathers through the prophets, and finally in his Son. These two stages of divine revelation correspond to the Old and New Testaments respectively. Divine revelation is thus seen to be progressive—but the progression is not from the less true to the more true, from the less worthy to the more worthy, or from the less mature to the more mature. How could it be so when it is one and the same God who is revealed throughout? Human conceptions of God may change, but the evolution of the idea of God is quite a different thing from the progress of divine revelation. The progression is one from promise to fulfilment,[8] as is made abundantly clear in the course of this epistle: the men and women of faith in Old Testament days did not in their lifetime experience the fulfilment of the divine promise in which they had trusted, "because, with us in mind, God had made a better plan, that only in company with us should they reach their perfection" (11:40, NEB). The earlier stage of the revelation was given in a variety of ways: God spoke in his mighty works of mercy and judgment, and made known through his servants the prophets the meaning and

---

ῥήματι τῆς δυνάμεως in the fact that without it the participial phrase ends in the fourth paeonic foot δυνάμεως, the one meter which Aristotle (*Rhetoric* 3.8) commends as a clausula in rhetorical prose, and one which is found elsewhere in this epistle (*Text,* p. 285, where he cites W. B. Sedgwick).

5. Gk. τῶν ἀγγέλων. From the fact that τῶν is omitted by 𝔭[46] B and Clement of Rome, G. Zuntz infers that the anarthrous ἀγγέλων is the true reading (*Text,* p. 218).

6. Gk. τοσούτῳ κρείττων . . . ὅσῳ ("by so much better . . . as") is an example of the rhetorical figure called *synkrisis* (cf. p. 25, n. 111). See G. Zuntz, *Text,* p. 286; he refers to F. Focke, "Synkrisis," *Hermes* 8 (1923), pp. 327ff., especially 335ff. Cf. 3:3; 12:4, and the special uses of the *a fortiori* argument mentioned on p. 68, n. 4; p. 344, n. 74.

7. Job 26:14.

8. Cf. J. K. S. Reid, *The Authority of Scripture* (London, 1957), pp. 182-93.

purpose of these works; they were admitted into his secret council and learned his plans in advance.[9] He spoke in storm and thunder to Moses,[10] in a still small voice to Elijah.[11] To those who would not heed the gently flowing stream of Shiloah he spoke by means of the Euphratean flood.[12] Priest and prophet, sage and singer were in their several ways his spokesmen; yet all the successive acts and varying modes of revelation in the ages before Christ came did not add up to the fulness of what God had to say. His word was not completely uttered until Christ came; but when Christ came, the word spoken in him was indeed God's final word. In him all the promises of God meet with the answering "Yes!" which seals their fulfilment to his people and evokes from them an answering "Amen!"[13] The story of divine revelation is a story of progression up to Christ, but there is no progression beyond him. It is "in these last days" that God has spoken in him, and by this phrase our author means much more than "recently"; it is a literal rendering of the Hebrew phrase which is used in the Old Testament to denote the epoch when the words of the prophets will be fulfilled,[14] and its use here means that the appearance of Christ "once for all at the consummation of the ages" (9:26) has inaugurated that time of fulfilment. God's previous spokesmen were his servants, but for the proclamation of his last word to mankind he has chosen his Son.

2b-3   Seven facts are stated about the Son of God which bring out his greatness and show why the revelation given in him is the highest which God can give.

(a)   God has appointed him "heir of all things." These words no doubt echo the oracle of Ps. 2:8, addressed to one who is both the Lord's Anointed and acclaimed by God as his Son:

"Ask of me, and I will make the nations your heritage,
And the ends of the earth your possession."

Our author applies the preceding words of this oracle to Christ in v. 5 below. But in his mind the inheritance of the Son of God is not limited to earth;[15] it embraces the universe, and particularly the world to come.[16] This is restated

9. Cf. Jer. 23:18, 22; Amos 3:7.
10. Ex. 19:19; Deut. 5:22ff.
11. 1 Kings 19:12.
12. Isa. 8:6ff.
13. Cf. 2 Cor. 1:20.
14. Gk. ἐπ᾽ ἐσχάτου τῶν ἡμερῶν τούτων, a Septuagintalism, reflecting Heb. b^e'aḥărît hayyāmîm ("in the latter end of the days"), which according to the context may mean "hereafter," "ultimately," or "in the end-time." Cf. Gen. 49:1; Num. 24:14; Deut. 4:30; 31:29; Isa. 2:2; Jer. 23:20; 30:24; 48:27; 49:39; Ezek. 38:16; Dan. 10:14; Hos. 3:5; Mic. 4:1. The use of the phrase here implies an inaugurated eschatology. See p. 231 with nn. 160-63 (on 9:26).
15. Cf. the extension of Abraham's promised inheritance in 11:9f., 14-16.
16. Cf. 2:5, τὴν οἰκουμένην τὴν μέλλουσαν.

in fuller detail in 2:5-9, where Jesus, as the last Adam, has all things put under his feet.

(b) It was through him that God "made the universe." The Greek word here rendered "universe" is *aiōnes,* which primarily means "ages"; but its meaning cannot be restricted to "ages" either here or in 11:3, where it re-appears in a similar context.[17] The whole created universe of space and time is meant, and the affirmation that God brought this universe into being by the agency of his Son is in line with the statements of other New Testament writers that "all things were made through him; and without him was not anything made that was made" (John 1:3) and that "all things were created through him and for him" (Col. 1:16).[18] In these and other statements to the same effect we may trace the language of a primitive Christian hymn or con-fession of faith in which Christ, as the Word or Wisdom of God, is acknowl-edged as the Father's agent in the work of creation.[19] This conception of Christ is based (i) on such Old Testament passages as Prov. 8:22-31, where Divine Wisdom is personified and pictured as being the companion and assessor of the Almighty in the beginning, when he created heaven and earth,[20] and (ii) on a very early Christian identification of Christ with Divine Wisdom incarnate—an identification arising perhaps from the fact that Christ on occasion actually spoke in the rôle of Divine Wisdom.[21]

(c) He is the "effulgence" or "reflection" of God's glory. This state-ment, like the last, is involved in the identification of Christ with the Wis-dom of God. In the Alexandrian Book of Wisdom, a work with which our author may well have been acquainted, Wisdom is said to be:

> . . . a breath of the power of God,
> and a pure emanation of the glory of the Almighty;
> . . . a reflection of eternal light,

---

17. There is ample evidence for this later use of αἰών, in singular and plural alike, to de-note the world of space; cf. Ex. 15:18, LXX ("The Lord reigns over the world [βασιλεύων τὸν αἰῶνα] for ever and ever"); Wisdom 13:9; 14:6; 18:4, etc. The rabbis used Heb. *'ôlām,* Aram. *'ālam,* in the same sense after the beginning of the Christian era. See H. Sasse in *TDNT,* I, p. 204 *(s.v.* αἰών).

18. See F. F. Bruce, *The Epistles to the Colossians, to Philemon, and to the Ephesians,* NICNT (Grand Rapids, 1984), pp. 61-65. According to Philo, "the image (εἰκών) of God is the Word (λόγος) through whom the whole world was constructed" *(Special Laws* 1.81; cf. *Sacri-fices of Abel and Cain* 8; *Migration of Abraham* 6; *Immutability of God* 57).

19. The piling up of participial clauses embodying predications about God was charac-teristic of the liturgical style of the synagogue. Cf. E. Percy, *Probleme der Kolosser- und Epheserbriefe* (Lund, 1946), pp. 38f.

20. Cf. also Rev. 3:14, where the exalted Christ speaks as "the beginning of the creation of God" (another echo of Prov. 8:22).

21. Cf. J. R. Harris, *The Origin of the Prologue to St. John's Gospel* (Cambridge, 1917), pp. 57-62.

an unspotted mirror of the working of God,
and an image of his goodness. (Wisdom 7:25f.)

The word "reflection" or "effulgence" (Gk. *apaugasma*) used both there and here denotes the radiance shining forth from the source of light;[22] and Philo similarly uses it of the Logos in relation to God.[23] But while our author's language is that of Philo and the Book of Wisdom, his meaning goes beyond theirs. For them the Logos or Wisdom is the personification of a divine attribute; for him the language is descriptive of a man who had lived and died in Palestine a few decades previously, but who nonetheless was the eternal Son and supreme revelation of God. Just as the radiance of the sun reaches this earth, so in Christ the glorious light of God shines into the hearts of men and women.

(*d*) He is the very image of the essence of God—the impress of his being. Just as the image and superscription on a coin exactly correspond to the device on the die, so the Son of God "bears the very stamp of his nature" (RSV).[24] The Greek word *charaktēr,* occurring here only in the New Testament, expresses this truth even more emphatically than *eikōn,* which is used elsewhere to denote Christ as the "image" of God (2 Cor. 4:4; Col. 1:15).[25] Just as the glory is really in the effulgence, so the being (Gk. *hypostasis*)[26] of God is really in Christ, who is its impress, its exact representation and embodiment.[27] What God essentially is, is made manifest in Christ. To see Christ is to see what the Father is like.

(*e*) He upholds all things "by his enabling word."[28] This expression is probably an instance of the Hebraic adjectival genitive: "the word of his

22. Both an active sense ("effulgence," "radiance") and a passive sense ("reflection") are attested for ἀπαύγασμα. In later credal language, the Son of God is "light of light" (φῶς ἐκ φωτός), the effulgent light being "of the same substance" (ὁμοούσιος) as the source of light. This active sense is more appropriate to the context in Heb. 1:3 (and probably in Wisdom 7:25).

23. *The Making of the World* 146; *Noah's Planting* 50; cf. *Special Laws* 4.123, where he says that what God breathed into the first man (Gen. 2:7) was "an effulgence (ἀπαύγασμα) of his blessed, thrice-blessed nature."

24. Gk. χαρακτήρ (from the verb χαράσσω in the sense "engrave") is used especially of the impression or stamp on coins and seals. Philo uses it repeatedly of the image of God in human beings, stamped by the Logos as by the divine seal (e.g., *Noah's Planting* 18). See *New Docs.,* IV (1979), § 1.

25. It is εἰκών that is rendered "image" in Wisdom 7:26, quoted above ("an image of his goodness"). See *Colossians–Philemon–Ephesians,* NICNT, pp. 57f.; cf. also Heb. 10:1 (pp. 234f.).

26. Gk. ὑπόστασις occurs five times in the NT (the other four being 2 Cor. 9:4; 11:17; Heb. 3:14; 11:1); here it has the meaning "substance" or "real essence" (in contrast to what merely appears to be). See p. 101 with n. 67; cf. T. B. Strong, "The History of the Theological Term 'Substance,'" *JTS* 2 (1901), pp. 224-35, 3 (1902), pp. 22-40.

27. Cf. A. E. Garvie, "Shadow and Substance," *ExT* 28 (1916-17), p. 398.

28. See p. 44, n. 4. Cf. Zuntz, *Text,* p. 45, for the view that "his enabling word" is here an expression denoting the Logos.

power" may mean "his mighty word" or "his enabling word."[29] The creative utterance which called the universe into being[30] requires as its complement that sustaining utterance by which it is maintained in being. So Paul can write to the Colossians of Christ as the one in whom all things were created and also as the one in whom "all things hold together" (Col. 1:17). He upholds the universe not like Atlas supporting a dead weight on his shoulders, but as one who carries all things forward on their appointed course.

The words "the effulgence of God's glory and the very image of his being, who bears all things along by his enabling word" may be quoted from a hymnic formula; this is suggested by the introductory relative pronoun ("who"), the succession of participles ("being . . . bearing"), and the rhythmical structure.

(f) He has "made purification for our sins."[31] Here we pass from the cosmic functions of the Son of God to his personal relationship with mankind, to his work as his people's high priest, which is elaborated throughout the epistle. The reference here, as appears from its fuller development later, is to the cleansing efficacy of "his one oblation of himself once offered."[32] The wisdom which created the worlds and maintains them in their due order may well beget in us a sense of wondering awe; but the grace which has provided a remedy for the defilement of sin by a life freely offered up to God on our behalf calls forth a sense of personal indebtedness which the contemplation of divine activity on the cosmic scale could never evoke. The underlying emphasis here, however, is that by making purification for sins the Son of God has accomplished something incapable of achievement by anyone else. And this accomplishment has as its proper sequel the seventh in the present series of facts which bring out the unequaled greatness of the Son of God.

(g) He "sat down at the right hand of the Majesty on high." "The Majesty on high" is a periphrasis for God.[33] That Jesus is enthroned at the right

---

29. Cf. R. A. Knox's translation: "all creation depends, for its support, on his enabling word."

30. Cf. Heb. 11:3, "the universe has been fashioned by God's utterance"; there as here the Greek noun translated "word" ("utterance") is ῥῆμα.

31. Gk. καθαρισμὸν τῶν ἁμαρτιῶν ποιησάμενος. The absence of a perfect participle active in Latin (except for deponent verbs) has led to the use of the present participle here in the Vulgate as the equivalent of the Greek aorist participle ποιησάμενος (purgationem peccatorum faciens); this rendering, reflected in most translations based on the Vulgate (e.g., R. A. Knox, "making atonement for our sins"), has facilitated the view that during his present heavenly session Christ continues to make purification for sin. Cf. 10:12 (p. 245, n. 67).

32. From the Prayer of Consecration, Book of Common Prayer. If we retain the reading δι' ἑαυτοῦ, "by himself" (cf. p. 44, n. 4), the meaning may be not only that Christ made this purification by his own act, without assistance from others, but also that he made it by means of his own person—i.e., that he presented himself as the purificatory offering (which is, of course, repeatedly emphasized in this epistle). Cf. Zuntz, Text, p. 44.

33. Gk. τῆς μεγαλωσύνης ἐν ὑψηλοῖς (cf. 8:1 for a similar periphrasis with μεγαλωσύνη). Cf. the use of "The Power" (Gk. ἡ δύναμις) as a surrogate for the divine name in Mark 14:62.

hand of God is one of the earliest affirmations of Christian faith; it goes back to Jesus' own application to himself of the opening words of the divine oracle in Ps. 110: "Sit at my right hand."[34] That no literal location is intended was as well understood by Christians in the apostolic age as it is by us: they knew that God has no physical right hand or material throne where the ascended Christ sits beside him; to them the language denoted the exaltation and supremacy of Christ as it does to us. Paul can express the same thought in different language by saying that Christ has "ascended far above all the heavens, that he might fill all things" (Eph. 4:10), that "God has highly exalted him, and bestowed on him the name which is above every name" (Phil. 2:9). Ps. 110 provides the key text of this epistle, and the significance of Christ's being a *seated* high priest is explicitly set forth in the following chapters, especially in 10:11-14, where he is contrasted with the Aaronic priests who remained standing because their sacrificial service never came to an end. It may also be observed that the oracle of Ps. 110 is addressed to a prince of the house of David, and it was evidently a prerogative of the house of David to be seated in the divine presence, like David himself when he "went in, and sat before Yahweh" (2 Sam. 7:18).[35]

Thus the greatness of the Son of God receives sevenfold confirmation, and it appears, without being expressly emphasized, that he possesses in himself all the qualifications to be the mediator between God and the human race. He is the Prophet through whom God has spoken his final word; he is the Priest who has accomplished a perfect work of cleansing for his people's sins; he is the King who sits enthroned in the place of chief honor alongside the Majesty on high.

4 His exaltation to the right hand of God in itself marks him out as being superior to the angels[36]—a superiority which is further shown by the title which he bears. His name which is more excellent than theirs may be inferred from the context to be the title "Son."[37] If he is said to have "inherited" the name of Son, this does not mean that the name was not his before his exaltation. It was clearly his in the days of his humiliation: "Son though he was,

34. "From henceforth shall the Son of man be seated at the right hand of the power of God" (Luke 22:69). See pp. 63f. below.

35. In Ezekiel's vision of the new commonwealth the Davidic prince has the privilege of sitting in the temple "as prince" (i.e., only as prince, not as priest) "to eat bread before Yahweh" (Ezek. 44:3).

36. "Having become (γενόμενος) so much better," where γενόμενος may be a simultaneous aorist participle. In Philo the Logos is "the most senior of the angels, as it were an archangel" (*Confusion of Tongues* 146); the Son in this epistle has an even higher status. See A. Vanhoye, "Christologia a qua initium sumit Epistula ad Hebraeos," *Verbum Domini* 43 (1965), pp. 3-14, 49-61, 113-23.

37. Cf. v. 5. On the other hand, "the name which is above every name" in Phil. 2:9 is probably "LORD" (in the LXX sense of κύριος as equivalent of Heb. *Yahweh*).

50

he learned obedience by what he suffered" (5:8). It was his, indeed, ages before his incarnation: this is the plain implication of the statement in 1:2 that God has spoken to us in "his Son, . . . through whom he made the universe." He inherits the title "Son," as he inherits all things (v. 2), by the Father's eternal appointment.

The comparative adjective "better" is used thirteen times in Hebrews[38] to contrast Christ and his new order with what went before him. Here his superiority to angels is asserted, and elaborated by the following chain of Old Testament quotations, for two specific reasons—to show (i) that the final message of God, communicated by the Son, is safeguarded by even more majestic sanctions than those which attended the law, communicated by angels (2:2f.), and (ii) that the new world over which the Son is to reign as Mediator far surpasses the old world in which various nations were assigned to angels for administration (2:5). It may be that there was also a general reason for emphasizing the Son's superiority to angels, if "all sorts of strange teaching" against which these Hebrews are warned (13:9) included a doctrine of angel-worship such as seems to have been introduced among the Colossian Christians;[39] but this must remain uncertain.

B. CHRIST BETTER THAN ANGELS (1:5-14)

5 *For to which of the angels did God ever say,*
  "You are my Son;
    today I have begotten you"?[40]
 Or again,
    "I will be his Father,
    and he shall be my Son"?[41]
6 *And when, again, he brings the firstborn into the world, he says,*
    "And let all God's angels worship him."[42]
7 *With regard to the angels he says,*
    "He makes his angels winds,
    and his ministers a flame of fire";[43]
8 *but to the Son:*
    "Your throne, O God, is for ever and ever;[44]

---

38. Gk. κρείττων. Cf. 6:9; 7:7, 19, 22; 8:6 (bis); 9:23; 10:34; 11:16, 35, 40; 12:24.
39. Cf. T. W. Manson, "The Problem of the Epistle to the Hebrews," *Studies in the Gospels and Epistles* (Manchester, 1962), pp. 242-58.
40. Ps. 2:7.
41. 2 Sam. 7:14; 1 Chron. 17:13.
42. Deut. 32:43 LXX.
43. Ps. 104:4 (LXX 103:4).
44. Gk. εἰς τὸν αἰῶνα τοῦ αἰῶνος. A few authorities (B 33 lat^t) omit τοῦ αἰῶνος.

the scepter of righteousness is the scepter of your kingship.[45]

9   *You have loved righteousness and hated lawlessness;*[46]
    therefore your God has anointed you, O God,
    with the oil of exultation more than your companions."[47]

10 *And,*

   "It is you, O Lord, who founded the earth in the beginning;
   the heavens are your handiwork.

11 *They will perish, but you remain;*
   they will all wear out like a cloak;

12 *you will fold them up*[48] *like a mantle,*
   like a cloak,[49] *and they will be changed;*
   but you are the same:
   your years will not fail."[50]

13 *But to which of the angels has he ever said,*
   "Sit at my right hand,
   till I make your enemies a footstool for your feet"?[51]

14 *Are not all of them ministering spirits, sent to do service for those who*
   are to inherit salvation?

In these ten verses our author adduces seven Old Testament passages to corroborate his argument that the Son of God is superior to the angels. His use of them introduces us to his distinctive principles of biblical exegesis, which receive further copious illustration throughout the epistle. The general New Testament use of the Old Testament is a highly important and interesting study,[52] but the use of the Old Testament in the Epistle to the Hebrews, while

---

45. Gk. τῆς βασιλείας σου (so the LXX); but 𝔭46 ℵ B have αὐτοῦ instead of σου ("his kingdom" instead of "your kingdom"), and this is probably the true text here, the majority reading being the result of a very natural assimilation to the LXX.

46. Gk. ἀνομίαν, for which ℵ A 33 and a few other authorities have ἀδικίαν (a variant reading found also in some LXX authorities).

47. Ps. 45:6f. (LXX 44:7f.).

48. Gk. ἑλίξεις, for which ℵ* D* have "you will change" (ἀλλάξεις). Both variants are attested for the LXX, but ἀλλάξεις has the weight of authority there (cf. the MT), whereas ἑλίξεις has it here.

49. Gk. ὡς ἱμάτιον. These words are absent from the LXX, but are well attested for the present passage (𝔭46 ℵ A B D* 1739); as a result of assimilation to the LXX they are omitted from K L P with the majority of later manuscripts and the TR; hence they do not appear in the AV/KJV.

50. Ps. 102:25-27 (LXX 101:26-28).

51. Ps. 110:1 (LXX 109:1).

52. For work on this subject cf. C. H. Dodd, *According to the Scriptures* (London, 1952), and *The Old Testament in the New* (London, 1952); R. V. G. Tasker, *The Old Testament in the New Testament* (London, 1954); B. Lindars, *New Testament Apologetic* (London, 1961); M. Barth, "The Old Testament in Hebrews," in *Current Issues in New Testament Interpretation,* ed. W. Klassen and G. F. Snyder (New York, 1962), pp. 53-78; A. T. Hanson, *The Living Utterances of God* (London, 1983). See Introduction, p. 27, n. 116.

it has its place within that more general study, exhibits a number of features of its own. Among these is the prominence given to the Psalter;[53] more than once the writer interprets a passage from the other Old Testament books by way of exegesis of a passage from the Psalms.[54] Of the seven quotations here, five are taken from the Psalter; of the other two, one is taken from the Former Prophets and one from the Torah.

5   (a)   The first quotation is from Ps. 2:7. The words "You are my Son; today I have begotten you" were never addressed by God to any angel. The angels may be called collectively "the sons of God,"[55] but no one of them is ever called the son of God in terms like these, which single out the person addressed and give him a status apart.[56] The divine decree of Ps. 2:7b-9, which opens with these words, may, as has been suggested, "have preserved the text of a coronation liturgy used by the Davidic dynasty."[57] At any rate, they are cited in the psalm by the Lord's Anointed as the ground of his confidence in the face of the plottings of his enemies. But, like much else that was said with regard to the Davidic dynasty in its early days, it was believed in later days that these words would be most fully realized in the Messiah of David's line who would rise up in the time of fulfilment.[58] About the middle of the first century B.C., for example, they are quoted in the *Psalms of Solomon* with reference to the Davidic Messiah whose advent is ardently prayed for.[59] An allusion to them, too, may be found in Gabriel's annunciation to Mary about her coming child: "He will be great, and will be called the Son of the Most High: and the Lord God will give to him the throne of his father

53. Cf. S. Kistemaker, *The Psalm Citations in the Epistle to the Hebrews* (Amsterdam, 1961).

54. Cf. R. Rendall, "The Method of the Writer to the Hebrews in Using Old Testament Quotations," *EQ* 27 (1955), pp. 214-20.

55. Cf. Gen. 6:2, 4; Job 1:6; 2:1; 38:7 (in most of the places the LXX calls the "sons of God" angels).

56. Dan. 3:25 is not an exception, despite AV/KJV "the Son of God"; the ERV/ARV and the RSV rightly render the Aramaic phrase "a son of the gods" (i.e., a divine being or an angel).

57. E. Voegelin, *Order and History*, I (Oxford, 1956), p. 306. Cf. A. Bentzen, *King and Messiah*, E.T. (London, 1955), pp. 16-20; S. Mowinckel, *He That Cometh*, E.T. (Oxford, 1956), pp. 11, 64, et passim. So far as the form is concerned, we recognize here the language which was widely used in enthronement ceremonies throughout the ancient Near East. Thus Voegelin (*Order*, p. 305) quotes parallels from the Pyramid texts: "This is my son, my firstborn. . . . This is my beloved, with whom I have been satisfied" (1a-b), and "This is my beloved, my son; I have given the horizons to him, that he may be powerful over them like Harachte" (4a-b). See also J. Dupont, "Filius meus es tu," *RSR* 35 (1948), pp. 522-43.

58. A. R. Johnson (*Sacral Kingship in Ancient Israel* [Cardiff, 1955], pp. 118-20) finds in the original intention of the second psalm "the thought of the eventual fulfilment of this promise [that David would be made supreme over the kings of the earth] in the person of his descendant and ideal successor upon the throne, the true Messiah of the House of David."

59. Ps. Sol. 17:26.

David" (Luke 1:32). More important still is the fact that the heavenly voice which greeted Jesus at his baptism hailed him in the opening words of the decree of Ps. 2:7, "You are my Son" (Mark 1:11).[60] Indeed, the "Western" text of Luke 3:22 represents the heavenly voice as addressing to Jesus the fuller wording from Ps. 2:7 which is quoted here by the author of Hebrews: "You are my Son; today I have begotten you." The words were evidently in widespread use as a *testimonium* in the apostolic age, as Acts 13:33 bears witness;[61] and not only these words but the other parts of the psalm were given a messianic interpretation, as may be seen from the quotation and explanation of its first two verses in Acts 4:25-28.[62]

What did our author understand by the word "Today" in this quotation? In view of the emphasis laid throughout the epistle on the occasion of Christ's exaltation and enthronement, it is probable that he thought of this occasion as the day when he was vested with his royal dignity as Son of God.[63] It is certainly to this occasion that our author refers the divine acclamation of Christ as high priest in Ps. 110:4,[64] and the collocation of that acclamation with the present one in 5:5f.[65] suggests strongly that both are associated with the same occasion. The eternity of Christ's divine Sonship is not brought into question by this view; the suggestion rather is that he who was the Son of God from everlasting entered into the full exercise of all the prerogatives implied by his Sonship when, after his suffering had proved the completeness of his obedience, he was raised to the Father's right hand.

60. The following words spoken by the heavenly voice ("my beloved, in whom I am well pleased") echo the language in which the Servant of the Lord is introduced in Isa. 42:1. Jesus understood that his mission as the Messiah and divine Son of Ps. 2:7 was to be fulfilled in terms of the obedient, humble, suffering, and triumphant Servant of the Lord introduced in Isa. 42:1; and his understanding was in conformity with the original intention of the Servant Songs. See pp. 177-79, 217f., 232, 240f.

61. See F. F. Bruce, *The Book of the Acts*, NICNT (Grand Rapids, ²1988), pp. 259f.

62. See *Acts*, NICNT, pp. 98f. Cf. the application of the "rod of iron" of Ps. 2:9 to the Messiah in Rev. 12:5; 19:15, and to the Messiah's associates in Rev. 2:27.

63. Cf. Rom. 1:4, where Paul's words "designated Son of God in power . . . by the resurrection from the dead" have reference to that "particular event in the history of the Son of God incarnate by which he was *instated* in a position of sovereignty and invested with power, an event which in respect of investiture with power surpassed everything that could previously be ascribed to him in his incarnate state" (J. Murray, *The Epistle to the Romans*, NICNT, I [Grand Rapids, 1959], p. 10). We might also compare the comment on Ps. 2:7 in Midrash *Tehillim* (so also Midrash *Samuel*, ch. 19, with the readings of *Yalquṭ Shim'oni* 2.620): "Rabbi Huna says in the name of Rabbi Acha: The sufferings are divided into three parts: one for David and the fathers, one for our own generation, and one for King Messiah, as it is written, 'He was wounded for our transgressions. . . .' And when the hour comes, the Holy One—blessed be He!—says to them, I must create him a new creation, as it is said, 'Today I have begotten you.'" The implication here seems to be that Ps. 2:7 refers to the time when the Messiah, after suffering and death, is brought back to the realm of the living.

64. Cf. v. 13 below (pp. 63f.).

65. See pp. 122-26.

(b) The second quotation comes from 2 Sam. 7:14. There the prophet Nathan conveys the divine response to David's desire to build a house for the ark of God. God desires no house of cedar, but promises to establish David's house in perpetuity. Yet after David's death his son and successor will build a house for God, and his royal throne will endure forever. "I will be his father," says God, "and he shall be my son" (2 Sam. 7:14).[66]

Although David's immediate successor, Solomon, did build a temple for the God of Jacob, the event proved that the divine promises made to David regarding his son and heir were not exhausted in Solomon.[67] The later prophets looked forward to a greater son of David in coming days in whom "the sure mercies of David" would be adequately realized. This son of David is the peaceful ruler of Mic. 5:2-4, the prince of the four names of Isa. 9:6f., the "leader and commander to the peoples" of Isa. 55:4, the one "whose right it is" of Ezek. 21:27, Zion's king of Zech. 9:9. On the eve of Christ's coming the *Psalms of Solomon* and the Qumran texts alike attest the eagerness with which the son of David was expected. In a document from Cave 4 at Qumran, 4Q*Florilegium,*[68] a few biblical passages are brought together as describing the imminent restoration of David's house, including an abridged form of 2 Sam. 7:11-14, "The LORD declares to you that he will build you a house; and I will raise up your seed after you, and I will establish the throne of his kingdom for ever. I will be his father, and he shall be my son." This quotation is immediately followed by the comment: "He is the shoot of David, who is to arise with the Expounder of the Law . . . in Zi[on in the l]ast days."[69] The "shoot[70] of David" is, of course, the "righteous Branch" to be raised up for David in Jer. 23:5; 33:15—the Davidic Messiah. The fulfilment of the ancient promise made through Nathan is clearly celebrated in Gabriel's words of annunciation to Mary (Luke 1:32f.) and in Zechariah's thanksgiving (Luke 1:68f.):

"Blessed be the Lord God of Israel;
for he has visited and redeemed his people,

---

66. See also p. 93, n. 15. With this prose narrative are closely associated the poetic oracles of Pss. 89:19-37 (LXX 88:20-38) and 132:11-18 (LXX 131:11-18) as well as 2:7-9. On 2 Sam. 7:14 see also D. J. McCarthy, "2 Samuel 7 and the Structure of the Deuteronomic History," *JBL* 84 (1965), pp. 131-38; J. Becker, *Messianic Expectations in the Old Testament,* E.T. (Philadelphia, 1980).

67. Cf. *Acts,* NICNT, pp. 147ff., 255f. (on Acts 7:46f.; 13:22f.).

68. Cf. J. M. Allegro, "Further Messianic References in Qumran Literature," *JBL* 75 (1956), pp. 174-87, especially pp. 176f.; "Fragments of a Qumran Scroll of Eschatological Midrashim," *JBL* 77 (1958), pp. 350-54; cf. *DJD,* V (Oxford, 1968), § 174 (pp. 53-57).

69. These words are immediately followed by the quotation and messianic application of Amos 9:11a (cf. Acts 15:16).

70. Heb. *semah,* the word translated "Branch" in Jer. 23:5; 33:15.

and has raised up a horn of salvation for us
in the house of his servant David."

The general testimony of the New Testament to the bringing near of God's salvation in "his Son, who was born of the seed of David according to the flesh" (Rom. 1:3), provides sufficient justification for our author's referring to Jesus the language of 2 Sam. 7:14.

6 *(c)* The third quotation ("And let all God's angels worship him") is preceded by words which, especially as rendered in the ERV/ARV ("when he again bringeth in the firstborn into the world"), have been thought to refer to the second advent of Christ. If "again" is taken closely with "brings in," the meaning certainly appears to be: "And when he brings the firstborn into the world a second time." For this interpretation Westcott argues strongly. But the word order is not as conclusive as he maintains.[71] The RSV and the NEB have rightly reverted to the construction of the AV/KJV; a slight alteration would suffice to bring the ARV into line: "And when, again, he bringeth in the firstborn into the world." The adverb "again" marks this as a further quotation setting forth the preeminence of Christ.[72] The two previous quotations have marked him out as the Son of God; this one marks him out as one who is worshiped by angels. He is called "the firstborn" because he exists before all creation and because all creation is his heritage. The title may be traced back to Ps. 89:27 (LXX 88:28), where God says of David (and in general of the Davidic king):

"I will make him the firstborn,
The highest of the kings of the earth."[73]

The quotation "And let all God's angels worship him" bears a general resemblance to Ps. 97:7 (LXX 96:7), "Worship him, all you gods" (more especially in the Septuagint, "Worship him, all his angels"). But it bears an even closer resemblance to words from the longer Septuagint form of Deut. 32:43, the concluding words of the Song of Moses:

"Rejoice, O heavens, along with him,

---

71. Indeed, as soon as he has said *(ad loc.)* that "such a transposition of πάλιν [as is involved in the view that it simply introduces a fresh quotation] is without parallel" he adds a parenthesis calling attention to Wisdom 14:1 where just such a transposition is found (πλοῦν τις πάλιν στελλόμενος does not mean "one preparing to sail again" but, as the ERV and the RSV rightly render, "Again, one preparing to sail").

72. Following upon the πάλιν of v. 5b (cf. John 19:37; Rom. 15:10f.; 1 Cor. 3:20; Heb. 2:13; 4:5; 10:30). We need not think that δέ (in ὅταν δὲ πάλιν) is strongly adversative; the theme of this quotation is the same as that of the two preceding ones, the supremacy of Christ, but it is carried farther in this quotation by being set over against the inferior rôle of angels.

73. Quoted of Christ in Rev. 1:5; he is called the "firstborn" also in Rom. 8:29; Col. 1:15, 18 (see *Colossians–Philemon–Ephesians,* NICNT, pp. 58-61, 71f.).

And let the sons of God worship him;[74]
Rejoice, O nations, with his people,[75]
And let all the angels of God ascribe strength to him;
For he avenges the blood of his sons, and will avenge it,
    And will recompense punishment to his adversaries;
Even to those who hate him will he recompense it,
    And the Lord will cleanse his people's land."

Two questions arise with regard to the use of this quotation. Since in its original setting it is Yahweh, the God of Israel, whom all angels are to worship, why is their worship here said to be paid to the Son?[76] And why is it paid to him when God brings him into the world?

There is a rabbinic tradition to the effect that when Adam (who in one sense was God's "firstborn") was created (or "introduced into the world"), God invited the angels to worship him, but at Satan's instigation they refused. According to *The Life of Adam and Eve* (13f.), "God the Lord spoke: 'Here is Adam. I have made him in our image and likeness.' And Michael went out and called all the angels, saying: 'Worship the image of God as the Lord God has commanded.' And Michael himself worshipped first."[77] Here, however, it is not the first Adam but the last who is the object of angelic homage; our author was possibly acquainted with an interpretation of the words he quotes which represented the angels as called upon to pay allegiance to the heavenly Son of Man at the time of his public manifestation. However that may be, he would have cordially agreed with the statement of John 5:23, where the Father's purpose in committing judgment to the Son is said to be "that all may honor the Son, even as they honor the Father."

The moment intended by the conjunction "when" is probably neither the incarnation nor the second advent of Christ: it is not so much a question

74. The text of Deut. 32:43 known to our author may have varied somewhat from this. But his quotation, as it stands, conforms to l. 2 of this passage, except that the expression "the sons of God" has been replaced by "all the angels of God" from l. 4; we can well understand that such a substitution could have been deliberate in this context. A Hebrew manuscript (4QDt^q) with the longer text of Deut. 32:43 (previously known only from the LXX) has been identified in the material from Qumran Cave 4; cf. P. W. Skehan, "A Fragment of the 'Song of Moses' (Deut. 32) from Qumran," *BASOR* 136 (December 1954), pp. 12-15; F. M. Cross, *The Ancient Library of Qumran and Modern Biblical Studies* (Grand Rapids, [3]1980), pp. 182f.

75. This line is quoted by Paul in Rom. 15:10 as fulfilled in the extension of the gospel of Christ to the Gentiles.

76. See T. F. Glasson, "'Plurality of Divine Persons' and the Quotations in Hebrews 1.6ff.," *NTS* 12 (1965-66), pp. 270-72.

77. See J. H. Charlesworth (ed.), *The Old Testament Pseudepigrapha*, II (Garden City, NY, 1985), p. 262. Allusions to this story have been traced in TB *Sanhedrin* 59b; 2 Enoch 31:3; cf. *Ascension of Isaiah* 11:23ff., which may be influenced by our present passage. See W. Bousset, *Hauptprobleme der Gnosis* (Göttingen, 1907), pp. 198f.; C. H. Dodd, *The Bible and the Greeks* (London, 1935), pp. 156f.; W. D. Davies, *Paul and Rabbinic Judaism* (London, 1948), p. 42.

of his being brought into the world as of his being introduced to it as the Son of God, and we may think rather of his exaltation and enthronement as sovereign over the inhabited universe, the *oikoumenē*,[78] including the realm of angels, who accordingly are summoned to acknowledge their Lord. For (as is pointed out in 2:5) in the new age which his enthronement has inaugurated, it is to him, and not to angels, that the *oikoumenē* is made subject.

7 (d) The fourth quotation, from Ps. 104 (LXX 103):4, relates to the place of angels in the divine administration of the universe, in order to show that, high as that place may be, it is far inferior to the position of supremacy given to the Son. The quotation here conforms to the Septuagint,[79] and expresses an emphasis slightly different from the probable intention of the Hebrew text:

> Who makes winds his messengers;
> Flames of fire his ministers.

That is to say, in the Hebrew text the natural elements fulfil the commissions of God: the winds speed forth on his errands and fire renders him service.[80] Here, however, the meaning is different. It may be that the angels are portrayed as executing the divine commands with the swiftness of wind and the strength of fire. There is a parallel to this interpretation in the Latin version of 4 Ezra (2 Esdras) 8:21f., where Ezra addresses God as one "before whom the hosts of angels stand trembling, they whose service takes the form of wind and fire." But another interpretation is indicated by the Syriac and other eastern versions of this passage in 4 Ezra, according to which God is the one "before whom the hosts of angels stand trembling and at whose command they are changed to wind and fire."

> The Angels of Wind and of Fire
> Chant only one hymn and expire

78. The οἰκουμένη into which the firstborn is introduced here is probably the same as the οἰκουμένη of 2:5 over which the Son of Man is enthroned; the clause "of which we are speaking" in 2:5 could point back to this prior mention of the οἰκουμένη. So, in Rev. 5:6ff., when the slaughtered Lamb appears before the throne of God to assume his prerogatives as the Lion of the tribe of Judah, the heavenly beings fall down before him and pay him equal honor with God. If this is our author's meaning, then it could stand even if we followed Westcott in taking πάλιν closely with εἰσαγάγῃ, for the words would refer to God's bringing his firstborn back from death into the inhabited realm again. As for Westcott's further contention, that ὅταν . . . εἰσαγάγῃ must point to an event in the future, it may be said (i) that this is not the invariable force of ὅταν with the aorist subjunctive (cf. 1 Cor. 15:27, ὅταν δὲ εἴπῃ), and (ii) that even if this is its force here, the futurity may be with respect to the time when Deut. 32:43 was uttered. For the thought of Jesus' presentation to the angels cf. E. Schweizer's remarks on the schema "exaltation, presentation, enthronement," in *Lordship and Discipleship*, E.T., SBT 28 (London, 1960), pp. 65f.

79. Except that our LXX authorities have πῦρ φλέγον as the last two words and not πυρὸς φλόγα, as here.

80. Cf. Ps. 148:8. The storm winds and the lightnings correspond to the cherubim and seraphim respectively.

> With the song's irresistible stress;
> Expire in their rapture and wonder,
> As harp-strings are broken asunder
> By music they throb to express![81]

If this is the way in which our author understands Ps. 104:4, then he is contrasting the evanescence of angels with the eternity of the Son, which is stressed in the two quotations which follow.

8-9 *(e)* The fifth quotation, from Ps. 45:6f. (LXX 44:7f.), is set in contrast to the fourth.[82] The forty-fifth psalm celebrates a royal wedding; the poet addresses first the bridegroom and then the bride. The words here quoted form part of his address to the bridegroom. We cannot be sure whether the bridegroom was a king of the northern[83] or of the southern kingdom, but on balance it seems more probable that he was a prince of the house of David.[84] That he should be addressed as God "has seemed too daring to many commentators who seek to evade it or explain it away."[85] The marginal alternative "Thy throne is God"[86] is quite unconvincing, and whatever may be said in support of the RSV rendering of Ps. 45:6, "Your divine throne endures for ever and ever,"[87] still more can be said in sup-

---

81. H. W. Longfellow, *Sandalphon.* Cf. the comment on Dan. 7:10 ("a stream of fire . . . came forth from before him; a thousand thousands served him") in TB Ḥagigah 14a: "Every day ministering angels are created from the fiery stream, and utter song, and cease to be"; also (and more appositely) the angel's words to Manoah in *Yalquṭ Shim'oni* 2.11.3 (almost certainly a reference to Ps. 104:4): "God changes us hour by hour; . . . sometimes he makes us fire, and sometimes wind." Cf. also 1QH 1.10f.: "Thou hast appointed . . . the mighty winds according to their laws before they became holy angels."

82. Whatever be said of the force of δέ in v. 6, there is no doubt about its strongly adversative force here, where it harks back to μέν in v. 7 (καὶ πρὸς μὲν τοὺς ἀγγέλους . . . πρὸς δὲ τὸν υἱόν).

83. The reference to the daughter of Tyre with her gift in Ps. 45 (LXX 44):13 has been thought to point to the marriage of Ahab and Jezebel (cf. W. O. E. Oesterley, *The Psalms* [London, 1953], p. 250); but such a foundation, even when reinforced by a comparison of the "ivory palaces" of Ps. 45:8 (LXX 44:9) with Ahab's "ivory house" mentioned in 1 Kings (LXX 3 Kms.) 22:39, is too slender for such a superstructure.

84. It was certainly on the ground of its attachment to the Davidic monarchy that it was included in the temple collection of the "sons of Korah." In *Test. Judah* 24:5f. the language of Ps. 45:6 (along with that of Isa. 11:1 and Zech. 9:9) is used with reference to the coming Messiah of Judah's tribe. The Targum on Ps. 45:2 paraphrases: "You, O King Messiah, are fairer than the children of men." And no doubt the application of this psalm to the Davidic Messiah underlies our author's present use of it.

85. J. Paterson, *The Praises of Israel* (New York, 1950), pp. 26f.

86. Heb. 1:8, ARV mg. (cf. RSV mg., "God is thy throne"), but such an expression would not "be consistent with the religion of the psalmists" (T. K. Cheyne, *The Book of Psalms* [London, 1888], p. 127).

87. "Your divine throne" is a free rendering of *kis'ăkā 'ĕlōhîm,* construed as meaning "your throne (is like) God's" (cf. NEB, "Your throne is like God's throne"), after the analogy of Cant. 1:15; 4:1, where *'ênayik yônîm* is to be construed as "your eyes (are like those of) doves"

port of the Septuagint rendering reproduced by our author here. Indeed, our author may well have understood "God" in the vocative twice over in this quotation; the last clause could easily be construed "Therefore, O God, thy God has anointed thee with the oil of gladness above thy fellows."[88] This is not the only place in the Old Testament where a king, especially of the Davidic line, is addressed in language which could only be described as the characteristic hyperbole of oriental court style if interpreted solely of the individual so addressed. But to Hebrew poets and prophets a prince of the house of David was the vicegerent of Israel's God; he belonged to a dynasty to which God had made special promises bound up with the accomplishment of his purpose in the world. Besides, what was only partially true of any of the historic rulers of David's line, or even of David himself, would be realized in its fulness when that son of David appeared in whom all the promises and ideals associated with that dynasty would be embodied. And now at length the Messiah had appeared. In a fuller sense than was possible for David or any of his successors in ancient days, this Messiah can be addressed not merely as God's Son (v. 5) but actually as God,[89] for he is both the Messiah of David's line and also the effulgence of God's glory and the very image of his being.

All things created, even the angels, are subject to time and tide, change and decay, but the throne of God's Son endures forever; his is the kingdom that is to know no end. His, too, is the only kingdom characterized by perfect righteousness. The righteousness and justice which are the foundation of God's throne[90] are equally the foundation of Messiah's throne:[91] "righteousness shall be the girdle of his waist, and faithfulness

---

(cf. A. R. Johnson, *Sacral Kingship*, p. 27; he refers to earlier treatments of the passage by G. R. Driver in *The Psalmists*, ed. D. C. Simpson [Oxford, 1926], p. 124, and C. R. North, "The Religious Aspects of Hebrew Kingship," *ZAW* 50 [1932], pp. 29-38). The analogy with the construction in Cant. 1:15; 4:1 is criticized by Cheyne (*Psalms*, p. 127) as "very harsh"—"would a Hebrew reader," he asks, "have understood the phrase thus? A dove has really eyes, but God has only metaphorically a throne: would the reader have naturally thought of 'God's throne'?" See also J. A. Emerton, "The Syntactical Problem of Psalm xlv.7," *JSS* 13 (1968), pp. 58-63; L. C. Allen, "Psalm 45:7-8 (6-7) in Old and New Testament Settings," in *Christ the Lord . . . presented to D. Guthrie*, ed. H. H. Rowdon (Leicester, 1982), pp. 220-42.

88. Cf. NEB: "Therefore, O God, thy God has set thee above thy fellows, / By anointing with the oil of exultation" (with the alternative rendering in a footnote: "Therefore God who is thy God . . .").

89. Cf. "Mighty God" as a title of the coming king in Isa. 9:6. The analogy with similar compound expressions whose first element is *'Ēl* makes it unlikely that *'Ēl gibbôr* here is simply to be construed as "a god of a hero." See further B. B. Warfield, "The Divine Messiah in the Old Testament," *Biblical and Theological Studies* (Philadelphia, 1952), pp. 79-126.

90. Ps. 89:14 (LXX 88:15).

91. Messiah's throne, in fact, *is* God's throne (cf. the variant reading αὐτοῦ mentioned on p. 52, n. 45).

the girdle of his loins" (Isa. 11:5).[92] That is to say, the Messiah is personally devoted to those principles of equity and uprightness which it is his royal prerogative to maintain. His anointing with "the oil of exultation" refers not so much to his official inauguration as Messiah[93]—when "God anointed Jesus of Nazareth with the Holy Spirit and with power" (Acts 10:38)[94]—as to the joy with which God has blessed him in acknowledgment of his vindication of divine justice, "the joy that was set before him" mentioned in 12:3.[95]

But who are Messiah's "companions," whose joy is thus surpassed by his? In reference to a king of David's line they might be kings of neighboring nations, or members of his own family and court. In the present context, however, the term must have a special meaning—unless we say that our author has simply allowed the quotation to run on without attaching any particular significance to its closing words, which is improbable. The angels cannot be intended; their inferiority to the Son is so insisted on here that they could scarcely be described as his "companions." It is most likely that the reference is to the "many sons" of 2:10, whom the firstborn Son is not ashamed to call his "brothers" (2:11), and who are designated in 3:14 as the Messiah's *metochoi* ("partners")—the same Greek word as is here translated "companions."[96] Their joy is great because of their companionship with him, but his is greater still.

10-12 *(f)* The sixth quotation is taken from Ps. 102:25-27 (LXX 101:26-28). The psalm, which begins "Hear my prayer, O Yahweh," is truly described in its superscription as "a prayer of one afflicted, when he is faint, and pours out his complaint before Yahweh." Both he and Zion, his city, have experienced the judgment of God, but he makes confident supplication for mercy and restoration for himself and Zion, that men and women may assemble there once more to give praise to God. He is oppressed by a sense of the brevity of his personal span of life, with which he contrasts the eternal being of God. In comparison with his own short life, heaven and earth are long-lived; yet heaven and earth must pass away. They had their beginning when God created them, and they will grow old and disappear one day; but the God who created them existed before they did, and he will survive their disappearance. As one man in his lifetime outlives many successive suits of

92. Cf. also Isa. 9:7; 32:1.

93. "An official anointing (89:21) is not meant here; the phrase is symbolic for 'gladdened thee with prosperity'" (Cheyne, *Psalms*, p. 127).

94. That is to say, at his baptism (Mark 1:10; cf. Luke 4:18, quoting Isa. 61:1); see *Acts*, NICNT, pp. 213f.

95. Cf. the expression "the oil of gladness" in Isa. 61:3; the Hebrew is the same as in Ps. 45:7 *(šemen śaśôn)*.

96. See p. 101, n. 68.

clothes, so God has seen and will yet see many successive material universes, but he himself is eternal and unchanging.

The words in which the psalmist addresses God, however, are here applied to the Son, as clearly as the words of Ps. 45:6f. were applied to him in vv. 8 and 9. What justification can be pleaded for our author's applying them thus? First, as he has already said in v. 2, it was through the Son that the universe was made. The angels were but worshiping spectators when the earth was founded,[97] but the Son was the Father's agent in the work. He therefore can be understood as the one who is addressed in the words:

> Of old thou didst lay the foundation of the earth;
> And the heavens are the work of thy hands.

Moreover, in the Septuagint text the person to whom these words are spoken is addressed explicitly as "Lord"[98] ("Thou, Lord, in the beginning didst lay the foundation of the earth"); and it is God who addresses him thus. Whereas in the Hebrew text the suppliant is the speaker from the beginning to the end of the psalm, in the Greek text his prayer comes to an end with v. 22;[99] and the next words read as follows:

> He answered[100] him in the way of his strength:
> "Declare to me[101] the shortness of my days:
> Bring me not up in the midst of my days.
> Thy years are throughout all generations.
> Thou, Lord, in the beginning didst lay the foundation of the
>   earth. . . ."

This is God's answer to the suppliant; he bids him acknowledge the shortness of God's set time (for the restoration of Jerusalem, as in v. 13) and not summon him to act when that set time has only half expired, while he assures him that he and his servants' children will be preserved forever.[102] But to whom (a Christian reader of the Septuagint might well ask) could God speak

---

97. Job 38:7.

98. Gk. κύριε (omitted by א* in the LXX text, but restored by אc.a.).

99. Verse 23 in the MT and the LXX.

100. The LXX has treated Heb. 'innāh ("he afflicted," "he humbled") as 'ānāh ("he answered"); the difference is formally one of vocalization.

101. The LXX has treated Heb. 'ōmar 'ēlî ("I say, 'My God'") as 'ĕmôr 'ēlai ("say to me"); again, the difference is purely one of vocalization.

102. Cf. B. W. Bacon, "Heb. 1:10-12 and the Septuagint Rendering of Ps. 102:23," ZNW 3 (1902), pp. 280-85. Bacon suggested that the Hebrew, as well as the Greek, text of this psalm formed a basis for messianic eschatology, especially its reference to the "shortness" of God's days, i.e., of the period destined to elapse before the consummation of his purpose; he found here the OT background of Matt. 24:22, Mark 13:20, and Ep. Barn. 4:3 ("as Enoch says, 'For to this end the Master has cut short the times and the days, that his Beloved should make haste and come to his inheritance'").

in words like these? And whom would God himself address as "Lord," as the maker of earth and heaven?[103] Our author knows of one person only to whom such terms could be appropriate, and that is the Son of God.

That our author understood this quotation from Ps. 102 as an utterance of God seems plain from the way in which it is linked by the simple conjunction "and" to the preceding quotation from Ps. 45. Both quotations fall under the same rubric: "But to[104] the Son [God says]." If in the preceding quotation the Son is addressed by God as "God," in this one he is addressed by God as "Lord." And we need not doubt that to our author the title "Lord" conveys the highest sense of all, "the name which is above every name." No wonder that the Son has ascribed to him a dignity which surpasses all the names angels bear. Nor is our author the only New Testament writer to ascribe to Christ the highest of divine names, or to apply to him Old Testament scriptures which in their primary context refer to Yahweh.[105]

13 *(g)* The seventh quotation, which clinches the argument, consists of the opening words of Ps. 110 (LXX 109), "Yahweh's oracle to my lord."[106] The language of the oracle, "Sit at my right hand," has already been reflected in the wording of v. 3, where the Son of God is said to have "sat down at the right hand of the Majesty on high"; now it is expressly quoted. Like the first of these seven quotations ("You are my Son; today I have begotten you"), it refers to the king's enthronement, and carries with it the promise of victory over all his enemies. Whether Ps. 110 was composed against the background of some particular event in the history of the Hebrew monarchy,[107] such as Solomon's installation as king, or had its place in the national cult,[108] the New Testament uniformly interprets it as messianic, and applies it to Jesus. When Jesus asked how the scribes of his day could say that the Messiah was David's son, whereas the opening words of Ps. 110 acclaimed him as David's Lord, the messianic interpretation of the psalm was evidently

103. It is unlikely that this passage is primarily responsible for our author's description of the Son in v. 2 as the one through whom God made the universe—a description which probably owes more to Prov. 8:22-31 than to any other OT passage—but it could be taken as corroborative testimony for the identification of Wisdom in Prov. 8:22ff. with the Messiah.

104. While πρὸς τοὺς ἀγγέλους in v. 7 must be rendered "of (concerning) the angels," that is no reason for not rendering πρὸς τὸν υἱόν in v. 8 "to the Son." Cf. p. 170, n. 64.

105. Cf. the application to Christ of Isa. 45:23 in Phil. 2:10f. (see p. 50, n. 37), and of Isa. 8:13 ("Yahweh of hosts, him you shall sanctify") in 1 Pet. 3:15 ("sanctify in your hearts Christ as Lord").

106. Heb. *nᵉ'um yhwh la'ḏōnî* (LXX εἶπεν ὁ κύριος τῷ κυρίῳ μου).

107. The installation of Simon as "leader and high priest for ever" in 140 B.C. (1 Macc. 14:41) is certainly not the occasion which stimulated the composition of the psalm (cf. p. 125, n. 35).

108. Cf. A. R. Johnson, *Sacral Kingship*, pp. 120-22; H. Ringgren, *The Messiah in the Old Testament* (London, 1956), pp. 13-16.

common ground to him and them.[109] Its general messianic interpretation forms the background to its use in the apostolic preaching: the words "Sit at my right hand," which by common consent were addressed to the Messiah, must be regarded as addressed to Jesus, the apostles claimed, since his death and resurrection had shown that he was the Messiah.[110] Indeed, Jesus himself at his trial claimed to be the one addressed in these words when he told his judges that they would from then on see the Son of Man seated at the right hand of the Almighty.[111] This claim, condemned as blasphemy by the Sanhedrin, was held by the apostles to have been vindicated by the subsequent act of God; and the heavenly session of Christ has, from the earliest days of the church's existence, been maintained in Christian confession.[112] It remained for the writer to the Hebrews, however, to bring out further implications of the ascription of this psalm to Jesus, by taking along with the divine utterance of v. 1 ("Sit at my right hand . . .") the further divine utterance of v. 4 ("You are a priest for ever after the order of Melchizedek").[113]

14 The most exalted angels are those whose privilege it is to "stand in the presence of God" like Gabriel (Luke 1:19),[114] but none of them has ever been invited to sit before him, still less to sit in the place of unique honor at his right hand. Their standing posture betokens their promptness to execute his commands, or simply to abide his pleasure.

> Thousands at his bidding speed
> And post o'er land and ocean without rest:
> They also serve who only stand and wait.[115]

All of them, the highest angels as well as the lowest, are but servants of God, "ministering spirits" (a phrase which echoes the language of Ps. 104:4 as

109. Mark 12:35ff.

110. Cf. Acts 2:33ff., with *Acts*, NICNT, pp. 66f.

111. See p. 50, n. 34; in Mark 14:62 ("you shall see the Son of man sitting at the right hand of the Power, and coming with the clouds of heaven") there is a combined allusion to Ps. 110:1 and Dan. 7:13. For the figure of the Son of Man see below, pp. 72-75 (on 2:6ff.).

112. Cf. Acts 7:55f.; Rom. 8:34; Eph. 1:20; Col. 3:1; 1 Pet. 3:22; Rev. 3:21. See J. Daniélou, "La session à la droite du Père," in *The Gospels Reconsidered* (Oxford, 1960), pp. 68-77; J. Dupont, "'Assis à la droite de Dieu': L'interprétation du Ps 110, 1 dans le Nouveau Testament" (1970), in *Nouvelles Études sur les Actes des Apôtres* (Paris, 1984), pp. 210-95; D. M. Hay, *Glory at the Right Hand: Psalm 110 in Early Christianity* (Nashville/New York, 1973); M. Gourgues, *À la Droite de Dieu: Résurrection de Jesus et actualisation du Psaume 110 dans le Nouveau Testament* (Paris, 1978).

113. See 5:6, 10; 6:20; 7:1ff.; 10:12f. (pp. 123-33, 155-70, 244-46).

114. Cf. "the seven angels that stand before God" (Rev. 8:2). Their names are given in 1 Enoch 20:2-8. In Tobit 12:15 Tobias's fellow-traveler introduces himself as "Raphael, one of the seven holy angels who present the prayers of the saints and enter into the presence of the glory of the Holy One." In Daniel's vision of the Ancient of Days, however, "ten thousand times ten thousand stood before him" (Dan. 7:10).

115. John Milton, *Sonnet on his Blindness.*

quoted above in v. 7),[116] and not to be compared with the Son. More remarkable still, their service is performed for the benefit of a favored class of human beings, the heirs of salvation. That these should be the beneficiaries of angelic ministry may well be due to their close association with the Son of God, by whom they are being brought to glory (2:10).[117] These angels are clearly different beings from the hostile world-rulers and elemental spirits mentioned in Paul's epistles, whose influence has been broken over the lives of those who have died with Christ.[118]

The salvation here spoken of lies in the future; it is yet to be inherited, even if its blessings can already be enjoyed in anticipation. That is to say, it is that eschatological salvation which, in Paul's words, is "nearer to us now than when we first believed" (Rom. 13:11) or, in Peter's words, is "ready to be revealed in the last time" (1 Pet. 1:5).[119] Our author does not need to explain to his readers what he means by this salvation; the term and its meaning are familiar to them already. What they do need to understand is the fearful danger to which they will be exposed if they treat this salvation lightly.

The Son of God's ascendancy over angels has thus been asserted and confirmed by the testimony of Old Testament scripture. Some of the Old Testament passages adduced, and especially the first and the last (Pss. 2:7; 110:1), were already well established in the church as messianic testimonies, and were acknowledged as having met their fulfilment in Jesus. In them Jesus was addressed by God in terms that surpassed the honors enjoyed by the mightiest of archangels, who indeed are called upon to pay him homage in recognition of his sovereignty over them. And the authority of the gospel which the readers of this epistle had embraced was the authority of Jesus, the Son of God, supremely exalted by his Father. As God had no greater messenger than his Son, he had no further message beyond the gospel.

---

116. Gk. λειτουργικὰ πνεύματα (cf. v. 7, ὁ ποιῶν τοὺς ἀγγέλους αὐτοῦ πνεύματα, καὶ τοὺς λειτουργοὺς αὐτοῦ πυρὸς φλόγα). Cf. Philo's reference to "ministering angels" (ἄγγελοι λειτουργοί) in *Virtues* 73. In *Test. Levi* 3:5 the "archangels"—or "angels of the presence (πρόσωπον) of God"—are described as "those who minister (λειτουργοῦντες) and make propitiation before the Lord for all the sins of ignorance (ἄγνοιαι) of the righteous" (cf. below, 5:2; 9:7). There is no good reason to suppose that the "ministering spirits" here are the vanquished enemies of Ps. 110:1 (cf. 1 Cor. 15:24ff.), as does O. Cullmann (*Christ and Time*, E.T. [London, 1951], p. 196; cf. C. D. Morrison, *The Powers that be* [London, 1960], pp. 33f.).

117. In the light of ch. 11, we need not exclude from these heirs of salvation several persons in the OT record who received angelic ministry (cf. also 13:2). The fact that angels, though higher than human beings in the order of creation, render service to the heirs of salvation shows how the relation between the two is reversed in the order of grace.

118. Cf. Eph. 6:12; Col. 2:8, 15, 20 (also Rom. 8:38; 1 Cor. 2:8; 15:24).

119. Cf. 9:28, where Christ's second appearing will consummate his people's salvation (p. 233).

HEBREWS 2

C. FIRST ADMONITION: THE GOSPEL AND THE LAW (2:1-4)

1 *Therefore we must pay the more careful attention to what we have heard, so as not to drift away from it.*

2 *For, if the word spoken through angels was securely established, and every transgression and disobedient act received its just requital,*

3 *what escape will there be for us if we neglect a salvation so great? This salvation was first announced through the Lord; it was delivered to us with assurance by those who heard him,*

4 *while God at the same time confirmed the message with signs and wonders and a variety of mighty works and with gifts of the Holy Spirit distributed according to his will.*

1 The main reason why the Son's superiority to angels has been so emphasized now begins to appear. The older revelation, the law of Sinai, was communicated by angelic intermediaries, but God's final revelation was given in his Son and therefore demands correspondingly serious attention. The truth and teaching of the gospel must not be held lightly; they are of supreme moment, they are matters of life and death, and must be cherished and obeyed at all costs. The danger of drifting away from them, and so losing them, cannot be treated too gravely. ERV/ARV "lest haply we drift away from them" contemplates Christians as in peril of being carried downstream past a fixed landing place and so failing to gain its security. AV/KJV "lest at any time we should let them slip" reflects another use of the same verb, of allowing a ring to slip off the finger and so losing it.[1] Whatever be the precise metaphorical force of the verb here, our author is warning Christian readers, who have heard and accepted the gospel, that if they yield to the temptation to abandon their profession their plight is hopeless.

2 The sanctions which attended the law given at Sinai were severe and inescapable. Every commandment had the appropriate penalty prescribed for its infringement, and for those who deliberately and of set policy

---

1. Gk. μήποτε παραρυῶμεν. For the various meanings of παραρρέω (lit. "flow past") cf. LSJ, MM, and BAGD.

66

defied or disregarded the law of God there was no reprieve—for such behavior the death sentence was fixed in advance.[2] Yet the law was not imparted by such august mediation as the gospel; the law was "the word spoken
through angels."

The angelic mediation of the law is not recorded in the Old Testament.
The nearest thing to it is the description of the Sinai theophany at the beginning of the Blessing of Moses (Deut. 33:2):

> "Yahweh came from Sinai,
> and dawned from Seir upon us;
> he shone forth from Mount Paran,
> he came from the ten thousands of holy ones,
> with flaming fire at his right hand."

In the Septuagint this last clause is rendered: "At his right hand were angels
with him." This associates the angels more closely with the law-giving, but
does not make them mediators. Their mediatorship finds clearer expression
in the intertestamental and early Christian age, and is mentioned as a matter
of general knowledge in two other places in the New Testament. In Gal. 3:19
the fact that the law "was ordained by angels through an intermediary" is adduced by Paul to prove its inferiority to God's unmediated promise to
Abraham; and in Acts 7:53 Stephen charges the Jewish nation with having
repudiated the law from earliest days, even though they received it "as
delivered by angels."[3] For our author the mediation of the law by angels is
not bound up (as it was for Paul) with the tension between angels and their
world order on the one hand and Christ and his salvation on the other. In this
epistle, moreover, the law is not a principle set in opposition to the grace
manifested in Christ's saving work, but rather an anticipatory sketch of that
saving work. Here we find a concern with the sacrificial cultus rather than

---

2. Cf. Num. 15:30, "But the person that does anything with a high hand . . . reviles
Yahweh, and that person shall be cut off from among his people." Gk. μισθαποδοσία ("requital") is found in the NT only in this epistle—here of the penalty for wrongdoing, in 10:36 and
11:26 of the reward for faithfulness (cf. μισθαποδότης of God as a "rewarder" in 11:6).

3. John Calvin (*Harmony of the Last Four Books of the Pentateuch*, E.T., IV [Edinburgh,
1855], p. 381) suggested that the NT references to the angelic administration of the law were
based on Deut. 33:2, but the angels' attendance on God at the giving of the law does not make
them its administrators or mediators. Parallels which have been adduced from Jewish literature
(e.g., Jub. 1:29; *Mekhilta* on Ex. 20:18; *Sifre* on Num. 12:5; *Pesiqta rabbati* 21) refer to the angels' attendance on God, not to their administration of the law. Yet our author, like Paul and
Luke, refers to the angelic administration as though it were a commonly accepted tradition. The
earliest reference to it outside the NT may be in Josephus, *Ant.* 15.136, where King Herod says
that the Jewish doctrines and laws have been sent by God "through angels" (δι' ἀγγέλων), but
there the ἄγγελοι may be human messengers (prophets). See F. F. Bruce, *Galatians*, NIGTC
(Grand Rapids/Exeter, 1982), pp. 176-78; *Acts*, NICNT (Grand Rapids, 1988), p. 153, n. 99. Cf.
also the presence of angels in 12:22 (p. 358, n. 155).

with the "tradition of the elders," with the ritual law as a means of access to God rather than with the moral law as a way of life.

3 But the great salvation proclaimed in the gospel was brought to earth by no angel, but by the Son of God himself. To treat it lightly, therefore, must expose one to sanctions even more awful than those which safeguarded the law. Here we have the first of many warnings which recur throughout the epistle, which make it plain that our author was afraid that his readers, succumbing to more or less subtle pressures, might become liable to those sanctions—if not by an overt renunciation of the gospel, then possibly by detaching themselves increasingly from its public profession until it ceased to have any influence upon their lives. Hence his urgent monition: "what escape can there be for us if we ignore a deliverance so great?" (NEB). This is the first of several places in the epistle where an inference is drawn *a fortiori* from law to gospel.[4]

The great salvation of which the gospel speaks was, to begin with, "announced through the Lord." It had, of course, been proclaimed in advance by the prophets; but not until the coming of Christ, when promise gave place to fulfilment, could it be effectively brought near. The note of fulfilment was heard when Jesus came into Galilee after John the Baptist's imprisonment, "preaching the gospel of God, and saying, 'The time is fulfilled, and the kingdom of God is at hand; repent and believe in the gospel'" (Mark 1:14f.), and when, as in the synagogue at Nazareth, he read the words of Isa. 61:1f. which announce "good tidings to the poor" and "release to the captives," and proclaim "the acceptable year of the Lord," and followed them with the declaration: "Today this scripture has been fulfilled in your hearing" (Luke 4:18-21).[5] Neither our author nor his readers had heard the liberating message direct from the lips of the Lord, but depended on the sure testimony of those who had listened to him. Our author, unlike Paul, does not claim any direct revelation from Christ for himself or assert his independence of the apostles; in this respect he puts himself on the same level as his fellow-Christians who heard the gospel from those "who from the beginning were eyewitnesses and ministers of the word" (Luke 1:2).

4 The witness of their informants, however, was confirmed by the signs and wonders and mighty works which attended their proclamation of the message; these were tokens granted by God to attest the truth of what was proclaimed. The testimony of the New Testament writings to the regularity with which these phenomena accompanied the preaching and receiving of

---

4. See 7:21f.; 9:14; 10:28f. C. Spicq (*L'Épître aux Hébreux*, I [Paris, 1952], p. 53) adduces parallels from Philo. It is essentially the *a minori ad maius* argument, which the rabbis described as *qal wā-hōmer* ("light and heavy"). See p. 45, n. 6; p. 344, n. 74.

5. Cf. N. B. Stonehouse, *The Witness of Luke to Christ* (London, 1951), pp. 68-92.

the gospel in the early apostolic age is impressive in its range. The "mighty works and wonders and signs"[6] which marked the ministry of Jesus (Acts 2:22) continued to mark the ministry of the apostles from Pentecost onward (Acts 2:43). They were associated particularly with the bestowal of the Spirit, as indeed they are here: God's "distributions of the Holy Spirit"[7] to believers in accordance with his sovereign pleasure[8] formed the most conclusive demonstration and seal of the truth of the gospel. When Paul tries to recall the Galatian Christians to the simplicity of Christ, he reminds them that it was the message of faith and not the imposition of legal requirements that was confirmed among them in the beginning by God's supplying the Spirit to them and performing mighty works in their midst (Gal. 3:5). Similarly the recipients of Peter's first epistle are reminded how the gospel was first preached to them in the power of "the Holy Spirit sent from heaven" (1 Pet. 1:12).[9] The New Testament writers (including our author at this point) would not have appealed to the evidence of these miraculous manifestations if there was any possibility that their readers would reply that they had never seen or heard of such things.[10] They were matters of common knowledge and widespread Christian experience, and the reference to them here is calculated to restore the readers' faith in the gospel as God's authoritative message.

D. THE HUMILIATION AND GLORY OF THE SON OF MAN (2:5-9)

5 *It was not to angels that God subjected the coming world, of which we are speaking.*
6 *But someone has borne witness somewhere to this effect:[11]*
   "What is man,[12] that you should bear him in mind?

---

6. Gk. δυνάμεσι καὶ τέρασι καὶ σημείοις. The same three nouns are used in Acts 2:22 as here, in a different order (cf. *Acts*, NICNT, p. 63).

7. Gk. πνεύματος ἁγίου μερισμοῖς. The question arises whether πνεύματος ἁγίου is here subjective genitive, in which case 1 Cor. 12:11 would be a ready parallel ("all these are inwrought by one and the same Spirit, who apportions to each one individually as he wills"), or objective genitive, in which case one might compare Gal. 3:5 ("he who supplies the Spirit to you and works miracles [δυνάμεις] among you . . ."). The latter construction is probably the more natural in the present context; the reference then is to God's distribution of spiritual gifts to his people.

8. Gk. θέλησις, not found elsewhere in the NT.

9. Cf. also Acts 8:14-17; 10:44-46; 19:6; 1 Cor. 14:1-33.

10. Cf. W. L. Knox, *The Acts of the Apostles* (Cambridge, 1948), pp. 62, 89.

11. Ps. 8:4-6 (LXX 8:5-7).

12. Gk. τί ἐστιν ἄνθρωπος. In 𝔓[46] and a few less important authorities (C* P 104 917 1288 1319 1891 2127 d Vg[tol] boh) τίς ("who?") is read in place of τί ("what?"). G. Zuntz (*The Text of the Epistles* [London, 1953], pp. 48f.) argues that τίς is the original reading here, and that it has been assimilated to LXX τί in the majority of our authorities. He would then trans-

> *or the son of man, that you should consider him?*
>
> 7   *You have made him a little lower than the angels,*
>   *you have crowned him with glory and honor,*[13]
>
> 8   *you have subjected all things beneath his feet."*
>
> *In subjecting "all things" to him,*[14] *he left nothing unsubjected to him. But as it is, we do not yet see all things subjected to him.*
>
> 9 *But we see him who was made a little lower than angels in order to suffer death—that is, we see Jesus—crowned with glory and honor, in order that [by God's grace]*[15] *he should taste death for all.*

---

late: "Who is the man (ἄνθρωπος with rough breathing, by crasis for ὁ ἄνθρωπος) whom thou mindest? Truly (ἦ with circumflex accent in place of ἤ, 'or') the Son of Man, for him thou visitest." Our author, he thinks, has deliberately altered the LXX for his purpose, which is to show that God placed the coming world under the rule not of angels but of the Son of Man, the Messiah. For a little while, indeed, he made him lower than the angels (in his suffering and death), but even so he crowned him with glory and honor. Zuntz finds that this construction, with the reading τίς, "alone permits a coherent interpretation of this passage," and points out that incidentally it "makes an end of that chapter of New Testament theology which is headed 'The anthropology of Hebrews.'" See, however, the critique by R. V. G. Tasker in "The Text of the 'Corpus Paulinum,'" *NTS* 1 (1954-55), p. 185: "It is true that the *auctor ad Hebraeos* more than once makes deliberate changes in the text of the Septuagint, but that he should have played havoc with the parallelism of the psalmist in this way in the interests of a Son of Man Christology seems to me unlikely."

13. The additional clause from Ps. 8:7, "you have set him over the works of your hands," is inserted here in ℵ A C D* P Ψ 0121b and several minuscules, with the Latin and Coptic versions. It is missing from 𝔭46 and B and possibly from Tertullian's biblical text; it is omitted in a number of Peshiṭta codices and asterisked by the Harclean Syriac; it is marked for deletion by a corrector in D and is lacking in the majority of later Greek MSS. The shorter text is probably the original; the longer text represents a natural assimilation to the LXX. It is unlikely that the omission of the clause has any theological significance, although G. Zuntz (*Text,* p. 172) suggests that its retention would have been in conflict with our author's argument that "we see not yet all things subjected to him" (v. 8b). But this consideration would have dictated even more imperiously the omission of the following clause of the quotation.

14. In 𝔭46 B and a few other authorities "to him" (αὐτῷ) is omitted, probably rightly. Cf. G. Zuntz, *Text,* pp. 32f.

15. Gk. χάριτι θεοῦ. But the minuscule 1739 (with 0121b and 424**), one Vulgate codex (G) and several Peshiṭta codices, and many of the Fathers (Origen, Eusebius, Theodore of Mopsuestia, Theodoret, Jerome, Ambrose, and others) attest the reading χωρὶς θεοῦ ("apart from God"), which is so obviously *lectio ardua* as to call for consideration. It is easy to see how χωρίς would be changed to χάριτι here; it is difficult to see how χάριτι could ever have been changed to χωρίς. But if χωρὶς θεοῦ is earlier than χάριτι θεοῦ, how can it be accounted for? The best explanation is that a scribe or annotator, reading the words of v. 8, "he left nothing that is not subject to him," remembered Paul's remark on the same words in 1 Cor. 15:27b, "But when it says, 'All things are put in subjection,' it is evident that he is excepted who did subject all things to him," and added at this place in Hebrews a marginal note to the same effect: "[nothing, that is to say,] apart from God." The marginal note was later written into the text of v. 9, and subsequently changed to the unexceptionable χάριτι θεοῦ. If this was what happened, it must have happened early enough for 𝔭46 (c. A.D. 200) to exhibit the reading χάριτι θεοῦ. J. A. Bengel *(Gnomon, ad loc.)* accepts "apart from God" but construes it in its context with ὑπὲρ παντός, "for all apart from God." G. Zuntz, *Text,* p. 34, regards χωρὶς θεοῦ as having the same meaning as δι'

5 A further reason for emphasizing the superiority of Christ to the angels now appears. To angelic beings the present world has been entrusted for administration, but not so the world to come. The biblical evidence for the angelic government of the world is early: it goes back to the Song of Moses in Deut. 32. The Septuagint reading of Deut. 32:8 (which has claims to represent the original text) runs thus:

> "When the Most High gave to the nations their inheritance,
> when he separated the children of men,
> he set the bounds of the peoples
> according to the number of the angels of God."[16]

(The following verse goes on to say that Yahweh has reserved Israel as his own heritage.) This reading implies that the administration of the various nations has been parceled out among a corresponding number of angelic powers. At a later time this implication becomes explicit: in Daniel, for example, we meet the angelic "prince of Persia" and "prince of Greece" (Dan. 10:20), while Michael is "the great prince" who champions the people of Israel (Dan. 10:21; 12:1). In a number of places some at least of these angelic governors are portrayed as hostile principalities and powers—the "world-rulers of this darkness" of Eph. 6:12.[17] In Hebrews nothing is said about their possible hostility; all that matters in the argument of this epistle is that they are angels. "The world to come, which is our theme" (NEB) is the new world-order inaugurated by the enthronement of Christ at the right hand of God,[18] the world-order over which he reigns from that place of exaltation, the world of reality which replaces the preceding world of shadows.[19] It has been *inaugurated* by Christ's enthronement, although it is not yet present in its fulness; its consummation awaits the time when Christ will appear to bring his people into the final blessings of the salvation which he has procured for

---

ἑαυτοῦ in 1:3; he agrees with A. Harnack (*Studien zur Geschichte des Neuen Testaments*, I [Berlin/Leipzig, 1931], p. 236) that the change to χάριτι θεοῦ was made on dogmatic grounds. See R. V. G. Tasker, "The Text of the 'Corpus Paulinum,'" p. 184; he follows Tischendorf in thinking χωρὶς θεοῦ to be a correction "made in the light of I Cor. 15:27 to exclude God from the inclusiveness implied in ὑπὲρ παντός."

16. LXX ἀγγέλων θεοῦ at the end of the verse presupposes Heb. *bᵉnê ʾēl* or *bᵉnê ʾelōhîm*, lit. "sons of God," in place of MT *bᵉnê Yiśrāʾēl* ("sons of Israel"). Cf. the RSV. Since the publication of the RSV a Hebrew witness to this reading (4QDt⁹) has been identified among the biblical texts from Cave 4 at Qumran; see P. W. Skehan, "A Fragment of the 'Song of Moses' (Deut. 32) from Qumran," *BASOR* 136 (December 1954), p. 12; "Qumran and the Present State of Old Testament Text Studies: The Masoretic Text," *JBL* 78 (1959), p. 21.

17. Cf. G. B. Caird, *Principalities and Powers* (London, 1956), pp. ix, 81, etc.

18. Cf. 1:6 (see p. 58 with n. 78). Here as there οἰκουμένη (lit. "inhabited world") is used; here ἡ οἰκουμένη ἡ μέλλουσα is practically synonymous with the μέλλων αἰών of 6:5 (cf. p. 147 with n. 49).

19. Cf. 8:5; 10:1 (pp. 182-84, 234f.).

them;[20] but here and now they are experiencing "the mighty works of the coming age" (6:5), some of which have just been referred to in v. 4. If then this world to come has not been entrusted to angels for its administration, to whom has it been placed in subjection? To the Son of God, whom his Father has "appointed heir of all things" (1:2). It is not in the rôle of the Son of God that he now appears, however, but as the Son of Man, in accordance with the words which our author quotes from the eighth psalm.

6-8a The writer to the Hebrews is not careful to name the particular author of any scripture which he may quote. All the Old Testament is to him a divine oracle, the voice of the Holy Spirit; but as for the human author, the vaguest allusion will suffice: "someone has borne witness somewhere." With these words he introduces Ps. 8:4-6 according to the Septuagint, with the omission of one clause.[21] The one significant difference between the Septuagint and Hebrew texts comes in the first line of Ps. 8:5; whereas the Hebrew is most naturally translated "thou hast made him but little lower than God" (ERV/ARV), the Septuagint says "thou madest him a little [or for a little while[22]] lower than the angels."[23]

The psalmist is overcome with wonder as he thinks of the glory and honor which God has bestowed on mankind, in making them but little lower than himself and giving them dominion over all the lesser creation.[24] The language of the psalm is plainly based on the words of the Creator in Gen. 1:26: "Let us make man in our image, after our likeness: and let them have dominion over the fish of the sea, and over the birds of the heavens, and over every living thing that moves on the earth."[25] Our author, however, applies these words not to the first Adam but to Christ as the last Adam, the head of the new creation and ruler of the world to come. Here is probably a tacit identification of "the son of man" in Ps. 8:4 with the "one like a son of man" in Dan. 7:13, who receives from the Ancient of Days "an everlasting dominion,

---

20. Cf. 9:28 (p. 233).

21. For "somewhere" (Gk. που) cf. 4:4 (p. 107, n. 22). The sense "I suppose" (attested for που in Rom. 4:19) is inappropriate here.

22. Gk. βραχύ τι might have temporal force.

23. The LXX here translates Heb. mē'ĕlōhîm by παρ' ἀγγέλους. The question is whether Heb. 'ĕlōhîm here denotes God in the usual OT sense, or is a plural in sense as well as in form, meaning "divine beings" or "angels" (as in Ps. 82:1b, "in the midst of the gods he holds judgment").

24. "At first sight," says H. Ringgren (The Messiah in the Old Testament [London, 1956], p. 20), "these words seem to refer to man in general or to Adam, but there is reason to believe that they were originally said about the king." The truth of the matter is, as H. L. Ellison has put it: "The real prototype of the king was Adam, God's viceregent, with his dominion over the world" (The Centrality of the Messianic Idea for the Old Testament [London, 1953], p. 14).

25. Cf. Wisdom 9:2, "by thy wisdom [thou] hast formed man, to have dominion over the creatures thou hast made." See J. Jervell, Imago Dei: Gen. 1, 26f. im Spätjudentum, in der Gnosis und in den paulinischen Briefen, FRLANT 76 (Göttingen, 1960).

which shall not pass away." It is true that in the psalm "the son of man" stands in a relation of synonymous parallelism with "man" in the preceding line; but then it is equally true that "one like a son of man" in Dan. 7:13 simply means "one like a human being."[26] The fact remains that, ever since Jesus spoke of himself as the Son of Man, this expression has had for Christians a connotation beyond its etymological force, and it had this connotation for the writer to the Hebrews.[27]

The conception of Christ as the last Adam is certainly no innovation on our author's part, and it may not even be original with Paul[28]—especially if we can recognize in Phil. 2:6-11 a pre-Pauline hymn in which the faithfulness of the second man is contrasted with the fall of the first man.[29] God's man as the fulfiller of God's purpose meets us in the Old Testament;[30] he is "the man of thy right hand, . . . the son of man whom thou madest strong for thyself" for whose triumph another psalmist prays to God (Ps. 80:17). When one person fails in the accomplishment of the divine purpose (as, in some degree, all did in Old Testament times), God raises up another to take his place. But who could take the place of Adam? Only one who was capable of undoing the effects of Adam's fall and thus ushering in a new world-order. It is

26. Heb. *'ĕnōš . . . ben 'āḏām* (Ps. 8:4); Aram. *keḇar 'ĕnāš* (Dan. 7:13).

27. See P. Giles, "The Son of Man in the Epistle to the Hebrews," *ExT* 86 (1974-75), pp. 328-32, and (more generally on the Son of Man) C. Colpe, *TDNT,* VIII, pp. 400-477 (*s.v.* ὁ υἱὸς τοῦ ἀνθρώπου); T. W. Manson, *The Teaching of Jesus* (Cambridge, [2]1935), pp. 211-34; A. J. B. Higgins, *Jesus and the Son of Man* (London, 1964), and *The Son of Man in the Teaching of Jesus,* SNTSM 39 (Cambridge, 1980); I. H. Marshall, "The Son of Man in Contemporary Debate," *EQ* 42 (1970), pp. 67-87, and *The Origins of New Testament Christology* (Leicester, 1976), pp. 63-82; J. Jeremias, *New Testament Theology,* E.T., I (London, 1971), pp. 257-76; G. Vermes, *Jesus the Jew* (London, 1973), pp. 160-91, and "'The Son of Man' Debate," *JSNT* 1 (1978), pp. 19-32; C. F. D. Moule, "Neglected Features in the Problem of 'the Son of Man,'" in *Neues Testament und Kirche (für R. Schnackenburg),* ed. J. Gnilka (Freiburg, 1974), pp. 413-28, and *The Origin of Christology* (Cambridge, 1974), pp. 11-22; R. Pesch and R. Schnackenburg (eds.), *Jesus und der Menschensohn (für A. Vögtle)* (Freiburg, 1975); M. Black, "Jesus and the Son of Man," *JSNT* 1 (1978), pp. 4-18; M. Casey, *Son of Man* (London, 1979); S. Kim, *"The 'Son of Man'" as the Son of God,* WUNT 30 (Tübingen, 1983); B. Lindars, *Jesus: Son of Man* (London, 1983).

28. It may be implicit in the temptation narrative of Mark 1:13; cf. W. D. Davies, *Paul and Rabbinic Judaism* (London, 1948), pp. 42f.

29. Cf. E. Lohmeyer, *Kyrios Jesus: Eine Untersuchung zu Phil 2, 5-11* (Heidelberg, 1928, [2]1961); E. Käsemann, "A Critical Analysis of Phil. 2:5-11" (1950), E.T. in *JTC* 5 (1968), pp. 45-88; R. P. Martin, *Carmen Christi,* SNTSM 4 (Cambridge, 1967); I. H. Marshall, "The Christ Hymn in Philippians 2:5-11," *TynB* 19 (1968), pp. 104-27; C. F. D. Moule, "Further Reflexions on Philippians 2:5-11," in *Apostolic History and the Gospel,* ed. W. W. Gasque and R. P. Martin (Exeter/Grand Rapids, 1970), pp. 264-76; J. Murphy-O'Connor, "Christological Anthropology in Phil. 2:6-11," *RB* 83 (1974), pp. 25-50; M. D. Hooker, "Philippians 2:6-11," in *Jesus und Paulus (für W. G. Kümmel),* ed. E. E. Ellis and E. Grässer (Göttingen, 1975), pp. 151-64; O. Hofius, *Der Christushymnus Philipper 2, 6-11,* WUNT 17 (Tübingen, 1976).

30. Cf. H. L. Ellison, *The Centrality of the Messianic Idea,* pp. 7-9.

unnecessary to look for the origins of this conception in the idea of a Heavenly Man belonging, perhaps, to the Zoroastrian realm of thought.[31] The New Testament portrayal of Christ as the last Adam can be accounted for adequately on the basis of the Old Testament, interpreted in the light of the character and achievement of Christ. By his character and achievement he is immediately recognizable by his people as

> the Proper Man,
> Whom God Himself hath bidden.[32]

The quotation from Ps. 8 is linked with what has gone before in that the clause with which the quotation ends—"Thou hast subjected all things beneath his feet"—echoes the earlier quotation from Ps. 110:1, "Till I make your enemies a footstool for your feet."[33] Not his enemies only, but the whole creation, will ultimately be brought into manifest subjection to him.

It is as the true representative of humanity that Christ is viewed as fulfilling the language of the psalm, and as fulfilling therewith the declared purpose of the Creator when he brought the human race into being. As mankind's true representative, accordingly, he must share in the conditions inseparable from the human condition; only so could he blaze the trail of salvation for mankind and act effectively as his people's high priest in the presence of God. This means that he is not only the one in whom the sovereignty destined for humanity is realized, but also the one who, because of human sin, must realize that sovereignty by way of suffering and death. Therefore he who has already been introduced as "so much better than the angels" had to be "made a little lower than the angels," as the psalmist said. Why this should be our author proceeds to show.

8b The psalmist's words, "Thou hast subjected all things beneath his feet," had reference to things on earth as far as Adam was concerned; but the dominion of Christ knows no such limitation. "For in subjecting all things to him, he left nothing that is not subject" (NEB). Our author does not add, as Paul did, "it is evident that he is excepted who put all things under him" (1 Cor. 15:27); but this exception is, of course, implied. (A very early copyist or reader perhaps added a marginal note here to make explicit what our author left implicit.)[34] As things are, however, the subjection of the created

---

31. Cf. discussions in J. M. Creed, "The Heavenly Man," *JTS* 26 (1925), pp. 113-36; C. H. Dodd, *The Bible and the Greeks* (London, 1935), pp. 145-69; W. Manson, *Jesus the Messiah* (London, 1943), pp. 174-90; S. Mowinckel, *He That Cometh* (Oxford, 1956), pp. 346-450; further bibliography will be found in these publications.

32. From T. Carlyle's translation of Luther's *Ein' feste Burg;* Luther's wording is: "der rechte Mann / Den Gott selbst hat erkoren."

33. These two OT passages are similarly conjoined by Paul in 1 Cor. 15:25-27. Cf. Heb. 10:13 (p. 246).

34. See p. 70, n. 15.

world to mankind, declared by the psalmist to be God's ordinance, is not yet fully realized, and even the Man of God's right hand does not yet command the willing allegiance of all.[35] But the sovereignty which human beings have proved unable to exercise thus far is already wielded on their behalf by the true Son of Man; his suffering and triumph constitute the pledge of his eternal kingdom.

9 For there at God's right hand he sits enthroned, and "crowned with glory and honor." Jesus, who became man; Jesus, who was made "a little lower than the angels"; Jesus, who endured death—this Jesus has been raised to the place of highest exaltation, and reigns there until all opposition to his sovereignty comes to an end. Then indeed in the fullest degree will be seen "all things subjected to him."[36]

Moreover, it is precisely because of his humiliation, suffering, and death that he has been invested with heavenly glory. This interpretation of our author's argument at this point brings it into line with Paul's "Therefore God has highly exalted him" in Phil. 2:9. But very many commentators on Hebrews have found themselves obliged by the construction here to think of the crowning with glory and honor as something preceding the suffering of death, as a solemn preparation for it.[37] The transfiguration of Christ has been

---

35. Gk. νῦν δέ at the beginning of the sentence is not temporal but logical: "but as it is" (cf. 8:6; 9:26; 11:16). There is a minor *crux interpretum* in the sentence: when our author says that "we do not yet see all things subjected to him," does "to him" (Gk. αὐτῷ) mean "to man" or "to Christ"? The *crux* is only a minor one because in any case Christ is in view as the representative Man. But in the first instance the reference is probably to man (so Westcott, Moffatt; cf. NEB: "But in fact we do not yet see all things in subjection to man"). We do not see man exercising his God-given right as lord of creation, but we do see God's Man invested with universal sovereignty. The writer confesses that it is not easy to recognize in man the being whom the psalmist describes as "crowned with glory and honor" and enjoying dominion over all the works of the Creator's hands. "Man's unfulfilled promise, however, he sees fulfilled in Christ, and for mankind fulfilled through Christ" (A. E. Garvie, "Shadow and Substance," *ExT* 28 [1916-17], p. 461). For the view that αὐτῷ means "to Christ" cf. Spicq, *ad loc.*: "Jesus is still far from having been accepted and acclaimed as king by all the universe: 'unbelieving sinners and demons are not yet subject to him' (St. Thomas). The author must here be expressing the anguish, if not the discouragement, of the despised and persecuted Christians, vainly awaiting God's kingdom on earth (2 Pet. 3:4). The truth is that Christ's militant kingdom is progressive; he must put down his enemies (1:13) before its plenary and triumphant realization." Our author recognizes that, even in exaltation and enthronement, Christ is waiting "till his enemies be made the footstool of his feet" (10:13); this implies that while he is the rightful ruler of all, all do not yet acknowledge his sovereignty. So, while the human race is primarily indicated by αὐτῷ, the Son of Man, federal head of that race, cannot be excluded from its scope.

36. Our author does not add, as Paul does, that then the whole creation, which "has been groaning in travail together until now," will be "delivered from its bondage to decay into the liberty of the glory of the children of God" (Rom. 8:19-22); this cosmic aspect of the redemptive work of Christ falls outside his theme.

37. "The crowning with glory and honour must, on any natural rendering of the Greek, precede the death" (A. Nairne, *The Epistle of Priesthood* [Edinburgh, 1913], p. 70). Cf. A. B.

thought of as the occasion referred to;[38] it was then that "he received glory and honor from God the Father" (2 Pet. 1:17), and it was immediately thereafter that he set out upon the last journey to Jerusalem.[39] "The crowning," says Alexander Nairne, "marks the victim, or the hero going gallantly to his contest, not the victorious king."[40] Yet it is difficult to fit this interpretation into the context of the general argument of this epistle, in which the glory is consistently presented as the sequel to the passion.[41] The phrase "because of the suffering of death" more naturally suggests that the crowning followed the suffering as its divinely appointed end than that the crowning took place *with a view to* the suffering of death.[42] As for the clause "that . . . he should taste death for all," it does indeed express purpose—not, however, the purpose of the crowning by itself, but rather the purpose of the whole sequence of preceding events, the humiliation, passion, and glory combined.[43] Because the Son of Man suffered, because his suffering has been crowned by his exaltation, therefore his death avails for all.[44] Chrysostom's comment on Christ's tasting death for everyone has been frequently quoted: "As a physician, though not needing to taste the food prepared for the sick man, yet in his care for him tastes first himself, that he may persuade the sick man with confidence to venture on the food; so, since all men were afraid of death, in

---

Bruce, *The Epistle to the Hebrews* (Edinburgh, 1899), pp. 79-83. The clause ὅπως . . . ὑπὲρ παντὸς γεύσηται θανάτου need not, however, be closely dependent on ἐστεφανωμένον, but is rather epexegetic of διὰ τὸ πάθημα τοῦ θανάτου. See n. 43 below.

38. Cf. A. E. Garvie, "Shadow and Substance," p. 549: "He had this foretaste of heaven, however, only to confirm Him in and equip Him for the purpose to surrender the glory and honour He might have claimed as His right, to put Himself in man's place, and to share with man the doom of death, which in no way was His due."

39. Cf. Luke 9:31 (Moses and Elijah conversed with Jesus about his "exodus" which he was about to accomplish at Jerusalem), followed by v. 51: "when the days of his being received up were now reaching their fulfilment, he set his face steadfastly to go to Jerusalem." At the moment of his transfiguration he was "ripe for glory" (A. E. Garvie, "Shadow and Substance," p. 549), but instead of ascending from the holy mount to heaven he came down to the plain and set out for Jerusalem.

40. *Epistle of Priesthood*, p. 313. Nairne saw a reference here to the crown of thorns.

41. Cf. 12:2 (pp. 337-39).

42. Cf. Westcott, *ad loc.*, for the point that διά with the accusative in the NT expresses "the *ground* and not the *object: because* something is, and not *in order that* something may be realized."

43. "Thus ὅπως . . . θανάτου explains and expounds this idea of διὰ τὸ πάθημα (which consists in) τοῦ θανάτου, gathering up the full object and purpose of the experience which has just been predicated of Jesus" (Moffatt, ICC, *ad loc.*). Cf. also the comments *ad loc.* of Westcott, Spicq, and Michel.

44. It is because Christ has been exalted as supreme over all that his death is now seen to be effective ὑπὲρ παντός. So far as the form goes, παντός might be masculine ("everyone") or neuter ("everything"); but since our author's concern is with Christ's work for humanity, and not with the cosmic implications of his work (cf. p. 75, n. 36), it is more probably to be taken as masculine. Cf. NEB: "so that . . . in tasting death he should stand for us all."

persuading them to take courage against death, he tasted it also himself though he had no need so to do."[45] But the point of our author's argument is that Christ did have need so to do, if the purpose of his incarnation was to be accomplished; Chrysostom has been over-influenced by the verb "taste."[46] Calvin's comment is more penetrating than Chrysostom's: "By saying 'for every one,' he means not only that Christ might be an example to others, as Chrysostom says, when he adduces the example of a physician taking the first taste of a bitter draught, that the patient may consent to drink it; he means rather that Christ died for us, and that by taking on Himself what was due to us, He redeemed us from the curse of death."[47]

Whatever may be said of the textual warrant for the phrase "by God's grace,"[48] it is entirely appropriate in the context and makes for a smooth transition to the words which follow.

E. THE SON OF MAN THE SAVIOR AND HIGH PRIEST OF HIS PEOPLE (2:10-18)

10 *It was indeed fitting for the one for whom all things exist and through whom all things exist, in leading*[49] *many sons to glory, to perfect through sufferings the pioneer*[50] *of their salvation.*

11 *For the sanctifier and those who are sanctified all come from one stock. That is why he is not ashamed to call them "brothers,"*

12 *when he says,*
     "I will declare your name to my brothers;
     in the midst of the congregation I will sing your praise";[51]

---

45. *Homilies on Hebrews* 4.12.

46. Cf. Chrysostom's further refinement on the use of the verb "taste": "Moreover he rightly said '*taste* death for every man'; he did not say 'die'. For as if he were only *tasting* it [instead of swallowing the bitter draught, so to speak], when he had spent but a little time therein, he immediately arose." (For the correlative idiom "taste life," in the sense of making but a preliminary trial of it, see *New Docs.*, IV [1979], § 12, quoting *IG* 14.1607.1, of an infant dying before reaching the age of one year.)

47. *Commentary on Hebrews, ad loc.*

48. Cf. p. 70, n. 15.

49. Gk. ἀγαγόντα, to be construed as a simultaneous aorist participle, which, moreover, despite its accusative case (the result of its being conformed to the accusative-and-infinitive construction), is to be taken in sense with αὐτῷ ("him") and not with ἀρχηγόν ("pioneer"). See Westcott, *ad loc.*

50. So the RSV renders τὸν ἀρχηγὸν τῆς σωτηρίας αὐτῶν (NEB "the leader who delivers them"). Cf. Acts 3:15 for the similar title τὸν ... ἀρχηγὸν τῆς ζωῆς (with *Acts*, NICNT, p. 82, n. 30, and E. K. Simpson, "The Vocabulary of the Epistle to the Hebrews," *EQ* 18 [1946], pp. 35f.).

51. Ps. 22:22 (LXX 21:23). The LXX is followed except that ἀπαγγελῶ here takes the place of διηγήσομαι as the rendering of Heb. *'ăsapp^erāh*, "I will declare."

13 *and again,*
"I will place my trust in him";[52]
and again,
"Here am I—I and the children that God has given me."[53]

14 *Since then the children are sharers in flesh and blood,*[54] *he himself likewise partook*[55] *of the same, so that through death he might bring to nought the one who held the power of death—namely, the devil—*

15 *and deliver those who for fear of death were liable to lifelong bondage.*

16 *It is not, you see, of angels but of the offspring of Abraham that he takes hold.*[56]

17 *Therefore it was necessary for him to be made like his brothers in all respects, so as to become a merciful and faithful high priest where their responsibility to God is concerned, with a view to making atonement*[57] *for the people's sins.*

18 *For since he himself endured trial and suffering, he is able to help those enduring trial.*

---

52. Isa. 8:17, last clause (LXX); cf. also Isa. 12:2; 2 Sam. (LXX 2 Kms.) 22:3 // Ps. 18:2 (LXX 17:3).

53. Isa. 8:18a (LXX).

54. Lit. "blood and flesh" (αἵματος καὶ σαρκός); for this order cf. Eph. 6:12.

55. Gk. παραπλησίως μετέσχεν. With παραπλησίως (here only in the NT) cf. παραπλήσιον in Phil. 2:27 (see *New Docs.*, III [1978], § 57). To press a distinction between μετέχω here and κοινωνέω in the immediately preceding clause would be precarious: our author insists that Christ partook of flesh and blood in the same way as "the children," so that his humanity is as genuine as theirs (cf. v. 17: "he had to be made like his brothers in all respects"). Such significant distinction as there is between the two forms lies in the tenses: "the children are sharers in (κεκοινώνηκεν, perfect) flesh and blood" in the sense that that is their original and natural state; human beings are per se creatures of flesh and blood. Our Lord, however, existed before his incarnation; "flesh and blood" form no essential part of his eternal being; but at a fixed point in time, by his own choice, "he also himself in like manner partook (μετέσχεν, aorist) of the same" and so began to share fully the nature of those whom he chose thus to redeem.

56. Gk. ἐπιλαμβάνεται, "takes hold." So ERV: "For verily not of angels doth he take hold, but he taketh hold of the seed of Abraham." Cf. NEB: "It is not angels, mark you, that he takes to himself, but the sons of Abraham." E. K. Simpson (*Words Worth Weighing in the Greek New Testament* [London, 1946], pp. 27-29) protests against weakening the meaning of the verb here to "help" (so ARV, "not to angels doth he give help")—a rendering for which Sir. 4:11 ("Wisdom . . . gives help to those who seek her") has been invoked—but that, he says rightly, "can be otherwise construed." He adduces good Hellenistic evidence for the sense "take hold." Cf. its use in Heb. 8:9 (also Matt. 14:31).

57. Gk. εἰς τὸ ἱλάσκεσθαι. The renderings of the RSV ("to make expiation for") and the NEB ("to expiate") are justified here because the direct object of the verb is "sins" (ἁμαρτίας). True, if sins need to be expiated, it is because they are sins committed against someone who ought to be propitiated; but in the Greek Bible ἱλάσκομαι (or ἐξιλάσκομαι) is not found with the person propitiated as its object. The only other NT occurrence of the verb ἱλάσκομαι is in Luke 18:13, ἱλάσθητι, "be merciful" (lit. "be propitiated"); but here there is no thought of propitiation in the ordinary sense: the only "propitiation" in view is the tax-collector's penitent prayer. Cf. the substantive ἱλαστήριον ("place *or* means of propitiation") in 9:5 (see p. 204) and in Rom. 3:25 (unless in the latter place it is accusative singular masculine of the adjective ἱλαστήριος),

10 The one "for whom and by whom all things exist" (RSV)[58] must here be God the Father, of whose perfecting work the Son is object. There are many who are ready to tell us confidently what would and what would not be worthy of God; but in fact the only way to discover what is a worthy thing for God to do is to consider what God has actually done. The person who says, "I could not have a high opinion of a God who would (or would not) do this or that," is not adding anything to our knowledge of God; he is simply telling us something about himself. We may be sure that all that God does is worthy of himself, but here our author singles out one of God's actions and tells us that it was a fitting thing for him to do.[59] And what was that? It was his making Jesus, through his sufferings, perfectly qualified to be the Savior of his people. It is in the passion of our Lord that we see the

---

and the substantive ἱλασμός ("propitiation") in 1 John 2:2; 4:10. The NT use of these words follows the precedent of the LXX, where (together with other cognates, especially the intensive verb ἐξιλάσκομαι) they are chiefly used as equivalents of the Piʻel conjugation of Heb. *k-p-r* and its derivatives. Whether the etymological force of this Piʻel conjugation is "cover completely" or "wipe out," its cultic use denotes the restoration of a relationship between God and mankind which has been broken by man's sin, the mediator in this work being normally the priest. That this propitiatory work is far from resembling the placating of a vengeful or capricious power is evident from the way in which the OT and the NT alike represent God as taking the initiative in providing the means for restoring the broken relationship between himself and his people: cf. Lev. 17:11, "I have given it [the sacrificial blood] to you upon the altar to make atonement *(leḵappēr)* for your lives"; Rom. 3:25, "whom [i.e., Christ] God put forward as an atonement by his blood, to be received by faith." See S. R. Driver, *HDB,* IV (Edinburgh, 1902), pp. 128-32 (*s.v.* "Propitiation"); J. Herrmann and F. Büchsel, *TDNT,* III, pp. 301-23 (*s.v.* ἱλάσκομαι); C. H. Dodd, *The Bible and the Greeks,* pp. 82-95; *The Epistle to the Romans,* MNTC (London, 1932), pp. 54f.; *The Johannine Epistles,* MNTC (London, 1945), pp. 25-29; T. W. Manson, "ΙΛΑΣΤΗΡΙΟΝ," *JTS* 46 (1945), pp. 1-10; E. K. Simpson, *Words Worth Weighing in the Greek New Testament,* pp. 10-12; R. R. Nicole, "C. H. Dodd and the Doctrine of Propitiation," *WTJ* 17 (1954-55), pp. 117-57; L. Morris, *The Apostolic Preaching of the Cross* (London, ³1965), pp. 143-213; *NBD* (Leicester, ²1982), pp. 986f. (*s.v.* "Propitiation"); *New Dictionary of Theology* (Leicester, 1988), pp. 54-57 (*s.v.* "Atonement"); N. H. Young, "C. H. Dodd, 'Hilaskesthai' and his Critics," *EQ* 48 (1976), pp. 67-78, with reply by R. R. Nicole, "'Hilaskesthai' Revisited," *EQ* 49 (1977), pp. 173-77, and again N. H. Young, "'Hilaskesthai' and Related Words in the New Testament," *EQ* 55 (1983), pp. 169-76. W. M. Ramsay, "The Greek of the Early Church and the Pagan Ritual," *ExT* 10 (1898-99), pp. 55, 157f., and A. Deissmann, *Bible Studies,* E.T. (Edinburgh, 1909), pp. 224f., quote as a parallel to the use of ἱλάσκομαι with the direct object ἁμαρτίας the inscription *CIA* 3.74 from Laurium in Attica, set up by Xanthus, a Lycian slave, regarding a sanctuary which he had founded for the Anatolian deity Mēn Tyrannos: it says of a certain type of offender against this deity, "let him incur a debt of sin (ἁμαρτίαν ὀφ(ε)ιλέτω) against Mēn Tyrannos, which he will by no means be able to expiate (ἐξειλάσασθαι)." See *New Docs.,* III (1978), § 6.

58. The preposition διά is used first with the accusative and then with the genitive, denoting God as "the final Cause and the efficient Cause of all things" (Westcott, *ad loc.*).

59. Gk. ἔπρεπεν γὰρ αὐτῷ. Cf. 7:26, "such a high priest became (ἔπρεπεν) us." Spicq (*Hébreux,* I, p. 53) notes that the argument about what befits God is otherwise unknown in the Bible, but appears in Greek literature, and notably in Philo (*Leg. Alleg.* 1.48; *Age of the World* 41, etc.) and Josephus (*Against Apion* 2.168).

very heart of God laid bare; nowhere is God more fully or more worthily revealed as God than when we see him "in Christ reconciling the world to himself" (2 Cor. 5:19).

For the great salvation which the gospel proclaims was not only "first announced through the Lord," as we have been told above, but was procured for us by him through his passion. He is the Pathfinder, the Pioneer of our salvation; this is the meaning of the word *archēgos,* rendered "author" here in the ERV/ARV and "captain" in the AV/KJV.[60] He is the Savior who blazed the trail of salvation along which alone God's "many sons" could be brought to glory. Man, created by God for his glory, was prevented by sin from attaining that glory until the Son of Man came and opened up by his death a new way by which humanity might reach the goal for which it was made. As his people's representative and forerunner he has now entered into the presence of God to secure *their* entry there.

But what is meant by his being made "perfect" through his sufferings? If the Son of God is the effulgence of his Father's glory and the very impress of his being, how can he be thought of as falling short of perfection? The answer is this: the perfect Son of God has become his people's perfect Savior, opening up their way to God; and in order to become that, he must endure suffering and death. The pathway of perfection which his people must tread must first be trodden by the Pathfinder;[61] only so could he be their adequate representative and high priest in the presence of God. There is much in this epistle about the attainment of perfection[62] in the sense of unimpeded access to God and unbroken communion with him, but in this as in other things it is Christ who leads the way.

60. The word ἀρχηγός appears four times in the NT, the other three being in Heb. 12:2 (see pp. 337f.); Acts 3:15; 5:31. Cf. p. 77, n. 50. C. J. A. Hickling suggests that "the pioneer of their salvation" might be taken as "a summary of much of what John [in his Gospel] means by his distinctive use of the Son of Man title" ("John and Hebrews: The Background of Hebrews 2.10-18," *NTS* 29 [1983], p. 114). See also E. K. Simpson, "The Vocabulary of the Epistle to the Hebrews," pp. 35f.; P.-G. Müller, *Christos Archegos* (Bern/Frankfurt, 1973); G. Johnston, "Christ as Archegos," *NTS* 27 (1980-81), pp. 381-85.

61. "The many sons in being brought to glory are perfected through suffering; and so it is in accord with the divine method of dealing that the pioneer of salvation should pass through the same experience" (A. E. Garvie, "Shadow and Substance," p. 504).

62. See 5:9, 14; 6:1; 7:11, 19, 28; 9:9, 11; 10:1, 14; 11:40; 12:2, 23, with exposition and notes below. Cf. Westcott, *Hebrews,* pp. 66-68; Spicq, *Hébreux,* I, pp. 64f. (where Philonic parallels are adduced); P. J. du Plessis, *ΤΕΛΕΙΟΣ: The Idea of Perfection in the New Testament* (Kampen, 1959), pp. 206-33; A. Wikgren, "Patterns of Perfection in the Epistle to the Hebrews," *NTS* 6 (1959-60), pp. 159-67; C. E. Carlston, "The Vocabulary of Perfection in Philo and Hebrews," in *Unity and Diversity in New Testament Theology* (G. E. Ladd *FS*), ed. R. A. Guelich (Grand Rapids, 1978), pp. 133-60; L. K. K. Dey, *The Intermediary World and Patterns of Perfection in Philo and Hebrews,* SBLDS 25 (Missoula, MT, 1975); D. G. Peterson, *Hebrews and Perfection,* SNTSM 47 (Cambridge, 1982).

In order to be a perfect high priest, a person must sympathize with those on whose behalf he acts, and he cannot sympathize with them unless he can enter into their experiences and share them for himself. Jesus did just this. Moreover, in order to be a perfect high priest, a person must learn the lesson of obedience to God; if he failed in this, he would really need a priest for himself, to enter into God's presence for him with the assurance of being admitted there. Of Jesus' obedience there could be no question.[63] But a high priest had one specially solemn service to perform; he had to present an atonement to God on his people's behalf. And an atonement efficacious in itself could be presented only by a high priest whose sympathetic self-identification with his people was unreserved, and at the same time by a high priest whose obedience to God was unmarred by any reluctance—not to say refusal—to obey. There is only one who fulfils these conditions perfectly—the one whose obedience and death fitted him completely to be his people's representative. He suffered not only with them but for them; his suffering was both voluntary and vicarious. He who suffered was the Son of God, and the "many" for whom he suffered are thus led to glory as sons of God in their turn.

11   "For a consecrating priest and those whom he consecrates are all of one stock" (NEB). That is a general truth, and in this supreme instance it is exemplified by the fact that not only do he who consecrates and those who are consecrated share a common humanity but also he is the Son of God and they are sons and daughters of God.[64] It is by his sacrifice of himself in obedience to God's will that they are sanctified, as appears more fully later in the epistle—"sanctified once for all through the offering of the body of Jesus Christ" (10:10).[65] By his death they are consecrated to God for his worship and service and set apart for God as his holy people, destined to enter into his glory. For sanctification is glory begun, and glory is sanctification completed. And since those who are sanctified to God through his death are sons and daughters of God, the Son of God is not ashamed to acknowledge them as his brothers and sisters—not only as those whose nature he took upon himself, but those whose trials he endured, for whose sins he made atonement, that they might follow him to glory on the path of salvation which he himself cut.

12-13   Three Old Testament quotations are introduced here, in which his solidarity with his people is set forth.[66]

---

63. See 5:7f. (pp. 126-32).

64. The argument here apparently requires the "one" from whom the sanctifier and the sanctified alike have their being to be God—not Abraham (in the sense of v. 16 below) nor yet Adam (cf. O. Procksch in *TDNT*, I, p. 112, *s.v.* ἁγιάζω), although it is to Adam that the same phrase ἐξ ἑνός refers in Acts 17:26.

65. Cf. also 9:13f.; 10:14, 29; 13:12; see p. 247, n. 73.

66. The exegesis of these three quotations in their present context is greatly indebted to G. Vos, *The Teaching of the Epistle to the Hebrews* (Grand Rapids, 1956), pp. 60f.

(a) The first quotation (Ps. 22:22 [LXX 21:23]) is taken from a psalm in which no Christian of the first century would have failed to recognize Christ as the speaker. It is the psalm whose opening words Jesus took upon his lips as the expression of his own experience in the hour of dereliction on the cross: "My God, my God, why hast thou forsaken me?"[67] Practically the whole of the lament to which the first part of the psalm is devoted was used in the church from very early times as a *testimonium* of the crucifixion of Christ; not only is it expressly quoted, but its language has been worked into the very fabric of the New Testament passion narratives, especially in the First and Fourth Gospels.[68] It is most natural, then, that when the psalmist's lament gives way to the public thanksgiving of which the second part of the psalm consists, the same speaker should be recognized, and the once crucified, now exalted Christ should be heard saying: "I will declare your name to my brothers; in the midst of the congregation I will sing your praise."[69] Following the Septuagint, our author uses the word *ekklēsia* for "congregation" (the Hebrew of Ps. 22:22 has *qāhāl*). The employment of this word in synonymous parallelism with "brothers" in a Christian context indicates that those whom the Son of God is pleased to call his brothers are the members of his church. By virtue of his suffering he has now become "the representative Head of a new mankind."[70]

(b) If it is easy to see the relevance of the quotation of Ps. 22:22 here, it is less easy to see the relevance of the quotation which follows it. "I will place my trust in him" is taken from the Septuagint of Isa. 8:17b. This is a good example of C. H. Dodd's thesis that the principal Old Testament quotations in the New Testament are not isolated proof-texts, but carry their contexts with them by implication.[71] In the context of this quotation, Isaiah, find-

---

67. Matt. 27:46; Mark 15:34.

68. The parting of our Lord's garments among the soldiers appears to have been recognized very early (cf. Mark 15:24) as a fulfilment of Ps. 22:18 (LXX 21:19); in John 19:24 that passage is explicitly quoted as a *testimonium* of the incident. Cf. C. H. Dodd, *According to the Scriptures* (London, 1952), pp. 97f.; B. Lindars, *New Testament Apologetic* (London, 1961), pp. 88-93.

69. Cf. the adaptation of Ps. 22:22 in *Odes of Solomon* 31:3f.:

He [our Lord] opened his mouth and spoke grace and joy;
   and chanted a new (song of) praise to his name.
Then he lifted up his voice to the Most High,
   and offered to him those who had become sons through him.

See J. H. Charlesworth (ed.), *The Old Testament Pseudepigrapha*, II (Garden City, NY, 1985), p. 762.

70. C. H. Dodd, *According to the Scriptures*, p. 20. See also E. Schweizer, *Lordship and Discipleship*, E.T., SBT 28 (London, 1960), pp. 71-75, 88-90.

71. *According to the Scriptures*, p. 126 et passim. In accordance with this insight, we may recall Calvin's interpretation of the two Isaiah quotations here in association with the "rock" of Isa. 8:14 (a notable *testimonium* in the NT), and link it with 2 Sam. 22:3, "God, my rock, in

ing that his oracles of salvation and judgment meet with no response from either king or people, seals them up and hands them over to his disciples for safekeeping, in order that, when their fulfilment comes, it may be made apparent that what he had spoken was the true word of God. Meanwhile, he says, "I will wait for Yahweh, who is hiding his face from the house of Jacob, and I will hope in him." God's hiding of his face from the house of Jacob provides the link with Ps. 22, where his face is hidden from the righteous sufferer who (in the Christian interpretation) is the representative of the whole house of Jacob, enduring the dereliction which was due to them. If Isaiah, one of the prophets through whom God of old time spoke to the fathers, was rejected by those to whom he came, so was the Son in whom God more recently spoke his final word; if Isaiah nonetheless maintained his trust in God and waited for vindication from him, so did the Son of God. "Commit yourself to Yahweh," the righteous sufferer is exhorted in mockery in Ps. 22;[72] but when the suffering is past he gratefully bears witness to the faithfulness of the God in whom he trusted:

> For he has not despised or abhorred the affliction of the afflicted;
> and he has not hid his face from him;
> but has heard, when he cried to him.[73]

This recurring pattern of men and women's trust in God in days of darkness and their glad acknowledgment of God's faithfulness when he acts for their vindication is found in the lives of many biblical characters; but there is something quite outstanding in the case of Isaiah. For it is with him that we begin to see the historical emergence of the righteous remnant, the faithful Israel within the empirical Israel, the group in whose survival the hope of the future was assured, one might almost say the *ekklēsia* of the Messiah. Certainly, in Isaiah's prophetic ministry there is a close association between the coming King and the remnant—or, to use the language of Hebrews, between the Son and his brothers. Moreover, there is reason to believe that Isaiah himself took steps to give a conscious corporate existence to the embryonic remnant of his own day, partly in the circle of his disciples of whom he speaks in Isa. 8:16 and partly in his own family.

   (c)   Isaiah's family is referred to directly in the third quotation, which comes from Isa. 8:18a, and in the Old Testament text follows immediately upon the second quotation. One may wonder, then, why the two quotations are separated by "And again," but the reason no doubt is that two separate points are being made. In the Septuagint the words quoted from Isa. 8:18a

---

him will I take refuge" (LXX . . . πεποιθὼς ἔσομαι ἐπ' αὐτῷ), and its parallel in Ps. 18:2 (LXX 17:3).

72. Verse 8 (LXX 21:9, practically quoted in Matt. 27:43a).

73. Ps. 22:24 (LXX 21:24), echoed in Heb. 5:7 (see pp. 128f.).

form a separate sentence, as they do here: "Here am I, and the children God has given me" (RSV). But in the Hebrew text they form the first part of a longer sentence: "Behold, I and the children whom Yahweh has given me are signs and portents in Israel from Yahweh of hosts, who dwells on Mount Zion."[74] The people might pay no heed to Isaiah's oracles, but so long as Isaiah himself went about in Jerusalem, he was an abiding witness to the message of God which had been conveyed through him. Not only so, but his own significant name ("Yahweh is salvation") and the equally significant names of his two sons—Shear-jashub ("Remnant will return") and Maher-shalal-hash-baz ("Hasten booty, speed spoil")[75]—reminded the people of the dominant themes of his message. Indeed, his sons' names were the expression of his own obedient trust in God, his confidence that what God had said would surely come to pass.

That the Son of God's confidence in his Father had been vindicated by his exaltation was not yet a matter of public manifestation; it had been revealed to believers and was proclaimed by them as part of their witness. But the life and witness of these believers—members of the family of Christ—was a token to the world that it had not seen or heard the last of Jesus of Nazareth. If he represented his people at the right hand of God, they represented him on earth. Isaiah's words about his children might therefore be understood in an extended sense as the words of Christ about his people. Once again his solidarity with them is affirmed, not now by means of the term "brothers," as in vv. 11 and 12, but by means of the term "children." The description of Christians as the "children" of Christ is peculiar to this epistle among the New Testament writings; yet Old Testament precedent for it might be found not only in the words of Isa. 8:18 but in a statement about the Suffering Servant in Isa. 53:10: "when he makes himself an offering for sin, he shall see his offspring" (RSV). As for the thought of their being given by God to his Son, a close parallel appears in our Lord's prayer in John 17, where he repeatedly speaks of his disciples as "those whom thou gavest me out of the world" (v. 6, etc.).[76]

14 Who are those "children" whom God has given to Christ? Men and women, creatures of flesh and blood. But if his solidarity with them is to be real, he also must be a true human being, a genuine partaker of flesh and blood. Moreover, he must partake of flesh and blood "in like manner" with them—that is to say, by the gateway of birth. No docetic or Apollinarian Christ will satisfy their need of a Savior or God's determination to supply

---

74. The LXX starts a new sentence after "whom God has given me": "And there shall be signs and wonders in the house of Israel from the Lord of hosts. . . ."
75. Isa. 7:3; 8:3.
76. Cf. John 6:37, 39.

that need. And if they, entering this earthly life by birth, leave it in due course by death, it was divinely fitting that he too should die. Indeed, this is stated here as the purpose of his incarnation—that he should die, and in the very act of dying draw the sting of death.

It calls for an exceptional effort of mind on our part to appreciate how paradoxical was the attitude of those early Christians to the death of Christ. If ever death had appeared to be triumphant, it was when Jesus of Nazareth, disowned by the leaders of his nation, abandoned by his disciples, executed by the might of imperial Rome, breathed his last on the cross. Why, some had actually recognized in his cry of pain and desolation the complaint that even God had forsaken him. His faithful followers had confidently expected him to be the destined liberator of Israel; but he had died—not, like Judas of Galilee or Judas Maccabaeus, in the forefront of the struggle against the Gentile oppressors of Israel, but in evident weakness and disgrace—and their hopes died with him. If ever a cause was lost, it was his; if ever the powers of evil were victorious, it was then. And yet—within a generation his followers were exultingly proclaiming the crucified Jesus to be the conqueror of death and asserting, like our author here, that by dying he had reduced the erstwhile lord of death to impotence. The keys of death and Hades were henceforth held firmly in Jesus' powerful hand, for he, in the language of his own parable, had invaded the strong man's fortress, disarmed him, bound him fast, and robbed him of his spoil (Luke 11:21f.). This is the unanimous witness of the New Testament writers; this was the assurance which nerved martyrs to face death boldly in his name. This sudden change from disillusionment to triumph can only be explained by the account which the apostles gave—that their Master rose from the dead and imparted to them the power of his risen life.

The prince or angel of death is here identified with the devil—that is, Satan. It is not easy to parallel this outright identification,[77] but it is not inconsonant with the general teaching of the New Testament. "The reason the Son of God appeared," says another New Testament writer, "was to destroy the works of the devil" (1 John 3:8),[78] and while the particular work of the devil most prominent in that context is sin, the association between sin and death is close enough for the destruction of death to be included in the purpose of the Son of God's appearance.[79] Our author in all probability belonged

---

77. Cf. *Pesiqta rabbati* 36 (161a): when Satan saw the soul of the preexistent Messiah he said, "Truly this is the Messiah, who will plunge me and the angel princes of the nations into Gehinnom, as it is written: 'He will swallow up death for ever' [Isa. 25:8]."

78. Cf. Rev. 12:5ff., where the downfall of the dragon is the sequel to the birth and exaltation of the "man child."

79. Cf. 1 Cor. 15:26, where death is the last of the enemies to be destroyed (καταργεῖσθαι) by Christ, in ultimate fulfilment of Ps. 110:1. See p. 246.

to the circle from which the book of Wisdom came at an earlier date, and shared the sentiments on this subject which find expression there:

> God did not make death,
> and he does not delight in the death of the living.
> For he created all things that they might exist, . . .
> and the dominion of Hades is not on earth. (Wisdom 1:13f.)

> God created man for incorruption,
> and made him in the image of his own eternity,
> but through the devil's envy death entered the world,
> and those who belong to his party experience it. (Wisdom 2:23f.)

These quotations do not amount to a statement that the devil "had the power of death," but they come very near to it.[80] Jesus broke the devil's grip on his people when in death he became the death of death, when (in S. W. Gandy's words)—

> He hell in hell laid low,
> Made sin, he sin o'erthrew,
> Bowed to the grave, destroyed it so,
> And death, by dying, slew.

15 Only by becoming a human being could the Son of God conquer death, which mankind without him could never have done; until his conquest of death, death seemed to have the last word. The resurrection faith was cherished before he came, but his resurrection "brought life and immortality to light"[81] and gave that faith a firmer basis. His resurrection is not expressly mentioned here (or anywhere else in the epistle, for that matter, outside the doxology of 13:20f.), but it is implied nonetheless. If death had had the last word with him too, how would anyone have supposed that through death he had disabled the prince of death? The fear of death is a most potent fear. Through fear of death many will consent to do things that nothing else could compel them to do. Some braver souls, it is true, will accept death sooner than dishonor; but for the majority the fear of death can be a tyrannous instrument of coercion. And death is indeed the king of terrors to those who recognize in it the penalty of sin. But by the death of their Sanctifier, Christ's brothers and sisters are sanctified; his death has transformed the meaning of death for them. To them his death means not judgment, but blessing; not bondage, but liberation. And their own death, when it comes, takes its character from his death. If, then, death itself cannot separate the people of

---

80. Since Satan is chief prosecutor in the heavenly court, there is no difficulty in regarding him also as executioner-in-chief. Cf. 1 Cor. 5:5, "deliver this man to Satan for the destruction of the flesh."

81. 2 Tim. 1:10, where Christ is said already to have "abolished (καταργέω) death."

Christ from God's love which has been revealed in him, it can no longer be held over their heads by the devil or any other malign power as a means of intimidation.

16   He became man, then, in order to save men and women. When the Son of God, the Creator and Lord of angels, humbled himself, he passed by angelic estate and stooped lower still, taking to himself human nature for the redemption of the human family. Not of angels but of human beings he "takes hold": the verb is the same as that used in 8:9, where God recalls how he "took hold" of his people Israel by the hand to bring them out of Egypt, and in both places the "taking hold" carries with it the idea of help and deliverance. It unduly weakens the force of the word to translate with the RSV, "it is not with angels that he is concerned but with the descendants of Abraham."[82]

No one, moreover, can become a human being without thereby becoming a member of some particular human group or family. So when the Son of God took our nature upon himself, he became "the son of Abraham" (Matt. 1:1). In doing that, however, he became the helper and liberator of all the children of Abraham, and here quite certainly we are not to confine the scope of "the offspring of Abraham" to his natural descendants; we are rather to understand the whole family of faith.[83] Our author was in hearty agreement with Paul: "it is people of faith who are the children of Abraham" (Gal. 3:7). They are, in other words, the "many sons" whom God is bringing to glory through his first-begotten Son (v. 10).[84]

17   Having thus emphasized our Lord's solidarity with his brethren, our author now introduces that particular aspect of his solidarity with them which he is especially concerned to expound—his high-priestly ministry on their behalf. Any priest must be one with those whom he represents before God, and this is equally so with Christ as his people's high priest.[85] In order to serve them in this capacity, he was obliged to become completely like his brothers and sisters—apart from sin, of course, as is pointed out below (4:15). He suffered with them and for them, and through his sufferings was made perfect—qualified in every way to be their high priest. He is merciful be-

---

82. Cf. p. 78, n. 56.

83. OT believers, who could not attain perfection except in company with believers of NT times (11:40), are included in this family (cf. B. W. Newton, *The Old Testament Saints not to be Excluded from the Church in Glory* [London, 1887], pp. 12f.).

84. Christ's passing by angels in order that human beings might be saved may provide a further reason why the inferiority of angels is so much stressed in Heb. 1; human beings who inherit salvation are actually served by angels (1:14). On the Son of God's assimilation to humanity in order to be merciful it has been asked: "is the writer here consciously turning on its head the Platonic notion of ὁμοίωσις θεῷ (*Theaitetos* 176B)?" (*New Docs.*, II [1977], § 14.4).

85. Christ is called a "high priest," and not merely a "priest" (as in Ps. 110:4), because our author views his redemptive work as the antitypical fulfilment of the sacrificial ritual of the Day of Atonement, where the high priest in person was required to officiate (Heb. 9:7, 11f.).

cause through his own sufferings and trials he can sympathize with theirs; he is faithful because he endured to the end without faltering.[86] It is difficult to decide whether his faithfulness here is his steadfast loyalty to God (as in 3:2) or his utter trustworthiness as far as his people are concerned. Since in fact both aspects are essential in a perfect high priest, and are true of Christ, it may not be necessary to decide too narrowly between them.

His high priesthood is exercised "in matters for which they are responsible to God."[87] And most crucial among these matters is the matter of sin. How can sinners approach the holiness of God, either personally or through a representative? They can come to him with confidence only if their sin has been removed. And this above all else makes Jesus so incomparable a high priest and representative of his people; not only is he sinless himself, and therefore entitled to enter the presence of God on his own account, but he has dealt effectively with his people's sins, and can therefore enter the presence of God on their account too. The purpose of his incarnation was that through his death he might "make atonement for the people's sins"—do in effective reality what the sacrificial ritual of Old Testament times could do only in a token form. A high priest who has actually, and not merely in symbolism, removed his people's sins, and therewith the barrier which their sins erected between themselves and God, is a high priest worth having.[88]

18 He endured keen trials and temptations himself, not only the trials incidental to our human lot, but those subtle temptations which attended his messianic calling. Time and again the temptation came to him from many directions to choose some less costly way of fulfilling that calling than the way of suffering and death,[89] but he resisted it to the end and set his face

---

86. An echo of the words ἐλεήμων . . . καὶ πιστός appears in the Valentinian *Gospel of Truth* (Jung Codex 20:10): "This is why the merciful one, the faithful one, Jesus, was patient to endure the sufferings until he took that book, for he knows that this death of his means life for many" (cf. W. C. van Unnik in *The Jung Codex*, ed. F. L. Cross [London, 1955], pp. 108, 110; K. Grobel, *The Gospel of Truth* [London, 1960], pp. 62f.; G. W. MacRae in *The Nag Hammadi Library*, ed. J. M. Robinson [Leiden, 1977], p. 39). See pp. 221f., n. 118.

87. So τὰ πρὸς τὸν θεόν (cf. 5:1) is translated by T. W. Manson, *Ministry and Priesthood: Christ's and Ours* (London, 1958), p. 57; he illustrates this use of πρός from the formula ἔσται αὐτῷ πρὸς τὸν θεόν ("he will be answerable to God") occurring in an inscription from Western Phrygia, and refers to W. M. Calder, "The Eumeneian Formula," in *Anatolian Studies presented to W. H. Buckler* (London, 1939), pp. 15-26. A. Nairne renders the phrase "on the Godward side" (*The Epistle of Priesthood*, p. 45; in his preface he acknowledges indebtedness for this translation to a Cambridge sermon by G. H. Whitaker). Cf. also Josephus, *Ant.* 9.236: King Jotham was εὐσεβὴς μὲν τὰ πρὸς τὸν θεόν, δίκαιος δὲ τὰ πρὸς τοὺς ἀνθρώπους ("pious in matters relating to God, just in matters relating to human beings").

88. See R. A. Stewart, "The Sinless High Priest," *NTS* 14 (1967-68), pp. 126-35.

89. Cf. his friends' attempts to restrain him (Mark 3:21 [and 31?]) and Peter's well-meant remonstrance (Mark 8:32), in which he recognized another form of the temptation which he faced earlier in the wilderness and later in Gethsemane; hence his rebuke to Peter (Mark 8:33) took the same form as his reply to the tempter in the wilderness (Matt. 4:10).

steadfastly to accomplish the purpose for which he had come into the world. Now his people were not only enduring those trials which are common to mankind, but were being tempted in their turn to be disloyal to God and give up their Christian profession.[90] What a source of strength it was to them to be assured that in the presence of God they had as their champion and intercessor one who had known similar and even sorer temptations, and had withstood them victoriously![91]

90. On the general subject see K. G. Kuhn, "Temptation, Sin and Flesh," in *The Scrolls and the New Testament*, ed. K. Stendahl (London, 1958), pp. 94-113, especially pp. 96, 112.

91. On the presentation of Jesus in these first two chapters see especially the careful exposition by A. Vanhoye, *Situation du Christ*, LD 58 (Paris, 1969).

HEBREWS 3

II. THE TRUE HOME OF THE PEOPLE OF GOD
(3:1–4:13)

A. JESUS GREATER THAN MOSES (3:1-6)

1 *Therefore, you who are members of a holy brotherhood, partakers of a heavenly calling, consider the apostle and high priest whom we confess—consider Jesus.*

2 *He is faithful to the one who appointed him, just as Moses was faithful in all God's house.*[1]

3 *Jesus, in fact, has been deemed worthy of greater glory than Moses, inasmuch as the builder of the house has greater honor than the house.*

4 *For every house is built by someone, but the one who built all things is God.*

5 *Moses indeed was faithful in all God's house as a servant,*[2] *serving by way of testimony to the things which are about to be spoken of,*

6 *but Christ is faithful as a son over his house. Now it is we who are Christ's house,*[3] *if we maintain our confidence and the hope in which we boast.*[4]

---

1 To Jesus, then, the attention of the readers is directed. The terms in which

1. Gk. ἐν [ὅλῳ] τῷ οἴκῳ αὐτοῦ. The omission of ὅλῳ in 𝔭¹³ 𝔭⁴⁶ B and the Coptic versions with Cyril and Ambrose may well be original; in that case it has been supplied here in our other authorities on the basis of v. 5 (following the LXX).

2. Cf. Num. 12:7, where LXX πιστός renders Heb. *ne'ĕmān* ("entrusted").

3. Gk. οὗ οἶκος, "whose house." A few MSS (𝔭⁴⁶ D* 0121b 1739 and the Latin and Coptic versions) have ὅς οἶκος, "which house"; this reading is preferred by G. Zuntz as being "logically correct" (*The Text of the Epistles* [London, 1953], p. 93).

4. The added words "firm unto the end" (Gk. μέχρι τέλους βεβαίαν) are attested by ℵ A C D K P Ψ 0121b 33 81 629 1739 byz lat syrᵖᵉˢʰ copᵇᵒ; they are omitted in 𝔭¹³ 𝔭⁴⁶ B and the Sahidic (Coptic) and Ethiopic versions with Lucifer and Ambrose (μέχρι τέλους is omitted in 1022). They probably represent an insertion from the end of v. 14, as has been held by Mill, Bentley, Riggenbach, Windisch, Moffatt, Zuntz (*Text*, p. 33), and B. M. Metzger (*Textual Commentary on the Greek New Testament* [London/New York, 1971], p. 665); cf. the RSV and the NEB. One would have expected neuter βέβαιον here (in agreement with καύχημα), and not feminine βεβαίαν, which is appropriate in v. 14 (in agreement with παρρησίαν).

they are addressed—"brothers in the family of God, who share a heavenly calling" (NEB)—are calculated to remind them of the dignity with which God has invested them, a dignity which it would be insulting to God for them to treat lightly. Two common New Testament designations of Christians are joined together in the phrase "holy brothers,"[5] while the insistence on the heavenly character of their calling[6] marks them out as citizens of a realm not circumscribed by the conditions of earthly life. They are set apart by God for himself, made members of his family, and called to share in his eternal rest. The practical implications of all this become clear as the present phase of our author's argument proceeds.

When Jesus is designated as "the apostle and high priest of our confession,"[7] he is marked out as being both God's representative among human beings and their representative in the presence of God. The Old Testament writings tell the story of God's self-revelation to human beings and their response to that revelation; in both respects these writings find their fulfilment in Jesus. For he is not only, as has been emphasized already, the one in whom God has revealed himself finally and completely, but also the perfect embodiment of humanity's obedient response to God.

2 In both respects Jesus has proved himself faithful—a faithful high priest (cf. 2:17) and a faithful envoy. The faithfulness of an envoy consists in his loyal discharging of the commission with which he has been entrusted; and such faithfulness was manifested preeminently in the Sent One of God, who glorified his Father on earth by finishing the work which he had given him to do (cf. John 17:4).

The combining of the two rôles of divine envoy and priest in one person is not common in the Old Testament; it appears only in a few outstanding characters, among whom Moses occupies a special place. That Moses was an apostle of God to his people does not call for demonstration; it is equally true that he was his people's most effective intercessor with God.[8] It

---

5. Gk. ἀδελφοὶ ἅγιοι. Cf. Col. 1:2, ἁγίοις καὶ πιστοῖς ἀδελφοῖς (*Colossians–Philemon–Ephesians*, NICNT [Grand Rapids, 1984], p. 39). Cf. Heb. 6:10 (p. 151 with n. 65).

6. Elsewhere in the NT it is called a "holy calling" (2 Tim. 1:9) and an "upward calling" (Phil. 3:14); cf. also Rom. 1:7; 8:28, 30; 1 Pet. 1:15, etc. The church is the community of those whom God has called (Eph. 4:4; Col. 3:15; Heb. 9:15, etc.).

7. Gk. τὸν ἀπόστολον καὶ ἀρχιερέα τῆς ὁμολογίας ἡμῶν. Philo (*Life of Moses* 2.2ff.) describes Moses as filling the rôles of prophet and high priest, and also of king and legislator. The two possible ways of understanding ὁμολογία ("confession" either as "that which is confessed" or as "the act of confessing") are indicated respectively by the NEB text ("the Apostle and High Priest of the religion we profess") and margin ("him whom we confess as God's Envoy and High Priest"). The former is preferable; cf. BAGD ("the high priest of whom our confession speaks"). On "apostle and high priest" see also K. H. Rengstorf in *TDNT*, I (Grand Rapids, 1964), *s.v.* ἀπόστολος, pp. 416, 419, 423f. Justin calls Jesus "apostle" in his *First Apology* 12.9; 63.5.

8. In Philo, *Who Is Heir of Divine Things?* 205f., Moses is the primary λόγος who stands on the frontier between God and created beings as suppliant (ἱκέτης) for mortals and ambassa-

was his brother Aaron, and not he, who was high priest of Israel as far as title and investiture were concerned; but it was Moses, and not Aaron, who was Israel's true advocate with God. After the idolatrous festival in honor of the golden calf, in which Aaron himself was implicated, it was Moses whose prevailing plea procured pardon for his guilty people (Ex. 32:11-14, 31f.), as it did on a later occasion when the unfavorable report of the spies caused a rebellion in the camp and a resolution to return to Egypt (Num. 14:13-19). When Moses' unique position as the spokesman of God was challenged even by members of his own family, his faithfulness was vindicated by God. Other spokesmen of God might receive communications from him by vision or dream, but Moses enjoyed more direct revelation than they: "Not so with my servant Moses; he is entrusted with all my house: with him I speak mouth to mouth, clearly, and not in dark speech; and he beholds the form of Yahweh" (Num. 12:7f.).[9] Moses was acknowledged by God as chief steward[10] over his household,[11] and if "it is required in stewards, that one be found faithful" (1 Cor. 4:2), Moses certainly met this requirement. The "house" of Num. 12:7 in which Moses served so faithfully is not the tent of meeting but the people of Israel, the family of God.[12]

3-4 Yet, great as Moses was, his status was inferior to Christ's. The implication for the recipients of this epistle is plain: the old economy, inaugurated by Moses, is inferior to the new order introduced by Christ. Moses was a household servant[13] exalted by virtue of his outstanding faithfulness to the post of chief administrator of God's household; but Christ, the Son of God, through whom the universe was made and to whom it has been given by his Father as his heritage, is founder and inheritor of the household. In this regard

dor (πρεσβευτής) of the Ruler to his subjects, the mean between extremes (μέσος τῶν ἄκρων), a surety to both sides (ἀμφοτέροις ὁμηρεύων).

9. Quoted by Philo (*Leg. Alleg.* 3.103) to emphasize Moses' greatness. Cf. E. J. Young, *My Servants the Prophets* (Grand Rapids, 1952), pp. 38-55. On Moses as advocate and intercessor, see N. Johansson, *Parakletoi* (Lund, 1940), pp. 5, 67, 161, quoted by C. K. Barrett, *From First Adam to Last* (London, 1962), p. 61 n. See also A. T. Hanson, *Jesus Christ in the Old Testament* (London, 1965), pp. 48-57.

10. His position was that denoted by the Hebrew phrase *'al ha-bayit* (lit. "over the house," used, e.g., of Shebna in Isa. 22:15), although this phrase is not used in Num. 12:7.

11. Gk. οἶκος (like Heb. *bayit*) can mean both "house" ("dwelling") and "household" ("family"); it is the latter sense that is uppermost in the present passage (as in Num. 12:7). It must be further noted that "his house" in vv. 2, 5, and 6 means "*God's* house(hold)"—although in v. 6 the context shows that it is Christ's house(hold) also.

12. So the Targum of Onqelos at Num. 12:7 paraphrases *bêṯî* ("my house") as *'ammî* ("my people"). Cf. n. 15 below. In a comment on Gen. 28:17, Philo (*Migration of Abraham* 5) equates God's house with the Logos.

13. Gk. θεράπων (v. 5), as in Num. 12:7 (LXX); Wisdom 10:16 (cf. p. 308, n. 169). As a household servant Moses was a member of the household, and therefore lower in rank than the founder and master of the household. Justin Martyr (*First Apology* 20.5) refers to Menander and other writers for the sentiment that the builder (δημιουργός) is greater than what he builds.

the Son is one with the Father: God the Father, the Maker of all things,[14] is inevitably the founder of his own household, and it was through his Son that he brought into being all things in general and his own household in particular.

5-6a Moses' relation to God's household, then, was that of a servant; Christ's relation to it is that of the Son and heir. Moses administered the household as one who was himself part of the household; Christ rules over the household[15] as the Son whom his Father, the owner of the household, has appointed to exercise this rule. The Son's authority is greater than the servant's: Moses was not the *author* of the old economy as Christ is the author of the new. Yet God issued a solemn warning to any who might venture "to speak against my servant Moses" (Num. 12:8); more solemn still is the implicit warning against denying or ignoring the claims of Christ and the gospel. The claims of Christ and the gospel, indeed, are foreshadowed in the ministry which was committed to Moses: Moses' ministry was designed as "by way of testimony to the things which are about to be spoken of"[16]—or, in the language used later in this epistle, it was designed as "a shadow of the good things to come" (10:1), the good things which now have indeed come in Christ. In some sections of Jewish Christianity Christ's rôle was envisaged as primarily that of a second Moses; here he is presented as being much more than that.[17]

14. It is just possible to take the second clause of v. 4 to mean that "he who founded everything" (i.e., Christ, according to 1:2) is God (ὁ δὲ πάντα κατασκευάσας θεός)—in other words, to take it as an assertion of the deity of Christ. But it is simpler to regard the clause as an affirmation that God is the Creator of everything.

15. In a higher sense than that implied by Heb. *'al ha-bayit* (see p. 92, n. 10). S. Aalen ("'Reign' and 'House' in the Kingdom of God in the Gospels," *NTS* 8 [1961-62], pp. 215-40) points out that the Targum on 1 Chron. 17:14 (cf. 2 Sam. 7:16) reads: "I will maintain him [the son of David] faithful in my people and in my holy house for ever." He suggests that this interpretation, as well as Num. 12:7, stands behind our present passage, and finds here the explanation of our author's making both Christ and God builder of the house (vv. 3-4). "The motif of the faithful son who is the builder of God's house and is in God's house is exactly that which we find" in the Targum. Cf. vv. 6, 14 for the identification of the house and people of God; cf. also Heb. 1:5b for the application to Christ of 2 Sam. 7:14//1 Chron. 17:13.

16. In the word "testimony" (μαρτύριον) there may be an echo of the repeated references to the σκηνὴ τοῦ μαρτυρίου ("tent of testimony") in Num. 12:4f., 10 (cf. Acts 7:44); the typology of the tent is elaborated later in Heb. 9:1-10. Yet, if there is such an echo, it is no more than an echo; it is the prophetic and anticipatory character of Moses' rôle and ministry that is referred to, with the implication that the fulfilment which has now come in Christ surpasses the work of Moses. This work embraces not only the tent of testimony with its furniture and ritual but everything that was bound up with the wilderness covenant (8:6-13), including the Levitical priesthood (7:11-14).

17. E. L. Allen ("Jesus and Moses in the New Testament," *ExT* 67 [1955-56], pp. 104-6) suggests that our author is here refuting a "new Moses Christology," as he elsewhere refutes an "angel-Christology." It is principally among the Ebionites that a "Moses Christology" is attested (cf. *Clem. Recog.* 1.36ff., 4.5; *Clem. Hom.* 3.47ff., 8.5ff.; H.-J. Schoeps, *Theologie und Geschichte des Judenchristentums* [Tübingen, 1949], pp. 87-98); it goes back to the prophecy about the Prophet like Moses in Deut. 18:15-19. This prophecy, which played an important part

6b   If the household of God in which Moses served him so loyally was the people of Israel, what is the household of God today, over which the Son of God bears rule? That household comprises all believers:[18] "we are that household of his, if only we are fearless and keep our hope high" (NEB). The conditional sentences of this epistle are worthy of special attention.[19] Nowhere in the New Testament more than here do we find such repeated insistence on the fact that continuance in the Christian life is the test of reality. The doctrine of the final perseverance of the saints has as its corollary the salutary teaching that the saints are the people who persevere to the end. In the parable of the sower the seed sown on rocky ground made a fair showing at first, but could not withstand the heat of the sun "because it had no root"; and in the interpretation of the parable this is said to refer to people "who, when they have heard the word, immediately receive it with joy; and they have no root in themselves, but endure for a while; then, when tribulation or persecution arises on account of the word, immediately they fall away" (Mark 4:5f., 16f.). This is precisely what our author fears may happen with his readers; hence his constant emphasis on the necessity of their maintaining fearless confession[20] and joyful hope.[21] Christians live by faith and not by sight; but while their hope is in things unseen, it is something to exult in, not to be ashamed of. The waning of the first expectant enthusiasm of these "Hebrews,"[22] the apparent postponement of their hope, and various kinds of pressure brought to bear upon them,

---

in the eschatological thinking of the Samaritans and of the Qumran community, is applied to Christ in several places in the NT (cf. Mark 9:7; John 6:14; 7:20; Acts 3:22f.; 7:37), but does not occupy a central place in NT Christology (cf. O. Cullmann, *The Christology of the New Testament* [London, 1959], pp. 13-50); F. F. Bruce, *Biblical Exegesis in the Qumran Texts* [London, 1960], pp. 46-50; G. J. Brooke, *Exegesis at Qumran* (Sheffield, 1985), pp. 167f., 311f.

18. Under Christ, as in the time of Moses, there is but one continuous household of God; it goes back beyond Moses and even Abraham to embrace Abel and Enoch and Noah (11:4ff., 40). So, in Eph. 2:19 Gentile Christians are called "fellow-citizens with the saints [i.e., with Israel, God's holy people], and members of the household of God." The conception of the faithful community as the house of God is paralleled at Qumran; e.g., the inner council or nucleus of the Qumran community is described as "a holy house for Israel, a most holy assembly for Aaron, . . . a most holy dwelling for Aaron, . . . a house of perfection and truth in Israel" (1QS 8.5-10; cf. p. 193). See A. R. C. Leaney, *The Rule of Qumran and its Meaning* (London, 1966), pp. 214-20.

19. Cf. v. 14; 10:26.

20. On "boldness" (Gk. παρρησία, recurring in 4:16; 10:19, 35) cf. W. C. van Unnik, "De semitische Achtergrond van *ΠΑΡΡΗΣΙΑ* in het Nieuwe Testament," *Mededelingen der koninklijke Nederlandse Akademie van Wetenschappen (Afd. Letterkunde),* Nieuwe Reeks, Deel 25 (Amsterdam, 1962); "The Christian's Freedom of Speech in the New Testament," *BJRL* 44 (1961-62), pp. 466-88.

21. Cf. Rom. 5:2; 8:24f.; Eph. 1:18; Col. 1:23; 1 Pet. 1:13 for the relation between the maintenance of Christian hope and the attainment of final salvation. Rom. 5:2 (καυχώμεθα ἐπ' ἐλπίδι . . .) bears a special resemblance to the wording here (τὸ καύχημα τῆς ἐλπίδος).

22. Cf. A. Pott, *Das Hoffen im Neuen Testament* (Leipzig, 1915), pp. 84-87, for the view that the language here reflects a time when the first enthusiasm was in danger of being quenched. Cf. also 6:11; 10:23.

all combined to threaten the steadfastness of their faith. Hence our author, in deep concern, urges upon them that they have everything to gain by standing fast, and everything to lose by slipping back. He reinforces his warning by appealing to a familiar Old Testament precedent.

B. SECOND ADMONITION: THE REJECTION OF JESUS MORE SERIOUS THAN THE REJECTION OF MOSES (3:7-19)

7 *Therefore, as the Holy Spirit says,*[23]
　　"Today, if only you would listen to his voice![24]
8　　*Do not harden your hearts as in the rebellion,*
　　in the day of testing in the desert,
9　　*where your forefathers tried me*[25] *and put me to the test,*[26]
　　and saw my works for forty years.[27]
10　　*Therefore I was vexed with this*[28] *generation, and said,*
　　'They always go astray at heart,
　　they have not learned my ways';
11　　*As I swore in my wrath,*
　　'They shall not enter[29] *into my rest!' "*[30]
12 *See to it, brothers, that there is not in any of you an evil heart of unbelief, deserting the living God;*

---

23. The Holy Spirit is viewed as the author of the OT revelation not only in its words, as here (cf. 10:15), but also in its material content such as the plan for the construction of the wilderness tabernacle (9:8).

24. Gk. εἰ, representing Heb. *'im* ("if"), in Ps. 95 (LXX 94):7b, expresses a wish here as certainly as it expresses a strong negative in v. 11 below.

25. א² D¹ Ψ 0121b 1739, with the majority of later MSS, the Latin, Syriac, and Bohairic (Coptic) versions, add με after ἐπείρασαν.

26. Gk. ἐν δοκιμασίᾳ ("by way of proving"). The LXX has ἐδοκίμασαν, which is the reading probably represented in Heb. 3:9 by the Latin and Peshitta (Syriac) versions. K L and the bulk of later MSS have ἐδοκίμασάν με in 3:9.

27. In the MT and the LXX "forty years" belongs to the following clause ("Forty years long was I grieved with that generation"); but our author clearly attaches it to the words which precede by inserting διό ("Wherefore") before προσώχθισα ("I was displeased"). But see v. 17 with exposition and note (p. 102, n. 73).

28. Gk. ταύτῃ, in place of LXX ἐκείνῃ (there is no pronoun here in the MT). Our author perhaps replaced "that" by "this" in order to point the moral more tellingly for the generation which he himself was addressing. Cf. our Lord's repeated references to "this generation" (Matt. 11:16; 12:41f., 45; 23:36; 24:34 and parallels; cf. also Acts 2:40).

29. Gk. εἰ εἰσελεύσονται, following the LXX, represents an overliteral rendering of the Hebrew idiom *'im yᵉbō 'ûn*, rightly translated "They shall not enter." The AV/KJV gives the right rendering here, but in 4:3, 5 follows the Geneva and Bishops' Bibles with the misleading literalism, "if they shall enter into my rest"—the more surprisingly since Tyndale and Coverdale had already given the true idiomatic sense throughout.

30. Ps. 95 (LXX 94):7b-11, quoted according to the LXX apart from variations mentioned in nn. 26, 27, and 28 above.

13 *but encourage one another day by day, so long as it is called "Today,"*
lest any of you be hardened by the deceitfulness of sin.

14 *For we have become partners of Christ, if we maintain the beginning*
of our steadfastness firm to the end.

15 *When it is said,*[31]
"Today, if only you would listen to his voice!
Do not harden your hearts as in the rebellion" —

16 *who, I ask, rebelled against him when they heard him? Was it not all*
those who came out of Egypt under Moses' leadership?

17 *And with whom was he vexed for forty years?*[32] *Was it not with those*
who sinned, those whose corpses fell in the desert?[33]

18 *And to whom did he swear that they would not enter his rest, if not to*
those who disobeyed him?[34]

19 *We see, then, that it was because of unbelief that they were unable to enter.*

7-11 The New Testament bears witness, in a number of places, to a primitive and widespread Christian interpretation of the redemptive work of Christ in terms of a new Exodus.[35] In some of its features this interpretation may have originated during the Galilaean ministry of Jesus;[36] but after his resurrection it comes to present a reasonably fixed form. The death of Christ is itself called an "exodus";[37] he is the true passover, sacrificed for his people,[38] "a lamb without blemish and without spot."[39] They, like Israel in early days, are "the church in the wilderness";[40] their baptism into Christ is

---

31. "When it is said" (ἐν τῷ λέγεσθαι) should perhaps be taken as the beginning of a new sentence, as in NEB: "When Scripture says, 'Today if you hear his voice, do not grow stubborn as in those days of rebellion,' who, I ask, were those who heard and rebelled?" Here γάρ in τίνες γάρ (ERV/ARV "For who. . . ?") is taken as a particle of emphasis.

32. Here the construction of the MT and the LXX is presupposed (cf. n. 27 above).

33. Cf. Num. 12:29, 32.

34. Gk. ἀπειθήσασιν, for which 𝔭[46] has ἀπιστήσασιν ("who did not believe"), probably under the influence of ἀπιστία ("unbelief") in v. 19. Cf. similar variants in 4:6, 11; 11:31.

35. Cf. J. R. Harris, "Jesus and the Exodus," in *Testimonies*, II (Cambridge, 1920), pp. 51-57; H. Sahlin, "The New Exodus of Salvation according to S. Paul," in A. Fridrichsen, etc., *The Root of the Vine* (London, 1953), pp. 81-95; J. Daniélou, *From Shadow to Reality*, E.T. (London, 1960); R. E. Nixon, *The Exodus in the New Testament* (London, 1963); A. T. Hanson, *Jesus Christ in the Old Testament*, pp. 58-65; E. Käsemann, *The Wandering People of God*, E.T. (Minneapolis, 1984), pp. 68-87. At an earlier time the return of Israel from the Babylonian exile had been portrayed in terms of a new Exodus (cf. Isa. 41:17f.; 42:9; 43:16-21; 52:12).

36. Cf. H. W. Montefiore, "Revolt in the Desert?" *NTS* 8 (1961-62), pp. 135-41.

37. Luke 9:31 (Gk. ἔξοδος, ARV "decease").

38. 1 Cor. 5:7b (the same idea underlies the passion narrative of the Fourth Gospel).

39. 1 Pet. 1:19. The paschal and baptismal symbolism of 1 Pet. 1:3–4:11 is unmistakable, although it has been exaggerated in various directions by such writers as R. Perdelwitz, *Die Mysterienreligionen und das Problem des I. Petrusbriefes* (Giessen, 1911); B. H. Streeter, *The Primitive Church* (London, 1929), pp. 115-36; F. L. Cross, *I Peter: A Paschal Liturgy* (London, 1954).

40. Acts 7:38 (see *Acts*, NICNT [Grand Rapids, ²1988], p. 142); cf. also L. Cerfaux, *The Church in the Theology of St. Paul* (London, 1959), pp. 100ff.

the antitype of Israel's passage through the Red Sea;[41] their sacramental feeding on him by faith is the antitype of Israel's nourishment with manna and the water from the rock.[42] Christ, the living Rock, is their guide through the wilderness;[43] the heavenly rest which lies before them is the counterpart to the earthly Canaan which was the goal of the Israelites.[44] The moral implications of this typology are pressed upon Christian readers by more than one New Testament writer: Paul tells the Corinthians that the record of Israel's rebellion and punishment in the wilderness has been preserved "for our instruction," lest we should imitate their disobedience and be overtaken by comparable judgment;[45] Jude similarly draws practical lessons for his fellow-believers from the fact that "Jesus, having saved a people out of the land of Egypt, afterward destroyed those who did not believe."[46]

This typology was familiar to our author, and quite probably to his readers as well; he uses it, therefore, to warn them against giving up their faith and hope. After his fashion, he bases his argument on a passage from the Psalter, which he expounds in the light of the historical record.

Ps. 95 falls into two parts: the first (vv. 1-7a) consists of a call to worship God, while the second (vv. 7b-11), reproduced by our author here, is a warning against disobeying him, reinforced by a reminder of what happened to Israel in the wilderness for disobedience. The liturgical use of the psalm at this day by Jews (for whom it is one of the special psalms appointed for the inauguration of the sabbath[47]) and Christians (for whom it has been from very early times an integral part of the service of morning prayer[48]) no doubt perpetuates earlier practice, in which it was sung as part

---

41. 1 Cor. 10:1f.
42. 1 Cor. 10:3f.
43. 1 Cor. 10:4b.
44. This is the point of our author's argument in 3:7–4:11; it emerges clearly in 4:1ff.
45. 1 Cor. 10:6ff.
46. Jude 5. For "Jesus" the AV/KJV, the ARV, and the ERV/NEB have "the Lord" ([ὁ] κύριος), which is the reading of א C* and the majority of witnesses; but the textual evidence strongly supports the view that the original reading was "Jesus" (so A B with many minuscules and the Latin and Coptic versions. See B. M. Metzger, *Textual Commentary on the Greek New Testament*, pp. 725f. It is unlikely that "Jesus" in this place "might be understood as Joshua" (NEB mg.); Joshua played a minor rôle in the wilderness and became Israel's leader only on the eve of the entry into Canaan (see Heb. 4:8). It is much more probable that Jude's language reflects an identification of Jesus (the pre-incarnate Son of God) with the Rock which supplied Israel's need in the wilderness (so Paul in 1 Cor. 10:4b) or with the Angel of the Divine Presence who guarded and guided them from Egypt to the promised land—the one of whom God said, "My name is in him" (Ex. 23:21), and who was commissioned both to provide protection and to mete out judgment (Ex. 14:19; 23:20ff.; Isa. 63:9; cf. Acts 7:38).
47. Cf. S. Singer, *The Authorised Daily Prayer Book of the United Hebrew Congregations of the British Empire* (London, 1939), p. 108a.
48. Cf. "The Order for Morning Prayer," in the Anglican *Book of Common Prayer*, where Ps. 95 forms the Invitatory.

of the temple service for the sabbath day.[49] The two parts should not be dissociated from each other:[50] it is a good thing to worship God, but acts and words of worship are acceptable only if they proceed from sincere and obedient hearts.

"If only you would listen to his voice today!" says the psalmist, and then he introduces God himself as addressing his people: "Do not harden your hearts, as at Meribah. . . ." "The rebellion" (so the Septuagint,[51] followed by our author) is the equivalent of "Meribah" in the Hebrew text, as "the testing"[52] is the equivalent of "Massah." When the Israelites threatened revolt against Moses at Rephidim, because there was no water there, he asked them: "Why do you rebel[53] against me? why do you put Yahweh to the test?"[54] (Ex. 17:2)—and called the place Massah ("testing") and Meribah ("rebellion") because of their behavior (Ex. 17:7). But it was not on that occasion only, but repeatedly throughout the forty years of wandering, that they "tested" God, in the sense of trying to see how long his patience would hold out in face of their stubbornness of heart.

Of these other occasions the one which is uppermost in the psalmist's mind is that recorded in Num. 14:20ff. When the majority of the spies brought back to Kadesh-barnea an unfavorable report of the land of Canaan, the people revolted against the leadership of Moses and Aaron, and were on the point of choosing a new leader who would take them back to Egypt. In response to Moses' intercession on their behalf, God refrained from wiping the whole nation out by plague, but, said he, "None of the men that have seen my glory, and my signs, which I wrought in Egypt and in the wilderness, yet have put me to the test these ten times, and have not hearkened to my voice, shall see the land which I swore to give to their fathers, neither shall any of them that despised me see it" (Num. 14:22f.).[55] Therefore, instead of invading the promised land at once and taking possession of it, the people remained in the neighborhood of Kadesh-barnea thirty-eight years, "until the entire

49. Cf. W. E. Barnes, *The Psalms*, WC (London, 1931), pp. 456ff.

50. As is done, e.g., by T. K. Cheyne, *The Book of Psalms* (London, 1888), pp. 265f. In the *Deposited Prayer Book* of 1928 the Invitatory consisted of vv. 1-7a only (ending with "Let us kneel before the Lord our Maker"). Contrast the wise words of Leonard Hodgson: "The fact that God has sworn in His wrath that men who do certain things shall not enter into His rest enables the Church to open its worship each day with the words, 'Come, let us sing unto the Lord, let us heartily rejoice in the strength of our salvation'" (*The Doctrine of the Atonement* [London, 1951], p. 60). The unity of Ps. 95 is maintained by A. A. Anderson, *Psalms*, NCBC (London, 1972), pp. 676-80; he entitles it "No Worship without Obedience."

51. Gk. παραπικρασμός (cf. the verb παραπικραίνω in v. 16, with p. 101, n. 71).

52. Gk. πειρασμός.

53. Heb. *rîḇ*, the root of "Meribah." So again in Num. 20:13.

54. Heb. *nāśāh* (Pi'el conjugation), the root of "Massah." The same verb is used in Deut. 8:2, where God speaks of leading Israel forty years in the wilderness to "prove" them.

55. See p. 92. Cf. also Deut. 1:26, 34ff.

generation, that is, the men of war, had perished from the camp, as Yahweh had sworn to them" (Deut. 2:14). Of those who were already full-grown men when they came out of Egypt, none except Caleb and Joshua survived to enter Canaan, the "rest" or home which God had prepared for them.[56]

A later generation of Israelites was warned by the psalmist not to follow the bad example of their ancestors' refusal to listen to God, lest disaster should overtake them in turn; and now a still later generation has the same warning impressed upon it by the writer to the Hebrews. Although the writer does not say so in so many words, it may well be that he saw a special significance in the "forty years" of Ps. 95:10. We have evidence of a belief that God's dealings with Israel, which began with a probationary period of forty years, would be rounded off at the end-time by a probationary period of like duration;[57] and (if this epistle was written shortly before A.D. 70) it was nearly forty years now since Jesus had accomplished his "exodus" at Jerusalem. Hence the urgency of the present appeal to the readers to take heed "so long as it is called 'Today'" (v. 13).[58]

12 The judgment of the wilderness days befell the Israelite who rejected Moses. But just as Christ is greater in glory than Moses (v. 3), so the loss incurred in rejecting Christ is greater even than that incurred in rejecting Moses. The rebels in Moses' day missed the promised blessing of entry into an earthly Canaan, but latter-day rebellion would forfeit the greater blessings of the new age.[59] It was "an evil heart of unbelief"[60] that prevented

56. In Deut. 12:9 Canaan is called "the rest [Heb. *m^{c}nûḥāh*, as in Ps. 95:11] and the inheritance, which Yahweh your God gives you." The domestic sense of the word appears in Ruth 1:9, "may Yahweh grant that you find rest [Heb. *m^{c}nûḥāh*], each of you in the house of her husband" (similarly in Ruth 3:1, Heb. *mānôaḥ*).

57. Especially in the Qumran literature; cf. the interval of forty years between the death of the Teacher of Righteousness and "the consuming of all the men of war who returned with the Man of Falsehood" (CD 20.14f., echoing Deut. 2:14-16); the forty years after which the wicked are to be no more (4QpPs. 37, fragment A, 1.6ff.); the forty years' warfare of 1QM (further documentation in Y. Yadin, *The Scroll of the War . . .* [Oxford, 1962], p. 37, n. 1). In TB *Sanhedrin* 99a Eliezer ben Hyrcanus infers from Ps. 95:10 that the days of the Messiah will last forty years.

58. In this connection it is interesting to notice a messianic interpretation of the "Today" of Ps. 95:7b in TB *Sanhedrin* 98a: when Elijah sends a rabbi to interview the Messiah at the gates of Rome, the rabbi asks the Messiah, "Lord, when are you coming?" and receives the answer "Today." Elijah explains to him that this means "Today, if only you would hear his voice."

59. So in TB *Sanhedrin* 110b Rabbi Aqiba deduces from Ps. 95:11 (and Num. 14:35) that the generation of Israelites which perished in the wilderness will have no part in the age to come.

60. Their "unbelief" (ἀπιστία) involved disloyalty as well as the passive failure to believe. The whole expression (καρδία πονηρὰ ἀπιστίας) bears at least a verbal resemblance to one or two source-passages for the rabbinical doctrine of the "evil inclination" *(yēṣer hā-rā')*; cf. the "evil heart" and "evil root" of 4 Ezra (2 Esdras) 3:20-22 (with the "evil root" cf. Heb. 12:15, p. 349), the "grain of evil seed . . . sown in Adam's heart from the beginning" of 4 Ezra 4:30, and the "evil thought" of 4 Ezra 7:92.

the generation which witnessed the Exodus from enjoying the "rest" they had hoped to attain in Canaan; our author urges his readers to take heed lest such a heart be found in any of them. "Falling away from the living God" (ERV/ARV; cf. RSV) is a more positive activity than the English words themselves might suggest; it denotes rebellion against him.[61] When the Israelites at Kadesh-barnea repudiated the leadership of Moses and Aaron, they revolted in effect against God, who had appointed these two men to be their leaders. And for Christians to repudiate the apostle and high priest of their confession, similarly appointed by God, would be if possible an even more outrageous revolt against the living God. It has indeed been questioned whether a relapse from Christianity into Judaism could be described in such words; do they not denote a complete abandonment of faith in God in any form, whereas in Judaism the living God was acknowledged and worshiped? But a relapse from Christianity into Judaism would be comparable to the action of the Israelites when they "turned back in their hearts to Egypt";[62] it would not be a mere return to a position previously occupied, but a gesture of outright apostasy, a complete break with God. For those who had never been illuminated by God's final revelation of himself in Christ, Judaism provided a means of access to God—shadowy and imperfect as it might be.[63] But for those who had received the illumination of the gospel to renounce it in favor of the old order which the gospel had superseded would be a form of the irretrievable sin—the sin against light.[64]

13 Let them be vigilant therefore, and encourage one another with might and main to be steadfast in their faith, during the present time of probation. While this time lasts, each succeeding day is a fresh "Today" in which they may heed the psalmist's warning to hear the voice of God and render him heart-obedience. The exhortation to mutual encouragement was wise: in isolation from fellow-believers each individual among them was more liable to succumb to the subtle temptations which pressed in from so many sides, but if they came together regularly for mutual encouragement the devotion of all would be kept warm and their common hope would be in less danger of flickering and dying.[65] In isolation each was prone to be impressed by the specious arguments which underlined the worldly wisdom of a certain measure of compromise of their Christian faith and witness; in the healthy atmosphere of the Christian fellowship these arguments would be the more readily appraised at

---

61. Gk. ἀποστῆναι (whence ἀποστασία, "apostasy"). Hermas has an echo of this passage in *Shepherd*, Vision 2.3.2: "you are saved by not having fallen away (ἀποστῆναι) from the living God."

62. Cf. Acts 7:39 (echoing Num. 14:3).

63. Cf. 10:1.

64. Cf. 6:4-6.

65. Cf. 10:24f. (pp. 256-58).

their true worth, and recognized as being so many manifestations of "the deceitfulness of sin."[66] Where the right path lies clear before the eyes, a disinclination to follow it can be reinforced in the mind by many beguiling lines of rationalization; but to surrender to them results in a hardening of the heart, a reduced sensitivity of conscience, which makes it more difficult to recognize the right path on a subsequent occasion. But in a fellowship which exercised a watchful and unremitting care for its members the temptation to prefer the easy course to the right one would be greatly weakened, and the united resolution to stand firm would be correspondingly strengthened.

14 Again the paramount necessity of perseverance is stressed: only if they kept their original confidence[67] firm to the end could they be truly called partners of Christ. The word rendered "partners" (RSV "we share in Christ") is the word used at the end of the quotation from Ps. 45:6f. in Heb. 1:8f.—"God . . . has anointed you with the oil of exultation more than your companions."[68] The meaning of the phrase "partners of Christ" is probably not that of participation in him (as in the Pauline expression "in Christ"), but rather that of participation with him in his heavenly kingdom—the unshakable kingdom of 12:28.[69] To begin well is good, but it is not enough; it is only those who stay the course and finish the race that have any hope of gaining the prize.[70] The Israelites made a good beginning when they crossed the Sea of Reeds and praised God for their deliverance; but the good beginning was not matched by their later behavior.

15-18 When the scripture already quoted says, "Do not harden your hearts as in the rebellion," to whom is God speaking? Who were the people who turned a deaf ear to his voice and so provoked[71] him to anger? It was

66. Gk. τῇ ἀπάτῃ τῆς ἁμαρτίας (cf. Gen. 3:13; 2 Cor. 11:3).

67. Gk. ὑπόστασις, as in 11:1 (a different meaning from that in 1:3). This sense of "confidence," "assurance," "conviction," is readily derivable from the primary sense of "that which underlies" ("ground," "basis"); this confidence rests upon a stable foundation. Cf. H. Dörrie, "ΥΠΟΣΤΑΣΙΣ: Wort- und Bedeutungsgeschichte," *Nachrichten der Akademie der Wissenschaften in Göttingen*, philologisch-historische Klasse, 1955, No. 3, pp. 35-92. See pp. 276f., with nn. 4-8.

68. Gk. μέτοχοι (for its use in the sense of "business partners" see *New Docs.*, I [1976], § 40). Apart from Luke 5:7, where the sons of Zebedee are "partners" in fishing with Simon Peter and his brother (note the alternative use of κοινωνοί in the same sense in Luke 5:10), μέτοχοι in the NT is used only in Hebrews, its occurrences being (in addition to the present passage and 1:9) 3:1 ("sharers of a heavenly calling"), 6:4 ("sharers of the Holy Spirit"), and 12:8 ("sharers" in chastening).

69. This involves taking the genitive τοῦ Χριστοῦ here in a different way from the genitive πνεύματος ἁγίου in 6:4, but the context in either place must determine the precise force of the genitive. For the general idea here cf. Paul's words of encouragement and warning about inheriting the kingdom (e.g., 1 Cor. 6:9f.; Gal. 5:19-21; Eph. 5:5; cf. Rom. 8:17; 2 Tim. 2:12).

70. Cf. 12:1f.

71. Gk. παρεπίκραναν (for the cognate noun παραπικρασμός cf. vv. 8, 15); this verb παραπικραίνω, thought by Moffatt to be a Septuagintal coinage (ICC, *ad loc.*), is used of Israel's

those[72] who came out of Egypt under the leadership of Moses, those who had experienced God's redeeming power. When the writer asks, "And with whom was he vexed for forty years?"[73] to which generation does he refer? To that generation which witnessed his mighty works, and nevertheless rebelled against him—that "evil congregation" against which sentence was passed: "As I live, says Yahweh, what you have said in my hearing I will do to you: your dead bodies shall fall in this wilderness" (Num. 14:27). And who were the people to whom he swore in his wrath that "they would not enter his rest"? Those who, having covenanted to obey him, proved repeatedly disobedient, and showed themselves to be "a perverse generation, children in whom is no faithfulness" (Deut. 32:20).

19 It was unbelief,[74] faithlessness, then, that kept them out of the promised land. They had enjoyed God's delivering mercy in the Exodus, and had heard him speak when he gave the law at Sinai; but those initial experiences did not keep them from dying in the wilderness, or guarantee their safe arrival in Canaan. The moral must have been plain enough to the recipients of the epistle. For they too had experienced the redeeming power of God; they too had the promise of the homeland of the faithful to look forward to; but one thing could prevent them from realizing that promise, just as it had prevented the mass of the Israelites who left Egypt from entering Canaan— and that one thing was unbelief.

---

wilderness behavior in Deut. 31:27; 32:16; Pss. 78 (LXX 77):8, 17; 105 (LXX 104):28; cf. Ps 107 (LXX 106):11, etc.

72. "All they that came out (πάντες οἱ ἐξελθόντες) of Egypt," says our author, leaving out of view for the moment the two exceptions, Caleb and Joshua; contrast Paul in 1 Cor. 10:5, "with the majority of them (ἐν τοῖς πλείοσιν αὐτῶν) God was displeased."

73. The construction of the MT and the LXX is implied in v. 17; cf. p. 95, n. 27.

74. The juxtaposition of δι' ἀπιστίαν ("because of unbelief") in v. 19 and τοῖς ἀπειθήσασιν ("to them that were disobedient") in v. 18 (cf. p. 96, n. 34 for textual variant) emphasizes the close relation in the NT between ἀπιστία and ἀπείθεια (cf. ὁ πιστεύων over against ὁ δὲ ἀπειθῶν in John 3:36).

HEBREWS 4

C. THE TRUE REST OF GOD MAY BE FORFEITED (4:1-10)

1 *Let us therefore fear lest, when the promise of entering his rest has been left open,*[1] *any of you should turn out*[2] *to have fallen short of it.*
2 *For in truth we have heard the good news as they did, but the message which they heard*[3] *did them no good since it was not combined with faith on the part of the hearers.*[4]

1. Gk. καταλειπομένης, here in the sense of being "left open." The promise (ἐπαγγελία) is implied in the warning.

2. Gk. δοκῇ, "might be deemed." Cf. NEB: "one or another among you should be found to have missed his chance."

3. Gk. ὁ λόγος τῆς ἀκοῆς. Cf. Rom. 10:16f. The use of ἀκοή in the sense of the gospel message (based on the meaning of the word in Isa. 53:1, LXX) is illustrated by Rom. 10:16f., which the NEB renders: "For Isaiah says, 'Lord, who has believed our message?' We conclude that faith is awakened by the message, and the message that awakens it comes through the word of Christ."

4. Gk. μὴ συνκεκερασμένος τῇ πίστει τοῖς ἀκούσασιν, "it did not meet with faith in the hearers" (RSV). There is a bewildering diversity of readings here: for the masculine singular συνκεκερασμένος, agreeing with λόγος (ℵ d, the Sixto-Clementine Vulgate, Peshitta, some Sahidic texts, Lucifer, TR), a preponderant weight of authorities has the accusative plural συνκεκερασμένους, agreeing with ἐκείνους (𝔭[13] 𝔭[46] A B C D* 0121b and most later MSS, Vulgate MSS, Harclean Syriac, the Bohairic, Armenian, and Ethiopic versions, Chrysostom, Theodore of Mopsuestia, etc.). The latter reading (now approved by GNT[3] and NA[26]) was adopted by the ERV (not by the ARV): "because they were not united by faith with them that heard" (for a suggested explanation of this wording see p. 258, n. 119). Difficulty in making sense of this reading probably gave rise to the replacement of the active participle ἀκούσασιν by the passive ἀκουσθεῖσιν (1912, Theodore of Mopsuestia), which gives the smoother rendering "because they were not united by faith with the things that they heard." The replacement of the dative by the genitive ἀκουσάντων (D* 104 1611 2005 d, Harclean margin, Lucifer, etc.) yields the sense: ". . . united with the faith of the hearers"; this is intelligible only with the nominative συνκεκερασμένος. We are confronted here, in all probability, with "a variety of ancient conjectures vainly striving to heal a primitive corruption" (G. Zuntz, *The Text of the Epistle* [London, 1953], p. 16)—but "vainly" is perhaps not the right word; whoever thought of healing the corruption by changing -ους to -ος may have restored the original text by accident. Cf. B. F. Westcott, *The Epistle to the Hebrews* (London, ²1892), pp. 94f., 112f. See also B. M. Metzger, *Textual Commentary on the Greek New Testament* (London/New York, 1971), p. 665. But the sense is plain enough; the good news had to be appropriated or assimilated by faith if it was to bring any benefit to the hearers.

3 *It is we who have believed that enter[5] into that rest,[6] as God has said,*
> *"As I swore in my wrath,*
> *'they shall not enter my rest!' "[7]—*
and yet God's works have been finished since the world's foundation.[8]

4 *For this is what Scripture has said somewhere regarding the seventh day:*
> *"On the seventh day God rested from all his works. "[9]*

5 *And again in this passage it says,*
> *"They shall not enter my rest!"*

6 *Since then it is left open for some to enter it, and those who previously heard the good news failed to enter because of disobedience,[10]*

7 *he fixes a certain day again, namely "Today," when he says in (a psalm of) David after such a long lapse of time, as has been said before,[11]*
> *"Today, if only you would listen to his voice!*
> *Do not harden your hearts. "[12]*

8 *Now if Joshua had given them rest, God would not have spoken of another day after this.*

9 *So then, a sabbath rest[13] remains open for the people of God.*

---

5. Gk. εἰσεϱχόμεθα γὰϱ οἱ πιστεύσαντες. In place of γάϱ ("for"), οὖν (probably in a re-sumptive sense, "well then") is read by ℵ A C 1739 with a few minuscules and the Bohairic version.

6. Gk. εἰς τὴν κατάπαυσιν, but τήν is omitted by 𝔭[13] 𝔭[46] B D* (and this may well be the original reading).

7. Ps. 95:11 (LXX 94:11).

8. Gk. ἀπὸ καταβολῆς κόσμου. For the καταβολὴ κόσμου cf. 9:26; also Matt. 13:35; 25:34; Luke 11:50; John 17:24; Eph. 1:4; 1 Pet. 1:20; Rev. 13:8; 17:8. The attempt to render it "downfall of the world" and link it with the "catastrophic" interpretation of Gen. 1:2 cannot be sustained. For another usage of καταβολή see Heb. 11:11.

9. Gen. 2:2. The LXX simply has καὶ κατέπαυσεν τῇ ἡμέϱᾳ τῇ ἑβδόμῃ . . . ; here our author has inserted ὁ θεὸς ἐν after κατέπαυσεν (J. Moffatt, ICC, *ad loc.*, points out that the present form of the quotation corresponds to Philo's in *Cain's Posterity* 64). The LXX choice of καταπαύω here to render Heb. *šābat* eases our author's interpretation of the κατάπαυσις of Ps. 95:11 in terms of God's cessation from his works of creation. Philo (*Leg. Alleg.* 1.6, 16) takes κατέπαυσεν in Gen. 2:2 as transitive, "he caused to rest"; similarly Heb. 4:4 could be rendered "God caused (his people) to rest on the seventh day" and the κατάπαυσις of Ps. 95:11 would be the rest that God gives; but this is an awkward construction, and does not suit the context.

10. Gk. δι' ἀπείθειαν (so A B D with the majority of MSS and the Syriac version); 𝔭[46] ℵ* and the Latin, Coptic, and Armenian versions read δι' ἀπιστίαν ("because of unbelief"); cf. 3:18f. (p. 96, n. 34; p. 102, n. 74).

11. Gk. πϱοείϱηται (B 1739 read the active πϱοείϱηκεν, "he has said before").

12. Ps. 95 (LXX 94):7b-8a.

13. Gk. σαββατισμός, "sabbath-keeping"; this is the earliest attested occurrence of the word in extant Greek literature (it appears some decades later in Plutarch, *On Superstition* 3.166a, in a list of superstitious practices). The verb σαββατίζω, from which it is formed, is used in the LXX with the meaning "keep sabbath"—usually as the rendering of Heb. *šābat* (Ex. 16:30; Lev. 23:32; 26:35 [ter]; 2 Chron. 36:21 [bis]; 1 Esdras 1:58; 2 Macc. 6:6).

10 *For one who has entered God's rest has rested in turn from his own works, as God did from his.*

1   The promise of entering the "rest" of God remains open. The meaning of that "rest" was not exhausted by the earthly Canaan which was entered by the Israelites of the generation which had grown up to manhood in the wilderness; the spiritual counterpart of the earthly Canaan is the goal of the people of God today. Our author therefore urges his readers again to press on and attain that goal. It will not be reached automatically; they will do well to fear[14] the possibility of missing it,[15] just as the generation of Israelites which died in the wilderness missed the earthly Canaan, although that was the goal which they had before them when they set out from Egypt.

2   The parallel between those Israelites and the people of God in the new age is impressive enough for the disaster which befell the former to serve as a warning to the latter. The Israelites of those earlier days had good news proclaimed to them, just as the readers of this epistle had good news proclaimed to *them*[16] (cf. 2:3f.). But the hearing of the good news brought no lasting benefit to those earlier Israelites; it did not ensure their attainment of the goal for which they set out. Why? Because they did not appropriate the good news by faith when they heard it. The good news which was proclaimed to them, summarized in such Old Testament passages as Ex. 19:3-6; 23:20-33, told them how the God of their fathers, who had delivered them from Egypt, would bring them safely to the promised land and give them possession of it, and would make them "a kingdom of priests, and a holy nation" to himself, if only they would obey his voice and keep his covenant.[17] The reason why this message did not do them as much good as it was designed to do was that, in spite of their serious undertaking, they did not obey his voice or keep his covenant: "they brought no admixture of faith to the hearing of it" (NEB). The practical implication is clear: it is not the hearing of the gospel

---

14. Fear of the consequences of apostasy is a recurrent note in this epistle (cf. especially 10:27, 31), but those who have a proper fear of God (12:28f.) need fear none else (13:6).

15. Gk. ὑστερηκέναι, "to have fallen short." W. M. Ramsay, "The Greek of the Early Church and the Pagan Ritual," *ExT* 10 (1898-99), pp. 57f., draws attention to the same form in a Greek inscription from the Middle Maeander valley of Asia Minor (*Cities and Bishoprics of Phrygia*, I [Oxford, 1895], no. 42), where a man has failed in his duty of attendance at a temple of Apollo (διὰ τὸ ὑσ[τερηκέν]ε καὶ μὴ παραγεγον[ένε]).

16. Gk. ἐσμεν εὐηγγελισμένοι, "we have been evangelized" (cf. v. 6, οἱ πρότερον εὐαγγελισθέντες, "those who had formerly been evangelized"). The noun εὐαγγέλιον is not used in this epistle.

17. A. T. Hanson argues that the gospel which the Israelites received in the wilderness was the identical gospel of Christ received by the recipients of this epistle (*Jesus Christ in the Old Testament* [London, 1965], pp. 58-65).

by itself that brings final salvation, but its appropriation by faith; and if that faith is a genuine faith, it will be a persistent faith.

3-5 It is for those who have accepted the saving message by faith, then, that entry into the "rest" of God is intended—that rest which, in Ps. 95:11, he refers to as "my rest." But in what sense does God speak of "my rest"? Does it simply mean "the rest which I bestow" or does it also mean "the rest which I myself enjoy"? It means the latter: the "rest" which God promises to his people is a share in that rest which he himself enjoys. Here, then, our author proceeds to bring out the underlying meaning of the reference to God's "rest" in Ps. 95:11 by relating it to Gen. 2:2f., where God is said to have "rested on the seventh day from all his work which he had done" in the course of the preceding six days. The Septuagint uses the same Greek word for God's "resting" or "desisting" on the sabbath day from his creative work (Gen. 2:2f.; Ex. 20:11) as for the "rest" of God in Ps. 95:11 (in the former case, the verb *katapauō;* in the latter, the substantive *katapausis*), although the Hebrew words are different (in the former case, the verb *šābat,* explaining the sense of *šabbāt,* "sabbath"; in the latter, the substantive *mᶜnûḥāh*).

It was not because the "rest" of God was not yet available that the wilderness generation of Israelites failed to enter into it; it had been available ever since creation's work was ended. When we read that God "rested on the seventh day from all his work which he had done" (Gen. 2:2), we are to understand that he *began* to rest then; the fact that he is never said to have completed his rest and resumed his work of creation implies that his rest continues still, and may be shared by those who respond to his overtures with faith and obedience. This interpretation which views the divine sabbath as beginning from the moment when creation's work came to an end and going on to the present time is paralleled in Philo[18] and is implied by our Lord's words in John 5:17, "My Father is working still, and I am working."[19] It differs from another interpretation which was widespread in the early church, according to which the seventh day of Gen. 2:2f. is a type of the seventh age of righteousness which is to follow six ages of sin's domination.[20] The iden-

18. J. Moffatt (ICC, p. 53) refers to Philo, *On the Cherubim* 26, and *On the Sacrifices of Abel and Cain* 8, for his treatment of the sabbath as the rest of God, but points out rightly that all such speculations as we find in Philo "are remote from our author." On the biblical basis of our author's thought see G. von Rad, "There Remains Still a Rest for the People of God," E.T. in *The Problem of the Hexateuch and Other Essays* (Edinburgh, 1966), pp. 94-102.

19. The point of this reply to the charge that Jesus had broken the sabbath by performing an act of healing on that day is this: "You charge me with breaking the sabbath by working on it. But although God's sabbath began after the work of creation was finished, and is still going on, he continues to work—and therefore so do I."

20. Cf. *Ep. Barn.* 15:4f., 8: "Pay attention, children, to the meaning of the words: 'He

tification of the rest of God in the Epistle to the Hebrews with a coming millennium on earth has, indeed, been ably defended;[21] but it involves the importation into the epistle of a concept which in fact is alien to it.

The vagueness of the terms with which the quotation from Gen. 2:2 is introduced is characteristic of our author: "he/it has said somewhere[22] with regard to the seventh day." The subject of the verb "has said" is not made explicit: "he" would be God, the subject of the preceding "has said" in v. 3, while "it" would refer to "Scripture" (cf. NEB: "does not Scripture somewhere speak thus of the seventh day. . . ?"). The fact that Gen. 2:2 is part of the creation narrative, and not reported as an utterance of God, might suggest that "Scripture," not "God," is the subject of "has said"; but this cannot be regarded as a conclusive argument. The repetition of the warning words of Ps. 95:11b after the Genesis quotation emphasizes the identification of the one rest with the other: God's rest has remained open to his people since the work of creation was finished, but it will be forfeited by disobedience.

6-7 It was disobedience, as we have seen, that kept the generation of the Exodus out of God's promised rest, in spite of the good news which was announced to them. But that same promised rest was still open for the people of God centuries after the wilderness period, for the writer of Ps. 95 urges his contemporaries to listen to the voice of God "today," instead of hardening their hearts in obstinacy like their ancestors and being debarred from entering into the rest of God as they had been. Ps. 95 is anonymous in the Masoretic text, but the Septuagint assigns it to David.[23] Our author's phrase "in

---

finished it in six days.' It means that in 6,000 years the Lord will bring everything to completion. For the 'day' with him is a thousand years, of which he himself bears me witness when he says: 'Behold, the day of the Lord shall be as a thousand years.' Therefore, children, in six days— that is in 6,000 years—everything will be brought to completion. 'And he rested the seventh day.' This means: when his Son comes and brings to nought the period of the Lawless One and judges the ungodly and changes the sun and moon and stars, then he will rest properly on the seventh day. . . . Finally he says to them: 'Your new moons and your sabbaths I cannot endure.' See what he means: it is not your present sabbaths that are acceptable, but the sabbath that I have made, in which, when I have put everything to rest, I will make a beginning of the eighth day, that is, the beginning of a new world." The sabbath of God is here the seventh millennium of the present creation, which is to be followed by the eternal age of the new creation. (Barnabas has confused the issue by superimposing on the Jewish schema of the millennial sabbath or seventh "day" the Christian concept of an eighth millennium corresponding to the resurrection day.)

21. Notably by G. H. Lang, *The Epistle to the Hebrews* (London, 1951), pp. 73-80. See p. 352, n. 121.

22. Gk. που, as in 2:6 (perhaps to be translated not "somewhere" but more generally "as we know" or "to quote familiar words"; cf. Westcott, *ad loc.*).

23. The LXX title to this psalm is Αἶνος ᾠδῆς τῷ Δαυείδ.

David" (v. 7)[24] may mean simply "in the Psalter"; whether he thought of David as the composer of this particular psalm or not is immaterial to his argument, which is that the wording of the psalm implies that entry into the "rest" of God is still available "so long a time"[25] after the age of the Exodus and wilderness wanderings. Whether the psalm is the composition of David or not, the point of paramount importance is that it was God who spoke "in David" (cf. 3:7) and his word remains effectively vital long after it was uttered, addressing the heart and conscience of hearers in the Christian era with the same convicting relevance as characterized it when first it was spoken. By dint of repetition our author endeavors to bring home to his readers the fact that the divine warning is as applicable to them as it was in the days of Moses or David. If they treat the saving message lightly, if they "tempt" God by trying to see how far they can presume upon his patience, they in their turn will forfeit his "rest." Therefore to them, as to the psalmist's contemporaries, the urgent appeal goes forth:

> While it is called Today, repent
> And harden not your heart.

8 It is plain (our author implies) that the "rest" spoken of in Ps. 95:11 is not the earthly Canaan. For that land of rest was occupied by the Israelites of the second generation, who entered it under the command of Joshua. The people addressed in the ninety-fifth psalm were already living in the land of Canaan, as their ancestors had been for generations now. Likewise, the "rest" which they were in danger of forfeiting through stubbornness of heart must have been something different from the "rest . . . from all their enemies round about" which God had given to Israel in Joshua's day (Josh. 23:1; cf. 21:44).[26]

We must, of course, use the personal name "Joshua" here instead of "Jesus" which appears in the AV/KJV (the revisers of 1611 would have done better to follow the precedent of Tyndale, Coverdale, and Whittingham, all of whom had used "Joshua").[27] Yet it must be recognized that the reader of the Greek Bible had (and still has) an advantage over the reader of the English Bible because to him "Joshua" and "Jesus" are not two names but one;

---

24. Cf. Rom. 11:2, ἐν 'Ηλείᾳ (where authorship is not implied); 9:25, ἐν τῷ 'Ωσηέ.

25. Gk. μετὰ τοσοῦτον χρόνον. Our author takes historical perspective into account.

26. In both these places the LXX uses καταπαύω, rendering the Hiph'il of Heb. nûaḥ (the root whence mᵉnûḥāh of Ps. 95:11 is derived).

27. The Geneva and Bishops' versions have "Jesus." In the LXX Joshua the son of Nun appears as 'Ιησοῦς Ναυῆ. Cf. Acts 7:45 (RSV rightly "Joshua"; AV/KJV "Jesus"). It was probably because Greek-speaking Christians saw a divinely designed coincidence between the names of the great OT "Jesus" and of their own Savior that Aquila in his second-century Greek version of the OT avoided the use of 'Ιησοῦς for "Joshua," preferring the more exact transliteration 'Ιωσούα.

he could distinguish between our Lord and his most illustrious namesake of Old Testament days, and at the same time appreciate some of the implications of the fact that they *are* namesakes. The parallel between the Old Testament "Jesus," who led his followers into the earthly Canaan, and Jesus the Son of God, who leads the heirs of the new covenant into their heavenly inheritance, is a prominent theme of early Christian typology,[28] and could scarcely have been absent from our author's mind. Yet he does not dwell on it here; he is more concerned to point the contrast between the temporal "rest" which Israel entered under Joshua and the true rest which is still reserved for the people of God.

9-10   This rest which is reserved for the people of God is properly called a "sabbath rest"—a *sabbatismos* or "sabbath keeping"[29]—because it is their participation in God's own rest. When God completed his work of creation, he "rested"; so his people, having completed their service on earth, will enter into his rest.[30] Verse 10, with its initial conjunction "for," explains the description of the believers' coming rest as a "sabbath keeping" in v. 9. Some ambiguity is occasioned by the threefold "his" in v. 10 of the ERV/ARV, where the Greek wording is rendered rather literally;[31] the meaning is brought out clearly in the NEB rendering: "Therefore, a sabbath rest still awaits the people of God; for anyone who enters God's rest, rests from his own work as God did from his."[32] In other words, he has completed his appointed work in accordance with God's will.

---

28. Cf. *Ep. Barn.* 6:8f.; Justin, *Dialogue with Trypho* 113, 132. J. R. Harris (*Testimonies,* II [Cambridge, 1920], pp. 51-57) shows how in early Christian apologetic Jesus is regarded as the antitype not only of the earlier Joshua but also of the later Joshua (or Jeshua), the first post-exilic high priest (Ezra 3:20; Hag. 1:1; Zech. 3:1; 6:11ff., etc.; cf. p. 116, n. 68; p. 121; pp. 124f., n. 33; p. 253, n. 97); he traces a threefold typological pattern: "Jesus the Guide to the Land of Rest; Jesus the new Circumciser (cf. p. 113, n. 51); Jesus the great High-Priest" (p. 91). Harris went so far as to deprecate the alteration of AV/KJV "Jesus" to "Joshua" in the ERV/ARV as obscuring the typology and altering the proper emphasis of the conditional clause with which v. 8 begins; he argued that the sense was "If it was *to them* that Jesus gave rest"—our author's point being, in his judgment, that Jesus gave rest, not to the Israelites of wilderness days, but to believers of the Christian age. But this is to read into our author's argument the more farfetched typology of later *testimonia*. (Cf. the reference to Jude 5 on p. 97, n. 46.)

29. See p. 104, n. 13. See E. Lohse in *TDNT,* VII, pp. 34f. (*s.v.* σαββατισμός). In Mishnah *Tamid* 7.4 the title of Ps. 92 is interpreted: "a psalm, a song for the time that is to come, for the day that shall be all sabbath and rest in the life everlasting." Cf. Jub. 2:30; 6:8.

30. Compare the remarkable parallel in Rev. 14:13, where the Spirit confirms the blessedness of "the dead who die in the Lord" with the words, "Blessed indeed, ... that they may rest (ἀναπαύομαι, 'have relief') from their labors; for their deeds (ἔργα, as here) follow them."

31. The first two occurrences of "his" represent Gk. αὐτοῦ, the third represents Gk. ἴδιος (ἀπὸ τῶν ἰδίων, "from his own").

32. So E. Nestle, "Heb. iv.10," *ExT* 9 (1897-98), pp. 47f.: "Here there can be no doubt that the first αὐτοῦ refers to God, the second αὐτοῦ and αὐτός [ERV/ARV "himself"] to man."

What then is this sabbath rest which awaits them? It is evidently an experience which they do not enjoy in their present mortal life, although it belongs to them as a heritage, and by faith they may live in the good of it here and now.[33] How they may do so is illustrated with a wealth of biographical detail in ch. 11. And in that chapter we have further references to the eternal homeland which is the heritage of believers, the saints' everlasting rest—the "better country, that is, a heavenly one" which they desire, the "city" which God has prepared for them, the well-founded city of which he is both architect and builder (11:10, 16). Of this city of God men and women of faith are citizens already, although the full exercise of their civic privileges in it is reserved for the future. Do they, then, receive these privileges and enter into the rest of God at death or at resurrection? Our author gives us no explicit answer to this question. So far as believers of Old Testament days are concerned, however, it appears that they did not attain their heavenly homeland immediately at death. When we are told that "they did not enter upon the promised inheritance, because, with us in mind, God had made a better plan, that only in company with us should they reach their perfection" (11:39f., NEB),[34] the meaning must be that they had to wait until the time of fulfilment was introduced by Christ before they could realize completely those promised blessings whose prospect enabled them to live as they did. It may be, then, that in resurrection they, "in company with us," are to attain this perfection and enter into God's rest; but in the absence of an express statement to this effect (there is but little reference to resurrection throughout this epistle), we cannot be certain that this was our author's understanding of the matter. It is, indeed, perfectly conceivable that in his view the Old Testament believers entered into the rest of God as soon as Christ had accomplished his redemptive work, while believers of the New Testament age enter it at death. One way or the other, this blissful rest in unbroken fellowship with God is the goal to which his people are urged to press forward; this is the final perfection which has been prepared for them by the sacrifice of their heavenly high priest. "It is for you," our author might well have told them (in the words of a younger contemporary of his),[35] "that paradise is opened, the tree of life is planted, the age to come is prepared, plenty is provided, a city is built, rest is appointed, goodness is established and wisdom perfected beforehand" (4 Ezra 8:52).

33. Cf. C. K. Barrett, "New Testament Eschatology," *SJT* 6 (1953), pp. 136-55, 225-43; "The Eschatology of the Epistle to the Hebrews," in *The Background of the New Testament and its Eschatology,* ed. W. D. Davies and D. Daube (Cambridge, 1956), pp. 363-93; O. Hofius, *Katapausis: Die Vorstellung vom endzeitlichen Ruheort im Hebräerbrief,* WUNT 11 (Tübingen, 1970).

34. See pp. 330f.; cf. also pp. 358-60 (on 12:23).

35. 4 Ezra (2 Esdras) is probably to be dated somewhere within the last thirty years of the first century A.D.

D. EXHORTATION TO ATTAIN GOD'S REST (4:11-13)

11 *Let us make every effort, then, to enter that rest, so that no one falls through the same example of disobedience.*[36]

12 *For the word of God is living and active.*[37] *It is sharper than any two-edged sword: as it pierces, it divides soul from spirit, joints from marrow; it discerns the thoughts and purposes*[38] *of the heart.*

13 *No created being is hidden from it: all things lie bare and exposed in the sight of him to whom our account must be rendered.*

11 In view of all the glory which is accessible to faith, in view of the disaster which follows upon unbelief, our author urges his readers once more to make it their earnest endeavor[39] to attain the eternal home of the people of God, and not miss it through disobedience like that of the Israelites in the wilderness. Zeal and perseverance are called for; no one can

> be carried to the skies
> On flowery beds of ease.[40]

God is not to be trifled with; his word cannot be ignored with impunity, but must be received in faith and obeyed in daily life. God's "Today" has arrived; let us take his word seriously and make haste to enter his rest.[41]

12 For God's word—that word which fell on disobedient ears in the wilderness and which has been sounded out again in these days of fulfilment—is not like the word of man; it is living, effective, and self-fulfilling; it diagnoses the condition of the human heart, saying "Thou ailest here, and here"; it brings blessing to those who receive it in faith and pronounces judgment on those who disregard it.

All that our author says here about the word *(logos)* of God is in line with the Old Testament witness. There are verbal links with Philo, who can, for example, speak of the Logos as the "cutter"[42]; but Moffatt rightly says

---

36. Gk. ἀπειθείας, for which ἀπιστίας ("of unbelief") is read by 𝔓46 1611 2005 with the Latin, Sahidic, Coptic, and Armenian versions. Cf. 3:8; 4:6; 11:31 (p. 96, n. 34; p. 104, n. 10; p. 315, n. 212).

37. Gk. ἐνεργής, for which B reads ἐναργής ("manifest," "clear-shining")—a reading known to Jerome. Cf. Mangey's conjectural but certain emendation ἐνάργειαν for ἐνέργειαν in Philo, *Migration of Abraham* 35, ἐνάργειαν τῶν πραγμάτων ἀριδηλοτάτην ("the most distinct clarity of things").

38. Gk. ἐνθυμήσεων καὶ ἐννοιῶν, for which D* reads ἐνθυμήσεως ἐννοιῶν τε and C* I (and possibly Origen in one out of two instances) ἐνθυμήσεως καὶ ἐννοιῶν.

39. Gk. σπουδάσωμεν ("Let us then make every effort," NEB; "Let us therefore strive," RSV).

40. I. Watts (1674-1748).

41. Cf. C. H. Dodd, *According to the Scriptures* (London, 1952), pp. 20f.

42. He explains the dividing of the covenant victims in Gen. 15:10 as performed by God

that "our author is using Philonic language rather than Philonic ideas." With the "living" word we may compare Stephen's reference to the "living oracles" received by Moses at Sinai (Acts 7:38), and Peter's description of "the word of God, which lives and abides" (1 Pet. 1:23). The word is "active" in the sense that it speeds to fulfil the purpose for which it has been uttered: this self-fulfilling character which it possesses is well summed up in Isa. 55:11 where the God of Israel says of "my word . . . that goes forth from my mouth": "it shall not return to me empty, but it shall accomplish that which I purpose, and prosper in the thing for which I sent it."[43]

If the word of God is personified here, the personification is slight— slighter, for instance, than in Wisdom 18:15f., where the Logos is not simply compared to a sharp sword, but is portrayed as the personal wielder of the sword:

> Thy all-powerful word leaped from heaven, from the royal throne,
> into the midst of the land that was doomed,
> a stern[44] warrior carrying the sharp sword of thy authentic command,
> and stood and filled all things with death,
> and touched heaven while standing on the earth.

The "word of God" in this Hebrews passage is parallel not so much to "thy all-powerful word"[45] as to "thy authentic command"[46] in the Wisdom passage, for it is God's "authentic command" that is described as a sharp sword.[47]

Here, however, the divine word is not merely described as a sharp sword, but as sharper than the sharpest sword. The expression "a two-edged sword"[48] occurs a few times in the Old Testament,[49] but there is no particular reference here to any one of its Old Testament occurrences, nor yet (in all probability) to other Old Testament passages which have been suggested as

---

"by means of his word, the cutter of everything (τῷ τομεῖ τῶν συμπάντων ἑαυτοῦ λόγῳ)" (*Who Is the Heir of Divine Things?* 130).

43. Cf. Jer. 23:29, "Is not my word (LXX οἱ λόγοι μου) like fire? . . . and like a hammer that breaks the rock in pieces?"

44. Gk. ἀπότομος (cf. here τομώτερος, "sharper").

45. Gk. ὁ παντοδύναμός σου λόγος. See p. 314, n. 206.

46. Gk. τὴν ἀνυπόκριτον ἐπιταγήν σου.

47. Gk. ξίφος ὀξύ (as against τομώτερος ὑπὲρ πᾶσαν μάχαιραν here); cf. Isa. 49:2, where God makes the Servant's mouth "like a sharp sword." (See p. 314, n. 206.)

48. Gk. δί-στομος (lit. "two-mouthed"), not δισ-τόμος ("twice-cutting"). The word is classical; cf. Euripides, *Helena* 983, δίστομον ξίφος ("two-edged sword").

49. Judg. 3:16; Ps. 149:6; Prov. 5:4; Sir. 21:3. Its other NT occurrences are in Revelation (1:16; 2:12, and in some authorities 19:15), of the "sword" (Gk. ῥομφαία) proceeding from the mouth of the glorified Christ. In the Valentinian *Gospel of Truth* (Jung Codex 26:2) the judgment (κρίσις) which comes from heaven is described as "a drawn sword of two edges cutting this way and that." There may be an allusion there to the sword at the east of Eden (Gen. 3:24), which Philo (*On the Cherubim* 28) interprets as the Logos.

being in our author's mind here, such as the dividing of the carcasses in Gen. 15:10[50] or the circumcising of the Israelites with flint knives in Josh. 5:2ff.[51] The words which follow—"as it pierces, it divides soul from spirit, joints from marrow"—are to be understood as a "rhetorical accumulation of terms to express the whole mental nature of man on all its sides"; so A. B. Davidson, who further points out that since "the idea of dividing the soul and spirit suggests the division of a body into its members, hence joints and marrow are attributed to them, expressing the subtle articulations of the spiritual being and the innermost nature and substance of it."[52] It would indeed be precarious to draw any conclusions from these words about our author's psychology, nor is it necessary to understand them in the sense of the Pauline distinction between soul and spirit.[53] That the word of God probes the inmost recesses of our spiritual being and brings the subconscious motives to light is what is meant; we may compare Paul's language about the coming day when the Lord "will both bring to light the hidden things of darkness, and make manifest the counsels of the hearts" (1 Cor. 4:5). It is not surprising, accordingly, that a judicial function is here attributed to the word of God.[54] It is "discriminative of the heart's thoughts and intents"; this is the rendering of

50. Cf. Philo's treatment of this narrative (pp. 111f., n. 42 above).

51. Justin Martyr, drawing out the parallel between Joshua and Jesus (see p. 109, n. 28 above), says: "Jesus Christ circumcises all who will with knives of stone" (*Dialogue with Trypho* 24). This becomes a commonplace interpretation of Josh. 5:2 in early Christian literature; the Syriac father Aphrahat in his treatise *On Circumcision* puts it thus: "Jesus our Saviour circumcised a second time, with the circumcision of the heart, the people who had been baptized by baptism, and they were circumcised *with the scimitar which is sharper than a sword with two edges*" (J. R. Harris, *Testimonies*, II, pp. 55f.). Aphrahat evidently thinks of the "word of God" (as described in this passage of Hebrews) as the means by which our Lord effects the circumcision of the heart. But it is going too far to suppose with Rendel Harris (*loc. cit.*) that Aphrahat's language reflects a use of the *testimonium* (Josh. 5:2) which was already accessible to the author of Hebrews, and that accordingly the heart-discerning power of the Logos in our present passage is another way of expressing the circumcision of the heart.

52. A. B. Davidson, *The Epistle to the Hebrews* (Edinburgh, 1882), p. 96. Cf. E. Schweizer, *TDNT*, IX, p. 651 (*s.v.* ψυχή).

53. C. Spicq, however, following A. J. Festugière (*L'idéal religieux des Grecs et l'Évangile* [Paris, 1932], pp. 212ff.), sees here the Philonic dichotomy between ψυχή and πνεῦμα, the latter being the higher part which apprehends divine philosophy (*L'Épître aux Hebreux*, I [Paris, 1952], pp. 52f.). (Cf. G. H. Lang, *Hebrews*, pp. 82f.: "It is of the highest importance to recognize these two types of life, the soulish and the spiritual.") More characteristic of Philo, however, is his depiction of the Logos as the "cutter" (τομεύς) which divides the tripartite soul of Platonism into its components, and then further divides each of these components into two (*Who Is the Heir of Divine Things?* 225).

54. With the application to the word of God of the epithet κριτικός here may be compared Philo's comment on Gen. 14:7, where the same place is called En-mishpat ("the spring of judgment," LXX τὴν πηγὴν τῆς κρίσεως) and Kadesh ("holy place"): "The wisdom of God is both holy . . . and the judgment (κρίσις) of all things, by which all opposites are disjoined" (*On Flight* 196).

E. K. Simpson, who, in a survey of the use of the adjective *kritikos* (ARV "quick to discern")[55] by Aristotle and others, says: "In all these examples it is a sifting process that is at work; and what winnowing-fan can vie with the gales of the Spirit blowing through the Word?" With the function here ascribed to the word of God we may compare the epithet "heart-knowing" applied to God himself in Acts 1:24; 15:8.[56]

13 We may conceal our inner being from our neighbors, and we can even deceive ourselves; but nothing escapes the scrutiny of God; before him everything lies exposed and powerless.[57] And it is to him, not to our fellow-men or to our own conscience, that our final account[58] must be rendered. Stripped of all disguise and protection, we are utterly at the mercy of God, the Judge of all. Therefore, "let us make every effort. . . !"

With these words, the second admonition of the epistle is concluded.

III. THE HIGH PRIESTHOOD OF CHRIST (4:14–6:20)

A. CHRIST'S HIGH PRIESTHOOD AN ENCOURAGEMENT TO HIS PEOPLE (4:14-16)

14 *Since, then,[59] we have a great high priest who has passed through the heavens, Jesus, the Son of God, let us maintain our confession.*

15 *Our high priest is not one who cannot sympathize with our frailties; he has endured trial in all respects like ourselves, while remaining free from sin.*

16 *So let us approach the throne of grace with confidence, in order to receive mercy and find[60] grace for timely help.*

---

55. "The Vocabulary of the Epistle to the Hebrews," *EQ* 18 (1946), pp. 37f.

56. Gk. καρδιογνώστης.

57. Gk. τετραχηλισμένος, perfect participle passive of τραχηλίζω, which appears to denote bending back the neck (τράχηλος) or seizing by the throat. The former sense is quoted from Theophrastus (bending back the sacrificial victim's neck for the fatal stroke). E. K. Simpson quotes examples from Philo and Josephus in support of the rendering "exhausted": "in the wrestler's art τραχηλισμός was a grip of the antagonist's throat akin to the bandit's *garrote*, rendering him limp and powerless. . . . This characteristic figure then may be held to represent either the denuded or helpless plight of all created persons or forces when brought face to face with their Creator and Lord" ("The Vocabulary of Hebrews," p. 38). For the thought cf. 1 Enoch 9:5, where the chief angels say to God, "Everything is naked and open before you" (πάντα ἐνώπιόν σου φανερὰ καὶ ἀκάλυπτα).

58. Gk. λόγος, in a different sense from that in which it is used at the beginning of v. 12. Cf. 13:17 (p. 385 with n. 99). The idiom is classical.

59. In the versions of Tyndale and Coverdale (following Luther) 4:14 appears as 5:1 — a more logical arrangement than our conventional chapter-division. See G. Friedrich, "Das Lied vom Hohenpriester im Zusammenhang von Hebr 4,14–5,10," *TZ* 18 (1962), pp. 95-115.

60. Gk. εὕρωμεν, omitted from B; according to Zuntz (*Text,* p. 41) its omission means

14 With admonition is coupled positive encouragement. Jesus has already been presented to the readers as "a merciful and faithful high priest" (2:17), and they are now shown how he is the one from whom they can receive all the strength they need to maintain their confession and resist the temptation to let go and fall back. "Jesus, the Son of God" is not disqualified by his divine origin from sharing in his people's troubles and sympathizing with their weakness. He himself endured every trial that they are likely to undergo, but remained steadfast throughout, and has now "passed through the heavens" to the very throne of God. In him, then, his people have a powerful incentive to perseverance in faith and obedience.

"The heavens" through which Jesus passed are the heavenly regions in general; we need not try to enumerate the successive "heavens" involved and determine whether he is envisaged as passing through three or seven of them.[61] The plural "heavens," as regularly in the New Testament and Septuagint, reflects the Hebrew word used in the Old Testament, which is always plural. What is emphasized here is his transcendence; he is "exalted high above the heavens," as we are told later in the epistle (7:26), or, as it is put in Eph. 4:10, he "ascended far above all the heavens, that he might fill all things."[62] It is because he has been so highly exalted that he is such a "great" high priest;[63] there is already the implied contrast here (which is brought out in explicit detail later) between him and the earthly high priests of Aaron's line, whose highest privilege was to pass once a year through the inner veil into the holy of holies in a material and temporary sanctuary, there to appear for a few moments before God on behalf of their people. With him as their permanent helper, the people of Christ might well hold fast the "confession"[64] in which he played a central part.

15 His transcendence, however, has made no difference to his humanity. Our author has already stated that, in order to "become a merciful and faithful high priest," the Son of God had to be "made like his brothers in all respects," and that "he is able to help those enduring trial" because "he himself endured trial and suffering" (2:17f.). So here he repeats that Chris-

---

that we have as the object of the remaining verb λάβωμεν the typical LXX expression ἔλεος καὶ χάριν ("mercy and grace").

61. For the enumeration of heavens (three or seven) cf. 2 Cor. 12:2; *Test. Levi* 2:7ff.; *Ascension of Isaiah* 6:13; 7:13ff.; TB *Ḥagigah* 12b (see p. 356, n. 150); 3 Enoch 1:1-12. For the view that "the heavens" through which Christ has passed are symbolized by the outer compartment of the earthly sanctuary see p. 208, n. 57.

62. Cf. Eph. 1:21.

63. In the OT "high priest" is literally (for the most part) "great priest" (Heb. *kōhēn gāḏôl*); so in 10:21 (p. 253 with n. 97). The unusually full expression here (Gk. ἀρχιερεὺς μέγας) probably marks Jesus out as greater than the Aaronic high priests; it is used in 1 Macc. 13:42 (of Simon Maccabaeus) and in Philo, *On Dreams* 1.214, 219; 2.183 (of the Logos).

64. Gk. ὁμολογία, as in 3:1.

tians have in heaven a high priest with an unequaled capacity for sympathizing with them in all the dangers and sorrows and trials which come their way in life, because he himself, by virtue of his likeness to them,[65] was exposed to all these experiences. Yet he endured triumphantly every form of testing that mankind could endure, without any weakening of his faith in God or any relaxation of his obedience to him. Such endurance involves more, not less, than ordinary human suffering: "sympathy with the sinner in his trial does not depend on the experience of sin but on the experience of the strength of the temptation to sin which only the sinless can know in its full intensity. He who falls yields before the last strain."[66] The phrase "free from sin"[67] does not mean that our Lord experienced every kind of human temptation except temptation to sin; like the Israelites in Moses' day, he too had his day of trial in the wilderness, and any compromise with the tempter's suggestions, any inclination to put God to the test, would have been as certainly sin as his refusal to countenance these suggestions or abate one iota of his confidence in his Father meant spiritual victory—victory for himself and also for his people.[68]

16 Therefore, says our author, let us come with full confidence[69] to the throne of grace. This throne of grace is the throne of God, where Jesus, as his people's high priest, sits exalted at the Father's right hand. It is the antitype, in our author's mind, to the "mercy-seat" in the earthly sanctuary, of which he speaks below in 9:5; in Tyndale's New Testament and the Great Bible (1539) the same rendering, "the seat of grace" (following Luther's *Gnadenstuhl*), is used both there and here. It was at the earthly mercy-seat that the work of atonement was completed in token on the Day of Atonement and the grace of God extended to his people; the presence of the Christians' high priest on the heavenly throne of grace bespeaks a work of atonement

65. Gk. καθ' ὁμοιότητα, lit. "according to likeness" (RSV "as we are"). The NEB brings out the meaning well: "one who, because of his likeness to us, has been tested every way, only without sin."

66. B. F. Westcott, *ad loc.*

67. Gk. χωρὶς ἁμαρτίας. Cf. B. F. C. Atkinson, *The Theology of Prepositions* (London, 1944), p. 5 ("His sinless nature contained nothing that responded to temptation, as does ours"); J. Moffatt, ICC, *ad loc.* ("The special reference is to temptations leading to apostasy or disobedience to the will of God. It is true that χωρὶς ἁμαρτίας does exclude some temptations . . . a number of our worst temptations arise out of sin previously committed").

68. J. R. Harris ("The Sinless High Priest," *ExT* 33 [1921-22], pp. 217f.) sees an allusion here to the typological parallel between Jesus and Joshua the high priest of Zech. 3:1ff. (p. 109, n. 28; p. 253, n. 97); the parallel is incomplete in that Joshua needed to be cleansed from his own sins (cf. Heb. 7:27), whereas Jesus was χωρὶς ἁμαρτίας. On the general subject which our author treats here cf. J. K. S. Reid, "Tempted, yet without sin," *EQ* 21 (1949), pp. 161-67; A. H. Curtis, *The Vision and Mission of Jesus* (Edinburgh, 1954), pp. 131ff.

69. Gk. παρρησία (cf. p. 249 with n. 82, on 10:19). See W. C. van Unnik, "The Christian's Freedom of Speech in the New Testament," *BJRL* 44 (1961-62), pp. 484f.

completed not in token but in fact, and the constant availability of divine aid in all their need. Thanks to him, the throne of God is a mercy-seat to which they have free access and from which they may receive all the grace and power required "for timely help"[70] in the hour of trial and crisis.[71]

---

70. Gk. εἰς εὔκαιρον βοήθειαν. F. Büchsel, *TDNT,* I, p. 629 (*s.v.* βοηθέω), cites a close parallel from a Greek inscription: βοηθεῖτο κατὰ τὸ εὔκαιρον, "received timely help" (*OGIS* 693.12).

71. See on this paragraph W. Schrenk, "Hebräerbrief iv.14-16: Textlinguistik als Kommentierungsprinzip," *NTS* 26 (1979-80), pp. 242-52.

HEBREWS 5

B. QUALIFICATIONS FOR HIGH PRIESTHOOD (5:1-4)

1 *Every high priest, being taken from human stock, is appointed[1] on be-*
half of human beings where their responsibility to God is concerned,
to offer gifts and sacrifices[2] for sins.[3]
2 *He must be able to deal considerately with the ignorant and erring,*
since he himself is also beset by frailty,
3 *because of which he must bring a sin offering[4] for himself as well as*
for the people.
4 *No one takes this honor on himself—only one who is called by God,*
as Aaron was.

Our author makes two points about the general qualifications which any high priest must satisfy, before he goes on to speak more particularly of Christ's qualifications to be his people's high priest. A high priest must be *(a)* able to sympathize with those whom he represents, and *(b)* divinely appointed to his office. How these two conditions apply to the Aaronic high priesthood is briefly set out.

1 *(a)* A high priest represents men and women "where their responsibility to God is concerned";[5] it is necessary therefore that he should be a human being himself. Aaron and his successors, who represented the nation of Israel in the presence of God, were Israelites themselves, conversant

---

1. Gk. καθίσταται. That it is to be construed here (and in 8:3) as a passive is confirmed by the corresponding use of the active καθίστησιν in 7:28 ("the law appoints as high priests men who are subject to frailty"). It might be parsed as middle and transitive, and is so interpreted by Calvin *(ad loc.)*, its object being regarded as τὰ πρὸς τὸν θεόν ("every high priest ordains the things which pertain to God"); but τὰ πρὸς τὸν θεόν is an adverbial phrase (cf. 2:17).

2. Gk. δῶρά τε καὶ θυσίας. The particle τε ("both") is omitted by 𝔭⁴⁶ B Dᶜ; for its retention cf. G. Zuntz, *The Text of the Epistles* (London, 1953), p. 62.

3. Gk. ὑπὲρ ἁμαρτιῶν, for which 𝔭⁴⁶ 1739 read περὶ ἁμαρτιῶν (probably under the influence of v. 3). For περὶ ἁμαρτιῶν cf. 1 Pet. 3:18. This is not precisely the idiomatic LXX use of περὶ ἁμαρτίας as the equivalent of Heb. *ḥaṭṭā't / ḥăṭā'āh*, for which see 10:6 (p. 241, n. 42).

4. Gk. περὶ ἁμαρτιῶν, for which the Byzantine text has ὑπὲρ ἁμαρτιῶν (cf. v. 1, and n. 3 above).

5. Cf. p. 88, n. 87.

118

with the conditions under which their people lived, exposed to the same pressures and trials.

The high priest's duties are here said to be the presenting of his people's gifts and sin offerings to God.[6] "Gifts" is the more comprehensive term; it would normally include "sacrifices" but not be coextensive with them. But "gifts and sacrifices" appears to be used by our author as a general expression in the sense of "offerings"; here the particular class of offerings intended is indicated by the added words "for sins."[7] And it emerges clearly in the course of his later argument that the particular sin offerings which he has in mind are those presented annually on the Day of Atonement; that was the occasion above all others on which the high priest in person was required to discharge the sacrificial functions.[8]

2 In order to fulfil these duties worthily, a high priest needs not only to pay heed to the precise performance of the several ritual details, but also to have inward feelings which are in keeping with his sacred work. This is something which commands our instant approval. No one can read the history of the Second Temple without being conscious of the preposterous situation which made a man like Alexander Jannaeus[9] his subjects' representative before God in the most solemn moments of national worship. Even if his ritual acts had been more punctiliously correct than many of the worshipers thought them to be,[10] the character of the man made him hopelessly unsuitable for the high priesthood. No man in Israel was less disposed to "deal considerately with the ignorant and erring"—or with anyone else. And indeed, from the fall of the house of Zadok[11] to the destruction of the temple 240 years later there were few high priests in Israel who manifested the per-

---

6. The linking of "gifts" (Gk. δῶρα) and "sacrifices" (Gk. θυσίας) by "both . . . and" (Gk. τε καί) suggests that the two terms are not sharply disjoined, as though the sense were: "that he may offer *(a)* gifts and *(b)* sacrifices for sins"; ὑπὲρ ἁμαρτιῶν probably qualifies δῶρά τε καὶ θυσίας and not θυσίας alone. The phrase "gifts and sacrifices" may be a generic term current in Alexandrian Judaism; cf. *Epistle of Aristeas* 234: "to honor God, not with gifts or sacrifices (οὐ δώροις οὐδὲ θυσίαις), but with purity of soul . . ." (cf. 8:3; 9:9).

7. Cf. the very different tone of Philo's summary of the high priest's functions: since his vestments symbolize the cosmos, "he who has been consecrated to the Father of the cosmos must needs have that Father's son [the cosmos] with all his fulness of excellence to plead his cause, that sins may be remembered no more and good things be supplied in most lavish abundance" (*Life of Moses* 2.134).

8. Cf. 9:7 (pp. 206-08).

9. Hasmonaean king and high priest, 103-76 B.C.

10. By combining the indications from Josephus, *Ant.* 13.372f., and TB *Sukkah* 48b, we learn that once, at the Feast of Tabernacles, the populace pelted him with citrons because he insisted on performing the ceremony of water-pouring in a way which did not commend itself to them as proper (pouring the water on the ground beside the altar, after the Sadducean manner, and not on the altar itself, in the Pharisaic manner).

11. When Onias III was assassinated (171 B.C.); cf. Dan. 9:26a; 11:22; 2 Macc. 3:34.

sonal qualities so indispensable for their sacred office. Our author, however, in all that he has to say about Israel's priesthood and sacrificial worship has the literary data of the Pentateuch in mind and not the facts of more recent history.

The Greek verb translated "deal considerately" denotes in general "the golden mean between indifference and mawkish sentimentality";[12] here it indicates more particularly forbearance and magnanimity on the part of people who are subject to great provocation and who could, if they wished, give way to unmoderated anger and meet the provocation with the utmost severity. A high priest could not make fitting expiation for sins which filled him, at that very time, with feelings of indignation and exasperation against those who were guilty of them. Aaron is credited with exemplary forbearance in face of the repeated provocation and envy of those on whose behalf he served as high priest[13]—although in this respect, as in most others, he falls behind his brother Moses.[14]

The objects of his gentle forbearance are those who are ignorant and going astray—probably we should understand a hendiadys here and take the phrase to mean "those who go astray through ignorance."[15] It was for such people—for those who succumbed to the moral infirmities which are common to mankind—that sin offerings were prescribed in the law: "and the

---

12. Gk. μετριοπαθεῖν. "This striking expression," says E. K. Simpson ("The Vocabulary of the Epistle to the Hebrews," *EQ* 18 [1946], pp. 36f.), "traces its genesis to the Peripatetic philosophy, in contradistinction from the Stoic's affectation of a marble apathy of demeanour. Within the bounds of self-respect it advocates a tolerant or sympathetic posture of mind in respect of provocations from others or misfortunes that may have overtaken them. The term μετριοπάθεια is accordingly coupled with πραότης and ἐπιείκεια, especially by Plutarch, with whom it is a favourite locution. The noble portrait of Achilles limned by Euripides in the *Iphigeneia in Aulis* (920f.) presents its prototype:

ἐπίσταμαι δὲ τοῖς κακοῖσί τ' ἀσχαλᾶν
μετρίως τε χαίρειν τοῖσιν ἐξωγκωμένοις.

Such a blend of forbearance and condolence was ideally requisite in God's high priest under the old dispensation, both in his sacerdotal and judicial functions. But human infirmity marred the fair vision, till the Eternal Priest, Perfection's real Counterpart, trod the scene. For (and this renders the word almost untranslatable) μετριοπάθεια is the golden mean between indifference and mawkish sentimentality. Aaron's fond compliance with Israel's masked idolatry and Eli's lax indulgence of his profligate sons were gross abuses of their lofty office. The true high priest's long-suffering will be *duly* measured, proportionate to the case in hand and the ignorance or waywardness he has to deal with; it will be adjusted to an equitable standard and free from extravagance no less than insensibility; not gushing, yet unfeignedly gracious (cf. Aristeas, 256: τὰ πρὸς τὸν καιρόν πράσσειν δεόντως μετριοπαθῆ καθεστῶτα). . . . *To treat considerately* is an inadequate rendering, yet we can devise no better." Cf. also C. Spicq, *L'Épître aux Hébreux*, I (Paris, 1952), p. 43; he mentions several occurrences in Philo.

13. Cf. Num. 14:5; 16:22, 47f.; Ps. 106:16.

14. Cf. Num. 12:3 (see also pp. 91f.).

15. Gk. τοῖς ἀγνοοῦσιν καὶ πλανωμένοις.

priest shall make atonement before Yahweh for the person who commits an error, when he sins unwittingly, to make atonement for him; and he shall be forgiven" (Num. 15:28).[16] No such provision was made for the deliberate and defiant lawbreaker.[17]

But with those who erred through ignorance the high priest might well sympathize, for he was prone to the same weaknesses himself. This was manifest from the records of several priests of Old Testament times (not to speak of those of the Hellenistic and Roman eras). Outstanding examples of high priests "beset by frailty" were Joshua the son of Jehozadak, whose unfitness for the office had to be removed by the cleansing pronouncement of God (Zech. 3:3-9), and Aaron himself, whose feeble yielding to the people's demand for a visible symbol of deity is matched only by the ineptitude of his excuse to Moses: "I said to them, 'Let any who have gold take it off'; so they gave it to me; and I threw it into the fire, and there came out this calf" (Ex. 32:24). Aaron was in no condition to make priestly intercession to God for the people on whom he had brought this great sin; it was Moses who went into the presence of God to make atonement for their sin and procure his pardon for them.[18]

3   No wonder, then, that the high priest had to present a sin offering for himself as well as for his people. This is specifically provided for in the directions for the Day of Atonement. Only after Aaron had presented a bullock as a sin offering to make atonement for himself and his family, in accordance with the prescription of Lev. 16:6, could he proceed with the atoning ritual on the people's behalf. As our author points out later in the epistle (7:27), this is one of the features which distinguish the Christians' high priest from those of the Aaronic succession: Jesus, being "holy, free from guile and defilement," had no need to offer a preliminary sacrifice for himself. It is by enduring the common weaknesses and temptations of the human lot, not by yielding to them, that he has established his power not only to sympathize with his people but to bring them help, deliverance, and victory.

4   *(b)*   If one qualification in a high priest is his ability to sympathize, another is his being called by God to this honorable service. No person can

---

16. Cf. Lev. 4:2 et passim; 5:17. The guilt offering of Lev. 6:1-7, making provision for cases of fraud in civil negotiations which involve "a breach of faith against Yahweh," implies less inadvertence than does the sin offering of Lev. 4; the case of Lev. 5:17 "appears when someone feels an obscure sense of guilt weighing upon him through the unintentional transgression of a divine commandment, without being able to give a more exact account of the matter; in this case too he is to bring a guilt-offering, because the transgression might conceivably consist of a 'breach of faith' or 'trespass' [of the kind mentioned in Lev. 5:15]; but as the extent of the trespass cannot be gauged, there can naturally be no question of making restitution in the proportion of six parts to five" (A. Dillmann, in A. Dillmann and V. Ryssel, *Die Bücher Exodus und Leviticus* [Leipzig, [3]1897], p. 478, on Lev. 5:17).

17. Cf. Num. 15:30 (p. 67, n. 2).

18. Ex. 32:11-14, 31f.

of his own accord set himself up as high priest, nor can he hold office validly by the gift of any earthly authority. (Had our author been minded to review the history of the Jewish high priesthood during the last two centuries or so of its existence, he could have illustrated this last point very effectively!)[19] Aaron, the first of Israel's high priests, occupied his office by divine appointment (Ex. 28:1ff.; Lev. 8:1ff.; Num. 16:5; 17:5; 18:1ff.; Ps. 105:26), and so did his heirs and successors (Num. 20:23ff.; 25:10ff.). And others who were not of Aaronic descent, but in a time of emergency exercised an intercessory and sacrificial ministry like that of the Aaronic priests, did so by a direct and special call from God, as did Samuel (1 Sam. 7:3-17).[20] If our author is to sustain his thesis that Jesus is his people's great high priest, he must produce comparable evidence of a divine call in his case.

C. CHRIST'S QUALIFICATIONS FOR HIGH PRIESTHOOD (5:5-10)

5 *In the same way Christ also did not exalt himself to the dignity of high priesthood; he was exalted to it by the one who said to him,*
    "You are my Son,
    today I have begotten you"[21] —
6 *as he says also in another place,*
    "You are a priest for ever,
    after the order of Melchizedek."[22]
7 *In the days of his flesh Christ offered up entreaties and supplications,*[23] *with loud cries and tears, to the one who was able to save him from death, and was heard because of his humble devotion.*

19. After the deposition of Onias III in 174 B.C., Jason and later Menelaus were appointed to the high priesthood by Antiochus IV; Alcimus was appointed by Demetrius I in 162 B.C.; the Hasmonaean Jonathan was appointed by Alexander Balas, putative son of Antiochus IV, in 152 B.C.; his brother Simon and his successors were appointed by decree of the Jewish people in 140 B.C. (1 Macc. 14:41). With the fall of the Hasmonaean house the high priests were appointed successively by Herod the Great (37-4 B.C.), Archelaus (4 B.C.–A.D. 6), Roman governors (A.D. 6-41), and members of the Herod family (A.D. 41-66). The last high priest, Phanni, son of Samuel, was appointed by popular ballot during the war against Rome (cf. Josephus, *War* 4.155-57).

20. Note the collocation of Samuel with Moses in Jer. 15:1; cf. Ps. 99:6 (LXX 98:6). See p. 322 (on Heb. 11:32).

21. Ps. 2:7 (cf. Heb. 1:5a, pp. 53f.).

22. Ps. 110:4 (LXX 109:4). The verb εἶ ("are"), present in the LXX, is left to be understood here (it is supplied in 𝔭⁴⁶ P 629 *pc*).

23. Gk. δεήσεις τε καὶ ἱκετηρίας. The collocation of the two words is quoted from Isocrates, Polybius, and Philo (cf. BAGD, *s.v.* ἱκετηρία; Spicq, *Hébreux*, I, p. 45; II, pp. 112f.). Whereas δέησις is common in the NT, ἱκετηρία occurs here only (it occurs in the LXX in Job 40:22 [conjoined with δέησις]; 2 Macc. 9:18); it is originally the feminine of the adjective ἱκετήριος, and such a substantive as ἐλαία or ῥάβδος is implied along with it, the olive branch being the regular token of supplication.

8 *Son though he was,* [24] *he learned obedience by what he suffered;*

9 *and having thus been made perfect, he became the source of eternal salvation to all those who obey him,*

10 *acclaimed by God as high priest after the order of Melchizedek.*

The same two qualifications as are requisite in any high priest are present in Christ; in his case, however, our author presents them in the reverse order: *(a)* his divine appointment and *(b)* his ability to sympathize with his people.

5 *(a)* Even Christ, the Son of God, did not assume the high-priestly dignity by his own initiative; he was called to it by God, who acclaimed him as his Son in the words of Ps. 2:7. The words "You are my Son; today I have begotten you," have already been quoted in Heb. 1:5. It was suggested in the exposition of that verse (largely on the basis of the present context of the quotation) that "today" in our author's mind is the day of Christ's enthronement—the day when the Most High gave public notice that he had exalted the crucified Jesus as "both Lord and Christ" (Acts 2:36). And, says our author, the same God who acclaimed Jesus as his Son has also acclaimed him as perpetual high priest.[25]

6 The opening words of Ps. 110, as we have seen already in our study of their quotation in Heb. 1:13, form one of the earliest Christian *testimonia* to the Messiahship of Jesus. But our author takes up v. 4 of that psalm and applies it to Jesus in a way which, so far as we can tell, was unprecedented in the early church. In some strands of Jewish expectation, a distinction was made between the lay Messiah (the "Messiah of Israel" or prince of the house of David) and the priestly Messiah (the "Messiah of Aaron").[26] It has indeed been argued that the people to whom this epistle was addressed were related to those groups which held a twofold messianic hope of this kind.[27] But here they are assured that Jesus, who was acclaimed by God as the Davidic Messiah in Ps. 2:7, was also acclaimed by God as high priest in Ps. 110:4. Chris-

24. Gk. καίπερ ὢν υἱός. On the rendering "Son though he was" see p. 130.

25. On the significance for our author of the fact that one and the same person is Son of God and high priest see M. C. Parsons, "Son and High Priest: A Study in the Christology of Hebrews," *EQ* 60 (1988), pp. 195-215.

26. This distinction, known from the *Testaments of the Twelve Patriarchs* (cf. G. R. Beasley-Murray, "The Two Messiahs in the Testaments of the Twelve Patriarchs," *JTS* 48 [1947], pp. 1-12), appears most clearly in the Qumran literature (e.g., 1QS 9.11); cf. A. S. van der Woude, *Die messianischen Vorstellungen der Gemeinde von Qumran* (Assen, 1957), passim; K. G. Kuhn, "The Two Messiahs of Aaron and Israel," *The Scrolls and the New Testament*, ed. K. Stendahl (London, 1958), pp. 54-64; F. F. Bruce, *Biblical Exegesis in the Qumran Texts* (London, 1960), pp. 41-55. See also A. J. B. Higgins, "Priest and Messiah," *VT* 3 (1953), pp. 321-36; "The Priestly Messiah," *NTS* 13 (1966-67), pp. 211-39.

27. Cf. Y. Yadin, "The Dead Sea Scrolls and the Epistle to the Hebrews," *Scripta Hierosolymitana* 4 (1958), pp. 36-55; H. Kosmala, *Hebräer-Essener-Christen* (Leiden, 1959). See pp. 7-9.

tians acknowledge not two Messiahs, but one, and that one is both king and priest.[28] But if the Messiah of David's line is high priest as well as king, he cannot be a "Messiah of Aaron"; Aaron belonged to the tribe of Levi, whereas David and his house belonged to the tribe of Judah, "a tribe of which Moses said nothing in connection with priests" (Heb. 7:14). No appeal can be made to those scriptures which establish the Levitical and Aaronic priesthood to support the claim that Jesus the son of David exercises a high-priestly ministry on his people's behalf.[29] But there is no need to appeal to those scriptures, for here is another scripture which speaks of another priestly order, and designates the Davidic king as priest of this order.

Melchizedek makes his appearance in Gen. 14:18 as king of Salem (traditionally, and in all probability rightly, identified with Jerusalem[30]) and priest of God Most High (*'Ēl 'Elyôn*).[31] When, centuries later, Jerusalem fell into David's hands and became his capital city (2 Sam. 5:6ff.), he and his heirs became successors to Melchizedek's kingship, and probably also (in a titular capacity at least) to the priesthood of God Most High.[32] But in the Hebrew monarchy "fundamentally, the union of religious and civil leadership seen in the 'divine kingship' of the fertile crescent was dissolved."[33] The chief priest-

---

28. Cf. B. Lindars, *New Testament Apologetic* (London, 1961), p. 142.

29. The attempt to establish a Levitical relationship for Jesus through his mother's kinswoman Elizabeth, who was "of the daughters of Aaron" (Luke 1:5), cannot be traced earlier than Hippolytus. According to Hippolytus (on Gen. 49:8) Jesus was descended from Levi as well as from Judah (an inference apparently drawn from *Test. Simeon* 7:2); he also interprets Moses' blessing of Levi (Deut. 33:8ff.) with reference to Jesus (cf. M. Brière, L. Mariès, and B. C. Mercier, *Hippolyte de Rome sur les Bénédictions d'Isaac, de Jacob et de Moïse*, in *Patrologia Orientalis* 27 [1954], pp. 72, 144ff.; also L. Mariès, "Le messie issu de Lévi chez Hippolyte de Rome," *Recherches de science religieuse* 39-40 [1951-52], *Mélanges Lebreton*, pp. 381ff.). See also J. L. Teicher, "The Damascus Fragments and the Origin of the Jewish Christian Sect," *JJS* 2 (1951), pp. 115-43, especially pp. 134ff.

30. Cf. Ps. 76:2, where "Salem" stands in synonymous parallelism with "Zion"; also the interpretation of Salem as Jerusalem in 1Q *Genesis Apocryphon* 22.13 (1st cent. B.C.) and in Josephus, *Ant.* 1.180. Others would identify Melchizedek's Salem with Shalem near Shechem (Gen. 33:18, AV/KJV, ERV/ARV mg.; cf. John 3:23, Salim). See p. 159, n. 16.

31. *'Ēl 'Elyôn* is identified with *Yahweh* in Gen. 14:22 (MT); *'Elyôn* and *Yahweh* also appear repeatedly as synonyms in poetic parallelism in the Psalms and elsewhere (e.g., Ps. 18:13). According to Philo of Byblus, *Elioun* ("Υψιστος, "Most High") was the chief deity among the Phoenicians.

32. Cf. A. R. Johnson, *Sacral Kingship in Ancient Israel* (Cardiff, 1955), pp. 24-33, 42-46; H. Ringgren, *The Messiah in the Old Testament*, SBT 18 (London, 1956), p. 15; A. Serina, *La figura di Melchisedeq nel Salmo CX,4: Il Sacerdozio e il Messianismo Sacerdotale del Re Davide* (Trapani, 1970).

33. H. L. Ellison, *The Centrality of the Messianic Idea for the Old Testament* (London, 1953), p. 11. He continues: "In Ps. 110:4 we see the union re-created." Even if the oracle of Ps. 110:4 was repeated regularly in the coronation ritual of the southern monarchy, it expressed a future ideal rather than a present fact. Zech. 6:13 has frequently been regarded as portraying a Davidic priest-king (so AV/KJV, ERV/ARV, "he ['the man whose name is the Branch'] shall be a priest upon his throne"), but the RSV is preferable: "there shall be a priest by his throne"

hood in the Jerusalem temple was exercised throughout the period of the monarchy, and for long afterward, by the family of Zadok—a family quite distinct from the Davidic line, and one that laid no claim to the succession of "the order of Melchizedek."[34] Under the Hasmonaeans, from Jonathan Maccabaeus onward, the chief priesthood and the chief civil power in Israel were combined in one person; but even if some justification for this unwonted combination was sought in the tradition of Melchizedek's royal priesthood,[35] the justification was empty, for the Hasmonaeans had nothing to do with Melchizedek. Indeed, the most pious groups in Israel strongly disapproved of the Hasmonaeans' assumption of the high priesthood,[36] and some of them—in particular, the community of Qumran—refused to recognize their usurpation of the sacred office, preferring to cherish the hope of a day when the legitimate line of Zadok would again be invested with the high-priestly dignity in a purified temple in a new Jerusalem.[37] But even so, this hope did not envisage the union of priesthood and kingship; it maintained a distinction, as has just been said, between the anointed priest and the anointed king of the new age.[38] For aught we know to the contrary, the writer to the Hebrews was the first to identify these two eschatological personages in such a way as to provide the fulfilment of the divine

---

(cf. LXX, "there shall be a priest at his right hand"). The recognition of two separate persons, a royal governor and a priest, is required by the following clause ("and the counsel of peace shall be between them both"); the reference would be to Zerubbabel and Joshua, "the two anointed ones" of Zech. 4:14.

34. See, however, H. H. Rowley, "Zadok and Nehushtan," *JBL* 58 (1939), pp. 113-41; "Melchizedek and Zadok," in *Festschrift für A. Bertholet*, ed. W. Baumgartner (Tübingen, 1950), pp. 461-72; "Melchizedek and David," *VT* 17 (1967), p. 485.

35. The language of the decree of the Jewish people in 1 Macc. 14:41, "that Simon should be their leader and high priest for ever," is probably based on Ps. 110:4 ("high priest for ever" here denoting an hereditary high priesthood). The view that Ps. 110 was actually composed in honor of Simon has now been generally abandoned, together with the attempt to find an acrostic of his name in its opening verses (so G. Margoliouth in *Academy*, February 20, 1982; G. W. H. Bickell, *ibid.*, April 9, 1982; R. H. Charles, "The Christ of the New Testament," *Exp.* VI.v [1902], pp. 252f.; B. Duhm, *Die Psalmen*, KHC [Tübingen, 1922], pp. 254ff.; R. H. Pfeiffer, *Introduction to the Old Testament* [New York, 1941], p. 630). "The contention held by some that the psalm belongs to the Maccabaean age because the letters composing the name of Simon, the Maccabaean leader, are the initial ones of the first four lines, can only be described as fantastic; for the fact is that these letters are not the initial ones of the lines in question, and can be made so only by arbitrary manipulation" (W. O. E. Oesterley, *The Psalms* [London, 1953], p. 461). Cf. H. Gunkel, *Die Psalmen* (Göttingen, 1926), p. 485. If the Hasmonaeans used this psalm to support their own high-priestly claims, that in itself might account for its nonappearance among the Qumran *testimonia*.

36. For the Pharisees' attitude cf. Josephus, *Ant.* 13.288-98; TB *Qiddushin* 66a.

37. CD 4.1ff.; in the Qumran commentaries the holder of the Hasmonaean high priesthood is referred to as "the wicked priest."

38. So later, during the war of liberation led by the messianic claimant Simeon Ben-Kosebah (A.D. 132-135), the otherwise unknown "Eleazar the priest" is named on the national coinage alongside "Simeon, prince of Israel."

oracle in Ps. 110:4.[39] The promised prince of the house of David is, by the same divine right, perpetual priest of Melchizedek's order. The implications of this are unfolded in detail in Heb. 7; but for the present our author, having established Jesus' qualification to be his people's high priest in terms of his divine appointment, turns to speak of a second qualification.

7 *(b)* His second qualification is his ability to sympathize with those whose cause he maintains. We have already been assured that Jesus is faithful and merciful as his people's high priest because he was made like his brothers in every respect—that he sympathizes with his people's weaknesses because he was exposed to all the tests and trials which they have to endure.[40] Now these statements are elaborated. These tests and trials befell him "in the days of his flesh"[41]—an expression which emphasizes the conditions of human weakness of which he partook during his earthly life and which does not imply that his human condition came to an end with his exaltation to the right hand of God. If the expression did have this meaning, it would seriously weaken our author's argument that Christians have right now a high priest who feels for them and with them in all their temptations and sorrows.

It would be a matter of great interest to discover something about the form in which our author knew the gospel story. He certainly does not dismiss the details of our Lord's earthly life or his inward experiences up to and including his passion as possessing no relevance for the "post-Easter" faith of the church.[42] On the contrary, he draws from those details and experiences lessons of great practical import for his readers' Christian life. He probably knew of a number of incidents in the life of Jesus when he "offered up[43] entreaties and

---

39. Whatever may be said about the provenience of the *Testaments of the Twelve Patriarchs,* there can be little doubt about the Christian origin of such a passage as that in *Test. Levi* 8:14: "a king shall arise out of Judah and shall establish a new priesthood . . . for all Gentiles." This is dependent on the Epistle to the Hebrews, and not vice versa (cf. also Heb. 7:14, pp. 165-67, with nn. 46, 50). The converse prediction in *Test. Reuben* 6:7ff., where kingship as well as priesthood is granted to the tribe of Levi, suggests a very different provenience. Elsewhere in the *Testaments* the kingship of Judah and the priesthood of Levi are kept distinct, the kingship being subordinate to the priesthood (as at Qumran). Cf. also Jub. 31:14f. (See p. 123, n. 26.)

40. Cf. 2:17f.; 4:15f.

41. Gk. ἐν ταῖς ἡμέραις τῆς σαρκὸς αὐτοῦ (NEB, "in the days of his earthly life").

42. And, for that matter, neither does Paul, whose words about not knowing Christ "after the flesh" in 2 Cor. 5:16 have been misinterpreted in this way (his meaning is excellently reproduced in the NEB: "With us therefore worldly standards have ceased to count in our estimate of any man; even if once they counted in our understanding of Christ, they do so now no longer"). It is unfortunate that the ministry of Christ is given so little place in early Christian confessions of faith: H. B. Swete speaks of the words "and lived among men" in the Creed of Caesarea (Socrates, *HE* 1.8) as standing alone in such documents as a reference to our Lord's career between his incarnation and passion (*The Ascended Christ* [London, 1912]; p. xv n.). See also A. M. Ramsey, "The Gospel and the Gospels," in *SE* = *TU* 73 (Berlin, 1959), pp. 39f.

43. Gk. προσενέγκας, from προσφέρω, rendered "offer" also in vv. 2 and 3. But it has no such sacrificial sense here, as though Christ's Gethsemane experience were somehow the coun-

supplications, with loud cries and tears, to the one who was able to save him from death"; but for us, restricted as we are to the Gospel narratives, "Gethsemane seems to offer the most telling illustration"[44] of these words. Mark tells us how "horror and dismay came over him" there, and he said to the three disciples who accompanied him: "'My heart is ready to break with grief; stop here, and stay awake.' Then he went forward a little, threw himself on the ground, and prayed that, if it were possible, this hour might pass him by. 'Abba, Father,' he said, 'all things are possible to thee; take this cup away from me. Yet not what I will, but what thou wilt'" (Mark 14:33b-36, NEB).

Some curious interpretations of the Gethsemane agony and prayer have been offered, with the well-meant intention of doing justice to our author's words. It has been suggested that what our Lord prayed for in Gethsemane was that he might be saved from dying there and then, either through physical exhaustion or by satanic assault.[45] But the reader of the Gospel accounts knows already what our Lord means by "this cup"; it cannot be anything other than "the cup which I drink" which he warned James and John that they also would have to drink if they desired to share his glory (Mark 10:38f.). For him, indeed, the cup was more bitter than for them, or for any of his other followers who have drunk it since; they have known that he shared it with them, but he drank it alone.[46] Our author's words here are further illustrated by the Johannine counterparts to the Gethsemane narrative of the Synoptic records. According to John, a day or two before his arrest in the garden Jesus said: "Now is my soul troubled. And what shall I say? Father, save me from this hour.[47] No, for this purpose I have come to this hour. Father, glorify thy name." The

---

terpart to the Aaronic high priest's offering for himself in v. 3 (so, e.g., A. B. Bruce, *The Humiliation of Christ* [Edinburgh, [4]1895], p. 277). See also A. Vanhoye, "L'oblation sacerdotale du Christ dans l'Épître aux Hébreux," *Didaskalia* 14 (1984), pp. 11-30, especially 12-19.

44. A. E. Garvie, "The Pioneer of Faith and of Salvation," *ExT* 26 (1914-15), p. 549: "While we must not limit the reference to Gethsemane, yet there this element in the passion is most clearly and fully presented to us." See also T. Lescow, "Jesus in Gethsemane bei Lukas und im Hebräerbrief," *ZNW* 58 (1967), pp. 215-39.

45. In *ExT* 6 (1894-95), p. 433, A. F. Schauffler is quoted (in an editorial note) for the view that "the 'cup' from which He prayed to be delivered was not the death on the Cross, but death in Gethsemane itself. He was praying for strength to reach the Cross, not for grace to escape it." Similarly T. Hewitt in *The Epistle to the Hebrews*, TNTC (London, 1960), pp. 97-101: "If Christ had died in the Garden, no greater calamity could possibly have fallen on mankind" (p. 100). But why? Once he had said "Not my will, but thine, be done," the offering up of his life at any subsequent moment must have constituted "a ransom for many," as he had said it would (Mark 10:45). See the more satisfactory treatment by D. Guthrie, *The Letter to the Hebrews*, TNTC (Leicester, 1983), pp. 129f.

46. Moreover, the drinking of the cup involved for him the bearing of the world's sin, as it could have done for no one else.

47. The construing of this prayer as a question ("Shall I say, 'Father, save me from this hour'?") may be felt to import a slightly histrionic element out of keeping with the spiritual intensity of the moment.

response came immediately from heaven: "I have glorified it, and I will glorify it again" (John 12:27f.).[48] Later in the same Gospel, Jesus at the moment of his arrest rebukes Peter's impetuous attempt to defend him: "Put your sword into its sheath: shall I not drink the cup which the Father has given me?" (John 18:11). The Father's name was glorified by the Son's willing acceptance of the cup of suffering from his hand. "The point to be emphasised is, not so much that the prayer of Jesus was heard, as that it *needed* to be heard: that He needed heavenly aid to drink the appointed cup."[49]

A difficulty has sometimes been felt in referring our author's words here to Jesus' Gethsemane experience, since he was not delivered from death[50]—the cup was not removed from him. Attempts to relieve the difficulty by insisting that the prepositional phrase here is not "from death" but "out of death"[51] do not touch the heart of the matter. But while Gethsemane provides "the most telling illustration" of our author's words, they have a more general reference to the whole course of our Lord's humiliation and passion. More than that: they have been influenced by the language of the twenty-second psalm, a psalm whose currency as a primitive Christian *testimonium* we have already noted.[52] "Loud cries and tears" might well describe the supplication and complaint of the first part of the psalm, while the statement that Christ was "heard[53] because of his humble devotion" echoes Ps. 22:24: "when he cried to him, he heard."[54] In the detailed Christological in-

48. Cf. also John 13:31f.; 17:1, 4f.

49. A. B. Bruce, *The Epistle to the Hebrews* (Edinburgh, 1899), p. 186.

50. It certainly does less than justice to our author's language to regard "the one who was able to save him from death" as little more than a circumlocution for "God" (in the sense of 1 Sam. 2:6, "Yahweh kills and brings to life; he brings down to Sheol and raises up").

51. A. E. Garvie ("The Pioneer of Faith . . . ," p. 549), G. H. Lang (*The Epistle to the Hebrews* [London, 1951], pp. 91f.), K. S. Wuest (*Hebrews in the Greek New Testament* [Grand Rapids, 1947], p. 99), and others emphasize that our Lord prayed to be delivered ἐκ θανάτου, "out of the midst of the death state" (after having entered into it), and not ἀπὸ θανάτου, "from death" (in the sense that he prayed that he might not die). But in fact no such clear-cut distinction can be made between the two prepositional phrases; Westcott *(ad loc.)* makes it quite clear that ἐκ θανάτου can cover both these distinct ideas; the prayer was not answered in the one sense, that it might be answered in the other. It is possible that ἐκ θανάτου here is an echo of Hos. 13:14 (LXX), ἐκ χειρὸς ᾅδου ῥύσομαι, καὶ ἐκ θανάτου λυτρώσομαι αὐτούς ("from the power of Hades I will rescue, and from death I will redeem them").

52. Cf. 2:12 with exposition and notes (pp. 82f.).

53. Gk. εἰσακουσθείς, with which cf. also Ps. 22:2 (21:3, LXX), οὐκ εἰσακούσῃ ("thou wilt not hear"). A. Harnack emended our text unnecessarily by inserting οὐκ before εἰσακουσθείς ("Zwei alte dogmatische Korrekturen im Hebräerbrief," in *Studien zur Geschichte des Neuen Testaments und der alten Kirche* [Berlin and Leipzig, 1931], pp. 245ff., reprinted from *Sitzungsberichte der preussischen Akademie der Wissenschaften*, phil.-hist. Klasse, 1929, pp. 62ff.); the emendation has been adopted by R. Bultmann in *TDNT*, II, p. 753 (*s.v.* εὐλαβής, etc.); cf. H. Windisch, *Der Hebräerbrief*, HNT (Tübingen, 1931), *ad loc.*, pp. 43f.

54. Gk. εἰσήκουσέ μου (LXX 21:25). Cf. also the occurrence of δέησις (cf. p. 122, n. 23) earlier in this verse of the psalm (LXX). Other passages in the Psalter which may have influ-

terpretation of the psalm, these words were understood as a reference to the resurrection of Christ;[55] our author may well have understood them thus, but he does not go into this question, which would have taken him beyond his present intention. His present intention is to insist that Jesus has been qualified for his high-priestly service by his agony and tears, his supplication and suffering, throughout which his trust in God never failed.[56]

That he was "heard for his godly fear" (RSV)[57] is the best interpretation of a phrase which has been understood in a variety of ways;[58] other interpretations are that he was "heard (and delivered) from the fear (of death)"[59] or that he was "heard by (the Object of) his godly fear."[60] The general New Testament usage of the word here rendered "godly fear" and of its cognates (and not least the usage in this epistle itself)[61] makes it improbable that fear

---

enced our author here are Pss. 31:22 (LXX 30:23); 39:12f. (LXX 38:13f.); 69:1-3 (LXX 68:2-4), and especially Ps. 116 (LXX 114 and 115), passim (for parallels in the last-named psalm cf. A. Strobel, "Die Psalmengrundlage der Gethsemane-Parallele, Hbr. 5, 7ff.," *ZNW* 45 [1954], pp. 252-66).

55. Cf. Justin Martyr, *Dialogue with Trypho* 106 (in section 99 Justin has interpreted Ps. 22:2 [LXX 21:3] of the agony in Gethsemane).

56. "What gives the reality to the priesthood is that it is no external office, inherited, usurped, or granted by favour, but it is an inward vocation and qualification in experience and character" (A. E. Garvie, *ExT* 28 [1916-17], p. 463, in an article "Shadow and Substance").

57. Gk. ἀπὸ τῆς εὐλαβείας.

58. Cf. Spicq, *ad loc.;* O. Michel, MK, *ad loc.* See also C. Maurer, "'Erhört wegen der Gottesfurcht' Heb 5,7," in *Neues Testament und Geschichte* (O. Cullmann *FS*), ed. H. Baltensweiler and B. Reicke (Zürich/Tübingen, 1972), pp. 275-84.

59. So Calvin, Beza, and many commentators since. R. Bultmann (*TDNT,* II, p. 753) conceded that this ("He was heard out of His anxiety, so that He was liberated from anxiety") was the best interpretation of the text as it stands, but as it does not suit the context he preferred Harnack's emendation (see p. 128, n. 53).

60. Cf. the OT designation of God as "the Fear of Isaac" (Gen. 31:42). MM (*s.v.* εὐλάβεια) cite a papyrus of A.D. 505 for the use of the word in the sense of "Your reverence" as a courtesy title.

61. The substantive εὐλάβεια appears in 12:28 (see p. 362, n. 190) and the verb εὐλαβέομαι in 11:7; the consistent meaning is reverence toward God. The substantive and the verb do not appear in the NT outside this epistle; the adjective εὐλαβής appears in the Lukan writings only, and always of devout Jews (Luke 2:25; Acts 2:5; 8:2; 22:12). "Trench has rescued this noun [εὐλάβεια] from detraction by showing that the Stoics reckoned it a positive virtue, the golden mean between rashness and poltroonery. According to Diogenes Laertius it is the very antithesis of fearfulness. In Luke's diction εὐλαβής is the devout, god-fearing soul, and later on in this Epistle the cognate verb is predicated in commendation of Noah's watchfulness. It corresponds with Cicero's *cautio,* defined in his *Tusculans* (iv. 6) as *a malis declinatio, si cum ratione fit,* and is summed up by Plutarch in the dictum: τὸ εὐλαβεῖσθαι σοφῶν ἴδιον (*Mor.* 1038). Philo uses the term of Eve's initial scruple to eat of the forbidden tree. It stands then for *circumspection, heedfulness,* the German *Behutsamkeit.* Πρὸς τὸ θεῖον εὐλάβεια is Plutarch's standing phrase for religious punctiliousness, and γεροντικὴ εὐλάβεια (*Brut.* 12) a praiseworthy feature of old age, namely *wariness*" (E. K. Simpson, *Words Worth Weighing in the Greek New Testament* [London, 1946], p. 19). See also Westcott, *ad loc.* The sense of the phrase ἀπὸ τῆς εὐλαβείας is exactly conveyed by the Vulgate rendering *pro sua reuerentia.*

of death is in view here; what is in view is rather our Lord's devotion and submission to the will of God. The fact that the cup was not removed qualifies him all the more to sympathize with his people; when they are faced with the mystery and trial of unanswered prayer they know that their high priest was tested in the same way and did not seek a way of escape by supernatural means of a kind that they do not have at their disposal.[62] At no point can the objection be voiced that because he was the Son of God it was different, or easier, for him.[63] He who would not have recourse to miraculous means to relieve his hunger in the wilderness refused to summon angelic forces to rescue him from his enemies.[64] He recognized the path of the Father's will, and followed it to the end; herein lay his "godly fear"—his "humble submission," as the NEB renders it.

8 "Though he was a Son," the rendering of the ERV/ARV (following the AV/KJV and followed by the RSV), fails to bring out the force of the clause. The absence of the definite article before the substantive "Son" in the Greek text here[65] should not be expressed by the indefinite article in English. It is the most natural thing in the world for a son to learn obedience by suffering; indeed, our author makes this very point in 12:5ff. But it is not any ordinary son that he is speaking about here, but the Son of God: "Son though he was"[66]—that is to say, Son of God though he was—even he was granted no exemption from the common law that learning comes by suffering.[67] The construction of the clauses and participial phrases in the ERV/ARV of vv. 7 and 8 suggests that the clause "though he was a Son" goes more closely with what precedes than with what follows. This would be in keeping with classical purity, so far as the laws governing concessive clauses of this type are concerned;[68] but in Hellenistic Greek there is ample precedent for placing

---

62. Cf. M. Rissi, "Die Menschlichkeit Jesu nach Hebr. 5,7 und 8," *TZ* 11 (1955), pp. 28-45.

63. This was precisely what he refused at his first temptation in the wilderness; having been so recently hailed by the heavenly voice as the Son of God, he was invited to exploit his divine Sonship for his personal advantage in a way that was not open to his people, but would not entertain the suggestion for a moment (Matt. 4:2-4; Luke 4:2b-4).

64. Cf. Matt. 26:53.

65. As in 1:2.

66. Gk. καίπερ ὢν υἱός. NEB "son though he was" would be the perfect translation if only "son" were given an initial capital.

67. Gk. ἔμαθεν ἀφ' ὧν ἔπαθεν. The rhyming relation of παθεῖν-μαθεῖν (πάθος-μάθος) gave rise to many epigrams in Greek literature to the effect that learning comes by suffering; so, e.g., in Aeschylus, *Agamemnon* 176ff., Zeus is described as the one "who has marked out the path of wisdom for mortals, and decreed as a sure law that learning comes by suffering (πάθει μάθος)." Cf. H. Dörrie, *Leid und Erfahrung: Die Wort- und Sinn-Verbindung παθεῖν-μαθεῖν im griechischen Denken* (Wiesbaden, 1956). Spicq (*Hébreux,* I, pp. 46f.) lists some Philonic parallels.

68. This is the main reason for Harnack's emendation (p. 128, n. 53), which yields the sense: "He was not heard, for all his godly fear, Son though he was." BDF (§ 211) take ἀπὸ τῆς

such a clause before the principal clause to which it belongs,[69] and this certainly gives better rhythm and sense here.

In what sense, then, did the Son of God learn obedience "by what he suffered"? We know the sense in which the words are true of us; we learn to be obedient because of the unpleasant consequences which follow disobedience. It was not so with him. As we are told later (10:7), he announced his dedication to the doing of God's will at his coming into the world. He set out from the start on the path of obedience to God, and learned by the sufferings which came his way in consequence just what obedience to God involved in practice in the conditions of human life on earth. Perhaps the obedient Servant of the Lord in Isa. 50:4-9 was in our author's mind. The Servant's eagerness to pay heed to the voice of God exposes him to ridicule and ill-treatment, but he accepts this as something inseparable from his obedience: "The Lord Yahweh has opened my ear, and I was not rebellious, I turned not backward. I gave my back to the smiters, and my cheeks to those who pulled out the beard; I hid not my face from shame and spitting" (Isa. 50:5f.). So the sufferings which Jesus endured were the necessary price of his obedience—more than that, they were part and parcel of his obedience, the very means by which he fulfilled the will of God. At the threshold of his public ministry, he silenced the Baptist's objections to baptizing him with the words "thus it is fitting for us to fulfil all righteousness"—or, as the NEB puts it, "we do well to conform in this way with all that God requires" (Matt. 3:15). Unlike those others who were baptized by John in the Jordan, confessing their sins, it was with no consciousness of sin that he accepted baptism, but with the resolution to place himself unreservedly at God's disposal for the accomplishment of his saving purpose—and if, in doing so, he associated himself publicly with sinners, that was something which he was going to do throughout his ministry, until he was "numbered with the transgressors" on the cross. It is not by accident that he spoke of his impending passion not only as the cup which he was going to drink but also as the baptism with which he was going to be baptized (Mark 10:38f.; Luke 12:50); the career of public obedience which was inaugurated in the earlier baptism was crowned by the second baptism—the fulfilment of "all righteousness" by the utmost endurance of trial and suffering as the first baptism had been by anticipation.

The Christians for whom this letter was intended found that the main-

---

εὐλαβείας with the following clause: "because of His godly fear, Son though He was, (and) because of the things which He suffered, He learned obedience . . ." (even though he was Son, he had to exercise godly fear)—a construction which weights v. 8 too heavily.

69. Especially in the LXX; cf. J. Jeremias, "Hbr. 5,7-10," *ZNW* 44 (1952-53), pp. 107-11, reprinted in *Abba* (Göttingen, 1966), pp. 319-23.

tenance of their faith and loyalty exposed them to trial and suffering which they could escape by renouncing their confession—or possibly even by drawing less public attention to it. But the question for them to face was: were they to fall back and lose everything or press on to perfection? Our author urges them to press on, in spite of all the suffering it may involve, and he sets before them the example of Jesus, who set his face "like a flint," refusing to turn back, and was thus made "perfect through sufferings." His example and his present aid might well encourage them too to persevere; no hardship could befall them in which he did not sympathize with them.

9-10 As we have already been told in 2:10, it was through sufferings that he was made perfect—fully qualified to be the Savior and High Priest of his people. To suffer death for God's sake is itself described as the attainment of perfection,[70] and the death of Christ is of course bound up with his being "made perfect" in the present context; but the essence of the perfection which our author has in mind consists in the twofold fact that by his suffering and death Christ *(a)* became to all who obey him "the source of eternal salvation" and *(b)* was "acclaimed by God as high priest after the order of Melchizedek." One can clearly recognize the motif of humiliation and suffering followed by exaltation in glory which pervades the primitive *kerygma.*

The expression translated "the source [or 'cause,' or 'author'] of salvation"[71] is found in classical Greek;[72] Philo also uses it—with regard to Noah, for example, and to the brazen serpent of wilderness days.[73] Here it has practically the same meaning as "the pioneer of their salvation" in 2:10. The salvation which Jesus has procured is an "eternal" one. The phrase "eternal salvation" appears in the Old Testament: "Israel is saved by Yahweh with everlasting salvation" (Isa. 45:17). Here, however, the Christian salvation is eternal, like the "eternal redemption" of 9:12, the "eternal inheritance" of 9:15, and the "eternal covenant" of 13:20, because it is based on the sacrifice of Christ, once for all accomplished, never to be repeated, and permanently valid. The salvation which Jesus has procured, moreover,

---

70. So Eusebius says of the martyr Marinus, "having been led off to death, he was perfected (τελειοῦται)" (*HE* 7.15.5). Cf. Heb. 12:23; Luke 13:32.

71. Gk. αἴτιος σωτηρίας αἰωνίου.

72. E.g., in Aeschines, *Against Ctesiphon* 57: "the gods have become the authors of salvation (τῆς μὲν σωτηρίας . . . αἰτίους) for the city." Cf. Josephus, *Ant.* 14.136: "Antipater was the author of their victory and also of their safety (ἅμα καὶ τῆς σωτηρίας αἴτιον)."

73. Noah's son Ham is reproached for his unfilial conduct toward his father, "the author of his salvation (τὸν αἴτιον τῆς σωτηρίας)" (*On the Virtues* 202); the brazen serpent was "the author of complete deliverance" (αἴτιος σωτηρίας . . . παντελοῦς) to those who beheld it (*Agriculture* 96); so also the Red Sea was a means of preservation (σωτηρίας αἴτιον) to the Israelites but of destruction to the Egyptians (*Contemplative Life* 86), and God himself is the author of his people's salvation (τῆς σωτηρίας αἴτιον) (*Special Laws* 1.252).

is granted "to all those who obey him." There is something appropriate in the fact that the salvation which was procured by the obedience of the Redeemer should be made available to the obedience of the redeemed. Once again the readers are encouraged to persevere in their loyalty to Christ, in whom alone eternal salvation is to be found—in whom also they have a high priest designated for them by God himself, "after the order of Melchizedek." Our author reverts to Melchizedek at the end of this section of his argument because he intends to go on now and elaborate the significance of his high-priestly order.

D. THIRD ADMONITION: SPIRITUAL IMMATURITY (5:11-14)

11 *Concerning this Melchizedek there is much that we have to say,[74] much that is hard to interpret, since you have become sluggish in your hearing.*

12 *Indeed, when you ought to be teachers because of the passage of time, you need to have someone teach you[75] the preliminary ABC of the oracles of God all over again. You have come to require milk instead of solid food.*

13 *Any one who is being fed on milk is unskilled in the word of righteousness; such a person is an infant.[76]*

14 *Solid food, on the other hand, is for those who are mature, those who through practice have had their senses trained to distinguish between good and evil.*

11 With the repeated reference to Ps. 110:4 in v. 10, the logical sequence of our author's argument would have led him on to expound the significance of Christ's being a priest "after the order of Melchizedek." This he does in Heb. 7:1ff., but first he turns aside (as he has done before[77]) to address some words of practical admonition to his readers' spiritual condition. Mel-

---

74. Gk. πολὺς ἡμῖν ὁ λόγος . . . λέγειν, but ὁ is omitted in 𝔓⁴⁶* D* P 1319. Zuntz (*Text*, p. 118) prefers the anarthrous reading, and takes the sense to be: "on this subject there is much to say but it would be obscure."

75. Gk. τοῦ διδάσκειν ὑμᾶς τινα. For διδάσκειν ὑμᾶς some authorities (462 1912 with the Latin versions and margin of the Harclean Syriac) have διδάσκεσθαι (ὑμᾶς), "you have need to be taught"; this may have been a change consequential upon the reading of τινα ("someone") as τίνα ("what [are the elements]"), a reading found in B² D² L and the majority of Byzantine witnesses with the Latin and Coptic versions (it is the reading of the TR, whence AV/KJV "which be the first principles of the oracles of God"). In 424** 1739 τινα in either form is absent; cf. Zuntz, *Text*, p. 75.

76. Gk. νήπιος γάρ ἐστιν. D* has the amplified reading "for he is still (ἀκμήν) a babe"— a reading attested also by Origen. For ἀκμήν in this sense (cf. Matt. 15:16) see *New Docs.*, II (1977), § 21.

77. E.g., in Heb. 3:7–4:13.

chizedek's person and office are subjects of deep import,[78] he says, but his readers may not be in a position to grasp what he has to say in this regard because their minds are so sluggish.[79]

12 You have been Christians for such a long time now, he goes on,

---

78. Gk. δυσερμήνευτος. Melchizedek was a subject of much speculation among Jews, as later among Christians. One line of Jewish tradition identified him with Shem (whose life, according to the Masoretic chronology, overlapped Abraham's by more than a century); this removed the difficulty of supposing that outside the line of the holy seed there should be one whom Abraham treated with such veneration. Another line thought of him as the prototype of the great priest of the age to come, but in a way which distinguished him from the Messiah of Ps. 110:1. As a result of polemic with the Christians, however, Judaism tended to take a less favorable view of Melchizedek. His blessing Abraham before he blessed God (Gen. 14:19f.) was reprobated, and it was held that on this account his priesthood was taken away from him and conferred on Abraham. See Justin, *Dialogue with Trypho* 19; M. R. James, *The Lost Apocrypha of the Old Testament* (London, 1920), pp. 17ff.; Strack-Billerbeck, IV (Munich, 1928), pp. 452ff.; M. Friedlaender, "La secte de Melchisédeq et l'Épître aux Hébreux," *RÉJ* 5 (1882), pp. 1ff., 188ff., 6 (1882), pp. 187ff.; G. Wuttke, *Melchisedech der Priesterkönig von Salem*, BZNW 5 (Giessen, 1927); M. Simon, "Melchisédech dans la polémique entre juifs et chrétiens et dans la légende," *RHPR* 17 (1937), pp. 58ff.; J. Klausner, *The Messianic Idea in Israel* (London, 1956), pp. 456, 515; J. J. Petuchowski, "The Controversial Figure of Melchizedek," *HUCA* 28 (1957), pp. 127-36; O. Cullmann, *The Christology of the New Testament* (London, 1959), pp. 83-85 (with a useful bibliographical apparatus in the footnotes); R. A. Stewart, *Rabbinical Theology* (Edinburgh, 1961), pp. 112-18; J. Fitzmyer, "Now this Melchizedek . . . (Heb. 7:1)," *CBQ* 25 (1963), pp. 305ff., reprinted in *Essays on the Semitic Background of the New Testament* (London, 1971), pp. 221-43; M. Delcor, "Melchizedek from Genesis to the Qumran Texts and the Epistle to the Hebrews," *JSJ* 2 (1971), pp. 115-35; F. L. Horton, *The Melchizedek Tradition*, SNTSM 30 (Cambridge, 1976); R. N. Longenecker, "The Melchizedek Argument of Hebrews," in *Unity and Diversity in New Testament Theology*, ed. R. A. Guelich (Grand Rapids, 1978), pp. 161-85. The fragmentary Qumran text 11QMelch has little enough in common with our author's exposition. The Qumran text quotes the regulations for the Year of Jubilee (Lev. 25:13) and the Year of Release (Deut. 15:2) and relates both to the eschatological return from exile. The proclamation of restoration and liberty at that time (cf. Isa. 61:1f.) is the responsibility of Melchizedek, "for that is the epoch of Melchizedek's acceptable year." Ps. 82:1 provides a biblical basis for assigning this proclamation to Melchizedek: Melchizedek is the *'ĕlōhîm* who stands there in the congregation of *'Ēl* and judges among the *'ĕlōhîm* (he is also the *'ĕlōhîm* who judges the nations in Ps. 7:8). Melchizedek is here promoted to be head of the heavenly court, judging the spirits of Belial's lot, and fulfilling a ministry of liberation for the people of his own lot, the children of light (to whom it is said of him in Isa. 52:7, "your *'ĕlōhîm* reigns!"). See A. S. van der Woude, "Melchisedek als himmlische Erlösergestalt in den neugefundenen eschatologischen Midraschim aus Qumran Höhle XI," *OTS* 14 (1965), pp. 354-73 *(editio princeps);* M. de Jonge and A. S. van der Woude, "11Q Melchizedek and the New Testament," *NTS* 12 (1965-66) pp. 301-26; J. A. Fitzmyer, "Further Light on Melchizedek from Qumran Cave 11," *JBL* 86 (1967), pp. 25-41, reprinted in *Essays on the Semitic Background of the New Testament*, pp. 245-67; J. Carmignac, "Le document de Qumran sur Melchisédeq," *RQ* 7 (1970), pp. 343-78. In the Nag Hammadi text *Melchizedek* (E.T. by B. A. Pearson and S. Giversen in *The Nag Hammadi Library*, ed. J. M. Robinson [Leiden, 1977], pp. 399-403) Melchizedek is portrayed as high priest and messianic warrior of the end-time. See pp. 159f., n. 20; p. 161, n. 26.

79. Gk. νωθρός, in the NT only here and in 6:12; in the LXX, Prov. 22:29 (of "slothful men"); Sir. 4:29; 11:12. See p. 151, n. 67.

that you ought to be able to teach others;[80] but as it is, you yourselves need to be taught—not only do you need to learn mysteries of deep import like the priestly order of Melchizedek, but the very ABC[81] of divine revelation. In view of the time that has elapsed since your conversion to Christianity, you ought to be taking solid food, like grown-up men and women; in fact, however, you are still unable to digest anything stronger than milk, the food of infants.

The contrast between milk and solid food in this spiritual sense appears to have been commonplace in the early church, as it was in Greek moral philosophy.[82] Paul makes it in 1 Cor. 3:1ff., where he tells the Corinthian Christians that, for all their claim to be "spiritual," they cannot be treated as such, since their fostering of party spirit in the church shows them to be still "carnal." They must therefore be treated as spiritual infants, and fed on the "milk" of elementary Christian ethics. There is indeed further wisdom to be imparted to those who have attained spiritual maturity—the "hidden wisdom in a mystery" decreed by God before all ages for his people's glory (1 Cor. 2:7)—but the Corinthians will not be able to assimilate this "meat" until they have grown up more, not in knowledge but in charity. (Was our author influenced here by that passage in 1 Corinthians? It would be interesting if he was, in view of Apollos's association with Corinth and Paul's mention of him in that same context.) The "milk" figure is used, without the contrast between it and strong meat, in 1 Pet. 2:2, where Peter exhorts his readers to acquire an appetite for pure spiritual milk, "so that you may thrive upon it to your souls' health" (NEB). But Peter is addressing "newborn babes," that is to say, people who have only recently been converted to Christianity.

13-14 The immaturity of the people addressed by our author, which caused him to doubt whether they were able to appreciate his teaching about

---

80. The statement that the recipients of this letter ought by now to have qualified as teachers of others has been made to bear an excessive weight of exegesis; K. Bornhäuser used it as one of his arguments for identifying the recipients with the converted priests of Acts 6:7 (*Empfänger und Verfasser des Briefes an die Hebräer* [Gütersloh, 1932], pp. 16ff.). The idea that ordinary Christians would not be expected to become teachers is quite unwarranted; the word διδάσκαλος is used here in quite an informal sense, and not of trained catechists or anything like that. It was an axiom of Stoicism that anyone who had mastered true learning was in a position to impart it to others; and it is equally a Christian axiom.

81. Cf. the NEB; Gk. στοιχεῖα (ARV "rudiments"). In addition to this primary sense of the letters of the alphabet, στοιχεῖα is used in the NT of the "elements" which make up the material universe (2 Pet. 3:10, 12) and of the "elemental spirits" of the world which seek to bring men into bondage and from which the gospel delivers them (Gal. 4:3, 9; Col. 2:8, 20). Cf. F. F. Bruce, *Galatians*, NIGTC (Grand Rapids/Exeter, 1982), pp. 193f., 203-5; *Colossians–Philemon–Ephesians*, NICNT (Grand Rapids, 1984), pp. 99f., 125f.

82. For details see Moffatt, Michel, and Spicq, *ad loc.;* also Spicq, I, pp. 53-56. For the periphrasis γεγόνατε χρείαν ἔχοντες γάλακτος, lit. "you have become having need of milk" (cf. 2 Cor. 6:14a), see BDF § 354 (p. 180).

the Melchizedek priesthood of Christ, was due to a disinclination to press on in the Christian way. Their sluggishness showed itself in a disposition to settle down at the point which they had reached, since to go farther would have meant too complete a severing of old ties. To such people the exposition of the high-priestly service of Christ, with the corollary that the old order of priesthood and sacrifice had been abolished once for all, might well have been unacceptable; the intellect is not over-ready to entertain an idea that the heart finds unpalatable.

The "milk" corresponds to the ABC of the divine oracles; some of the "first principles"[83] of which the ABC consists are mentioned in 6:1f. Those who have not proceeded beyond this stage are still infants, "unskilled in the word of righteousness"—or, as it may be rendered, "a principle of righteousness."[84] It is ethically mature people, those "who through practice have had their senses trained to distinguish between good and evil," who have built up in the course of experience a principle or standard of righteousness by which they can pass discriminating judgment on moral situations as they arise. The general idea is widespread among contemporary writers on ethics, although our author uses it for a purpose of his own.

---

83. Gk. ἀρχή, here and in 6:1. In the phrase τὰ στοιχεῖα τῆς ἀρχῆς here, τῆς ἀρχῆς may be taken as a genitive of definition; one cannot well press a distinction between the στοιχεῖα and the ἀρχή.

84. Gk. λόγος δικαιοσύνης (cf. the ὀρθὸς λόγος of Philo and Marcus Aurelius). The rendering "a principle of righteousness" is suggested by H. P. Owen, "The 'Stages of Ascent' in Hebrews v. 11–vi. 3," NTS 3 (1956-57), pp. 243-53. He distinguishes two phases in the stage of full growth: (a) the phase of ethical maturity, in which a "principle of righteousness" is acquired through experience; (b) the phase in which those who have thus had "their senses exercised to discern good and evil" are supplied with solid food such as the doctrine of Christ's high priesthood (this latter phase being the "perfection" of 6:1). This threefold ascent (infancy, moral maturity, spiritual illumination) he finds paralleled in Philo and the Stoics (but not Epictetus, who makes no room for the last phase). Cf. E. Percy, Probleme der Kolosser- und Epheserbriefe (Lund, 1946), p. 323. See further on 6:1 (p. 138). G. Delling (TDNT, I, p. 188, s.v. αἰσθάνομαι) takes the meaning to be that only to Christians of developed moral character can the doctrine of justification by faith (λόγος δικαιοσύνης) be imparted; νήπιοι so easily misunderstand it. This does not suit the context.

85. Gk. διὰ τὴν ἕξιν. The ἕξις is the habitus, experience, or skill acquired through practice.

HEBREWS 6

E. NO SECOND BEGINNING POSSIBLE (6:1-8)

1 *Therefore let us leave the preliminary stage of Christ's message[1] and press on[2] to perfection. Let us not lay the foundation all over again—the foundation of repentance from dead works and faith in God,*
2 *which consists in teaching about ablutions,[3] about laying on of hands, resurrection of the dead, and eternal judgment.*
3 *This then is what we shall do,[4] God permitting.*
4 *For it is impossible to renew again to repentance those who have once been enlightened, who have tasted the heavenly gift and partaken of the Holy Spirit,*
5 *who have experienced the goodness of God's word[5] and the mighty works of the coming age,[6]*
6 *if then they have fallen away. It is impossible, I say, because on their*

1. Lit. "the word of the beginning of Christ" (ERV/ARV mg.).
2. Gk. φερώμεθα, of swift and energetic movement.
3. The reading adopted is βαπτισμῶν διδαχήν (𝔭46 B latd(e) syrpesh), although the reading βαπτισμῶν διδαχῆς is much more widely attested (ℵ A C D K P 0122 byz latvg syrhcl arm). It is more likely that an original accusative (διδαχήν) was assimilated to the adjacent genitives than that an original genitive was altered to an accusative. If the accusative be preferred (so G. Zuntz, *The Text of the Epistles* [London, 1953], p. 93), it is parallel, and probably in apposition to θεμέλιον ("foundation"); and the following genitives ἐπιθέσεως ("imposition"), ἀναστάσεως ("resurrection"), and κρίματος ("judgment") are probably, like βαπτισμῶν ("baptisms"), dependent on διδαχήν. Cf. F. W. Beare, "The Text of the Epistle to the Hebrews in 𝔭46," *JBL* 63 (1944), p. 394; R. V. G. Tasker, *The Gospel in the Epistle to the Hebrews* (London, 1950), p. 25; B. M. Metzger, *A Textual Commentary on the Greek New Testament* (London/New York, 1971), p. 666.
4. Gk. ποιήσομεν, for which a handful of authorities (notably A C D) have ποιήσωμεν ("let us do").
5. Lit. "have tasted. . . ," an echo of Ps. 34 (LXX 33):8 (cf. 1 Pet. 2:3). What the psalmist says of God is here predicated of his word.
6. Gk. δυνάμεις τε μέλλοντος αἰῶνος. A Greek text having δύνοντος in place of μέλλοντος seems to be implied by Tertullian's quotation of this passage in *On Modesty* 20: "For it is impossible that those who . . . have tasted the word of God and found it sweet, when—their age already setting *(occidente iam aeuo)*—they have fallen away, should be recalled again unto repentance"; but this reading probably arose through the accidental omission of letters in δυν(άμεις τε μέλλ)οντος.

> *own account they are crucifying[7] the Son of God and exposing him to public shame.*
>
> 7 *The ground which drinks up the rain which frequently falls on it, and produces plants serviceable for those on whose account it is cultivated, has a share in God's blessing;*
>
> 8 *but that which brings forth thorns and thistles is worthless; it is on the point of being cursed, and will at last be burned.*

1 The opening words of this section are surprising. Our author has just told his readers that they are not really able to assimilate the solid food which he would like to give them—the teaching about the priestly order of Melchizedek—because they are immature. We might have expected him to say, as Paul says to the Corinthians[8] in a similar situation: "Therefore I must continue to feed you with milk." But he does not say this; he says: "let us press on." He judged that no good purpose would be served by going over the first principles again. That being so, we might have expected him to say: "You are not ready for solid food yet, you still need milk; *nevertheless* I am going to press on with the provision of solid food." But he does not say "nevertheless"; he says "therefore." "*Therefore* let us leave the elementary doctrines of Christ and press forward to maturity." Why "therefore"? Probably because their particular condition of immaturity is such that only an appreciation of what is involved in Christ's high priesthood will cure it. Their minds need to be.stretched, and this will stretch them as nothing else can. They have remained immature too long; *therefore* he will give them something calculated to take them out of their immaturity.[9]

"So," he says, "let us stop discussing the rudiments; do not let us start laying our foundations all over again." The rudiments ("the elementary doctrines of Christ," RSV) and the foundation are the same thing described in two different figures. Before he goes on, however, he lists some of the rudiments, quoting perhaps from a catechesis familiar to himself and his readers.[10] Six matters are listed, which fall naturally into three pairs: *(a)* "repentance from

7. AV/KJV and ERV/ARV "crucify . . . afresh," where the adverb "afresh" is intended to convey the force of the prefix ἀνα- in ἀνασταυροῦντας. But it is more probable that ἀνασταυρόω (not found elsewhere in biblical Greek) has the meaning "crucify" here which it has in nonbiblical writers (ἀνα- denoting "up," not "again"). So the RSV ("they crucify the Son of God on their own account") and the NEB ("with their own hands they are crucifying the Son of God"). The dative ἑαυτοῖς ("to themselves") may mean "to their own hurt" (cf. pp. 322f., n. 5, on 12:3). But the sense "crucify again" was accepted here by the Greek fathers and ancient versions (cf. Vg. *rursum cruci figentes*), possibly because of a feeling that this sense was especially appropriate to *Jewish* Christians (see also p. 149, n. 57).

8. 1 Cor. 3:2.

9. Cf. H. P. Owen, "The 'Stages of Ascent' in Hebrews v. 11–vi. 3," *NTS* 3 (1956-57), pp. 243-53.

10. Cf. O. Michel, MK, *ad loc.*

dead works" goes closely with *(b)* "faith in God"; *(c)* "instruction about ablutions" (RSV) goes with *(d)* "laying on of hands"; while there is a patent association between *(e)* "resurrection of the dead" and *(f)* "eternal judgment." But the connection between these six subjects is more complicated than that. On the most probable reading of the text, "teaching" in v. 2 appears to be in apposition to "foundation" in v. 1;[11] this suggests that the laying of a "foundation of repentance . . . and faith" consists in instruction about (i) ablutions, (ii) laying on of hands, (iii) resurrection, and (iv) judgment.[12]

We are thus given some insight into what was regarded as a suitable foundation of Christian teaching in a non-Pauline church, and one which had a Jewish basis. When we consider the "rudiments" one by one, it is remarkable how little in the list is distinctive of Christianity, for practically every item could have its place in a fairly orthodox Jewish community. Each of them, indeed, acquires a new significance in a Christian context; but the impression we get is that existing Jewish beliefs and practices were used as a foundation on which to build Christian truth. "It is significant," wrote Alexander Nairne, "that the points taken as representing the foundation of penitence and faith are all consistent with Judaism. 'Doctrines of washings'—how unnatural are the attempts to explain this plural as referring to Christian Baptism; 'imposition of hands, resurrection of dead, eternal judgement'—all this belonged to the creed of a Pharisaic Jew who accepted the whole of the Old Testament."[13] Very true; but it belonged equally to the creed of a nonconformist Jew of Essene or comparable outlook.

(a) Repentance from dead works. "Dead works" are works which must be repented of; in 9:14 they are works from which the conscience needs to be cleansed. Therefore they are probably not the works of the law, not even the sacrificial ceremonies prescribed by the cultic law,[14] although our author

---

11. See p. 137, n. 3.

12. "This renouncing of a past way of life, whether it be a Jewish or a pagan way, and this turning to God in faith to receive new power from him were symbolized, in early Christian practice, in the initiation ceremonies of 'baptism and the laying-on-of-hands'; and the outstanding characteristics of the new life that a Christian sought to live were the new sense of purpose and the increased sense of seriousness which were imparted to it by the certainty that, because Christ had been raised from the dead, there would be 'a resurrection of the dead' followed by a 'judgment' which would have eternal consequences" (R. V. G. Tasker, *Gospel in Hebrews*, p. 25). According to G. Zuntz (*Text*, p. 93), "διδαχήν is defined by the genitives βαπτισμῶν and ἐπιθέσεως, just as θεμέλιον is defined by μετανοίας and πίστεως. The two concluding genitives, 'resurrection' and 'judgment', denote the main subjects of the teaching."

13. *The Epistle of Priesthood* (Edinburgh, 1913), p. 15. Cf. G. H. Lang, *The Epistle to the Hebrews* (London, 1951), pp. 95f.

14. They have been taken in this sense, however, by able expositors, such as A. B. Bruce, *The Training of the Twelve* (Edinburgh, 1883), p. 81; cf. also R. V. G. Tasker, *Gospel in Hebrews*, p. 25 (where he describes this repentance as "an abandonment of the attempt to obtain righteousness by seeking to obey the precepts of a lifeless moral code").

does regard these as obsolete and moribund. They are works which issue in death because they are evil; they belong to the way of death and not the way of life. One could well believe that the catechesis on which the readers of this epistle had been trained included a version of the "Two Ways" teaching incorporated in the *Didachē* and the *Epistle of Barnabas,* but certainly earlier in date than either of these documents.[15] The *Didachē* begins its account of the way of death (which, it says, is "evil and fraught with a curse") with a catalog of the sins which belong to it: "murders, adulteries, lusts, fornications, thefts, idolatries, magic arts, sorceries, robberies, false depositions, hypocrisies, a double heart, fraud, arrogance, malice, obstinacy, covetousness, filthy language, envy, audacity, haughtiness, boastfulness. . . ."[16] It was with regard to precisely such vices that Paul told the Roman Christians that "the end of those things is death" (Rom. 6:21); very appropriately, therefore, might they be called dead works. Repentance from such things was insisted upon in the Old Testament, and in all the strains of Jewish thought and life which were derived from the Old Testament. The sectaries of Qumran, for example, described themselves as "the repentant of Israel";[17] and they were by no means the only Jews to think and speak in such terms. The keynote of John the Baptist's preaching was a call to repentance (cf. Mark 1:4; Matt. 3:2, 8 par. Luke 3:8); and when Jesus began to proclaim the kingdom of God in Galilee, he called upon his hearers to "repent, and believe in the gospel" (Mark 1:15). So too the Lukan Paul could remind the elders of the Ephesian church how he had spent over two years in their city "testifying both to Jews and to Greeks of repentance to God and of faith in our Lord Jesus Christ" (Acts 20:21).[18]

(b) Faith in God. The last two quotations illustrate the close association between repentance and faith. The foundation of faith in God was, of course, well and truly laid in the Old Testament. Throughout the volume faith is marked out as essential to true religion, from the statement that Abraham "believed Yahweh, and he reckoned it to him as righteousness" (Gen. 15:6)

---

15. *Didachē* 1:1–5:2; *Ep. Barn.* 18:1–20:2. As it appears in these documents, the ethical treatise of the "Two Ways"—the Way of Life and the Way of Death (or the Way of Light and the Way of Darkness)—is a slightly Christianized edition of an originally Jewish manual, going back to the pre-Christian era. Traces of it appear in the *Testaments of the Twelve Patriarchs* (*Judah* 20:1-5; *Asher* 1:3–6:6) and in the Qumran literature (1QS 3.18–4.26). On the use of the "Two Ways" in early Judaeo-Christian baptismal instruction see J. V. Bartlet, *The Apostolic Age* (Edinburgh, 1929), pp. 250-59, 313.

16. *Didachē* 5:1.

17. CD 4.2.

18. In Paul's epistles repentance does not figure soteriologically as faith does; other language is used to express the same "responding in kind to the creative effort of reconciliation" (C. F. D. Moule, "Obligation in the Ethic of Paul," *Essays in New Testament Interpretation* [Cambridge, 1982], pp. 271f.).

to Habakkuk's testimony that "the righteous shall live by his faith" (Hab. 2:4).[19] The readers of this epistle had already been reminded that it was unbelief that kept the generation of the Exodus from entering the promised land, and they were urged to apply this lesson to their own situation. Faith in God must include faith in his messengers, and in the gospel faith in God included—or indeed became tantamount to—faith in Christ. These "Hebrews" had certainly been taught the way of faith in Christ, but this way had been prepared for them in advance by the Old Testament insistence on faith in God: "if you will not believe, surely you shall not be established" (Isa. 7:9).

2 *(c) Teaching about ablutions.* This has commonly been regarded as a reference to Christian baptism, but it is doubtful whether Christian baptism is directly in view here at all. Apart from the fact that the word translated "ablutions" is in the plural *(baptismoi),* it may be significant that our author does not use *baptisma,* the Greek noun regularly employed in the New Testament to denote Christian baptism (and the baptism of John), but *baptismos,* which in its two other indubitable New Testament occurrences refers to Jewish ceremonial washings.[20] "Instruction about ablutions" (RSV) or "instruction about cleansing rites" (NEB) expresses the sense more adequately than "the teaching of baptisms" (ERV/ARV). There is no lack of instruction about ablutions in the Old Testament, and this provided a further foundation on which the Christian truths could be erected. Later in the epistle (9:13) the ritual of the red heifer in Num. 19, one of the most important of the ceremonial purifications prescribed in the Old Testament, is treated as a counterpart in the temporal order to the cleansing efficacy of the sacrifice of Christ in the spiritual order. The prophet Ezekiel in earlier days had used the terminology of the old ceremonial ablutions to describe God's inward cleansing of his people in the age of restoration: "I will sprinkle clean water upon you, and you shall be clean from all your uncleannesses, and from all your idols I will cleanse you" (Ezek. 36:25). In language like this the baptist groups which flourished in Judaism at the beginning of the Christian era found scriptural authority for their ceremonial washings, which went beyond what the letter of the law required.[21] Formerly our knowledge about these groups was derived from ancient writings which described them from the outside; but the discovery and decipherment of the Qumran texts have introduced us to

---

19. Quoted in 10:38 (see pp. 272-75).

20. The form βάπτισμα is peculiar to Christian writers. In 9:10 βαπτισμός is used in the plural of ablutions associated with the OT cultus; in Mark 7:4 of the Jewish purification of "cups and pots and vessels of bronze." In Col. 2:12 there is weighty textual evidence for βαπτισμῷ (𝔭[46] ℵ[2] B D* G) as against βαπτίσματι (ℵ* A C[2] D[2] Ψ byz) in the sense of Christian baptism. But the plural speaks against a straightforward interpretation in terms of Christian baptism in Heb. 6:2.

21. Cf. also Zech. 13:1. See W. Brandt, *Die jüdischen Baptismen,* BZAW 18 (Giessen, 1910); J. Thomas, *Le mouvement baptiste en Palestine et Syrie* (Gembloux, 1935).

one such group from the inside. The members of the Qumran community practiced ceremonial ablution in terms of Num. 19 and Ezek. 36; but they did not regard such ablution as a means of removing iniquity from the heart. Only by submission to the commandments of God, they believed, could one be inwardly purified, and not until then would ceremonial washings have any value.[22] There is evidence that such baptist groups of Jews were found in the lands of the Dispersion as well as in their homeland; the Jewish community in Rome, in particular, probably preserved some characteristic features of this nonconformist Judaism—features which were carried over into Roman Christianity, if the Hippolytean *Apostolic Tradition* may be trusted. According to Hippolytus, for example, baptism, as the central act of Christian initiation, took place on Easter Day, but on the preceding Thursday the candidate was required to have a ritual bath for the removal of impurity.[23] This prebaptismal bath has no warrant in the New Testament, but it may well have been a legacy from Roman Judaism.[24] If this epistle was sent to a group of believing Jews in Rome, the reference to "teaching about ablutions" may have had a more direct significance than meets the eye of the twentieth-century reader.[25]

(d) Laying on of hands. The imposition of hands (Heb. $s^e m\hat{\imath}\underline{k}\bar{a}h$) was an early Christian practice,[26] associated especially with the impartation of the Holy Spirit,[27] and that is most probably its significance here.[28] But it too was inherited from the Old Testament, where it is used especially in com-

22. 1QS 3.4-9; 5.13f. Josephus's account of the baptism of John is evidently colored by the historian's knowledge of Essene doctrine and practice: according to him, John "taught that baptism would be regarded as acceptable by God provided that people underwent it not to procure pardon for certain sins but for the purification of the body when once the soul had been purified by righteousness" (*Ant.* 18.117). Cf. p. 210, n. 65; p. 215, n. 88.

23. "And let those who are to be baptized be instructed to wash and cleanse themselves on the fifth day of the week" (*The Apostolic Tradition of St. Hippolytus*, ed. G. Dix [London, [2]1968], p. 31). Cf. R. J. Zwi Werblowsky, "On the Baptismal Rite according to St. Hippolytus," *Studia Patristica* 2 = *TU* 64 (Berlin, 1957), pp. 93-105.

24. Cf. J. Daniélou, "La communauté de Qumrân et l'organisation de l'Église ancienne," *RHPR* 35 (1955), pp. 104-16; M. Black, *The Scrolls and Christian Origins* (London, 1961), pp. 99-101, 114f.

25. D. Daube, *The New Testament and Rabbinic Judaism* (London, 1956), p. 109, points to the high importance attached to baptism among leading first-century members of the school of Hillel, some of whom were prepared to say that baptism alone (not as a ceremonial purification but as a rite with a deep moral and spiritual meaning) was sufficient to make a Gentile (whether male or female) a Jewish proselyte. M. Black (*Scrolls*, p. 51) compares Justin Martyr's "baptizing Pharisees" (*Dialogue with Trypho* 80).

26. Cf. Acts 6:6; 8:17; 9:12, 17; 19:6, with accompanying exposition and notes in NICNT.

27. Cf. G. W. H. Lampe, *The Seal of the Spirit* (London, 1951), pp. 70-93; T. W. Manson, "Entry into Membership of the Early Church," *JTS* 48 (1947), pp. 25-35; R. E. O. White, *The Biblical Doctrine of Initiation* (London, 1960), pp. 195-99.

28. Cf. references to the Holy Spirit in v. 4; 2:4; 10:29.

missioning someone for public office,[29] or as part of the sacrificial ritual.[30] In later Judaism the term appears regularly in the sense of ordination (of rabbis).[31]

(e) *Resurrection of the dead.* The resurrection of Jesus gave special importance to this doctrine in the church, but the doctrine as such was no innovation in New Testament times. It was held, as we know, by the Pharisees,[32] who found in it the guarantee that Israel's ancestral hope would be realized in perpetuity; it was taught expressly in the Old Testament (cf. Isa. 26:19; Dan. 12:2), and, as Jesus pointed out, it was taught implicitly at an earlier stage, when God, who is the God of the living, not of the dead, proclaimed himself to be the God of Abraham, Isaac, and Jacob (Ex. 3:6; cf. Mark 12:26f.).

(f) *Eternal judgment.* The Jewish belief in resurrection was closely associated with the expectation of judgment to come. That the God of Israel is Judge of all the earth in general and of his people in particular is an essential part of the Old Testament revelation (Gen. 18:25; Isa. 33:22); his recurring judgments in history will be summed up in the eschatological judgment of Dan. 7:9-14.[33] In Christian belief the "one like a son of man" through whom the eschatological judgment is carried out is identified with Jesus (Matt. 25:31ff.; John 5:22, 27; Acts 17:31, etc.).

3 It was on a foundation already laid in the Old Testament, then, and one on which their way of life was already based, that these people had received the gospel. All these things were now given a fresh and fuller significance because of the coming of Christ into the world. But the "Hebrews" were exposed to a subtle danger which could not be experienced by converts from paganism. If a convert from paganism gave up Christianity and reverted to paganism, there was a clean break between the faith which he renounced and the paganism to which he returned. But it was possible for the recipients of this letter, yielding gradually to pressures from various quarters, to give up more and more those features of faith and practice which were distinctive of Christianity, and yet to feel that they had not abandoned the basic principles of repentance and faith, the realities denoted by religious ablutions and the laying on of hands, the expectation of resurrection and the judgment of the age to come. For the writer to go on insisting on these things, therefore,

29. Cf. Num. 27:18, 23; Deut. 34:9.

30. Cf. Lev. 1:4; 3:2; 4:4; 8:14; 16:21, etc. See also p. 207, n. 56.

31. Cf. Mishnah, *Sanhedrin* 4.4. See J. Behm, *Die Handauflegung im Urchristentum* (Leipzig, 1911); J. Newman, *Semikhah* (Manchester, 1950); A. A. T. Ehrhardt, "Jewish and Christian Ordination," in *The Framework of the New Testament Stories* (Manchester, 1964), pp. 132-50.

32. Cf. Acts 23:8, with exposition and notes *ad loc.* in NICNT.

33. It is here called "eternal judgment" (κρίμα αἰώνιον) because it is the judgment which is valid for the whole coming age (αἰών), as distinct from the temporal judgments of the present age.

would not really help them; it would be better to press on to those teachings which belonged to spiritual maturity, in the hope that the maturity would come with the teachings. "This, then, we will do, God permitting"[34]—that is to say, not merely will our author go on to give his mature teaching about the Melchizedek priesthood, but he and his readers together will advance to full growth in Christ, please God.

4-6 The reason why there is no point in laying the foundation over again is now stated: apostasy is irremediable. Once more our author emphasizes that continuance is the test of reality. In these verses he is not questioning the perseverance of the saints; we might say that rather he is insisting that those who persevere are the true saints. But in fact he is stating a practical truth that has verified itself repeatedly in the experience of the church. Those who have shared the covenant privileges of the people of God, and then deliberately renounce them, are the most difficult persons of all to reclaim for the faith. It is indeed impossible to reclaim them, says our author. We know, of course, that nothing of this sort is ultimately impossible for the grace of God, but as a matter of human experience the reclamation of such people is, practically speaking, impossible.[35] People are frequently immunized against a disease by being inoculated with a mild form of it, or with a related but milder disease. And in the spiritual realm experience suggests that it is possible to be "immunized" against Christianity by being inoculated with something which, for the time being, looks so like the real thing that it is generally mistaken for it. This is not a question of those who are attached in a formal way to the profession of true religion without ever having experienced its power; it is blessedly possible for such people to have an experience of God's grace which changes what was once a matter of formal attachment into a matter of inward reality. It is a question of people who see clearly where the truth lies, and perhaps for a period conform to it, but then, for one reason or another, renounce it.[36]

---

34. Gk. ἐάνπερ ἐπιτρέπῃ ὁ θεός, in which we should see more than a conventional expression of piety.

35. According to C. Spicq, ἀδύνατον in Philo, "when understood of man and in relation to the moral plane, should be translated by 'incapable'; the impossibility in question is subjective and relative, due reservation being made with regard to divine intervention, and it is in this sense that *Hebrews* conceives the impossibility, not of the apostate's pardon, but of his turning" (*L'Épître aux Hébreux* [Paris, 1952], I, pp. 57f.). There is a closer parallel in Hermas, *Shepherd*, Similitude 9.26.6 ("it is impossible [ἀδύνατον] for him who will now deny his Lord to be saved"); but this is probably dependent on our present passage in Hebrews. According to J. Behm (*TDNT*, III, p. 451, n. 1, *s.v.* ἀνακαινίζω), the point is that it is impossible for a Christian teacher like the author to bring back such an apostate to repentance—not for God or for the apostate himself.

36. Comparisons have been drawn with our Lord's words about the unpardonable sin against the Holy Spirit (Mark 3:29) and John's words about a "sin unto death" for which prayer should not be offered (1 John 5:16). The sin spoken of by our Lord cannot be apostasy in the ordinary sense; it was rather a deliberate closing of eyes to the light, resisting the kingdom of God,

144

In our Lord's parable of the sower, no difference might have been seen for a time between what had sprouted on rocky ground and what was growing on good ground. It was only when a time of testing came that the difference became evident.[37] It was a time of testing now for the recipients of the epistle, and our author is anxious that they should respond triumphantly to the test and prove that in their case the seed had fallen into good ground.

From his description of the experiences of those who may nevertheless fall away, it would certainly be difficult to distinguish them at the outset from those who are going to stay the course. For they have *(a)* been enlightened, *(b)* tasted the heavenly gift, *(c)* partaken of the Holy Spirit, *(d)* experienced the goodness of the word of God and the mighty works of the age to come. Just as the Hebrew spies who returned from their expedition carrying   ible tokens of the good land of Canaan nevertheless failed to enter the land be   use of their unbelief, so those who had come to know the blessings of the new covenant might nevertheless in a spiritual sense turn back in heart to Egypt and so forfeit the saints' everlasting rest.[38]

(a)   They had been enlightened. It is tempting to understand the verb here in the sense of baptism—a sense which it bore among Christians in Rome in the middle of the second century.[39] The use of "enlightenment" in the sense of baptism need not be a borrowing from the language of the mysteries; it is quite in line with New Testament teaching.[40] At any rate, the

---

refusing to accept the evidence of God's visitation and ascribing the work of the Spirit of God to the power of Beelzebul. The sin of 1 John 5:16 could well be apostasy; cf. C. H. Dodd, *The Johannine Epistles*, MNTC (London, 1946), pp. 135-37, for the view that John, like the writer to the Hebrews, "is thinking of apostasy or denial of Christ as the sin that places a man beyond the pale. We know that he traced the presence and power of Antichrist in the denial of the Incarnation (4:2-5), and if a man had become identified with Antichrist it was perhaps natural to feel that he was past praying for."

37. Mark 4:3-8 and parallels. See p. 94 above.

38. Cf. the lessons drawn from the Israelites' day of testing in the wilderness in 3:7ff. It may be that the wilderness narrative is still in our author's mind. The Israelites who failed to enter Canaan failed in spite of the fact that they had been baptized in the Red Sea and had their camp illuminated by heavenly light, in spite of the provision of bread from heaven and water from the rock, and God's "good Spirit to instruct them" (cf. Neh. 9:20), in spite of their hearing the oracles of God and seeing his mighty works in their midst (cf. G. H. Lang, *Hebrews*, pp. 98-107).

39. It is so translated in the Syriac Peshitta here and in 10:32. Justin (*First Apology* 61:12f.; 65:1) uses the verb φωτίζω and the noun φωτισμός to describe baptism, and does so in a way which indicates that this was a current usage among the Christians of his acquaintance.

40. Especially with Johannine teaching about Christ as the Light. Cf. the quotation in Eph. 5:14, frequently taken to be a snatch of a baptismal hymn, in which the convert is invited to wake up from the darkness of spiritual death into the light of Christ. The rhythm of the words was the characteristic rhythm of initiation chants in the Greek world (see F. F. Bruce, *Colossians–Philemon–Ephesians*, NICNT [Grand Rapids, 1984], pp. 376-78). The Greek text of Ps. 34:5a (LXX 33:6a), "Come to him and be enlightened (φωτίσθητε)," was early used in the Christian baptismal liturgy (it is probably reflected in 1 Pet. 2:4).

enlightenment here is something which has taken place once for all—like baptism itself, which is unrepeatable for the simple reason that its repetition would contradict its whole significance.[41] The light of the gospel has broken in upon these people's darkness, and life can never be the same again; to give up the gospel would be to sin against the light, the one sin which by its very nature is incurable.

(b)   They had tasted the heavenly gift. As enlightenment suggests baptism, so the tasting[42] of the heavenly gift may suggest the Eucharist; certainly the people in question have partaken of communion in addition to being baptized.[43] And certainly it is possible for people who have experienced both the gospel sacraments to commit apostasy nonetheless. But the "heavenly gift" need not be restricted to the Eucharist; it may indicate the whole sum of spiritual blessings which are sacramentally sealed and signified in the Eucharist.[44]

(c)   They had become partakers of the Holy Spirit. It is precarious to argue that the personal Holy Spirit is not intended here, but rather his gifts or operations, on the sole ground that the definite article is lacking in the Greek. The presence or absence of the article is not in itself sufficient to decide whether the Giver or his gifts are in question. Whether it is possible for one who has been in any real sense a partaker of the Holy Spirit[45] to commit apostasy has been questioned, but our author has no doubt that it is possible in this way to "outrage the Spirit of grace" (10:29). The people whom he has in mind had not only been baptized and received the Eucharist, but had experienced the laying on of hands. Early apostolic history has a record of one

41. Cf. Origen, *On Martyrdom* 30, for the point that one cannot be baptized a second time. See also J. A. T. Robinson, "The One Baptism," in *Twelve New Testament Studies*, SBT 34 (London, 1962), p. 162.

42. For γεύομαι ("taste") in a eucharistic context cf. Acts 20:11. There is ample evidence of the eucharistic association of Ps. 34:8 (LXX 33:9) in the early church (cf. *Apostolic Constitutions* 8.13; Cyril of Jerusalem, *Catechetical Lectures* 23.20; Jerome, *Ep.* 71.6); the earliest instance of this association may be 1 Pet. 2:3. C. Spicq (*Hébreux*, I, p. 57) adduces examples in an attempt to show that "to taste the heavenly gift (Heb. 6:4) is an Alexandrinism, and to taste the word of God (Heb. 6:5) is a Philonism." On the former point he refers to Wisdom 16:3, where the quails of Num. 11:31ff. are described as ξενὴ γεῦσις, "an unaccustomed delicacy." This is not a very impressive parallel, but it might be added to the wilderness parallels mentioned on p. 145, n. 38.

43. Moffatt *(ad loc.)* draws attention to Philo, *On Flight and Finding* 139, for the food-metaphor following upon the light-metaphor (as here): "The divine ordinance both enlightens and sweetens the soul that has vision, flashing forth the beam of truth, and with persuasion, that sweet virtue, imparting sweetness to those who hunger and thirst after nobility of character." Philo has immediately before *(ibid.,* 137) explained the manna as being the "utterance of God and divine Word" (ῥῆμα θεοῦ καὶ λόγον θεῖον).

44. Cf. Paul's application of the spiritual food and drink of the wilderness wanderings in 1 Cor. 10:3ff.

45. "Partakers" represents Gk. μέτοχοι (cf. 3:1, 14). Cf. the "distributions of the Holy Spirit" in 2:4.

outstanding character who believed when he heard the gospel, was baptized, attached himself to the evangelist whose preaching had convinced him, and presumably received the Spirit when apostolic hands were laid upon him— yet Simon Magus was pronounced by Peter to be still "in the gall of bitterness and in the bond of iniquity" (Acts 8:9ff., 18ff.), and showed himself in the following decades to be the most determined opponent of apostolic Christianity.[46] If we ask in what sense a man like that could have partaken of the Holy Spirit, the words which follow here may point the way to an answer.

(d)   They had experienced the goodness of God's word[47] *and the powers of the age to come.* Simon Magus realized how good the word of God was when he heard it from Philip's lips, and he was amazed at the signs and great "powers"[48] which accompanied the reception of the gospel, proclaimed by a man who was "full of the Spirit" (Acts 6:3). Those "powers" or mighty works were "signs" that the age to come had broken in already on the present age; Jesus' words about the mighty works of his ministry remained true of the mighty works performed in his name in the apostolic age: "if it is by the Spirit of God that I cast out demons, then the kingdom of God has come upon you" (Matt. 12:28).[49] But Jesus also spoke of a day when many would say to him, "Lord, Lord, did we not prophesy in your name, and cast out demons in your name, and do many mighty works[50] in your name?"—only to be told, "I never knew you; depart from me, you evildoers" (Matt. 7:22f.). The Scriptures contain encouragement enough and to spare for the feeblest believer, but are full of solemn warnings to those who think they stand to beware lest they fall. A credible profession of faith must be accepted as genuine, but ultimately it is only the Lord who knows those who are his.

For it is possible for people who can be described in the language of vv. 4 and 5 to "fall away" irretrievably. This warning has been both unduly minimized and unduly exaggerated. It has been unduly minimized as when K. S. Wuest assures us that "having fallen away"[51] is "a conditional participle here

___

46. Cf. exposition and notes in *Acts*, NICNT, pp. 165-68, 170-72; A. Ehrhardt, "Christianity before the Apostles' Creed," in *The Framework of the New Testament Stories*, pp. 151-99 (especially p. 161).

47. Gk. καλὸν γευσαμένους θεοῦ ῥῆμα, with the adjective in predicative position. Cf. Philo's interpretation of the manna, quoted on p. 146, n. 43.

48. Gk. δυνάμεις, used in this sense here as in Acts 8:13; cf. Heb. 2:4 (pp. 68f.), from which it is evident that these "Hebrews" all had experience of such δυνάμεις in the days when the gospel was first brought to them.

49. The parallel passage in Luke 11:20 has "finger of God" where Matthew has "Spirit of God." In the apostolic age such δυνάμεις continue to be ministered by the Spirit (Gal. 3:5), who is the firstfruits of the coming age (Rom. 8:23). Cf. p. 71, n. 18 (on 2:5).

50. Gk. δυνάμεις.

51. Gk. παραπεσόντας. The verb παραπίπτω, found here only in the NT (by contrast with the cognate noun παράπτωμα, which is frequent in the sense of "trespass"), means "fall aside" or "go astray"; it is not its root meaning but its context which indicates that its reference here is

presenting a hypothetical case, a straw man" and that the sin in question "cannot be committed today since no temple and no sacrifices are in existence, and no transition period obtains."[52] It does not require temple and sacrifices, or a transitional period of the kind allegedly implied in this epistle, for men and women who have taken Christ's name upon themselves to commit apostasy; and biblical writers (the writer to the Hebrews being no exception) are not given to the setting up of men of straw. The warning of this passage was a real warning against a real danger, a danger which is still present so long as "an evil heart of unbelief" can result in "deserting the living God" (3:12).

On the other hand, our author's meaning can be exaggerated to the point of distortion when he is understood to say that for sins committed after baptism there can be no repentance. "The author of Hebrews," wrote F. C. Burkitt, "will allow no forgiveness for Christian sinners."[53] In this he was following the rigorist interpretation of Tertullian,[54] who quotes the opening verses of Heb. 6 to prove that there can be no pardon or restoration to communion for postbaptismal sin. Tertullian had one particular kind of sin in mind, and one which actually does not enter into our author's argument here: according to Tertullian, the writer of this warning passage (identified by him with Barnabas), "who learnt this *from* apostles, and taught it *with* apostles, never knew of any second repentance promised by apostles to the adulterer and fornicator."[55]

But the writer to the Hebrews himself distinguishes (as did the Old Testament law) between inadvertent sin and wilful sin,[56] and the context here

---

to apostasy—the same sin as is expressed by ἀποστῆναι in 3:12. See G. C. Berkouwer, *Faith and Perseverance,* E.T. (Grand Rapids, 1958); I. H. Marshall, *Kept by the Power of God* (London, 1969), especially pp. 135-41; P. E. Hughes, "Hebrews 6:4-6 and the Peril of Apostasy," *WTJ* 35 (1972-73), pp. 37-55; R. R. Nicole, "Some Comments on Hebrews 6:4-6 and the Doctrine of the Perseverance of God with the Saints," in *Current Issues in Biblical and Patristic Interpretation* (M. C. Tenney *FS*), ed. G. F. Hawthorne (Grand Rapids, 1975), pp. 355-64; N. Weeks, "Admonition and Error in Hebrews," *WTJ* 39 (1976-77), pp. 72-80.

52. "Hebrews Six in the Greek New Testament," *Bibliotheca Sacra* 119 (1962), pp. 45-53 (quotation on p. 52); cf. his *Hebrews in the Greek New Testament* (Grand Rapids, 1947), pp. 113ff.

53. In a review of A. E. Brooke's commentary on *The Johannine Epistles* (ICC) in the *Cambridge Review,* November 14, 1912, quoted with disapproval by A. Nairne, *The Epistle of Priesthood,* p. 130.

54. Burkitt, of course, unlike Tertullian, did not adopt as his own viewpoint what he believed the writer to the Hebrews to mean.

55. *On Modesty* 20. Tertullian is here criticizing the *Shepherd* of Hermas (the "*Shepherd* of the adulterers,*" as he scathingly calls it), which conceded one (but only one) opportunity of repentance and forgiveness for postbaptismal sin. See the exposition of 10:26ff. on p. 263, with nn. 144-46. On our author's perspective here see C. E. Carlston, "Eschatology and Repentance in the Epistle to the Hebrews," *JBL* 78 (1959), pp. 296-302; N. H. Young, "Hebrews 6:1-8: Pastoral Nonsense?" *Colloquium* 15 (1982-83), pp. 52-57.

56. Cf. 2:2; 5:2 (with exposition and notes).

shows plainly that the wilful sin which he has in mind is deliberate apostasy. People who commit this sin, he says, cannot be brought back to repentance; by renouncing Christ they put themselves in the position of those who, deliberately refusing his claim to be the Son of God, had him crucified and exposed to public shame.[57] Those who repudiate the salvation procured by Christ will find none anywhere else.

The margin of the ERV/ARV suggests an alternative rendering which may appear to moderate the gravity of our author's words: "it is impossible to renew them again unto repentance, *the while* they crucify to themselves the Son of God. . . ." By suggesting that these people cannot be brought back to repentance so long as they repudiate Christ, this rendering might be thought to imply that when they cease to repudiate him repentance will be possible. But this is certainly not what is meant. To say that they cannot be brought to repentance so long as they persist in their renunciation of Christ would be a truism hardly worth putting into words. The participle "crucifying" is much more appropriately taken as causal than as temporal in force; it indicates *why* it is impossible for such people to repent and make a new beginning. God has pledged himself to pardon all who truly repent, but Scripture and experience alike suggest that it is possible for human beings to arrive at a state of heart and life where they can no longer repent.

7-8 Such people are compared to land which, in spite of all the care expended in its cultivation, refuses to produce a good crop. The figure here is to much the same effect as Isaiah's vineyard song (Isa. 5:1-7). That vineyard received all the attention that any vineyard could have received, but when the time came for it to produce grapes, it produced nothing but wild grapes.[58] It was clearly reprobate[59] land, which would never respond to cul-

---

57. Cf. E. Ménégoz, *La théologie de l'Épître aux Hébreux* (Paris, 1894), pp. 21f. On the question whether ἀνασταυρόω here means "crucify" or "crucify again" see p. 138, n. 7. Taking it to mean "crucify again," J. A. T. Robinson ("One Baptism," p. 172) says: "Baptism means being put on the Cross once with Christ: it is absurd to think of renewing it for those who for their own ends are actually crucifying the Son of God again (*cf.* 10:29)." Among the LXX occurrences of παραδειγματίζω ("put to an open shame") is Num. 25:4, where it is used of the leaders of the Baal-peor apostasy who were hung up "in the sun before Yahweh." See A. T. Hanson, *Studies in Paul's Technique and Theology* (London, 1974), pp. 4-7.

58. Cf. Hermas, *Shepherd* (Mandate 10.1.5): "Even as good vineyards when they are neglected become unfruitful because of the thorns and various kinds of weeds, so men who have believed and fall into the many aforementioned preoccupations [secular business, moneymaking, pagan friendships, etc.], wander from a right mind and have absolutely no understanding of righteousness."

59. Gk. ἀδόκιμος (ERV/ARV "rejected"; RSV, NEB "worthless"). Compare those people who are described in Tit. 1:16 as "unfit for any good deed." E. K. Simpson, discussing the meaning of ἀδόκιμος in 1 Cor. 9:27 (cf. 2 Cor. 13:5), says, "Paul is thinking of spurious pretensions . . . we might construe: 'lest, after preaching to others, I myself should prove *base metal*'" (*Words Worth Weighing in the Greek New Testament* [London, 1946], pp. 17f.).

tivation; it must simply be allowed thenceforth to lie untended and become derelict. So our author compares those believers who persevere in faith to fertile land which produces fruit, while those in whose lives the fruits of righteousness do not appear are compared to land which will never produce anything but thorns and thistles,[60] to be kept down by burning, "for our God is a consuming fire" (12:29).

F. ENCOURAGEMENT TO PERSEVERE (6:9-12)

9 *But even if we speak like this, dear friends, we are convinced that you are in a better condition, showing the signs that go along with salvation.*[61]

10 *God is not unrighteous: he will not forget your work and the love*[62] *which you display for his name, serving his holy people as you have done and continue to do.*

11 *Our desire is that each of you should display the same eagerness for the fulfilment of your hope right on to the end,*[63]

12 *so that you may not grow sluggish but imitate those who through faith and steadfastness inherit the promises.*

9 Our author makes haste to reassure his readers, after his words of solemn warning: he does not believe that there are apostates, or even potential apostates, among them. He was encouraged to believe and hope the best of them because the fruits of righteousness had beyond all question manifested themselves in their lives. Those fruits, being the natural concomitants of salvation, bore witness that the people in whom they appeared were genuine heirs of salvation. His desire to reassure them, his concern that what he has just said should not discourage them, may have prompted his affectionate language here: this is the only place in the epistle where he calls them "beloved"—his "dear friends."

10 The fruits of righteousness which have shown themselves in their lives are the acts of service performed for their fellow-Christians. There is no good reason for restricting God's "holy people" ("saints") here to those

60. And therefore "on the point of being cursed" (Gk. κατάρας ἐγγύς), for in Gen. 3:17f. thorns and thistles are a consequence of the cursing of the land for sake of the human race. So in the "Two Ways" the way of death is κατάρας μεστή, "fraught with a curse" (*Didachē* 5:1; *Ep. Barn.* 20:1). Cf. Luke 13:6ff.; John 15:6.

61. Gk. ἐχόμενα σωτηρίας, "things that belong to salvation" (RSV); the presence of those things in the readers' lives was a token of the presence of salvation too, since they were so closely and invariably bound up with salvation.

62. AV/KJV "your work and labour of love" represents an assimilation to the text of 1 Thess. 1:3, found in K L with most minuscules and the TR.

63. Gk. ἄχρι τέλους, with which cf. 3:14, μέχρι τέλους.

in Jerusalem because of the similar language in Rom. 15:25; 1 Cor. 16:1; 2 Cor. 9:1—in those passages it is the context that shows that Jerusalem believers are intended. The "holy people" are as general here as are the "holy brothers" of Heb. 3:1. As for the acts of service referred to here, further details of the circumstances in which they were rendered are given later, in 10:32-34. If the recipients of the letter were resident in Rome, then the behavior for which our author commends them was a precedent for the reputation for Christian charity which the Roman church enjoyed in later times. We may think of Ignatius's description of that church as "having the presidency of love";[64] or the words of Dionysius, bishop of Corinth, in his letter to Soter, bishop of Rome (c. A.D. 170): "This has been your custom from the beginning, to do good in manifold ways to all the brothers, and to send contributions to the many churches in every city, in some places relieving the poverty of the needy, and ministering to the brothers in the mines."[65] The point here, however, is that deeds of kindness done to the people of God are reckoned by God as done to himself, and will surely receive their reward from him.

11-12 But let them go on as they have begun. Our author's insistence on the grace of continuance appears again as he assures them of his affectionate longing[66] that they should go on exhibiting the same zeal as marked them in the beginning, until the final and full realization of their hope. "Don't become sluggish,"[67] he urges them; "follow the example of those who have gone before, those who are now entering into the enjoyment of things which God promised them long ago, because they believed his word and persevered in hope." This exhortation to imitate the faith of the men and women of old anticipates the argument of ch. 11; that the reference is to God's people in Old Testament times is clear from the words that follow.

G. THE STEADFASTNESS OF GOD'S PROMISE (6:13-20)

13 *Such a person was Abraham. When God gave him a promise, he swore by himself, since he had no one greater to swear by:*

---

64. Ignatius, *To the Romans,* preface.

65. Eusebius, *Hist. Eccl.* 4.23.10.

66. Chrysostom (*Homilies on Hebrews* 10.5) draws attention to the writer's "fatherly affection" here.

67. Gk. νωθϱός (cf. 5:11). The warning here is against the deadly sin of *accidie* (ἀκήδεια), described in Dante's *Purgatorio* 17.76–18.145. Dorothy L. Sayers, in her edition of Dante, mentions such modern forms of it as false tolerance, "disillusionment," and escapism. Cf. Sir John C. Hawkins, "The Use of Dante as an Illustrator of Scripture," *ExT* 16 (1904-5), pp. 548f. The antidote to νωθϱεία is μαϰϱοθυμία, "perseverance." In this context (cf. v. 12) the forms μαϰϱοθυμέω/μαϰϱοθυμία are used for perseverance; later (10:32–12:7) our author prefers ὑπομένω/ὑπομονή. See O. Michel, *Der Brief an die Hebräer,* MK (Göttingen, 1949), p. 155 with n. 3.

14 *"Truly," he said, "I will bless you greatly and multiply you greatly."*[68]

15 *And thus, having shown steadfastness, he obtained the promise.*

16 *Human beings swear by what is greater than themselves, and an oath puts an end to all dispute for purposes of validation.*

17 *In this matter God wished to show the heirs of the promise the unchangeableness of his purpose even more convincingly, so he communicated it*[69] *with an oath.*

18 *His purpose was that by means of*[70] *two unchangeable things, in which it is impossible for God*[71] *to lie, we who have fled for refuge to take hold of the hope set before us might have strong encouragement.*

19 *We have*[72] *this hope as an anchor of the soul, secure and stable, entering into the inner side of the sanctuary curtain,*

20 *where Jesus*[73] *has entered on our behalf as forerunner—Jesus, who has become our high priest for ever after the order of Melchizedek.*

13-15 The example of Abraham, as father of all who have faith in God, was invoked in many strands of primitive Christianity. Even before the Christian message began to be proclaimed, John the Baptist pointed out that something more than biological descent from Abraham was necessary for acceptance with God; God did indeed desire "children of Abraham," but if need be he could bring them into being by his own creative act (Matt. 3:9 par. Luke 3:8). Paul justifies his claim that the way of righteousness opened up in the gospel is attested by the law and the prophets by pointing to the testimony of Scripture about Abraham, who "believed Yahweh; and he reckoned it to him as righteousness" (Gen. 15:6; quoted in Rom. 4:3; Gal. 3:6). James quotes the same testimony, but relates it to Abraham's offering up of Isaac in support of his insistence that "faith apart from works is barren" (Jas. 2:21-26). Our author here, and more fully in 11:8-19, presents Abraham as the supreme example of a man who received promises from God, and lived in the good of these promises, persevering to the end in faith and hope.

To our author Abraham was a significant figure, not only because of

---

68. Gen. 22:16f.

69. Gk. ἐμεσίτευσεν, lit. "mediated" (this is the only NT occurrence of the verb; for the noun μεσίτης from which it is derived cf. 8:6; 9:15; 12:24).

70. Gk. διά, for which 𝔓[46] and D have μετά, probably under the influence of μετά in the following ἀμεταθέτων, and possibly independently in the two MSS (cf. Zuntz, *Text*, p. 41).

71. Gk. θεόν, according to B D and the majority of later authorities, but 𝔓[46] ℵ* A 1739 and a few other minuscules, with citations in Eusebius (2/4), Didymus (2/2), Chrysostom, Cyril, and Theodoret (1/4), have the articulated τὸν θεόν. According to Zuntz (*Text*, p. 130), the addition of the article is an early Alexandrian corruption from which, however, B is free; the force of the anarthrous reading is that "it is impossible for one who is God to lie."

72. Gk. ἔχομεν, for which D (Gk., not Lat.) and a few other authorities have the subjunctive ἔχωμεν, probably under the influence of the subjunctive after ἵνα in the previous verse.

73. D* adds "Christ."

his faith in the promise of God, but also because of the part he plays in the story of Melchizedek. God's faithfulness to his promise to Abraham is a token of his faithfulness in regard to another of his promises, that concerning the Melchizedek priesthood. These two promises "hang together, and as Paul worked out the one in Galatians so our author will work out the other."[74]

The particular promise in view here is that made by God to Abraham after his offering up of Isaac: "By myself I have sworn. . . , 'I will indeed bless you, and I will multiply your descendants'" (Gen. 22:16f.).[75] But this was a recapitulation and elaboration of God's earlier promise to Abraham that he would bless him and make of him a great nation (Gen. 12:2f.). At the time when that earlier promise was made, Abraham was childless. As time went on, however, it was made clear to him that the promise would be fulfilled through the birth of a son to Sarah and himself when, by all natural reckoning, such a prospect would have been dismissed as impossible. Yet Abraham believed God, and in due course the promised child was born. On Isaac now hung every hope that the further promises of God regarding Abraham's descendants would be fulfilled; yet it was Isaac whom Abraham was commanded to offer up to God. When Abraham's faith and obedience were shown in his readiness to do even this, he received Isaac back from the dead, as it were (Heb. 11:19), and received at the same time a reaffirmation of the promises of God, reinforced on this occasion by the divine oath: "and thus, having patiently endured, he obtained the promise." There was much in God's promise to Abraham whose fulfilment lay in the distant future, but in the restoration to Abraham of the son upon whose survival the promise depended Abraham did, in a very substantial sense, "obtain the promise."[76]

16-17 Our author emphasizes the fact that when God repeated his promise to Abraham after the offering up of Isaac, he confirmed it with an oath. When human beings swear an oath in order to underline the certainty and solemnity of their words, they swear by someone or something greater than themselves. "As (surely as) Yahweh lives" was the supreme oath in Israel.

---

74. T. W. Manson, *Studies in the Gospels and Epistles* (Manchester, 1962), p. 249.

75. ERV/ARV more literally: "in blessing I will bless thee, and in multiplying I will multiply thy seed," where "in blessing" and "in multiplying" are intended as equivalents of the Hebrew absolute infinitive, which intensifies the force of the accompanying finite verb; cf. the present passage in the NEB ("I vow that I will bless you abundantly and multiply your descendants"). In the LXX (as in the MT) the divine promise is preceded by an explicit oath ("by myself I have sworn"); in the present quotation the oath is expressed simply by the Septuagintal asseverative εἰ μήν, "verily" (here only in the NT), preceding the verbal construction.

76. With "he obtained the promise" (Gk. ἐπέτυχεν τῆς ἐπαγγελίας [cf. 11:33]) here may be contrasted "not having received the promises" (Gk. μὴ λαβόντες τὰς ἐπαγγελίας) in 11:13 (cf. "these all . . . received not [οὐκ ἐκομίσαντο] the promise" in 11:39); but in 11:13 the reference is to the full realization of the promise of which the birth and, later, the restoration of Isaac were initial pledges. Cf. also 11:17 (pp. 302-05).

153

Abraham himself swore by God and made others do the same (Gen. 14:22; 21:23f.; 24:3). But, says our author, God has none greater than himself by whom to swear,[77] so when he wishes to confirm his promise in this way, he swears by himself (we may compare the recurring "as I live" in divine oracles throughout the Old Testament). This insistence on the divine oath in God's promise to Abraham prepares the readers for the significance of the fact that God's promise regarding the Melchizedek priesthood was similarly confirmed by an oath: "Yahweh has sworn, and will not change his mind" (Ps. 110:4).[78]

The bare word of God is guarantee enough in all conscience, but by confirming it thus he "makes assurance double sure." On this same passage from Genesis Philo remarks: "There is nothing amiss in God's bearing witness to himself. For who else would be capable of bearing witness to him? . . . He alone shall make any affirmation regarding himself, since he alone has unerringly exact knowledge of his own nature. God alone therefore is the strongest security first for himself, and in the next place for his deeds also, so that he naturally swore by himself when giving assurance regarding himself, a thing impossible for anyone else."[79]

Who are "the heirs of the promise" to whom God wished in this way "to show more convincingly . . . the unchangeableness of his purpose"? Not so much Abraham and the other patriarchs,[80] who for all their faith did not live to see it vindicated and in this sense "did not receive what they had been promised" (11:39); but those, like the writer and his readers, who experienced in the gospel the fulfilment of the oath which God swore to Abraham.

18-20 It is *we*, says our author, for whom this "strong encouragement" is intended. The "two unchangeable things" from which this encouragement is derived are *(a)* the promise of God (for "it is impossible for God to lie"), and *(b)* the oath by which his promise is confirmed. We are refugees from the sinking ship of this present world-order, so soon to disappear; our hope is fixed on the eternal order, where the promises of God are made good to his people in perpetuity. Our hope, based upon his promises, is our spiritual anchor. The figure of the anchor is not pressed; all that is meant is

---

77. Cf. Philo, *Leg. Alleg.* 3.203: "Well did he confirm his promise by an oath [Gk. ὅρκῳ βεβαιῶσαι, with which cf. πέρας εἰς βεβαίωσιν ὁ ὅρκος, "the oath is final for confirmation," v. 16], and by an oath worthy of God; for, you see, God does not swear by another, for there is nothing greater than he, but by himself, who is the best of all" (in reference to the oath of Gen. 22:16f.).

78. Cf. 7:20ff. (pp. 170f.).

79. *Leg. Alleg.* 3.205f.; cf. also *On Abraham* 273ff.; *On the Sacrifices of Abel and Cain* 91ff.

80. As in 11:9, where Abraham is described as a tent-dweller "with Isaac and Jacob, the heirs with him of the same promise"; they are so called because they came next to Abraham in the line of promise, but here those who have inherited the fulfilment of the promise are meant. See p. 153, n. 76. Cf. also the reference in 9:15 to "the promise of the eternal inheritance" realized under the new covenant.

that "we are moored to an immoveable object"[81]—and that immovable object is the throne of God himself, established (as is made clear in ch. 9) in the heavenly holy of holies, the counterpart in the eternal order to the inner sanctuary of the wilderness tabernacle, shut off from the outer sanctuary by the heavy curtain behind which dwelt the invisible presence of the God of Israel. And our hope is fixed there because Jesus is there, seated, as we have already been told, at "the right hand of the Majesty on high" (1:3). His presence there is a powerful corroboration of our hope. Abraham rested his hope in the promise and oath of God; but we have more than that to rest our hope upon: we have the fulfilment of his promise in the exaltation of Christ. No wonder that our hope is secure and stable.[82]

For Jesus has entered into the eternal world not only on his own behalf but on his people's too. He is there as our "forerunner," a word in which the conception of precedence prevails over that of speed, as E. K. Simpson tells us. "As applied to the Saviour," he continues, "it recalls His own care-quelling utterance: 'I go to prepare a place for you.' But the errand of this Forerunner embraces far wider ends than that of preparation. It proclaims an accomplished work of redemption and signalizes the first fruits of a mighty aftercrop. *Precursor* is a relative term implying a sequence. With their glorified Head, the members of His body must in due time be conjoined; and the sublime office of intercession above vested in the Eternal Priest constitutes the indispensable medium of its accomplishment. His advocacy is the safeguard of his church and the earnest of *her* glorification."[83]

He is there as his people's forerunner, the surety of their admission to the dwelling-place of God; he is there, too, as their perpetual high priest, "after the order of Melchizedek." With these words our author comes back to the point from which he digressed in 5:11; now he will go on and say what he has to say about the Melchizedek priesthood, "hard of interpretation" though it may be, in order that his readers may be educated to maturity of faith and life.[84]

---

81. A. B. Davidson, *ad loc.*; his comment on the anchor simile is a model of sanity. For the "veil" (καταπέτασμα) see p. 199, n. 14; pp. 250f., n. 87.

82. The adjectives "secure and stable" (ἀσφαλῆ τε καὶ βεβαίαν) might grammatically refer either to "hope" or to "anchor"; the construction slightly favors the latter (so probably the AV/KJV, and certainly the RSV and the NEB, as against the ERV/ARV). But since our hope is our "anchor," it is in reality our hope that is "secure and stable."

83. "The Vocabulary of the Epistle to the Hebrews," *EQ* 18 (1946), p. 187; he adduces instances from Arrian, Aristophanes, Euripides, Plutarch, Theophrastus, and the elder Pliny; and compares "Julius Caesar's *antecursores*, one of whose chief functions was that of selecting and staking out stations for encampment."

84. An attempt to identify Philonic affinities in the section now concluded is made by C. Spicq, "L'Épître aux Hébreux et Philon: Un Cas d'Insertion de la littérature sacrée dans la Culture profane du Ier siècle (Hébr. V,11–VI,20 et le 'De sacrificiis Abelis et Caini' de Philon)," *ANRW* II.25.4 (Berlin, 1987), pp. 3602-18.

HEBREWS 7

IV. THE ORDER OF MELCHIZEDEK (7:1-28)

A. MELCHIZEDEK THE PRIEST-KING (7:1-3)

1 *It was this Melchizedek, king of Salem, priest of God Most High,[1] who come to meet[2] Abraham when he was returning from the slaughter of the kings[3] and gave him his blessing.[4]*
2 *It was he to whom Abraham apportioned one tenth of everything.[5] His name is to be interpreted first of all as "king of righteousness," and then also[6] "king of peace."*
3 *He has neither father nor mother, he is without a genealogy, he has neither beginning of days nor end of life, but being made conformable to the Son of God he remains a priest in perpetuity.[7]*

1-2 In order to draw out the significance of Christ's being acclaimed as perpetual high priest "after the order of Melchizedek," our author goes back from his text, Ps. 110:4, to the only other place in the Bible where Melchizedek appears, the story of Abraham's rout of the four invading

---

1. Gk. τοῦ θεοῦ τοῦ ὑψίστου, the LXX rendering of Heb. *'el 'elyôn* (cf. p. 124, n. 31). Since (θεὸς) ὕψιστος was current as a divine title among Jews and Greeks alike (among the latter it was a designation of Zeus), it provided them with a common denominator in referring to the supreme God. Cf. Acts 7:48; 16:7; see also C. H. Dodd, *The Bible and the Greeks* (London, 1935), pp. 11-13. See *New Docs.*, I (1976), § 5.

2. Gk. ὁ συναντήσας (𝔭⁴⁶ C* Byz); the authority for the dittographic variant ὃς συναντήσας, however, is so weighty (א A B D and a few others) that the former (grammatical) reading was regarded as secondary, or as a successful Byzantine conjecture, until it was found in 𝔭⁴⁶.

3. The minuscules 456 and 460 add, "because he pursued the foreigners and rescued Lot with all the captivity" (ὅτι ἐδίωξεν τοὺς ἀλλοφύλους καὶ ἐξείλατο Λὼτ μετὰ πάσης αἰχμαλωσίας).

4. D* 330 440 823 continue, "and Abraham having been blessed by him . . ." (καὶ Ἀβραὰμ εὐλογηθεὶς ὑπ' αὐτοῦ . . .).

5. Gk. πάντων (for which 𝔭⁴⁶ B read the singular παντός).

6. Gk. ἔπειτα δὲ καί (𝔭⁴⁶ and a few other authorities omit δὲ καί).

7. Gk. εἰς τὸ διηνεκές (in the Greek Bible only in this epistle, the other occurrences being in 10:1, 12, 14), here synonymous with εἰς τὸν αἰῶνα of Ps. 110:4 (LXX 109:4, for Heb. *le'ôlām*). The adjective διηνεκής is classical from Homer onward. See *New Docs.*, II (1977), § 38.

kings from the east (Gen. 14). From the part played by Melchizedek in that narrative, it will be shown how aptly he prefigures the high priesthood of Christ.

According to that narrative (which belongs, as archaeological evidence indicates, to the Middle Bronze Age), Chedorlaomer, an Elamite king, with three allied rulers, raided Transjordan and the Negeb, defeated the city-states of the "circuit of Jordan"—Sodom and her neighbors—and carried off a large number of captives, including Lot, Abraham's nephew. When news of this came to Abraham at Mamre, near Hebron, he armed his own retainers, enlisted the aid of his neighbors, and set off in pursuit of the invaders. He overtook them near Damascus, launched a surprise attack on them, put them to flight, and recovered the captives and the plunder. On his homeward progress he was met by the grateful king of Sodom, who proposed that Abraham should return the captives to him but retain the material plunder as his proper spoils of war. Abraham declined to retain anything because of an oath he had just sworn to "God Most High, maker of heaven and earth."[8] For, immediately before the king of Sodom made his proposal to Abraham, Abraham had been greeted by another local ruler, Melchizedek.

> And Melchizedek king of Salem brought out bread and wine; he was priest of God Most High. And he blessed him, and said, Blessed be Abraham by God Most High, maker of heaven and earth: and blessed be God Most High, who has delivered your enemies into your hand. And he gave him a tenth of everything.[9] (Gen. 14:18-20)

This is all that the Genesis narrative has to say about Melchizedek, but it is enough for our author; more would have been superfluous. He finds as much significance in what is not said about Melchizedek as he does in what is said about him. It is indeed noteworthy that one of the things which is said about Melchizedek in the Genesis narrative is passed over by our author without mention—his bringing forth bread and wine for Abraham's refreshment.[10]

8. Heb. *'ēl 'elyôn qôneh šāmayim wā-'āreṣ* (where *qôneh* probably means "creator" or "maker"; so LXX ὅς ἔκτισε). A similar divine designation appears on a bilingual Hittite-Phoenician inscription (discovered by H. T. Bossert in 1946) of Azitawandas, king of Danuna (Karatepe) in the Taurus foothills (9th cent. B.C.): *b'l šmm w'l qwn 'rṣ* ("the lord *[ba'al]* of heaven and god *['ēl]* creator *[or* possessor] of earth"). Cf. R. Marcus and I. J. Gelb, "The Phoenician Stele Inscription from Cilicia," *JNES* 8 (1949), pp. 111-20; A. M. Honeyman, "Epigraphic Discoveries at Karatepe," *PEQ* 81 (1949), pp. 21-39.

9. This last clause is ambiguous as it stands—who gave whom a tenth of all?—but in the context, as our author has no difficulty in seeing, it must be Abraham who gives a tenth to Melchizedek. See p. 162, n. 27.

10. That the bread and wine were for Abraham's refreshment is more probable, in the circumstances, than that they constituted a sacrificial offering, being the food of the gods (so Spicq, *ad loc.*, citing A. Vincent, *La religion des judéo-araméens d'Éléphantine* [Paris, 1937], p. 129). In *Test. Levi* 8:5 a meal of bread and wine forms part of the consecration of the priest

Few typologists of early Christian or more recent days could have resisted so tempting an opportunity of drawing a eucharistic inference from these words![11]

Philo's treatment of the Melchizedek story presents points of comparison, but even more markedly points of contrast, with the treatment here. He contrasts Melchizedek's provision of bread and wine with the refusal of the Ammonites and Moabites (the descendants of Lot) to supply Israel in the wilderness with bread and *water:*[12] "but let Melchizedek bring forth wine instead of water, let him give souls unmixed wine to drink, that they may be seized by a divine intoxication which is more sober than sobriety itself; for he is a priest, even Reason *(logos),* and has as his portion the Existing One."[13]

The difference between Philo's allegorization and our author's typological exegesis is plain. The only substantial coincidence between their accounts of Melchizedek lies in their both pointing out the etymological sense of his name and title: "God has made him king of peace," says Philo, "for that is how 'Salem' is to be interpreted, and his own priest. He did not fashion any work of his beforehand, but made him from the first a king of this character, both peaceful and worthy of his own priesthood, for he is called 'righteous king.'"[14] Both authors, that is to say, connect *zedek,* the second element in Melchizedek's name, with the Hebrew word commonly translated "righteousness";[15] and both relate the name of his city to Hebrew *shālōm,*

(cf. G. Widengren, "Royal Ideology and the Testaments of the Twelve Patriarchs," in F. F. Bruce (ed.), *Promise and Fulfilment* [S. H. Hooke *FS,* Edinburgh, 1963], pp. 207f.). See pp. 378-80 (on 13:10).

11. Cf. Cyprian, *Epistle* 62:4: "For who is more a priest of God Most High than our Lord Jesus Christ, who offered a sacrifice to God the Father, and offered that same thing which Melchizedek had offered, namely bread and wine—that is, his body and blood?" So also Ambrose, *Mysteries* 45f.; *Christian Faith* 3.87f.; cf. Canon of the Roman Mass (quoted p. 14, n. 55 above). More recently a Lutheran scholar, W. Vischer, has seen in Melchizedek's bread and wine a pointer to the sacrament of the new covenant (*Das Christuszeugnis des Alten Testaments,* I [Zürich, 1943], p. 164).

12. Deut. 23:4.

13. *Leg. Alleg.* 3.82. "The Existing One" as in Ex. 3:14, LXX (ὁ ὤν).

14. *Leg. Alleg.* 3.79 (cf. Josephus, *War* 7.438; *Ant.* 1.180). Here Philo goes on to say that Melchizedek (i.e., Reason) is a king, not a tyrant, the author of laws, not of lawlessness (ὀρθὸς νοῦς [cf. p. 136, n. 84], not τύραννος νοῦς). Elsewhere he interprets the five "kings" of the circuit of the Jordan as denoting the five senses and the four kings who conquered them as the four passions: pleasure, desire, fear, and grief (*On Abraham* 236-44).

15. Heb. *ṣedeq.* Cf. the name of Adonizedek, king of Jerusalem (Josh. 10:1ff.). It is debated whether in these names the first element ("my king is righteous"; "my lord is righteous") or the second ("Zedek is my king"; "Zedek is my lord") should be regarded as the divine title (cf. the Phoenician deity *Sydyk* mentioned by Philo of Byblus); see A. R. Johnson, *Sacral Kingship in Ancient Israel* (Cardiff, 1955), pp. 31-34, where the words of another king of Jerusalem, Abdi-ḫiba, are quoted from Tell el-Amarna Tablet No. 287, ll. 32f.: "Behold, my lord the king, I am in the right *(ṣaddûq)* with regard to the Kashi people."

"peace."[16] There is a fitness in this collocation of righteousness and peace both in the natural order and preeminently in our author's explanation of Melchizedek in terms of the gospel, where peace with God is based upon the righteousness of God.[17]

3 The words which follow present an outstanding example of the argument from silence in a typological setting.[18] When Melchizedek is described as having "neither father nor mother,[19] without a genealogy," and having "neither beginning of days nor end of life," it is not suggested that he was a biological anomaly, or an angel in human guise.[20] Historically Mel-

16. βασιλεὺς τῆς εἰρήνης (Philo). The name Jerusalem (MT *yᵉrûšalaim*, Akk. *uru-salim*) may mean originally "Shalem has founded," Canaanite *warawa-šalem* (J. Gray, *The Canaanites* [London, 1964], p. 125). Shalem is attested as a divine name at Ugarit (cf. A. R. Johnson, *Sacral Kingship*, p. 46); even so it is cognate with Heb. *šālôm* ("peace"), and our author's etymology is well founded. Cf. Ps. 85:10 (LXX 84:11), where *ṣedeq* and *šālôm* kiss each other. A later etymology, connecting the first element in Jerusalem with Heb. *rā'āh* ("see"), explains the name as "vision of peace"; compare the hymn *urbs beata uera pacis uisio Ierusalem* ("Blessed city, vision bright/Of true peace, Jerusalem!"). W. F. Albright suggested that we should read in Gen. 14:18 not *melek šālēm* ("king of Salem") but *melek šᵉlōmōh* ("king of his peace," i.e., "a king allied to him"); the emendation, even if it be, as he says, "the simplest possible haplography," seems quite unnecessary ("Abram the Hebrew," *BASOR* 163 [October 1961], p. 52). Cf. p. 124, n. 30).

17. Cf. Isa. 32:17 ("the work of righteousness shall be peace"); Rom. 5:1 ("having therefore been justified by faith, we have peace with God").

18. The argument from silence plays an important part in rabbinical interpretation of Scripture where (for exegetical purposes) nothing must be regarded as having existed before the time of its first biblical mention (cf. Strack-Billerbeck, *Kommentar zum Neuen Testament aus Talmud und Midrasch*, III [Munich, 1926], pp. 694f.). The argument is used extensively by Philo for allegorical purposes; thus Sarah is "without mother" (ἀμήτωρ, the word here used of Melchizedek) because her mother is nowhere mentioned (cf. Gen. 20:12, where Abraham says: "she is . . . not the daughter of my mother"); this means that Sarah, "the virtue-loving mind," was not born "from perceptible matter which is always in a state of formation and dissolution, . . . but from the Author (αἴτιος) and Father of all" (*On Drunkenness* 59ff.). See G. Quell, *TDNT*, V, pp. 1019-21 (*s v.* ἀπάτωρ).

19. The meaning of ἀπάτωρ ἀμήτωρ here is well brought out in the Syriac Peshiṭta: "his father and mother are not listed in genealogies." Attempts have been made to link this description of Melchizedek with the words used of himself by Abdi-ḥiba, king of Jerusalem (14th cent. B.C.), in Amarna Tablet No. 288, ll. 14f. (cf. p. 158, n. 15): "Neither my father nor my mother but the mighty arm of the king [of Egypt] set me in the house of my father." There is no connection at all bet᠁᠁en the two documents. Abdi-ḥiba means that his sacral kingship was not so much hereditary as conferred by his overlord. There is not even any real connection between this passage and Philo's statement that "the high priest is not a human being but a divine *logos*, having no part in any unrighteousness whether intentional or otherwise; for Moses says that he cannot be defiled either for his father, the mind, or for his mother, sense-perception [Lev. 21:11], because, to my mind, he has parents most pure and incorruptible, his Father being God, who is also the Father of all, and his mother Wisdom, through whom the universe came into being" (*On Flight and Finding* 108f.). There is a contact in these words of Philo with Melchizedek, whom he elsewhere (see p. 158) explains as being Reason *(logos);* but our author attaches to the fatherless and motherless condition of Melchizedek quite another significance, which appears plainly from the course of his argument.

20. In the early centuries A.D. some gnostic circles regarded Melchizedek as an angelic

chizedek appears to have belonged to a dynasty of priest-kings in which he had both predecessors and successors. If this point had been put to our author, he would have agreed at once, no doubt; but this consideration was foreign to his purpose. The important consideration was the account given of Melchizedek in holy writ; to him the silences of Scripture were as much due to divine inspiration as were its statements. In the only record which Scripture provides of Melchizedek—Gen. 14:18-20—nothing is said of his parentage, nothing is said of his ancestry[21] or progeny, nothing is said of his birth, nothing is said of his death. He appears as a living man, king of Salem and priest of God Most High; and as such he disappears. In all this—in the silences as well as in the statements—he is a fitting type of Christ; in fact, the record by the things it says of him and by the things it does not say has assimilated him to the Son of God. It is the eternal being of the Son of God that is here in view; not his human life. Our author has no docetic view of Christ; he knows that "our Lord has sprung from Judah" (v. 14). But in his eternal being the Son of God has really, as Melchizedek has typically, "neither beginning of days nor end of life"; and more especially now, exalted at the right hand of God, he "remains a priest in perpetuity." Melchizedek remains a priest continually for the duration of his appearance in the biblical narrative; but in the antitype Christ remains a priest continually without qualification. And it is not the type which determines the antitype, but the antitype which determines the type; Jesus is not portrayed after the pattern of Melchizedek, but Melchizedek is "made conformable to the Son of God."[22]

---

power superior to all others (Hippolytus, *Refutation* 7.36; Epiphanius, *Panarion* 55). In *Pistis Sophia* Melchizedek rules the realm of light as the Receiver (παραλήμπτωρ) of Light (33a-35a, 179b-180a, 265b-266a, 295b, 302a-b, 324b-325a). Orthodox Christians had little difficulty in identifying him with the Son of God before his incarnation; for the persistence of this view cf. J. B. McCaul: "Cunaeus . . . believes, as Ewald does, and I do, that Melchizedek was the second person in the Ever Blessed Trinity, the Divine *angel of the Lord,* who continually appeared to the Fathers under the Old Testament dispensation . . . if Melchizedek was 'without beginning of days or end of life,' but 'abideth a priest continually,' how can it be believed of him that he was a mere mortal? . . . Melchizedek, as the Divine *Logos,* existed from eternity" (*The Epistle to the Hebrews* [London, 1871], pp. 75, 80). A. T. Hanson argues that the writer to the Hebrews himself made this identification (*Jesus Christ in the Old Testament* [London, 1965], pp. 65-82)—but Melchizedek, "resembling the Son of God" (Heb. 7:3), is distinguished from him as certainly as Aaron is (cf. Heb. 7:11).

21. For the Aaronic priest, on the other hand, the establishment of proper parentage was an essential qualification; as late as the Hasmonaean dynasty any uncertainty on this score could invalidate a man's claim to the office (Lev. 21:13f.; Ezra 2:62; Neh. 7:64; Josephus, *Ant.* 13.292; TB *Qiddushin* 66a). It was therefore necessary that the identity of an Aaronic priest's father and mother should be publicly known. This contrast between the two orders of priesthood may have been present to our author's mind.

22. There is no real analogy here with Dan. 3:25 (Gk. 3:92), where the fourth man in the furnace is simply "like an angel" ("like a son of the gods"). The Son of God at his coming into the world had to be "made like (ὁμοιωθῆναι) his brothers" (Heb. 2:17) because they were al-

B. THE GREATNESS OF MELCHIZEDEK (7:4-10)

4 *See how great this man[23] is! To him[24] the patriarch Abraham gave a tenth of the spoils.*

5 *Now those descendants of Levi who receive the priesthood are entitled according to the law to be paid tithes by the people—that is, their own brothers—although they too are Abraham's offspring.*

6 *But Melchizedek, who does not belong to their genealogy, has been paid tithes by Abraham, and has bestowed his blessing on the recipient of the promises.*

7 *Beyond all dispute it is the inferior who is blessed by the superior.*

8 *Again, in our situation it is mortal human beings who are paid tithes, but in that situation they are paid to one who is attested as being alive.*

9 *One might almost say that,[25] by the agency of Abraham, Levi, who is paid tithes, paid tithes to Melchizedek,*

10 *for he was still in his forefather's body when Melchizedek came to meet him.*

4 The surpassing dignity of Melchizedek's priestly order will be appreciated the more if one considers the tokens of Melchizedek's greatness. Abraham was a great man indeed—"a prince of God" to his neighbors, called "my friend" by God himself—but in the account of his interview with Melchizedek, it is Melchizedek who appears as the greater of the two.[26] And if

---

ready "sharers in flesh and blood" before his incarnation; but as regards his eternal person Melchizedek was "made like" (ἀφωμοιωμένος) him, because he already existed before Melchizedek came on the scene. The language here rules out the idea that Melchizedek *was* the pre-existent Christ"—an idea which A. T. Hanson thinks our author did not express outright "because he did not have quite the courage to do so" (*Jesus Christ in the Old Testament,* pp. 69, 71).

23. Gk. οὗτος, omitted by D* 1739 424** (perhaps by the independent operation of homoeoteleuton; cf. G. Zuntz, *The Text of the Epistles* [London, 1953], p. 87). This shorter text is perhaps implied in RSV "See how great he is!" and NEB "Consider how great he must be...."

24. Gk. ᾧ ("to whom"), to which ℵ A with the Latin versions, the Harclean Syriac, the bulk of the later MSS, and the TR add καί ("to whom indeed"), influenced perhaps by ᾧ καί at the beginning of v. 2.

25. Gk. ὡς ἔπος εἰπεῖν, a classical phrase qualifying what might otherwise be an exaggeration, not found elsewhere in the Greek Bible, but common in Philo.

26. That Melchizedek should be greater than Abraham, as Gen. 14 so clearly indicates, constituted a problem for Jewish exegetes. Some of them identified him with Shem, whose life, according to the MT, overlapped Abraham's—he survived the Flood by some 500 years (Gen. 11:11), and may even have been reckoned to have outlived Abraham. If Abraham paid respect to such a venerable ancestor by giving him tithes and accepting his blessing, no offense would be caused to any reader, however great Abraham might appear in his eyes. But later it was felt necessary to modify the honor thus implicitly ascribed to Shem. So Rabbi Zechariah said in the name of Rabbi Ishmael: "God wanted to derive the priestly line from Shem, as it is said, 'He was priest of God Most High.' But God derived it [the priestly line] from Abraham, when Shem placed the blessing of Abraham before the praise of God, as it is said, 'Blessed be Abram . . . and blessed be God Most High . . .' (Gen. 14:19). Abraham said to him: 'Does one place the

Melchizedek was greater than Abraham, his priesthood (our author argues) must be greater than a priesthood which traces its descent from Abraham. The superior greatness of Melchizedek appears in two important respects: he accepted tithes from Abraham and bestowed his blessing on Abraham.

5-6a The tithes which he received from Abraham evidently amounted to one tenth of all the spoils of war[27] which Abraham had recovered from the invading kings. The dedication of one tenth of the spoils of war to a deity (on whose behalf his priest acted) was practiced among the Greeks and other nations,[28] but is not attested for Israel. As far as the institution of the "holy war" in Israel was concerned, it was not one tenth only, but all that was captured, which was devoted to God according to the law of the *ḥērem* or "ban."[29] In Israel agricultural produce was tithed year by year and the tithe was allocated to the tribe of Levi "for an inheritance" (Lev. 18:21, the "commandment" of v. 5), and one tenth of that tithe was further earmarked for the priesthood (Num. 18:26).[30] In Nehemiah's time the Levites received the tithes under the supervision of the priests and brought the "tithe of the tithes"

---

blessing of a servant before that of his master?' Straightway it [the priesthood] was given to Abraham, as it is said, 'The LORD said to my Lord, Sit at my right hand, until I make your enemies your footstool' (Ps. 110:1). And after this it is written, 'The LORD has sworn, and will not repent: You are a priest for ever after the order of Melchizedek,' *'al dibrātî malkî-ṣedeq* (Ps. 110:4). This means: 'on account of what Melchizedek had said.' And hence it is written, *'he* was priest of God Most High' —he was priest, but his descendants were not priests" (TB *Nedarim* 32b). This remarkable exegesis, which takes "You are a priest for ever" as addressed to Abraham, and regards Melchizedek's priesthood as superseded by Abraham's (and consequently by that of Levi, who "was still in his forefather's body when Melchizedek came to meet him"), might almost have been designed as a deliberate rebuttal of the argument in Heb. 7:4-10. See p. 134, n. 78, with bibliography at the end of that note.

27. Gk. ἀϰϱοθίνια. That the "tenth of all" which Abraham gave Melchizedek (Gen. 14:19) was the tenth part of the spoils is implied, but not stated, in the Old Testament narrative. According to the *Genesis Apocryphon* from Qumran Cave 1, Abraham "gave him a tithe of all the goods of the king of Elam and his companions" (col. 22, l. 17). Philo says that Abraham, "being declared the winner of the trophies by God, the giver of victory, dedicated the tithes to him as a thank-offering for his victory" (*Preliminary Studies* 93), and that "when the great priest of the all-great God saw him approaching, bearing his trophies . . . he honored him with prayers and offered up sacrifices in celebration of the victory (ἐπινίϰια)" (*On Abraham* 235). So too Josephus says that Abraham offered Melchizedek "the tithe of the plunder" (*Ant.* 1.181). But according to Eupolemus and other Jewish writers it was Melchizedek who paid tithes to Abraham. See R. H. Smith, "Abram and Melchizedek," *ZAW* 77 (1965), pp. 129-52: Melchizedek surrenders his city to the conquering Abram; cf. Merneptah's victory stele, where "the princes lie prostrate, saying 'Salaam!' " (*DOTT*, p. 139).

28. See Herodotus, *History* 1.89; Xenophon, *Anabasis* 5.3; *Hellenica* 4.3 (for Greek practice); Livy, *History* 5.21 (for Roman practice); cf. also Pindar, *Olympian Odes* 11.51; Xenophon, *Cyropaedia* 7.5.

29. Cf. Deut. 20:16-18; Josh. 6:21, 24. See G. von Rad, *Der heilige Krieg im alten Israel* (Zürich, 1951), pp. 13f.; C. H. W. Brekelmans, *De Ḥerem in het Oude Testament* (Nijmegen, 1959); R. de Vaux, *Ancient Israel*, E.T. (London, 1961), pp. 260f.

30. Cf. R. de Vaux, *Ancient Israel*, pp. 140f., 360, 380-82, 403-5.

to the temple to be handed over to the priests (Neh. 10:38f.). By the first century A.D., however, there is reason to think that the administration of the tithes was carried out by the priests.[31] It may have been knowledge of the actual practice at that time that led our author to say that it was "those descendants of Levi who receive the priesthood" who tithed the people in accordance with the commandment—although in general his description of the laws relating to the priesthood and sanctuary is based on the Pentateuch and not on contemporary custom.

Our author's argument, however, does not rest upon the details of the administration of the tithe according to the Old Testament law, but on the fact that whereas the members of the tribe of Levi received tithes from their fellow-Israelites, who were children of Abraham like themselves, Abraham—ancestor alike of the Levites and of their kinsfolk who paid them tithes—recognized the superiority of Melchizedek by paying tithes to *him*. The priesthood of Melchizedek's order is thus shown to enjoy higher status than the Levitical priesthood;[32] Melchizedek, like Christ, who has been acclaimed high priest after his order, does not have his genealogy reckoned among the sons of Levi.

6b-7   Moreover, great as Abraham's privileges were by virtue of the promises which he received from God, he recognized the superiority of Melchizedek by accepting a blessing at his hands—"and beyond all dispute the lesser is always blessed by the greater" (NEB).

8   Another token of Melchizedek's superiority to the Levitical priesthood is this: nowhere is it related that Melchizedek lost his priestly office by death, whereas we have the record, generation after generation, of Levitical priests who died and had to hand on their dignity and duty to their heirs. The tithe prescribed by Israelite law is paid to mortal men; the tithe which Abraham gave Melchizedek was received by one who, as far as the record goes, has no "end of life." As far as the record goes, for our author is not interested in anything that might be known or inferred about Melchizedek outside the biblical narrative. But what was true of Melchizedek in this limited and "literary" sense is true absolutely of him who serves his people as high priest in the presence of God. Melchizedek "is attested as being alive" in the sense that we never read of him otherwise than as a living man; Christ can be said to live in the sense that, having died once for all and risen from the dead, he is alive forevermore (cf. v. 16 below; Rom. 6:9; Rev. 1:18). The practical implications of this are drawn out more fully in vv. 23-25 of the present chapter.

---

31. So E. Schürer, *History of the Jewish People in the Age of Jesus Christ,* II (Edinburgh, 1979), p. 270, infers from Josephus, *Life* 63, 80; *Ant.* 20.181, 206f.

32. That this higher status is permanent may be indicated by the two perfect tenses of v. 6: Melchizedek "has taken tithes" (δεδεκάτωκεν) and "has blessed" (εὐλόγηκεν).

9-10 Reverting for a moment to the tithe-receiving tribe of Levi, our author points out that Levi, the ancestor of that priestly tribe and the embodiment of its corporate personality, may be said himself to have paid tithes to Melchizedek (thus conceding the superiority of the Melchizedek priesthood) in the person of his ancestor Abraham. Levi was Abraham's great-grandson, and was yet unborn when Abraham met Melchizedek; but an ancestor is regarded in biblical thought as containing within himself all his descendants.[33] That Levi may be thought of thus as paying tithes to Melchizedek is an afterthought to what has already been said about the significance of this particular payment of tithes; lest it should be criticized as farfetched, our author qualifies it with the phrase "one might almost say" ("it might even be said," NEB).[34]

C. IMPERFECTION OF THE AARONIC PRIESTHOOD (7:11-14)

11 *Now if perfection were attainable through the Levitical priesthood[35] (under which the people have received the law),[36] what further need would there be for another priest to arise after Melchizedek's order, instead of being called after Aaron's?*

12 *With the change of priesthood, of course, there takes place necessarily[37] a change[38] of law also.*

13 *The man with a view to whom these things are said belongs to[39] another tribe, from which no one ever ministered[40] at the altar.*

---

33. Cf. Jacob and Esau (Gen. 25:23; Mal. 1:2f.; Rom. 9:11ff.), and preeminently Adam (Rom. 5:12, where "all sinned" is a way of indicating what happened when Adam sinned). (Adam, however, incorporates his posterity as no other biblical figure does.)

34. On these ten verses see B. A. Demarest, *A History of Interpretation of Hebrews 7,1-10 from the Reformation to the Present*, BGBE 19 (Tübingen, 1976).

35. Gk. διὰ τῆς Λευιτικῆς ἱερωσύνης. The adjective occurs in the LXX only in the title of the book of Leviticus; it is used by Philo (e.g., he refers to "the Levitical tribe" in *On Flight and Finding* 93). Here and in vv. 12, 24, ἱερωσύνη is used for "priesthood"; in v. 5 ἱερατεία was used (there only in this epistle; cf. Luke 1:9). Both words are used in the LXX, ἱερατεία being the commoner. Cf. p. 171, n. 72.

36. ὁ λαὸς γὰρ ἐπ' αὐτῆς νενομοθέτηται. 𝔭⁴⁶ omits γάρ. For ἐπ' αὐτῆς (𝔭⁴⁶ ℵ A B C D* L P Ψ *al*) D² byz read ἐπ' αὐτῇ (see G. Schrenk, *TDNT*, III, p. 277, *s.v.* ἀρχιερεύς); a few minuscules read ἐπ' αὐτήν. For the perfect νενομοθέτηται (so also at 8:6) D² K L Ψ byz read the pluperfect ἐνομοθέτητο. Since νομοθετέω means "legislate," its passive use with ὁ λαός as the subject is curious; BAGD can cite only one instance of the active verb with a personal object, and that from Pseudo-Galen. See *New Docs.*, I (1976), § 2.

37. Gk. ἐξ ἀνάγκης καί, a Philonic formula (cf. Spicq, *Hébreux*, I, p. 42).

38. Gk. μετάθεσις, which here (as in 12:27) implies not merely change but abrogation (cf. ἀθέτησις in v. 18).

39. Gk. μετέσχηκεν, "has partaken of"; cf. 2:14 for the aorist μετέσχεν, which is read here in 𝔭⁴⁶. (See p. 78, n. 55).

40. Gk. προσέσχηκεν ("has attended to"), so ℵ B D and the majority of MSS, as against

14 *It is known to all*[41] *that our Lord has sprung*[42] *from Judah, a tribe of which Moses said nothing in connection with priests.*[43]

11 It could not be argued that the later priesthood (of Aaron) superseded the earlier (of Melchizedek),[44] for the priesthood of Aaron was already well established when the divine oracle was uttered which hailed the Messiah of David's line as "a priest for ever after the order of Melchizedek." What the oracle implies, our author argues, is that the Aaronic priesthood did not exhaust the mediatorial functions which, in God's purpose, were to be discharged between him and the human race. If God had intended the Aaronic priesthood to inaugurate the age of perfection, the time when men and women would enjoy unimpeded access to him, why should he have conferred on the Messiah a priestly dignity of his own—different[45] from Aaron's and by implication superior to Aaron's? In fact, as is argued below in manifold detail, the Aaronic priesthood was neither designed nor competent to inaugurate the age of fulfilment; that age must be marked by the rise of another priest, whose priesthood was of a different order and character from Aaron's. Some phases of Jewish expectation did look forward to a new age—the age of restoration—when a worthy priest would preside over the state;[46] but this coming priest of the tribe of Levi could at

---

προσέσχεν, the reading of 𝔭[46] 1739 A C 33 1288 2004 (the "minor Alexandrians"). G. Zuntz prefers the aorist here after the perfect μετέσχηκεν in the preceding clause: "the differentiation is excellent; it intimates that no one of the tribe of Judah *had ever attended* to the altar (προσέσχε) and that Jesus 'has permanently a share in' (μετέσχηκε, 'belongs to') that tribe" (*Text*, p. 79).

41. Gk. πρόδηλον, "obvious."

42. Or "has risen": Gk. ἀνατέταλκεν, here a synonym of ἀνίστασθαι in v. 11, but chosen perhaps because it echoes the rising of the star out of Jacob in Num. 24:17 (where, interestingly enough, LXX ἀνατελεῖ appears in parallelism to ἀναστήσεται in the following clause); cf. also the messianic associations of ἀνατολή in Zech. 6:12 (for Heb. ṣemaḥ, ARV "branch"), identified with the Logos by Philo (*Confusion of Tongues* 62f.). Num. 24:17 probably also underlies Matt. 2:2, "we have seen his star at its rising" (ἐν τῇ ἀνατολῇ). Cf. the reproduction of ἀνατέλλω from Num. 24:17 in *Test. Judah* 24:1 (cf. *Test. Dan* 5:10; *Test. Gad* 8:1).

43. D^c K L with TR "priesthood" (ἱερωσύνης); cf. AV/KJV.

44. For such an argument cf. p. 161, n. 26.

45. The new priest is designated in v. 11 ἕτερον . . . ἱερέα ("a different priest") and not merely ἄλλον ("another"), if one may press the distinction between ἕτερος and ἄλλος. See A. Vanhoye, *Prêtres anciens, prêtre nouveau selon le Nouveau Testament*, Parole de Dieu 20 (Paris, 1980).

46. Such an expectation finds expression in Qumran literature, influenced probably by the description of the new commonwealth in Ezek. 40–48, where the priesthood takes practical precedence over "the prince." The Qumran community evidently envisaged the high priest (the "Messiah of Aaron") as head of state in the coming age of restoration, taking precedence over the Davidic prince (the "Messiah of Israel"). Thus in 1QSa, col. 2, l. 12, precedence over "the Messiah of Israel" is accorded to "the priest who is head of the whole congregation of Israel." But he is a Levitical (probably Zadokite) priest, and fulfils Moses' blessing of Levi in Deut. 33:8-11 (cf. 4Q *Testimonia*, ll. 14ff.). We might compare the "new priest" of *Test. Levi* 18:2ff.,

best be actually what the Aaronic high priest was ideally and could not bring in perfection in the sense intended by our author. For that, another priest of a different kind was called for.

The words "Now if perfection were attainable through the Levitical priesthood" have a bearing on the class of readers at whom our author's argument was aimed. If they were Gentile converts, in danger of abandoning their Christian faith, their only response to these words would have been: "We never thought there *was* perfection through the Levitical priesthood"— they certainly never thought so in their pagan days and they would have received no encouragement to think so in their Christian days. But if they were Jews by birth, now in danger of giving up the distinctive features of their Christian confession and merging once more in their former Jewish environment, the situation was quite different. Before their conversion they had envisaged no priesthood beyond the Levitical priesthood; even if they looked for a new priest to arise in the age to come, he was still a Levitical priest. Their Christian teachers would have encouraged them to think of the Levitical priesthood as something belonging to the age of preparation, which had now given way to the age of fulfilment; but they were in danger of concluding that, after all, the old order (including the Levitical priesthood and everything else that went with it) had still much to be said in its favor. To such people our author's assurance that the supersession of the Levitical priesthood by another had been decreed by God long before would have had practical relevance.

12 Nor is it only the Aaronic priesthood which must be superseded. That priesthood was instituted under the Mosaic law, and was so integral to it that a change in the priesthood carries with it inevitably a change in the law. If the Aaronic priesthood was instituted for a temporary purpose, to be brought to an end when the age of fulfilment dawned, the same must be true of the law under which that priesthood was introduced. So by his own independent line of argument our author reaches the same conclusion as Paul: the law was a temporary provision, "our custodian until Christ came" (Gal. 3:24). Paul, indeed, thinks of the law as an institution designed to arouse men and women's awareness of sin and not (as he had once believed) to promote their justification before God, whereas our author thinks rather of the sacrificial cultus as

---

but the recensions in which the *Testaments of the Twelve Patriarchs* have come down to us (apart from the recently discovered Qumran fragments) have been so thoroughly worked over in a Christian sense that it is highly precarious to draw firm conclusions from them about Jewish expectations. M. de Jonge has good reason for concluding that the purport of *Test. Levi* 18:2ff., and of other passages which describe the priest of the new age (see p. 167, n. 50), in their present form, is to "glorify Jesus Christ" (*The Testaments of the Twelve Patriarchs* [Assen, 1953], p. 90). Cf. M. Black, "The Messiah in the Testament of Levi xviii," *ExT* 60 (1948-49), pp. 321f., 61 (1949-50), pp. 157f.; *The Scrolls and Christian Origins* (London, 1961), pp. 145-57.

something which could never effectively remove sin.[47] If we like, we may say that Paul has the moral law mainly in mind, whereas the author of Hebrews is concerned more with the ceremonial law—although the distinction between the moral and ceremonial law is one drawn by Christian theologians, not by those who accepted the whole law as the will of God, nor yet by the New Testament writers.[48] But in principle Paul and our author are agreed that the law was a temporary dispensation of God, valid only until Christ came to inaugurate the age of perfection. Its supersession is here seen to be implied in the acclamation of Messiah as a priest after the order of Melchizedek.

13-14 How radical is the change in the law which is involved in the announcement of a priesthood after Melchizedek's order may be appreciated when it is considered that the person to whom this announcement refers has nothing to do with the tribe of Levi, to which the priesthood was restricted by the law. It is a matter of common knowledge that our Lord belonged to the tribe of Judah. This, it may be remarked, could be a matter of common knowledge only if it was generally accepted that he was born of the royal line of David—that he was so born was a commonplace of primitive Christian preaching and confession.[49] But whatever hopes and promises were attached in the Pentateuch to the tribe of Judah, priestly service found no place among them.[50] No member of the tribe of Judah was appointed to officiate at the altar.[51] The attempts which were made at a later date to justify the doctrine of the priesthood of Christ by providing him with a Levitical lineage[52] would have been dismissed by our author (had he known anything about them) not only as irrelevant but as perverse, because they blunted the point of his argument—the calculated supersession of the Levitical priesthood by one of a different kind. Nor would he have looked with any greater favor on attempts to

---

47. Cf. H. Windisch: Hebrews views the law "not as a prescription for the behavior of the individual, but as the sum of sacrificial regulations for the ancient cultic community" (*Der Hebräerbrief,* HNT [Tübingen, 1931], p. 66).

48. This does not mean that the distinction is not a valid one, but it does not come to the fore in either the OT or the NT.

49. Cf. Acts 2:29-31; 13:23; Rom. 1:3; 2 Tim. 2:8; Rev. 22:16 (not to mention the Matthaean and Lukan nativity narratives).

50. If the *Testaments of the Twelve Patriarchs* speak of a priest of the tribe of Judah (*Test. Levi* 8:14), that is one of the clearest signs of Christian influence in the extant recensions (cf. p. 166, n. 46). The normal arrangement is that expressed by Judah when he says of himself and Levi: "To me the Lord gave the kingdom, and to him the priesthood, and he set the kingdom beneath the priesthood" (*Test. Judah* 21:2). Cf. p. 126, n. 39).

51. As far as the Pentateuchal legislation is concerned, at least. David and Solomon are said to have offered sacrifice on various occasions (cf. 2 Sam. 6:13, 17f.; 24:25; 1 Kings 3:4; 8:62-64), and "David's sons were priests" (2 Sam. 8:18).

52. Cf. p. 124, n. 29. Our author's position is much more satisfactory, and could have been established on historical grounds as well as by the arguments he uses, had he been minded to appeal to the former (Jesus, as Son of David, is the true heir to Melchizedek's office).

establish a new *earthly* priesthood to be exercised by members of the holy family,[53] although the holy family undoubtedly belonged to the tribe of Judah. The priesthood in which he is interested is different not only because it is exercised by one who came from another tribe than Levi, but also because it is not exercised on earth: it belongs to the eternal order, not to the material world.

D. SUPERIORITY OF THE NEW PRIESTHOOD (7:15-19)

15 *Our argument is clearer still, if another priest is to arise after the fashion of Melchizedek,*

16 *a priest who has come not according to the law of an earthly commandment but according to the power of an indissoluble[54] life.*

17 *For God's testimony is:*
   "You are a priest for ever,
   after the order of Melchizedek."[55]

18 *Here we have the cancellation[56] of the previous commandment, because it was weak and unprofitable*

19 *(for the law made nothing perfect), and the introduction[57] of a better hope, by which we approach God.*

---

53. In some Jewish Christian circles James the Just and his successors appear to have been regarded as constituting a new priestly line by virtue of their relation κατὰ σάρκα to Jesus. It is this situation that probably underlies the curious statement of Hegesippus that James the Just "alone was accustomed to enter the sanctuary (ναός) and be found kneeling and praying for the people's forgiveness" (Eusebius, *Hist. Eccl.* 2.23.6). He certainly did not have the entrée into the literal sanctuary. See A. Ehrhardt, *The Apostolic Succession in the First Two Centuries of the Church* (London, 1953), p. 1 et passim.

54. Gk. ἀκατάλυτος (ARV mg. "indissoluble"; RSV "indestructible"; NEB "that cannot be destroyed").

55. Ps. 110:4 (LXX 109:4).

56. Gk. ἀθέτησις, a stronger word than μετάθεσις in v. 12. "The earlier rules are cancelled" (NEB). The noun occurs once again in the NT, in Heb. 9:26, of the cancellation of sin by the self-oblation of Christ (see p. 231 with n. 165). See A. Deissmann, *Bible Studies*, E.T. (Edinburgh, 1902), pp. 228f.; *New Docs.*, II (1977), § 29. The verb ἀθετέω appears about a dozen times (cf. Heb. 10:28), being used, e.g., in Mark 7:9 of those who "set aside the commandment of God" (NEB) in order to maintain their own tradition. E. K. Simpson points out that its Hellenistic sense of "an act of supersession or setting aside" appears in its technical use by "the Alexandrian grammarians to signify the obelizing of a suspected passage counted spurious (Luc. *V.H.* ii.20) and therefore to be expunged from an author's text. In this sense of deletion we find it in the papyri with reference to annulled decrees and even paid-off loans. The Palestinian writer Philodemus (*Rhet.* i.43) writes of certain locutions 'not easily to be discarded' (οὐκ ἂν ῥαδίως ἀθετῆσαι); and there are passages such as Gal. 2:21; 3:15, in the New Testament where this translation would be plausible" ("The Vocabulary of the Epistle to the Hebrews," *EQ* 18 [1946], p. 190).

57. Gk. ἐπεισαγωγή, where the prefix ἐπί may retain something of its classical force "in addition," "over and above" (Moffatt, ICC, *ad loc.* quotes its use by Josephus in *Ant.* 11.196 for the "replacement" of Vashti by another wife in the Persian king's affections).

15-17   A further token of the imperfection of the old priesthood and the superiority of the new lies on the face of our author's Old Testament text, "You are a priest *for ever*." These words are quite inapplicable to the old order; no priest of Aaron's line could have been described as "a priest for ever,"[58] for the simple reason that each one of them died in due course. But the Christians' high priest is immortal; having died once for all and risen from the dead, he discharges his ministry on his people's behalf in the power of a life which can never be destroyed. The law which established the Aaronic priesthood is called a "carnal commandment" (AV/KJV, ERV/ARV) because it is "a system of earth-bound rules" (NEB); it is concerned with the externalities of religion—the physical descent of the priests,[59] a material shrine, animal sacrifices, and so forth. Like everything else in the Levitical régime, the Aaronic order of priesthood was marked by transience; it stands thus in contrast to the permanence and effectiveness of the priestly office of Christ.

18-19   The declaration "You are a priest for ever, after the order of Melchizedek" thus announces the abrogation of the earlier law which instituted the Aaronic order. It was inevitable that the earlier law should be abrogated sooner or later; for all the impressive solemnity of the sacrificial ritual and the sacerdotal ministry, no real peace of conscience was procured thereby, no immediate access to God. That is not to say that faithful men and women in Old Testament times did not enjoy peace of conscience and a sense of nearness to God; the Psalter provides evidence enough that they did. The psalmist who cried, "Blessed is he whose transgression is forgiven, whose sin is covered; blessed is the man to whom Yahweh imputes no iniquity" (Ps. 32:1f.), knew the blessedness of a peaceful conscience; and his colleague who said, "it is good for me to be near God" (Ps. 73:28), knew that access to the divine presence was always available to the man or woman of faith. But these experiences had nothing to do with the Levitical ritual or the Aaronic priesthood. The whole apparatus of worship associated with that ritual and priesthood was calculated rather to keep people at a distance from God than to bring them near. But the "hope set before us" in the gospel is better because it accomplishes this very thing which was impossible under the old ceremonial; it enables Christians to "draw near to God." How it enables them to do so is explained in greater detail later on;[60] but the fact that the gospel, unlike the law, has opened up a way of free

---

58. The Aaronic priesthood itself is described as "an everlasting priesthood" (Ex. 40:15; cf. Jer. 33:18), but no individual member of the priesthood is described as an everlasting priest. When the language of Ps. 110:4 was applied to Simon the Hasmonaean (1 Macc. 14:41), "a priest for ever" was evidently understood in the weaker sense of "founder of an hereditary priesthood." See p. 125, n. 35; cf. also p. 172.

59. Cf. the RSV rendering of v. 16: "not according to a legal requirement concerning bodily descent."

60. Cf. 10:19-22 (pp. 249-56).

access to God is our author's ground for claiming that the gospel has achieved that perfection which the law could never bring about.

E. SUPERIOR BECAUSE OF THE DIVINE OATH (7:20-22)

20 *Moreover, insofar as the new priesthood is not unaccompanied by the swearing of an oath[61] (for those of the Levitical order have been made[62] priests without the swearing of an oath,*
21 *but this one with the swearing of an oath by[63] him who says to him,[64] "The Lord has sworn and will not change his mind: 'You are a priest for ever' "),[65]*
22 *to that extent also Jesus has become guarantor of a better covenant.*

20-21 Our author continues to examine his text, so as to extract from it its last degree of significance for the character of the new priesthood. He now draws his readers' attention to the fact that the acclamation of Messiah as a perpetual priest was confirmed by a divine oath: "The LORD has sworn and will not change his mind: 'You are a priest for ever.'" What he has said about God's oath to Abraham in 6:13ff.[66] is equally true about God's oath here. The bare word of God is assurance enough, but God, "desiring to show even more clearly . . . how unchanging was his purpose, guaranteed it by oath" (6:17, NEB). The inauguration of the Aaronic priesthood rested on a divine command: "bring near to you Aaron your brother," said God to Moses, "and his sons with him, from among the people of Israel, to serve me as priests" (Ex. 28:1). But there is no mention of a divine oath in the record of their appointment as there is in Ps. 110:4, where a new priest "after the order of Melchizedek" is introduced. This suggests the superior dignity of the Melchizedek priesthood.[67]

61. Gk. ὁρκωμοσία (rendered "oath" twice in v. 21); this word was a neuter plural in classical Greek (with proparoxytone accent) but appears as a feminine singular in the Hellenistic idiom (three instances are quoted from the LXX).

62. Our author uses the elegant periphrasis εἰσὶν . . . γεγονότες (cf. v. 23).

63. Gk. διά with the genitive (ERV/ARV mg. "through"), but nevertheless it is the agent, not the intermediary (God, not the psalmist), that is intended.

64. See p. 63, n. 104.

65. The Western and Byzantine texts complete the quotation from Ps. 110:4 by adding "after the order of Melchizedek" (cf. AV/KJV).

66. Cf. p. 154, with n. 77.

67. Moffatt points out (*ad loc.*) that "Roman readers could understand from their former religion how oaths were needful in such a matter," quoting Suetonius (*Life of Claudius* 22) to the effect that the Emperor Claudius nominated no one to membership of the priestly colleges without swearing (*nisi iuratus*) that he was suitable. The parallel is worth recording, but the present commentary (unlike Moffatt's) is not written in the belief that the "former religion" of the addressees of this epistle was the old Roman religion.

22   And since it is Jesus who is acclaimed as priest after the order of Melchizedek, it is Jesus whose superior dignity is thus confirmed. Our author emphasizes this by arranging the construction of this long sentence,[68] vv. 20-22, so that the weight of the argument falls on its last word, "Jesus." And when he does so, he introduces a further aspect of the priesthood of Jesus which will be developed in the following chapters—Jesus' rôle as guarantor and mediator of a covenant which is as much superior to the covenant of the *ancien régime* as his priesthood is superior to that of Aaron. This is the first occurrence of the term "covenant" in this epistle, but the term is about to play such a central part in the argument to follow that the whole epistle has been described as "The Epistle of the *Diatheke*."[69] For the moment, however, the designation of Jesus as "the guarantor[70] of a better covenant" prepares the reader for what is to come; there are still two further tokens of the superiority of the Melchizedek priesthood which must be mentioned.

F. SUPERIOR BECAUSE OF ITS PERMANENCE (7:23-25)

23   *Again, those high priests have been[71] many in number because death prevented them from continuing,*
24   *but this one, because he continues "for ever," has a priesthood[72] which is untransferable.[73]*

68. The construction of this long sentence, with the parenthesis and inserted quotation of v. 21, is characteristically Philonic. For the *a fortiori* argument cf. 2:1-3 (p. 68, n. 4).

69. Gk. διαθήκη ("settlement"). Cf. the title of articles by G. Vos, "Hebrews, the Epistle of the Diatheke," *PTR* 13 (1915), pp. 587-632, 14 (1916), pp. 1-61. See p. 221 with nn. 115-17.

70. Gk. ἔγγυος, here only in the NT; it occurs three times in the LXX (Sir. 29:15f.; 2 Macc. 10:28). In common Greek it is found frequently in legal and other documents in the sense of a surety or guarantor. The ἔγγυος undertakes a weightier responsibility than the μεσίτης or mediator (cf. Heb. 8:6; 9:15; 12:24); he is answerable for the fulfilment of the obligation which he guarantees. Moffatt (ICC, *ad loc.*) draws attention to the close association between the rôles of surety and savior in Sir. 29:15f.:

> Do not forget all the kindness of your surety,
> for he has given his life for you.
> A sinner will overthrow the prosperity of his surety,
> and one who does not feel grateful will abandon his rescuer.

The old covenant had a mediator (cf. Gal. 3:19) but no surety; there was no one to guarantee the fulfilment of the people's undertaking: "All that Yahweh hath spoken will we do, and be obedient" (Ex. 24:7). But Jesus guarantees the perpetual fulfilment of the covenant which he mediates, on the manward side as well as on the Godward side. As the Son of God, he confirms God's eternal covenant with his people; as his people's representative, he satisfies its terms with perfect acceptance in God's sight.

71. Gk. εἰσιν γεγονότες, as in v. 21.

72. Gk. ἱερωσύνην (ἱερατείαν in D*); cf. p. 164, n. 35.

73. ERV/ARV mg.: "hath a priesthood that doth not pass to another." The Greek adjective is ἀπαράβατος (see p. 172, n. 76).

25 *Therefore indeed he is able to bring complete and final salvation to those who approach God through him, since he lives continuously to intercede for them.*

23 It has already been pointed out (vv. 16f.) that our Lord's indissoluble life makes it possible for him to fulfil to the letter the words "You are a priest *for ever*." If these words were applied to a dynasty of priests, "for ever" could be understood only of a hereditary succession of indefinite duration.[74] The Aaronic priests were indeed appointed on the hereditary principle (not, of course, on the basis of Ps. 110:4); but none of them could enjoy the priestly dignity in perpetuity. Aaron, the first of the line, served his people in the high priesthood throughout the wilderness wanderings; but the day came when Aaron and his son Eleazar were taken by Moses to the summit of Mount Hor. There "Moses stripped Aaron of his garments, and put them upon Eleazar his son; and Aaron died there on the top of the mountain. Then Moses and Eleazar came down from the mountain" (Num. 20:28). Later, after the settlement in the land of Canaan, Eleazar died in his turn (Josh. 24:33) and was succeeded by his son Phinehas; and so the tale went on. In generation after generation the high priest died and his office passed to another, until in all (so Josephus reckons[75]) eighty-three high priests officiated from Aaron to the fall of the Second Temple in A.D. 70. Our author has good reason for what he here says of them: "Those other priests are appointed in numerous succession, because they are prevented by death from continuing in office" (NEB).

24 "But the priesthood which Jesus holds is perpetual, because he remains for ever" (NEB). Our author, says E. K. Simpson, "has already dwelt on the perpetuity of Christ's priesthood as in keeping with the unprocessionate type of Melchizedek, and stressed its intransmissibility in the ascription of 'an indissoluble life' to the ideal Priest he is setting forth. But he now affirms that it is in its very nature unsupersedable, that finality inheres in it. The high-priestly Son, in contrast with mortal intermediaries, is described at the close of the chapter as 'perfected for evermore.' Perhaps *indefectible* would be a suitable translation. . . . In the one flawless Mediator we descry priesthood at its summit-level. His unique endowments exhaust the requisites of the office and invest it with ineffaceable validity."[76]

Here no high allegorical interpretation of the mortality of Old Testa-

---

74. As in Ex. 40:15; Num. 25:13. Cf. p. 125, n. 35.

75. *Ant.* 20.227.

76. "Vocabulary of Hebrews," pp. 187f., on the word ἀπαράβατος (see p. 171, n. 73). Simpson (p. 188) points out that "Epictetus (*Enchir.* 51) urges his pupil to let all that is best be to him a νόμος ἀπαράβατος and Josephus (*Contra Ap.* ii.41) asks what is a fairer spectacle than εὐσέβεια ἀπαράβατος; moreover, the adverb equals *without fail* in Vettius Valens."

ment priests is offered such as we find in Philo. According to him, the death of the high priest means the departure of "the most sacred Logos" from the soul of man, in consequence of which all kinds of inadvertent errors find an entrance there.[77] But to our author the death of the high priest (or of any other priest) means that he is no longer available to those who counted upon him to intercede for them with God. Of course, as long as the old order endured, a new priest was always at hand to step into the place of his predecessor, but people might feel that because of certain personal qualities which he possessed over and above the sacredness of his office, the late priest was a more effective intercessor with God than his successor could ever be. No such misgivings could be entertained with regard to the high priesthood of Christ, however. He would never have to hand it over to someone less well qualified to discharge its mediatorial functions. Those who entrusted their cause to him knew therefore that it was permanently secure in his hands.

25 Those who have Christ as their high priest and mediator with God have in him a Savior whose saving power is available without end,[78] not liable to the mischances of mortal life. He lives eternally, eternally engaged to bless and protect those who have committed themselves to him. The way of approach to God through him is a way which is always open, because in the presence of God he represents his people as "a priest for ever." He is no mediator in the ordinary sense, a go-between who places his good offices at the disposal of two parties in the hope of bringing them to agreement. He is the unique Mediator between God and mankind because he combines Godhead and manhood perfectly in his own person; in him God draws near to men and women and in him men and women may draw near to God, with the assurance of constant and immediate access.

What is our Lord's special function as his people's high priest with God, apart from ensuring their never-failing acceptance before God? In 2:17f. we have been told that he became high priest to make atonement for his people's sins and strengthen them in temptation; in 4:15f. we have been told that he sympathizes with their weakness and supplies the mercy and grace to help them in time of need. Here his high-priestly function is summed up in terms of intercession: "he lives continuously to intercede for them." The intercessory work of Christ at the right hand of God is not a doctrine peculiar to our author; it appears in one of Paul's great lyric outbursts:

Who shall bring any charge against God's elect?
It is God who justifies; who is to condemn?

77. *On Flight and Finding* 116f., in a discussion of Num. 35:25, where the unintentional homicide stays in the city of refuge until the death of the high priest.

78. Gk. εἰς τὸ παντελές, "completely" (ERV/ARV mg.), "absolutely" (NEB), "for all time" (RSV); the phrase appears in one other place in the NT (Luke 13:11).

> It is Christ Jesus who died,
> yes, who was raised from the dead,
> who is at the right hand of God,
> who indeed intercedes for us. (Rom. 8:33f.)

In these words we may trace the echo of an early Christian confession of faith, which, in addition to acknowledging the death, resurrection, and enthronement of Christ, made mention also of his intercessory ministry. We may also trace the echo of the fourth Servant Song, where the Servant of the LORD, once humbled and put to shame but now highly exalted, is said to have made, or to be making, "intercession for the transgressors."[79] This is one of the statements about the Servant which indicate that his ministry is priestly, as well as prophetic and royal.

But the teaching and action of Jesus on earth must have encouraged his disciples to recognize in him their all-prevailing intercessor. "I have prayed for you," he said to Simon Peter at the Last Supper, "that your faith may not fail; and when you have turned again, strengthen your brothers" (Luke 22:32). If it be asked what form his heavenly intercession takes, what better answer can be given than that he still does for his people at the right hand of God what he did for Peter on earth? And the prayer recorded in John 17, also belonging to the same night in which he was betrayed, is well called (after David Chytraeus) his high-priestly prayer, and (such is the affinity of mind between the Fourth Evangelist and our present author) a careful study of John 17 will help us considerably to understand what is intended here when our Lord is described as making intercession for those who come to God through him.

It is important to emphasize this, for the character of our Lord's intercession has at times been grotesquely misrepresented in popular Christian thought. He is not to be thought of "as an orante, *standing* ever before the Father with outstretched arms, like the figures in the mosaics of the catacombs, and with strong crying and tears pleading our cause in the presence of a reluctant God; but as a *throned* Priest-King, asking what he will from a Father who always hears and grants his request. Our Lord's life in heaven is his prayer."[80]

---

79. Isa. 53:12. An intercessory ministry is implied in Acts 7:56, where Stephen sees the Son of Man standing at God's right hand as his witness or advocate (cf. *Acts*, NICNT, p. 155 with n. 106). Cf. Luke 12:8, where the Son of Man confesses in heaven those who confess him on earth. Cf. p. 30.

80. H. B. Swete, *The Ascended Christ* (London, 1912), p. 95. See further G. Rupp, "The Finished Work of Christ in Word and Sacrament," in *The Finality of Christ*, ed. D. Kirkpatrick (Nashville/New York, 1966), pp. 175-92, especially pp. 187-90; P. Giles, *Jesus, the High Priest* (Bognor Regis, 1984). The significance and efficacy of our Lord's intercessory presence in heaven have never been better expressed than in Charles Wesley's hymn, "Arise, my soul, arise"—especially in the stanza:

> Five bleeding wounds he bears,
> Received on Calvary;

But our Lord's life in heaven is the life of one who has been brought back from the death which he endured when he gave himself as a sacrifice for his people's sins. In the language of the Apocalypse, it is as the Lamb once slain that he exercises world dominion from the heavenly throne (Rev. 5:6-14). The appearance in God's presence of the Crucified One constitutes his perpetual and prevalent intercession. His once-completed self-offering is utterly acceptable and efficacious; his contact with the Father is immediate and unbroken; his priestly ministry on his people's behalf is never ending, and therefore the salvation which he secures to them is absolute.

G. SUPERIOR BECAUSE OF THE CHARACTER OF JESUS (7:26-28)

26 *A high priest like this, in fact, suited our case: one who is holy, free from guile and defilement, separated from sinners, exalted high above the heavens.*[81]

27 *He is under no daily necessity, like those high priests, to offer sacrifices first for his own sins and then for those of the people: he did the latter once for all*[82] *when he offered up himself.*

28 *The law appoints as high priests*[83] *men who are subject to frailty, but the sworn word which was spoken after the law appoints one who is Son, one who has been made perfect for ever.*

26 But whatever other reasons may be adduced to demonstrate the superiority of the new priesthood, there is one final argument. The new priesthood is better because the new priest is Jesus. Jesus, who endured sore temptations

---

They pour effectual prayers,
  They strongly speak for me:
"Forgive him, O forgive," they cry,
"Nor let that ransomed sinner die!"

81. These words have the solemn style of a cultic hymn; O. Michel suggests that in "such a high priest became us, / holy, guileless, undefiled, / separated from sinners, / made higher than the heavens" we have a quatrain from an early hymn in praise of Christ (MK, p. 177; cf. H. Windisch, HNT, p. 67). The last phrase, ὑψηλότερος τῶν οὐρανῶν γενόμενος, has been compared with words about the divine Logos in the Orphic fragment 274, 1. 34: αὐτὸς ἐπουράνιος καὶ ἐπὶ χθονὶ πάντα τελευτᾷ, "he himself being above the heavens also accomplishes all upon earth"— but these words may reflect Jewish or Christian influence; see H. Traub, *TDNT,* V, pp. 538f. (*s.v.* ἐπουράνιος); cf. A. Ehrhardt, "Goethe, Johannes und Palaiphatos," *EvTh* 30 (1960), pp. 579f., and *The Beginning* (Manchester, 1968), p. 13.

82. Gk. ἐφάπαξ (cf. 9:12; 10:10), a more emphatic form of ἅπαξ (6:4; 9:7, 26, 27, 28; 10:2; 12:26, 27), "once for all"—used repeatedly in this epistle to convey the finality and perfection of the self-offering of Christ.

83. A few authorities, including 𝔓⁴⁶ (apparently) and D, read "priests" instead of "high priests."

on earth; Jesus, who poured out his heart in earnest prayer to God; Jesus, who learned by suffering how hard the way of obedience could be; Jesus, who interceded for his disciples that their faith might not fail when the hour of testing came; Jesus, who offered up his life to God as a sin offering on their behalf—this same Jesus is the unchanging high priest and helper of all who come to God through him. "Such a high priest does indeed fit our condition" (NEB). He has the unique qualification of having experienced the full force of temptation without once yielding to it. There is no question of his fitness to appear in the presence of God; he is the Holy[84] One of God, free from all guile[85] and defilement. Philo can speak of the Logos as the ideal high priest, free from all defilement;[86] but Christians have as their high priest one who does not remain in the realm of ideas but is the incarnate Logos, one who preserved his purity while treading the common ways of this world and sharing our human lot. Although he came to earth "in the likeness of sinful flesh,"[87] lived among sinners, received sinners, ate with sinners, was known as the friend of sinners, yet he is set apart from sinners,[88] "in a different class from sinful men";[89] and is now exalted above all the heavens to share the throne of God.

27 Aaron and his successors, before they presented a sin offering on behalf of the people, had to present one for themselves. This was preeminently true on the annual Day of Atonement: before the ritual of the two goats

---

84. Gk. ὅσιος, used of Christ also in Acts 2:27; 13:35. In both these places the words of Ps. 16:10 (LXX 15:10), "Neither wilt thou suffer thy holy one to see corruption," are viewed as fulfilled in the resurrection of Christ. In the LXX ὅσιος most often represents Heb. ḥāsîd, a word which can be used both of the godly person (as in Ps. 16:10) and of God himself (as in Ps. 145 [LXX 144]:17; cf. ὅσιος in Rev. 15:4; 16:5). The Hebrew word is cognate with ḥesed ("lovingkindness," "steadfast love") and has the basic sense of "loyal to covenant obligations."

85. Gk. ἄκακος (cf. Rom. 16:18, where it has the sense, not present here, of being so guileless as to be unsuspecting and easily led astray). According to W. Grundmann, if ὅσιος denotes Christ's "religious qualification—being ὅσιος He is the true priest before God—and ἀμίαντος the cultic—no μίασμα attaches to Him to cause cultic disqualification—ἄκακος is the moral. As High-priest He is one who has done no evil. The sense here is active; ἀμίαντος expresses the passive side" (*TDNT*, III, p. 482, *s.v.* ἄκοκος).

86. Gk. ἀμίαντος, the same word as our author uses here (cf. Philo, *Special Laws* 1.113; similarly *On Flight and Finding* 108-12). But Philo is concerned to present the undefiled character of the Logos as the truth denoted allegorically by the law forbidding the high priest to touch a corpse or mourn for the dead (Lev. 21:10f.).

87. Rom. 8:3; cf. exposition by C. E. B. Cranfield, *The Epistle to the Romans*, ICC (Edinburgh, 1975), pp. 379-82.

88. Gk. κεχωρισμένος ἀπὸ τῶν ἁμαρτωλῶν. The high priest of Israel, while not personally free from sin, was ceremonially set apart from his fellows for the proper discharge of his sacred functions. But Jesus has no need to be set apart in any such ceremonial manner; his separation is, on the one hand, inward and moral, and, on the other hand, the consequence of his being now exalted to the right hand of God, withdrawn from the midst of a sinful world.

89. W. Manson, *The Epistle to the Hebrews* (London, 1951), pp. 116f.

was enacted, to cleanse the nation from the accumulated sin of the past twelve months, the direction ran: "Aaron shall offer the bull as a sin offering for himself, and shall make atonement for himself and for his house" (Lev. 16:6). But there were other occasions on which a similar atonement had to be made: "if it is the anointed priest who sins, thus bringing guilt on the people, then let him offer for the sin which he has committed a young bull without blemish to Yahweh for a sin offering" (Lev. 4:3). This occasional sin offering may have been in our author's mind when he used the expression "daily" in this connection. There is indeed no explicit command for a daily sin offering to be presented by the high priest on his own account; but inadvertent sinning, of the kind provided for in Lev. 4:1ff., could well have been a daily hazard. And the high priest occupied a special position; an inadvertent sin on his part brought guilt on the people. It was wise therefore to take precautions against the very possibility of his having committed an inadvertent sin. According to Philo, "the high priest . . . day by day offers prayers and sacrifices and asks for blessings . . . that every age and every part of the nation, as of a single body, may be joined harmoniously into one and same fellowship, having peace and good order as their aim."[91] But these daily or occasional sacrifices, whether offered for his own sins or for those of the people, were summed up and "raised, so to speak, to a higher power"[92] by the special ceremonies of the Day of Atonement.

But Jesus has no need to present a daily sacrifice—or, for that matter, a yearly sacrifice—for his people's sins. He presented a permanently valid sin offering on their behalf when he offered up his own life—an offering so perfect and efficacious that it needs no repetition. Still less has he any need to present such a sacrifice for himself; he is "holy, free from guile and defilement." For all the completeness of his identification with his people and his sympathetic entering into their trials and sufferings, he is personally free

---

90. Cf. 9:7 (pp. 206-08).

91. *Special Laws* 3.131; cf. his reference in *Who Is the Heir of Divine Things?* (174) to "the permanent sacrifices, both the oblation of flour which the priests offer for themselves and the oblation of two lambs which they are directed to offer on behalf of the nation." The oblation of flour which the priests were directed to offer for themselves (Lev. 6:19ff.) was not a *pro forma* sin offering, and indeed it might be inferred from the terms of the prescription that it was presented only on the day of their anointing (in that case "perpetually" in Lev. 6:20 would mean "when each new priest is anointed in his turn"). But quite clearly it came to be observed as a daily ceremony, whatever its original intention was; cf. Sir. 45:14, concerning Aaron: "His sacrifices (θυσίαι) shall be wholly burned twice every day continually" (καθ' ἡμέραν ἐνδελεχῶς δίς).

92. A. B. Davidson, *The Epistle to the Hebrews* (Edinburgh, 1882), p. 144. It is doing violence to the natural sense of the Greek to interpret it, with Westcott *(ad loc.)*, as meaning: "The characteristic High-priestly office of the Lord is fulfilled 'daily,' 'for ever,' and not only, as that of the Levitical High-priest, on one day in the year." That is true, but it is not what our author says here. Cf. "daily" (καθ' ἡμέραν, as here) in 10:11.

from the guilt and tyranny of sin, and for that very reason is the more able to be their effective high priest. We have already been told that he "made purification for sins" (1:3), that he was appointed "to make atonement for the people's sins" (2:17), since it is the function of every high priest to "offer gifts and sacrifices for sins" (5:1). But now we are told expressly the nature of the sacrifice which our Lord offered: "he offered up himself." There is an Old Testament adumbration of such a self-offering in the portrayal of the Suffering Servant who "makes himself an offering for sin" (Isa. 53:10).[93] The martyrs of Maccabaean days yielded up their lives with the confidence that they would be accepted as an atonement on their fellow-Israelites' behalf (2 Macc. 7:37f.; 4 Macc. 6:27ff.; 17:22; 18:4);[94] and it was similarly the belief of the Qumran sectaries that their piety and privations would make expiation for the land of Israel.[95] But there is no need for our author to look for precedents to enable him to interpret the death of Jesus in terms of a voluntary sin offering; this was how Jesus himself envisaged his death. When he said that the Son of Man had come "to give his life a ransom for many" (Mark 10:45) and spoke of his covenant blood as "poured out for many" (Mark 14:24), he indicated clearly that he was presenting himself to God as a sacri-

---

93. See W. Zimmerli and J. Jeremias, *TDNT*, V, pp. 654-717 (*s.v.* παῖς θεοῦ). See further on 9:28 (p. 232 with nn. 169-72). The word translated "offering for sin" in Isa. 53:10 is Heb. *'āšām*, the reparation offering or "guilt offering" (RSV) of Lev. 5:6ff.; 7:1ff. This passage may form the OT background for Paul's statements that Jesus was sent "as an offering for sin" (Rom. 8:3) and that he was "made to be sin on our behalf" (2 Cor. 5:21); perhaps also for our Lord's own words about giving his life "a ransom for many" (Mark 10:45). On the relation of the Isaianic Servant of the Lord to Jesus see *Acts*, NICNT, pp. 174-76 with nn. 66-70.

94. See M. de Jonge, "Jesus' Death for Others and the Death of the Maccabean Martyrs," in *Text and Testimony: Essays in Honour of A. F. J. Klijn*, ed. T. Baarda and others (Kampen, 1988), pp. 142-51. In his article "The Background of Mark 10:45," in *New Testament Essays: Studies in Memory of T. W. Manson*, ed. A. J. B. Higgins (Manchester, 1959), pp. 1-18, C. K. Barrett quotes these passages from 2 and 4 Maccabees as containing the doctrine of *kappārāh*, and suggests that a creative mind working upon such a background as these passages provide could produce a saying like that recorded in Mark 10:45. He concludes also "that the connection between Mark 10:45 and Isa. 53 is much less definite and more tenuous than is often supposed" (p. 15). It is indeed an exaggeration of that connection to speak and write, as some have done, as though Mark 10:45 were practically a quotation from Isa. 53. But Jesus and the Evangelists certainly knew and were influenced by the book of Isaiah; there is little if any evidence for their acquaintance with 2 and 4 Maccabees. Moreover, that the Son of Man "should suffer many things and be treated with contempt" is something which is *written* (Mark 9:12; cf. 14:21). This expression implies canonical Scripture; Isa. 52:13–53:12 will satisfy the terms of reference, but scarcely the martyrologies of Maccabees. True, when Jesus spoke of his life as being λύτρον ἀντὶ πολλῶν he did not say so simply because this was written "in the volume of the book" but because it was his own fixed purpose and ardent desire in accordance with what he knew to be God's will. Indeed, it may be held, not only did he by his acceptance of the death of the cross fulfil the prophecy of Isa. 52:13–53:12 but he knew that he was fulfilling it.

95. Cf. 1QS 3.6-12; 4.20f.; 5.6f.; 9.3-5; see F. F. Bruce, *Biblical Exegesis in the Qumran Texts* (London, 1960), pp. 57-63. Cf. p. 193 with n. 66; pp. 209f., n. 63.

fice for others. And when the hour came and he was stretched upon the cross, instead of having his heart filled with bitter resentment against his executioners or with feelings of reproach against God for allowing this to happen to him, he offered up his life to God as a sin offering in his people's stead. How acceptable to God this sacrifice was, or how effective in the purifying of heart and life, let those bear witness who have found through faith in him that peace with God and release from sin which nothing else could have brought about.[96]

28 Under the ancient law, as we have already been told, the high priest is "beset by frailty, because of which he must bring a sin offering for himself as well as for the people" (5:2f.). But the divine acclamation, given under oath, of a new and perpetual priesthood after Melchizedek's order, was designed to supersede the earlier priesthood established by the law. This supersession came into effect when the Messiah appeared and vindicated his high-priestly title on the basis of a perfect sacrifice. Fully equipped to discharge an intercessory ministry at the right hand of God, this is no high priest subject to all the conditions of earthly frailty; this is the one whom God addresses as Son, whose high priesthood is absolutely efficacious[97] and eternally suited to meet his people's need.[98]

---

96. The self-offering of Christ, as Priest and Sacrifice, Victor and Victim, in one, is further elaborated in 9:11-14; 10:5-14.

97. This is the sense of his being "perfected" (τετελειωμένον); cf. 2:10; 5:9.

98. As in 5:5f., our author brings together Ps. 2:7 and 110:4 (LXX 109:4) in the collocation of the words "Son . . . for evermore" (Gk. υἱὸν εἰς τὸν αἰῶνα). For the anarthrous "Son" cf. Heb. 1:2; 5:8.

HEBREWS 8

V. COVENANT, SANCTUARY, AND SACRIFICE (8:1–10:18)

A. PRIESTHOOD AND PROMISE (8:1-7)

1 *This is the sum of our argument thus far:*[1] *this is the kind of high priest we have—one who has taken his seat at the right hand of the throne of the Majesty in heaven,*[2]

2 *a minister of the sanctuary,*[3] *that is, of the true tent, pitched by the Lord,*[4] *not by any human hand.*

1. Or, "Now to sum up what we are saying" (ARV mg.). Moffatt *(ad loc.)* aptly refers to Coverdale's rendering: "Of the thinges which we haue spoken, this is the pyth." The question is whether κεφάλαιον should be understood here as meaning "chief point" (so in the classical writers and Philo) or "sum," "summary" (Coverdale's "pith"). The former rendering is preferred by the RSV and the NEB. But our author may feel that his argument about the superiority of the Melchizedek priesthood has been too involved for some of his readers to follow, so he sums it up by saying: "What all this amounts to, what it all leads up to, is this: it is a high priest of this superior order and quality that we have." W. Manson, on the other hand, thinks that the rendering "point," or even "sum" or "gist," "throws us too much back on the past course of the argument, and fails to bring out the transcendent character of the vista which here opens to our eyes"; he offers the paraphrase "to crown the argument"—which certainly does justice to the preposition in the phrase ἐπὶ τοῖς λεγομένοις (*The Epistle to the Hebrews* [London, 1951], p. 123).

2. "The Majesty in heaven" (Gk. ἡ μεγαλωσύνη ἐν τοῖς οὐρανοῖς) is a reverential periphrasis for the name of God, like "the Majesty on high" in 1:3. (See p. 49, n. 33.) The expression used here is fuller than that in 1:3 because of the addition of "the throne" between "right hand" and the surrogate for the divine name; for the fuller expression cf. also 12:2 ("the right hand of the throne of God").

3. Gk. τῶν ἁγίων λειτουργός, which might equally well be rendered "a minister of the holy things"; the principal reason for preferring the rendering "sanctuary" is that this is the regular sense of the neuter plural (τὰ) ἅγια in this epistle (cf. 9:2, 8, 12, 24, 25; 10:19; 13:11). The substantive λειτουργός (which refers to angels in 1:7) is used in Rom. 13:6 of civil rulers as servants of God, in Rom. 15:16 of Paul in his apostleship to the Gentiles, in Phil. 2:25 of Epaphroditus ministering to Paul's need as the Philippian church's representative; in the LXX the verb λειτουργέω and the *nomen actionis* λειτουργία (cf. v. 6) are frequently used in the Pentateuch of the ministration of the priests and Levites in the wilderness tabernacle.

4. Gk. ἣν ἔπηξεν ὁ κύριος, an echo of Num. 24:6, LXX, where Balaam describes the Israelite encampment as being "like tents which the Lord pitched" (ὡσεὶ σκηναὶ ἃς ἔπηξεν κύριος).

3 *Every high priest is appointed[5] to offer gifts and sacrifices;[6] therefore this one also must have had an offering to make.*

4 *Now if[7] he were on earth, he would not be a priest at all, seeing that according to the law there are already those who offer[8] the (prescribed) gifts.*

5 *The place where they minister is a shadow and copy of the heavenly reality, as the oracle said to Moses[9] when he was about to erect[10] the tent: "See to it," said God, "that you make everything according to the pattern which was shown you on the mountain."[11]*

6 *But as it is, Christ has received[12] a better ministry,[13] inasmuch as he is mediator of a better covenant, enacted[14] on the basis of better promises.*

7 *For if the first covenant had been faultless, no place would have been sought for a second one.[15]*

1-2 Having established the superiority of the high priesthood of Christ, our author now proceeds to relate his high priesthood to the themes of covenant, sanctuary, and sacrifice, with which the Aaronic priesthood was closely bound up. As the Aaronic priesthood gives place to the priesthood after the order of Melchizedek, so the old covenant gives place to the new, the earthly sanctuary gives place to the heavenly, and sacrifices which were but temporary tokens give place to one which is effective and of eternal validity. "To crown the argument," then, the great high priest whom Christians have

5. Gk. καθίσταται, as in 5:1 (cf. p. 118, n. 1).

6. The "gifts and sacrifices" (δῶρά τε καὶ θυσίαι) are not distinguished here any more than they are in 5:1 (see p. 118).

7. Gk. εἰ μὲν οὖν, for which K L with the majority of later MSS and TR have εἰ μὲν γάρ (whence AV/KJV "For if . . .").

8. Gk. ὄντων τῶν προσφερόντων. K L, with the majority of later MSS, the Peshiṭta, and the TR, add ἱερέων after ὄντων (whence AV/KJV, "seeing that there are priests that offer . . .").

9. Gk. κεχρημάτισται Μωϋσῆς. Cf. Heb. 11:7; 12:25; Matt. 2:12, 22; Luke 2:26; Acts 10:22 for χρηματίζω meaning "give a divine oracle" (cf. also χρηματισμός in Rom. 11:4). The perfect tense probably implies that the oracle, once given, now stands on permanent record (compare the perfects εἴρηκεν, γέγραπται, used to introduce OT quotations, e.g., in Heb. 4:4; 10:7).

10. Gk. ἐπιτελεῖν (ARV mg., "complete").

11. Ex. 25:40, LXX. Here πάντα, "all things," is added to the LXX text (as in Philo, *Leg. Alleg.* 3.102); LXX Cod. F (Ambrosianus), which includes πάντα, is probably influenced by the text of our present passage. This quotation has the aorist participle δειχθέντα as against the perfect δεδειγμένον of the LXX.

12. Gk. τέτυχεν (𝔭46 ℵ* A D* K L and 9 minuscules), for which B and many Byzantine witnesses have τέτευχεν, and P Ψ 33 1739 and many other minuscules τετύχηκεν (see G. Zuntz, *The Text of the Epistles* [London, 1953], pp. 119f.).

13. Gk. λειτουργία. Cf. p. 180, n. 3.

14. Gk. νενομοθέτηται. Cf. 7:11 (p. 164, n. 36), where the subject of the verb (in the passive, as here) is "the people."

15. Gk. δευτέρας, for which B* reads ἑτέρας ("another"), a reading "unbelievable in the context," according to Zuntz (*Text*, p. 41).

is one who is enthroned at the right hand of God, who discharges his ministry in no earthly shrine but in the heavenly dwelling-place of God, a tabernacle pitched by no human hands.[16] By contrast with all material sanctuaries, this one is called the true or "real[17] sanctuary" (NEB), the only one which is not an imitation of something better than itself, the only one whose durability comes anywhere near to matching the eternity of the living and true God whose dwelling-place it is. This "real sanctuary" belongs to the same order of being as the saints' everlasting rest of chs. 3 and 4, the better country and well-founded city of 11:10, 16, the unshakable kingdom of 12:28. What its essential character is will appear more clearly in the course of our exposition.[18]

3 But if Jesus ministers as high priest in this authentic sanctuary, what is the nature of his ministry? A high priest, as has been said before (5:1), is appointed to present "gifts and sacrifices for sins";[19] therefore this high priest must also have something to offer. The nature of his offering, however, is not stated until 9:14 (although it has been mentioned already in 7:27), because in the meantime there are further points of contrast between the old order of worship and the new which have to be elucidated. In passing we may note that it is not implied that Jesus is continually or repeatedly presenting his offering; this is excluded by 7:27, which contrasts the daily sacrifices of the Aaronic high priests with the offering which the Christians' high priest has already presented once for all. The tense and mood of the Greek verb "to offer" in this clause also exclude the idea of a continual offering;[20] indeed, the NEB suggests in a footnote a rendering which would make the situation

---

16. Cf. 9:11, 24. In early Christian usage "not made with hands" (ἀχειροποίητος, or an equivalent phrase), as distinct from "made with hands" (χειροποίητος, or an equivalent phrase), is used to distinguish the new order inaugurated by Christ from all earlier religious entities, whether objects of worship (Acts 19:26), sacred buildings (Mark 14:58; Acts 7:48; 17:24), ordinances (e.g., circumcision, as in Col. 2:11; Eph. 2:11), the resurrection body as distinct from the body of flesh and blood (2 Cor. 5:1).

17. Gk. ἀληθινός. Cf. 9:24 (and 10:22, which is not such an apt parallel). While the classical distinction is that ἀληθής means "true" as opposed to "false," and ἀληθινός "real" as opposed to merely "apparent," it would be precarious to press this distinction in the NT, as a comparison of the two adjectives in John's Gospel will show. In this epistle ἀληθής is not found. As God himself is real—τὸν μόνον ἀληθινὸν θεόν of John 17:3 (cf. Paul's solitary use of ἀληθινός, in relation to God, in 1 Thess. 1:9)—so other entities are real insofar as they are associated with his reality.

18. Cf. especially 10:19-25 (pp. 249-60); 12:22-24 (pp. 355-61).

19. The additional phrase "for sins" (cf. p. 118, n. 3) is missing here; but it is our Lord's presenting of himself as a sin offering that our author has principally in mind (cf. 1:3; 7:27).

20. The infinitive "to offer" at the end of v. 3 (unlike the identical phrase in the first clause of the verse, which represents Gk. εἰς τὸ προσφέρειν), renders the adjective clause ὃ προσενέγκῃ with its antecedent τι ("something"). The fact that προσενέγκῃ is aorist (subjunctive) is consistent with our author's repeated emphasis on the singularity of the sacrifice which Christ offered (cf. 7:27; 10:12).

completely unambiguous: "this one too must have had something to offer."[21] It is a pity that the nuance of meaning here should be obscured in a well-known and generally admirable private version which renders the passage: "It follows, therefore, that in these holy places this man has something that he is offering."[22]

4 That Jesus' high-priestly ministry must be exercised in the heavenly sanctuary is further shown by the fact that there would be no room for him to exercise it in the earthly sanctuary. In the earthly sanctuary, whether we think of the earlier tent-shrine or the later temple in Jerusalem, the high priesthood was confined to one family; and far from belonging to that family, Jesus did not even belong to the tribe from which it came.[23] On earth Jesus was a layman, excluded by the law from all priestly functions. The "Rightful Teacher" of the Qumran community was a priest,[24] even if for one reason or another he was excluded from performing priestly functions in the Jerusalem temple; but the founder of Christianity was not, and the Essenes would no more have looked upon him as a priest than the Jerusalem hierarchy did. But to our author, this simply emphasizes the dignity of Jesus' high priesthood; for a high priesthood exercised in any earthly shrine is far inferior to that heavenly high priesthood which depends for its exercise on a perfect sacrifice offered once for all and consequent admission to the sanctuary above.

5 For the earthly sanctuary from the outset was designed to be nothing more than a "copy[25] and shadow"[26] of the heavenly reality. This is how our author understands the divine injunction to Moses, regarding the details

---

21. Gk. ἀναγκαῖον ἔχειν τι καὶ τοῦτον ὃ προσενέγκῃ. The verb "to be" is not expressed here with the adjective "necessary" (ἀναγκαῖον); this is indicated in the AV/KJV (but not in the ERV/ARV) by the italicization of "*it is.*" One might therefore translate "it was necessary" as readily as "it is necessary" ("it was necessary" referring to the once-for-all self-offering of Calvary).

22. J. B. Phillips, *Letters to Young Churches* (London, 1947), p. 170; *The New Testament in Modern English* (London, 1958), *ad loc.* But Phillips cannot be charged with any ulterior motive in so translating. (The wording was corrected to "something to offer" in the revised edition of 1972.)

23. Cf. 7:14.

24. Cf. 1QpHab 2.6-10, where "the priest into whose heart God has put wisdom to interpret all the words of his servants the prophets" is probably the Rightful Teacher.

25. Gk. ὑπόδειγμα, used in 9:23 in a similar sense to this, and in 4:11 in the sense of a moral example (so also in all its other NT occurrences, John 13:15; Jas. 5:10; 2 Pet. 2:6). In Ezek. 42:15 (LXX) the prophet's angel-guide is said to have "measured the plan (ὑπόδειγμα) of the house [the temple of the new commonwealth] round about in order." In Attic Greek παράδειγμα was preferred to ὑπόδειγμα, but whereas here it is the earthly copies of the heavenly realities that are the ὑποδείγματα, in Attic Greek the heavenly exemplars themselves are called the παραδείγματα (cf. pp. 184f., n. 32). Cf. T. F. Torrance, *Royal Priesthood* (Edinburgh, 1955), pp. 20f.

26. Gk. σκιά (cf. 10:1 and see pp. 184f., n. 32).

of the tabernacle in the wilderness: "And see that you make them after the pattern for them,[27] which is being shown you on the mountain" (Ex. 25:40). This "pattern" (referred to also in Ex. 25:9; 26:30; 27:8) was something visible;[28] it did not consist merely of the verbal directions of Ex. 25–30. It may have been a model for which the verbal directions served as a commentary; it may have been the heavenly dwelling-place of God which Moses was permitted to see.[29] The tabernacle was intended to serve as a dwelling-place for God in the midst of his people on earth, and it would be completely in keeping with current practice that such an earthly dwelling-place should be a replica of God's heavenly dwelling-place.[30] This, of course, is how our author understands the situation. The high priests of Aaron's line ministered[31] in the earthly sanctuary; Jesus exercises his high-priestly ministry in the heavenly sanctuary, of which the earthly one was but a replica. There is indeed some affinity with Platonic idealism here, but it is our author's language, and not his essential thought, that exhibits such affinity. For him, the relation between the two sanctuaries is basically a temporal one. If the earthly sanctuary is a "shadow" of the heavenly, it is because the whole Levitical order *fore-shadowed* the spiritual order of the new age. Here as in 10:1 the old order has "a shadow of the good things to come."[32]

---

27. Gk. τύπος, rendering Heb. *tabnît* ("building," "construction"); the implication is that Moses was shown something like a scale model of the sanctuary which was to be erected.

28. In the Hebrew text of Ex. 25:40 the phrase "which is being shown you" means literally "which you are caused to see" (*'ăšer 'attāh mor'eh*, where *mor'eh* is the Hoph'al participle of *rā'āh*, "see").

29. Cf. F. M. Cross, Jr.: "Probably the conception of the *tabnîth*, the 'model' (Exodus 25:9), also goes back ultimately to the idea that the earthly sanctuary is the counterpart of the heavenly dwelling of a deity" ("The Tabernacle," *BA* 10 [1947], pp. 45-68, esp. p. 62). In Wisdom 9:8 Solomon's temple is "a copy (μίμημα) of the holy tent which thou didst prepare from the beginning." (Cf. 1 Chron. 28:19.) See also G. E. Wright, "The Temple in Palestine and Syria," *BA* 7 (1944), pp. 66-88.

30. As early as the Babylonian *Enuma elish* there is a heavenly *ubšukkinaku* or "court of assembly" corresponding to the earthly temple (3.61, 119, 131). Cf. W. F. Albright, *Archaeology and the Religion of Israel* (Baltimore, ³1953), pp. 142ff. (where cosmic significance is attached to the pillars, sea, altar-base, etc., of the temples of Solomon and Ezekiel); also p. 88, for the point that in Phoenician "it would seem that the words *bêtu*, 'house,' and *hêkalu*, 'temple,' refer both to a residence in heaven and to temples on earth." The antiquity of the cosmic interpretation of the tabernacle and temple is illustrated by its appearance in Josephus (*Ant.* 3.123; *War* 5.212f.); cf. 2 Baruch 4:2-7; *Ascension of Isaiah* 7:10. See also E. Burrows, "Some Cosmological Patterns in Babylonian Religion," in *The Labyrinth*, ed. S. H. Hooke (London, 1935), pp. 45ff., especially 59ff.; R. E. Clements, *God and Temple* (Oxford, 1965). On the other hand, R. de Vaux expresses considerable skepticism with regard to the cosmic symbolism of the sanctuary in Israel (*Ancient Israel,* E.T. [London, 1961], pp. 328f.). See 12:22 (pp. 355-58).

31. Gk. λατρεύω, preeminently of worship or priestly service (cf. 9:9, 14; 10:2; 12:28; 13:10, with the related substantive λατρεία in 9:1, 6).

32. Cf. Paul's description of the Jewish laws regarding food and festivals as "only a shadow of what is to come; but the substance belongs to Christ" (Col. 2:17). This is a different

How the pattern which Moses saw on Mount Sinai could be handled by a thoroughgoing Platonist is seen in Philo's treatment of the Exodus passage: Moses "saw with the soul's eye the immaterial forms ('ideas') of the material objects which were about to be made, and in accordance with these forms copies perceptible to the senses had to be reproduced, as from an archetypal drawing and patterns conceived in the mind."[33] Moses, in other words, was enabled to grasp with his mind the invisible "ideas" laid up eternally in the "place above the heavens"[34] (much as Plato envisaged a pattern of his republic laid up in heaven, so that it was a matter of minor importance whether an earthly copy of it ever came into existence or not),[35] and commanded to give material expression to these "ideas" in a tabernacle on earth.

6 It is, then, in no earthly replica of the heavenly dwelling-place of God that Jesus ministers as his people's high priest, but in the heavenly dwelling-place itself; his ministry accordingly is far superior to any earthly ministry. And it is superior besides because of the superiority of the covenant in the power of which it is exercised—the covenant of which Jesus is himself the Mediator. He has already been called, in passing, the "guarantor of a better covenant" (7:22); the present description of him as "mediator of a better covenant" (repeated with variations in 9:15; 12:24) "presents an instance," as E. K. Simpson says,[36] "of the profound enhancement conferred on expressions already in vogue by the Christian revelation." For, he continues, the Greek word translated "mediator"[37] is shown by the papyri to have been a common business term "in the sense of *arbitrator* or *go-between*. . . . The somewhat wider usage for any *internuntius* occasionally met with prepared the way for its loftiest connotation. Thus Moses is styled in Philo as well as by St. Paul *mesitēs,* the 'middleman' of the old covenant. But Christ is the Mediator *par excellence,* not with that merely metaphysical application by which Plutarch (*Mor.* 369) alludes to Mithras as the *mesitēs* between Ormuzd and Ahriman in Persian theosophy, but in its su-

---

use of the "shadow" concept from Philo's: he interprets the name Bezaleel as "in the shadow of God" and explains that Bezaleel constructed the copies (μιμήματα) whereas Moses constructed the exemplars (παραδείγματα); "therefore the one drew an outline as it were of shadows (οἷα σκιὰς ὑπεγράφετο), whereas the other fashioned no shadows, but the archetypal entities themselves" (*On Dreams* 1.206; cf. *Leg. Alleg.* 3.101-3). (Cf. Plotinus, *Enneads* 1.6.8.) For the conception of the earthly sanctuary as a copy of the sanctuary in heaven cf. also Rev. 11:19; 14:17; 15:5f. (in Rev. 4–7 heaven itself is the temple of God). The conception, while much earlier than Plato, lends itself to a Platonic interpretation. Cf. O. Procksch in *TDNT,* I, pp. 96f. (*s.v.* ἅγιος).

33. *Life of Moses* 2.74.

34. Gk. ὑπερουράνιος τόπος (Plato, *Phaedrus* 247c). See p. 33 with n. 136.

35. Plato, *Republic* 9.592b.

36. "The Vocabulary of the Epistle to the Hebrews," *EQ* 18 (1946), p. 188.

37. Gk. μεσίτης (once in the LXX, in Job 9:33, where Job wishes that there were such an intermediary between himself and God). See p. 152, n. 69.

preme ethical significance, typified in the 'reconciling rainbow' encircling the throne, or in the ladder of Jacob's vision conjoining sundered heaven and earth—one, to borrow a fine coinage of Tyndale, who is the perfect *Atonemaker*, conserving the interests of both parties for whom He acts. Intensely zealous that God's honour should contract no stain, this ideal Mediator, having secured that supreme end, will with equal zeal seek the offender's rescue and reclamation. Such an unique Intermediary evangelical faith recognizes in her beloved Lord."[38]

What the better promises are on which this better covenant is established will appear in the quotation from Jer. 31:31-34 which follows in vv. 8-12. For the better covenant of which our Lord is Mediator is the new covenant foretold by Jeremiah. From the words of the quotation, too, it will be possible to gather something of the meaning which the term "covenant" has in this epistle.

7 But indeed, the covenant of which Jesus is Mediator may be inferred to be a better covenant from the simple fact that it is a *new* covenant. If the old covenant had been perfect, it would not have needed to be superseded by a new one. And the new one must be better, for there would have been no point in replacing the old covenant by another no better than itself.

B. THE OLD COVENANT SUPERSEDED (8:8-13)

8 *But God, finding fault with the people, says,*[39]
    "See, the days are coming, says the Lord,
    when I will make[40] a new covenant with the house of Israel
    and the house of Judah,
9   *not like the covenant which I made with their forefathers,*
    on the day I took them by the hand to bring them out of the land of Egypt,
    for they did not continue in my covenant,
    and I disregarded them,[41] says the Lord.

---

38. Cf. pp. 173-75 (on 7:25). See also R. H. Nash, "The Notion of Mediator in Alexandrian Judaism and the Epistle to the Hebrews," *WTJ* 40 (1977-78), pp. 89-115.

39. Jer. 31:31-34 (LXX 38:31-34).

40. LXX διαθήσομαι ("I will covenant") is replaced here by συντελέσω ("I will accomplish"); in v. 10 below (as in 10:16) it is retained. In Jer. 34:8, 15 (LXX 41:8, 15) συντελεῖν διαθήκην is used of a covenant made under Zedekiah, by which Hebrew slaves were to be set free. In all these places, whatever the Greek rendering may be, the Hebrew idiom *kārat bᵉrît* (lit. "to cut a covenant") is used (cf. p. 222, n. 124).

41. LXX κἀγὼ ἠμέλησα αὐτῶν as against Heb. *wᵉ'ānōkî bā'altî bām*, "although I was a husband unto them"—or perhaps "although I was their master" (H. L. Ellison, "The Prophecy of Jeremiah," *EQ* 37 [1965], p. 23). The LXX may presuppose *gā'altî* ("I rejected") for *bā'altî*. The Peshitta follows the LXX; the Vg. follows the MT.

10   *This, then, is the covenant*[42] *I will make with the house of*
        Israel
        in days to come, says the Lord:
        I will put my laws in their mind
        and write[43] *them on their heart,*
        and I will be their God,
        and they shall be my people.
11   *Neither will each teach his neighbor,*[44]
        or each his brother, saying, 'Know the Lord';
        for they will all know me,
        from the least to the greatest of them.
12   *For I will be merciful*[45] *to their iniquities,*
        and remember their sins[46] *no more."*
13   *Now, in saying "A* new *covenant," he has made the first one old. And*
     that which is growing old and aging will soon disappear.

8-12   The speaker in this oracle of the new covenant is God: it is to him that
the repeated pronouns of the first person singular—I, me, my—refer. The
oracle itself is punctuated by the phrase "oracle of Yahweh" (here rendered
"says the Lord"). So our author, as is his custom, ignores the fact that it was
delivered through Jeremiah; the divine authorship is all that he is concerned
with. "He says" in the sentence which introduces the quotation means "God
says" (cf. 10:15, where the same oracle is introduced as the Holy Spirit's
witness); "finding fault with the people" refers to the terms in which the
oracle itself charges the Israelites with breaking God's earlier covenant.

The new covenant foretold by Jeremiah is set in contrast with the
covenant which Yahweh made with the people of Israel when he delivered
them from the land of Egypt. The ratification of that earlier covenant is recorded in Ex. 24:1-8, a passage to which specific reference is made in 9:18-
20.[47] At that time, as Jeremiah on a previous occasion reminded his hearers,
the essence of God's covenant with Israel was: "Obey my voice, and I will
be your God, and you shall be my people; and walk in all the way that I command you, that it may be well with you" (Jer. 7:23). But his commandment

---

42. Codd. A D Ψ have "this is my covenant."

43. Gk. ἐπιγράψω ("I will inscribe"), for which 𝔭⁴⁶ B Ψ have the simple verb γράψω ("I
will write").

44. Gk. πολίτην, for which P 1912 with the Latin versions, the margin of the Harclean
Syriac, and the TR have πλησίον (AV "neighbour"), by way of assimilation to the sense of the
Hebrew text.

45. Gk. ἵλεως ἔσομαι, translating Heb. *'eslaḥ,* "I will forgive."

46. A D and the bulk of later manuscripts, followed by the TR, insert καὶ τῶν ἀνομιῶν
αὐτῶν after τῶν ἁμαρτιῶν αὐτῶν (cf. AV/KJV "their sins and their iniquities will I remember no
more"), following the homiletic expansion of 10:17.

47. See pp. 224-26.

was disregarded; his charge against his people, reiterated in Jeremiah's day, was: "But they did not obey or incline their ear, but walked in their own counsels and the stubbornness of their evil heart,[48] and went backward and not forward. From the day that your fathers came out of the land of Egypt to this day, I have persistently sent all my servants the prophets, day after day; yet they did not listen to me, or incline their ear, but stiffened their neck. They did worse than their fathers" (Jer. 7:24-26).

Prophet after prophet came to Israel and Judah, recalling the people to their covenant loyalty; Jeremiah himself was no exception. "Hear the words of this covenant, and do them," was his call (Jer. 11:6); and with that call went the assurance that the blessings attached to the keeping of the covenant would still be theirs if they were obedient, while persistent disobedience to it would bring a curse upon them as it had done upon their fathers.

The covenant theme was all the more topical in Jeremiah's day because of the solemn covenant which had been made by the king and the leaders of the nation in the eighteenth year of Josiah. The discovery by Hilkiah the priest of "the book of the law"—probably the law of Deuteronomy[49]—in the temple in that year (621 B.C.) was followed by a solemn act of national repentance and rededication. The newly discovered lawbook was read at a great gathering in the temple, "and the king stood by the pillar and made a covenant before Yahweh, to walk after Yahweh and to keep his commandments and his testimonies and his statutes, with all his heart and all his soul, to perform the words of this covenant that were written in this book: and all the people joined in the covenant" (2 Kings 23:3).

The king's repentance and covenant were genuine enough; but the others who took part in this ceremony and in the accompanying reformation of national religion did so largely by way of conforming to the royal will. Jeremiah was quick to perceive this, and to recognize that there was no ground for expecting this covenant to be kept any more than the covenant of Deut. 29:1 of which it was essentially a reaffirmation. Jeremiah's attitude and relation to King Josiah's covenant and reformation have often been discussed;[50] but there is very little in his recorded words that can be interpreted as a direct reference to these events, apart from the damning indictment of

---

48. Heb. *šᵉrîrût libbām (hārā')*, a characteristic Jeremianic phrase (elsewhere in the OT only in Deut. 29:29 and Ps. 81:12), used of those who disregard the divine covenant; found also repeatedly in the Qumran texts, e.g., CD 3.5, etc., in the context of the new covenant established "in the land of Damascus." Cf. p. 350, n. 107.

49. A view expressed as early as Jerome (*Commentary on Ezekiel* 1:1).

50. Cf. J. Skinner, *Prophecy and Religion* (Cambridge, 1922), pp. 89-107; G. A. Smith, *Jeremiah* (London, ⁴1929), pp. 134-61; H. H. Rowley, "The Prophet Jeremiah and the Book of Deuteronomy," in *Studies in Old Testament Prophecy presented to T. H. Robinson*, ed. H. H. Rowley (Edinburgh, 1950), pp. 157-74; W. Rudolph, *Jeremia*², HAT (Tübingen, 1958), p. 73; J. Bright, *Jeremiah*, AB (Garden City, NY, 1965), pp. xci-xcvi.

Jer. 3:10, where a divine oracle, explicitly uttered "in the days of Josiah the king," reprobates the kingdom of Judah for not taking warning from the fate of its sister-nation Israel: "for all this her false sister Judah did not return to me with her whole heart, but in pretence, says Yahweh." "I do not doubt," says H. L. Ellison, "that the first impulse of Jeremiah's heart was to leap with joy, when the news of a clean sweep of all heathenism was first received. But as a prophet, viewing it from God's standpoint, he could see that it never had any chance of success. It was not that it stayed superficial; there never was any question of its being anything else."[51] No reaffirmation of the Deuteronomic covenant, or even of that earlier covenant made on the morrow of the Israelites' escape from Egypt, could meet the situation. A new covenant, new in character as well as in time, was called for, and such a new covenant Jeremiah proclaimed.

We do not stay to argue that the oracle of the new covenant is an authentic utterance of Jeremiah[52]—although, to be sure, the identity of the prophet through whom these words of God were spoken would probably have been a matter of small importance to the author of this epistle. It is precisely in Jeremiah's prophetic ministry that the oracle finds its proper life-setting. The days were dark; national life was in collapse; it was "the time of Jacob's trouble" (Jer. 30:7).[53] But the people's life would be reconstituted on a new basis, and a new relationship between them and their God would be brought into being. This new relationship would involve three things in particular: (a) the implanting of God's law[54] in their hearts; (b) the knowledge of God as a matter of personal experience; (c) the blotting out of their sins.

(a)   The implanting of God's law in their hearts means much more than their committing of it to memory. Ample provision for memorizing it had already been made in the prescriptions of Deuteronomy: "these words which I command you this day shall be upon your heart; and you shall teach

---

51. "The Prophecy of Jeremiah," *EQ* 34 (1962), p. 162.

52. Its authenticity was denied by B. Duhm, on the ground that there is nothing here worthy of Jeremiah—that this "new covenant" does not go beyond that of Deuteronomy, and that even the promise that Israel and Judah would know it by heart does not add anything to the provision for memorizing the ancient law laid down in Deut. 6:6ff. (*Das Buch Jeremia Erklärt* [Tübingen/Leipzig, 1901], pp. 36ff.); for its authenticity cf. J. Skinner, *Prophecy,* pp. 325-34; G. A. Smith, *Jeremiah,* pp. 374-80; J. A. Bewer, *The Prophets* (New York/London, 1955), p. 260 ("Its Jeremian authorship has been validated over against critical doubts"); J. Bright, *Jeremiah,* p. 287 ("its authenticity . . . ought never to have been questioned . . . it represents what might well be considered the high point of his [Jeremiah's] theology").

53. G. A. Smith may be right in dating the oracle in the brief period of Gedaliah's governorship at Mizpah (*Jeremiah,* pp. 292f.).

54. The original wording of Jer. 31:33 is: "I will put my *tôrāh* within them." Heb. *tôrāh* means more than statutory law; it embraces the ideas of guidance, direction, and instruction. The NT fulfilment of this promise is nowhere better expressed than in Paul's words in Rom. 8:1-4 of the work of the indwelling Spirit of God in the believer.

them diligently to your children, and shall talk of them when you sit in your house, and when you walk by the way, and when you lie down, and when you rise. And you shall bind them as a sign upon your hand, and they shall be as frontlets between your eyes. And you shall write them on the door-posts of your house and on your gates" (Deut. 6:6-9). Even the memorizing of the law of God does not guarantee the performance of what has been memorized. Jeremiah's words imply the receiving of a new heart by the people—as is expressly promised in the parallel prophecy of his younger contemporary Ezekiel: "I will give them one heart, and put a new spirit within them; I will take the stony heart out of their flesh and give them a heart of flesh, that they may walk in my statutes and keep my ordinances and obey them; and they shall be my people, and I will be their God" (Ezek. 11:19f.; cf. 36:26f.). When first they heard the covenant-law they said: "All that Yahweh has spoken we will do, and we will be obedient" (Ex. 24:7). But they did not have the moral power to match their good intention. Hence the necessity arose of repeatedly returning to their God and his covenant, only to turn aside to their own ways once again. The defect did not lie in the covenant-law; it was good in itself but, to borrow Paul's language, "it was weakened by the flesh" (Rom. 8:3)— by the inadequacy of the human material which it had to work upon. What was needed was a new nature, a heart liberated from its bondage to sin, a heart which not only spontaneously knew and loved the will of God but had the power to do it.

The new covenant was a new one in that it could impart this new heart. It was not new in regard to its own substance: "I will be their God, and they shall be my people," quoted here from Jer. 31:33, was the substance of the covenant of Moses' day. "I will take you for my people, and I will be your God" was God's promise to the Israelites while they were still in Egypt (Ex. 6:7); "I ... will be your God, and you shall be my people" was his promise to them when he had given them his law in the wilderness (Lev. 26:12), a promise taken up and applied in apostolic days to the people of the new covenant (2 Cor. 6:16).[55] And in the New Testament Apocalypse, when a new heaven and earth come into being, and God's dwelling-place is established with his people, the ancient covenant-promise is repeated: "they shall be his peoples,[56] and God himself shall be with them [and be their God]" (Rev. 21:3). But while the "formula" of the covenant remains the same from age to age, it is capable of being filled with fresh meaning to a point where it can be described as a *new* covenant. "I will be your God" acquires fuller meaning with every further revelation of the character of God; "you shall be

---

55. Cf. Ex. 29:45; Jer. 7:23; 30:22; Ezek. 11:20; Hos. 2:23; Zech. 8:8; 13:9.

56. Note the plural (Gk. λαοί); for in the event the new covenant is not restricted to Israel and Judah.

my people" acquires deeper significance as the will of God for his people is more completely known.

(b)   The knowledge of God as a matter of personal experience is evidently regarded in Jeremiah's oracle as something beyond what the old covenant provided. There was a sense in which the people of Israel knew their God, because he had revealed himself to them, by contrast with the nations which did not know him; but even Israel tended to forget him.[57] Thus, when the generation which entered Canaan under Joshua died out, "there arose another generation after them, who did not know Yahweh, nor yet the work which he had done for Israel" (Judg. 2:10). At a later date, the prophet Hosea lamented the fact that there was no "knowledge of God in the land" of Israel and that disaster was fast overtaking the people on this account (Hos. 4:1, 6); "knowledge of God," which was closely coupled with covenant-loyalty, was the one thing needful, more desirable in God's sight than the costliest burnt offerings (Hos. 6:6). Jeremiah himself, in his tribute to King Josiah as one who did "justice and righteousness" and "judged the cause of the poor and needy," equates such behavior with the knowledge of God (Jer. 22:15f.). Josiah was a king, that is to say, who was mindful of his covenanted obligations. But now it is not simply a national acknowledgment of God and his covenant that is envisaged, nor yet such acknowledgment on the part of those in positions of high responsibility. It is a personal knowledge of God such as marked Jeremiah himself, a personal knowledge of God to be possessed by each individual member of the covenant community, because of the new heart received by each. Such knowledge of him by whom they are known, increasing until it attains its consummation in knowing even as they are known,[58] is of the essence of that "perfection" to which our author invites his readers to press forward.

(c)   The blotting out of his people's sins is essential to this new relationship into which God calls them with himself.[59] This indeed was not a novel idea when Jeremiah proclaimed it: the God of Israel was incomparably a pardoning God, passing over transgression, unwilling to retain his anger, delighting in loving-kindness, treading his people's iniquities underfoot, casting all their sins into the depths of the sea.[60] These are the words of Micah,

57. In the OT knowledge of God frequently connotes acknowledgment of his holiness and obedience to his will. When it is said (1 Sam. 3:7) that "Samuel did not yet know Yahweh," the reason is simply that he had not yet revealed himself to Samuel; but when it is said (1 Sam. 2:12) that the sons of Eli "did not know Yahweh," it is a reflection on their character and conduct: as the RSV has it, "they had no regard for the LORD."

58. Cf. Gal. 4:9 ("now that you have come to know God, or rather to be known by God"); 1 Cor. 8:3 ("but if one loves God, one is known by him"); 13:12 ("now I know in part; then I shall understand fully, even as I have been fully understood").

59. Cf. Isa. 43:25; 44:22.

60. Mic. 7:18f.

a century and more before the time of Jeremiah; but the idea was not original with Micah. When the God of Israel proclaimed his "name" in the ears of Moses, this note of forgiveness was emphasized, alongside the note of retribution for the impenitent: "Yahweh, a God merciful and gracious, slow to anger, and abounding in lovingkindness and truth; keeping lovingkindness for thousands, forgiving iniquity and transgression and sin; but who will by no means clear the guilty, visiting the iniquity of the fathers upon the children and the children's children, to the third and the fourth generation" (Ex. 34:6f.). But now the assurance of forgiveness of sins is written into the very terms of the covenant in the most unqualified fashion: "I will forgive their iniquity, and I will remember their sin no more." For the Hebrew, "remembering" was more than a mental effort; it carried with it the thought of doing something to the advantage, or disadvantage, of the person remembered.[61] When Cornelius's prayers and alms ascended as a memorial before God, God took action to Cornelius's advantage and sent his servant to him with a message which brought salvation to him and his household (Acts 10:4, 31; 11:13f.). When, on the other hand, "Babylon the great was remembered in the sight of God," it was "to make her drain the wine-cup of the fury of his wrath" (Rev. 16:19; cf. 18:5). If people's sins are remembered by God, his holiness must take action against them; if they are not remembered, it is because his grace has determined to forgive them—not in spite of his holiness, but in harmony with it. Under the old sacrificial system, there was "an annual reminder of sins" (Heb. 10:3); if there is no such recalling of sins to mind under the new covenant, it is because of a sacrifice offered up once for all (7:27).

Here, then, are the "better promises" on which the new covenant is established: (a) "I will put my laws in their mind"; (b) "they will all know me"; (c) "I will remember their sins no more." The covenant at Sinai involved divine promises, but not promises like these. The fulfilment of such promises gives a new meaning to the ancient covenant-words: "I will be their God, and they shall be my people." It has, indeed, been maintained more than once that the covenant concept, with its suggestion of a contractual obligation, is inadequate to convey the religious relationship subsisting between God and his people. This, however, is to concentrate on the form to the exclusion of the substance. It is true, no doubt, that as far as its form is concerned the early biblical covenant has close affinities with the treaties which bound vassal-states to their imperial overlords in the second millennium B.C. But it makes all the difference in the world to the substance of the covenant when it is God who takes the initiative in his grace, bestowing his promises freely on those whom he has called to be his people, and binding them to himself with bands

---

61. See O. Michel, *TDNT*, IV, pp. 675-78 (*s.v.* μιμνήσκομαι).

of love.[62] When analogies are drawn from human life to illustrate God's covenant with his people, it is from the family circle and not from the field of international politics that they are drawn—from the relation between husband and wife, or that between a father and his children.[63]

We know of at least one community of Israelites which, in the second century B.C., endeavored to realize the promise of the new covenant. The members of the Qumran community are described as "entering the new covenant in the land of Damascus"[64]—the "land of Damascus" being possibly their wilderness retreat on the shores of the Dead Sea.[65] They were to constitute "a holy house for Israel, a most holy assembly for Aaron . . . the foundation of a holy spirit according to eternal truth, to make atonement for the guilt of rebellion and for sinful disloyalty, and to obtain favor for the land apart from the flesh of burnt-offerings and the fat of sacrifice."[66] But our author would not have recognized in this community the fulfilment of Jeremiah's oracle. The men of Qumran might regard their obedience and endurance as an acceptable substitute for the sacrificial ritual while the temple and its services were polluted by an unworthy priesthood; but they looked forward to a new age which would revive the highest ideals of the old age; they looked forward to a renovated temple which would still be a temple made with hands, to a pure sacrificial worship which would still involve the slaughter of bulls and goats, to a worthy priesthood which would still be confined to the family of Aaron—or, more precisely, to the family of Zadok, which had ministered in the Jerusalem temple from its foundation in Solomon's day to 171 B.C. To our author, the new covenant involves the abolition[67] of the old sacrificial order because of a perfect and unrepeatable sacri-

62. For vassal treaties see G. E. Mendenhall, *Law and Covenant in Israel and the Ancient Near East* (Philadelphia, 1955); J. A. Thompson, *The Ancient Near Eastern Treaties and the Old Testament* (London, 1964); D. J. McCarthy, *Treaty and Covenant*, AnBib 21A (Rome, 1978). But Jeremiah's prophecy and the NT fulfilment give a new depth of meaning to the old term "covenant." In any case, the biblical covenant is much more than "a compact between God and man" (Skinner, *Prophecy*, p. 333); it is not a συνθήκη, an agreement between parties who are more or less equal in status, but a διαθήκη, a settlement by a superior on inferiors, "tendered on the one hand for acceptance on the other" (E. K. Simpson, "Vocabulary of Hebrews," p. 189). See further on 9:15-20 (pp. 220-24 with nn. 114-33).

63. Perhaps both these analogies are present in Jer. 31:32 (MT); "on the day I took them by the hand" may suggest a father leading his children (cf. Hos. 11:1, 3f.); "although I was a husband to them" suggests the marriage relationship (cf. Jer. 2:2; Hos. 2:7, 14-20).

64. CD 6.19; 8.21; cf. 20.12.

65. Cf. R. North, "The Damascus of Qumran Geography," *PEQ* 87 (1955), pp. 34-48.

66. 1QS 8.5f.; 9.3f. (for the former context see also p. 94, n. 18; for the latter context see also pp. 383f.).

67. This is the plain force of the words παλαιόω and ἀφανισμός in v. 13. Tyndale does not go beyond the due sense of the former word in his rendering: "In that he sayth a new testament he hath abrogat the olde." The latter word (with the verb ἀφανίζω) is used in classical Greek of legislation which becomes inoperative because it is no longer relevant to the changed circumstances.

fice, and a high-priestly ministry discharged in the heavenly, no longer in an earthly, sanctuary on the basis of that sacrifice by a priest of a different line from Aaron's. True worship, "in spirit and in truth,"[68] is thus released from dependence on the externalities of religion.

When Jesus, on the night in which he was betrayed, gave his disciples the cup and said, "This is my blood of the covenant, shed for many"[69] (Mark 14:24, NEB), the paschal context of the incident would surely have made them link his words with "the blood of the covenant" which God established with his people Israel in the days of Moses on the basis of the Ten Commandments (Ex. 24:8). Nor can we doubt that Jesus' intention was to announce that now at length that earlier covenant was to be replaced by the "new covenant" foretold by Jeremiah midway between Moses' day and his own.[70] Whether, in fact, the sacrifice of Jesus has had the effect which Jeremiah said the new covenant would have, let those tell who have proved its saving power. Or let one tell for all: "What the law could never do, because our lower nature robbed it of all potency, God has done: by sending his own Son in a form like that of our own sinful nature, and as a sacrifice for sin, he has passed judgment against sin within that very nature, so that the commandment of the law may find fulfilment in us, whose conduct, no longer under the control of our lower nature, is directed by the Spirit" (Rom. 8:3f., NEB).[71]

In Jeremiah's oracle the new covenant is to be made "with the house of Israel and with the house of Judah." In the New Testament fulfilment it is not confined to them, but extends to all believers of every nation—and indeed, in the Old Testament itself indications are not lacking that it was to have this all-embracing character.[72] Whether Jeremiah consciously en-

68. John 4:23f., another passage where worship is liberated from external restrictions of time and place.

69. Matt. 26:28 adds, "for the forgiveness of sins." Neither Mark nor Matthew (according to the most probable reading) records the adjective "new" before "covenant" in this word of institution, as is done by Paul (1 Cor. 11:25) and the longer text of Luke (Luke 22:20); but the new covenant is intended, whether "new" is expressed or only implied. The phrase "for many" may echo Isa. 53:11f. (cf. the phrase "a covenant of the people" in association with the first and second Servant Songs, Isa. 42:6; 49:8); J. Jeremias (*The Eucharistic Words of Jesus*, E.T. [Oxford, 1955], p. 151) interprets the phrase as meaning "for the whole world," Gentiles as well as the house of Israel (cf. John 6:51; 1 John 2:2). Cf. also H. Kosmala, *Hebräer–Essener–Christen* (Leiden, 1959), pp. 174-91.

70. Cf. G. A. Smith, *Jeremiah*, p. 380.

71. On this passage see C. E. B. Cranfield, *The Epistle to the Romans*, ICC, I (Edinburgh, 1975), pp. 378-95.

72. Thus in Isa. 42:6 the Servant is given not only "for a covenant to the people" but also "for a light to the nations" (cf. Isa. 49:6). See also the catena of OT texts in Rom. 15:9-12 in which Paul finds the Gentile mission adumbrated; and, perhaps most impressive of all, Isa. 19:24f.: "In that day Israel shall be the third with Egypt and Assyria, a blessing in the midst of the earth, whom Yahweh of hosts has blessed, saying, 'Blessed be Egypt my people, and Assyria the work of my hands, and Israel my heritage.'"

visaged the wider extension of the new covenant or not, its wider extension is really implicit in his prophecy: national origin and racial descent must also be included among those externalities from whose control true religion is released by the new covenant. "It is one thing to say that Jeremiah was not given to see what the new covenant would mean for the world, it is entirely another to say that by Israel and Judah he really meant the Church. . . . On the other hand, we must not fall into the opposite error of supposing that the new covenant will mean something else for 'all Israel' than it does for the Church, that saved Israel will be saved in some other way than is the Church. God does not abolish physical Israel, but in saving it transcends it, just as He does not scrap this earth but renews it."[73]

13   The very words "a new covenant" antiquate the previous one. In saying this our author does not go beyond Jeremiah, who explicitly contrasts the new covenant of the future with the covenant made at the time of the Exodus, and implies that when it comes, the new covenant will supersede that earlier one. The moral of the situation had been appreciated already by Paul, who speaks of himself and his colleagues as "ministers of a new covenant; not in a written code, but in the Spirit"; and by contrast with this new covenant refers to that associated with Moses as "the old covenant" (2 Cor. 3:6, 14).[74] And if the covenant of Moses' day is antiquated, our author further implies, so must be the Aaronic priesthood, the earthly sanctuary, and the Levitical sacrifices, which were all established under that covenant. The age of the law and the prophets is past; the age of the Son is here, and here to stay.[75]

But, our author goes on, if the earlier covenant, with all that accompanied it, is antiquated, it is ready to vanish away: "anything that is growing old and ageing will shortly disappear" (NEB). It cannot be proved from these words that the Jerusalem temple was still standing and its sacrificial ritual still being carried on. They could simply mean that by predicting the inauguration of a new covenant Jeremiah in effect announced the impending dissolution of the old order. They do indeed have that meaning. But if in fact the Jerusalem temple was still standing, if the priests of Aaron's line were still discharging their sacrificial duties there, then our author's words would be all the more telling. Jesus,[76] and shortly after him Stephen,[77] had foretold the downfall of the temple. Thirty years and more had elapsed since then, and it

73. H. L. Ellison, *Men Spake from God* (London, 1958), p. 92.

74. See P. E. Hughes, *Paul's Second Epistle to the Corinthians*, NICNT (Grand Rapids, 1962), pp. 93-106; C. K. Barrett, *The Second Epistle to the Corinthians*, HNTC (New York, 1973), pp. 109-26; V. P. Furnish, *II Corinthians*, AB (Garden City, NY, 1984), pp. 201-33.

75. See J. de Vuyst, *Oud en Nieuw Verbond in de Brief aan de Hebreeën* (Kampen, 1964).

76. Cf. Mark 13:2; John 2:19.

77. Cf. Acts 6:14.

might have been thought that the event had belied their prediction. But now that prediction is taken up by another Christian, who in many respects stands within the tradition of Stephen,[78] and shown to be logically involved in Old Testament prophecy. If the end of the temple and its ministry had been imminent thirty years before, it was the more imminent now that the forty years of probation[79] were more than three-quarters of the way toward their end.

78. Cf. W. Manson, *Hebrews*, pp. 25-46.
79. See p. 99 (on 3:9).

HEBREWS 9

C. THE SANCTUARY UNDER THE OLD COVENANT (9:1-5)

1 *Now the first covenant [also] had ordinances[1] for worship[2] and a sanctuary of this world.[3]*

2 *A tent was set up—the first one, called the holy place[4]—in which were the lampstand,[5] the table, and the showbread.[6]*

3 *Then behind the second curtain was the tent called the holy of holies,[7]*

4 *which had a golden incense-altar, and the ark of the covenant overlaid all around with gold. In the ark was the golden urn with manna, together with Aaron's rod which budded and the tablets of the testimony,*

5 *while above it were the cherubim[8] of glory overshadowing the mercy seat. It is not possible here and now to deal with these things one by one.[9]*

---

1. Gk. δικαιώματα (cf. v. 10), "regulations."

2. "Worship" represents Gk. λατρεία (cf. the cognate verb λατρεύω in 8:5).

3. Gk. τό τε ἅγιον κοσμικόν, where κοσμικός means "mundane" or "material" (the temptation to render it "cosmic" and relate it to the cosmological symbolism referred to on p. 184, n. 30, should be resisted). The adjective κοσμικός indicates that the Mosaic tabernacle (unlike its heavenly archetype) did belong to "this creation" (v. 11). The only other NT occurrence of κοσμικός is in Tit. 2:12, of "worldly lusts." Both ἅγιον and κοσμικόν are adjectives in the neuter gender, but here one of them must be taken as filling the rôle of a substantive qualified by the other. By general agreement ἅγιον is taken as the substantive here, qualified by κοσμικόν, although elsewhere in this epistle it is not the neuter singular ἅγιον but the neuter plural ἅγια that is used in the sense of "sanctuary" or "holy place." In a letter dated March 9, 1959, Dr. B. F. C. Atkinson made the interesting suggestion that τό τε ἅγιον κοσμικόν might mean "and the holy ritual." "It seems to me," he wrote, "(i) to fit the immediate context much better, (ii) to agree better with the order of words, (iii) that κοσμικόν is not the right word to use for *earthly*."

4. Gk. ἅγια (neuter plural, as is plain from the reading of B, τὰ ἅγια). Elsewhere in the epistle the simple ἅγια is used for the holy of holies on earth and for its heavenly prototype.

5. Gk. λυχνία, "lampstand" (so the LXX for Heb. *menôrāh*).

6. Cod. B and the Sahidic Coptic version insert here "and the golden incense-altar" (transposing it from v. 4).

7. Gk. ἅγια ἁγίων (both neuter plural). ℵ^c B D^c K L read τὰ ἅγια τῶν ἁγίων. 𝔭^46 has ἅγια here and ἅγια ἁγίων in v. 2! This points to some primitive disturbance of the text.

8. The Hebrew plural -*îm* is preserved in the Greek transliteration χερουβείν.

9. Gk. κατὰ μέρος (RSV "in detail").

1 The inadequacy of the old order as compared with the new is now set forth with reference first to the arrangements of the sanctuary under the old covenant and then to the sacrificial ritual associated with that sanctuary. Provision was made under the old covenant for the people of God to worship him, but the sanctuary erected for this worship was a material one. The particular sanctuary which our author has in mind is plainly the wilderness tent described in detail in the book of Exodus. The fact that he makes the tent the basis of his argument here and not the Jerusalem temple may suggest that neither he nor his readers belonged to Jerusalem, but it cannot be treated as proof of this. Neither can it be treated as proof that the temple was no longer standing, nor yet that the readers were not Jews at all. What it does prove is that our author's argument is biblical through and through. Even Solomon's temple is not so apposite to his purpose as the Mosaic tabernacle, which is introduced (in Ex. 25:1ff.) immediately after the inauguration of the covenant (Ex. 24). It is not suggested here, as it is in Stephen's speech (Acts 7:44-50), that the mobile tabernacle of the wilderness wanderings was a more suitable shrine for a pilgrim people than the permanent house which Solomon built.[10] Our author's point is different: the sanctuary of the old covenant, in its very furnishings and sacrificial arrangements, proclaimed its own temporary character; and while this is shown with more special reference to the tabernacle, the principle holds good equally for the temple, whether Solomon's or Herod's.

2 The wilderness tent-shrine consisted of the court, the outer compartment, and the inner compartment. Although the successive temples which superseded it were much more elaborate, they preserved the same ground plan; the courts might be multiplied in number, but the holy house itself, standing toward the west side of the inmost court, consisted of the two essential compartments—the outer ("the holy place") and the inner ("the holy of holies"). Here each of the compartments of the wilderness sanctuary is called a "tent" or "tabernacle." The outer compartment was twenty cubits long, (approximately) ten cubits wide, and ten cubits high; here it is described simply in terms of its furniture. The "lampstand" was placed at the south side of the holy place; it was made of gold, with three branches springing from either side of the main stem; the main stem and all six branches each supported a flower-shaped lampholder (Ex. 25:31-39; 37:17-24). The seven-branched lampstands of the later sanctuaries appear to have been more elaborate than that prescribed for the wilderness tabernacle; some idea of their appearance may be obtained from representations on Hasmonaean coins and in a well-known relief on the Arch of Titus in Rome.[11] "The table, and

---

10. Cf. *Acts,* NICNT (Grand Rapids, [2]1988), pp. 146-49.

11. The seven-branched *menorah* on the Arch of Titus has been adopted as the coat of

the showbread" (a hendiadys for "the table of showbread") stood on the north side of the holy place. The table was made of acacia wood overlaid with gold; it was two cubits long, one cubit broad, and one and a half cubits high, and was equipped with golden plates, spoons, flagons, and bowls (Ex. 25:23-30; 37:10-16). The "showbread" (lit. "the setting forth of the loaves")[12] consisted of twelve cakes, baked of fine flour, placed fresh upon the table every sabbath day (Lev. 24:5-8); the old cakes, which were removed when the new cakes were placed on the table, became the perquisite of the priests, who ate them in the holy place; no layman might eat them, because they were "most holy" (Lev. 24:9).[13]

3 At the west end of the holy place hung a curtain of embroidered linen, suspended under the clasps which coupled together the two sets of linen curtains draped over the tabernacle framework (Ex. 26:31; 36:35f.). This curtain (Heb. *pārōkheth*) is here called "the second curtain"[14] to distinguish it from the linen screen through which one entered from the court into the holy place (Ex. 26:36f.; 36:37f.). Beyond the "second curtain" lay the inner compartment, the "holy of holies," which formed a cube on a side of ten cubits.

4 Two pieces of furniture are mentioned in connection with the holy of holies: the golden incense-altar and the ark of the covenant.

---

arms of the modern State of Israel. The appearance of non-Jewish figures in relief on the base of this *menorah* has occasioned some doubt as to its identity with the lampstand which stood in the temple; see, however, M. Kon, "The Menorah of the Arch of Titus," *PEQ* 82 (1950), pp. 25-30. Cf. also E. R. Goodenough, "The Menorah among Jews in the Roman World," *HUCA* 23.2 (1950-51), pp. 449-94. According to Philo, *Who is the Heir of Divine Things?* 221, and Josephus, *Ant.* 3.146, the seven branches of the *menorah* represent the seven planets.

12. Gk. ἡ πρόθεσις τῶν ἄρτων, a transposition of the LXX οἱ ἄρτοι τῆς προθέσεως ("the loaves of proposition," in the literal rendering of the Douay Bible in Ex. 25:30, etc.). The Hebrew expression is *lehem happānîm*, "bread of the face," i.e., bread set before the face or presence of God (Ex. 25:30; 35:13; 39:36, etc.), otherwise *lehem hattāmîd*, "the continual bread" (Num. 4:7), or *lehem hamma'āreket*, lit. "bread of setting in order" (1 Chron. 9:32, etc.).

13. Cf. 1 Sam. 21:1-6, where the priest of Nob gave David and his companions "holy bread" to eat: "for there was no bread there but the bread of the Presence, which is removed from before Yahweh, to be replaced by hot bread on the day it is taken away" (with our Lord's reference to this incident in Mark 2:25f.).

14. Gk. τὸ δεύτερον καταπέτασμα. In the LXX καταπέτασμα is also used for the screen at the entrance into the holy place (Ex. 26:37; 37:5 [corresponding to 36:37 of the MT and the EVV], etc., although in Ex. 26:36 another Greek word, ἐπίσπαστρον, is used); hence our author distinguishes the curtain at the entrance into the holy of holies as "the second curtain." Two distinct words are used in Hebrew; whereas "the second curtain" is the *pārōket*, the screen at the outer entrance is a *māsāk*. Philo distinguishes the two by reserving καταπέτασμα for the inner curtain and calling the outer screen a κάλυμμα (*Life of Moses* 2.101). The Mishnah tractate *Yoma* (5.1) records a dispute between rabbis on the nature of the inner curtain in the Second Temple: whereas one school of thought held that it was a single curtain (which is in agreement with such historical evidence as we have), another held that it was double, the two curtains of which it was composed being a cubit apart. Cf. the excursus by H. Laible in Strack-Billerbeck, III (Munich, 1926), pp. 733-36, with C. Schneider, *TDNT*, III, pp. 628-30 (*s.v.* καταπέτασμα). See also pp. 250f., n. 87.

The mention of the incense-altar raises two questions: *(a)* whether the reference actually is to the incense-altar and not rather to a "censer" (AV/KJV) or incense-shovel; *(b)* if the incense-altar is meant, how this statement relates to the Old Testament indications that the incense-altar stood in the holy place, not in the holy of holies.

(a) The Greek word *thymiatērion,* which our author employs here, is used in the Septuagint with the meaning "censer" but never with the meaning "incense-altar."[15] This fact, however, is not decisive for its meaning here. The word in itself simply means "a place where incense is put" or "a vessel for burning incense" and was used not only in the sense of "censer," but also in the general sense of "incense-altar"[16] and more particularly, by Philo[17] and Josephus,[18] of the incense-altar in the Israelite tabernacle or temple. We should expect some reference to the incense-altar here, along with the references to other articles of tabernacle furniture; there is no reason to expect a reference to a censer, since there is no mention of such an instrument in all the prescriptions for the construction and furnishing of the tabernacle in Ex. 25:1–31:11 or 35:1–40:33.[19] There was only one incense-altar, but there were several censers; and though it might be argued that the special reference here is to Aaron's censer, which he used on the Day of Atonement (Lev. 16:12; cf. Num. 16:46), this censer was scarcely distinctive enough to be mentioned separately; further, we are not told where it was kept, but since Aaron used it to carry fire into the holy of holies, to burn incense on it there, it is unlikely that it was kept in the holy of holies.[20] On the whole, it is more probable that the ARV is right (with the RSV and the NEB) in preferring "altar of incense" as the rendering here to "censer" of the AV/KJV and the ERV texts.[21]

---

15. It appears three times in the LXX: in 2 Chron. 26:19 and Ezek. 8:11 it represents Heb. *miqteret* ("censer"); and in 4 Macc. 7:11, where Aaron is described as being "equipped with a θυμιατήριον," the word plainly has the same sense. But Theodotion and Symmachus use it in Ex. 30:1 of the incense-altar (Heb. *mizbēah miqtar qᵉtōret*).

16. Cf. Herodotus, *Hist.* 2.162; Aelian, *Varia Historia* 12.51. It occurs in this sense in a Smyrnaean inscription of the first century A.D. (*CMRDM* 1.28); see *New Docs.,* III (1978), § 40.

17. *Who Is Heir of Divine Things?* 226f.; *Life of Moses* 2.94, 101 (in reference each time to the incense-altar in the Mosaic tabernacle).

18. *War* 5.218; *Ant.* 3.147, 198 (the former reference being to the incense-altar in the temple which fell in A.D. 70, the two latter references to the one in the Mosaic tabernacle).

19. The "firepans" of Ex. 27:3; 38:3, while designated by a Hebrew word (*mahtāh,* LXX πυρεῖον) which can also denote a censer (as in Lev. 10:1; 16:12), were not censers but utensils belonging to the altar of burnt offering in the tabernacle court.

20. According to TB *Yoma* 47a, the "censer heaped with incense" *(mahtāh gᵉdûšāh šel qᵉtōret)* was brought to the high priest on the Day of Atonement "out of the chamber in the house of Abtinas (Euthinos)" (cf. J. Jeremias, *Jerusalem in the Time of Jesus,* E.T. [London, 1969], p. 25).

21. Its interpretation as "altar of incense" certainly underlies its transposition in Cod. B and the Sahidic version to v. 2, among the furnishings of the holy place. In the one place in the NT where a "censer" is unambiguously mentioned (Rev. 8:3-5) the Greek term used is λιβανωτός.

(b) If that is so, the question of the location of the incense-altar arises. According to Ex. 30:6, it was to be put "before the veil that is by the ark of the testimony, before the mercy-seat that is over the testimony."[22] This does not make it altogether clear on which side of the veil dividing the holy place from the holy of holies the incense-altar stood, but the phrase "before the veil" does rather suggest that it stood in the holy place, not in the holy of holies.[23] This seems to be confirmed by Lev. 16:12, 18, where "the altar before Yahweh"[24] is on the outer side of the curtain (unless those are right who maintain that "the altar before Yahweh" of Lev. 16 is not the special incense-altar of Ex. 30:1-10 but the one altar of Ex. 27:1-8, as may be implied by Lev. 16:20). On the other hand, the incense-altar in Solomon's temple is described as "the whole altar that belonged to the inner sanctuary" (1 Kings 6:22).[25] It smacks of special pleading to argue that our author does not say that the incense-altar was situated *in* the holy of holies, but only speaks of the holy of holies as *"having* a golden altar of incense."[26] The participle "having" should naturally mean the same thing with reference to the incense-altar as with reference to the ark of the covenant. There was, however, a special con-

---

(O. Michel, MK, *ad loc.,* argues for "censer" as the meaning of θυμιατήριον here; so also E. Riggenbach, ZK, *ad loc.*)

22. The words "before the mercy-seat that is over the testimony" are absent from the LXX and the Samaritan Bible. In the Samaritan Bible, indeed, the whole section dealing with the incense-altar, Ex. 30:1-10, comes between vv. 35 and 36 of Ex. 26. P. E. Kahle has suggested that our author used a text of the LXX which had the same order as the Samaritan Bible, and that this explains his assigning the incense-altar to the holy of holies (*The Cairo Geniza* [London, ¹1947], pp. 146f.). It is true that in this order the incense-altar is brought into closer association with the inner curtain and the ark (for which directions are given in Ex. 26:31-34), but even so it is separated from them by Ex. 26:35, in which directions are given for the placing of the table and lampstand in the outer sanctuary.

23. On the other hand, it does suggest that the incense-altar stood near the curtain, whereas in the Second Temple it apparently was nearer the outer screen, since we are told that it was the first piece of furniture on which the priest came when he entered the holy place, before he came to the lampstand (TB *Yoma* 33a). Josephus, in his description of the Mosaic tabernacle, says that the incense-altar stood between the lampstand and the table of showbread (*Ant.* 3.147); both in this description and in his description of the Second Temple (*War* 5.216) he makes it clear that the incense-altar stood in the holy place.

24. The Samaritan Bible adds "before Yahweh" in Ex. 40:27, where incense is burned on the golden altar for the first time ("he burnt fragrant incense upon it before Yahweh"). On the problem of the altar in Lev. 16 see N. H. Snaith, *Leviticus and Numbers,* NCBC (London, 1967), pp. 114f.

25. This verse is absent from the LXX. In 2 Baruch 6:7 the incense-altar is included among the objects removed by an angel from the *holy of holies* before the destruction of Solomon's temple by the Chaldaeans. In a Canaanite temple of the Mosaic period excavated at Hazor the incense-altar was in the *dᵉbîr* or "holy of holies." In Rev. 8:3 the golden altar from which the prayers of the saints ascend as incense is "before the throne"; but there is no inner curtain separating two compartments in the heavenly sanctuary as portrayed in Revelation.

26. Gk. χρυσοῦν ἔχουσα θυμιατήριον. Cf. A. S. Peake, *The Epistle to the Hebrews,* CentB (Edinburgh/London, 1902), p. 175.

nection between the incense-altar and the holy of holies, no matter on which side of the veil the altar stood. On the one day in the year when the holy of holies was entered the incense-altar played a significant part; not only was the holy of holies never entered without incense from the incense-altar (Lev. 16:12f.), but the blood of the sin offering on the Day of Atonement was sprinkled on the horns of the incense-altar as well as on the mercy-seat (Ex. 30:10; Lev. 16:15).[27]

In any case, our author does not stay to answer the questions which his passing reference to the incense-altar may raise in his readers' minds; this is not the feature of the tabernacle to which he wishes to draw their attention more particularly, any more than the contents of the ark of the covenant, which he also passes over quickly.

The ark of the covenant was the principal, if not the only, article of furniture in the holy of holies in the tabernacle and in Solomon's temple. No more is heard of it after the destruction of the first temple by the Chaldaeans in 587 B.C. (although legend is more than willing to supply the lack of historical evidence);[28] it was not replaced in the postexilic temple, in which the holy of holies was completely empty, as Pompey found to his surprise when he insisted on forcing his way into it in 63 B.C.[29] The ark was a box of acacia wood plated with gold; it was called "the ark of the covenant" or "the ark of the testimony" (Ex. 25:22, etc.) because the covenant-terms, engraved on

---

27. Speculations on whether the directions about the incense-altar may have been a later addition to the description of the tabernacle in Exodus are irrelevant to the exegesis of this epistle, together with all other questions concerning the composition of the Pentateuch. The Pentateuch as our author knew it had the same contents as the Pentateuch known to us, although it was probably arranged in the LXX order (which in Ex. 35–40 particularly differs from the order of the MT). See D. W. Gooding, *The Account of the Tabernacle: Translation and Textual Problems of the Greek Exodus* (Cambridge, 1959); also the same writer's article "Tabernacle," in *NBD*[2].

28. Cf. the passage from 2 Baruch referred to in n. 25 above, where the ark and the curtain, with other objects belonging to the holy of holies, are removed by an angel. According to Tosefta *Yoma* 3.7 (cf. TB *Yoma* 52b; TJ *Soṭa* 3.22c, 6), the ark and the objects which accompanied it in the holy of holies (cf. p. 204, n. 37) were hidden at that time (since the pot of manna was one of these objects, the "hidden manna" of Rev. 2:17 may be recalled here); according to *Mekhilta* 59b (on Ex. 16:33), Elijah will bring them to light when he comes. In 2 Macc. 2:4-8 Jeremiah is said to have hidden "the tent and the ark and the altar of incense" in a cave in "the mountain where Moses had gone up and had seen the inheritance of God"; they will be revealed again by God when he "gathers his people together again and shows his mercy." In Samaritan tradition the ark and the holy vessels of the tabernacle were hidden on Mount Gerizim at the beginning of the epoch of divine displeasure *(fanuta);* they will be restored by the Taheb, the Prophet like Moses (Deut. 18:15-19), when he comes to inaugurate the new epoch of divine favor *(rahuta).* This belief was held by them in NT times, as is clear from the incident recorded in Josephus, *Ant.* 18.85-87.

29. Cf. Josephus, *War* 1.152f.; *Ant.* 14.71f.; Tacitus, *Hist.* 5.9; Ps. Sol. 2:1ff., 30f. In the postexilic holy of holies the position of the ark was marked by a slab called "the stone of foundation" (Heb. *'eḇen šattiyyāh*).

two stone tablets, were placed inside it (Ex. 25:16, 21).[30] When, at a later time, it was placed in the holy of holies in Solomon's temple, "there was nothing in the ark except the two tables of stone which Moses put there at Horeb, when Yahweh made a covenant with the people of Israel, when they came out of the land of Egypt" (1 Kings 8:9). "The very terms of this statement," according to Franz Delitzsch, "may almost seem to imply that other things had been there formerly."[31] By the "other things" he means more particularly the jar of manna and Aaron's rod, which the Old Testament does not place inside the ark. According to Ex. 16:33f. Moses commanded Aaron to put an omer of manna (about four pints, one-tenth of an ephah) in a jar,[32] "and place it before Yahweh, to be kept throughout your generations"; and Aaron accordingly "placed it before the testimony, to be kept." Similarly, when twelve rods or sceptres, one for each tribe of Israel, had been laid up "in the tent of meeting before the testimony," Aaron's rod, the rod of the tribe of Levi, was found the next day to have put forth buds, blossoms, and ripe almonds—a token that Aaron was the man whom God had chosen for the priesthood (Num. 17:1-10). Moses was then directed to "put back the rod of Aaron before the testimony, to be kept as a sign for the rebels" (Num. 17:10).[33] Does the phrase "before the testimony" imply that these objects were placed inside the ark, or simply that they were laid in front of it? Delitzsch thinks that the former "is a natural conclusion" from the phrases "before Yahweh" and "before the testimony";[34] this is by no means clear, especially as regards the phrase "before Yahweh," for this phrase is used of other installations in the tabernacle, which were certainly not inside the ark.[35] On the other hand, it will not do to say that the antecedent of "wherein" is not "the ark" but "the tent called the holy of holies" (v. 3);[36] this puts an intolerable strain on the natural construction of the sentence by the distance which it places between the relative and its antecedent. It is not to be doubted that our author represents the jar of manna and the rod as having been inside the ark along with the tables of the law. Since the Old Testament has noth-

---

30. Cf. Deut. 10:1-5; these tablets were the two which replaced those previously broken by Moses at the foot of Mount Sinai (Ex. 32:19). Cf. M. G. Kline, *Treaty of the Great King* (Grand Rapids, 1963), pp. 13-26.

31. *Commentary on the Epistle to the Hebrews*, E.T., II (Edinburgh, 1862), p. 57.

32. Heb. *ṣinṣenet* ("receptacle"), Gk. στάμνος ("jar," especially for racking off wine). This jar or "urn" (RSV) is said to have been of gold in the LXX (followed by Philo, *Preliminary Studies* 100), but not in the MT.

33. This incident belongs to the sequence of lessons prescribed for the season of Pentecost in the third year of the triennial synagogue lectionary (cf. A. E. Guilding, *The Fourth Gospel and Jewish Worship* [Oxford, 1960], p. 224; see p. 26 above).

34. *Hebrews*, p. 57.

35. For example, it is used of the incense-altar in Lev. 16:18 (see p. 201).

36. Cf. G. H. Lang, *The Epistle to the Hebrews* (London, 1951), p. 144.

ing to say of the jar of manna outside Ex. 16:33f., and nothing to say of Aaron's rod after it was used to strike the rock in Kadesh (Num. 20:8-11), it is open to anyone to surmise that, even if they were not originally in the ark, they were put there subsequently for safekeeping, and to surmise further that they were lost when the ark was captured by the Philistines (1 Sam. 4:11–6:16).[37] But this would simply be calling upon imagination to take the place of evidence, and on a par with rabbinical speculation about the disappearance of the ark and the objects which accompanied it when the first temple fell.

5 The lid of the ark was a golden slab called the "mercy seat" or place of atonement,[38] viewed by our author as the earthly counterpart of the "throne of grace" to which he has already exhorted his readers to draw near for help in the hour of need (4:16). It was given this name because of the part it played in the sacrificial ritual of the Day of Atonement; the blood both of the bullock which was offered to make atonement for the high priest and his family, and of the goat which was killed as a sin offering for the whole nation, was sprinkled on the mercy seat and in front of it, while the God of Israel undertook to "appear in the cloud upon the mercy seat" (Lev. 16:2; cf. vv. 14f.). The "cherubim of glory" were two gold figures of composite creatures which overshadowed the mercy seat (Ex. 25:18-22; 37:7-9) and served to support the invisible presence of Israel's God, who accordingly is repeatedly described as the one "who is enthroned on the cherubim" (1 Sam. 4:4, etc.). It was because of this function that they were called "cherubim of glory"; the glory is the *shekhînah,* the radiant presence of God dwelling in the midst of his people.[39] Originally the cherubim appear to have symbolized the storm winds,[40] on which the God of Israel was pictured as riding through the sky;

---

37. Cf. J. O. Boyd, "What was in the Ark?" *EQ* 11 (1939), pp. 165-68. Rabbinical tradition placed *in* the ark (in addition to the two tablets of stone) two silver columns belonging to the tablets of stone, the fragments of the original tablets of stone which Moses broke at the foot of Sinai, a copy of the Torah, and the names of God (TB *Baba Bathra* 14a). (The tradition about the copy of the Torah probably goes back to Deut. 31:26, where the Levites are commanded by Moses to "take this book of the law, and put it by the side of the ark of the covenant of Yahweh." Cf. CD 5.2, which speaks of "the sealed book of the law" as being "in the ark.") But in rabbinical tradition the jar of manna and Aaron's rod were not *in* the ark but stood beside it, along with the coffer of golden jewels which (according to 1 Sam. 6:4, 8, 11, 15) the Philistines sent as a guilt offering along with the ark when they returned it to Israel (Tosefta *Yoma* 3.7). On the general biblical significance of ark and sanctuary see G. von Rad, "The Tent and the Ark," E.T. in *The Problem of the Hexateuch and Other Essays* (Edinburgh, 1966), pp. 103-24.

38. Gk. ἱλαστήριον, so the LXX for Heb. *kappōret.* That Heb. *kappōret* means more than "lid" or "cover," and is akin in sense to the Pi'el conjugation *kipper,* "make atonement," is suggested by the emphasis which is placed upon it (in its own right) in the ritual for the Day of Atonement (Lev. 16:2, 13-16). Cf. Heb. 2:17 (p. 78, n. 57); 4:16 (pp. 116f.).

39. Cf. Rom. 9:4 ("who are Israelites, whose is . . . the glory").

40. Later they appear to have symbolized, more generally, the powers of creation. Ac-

thus in the theophany of Ps. 18:10 "he rode on a cherub, and flew; he came swiftly upon the wings of the wind" (cf. Deut. 33:26). Some idea of their composite character may be gained from Ezek. 10:10-14 (supplemented by 1:5-13), where they are portrayed as the supporters of the chariot-throne of God, which is not tied to his earthly shrine, but is capable of moving in any direction at will.[41] If it be asked why the golden cherubim did not come under the ban imposed by the Second Commandment on the making of images (as contrasted, for example, with the golden bull-calves of Dan and Bethel), the answer may lie in their symbolic nature;[42] they were not the "likeness of anything that is in heaven above, or that is in the earth beneath, or that is in the water under the earth" (Ex. 20:4; cf. Deut. 5:8).[43]

What our author would have had to say about the parabolic significance of the cherubim and the other installations which he mentions we can only imagine; when he says that he cannot now "deal with these things one by one," he leaves us with the impression that he could have enlarged at some length on their symbolism had he chosen so to do.[44] What he does proceed to enlarge upon is the use which was made of the ancient sanctuary on the annual Day of Atonement.

D. A TEMPORARY RITUAL (9:6-10)

6 *When these things have been set up thus, the priests go into the first tent continually in the discharge of their sacred offices;*[45]

---

cording to Philo the two cherubim "are allegorical representations of the two most august and highest potencies of Him Who Is, the creative and the kingly" (*Life of Moses* 2.99; cf. *Questions and Answers on Exodus*, no. 62). In his treatise *On the Cherubim* (which deals mainly with the cherubim of Gen. 3:24) he suggests alternatively that the two cherubim represent "the outermost sphere of the fixed stars" and "the inner contained sphere" in which are set the seven planetary zones; or the two hemispheres (23-26).

41. Cf. Ben Sira's encomium on Ezekiel (Sir. 49:8f.):

It was Ezekiel who saw the vision of glory
  which God showed him above the chariot of the cherubim;
for God remembered his enemies with storm,
  and did good to those who directed their ways aright.

42. Moreover, the bull-calves were associated with the fertility cults of Israel's nearest neighbors.

43. The much later golden cherubim from Herod's temple are said to have been exhibited on one of the gates of Antioch as trophies of the Roman triumph over Jerusalem; so John Malalas, *Chronographia*, book x. (Cf. W. L. Dulière, "Les Chérubins du troisième Temple à Antioche," *Zeitschrift für Religions- und Geistesgeschichte* 13 [1961], pp. 201-19.)

44. Philo does enlarge on them in various places, and especially in his *Life of Moses* 2.71-108.

45. Gk. λατρεία (in plural); cf. v. 1, where the singular is translated "worship" (p. 197, n. 2).

7 *but into the second goes the high priest only, and that once a year, not without blood, which he offers for himself and for the people's sins of ignorance.*[46]

8 *In this way the Holy Spirit shows*[47] *that, while the first tent still stands,*[48] *the way into the holy place has not yet been opened up.*

9 *This is a parable with a bearing on the present time: according to this*[49] *order of worship gifts and sacrifices*[50] *are offered which can never make the worshiper*[51] *perfect as regards the conscience.*

10 *Those gifts and sacrifices, in addition to matters of food and drink and various ablutions, are material ordinances*[52] *imposed until the time of reformation.*

6 In the tabernacle and in the temples which replaced it, the outer compartment, the holy place, was in continual use. Day by day, morning and evening, the appointed priests entered it to trim the lamps on the lampstand (Ex. 27:20f.) and at the same time to burn incense on the incense-altar (Ex. 30:7f.). The day on which the priest Zechariah was chosen by lot from among his fellow-priests of the course of Abijah to burn incense in the holy place (Luke 1:8-22) would have been in any case the most outstanding day in the whole of his priestly career; but the angelic vision and annunciation granted to him beside the incense-altar made the occasion more notable still. Again, week by week the appointed priests entered the holy place to put fresh loaves on the table of showbread (Lev. 24:8f.). These were the principal services which were discharged in "the first tent," and any member of the priesthood could discharge them.

7 But none except the high priest was permitted to enter "the second tent," the holy of holies; and even he was permitted to enter it only once a

---

46. Gk. ἀγνοήματα, "sins of ignorance" (cf. 5:2, pp. 120f., nn. 15, 16). The ARV mg. compares Sir. 23:2, where Ben Sira prays not to be spared in his ἀγνοήματα, lest they be multiplied and be his undoing. At Qumran sins of inadvertence incurred penance, but deliberate sins excommunication (cf. 1QS 9.1f.).

47. Gk. δηλοῦντος, "showing."

48. Gk. ἐχούσης στάσιν, lit. "having a standing," a literary phrase for "being in existence," or (more appropriately here) "retaining its status." It is not necessarily implied that the earthly sanctuary, as a material structure, no longer existed; what is implied is that, with Christ's passing "through the heavens" (4:14) into the presence of God, the earthly structure has lost its sanctuary status.

49. Gk. καθ᾽ ἥν (the antecedent being perhaps παραβολή), for which later manuscripts (e.g., D^c K L P) and the TR read καθ᾽ ὅν, as though the antecedent were καιρόν, "time."

50. For this phrase cf. 5:1; 8:3 (see p. 119, n. 6).

51. Gk. λατρεύω, as in 8:5 (see p. 184, n. 31); but there the priests are the subject, whereas here the ordinary worshiper is intended.

52. Gk. δικαιώματα, as in v. 1. They are δικαιώματα σαρκός, lit. "ordinances of flesh" (cf. v. 13), with which may be compared "the law of a 'fleshly' (σάρκινος) commandment" regulating the high-priestly succession in 7:16.

year, on the Day of Atonement, and the conditions of his entering it were strictly prescribed. These conditions are set out most fully in Lev. 16, where the holy of holies is called "the holy place within the veil" (v. 2). Aaron (and that means each successive high priest of Israel) might enter the holy of holies only on the tenth day of the seventh month (Tishri) in each year (around the time of the autumnal equinox). Attired not in his violet robe and its accessories,[53] but in vestments of white linen which were reserved for special sacrificial occasions,[54] he entered the holy of holies twice. On the first occasion he carried the blood of the bullock which had been sacrificed as a sin offering for himself and his household,[55] and sprinkled it on the front of the mercy-seat and before the mercy-seat, which all the time was shrouded in the cloud arising from the incense which burned on the golden altar. Then, when a goat had been slaughtered as a sin offering for the people at large, he brought its blood too into the holy of holies and sprinkled it on and before the mercy-seat. Having thus accomplished this part of the atoning ritual, he came out of the sanctuary and confessed the national sins over the head of the second goat, assigned by lot to "Azazel," which was then driven from the haunts of men into a "solitary land." In our author's typological application of the ritual of the Day of Atonement, however, no mention is made of this second goat;[56]

53. Ex. 28:31-35 (in the wider context of vv. 2-38).
54. Ex. 28:39-43; Lev. 6:10; 16:4.
55. Cf. 5:3; 7:27.
56. And therefore it is no part of the exegesis of this epistle to investigate the origin and purpose of the setting aside of a goat "for Azazel" (AV/KJV "scapegoat," Lev. 16:8, 10, 26). In the *Epistle of Barnabas* (7:7-11) the scapegoat is treated as a type of Jesus bearing the curse and yet wearing the crown (the crown being the fillet of scarlet wool said to have been placed on the scapegoat's head; cf. p. 225, n. 137). Justin Martyr (*Dialogue with Trypho* 40) regards the driving of the scapegoat into the wilderness as a type of the rejection of Jesus by the Jewish leaders. Some features of the scapegoat ceremony, especially the imposition of the high priest's hands on its head and the confession of the national sins over it, by which these sins were transferred to it (Lev. 16:21), have passed into the language of Christian devotion, as in Isaac Watts's lines:

My faith would lay her hand
    On that dear head of Thine,
While like a penitent I stand
    And there confess my sin.

There is also the classic account of Charles Simeon's conversion in 1779, as told by himself, which has had such a profound influence ever since on the thought and language of Anglican evangelicalism: "But in Passion Week, as I was reading Bishop Wilson on the Lord's Supper, I met with an expression to this effect—'That the Jews knew what they did, when they transferred their sin to the head of their offering.' The thought came into my mind, What, may I transfer all my guilt to another? Has God provided an Offering for me, that I may lay my sins on His head? Then, God willing, I will not bear them on my own soul one moment longer. Accordingly I sought to lay my sins upon the sacred head of Jesus" (H. C. G. Moule, *Charles Simeon* [London, (1892) 1948], pp. 25f.). (The work which Simeon was reading was *Short and Plain Instructions for the Better Understanding of the Lord's Supper*, by Thomas Wilson, bishop of Sodor and Man [London, 1736].) The relation of the scapegoat to the NT presentation of the atonement is he is concerned only with that part of the ritual which was associated with the sanctuary. And in this connection he emphasizes three points: (i) except on this annual occasion, the way into the throne room of God was barred for all Israelites, even for the high priest himself;[57] (ii) when the high priest did receive permission to enter, his entry was safeguarded by sacrificial blood; (iii) this sacrificial blood was not finally efficacious, for fresh blood had to be shed and a fresh entry made into the holy of holies year by year.

8 In the record of the tabernacle arrangements and the Levitical offerings the Holy Spirit had a lesson to teach, as in the other parts of Hebrew scripture. What lesson, then, does he teach in the prescriptions for the Day of Atonement? This, that throughout the age of the old covenant there was no direct access to God. "The way into the holy place" here means "the way into the holy of holies," which was barred by the inner veil. The use of "holy place" in the sense of "holy of holies" (recurring below in vv. 12, 24, 25) is probably based on the similar usage of Lev. 16:2 (where ambiguity is excluded by the added words "within the veil, before the mercy-seat"), 3, 16, 17, 20, 23, 27.[58] It is further to be noted that, whereas hitherto our author has used "the first tent" of the outer compartment of the sanctuary, here he uses it apparently to mean the sanctuary of "the first covenant," comprising the holy place and the holy of holies together.[59] And by "the first tabernacle" here we are to understand not merely the Mosaic tabernacle, but the other structures which replaced it from time to time, down to and including Herod's temple. The phrase "while the first tabernacle still stands" sheds no light, however, on the question whether or not Herod's temple was still in being when the epistle was written (AV/KJV renders the genitive absolute by the

---

discussed, among other questions of relevance to this section of Hebrews, by L. Morris in "The Day of Atonement and the Work of Christ," *RTR* 14 (1955), pp. 9-19. Cf. p. 376, n. 50.

57. Josephus (*Ant.* 3.123, 181) regards the holy of holies as symbolic of heaven, reserved for God alone, and the holy place (which in the tabernacle covered double the area of the holy of holies) as symbolic of earth and sea, which are accessible to human beings. So H. Koester, ("'Outside the Camp'; Heb. 13.9-14," *HTR* 55 [1962], p. 309) interprets the "tent" (i.e., the fore-tent) as "a symbol for the heavenly regions through which Christ was to pass to enter the heavenly sanctuary itself." This may well be our author's view. Cf. v. 11 below (pp. 211-13); also 4:14 (p. 115).

58. In Lev. 16 the outer compartment is called "the tent of meeting" in distinction from the inner compartment, which is there simply referred to as "the holy place" (vv. 16f., 20, 23) or "the holy sanctuary," *miqdaš haqqōdeš* (v. 33). N. H. Young ("The Gospel according to Hebrews 9," *NTS* 27 [1980-81], pp. 198-210, especially pp. 200-202) argues that "the first tent" is to be understood here in Heb. 9:8, as in vv. 2 and 6, of "the old covenant order now in process of dissolution."

59. Moffatt (ICC, *ad loc.*, p. 118) takes "the first tabernacle" in v. 8 in the same sense as in vv. 2, 6; according to him, our author "calls the fore-tent a παραβολή" (similarly N. H. Young, cited in n. 58 above). It is perhaps more likely, however, that the whole structure with its appropriate ritual is called a παραβολή.

past tense: "while as the first tabernacle was yet standing"). The phrase is part of a lengthy periodic sentence whose principal clause is "the priests go in continually into the first tabernacle . . . but into the second the high priest alone, once in the year." The present tense in this principal clause is a historic present, indicating primarily the procedure laid down by the Levitical law rather than the procedure which was still being enacted at Jerusalem while the author was writing, although the latter is not excluded. What he means is that unimpeded access to the presence of God was not granted until Christ came to accomplish his sacrificial ministry.

9 This state of affairs—the prohibition of general entry into the holy of holies—is parenthetically described as a parable or figure "for the time present" (ARV).[60] There is an ambiguity in these words: is "the present time" to be understood as "the time then present" (AV/KJV) or "the time now present" (ERV; cf. RSV, NEB)? If the former, then our author's meaning is that the presence of the veil was an "outward and visible sign" of the spiritual conditions then prevailing: the way to God had not yet been opened up. If the latter, then the veil, together with its significance, constituted "a parable bearing on the present crisis,"[61] emphasizing the contrast between the free access to God now guaranteed through Christ and the strictly limited access permitted by the structure and ceremonial of the earthly sanctuary. In the earthly sanctuary sacrifices were indeed offered, but their efficacy was sadly restricted; they could not bring "perfection" to the worshiper because they did not affect his conscience.[62] Now we see what our author wishes to teach his readers. The really effective barrier to a man or woman's free access to God is an inward and not a material one; it exists in the conscience. It is only when the conscience is purified that one is set free to approach God without reservation and offer him acceptable service and worship. And the sacrificial blood of bulls and goats is useless in this regard.[63] Animal sacrifice and

60. Gk. ἥτις παραβολὴ εἰς τὸν καιρὸν τὸν ἐνεστηκότα (the antecedent of ἥτις may be the whole situation of vv. 6-8, ἥτις being attracted to the gender and number of παραβολή).

61. W. Manson, *The Epistle to the Hebrews* (London, 1951), p. 132. That is to say, the real meaning of the tabernacle can only now be understood, in the light of the work of Christ.

62. Cf. v. 14; 10:2, 22; 13:18. Gk. συνείδησις ("conscience") is not a classical word. It belonged to vernacular Greek and only a short time before the beginning of the Christian era did it attain literary status; even then it was not generally adopted by philosophic writers. It was probably Paul who baptized it into its deeper sense of "moral conscience"; the word appears several times in his letters and was taken over from him by later NT and other Christian writers. We may compare Philo's use of τὸ συνειδός to denote a faculty which examines and passes judgment on conduct, "established in the soul like a judge" (*On the Creation* 128). See C. A. Pierce, *Conscience in the New Testament,* SBT 15 (London, 1955); J. Stelzenberger, *Syneidesis im Neuen Testament* (Paderborn, 1961).

63. This was appreciated by men and women of spiritual insight throughout Israel's history. That is plain enough from Ps. 51:16f., in the course of a prayer for forgiveness and restoration to fellowship with God. In later times the rabbis insisted that the repentance and confes-

other material ordinances which accompanied it could effect at best a ceremonial and symbolical removal of pollution.

10 What had regulations concerning food and drink and a variety of ritual washings to do with one's relation to God? The reference to "food and drink" probably has to do with the food-laws of Lev. 11.[64] Much more is said there about solid food than about drink; as far as drink goes, there is the direction that water may not be drunk from a vessel into which a dead animal has fallen (Lev. 11:34)—a sound hygienic direction, as no doubt were many of the food-laws, but having little enough to do with heart-religion. There were also the libations which accompanied several of the sacrificial offerings (cf. Num. 6:15, 17; 28:7f.). But for our author, as for Paul, these things were but "a shadow of the things to come" (Col. 2:17). As regards the "various ablutions," not only had the high priest to "bathe his body in water" after performing the ritual of the Day of Atonement (Lev. 16:24), but similar purifications were prescribed for a great variety of actual or ceremonial defilements.[65] Again, these purifications undoubtedly had great hygienic value, but when they were given religious value there was always the danger that those who practiced them might be tempted to think of religious duty exclu-

---

sion which attended the Day of Atonement were the real means by which atonement was made: "though no sacrifices be offered, the day in itself effects atonement" (*Sifra, 'Ēmōr* 14). But this relates rather to the situation after A.D. 70, when it was perforce impossible to perform the ancient ritual; while the temple was standing, the absence of confession and heart-repentance would indeed have invalidated the ritual, but it is hardly suggested that confession and heart-repentance could in themselves have sufficed, apart from the ritual. The whole implication of the tractate *Yoma*, which deals with the celebration of the Day of Atonement under the Second Temple, is that the detailed prescriptions of Lev. 16 are binding commandments of God, not one of which may be neglected. In the Qumran texts it is taught that the members of the community by their devotion to the law of God can procure atonement for the land of Israel "without the flesh of holocausts and the fat of sacrifices" (1QS 9.4); but they felt themselves conscientiously debarred from participation in the sacrificial services at Jerusalem because the temple was controlled by an unworthy and illegitimate priesthood; they looked forward to the day when acceptable sacrifices would be offered in a purified temple by a worthy priesthood. Their attitude was quite different from our author's; he regards the whole principle of an earthly sanctuary and animal sacrifices as a temporary expedient, now superseded forever. Cf. p. 384 with n. 92.

64. The expression "food and drink" (ἐπὶ βρώμασιν καὶ πόμασιν) denotes food-laws in general; we need not inquire too precisely which forms of "drink" our author had in mind (for πόμα cf. also 1 Cor. 10:4; 12:13 *v.l.*). Moffatt (ICC, *ad loc.*, p. 119) compares a few passages from the *Epistle of Aristeas:* "I suppose that most men feel some curiosity about the injunctions in the law with regard to meats and drinks and the animals which are considered unclean" (128); "our lawgiver . . . fenced us around on every side with prescribed purifications with regard to meats and drinks. . ." (142); "in the matter of meats and drinks he commands us first to offer a part as sacrifice, and only then to use the rest for ourselves" (158). For βρώματα cf. 13:9 (p. 377, n. 60).

65. Gk. διαφόροις βαπτισμοῖς (cf. 6:2). We may think also of the Qumran purifications in water; these indeed were of no avail for the man who was defiled at heart, but nonetheless they were obligatory for members of the community. (Cf. 1QS 3.4f.; see p. 142 with n. 22 and p. 215, n. 88.)

sively, or at least excessively, in terms of externalities. But all these things were "outward ordinances" (NEB), "regulations for the body" (RSV), not for the conscience, with a temporary and limited validity until the "time of reformation." By the rendering "reformation"[66] we might understand "reformation" in the sense of "reconstruction"; the coming of Christ involved a complete reshaping of the structure of Israel's religion. The old covenant was now to give way to the new, the shadow to the substance,[67] the outward and earthly copy to the inward and heavenly reality.

E. CHRIST'S ETERNAL REDEMPTION (9:11-14)

11 *But now Christ has appeared as high priest of the good things which have come to pass.[68] Through the greater and more perfect tent not made with hands—that is to say, not belonging to this creation—*

12 *and by virtue of his own blood, not the blood of goats and calves, he has entered the holy place once for all, having procured eternal redemption.*

13 *For if the blood of goats and bulls and the ashes of a heifer sprinkled on those who have been defiled have sanctifying power as far as bodily cleansing is concerned,*

14 *how much more will the blood of Christ, who through the eternal Spirit[69] offered himself to God as an unblemished sacrifice, cleanse[70] our[71] conscience from dead works so as to worship the living[72] God?*

11 But now the time of reformation has arrived; what used to be "the good things to come" are now "the good things that have come" (RSV), "the good

66. Gk. διόρθωσις, here only in the NT; we might render it "the new order."

67. In Hebrews the law is a pattern or preliminary blueprint of the redemptive order introduced by Christ; cf. Col. 2:17 (with E. Percy, *Die Probleme der Kolosser- und Epheserbrief.* [Lund, 1946], pp. 287f.).

68. The majority reading is τῶν μελλόντων ἀγαθῶν, "the good things that are to come," but the weight of the evidence favors τῶν γενομένων ἀγαθῶν, "the good things that have come" (so 𝔓46 B D* 1611 1739 2005 with the Syriac versions, Chrysostom, and Cyril of Jerusalem). "The combination of the oldest Greek and Latin with the Syriac evidence is in itself almost irresistible" in support of γενομένων rather than μελλόντων (G. Zuntz, *The Text of the Epistles* [London, 1953], p. 119); the reading μελλόντων is probably due to the influence of 10:1. See p. 235.

69. Gk. διὰ πνεύματος αἰωνίου (the ARV mg. suggests "his eternal spirit"). A few witnesses (D* P, with the Latin and Coptic versions) have "holy spirit" (πνεύματος ἁγίου) for "eternal spirit."

70. Codex B is not extant from this point onward.

71. The textual evidence is rather evenly divided between ὑμῶν ("your") and ἡμῶν ("our"); the latter is the reading of the ERV/ARV mg., the RSV mg., and the NEB.

72. A few witnesses add καὶ ἀληθινῷ ("and true") after ζῶντι ("living"), under the influence of 1 Thess. 1:9. (For "the living God" cf. Heb. 3:12; 10:31; 12:22.)

things already in being" (NEB). For Christ has appeared, and in him the shadows have given way to the perfect and abiding reality. And his appearance is properly announced with a triumphant trumpet-flourish; *his* entrance into the presence of God is not a day of soul-affliction and fasting,[73] like the Day of Atonement under the old legislation, but a day of gladness and song, the day when Christians celebrate the accession of their Priest-King.

The New Year, the Day of Atonement, and the Feast of Tabernacles[74] originally belonged to one festal complex at which the kingship of the God of Israel was annually celebrated. What part was played in this celebration by the king of Israel, God's vicegerent over his people, is a debated question.[75] But in the New Testament antitype of this festal complex the divine Priest-King fills the central and decisive rôle; by virtue of his perfect self-sacrifice he has taken his seat at the right hand of the throne of God, and reigns forevermore from the heavenly Zion, high priest of the new and eternal order. The sanctuary in which he ministers is the true tabernacle of which the Mosaic shrine was but a material copy; it is a sanctuary not made with hands, not belonging to the earthly creation.[76] The "greater and more perfect tent" through which he has passed to enter the heavenly holy of holies comprises "the heavens" of 4:14, the counterpart of the outer compartment in the earthly sanctuary. The idea of a sanctuary not made with hands goes back to the earliest forms of Christian teaching. Our Lord himself spoke of the time when the Jerusalem temple would be replaced by a temple "made without hands"[77] (Mark 14:58; cf. John 2:19-22), and Stephen and Paul insisted that no building "made with hands" could accommodate the Most High (Acts 7:48; 17:24).[78] What then is the nature of the spiritual temple in which God dwells? When Stephen maintained that "the Most High does not dwell in houses made with hands," he confirmed his statement by quoting Isa. 66:1f. But in that same prophetic context God declares that in preference to any material temple he chooses one "that is humble and contrite in spirit, and trembles at my word."

---

73. Cf. Lev. 16:29, 31; 23:26, 32.

74. The first, tenth, and fifteenth days of Tishri respectively.

75. See, e.g., S. Mowinckel, *He That Cometh,* E.T. (Oxford, 1956), pp. 21-95; and for a contrary view N. H. Snaith, *The Jewish New Year Festival* (London, 1947), pp. 195-203, 205-19.

76. See A. Vanhoye, "'Par la tente plus grande et plus parfaite . . .' Hé 9,11," *Biblica* 46 (1965), pp. 1-28. N. H. Young, "The Gospel according to Hebrews 9," pp. 202-5, argues that διά with σκηνῆς here has the same instrumental force ("by means of") as it has with αἵματος (twice) in v. 12. For the tent "not made with hands" (cf. p. 182, n. 16) see A. Cole, *The New Temple* (London, 1950); R. J. McKelvey, *The New Temple* (London, 1969); E. P. Sanders, *Jesus and Judaism* (London, 1985), pp. 77-90; I. H. Marshall, "Church and Temple in the New Testament," *TynB* 40.2 (1989), pp. 203-22.

77. While the words of Mark 14:58 are put into Jesus' mouth by "false witnesses," they are not a fabrication but a misrepresentation of something which he really said.

78. Cf. *Acts,* NICNT, pp. 149-51, 336.

And this means that he prefers to make his dwelling with people of that character, as is shown by the similar words of Isa. 57:15: "For thus says the high and lofty One who inhabits eternity, whose name is Holy: I dwell in the high and holy place, and with him also who is of a contrite and humble spirit." Our author stands right in this prophetic tradition when he affirms that the people of God are the house of God, "if we maintain our confidence and the hope in which we boast" (3:6). But how can the Son of God, who has "passed through the heavens" (4:14), be regarded as dwelling among his people? Because, as he has entered the heavenly sanctuary "by virtue of his own blood" (v. 12), his people, by virtue of that same blood, also enter it as "perfected" worshipers (10:19). Where he is, there are they.

12 Whereas Aaron and his successors went into the earthly holy of holies on the Day of Atonement by virtue of animal-sacrifices—"through the blood of goats and calves"[79]—Christ has entered the heavenly sanctuary "by virtue of[80] his own blood." It is unfortunate that the RSV says that he entered "taking not the blood of goats and calves but his own blood." Aaron certainly carried the sacrificial blood into the holy of holies,[81] but our author deliberately avoids saying that Christ carried his own blood into the heavenly sanctuary. Even as a symbolic expression this is open to objection. There have been expositors who, pressing the analogy of the Day of Atonement beyond the limits observed by our author, have argued that the expiatory work of Christ was not completed on the cross—not completed, indeed, until he ascended from earth and "made atonement 'for us' in the heavenly holy of holies by the presentation of his efficacious blood."[82] But while it was necessary under the old covenant for the sacrificial blood first to be shed in the

---

79. The plural is generalizing. "Calves" (Gk. μόσχος) is used here as a variation on "bulls" (Gk. ταῦρος, as in v. 13); the animal which Aaron was to sacrifice as a sin offering for himself and his house was "a young bull" (Lev. 16:3) and might therefore be designated in Greek either by μόσχος (so the LXX in Lev. 16) or by ταῦρος.

80. Gk. διά, with both occurrences of αἵματος.

81. Cf. v. 7 ("not without blood"), v. 25 ("with [ἐν] blood not his own"—where ἐν is probably instrumental in force, as in 10:19; 13:20, implying that the sacrificial blood carried by the high priest was his title to enter the inner sanctuary).

82. K. M. Monroe, *EQ* 5 (1933), p. 404 (in an article "Time Element in the Atonement," pp. 397-408, which was answered by T. Houghton, "The Atonement," *EQ* 6 [1934], pp. 137-46). Monroe argued that our Lord, after his resurrection, ascended immediately into heaven to sprinkle his blood on "the heavenly capporeth" and therefore could not allow Mary Magdalene to hinder him (John 20:17) until he had completed this essential stage of his atoning work. The ascension of John 20:17 is thus quite distinct from the ascension of Acts 1:9. This thesis had been sustained nearly half a century earlier by C. E. Stuart in a number of papers, especially *Propitiation by Blood* (London, 1887) and *A Few Remarks as to Atonement, Propitiation, and the Priesthood of the Lord Jesus Christ* (London, 1888). But it serves only to warn those who require such a warning against basing doctrines on types, instead of using types (if at all) to illustrate securely based doctrines. See also N. H. Young, "The Gospel according to Hebrews 9."

court and then to be brought into the holy of holies, no such division of our Lord's sacrifice into two phases is envisaged under the new covenant. When on the cross he offered up his life to God as a sacrifice for his people's sin, he accomplished in reality what Aaron and his successors performed in type by the twofold act of slaying the victim and presenting its blood in the holy of holies. The title of the Anglican Article XXXI speaks rightly "of the one oblation of Christ finished upon the cross." And then "through his own blood"—that is, by virtue of the infinitely acceptable oblation of his life— he could appear before God, not on sufferance but by right, as his people's prevailing representative and high priest. The Aaronic high priests had to present themselves before God repeatedly, because such redemption as their ministry procured bore but a token and temporary character; but Christ entered in once for all,[83] to be enthroned there in perpetuity, because the redemption procured by him is perfect in nature and eternal in effect.[84]

13 The blood of slaughtered animals under the old order did possess a certain efficacy, but it was an outward efficacy for the removal of ceremonial pollution. "The blood of goats and bulls" is a general term covering not only the sacrifices of the Day of Atonement but other sacrifices as well (we may compare the ironical question of Ps. 50:13, "Do I eat the flesh of bulls, or drink the blood of goats?"). The sin offerings presented on the Day of Atonement, or at any other time, had no effect on the consciences of those on whose behalf they were brought; they served merely in an external and symbolical manner to counteract the defilement of sin. Along with these offerings our author mentions "the ashes of a heifer[85] sprinkled on those who have been defiled." This is a reference to a ritual prescribed in Num. 19, for the removal of ceremonial impurity. A perfect red heifer, which had never borne the yoke, was to be slaughtered outside the camp of Israel in the presence of Eleazar the priest (representing his father Aaron, the high priest), who

---

83. Gk. ἐφάπαξ (as in 7:27; 10:10).

84. Cf. 5:9, where Christ is called "the source of eternal salvation." In the present verse "redemption" represents Gk. λύτρωσις, found elsewhere in the NT only in Luke 1:68; 2:38. The word is derived from λύτρον, "ransom" (used of the Son of Man in Matt. 20:28 par. Mark 10:45), whence also we have the derivatives λυτροῦσθαι, "to ransom" (Luke 24:21; Tit. 2:14; 1 Pet. 1:18), λυτρωτής, "redeemer," "ransomer" (Acts 7:35), and ἀντίλυτρον, "counter-ransom" (1 Tim. 2:6). The compound substantive ἀπολύτρωσις is more common in the NT than the simple λύτρωσις; it occurs in Heb. 9:15; 11:35, and in eight other NT passages, of which Rom. 3:24 is of outstanding importance for our understanding of the word as applied to the work of Christ. Cf. B. B. Warfield, *The Person and Work of Christ* (Philadelphia, 1950), pp. 325-48 ("'Redeemer' and 'Redemption'" [1916]), pp. 429-75 ("The New Testament Terminology of 'Redemption'" [1917]); F. Büchsel, *TDNT*, IV, pp. 340-56 (*s.v.* λύτρον, λύτρωσις, ἀπολύτρωσις, etc.); W. Mundle, J. Schneider, and C. Brown, *NIDNTT*, III, pp. 177-223 (*s.v.* "Redemption"); L. Morris, *The Apostolic Preaching of the Cross* (London, ³1965), pp. 11-62.

85. Gk. δάμαλις, as in the LXX of Num. 19, where the Hebrew word is simply *pārāh*, "cow." (The Targum of Pseudo-Jonathan has *'eglâ*, "heifer.")

was then to sprinkle its blood seven times in front of the tabernacle. The body of the heifer was then to be completely incinerated; Eleazar was to throw cedar wood, hyssop (marjoram), and scarlet thread into the burning fire. When all was consumed, the ashes were to be gathered up and stored outside the camp to be used as occasion required for the preparation of *mê niddāh*, "water for (the removal of) impurity." Anyone who contracted ceremonial defilement through touching or approaching a dead body was to be cleansed by being sprinkled with water containing some of the ashes of the heifer. Hence the allusion here to "the ashes of a heifer sprinkled on those who have been defiled" so as to "sanctify"[86] them in respect of "bodily cleansing"[87] (NEB, "to hallow those who have been defiled and restore their external purity"). The *mê niddāh* could be used for other purificatory purposes; according to Num. 31:21ff., metal vessels captured among the spoils of war could be cleansed from idolatrous contamination by being passed through fire and then sprinkled with this water. But while the water cleansed those who had incurred ceremonial defilement, it had the curious effect of rendering others who touched it (especially those who administered it) ceremonially unclean until sundown. The ritual of the red heifer is appropriately mentioned by our author at this point because, like the sacrifices on the Day of Atonement, "it is a sin offering" (Num. 19:9).[88] In course of time a closer connection seems

---

86. Here "sanctify" (Gk. ἁγιάζειν) means little more than "purify"; the person who had been defiled was by this means restored to a state in which he was no longer religiously tabu but could take part once more in the prescribed ordinances of worship. According to R. Yoḥanan (*Num. Rabba* 19.8), "neither does the dead body defile, nor does the water purify; but the Holy One, blessed be He, says, 'I have laid down a statute, I have issued a decree; you shall not transgress my decree'" (on Num. 19:2)—i.e., "This ritual is something that God has ordained, and so we carry it out."

87. Gk. πρὸς τὴν τῆς σαρκὸς καθαρότητα, "for the purification of the flesh." "Flesh" in this epistle denotes the outer and physical element in the human make-up in contrast to one's inner being, or conscience (vv. 9, 14). Cf. the "fleshly ordinances" of v. 9, the "fleshly commandment" of 7:16, and the contrast between "the fathers of our flesh" and "the Father of spirits" in 12:9. Cf. also 1 Pet. 3:21, where baptism is presented not as a "removal of dirt from the body" but as the Godward appeal or response of "a good conscience."

88. Heb. *ḥaṭṭā'ṯ hî;* hence the Mishnah repeatedly refers to the *mê niddāh* ("water for impurity") as *mê ḥaṭṭā'ṯ* ("water of sin offering" or "water for sin"), as in Num. 8:7, MT. The Mishnaic tractate *Parah* is devoted to this ritual. After A.D. 70 the slaying of the red heifer (which had previously taken place on the Mount of Olives, "outside the camp") was discontinued, and so the water for impurity could not be renewed once the existing stock of ashes was exhausted. According to Mishnah, *Parah* 3.5, the last priest to kill the red heifer was Ishmael ben Phabi (high priest *c.* A.D. 58-60). Among the Samaritans it was held that all that was necessary for the ritual was a valid priesthood, not a temple or altar; accordingly the slaying and burning of the red heifer was continued by them until 1348, the ashes of this last burning being preserved until *c.* 1600 (cf. M. Gaster, *Samaritan Traditions and Oral Law* [London, 1932], pp. 195f.). It has been suggested that the Qumran community also continued to carry out the ritual in spite of their separation from the temple, since they possessed a legitimate priesthood (cf. J. Bowman, "Did the Qumran Sect burn the Red Heifer?" *RQ* 1 [1958-59], pp. 73-84). Whether they carried out the

to have developed between the red heifer ceremony and the Day of Atonement than the written law prescribed: according to Maimonides[89] (who presumably had some traditional basis for his information) the high priest was sprinkled with the ashes of a heifer twice during the seven days[90] for which he was kept isolated in the temple before the Day of Atonement, in case he had inadvertently contracted ceremonial defilement.

Just how the blood of sacrificed animals or the ashes of the red heifer effected a ceremonial cleansing our author does not explain; it was sufficient for him, and no doubt for his readers, that the Old Testament ascribed this efficacy to them.

14 But it is no mere ceremonial cleansing that is effected by the sacrifice of Christ. Here our author presents us with one of the most impressive instances of his favorite "how much more" argument. Those earlier rituals might effect external purification, but the blood of Christ[91]—his offering up of himself to God—cleanses the conscience; it does the very thing that they could not do, since we have just been told that they could not, "as regards the conscience, make the worshiper perfect" (v. 9). They could restore him to formal communion with God and with his fellow-worshipers; but if it was an inward sense of guilt that kept him in heart at a distance from God, how could they possibly deal with that condition?

---

ritual or not, they certainly attached high importance to cleansing with *mê niddāh*, which nevertheless was of no avail to those whose heart remained impenitent (1QS 3.4-12). This probably explains Josephus's reference to the "purer lustrations" which the Essenes practiced (*Ant.* 18.19). (Cf. the account of John's baptism in Josephus, *Ant.* 18.117, quoted on p. 142, n. 22; see also p. 210, n. 65.) The *Epistle of Barnabas* (8:1-6) allegorizes the ritual of the red heifer, detail by detail, as a type of the cross and the gospel; cf. G. Allon, "Halakhah in the Epistle of Barnabas," *Tarbiz* 11 (1939-40), pp. 23ff. (summarized by S. Lowy, *JJS* 11 [1960], p. 24); R. A. Kraft (ed.), *The Didache and Barnabas* (New York, 1965), pp. 101-5. See also p. 255.

89. *Yad ha-Ḥazaqah* 1, *halakhah* 4 (quoted in full in F. Delitzsch, *Commentary on the Epistle to the Hebrews*, E.T., II [Edinburgh, 1872], p. 466). In his *Sepher Tohoroth* Maimonides expects that the burning of the red heifer will be resumed when Messiah comes, so that water for the removal of impurity can be prepared once more.

90. The isolation of the high priest for seven days preceding the Day of Atonement is laid down in Mishnah *Yoma* 1.1. According to Maimonides it was on the third and seventh days of this period that he was to be sprinkled; it is a matter of interest in this connection that the Qaraites, having no ashes of a heifer at their disposal, substituted for the sprinkling with *mê niddāh* in the situation envisaged by Num. 19 a purificatory bath on the third and seventh days (P. S. Goldberg, *Karaite Liturgy* [Manchester, 1957], p. 40).

91. "The blood of Christ" in v. 14 means his sacrificial death; "it is hard to envisage a reason for interpreting 'the blood' here in a sense other than that given by the words which follow, 'a death having taken place'" (L. Morris, *The Apostolic Preaching of the Cross*, p. 125). J. Behm, *TDNT*, I, pp. 172-77 (*s.v.* αἷμα); A. M. Stibbs, *The Meaning of the Word "Blood" in Scripture* (London, 1947); F. J. Taylor, *A Theological Word Book of the Bible*, ed. A. Richardson (London, 1950), pp. 33f. (*s.v.* "Blood"); L. L. Morris, "The Biblical Use of the Term 'Blood,'" *JTS* n.s. 3 (1952), pp. 216-27; F. Laubach, *NIDNTT*, I, pp. 220-24 (*s.v.* "Blood"). For the *a fortiori* argument cf. 2:1-3 (p. 68, n. 4).

Not all the blood of beasts
On Jewish altars slain
Could give the guilty conscience peace,
  Or wash away the stain:
  But Christ, the heavenly Lamb,
  Takes all our sins away,
A sacrifice of nobler name
And richer blood than they.[92]

Those earlier sacrifices were but token sacrifices; the sacrifice of Christ was a real self-offering, accomplished on the moral and spiritual plane. It was "through the eternal Spirit" that he offered himself to God. The phrase "through eternal spirit" (as it is literally, whether the substantive be spelled with a capital "S" or not) is extremely difficult to interpret with satisfactory precision. As regards the variant rendering of the ARV margin, "through his eternal spirit," it may be said that if our author had meant this, he could have said so quite simply. That our Lord's self-sacrifice is described as being "a spiritual and eternal sacrifice" (NEB) is clear, but perhaps even more is intended.[93] Behind our author's thinking lies the portrayal of the Isaianic Servant of the Lord, who yields up his life to God as a guilt offering for many, bearing their sin and procuring their justification. When this Servant is introduced for the first time, God says: "I have put my Spirit upon him" (Isa. 42:1). It is in the power of the Divine Spirit, accordingly, that the Servant accomplishes every phase of his ministry, including the crowning phase in which he accepts death for the transgression of his people, filling the twofold rôle of priest and victim, as Christ does in this epistle.[94] So, "in Christ's sacrifice we see the final revelation of what God is, that behind which there is nothing in God, so that the religion which rests on that sacrifice rests on the ultimate truth of the divine nature, and can never be shaken."[95]

The animals used for sacrifice in earlier days were required to be physically unblemished; the life which Christ presented to God on the cross was

92. I. Watts. His designation of Christ as "the heavenly Lamb" in this context is probably due simply to the NT designation of him as the Lamb of God, as in John 1:29 (cf. 1 Pet. 1:19).

93. A. Vanhoye takes the πνεῦμα αἰώνιον here to be the spiritual counterpart to the altar fire of the old order ("Esprit éternel et feu du sacrifice en Hé 9,14," *Biblica* 64 [1983], pp. 263-74; cf. "L'oblation sacerdotale du Christ dans l'épître aux Hébreux," *Didaskalia* 14 [1984], pp. 11-30, especially pp. 20-26).

94. Cf. v. 28 (p. 232 with nn. 169-72). The Servant's priestly rôle appears especially in Isa. 52:15, "so shall he sprinkle many nations" (for a vindication of this rendering cf. E. J. Young, *Studies in Isaiah* [Grand Rapids, 1954], pp. 199-206; H. L. Ellison, *The Servant of Jehovah* [London, 1953], pp. 29f.); the allusion may well be to the sprinkling of the water for the removal of impurity (cf. the sprinkling of 10:22; 12:24).

95. J. Denney, *The Death of Christ* (London, [6]1907), p. 208. The πνεῦμα is eternal because divine.

a life free from inward blemish; like the Servant of the Lord, "he had done no violence, and there was no deceit in his mouth" (Isa. 53:9).[96] Our Lord's complete holiness, his "active obedience" to God, is essential to the efficacy of his sacrifice. "Only one who knew no sin could take any responsibility in regard to it which would create a new situation for sinners. . . . Christ's offering of Himself without spot to God had an absolute or ideal character; it was something beyond which nothing could be, or could be conceived to be, as a response to God's mind and requirements in relation to sin. It was the final response, a spiritual response, to the divine necessities of the situation. . . . His sacrifice was rational and voluntary,[97] an intelligent and loving response to the holy and gracious will of God, and to the terrible situation of man."[98] How this particular response, and nothing else, could satisfy both the divine will and the human predicament becomes clearer in 10:5-10, where our author interprets the work of Christ in terms of Ps. 40:6-8.

It is not contact with a dead body, or anything of a material and external nature, that conveys real defilement or interrupts true communion with God. Our Lord made it plain on a memorable occasion that no one is defiled by anything outside himself; "but the things which come out of a man are what defile him. . . . For from within, out of the heart of man, come evil thoughts, etc. . . . All these evil things come from within, and they defile a man" (Mark 7:15, 21, 23). It is an inward and spiritual purification that is required if heart-communion with God is to be enjoyed. And therefore the "dead works" from which the conscience must be cleansed cannot be, as some commentators have held,[99] the unavailing ceremonial of Judaism; they must be things which convey inward and spiritual defilement. As in Heb. 6:1 (where "repentance from dead works" belongs to the rudiments of Christian teaching), they are those practices and attitudes which belong to the way of death, which pollute the soul and erect a barrier between it and God. But their pollution is removed from the conscience by the work of Christ, so that men and women, emancipated from inward bondage, can worship God in spirit and in truth. This is the "perfection" which the ancient ceremonial was unable to achieve.

F. THE MEDIATOR OF THE NEW COVENANT (9:15-22)

15 *For this reason, too, he is mediator of a new covenant, so that, now that there has been a death effective for the redemption of the trans-*

---

96. These actual words are applied to Christ in 1 Pet. 2:22.

97. Cf. Mark 14:36 ("not what I will, but what thou wilt"); John 17:19 ("for their sake I consecrate myself").

98. J. Denney, *Death of Christ*, pp. 227f.

99. Cf. p. 139, n. 14.

gressions committed under the first covenant, those who have been called may receive the promise of their eternal inheritance.

16 *For where there is a covenant—in this case, a testamentary covenant*[100]*—it is necessary that the testator's death should be registered.*[101]

17 *A testament is valid only when death has taken place;*[102] *has it ever*[103] *any force as long as the testator remains alive?*[104]

18 *Therefore, even the first covenant—or testament—has not been ratified*[105] *without blood.*

19 *For when every commandment*[106] *had been recited by Moses to all the people, in accordance with the law,*[107] *he took the blood of the calves [and goats],*[108] *with water, scarlet wool, and hyssop, and sprinkled both the book itself and all the people,*

20 *saying, "This is the blood of the covenant which God has enjoined on you."*[109]

21 *In the same way, too, he sprinkled with the blood the tent and all the vessels of divine service.*

22 *According to the law almost*[110] *everything is cleansed with blood, and there is no forgiveness apart from the shedding of blood.*

15 That Jesus is "mediator of a better covenant"—the new covenant foretold by Jeremiah—has already been stated in 8:6. But now the basis of his

100. "Testament" and "covenant" are variant renderings of the one Greek word διαθήκη.

101. Gk. φέρεσθαι, lit. "be brought," here probably used in the technical sense "be registered" (so *P. Oxy.*, II [London, 1899], no. 244, l. 12) or "be produced as evidence" (cf. J. J. Wettstein, *ad loc.*: "necesse est afferri testimonia de morte testatoris").

102. Gk. ἐπὶ νεκροῖς, lit. "over dead people," i.e., "with reference to dead people"; not "over the dead bodies" of the covenant victims, for they could not be classed as διαθέμενοι.

103. Gk. μήποτε, for which ℵ* D* have μὴ τότε ("not then").

104. In the ERV this clause is treated as a question: "for doth it ever avail while he that made it liveth?" This construction does best justice to the negative μή, which is appropriate in a question expecting the answer "No."

105. Gk. ἐγκεκαίνισται (from ἐγκαινίζω, "consecrate," used in the NT only here and in 10:20). See p. 250, n. 85.

106. Gk. πάσης ἐντολῆς, for which 𝔭⁴⁶ D* and Chrysostom read πάσης τῆς ἐντολῆς ("all the commandment").

107. Gk. κατὰ τὸν νόμον, but the article is omitted by ℵ* with the bulk of later manuscripts and the TR. Cf. 10:8 (p. 239, n. 29).

108. The phrase "and the goats" (Gk. καὶ τῶν τράγων) should probably be omitted with 𝔭⁴⁶ ℵᶜ K L Ψ 1739, about 30 Byzantine manuscripts, Chrysostom, and the Syriac versions; the addition, if such it be, probably is due to the influence of v. 12 (cf. Zuntz, *Text*, p. 55). (If, on the other hand, the words are accepted as authentic, their omission from 𝔭⁴⁶ and other authorities could be explained as due to harmonization with Ex. 24:5.)

109. Quoted from Ex. 24:8, where the LXX, following the Hebrew, has ἰδού ("behold") for τοῦτο ("this [is]") and διέθετο ("covenanted") for ἐνετείλατο ("commanded"). The initial "this is" may be influenced by the words of institution of the *new* covenant (cf. Mark 14:24; 1 Cor. 11:25). On the absence of eucharistic reference from Hebrews see pp. 379f.

110. Gk. σχεδόν, "I may almost say" (ERV/ARV), "it might almost be said" (NEB).

mediatorship is made plain; that basis is his sacrificial death. By virtue of his death redemption has been provided for those who had broken the law of God; the life of Christ was the costly price paid to liberate them from their sins.[111] The first covenant provided a measure of atonement and remission for sins committed under it, but it was incapable of providing "eternal redemption"; this was a blessing which had to await the inauguration of the new covenant, which embodies God's promise to his people: "I will forgive their iniquity, and I will remember their sin no more" (Jer. 31:34). The basing of the new covenant on the death of Christ is a New Testament doctrine not peculiar to our author; it finds clearest expression in the words of institution spoken by our Lord over the cup: "This is my blood of the covenant, which is poured out for many" (Mark 14:24) or, in their earliest recorded form, "This cup is the new covenant in my blood" (1 Cor. 11:25).[112] And now that this redemptive death has taken place, the "promise of their eternal inheritance" has been made good to those "who have been called"; the new covenant, and everything that the grace of God provides under it, is forever theirs. Christians have already been described in Heb. 6:17 as "the heirs of the promise"; the fulfilment of the promise is the "eternal inheritance" into which they have entered. "Eternal" is an adjective which our author associates especially with the new covenant; that covenant itself is eternal (13:20), and so the redemption which it provides and the inheritance into which it brings the people of God are likewise eternal (vv. 12, 15); the Mediator of this covenant, having offered himself up to God as "a spiritual and eternal sacrifice" (v. 14, NEB), has become to all who obey him the "source of eternal salvation" (5:9).[113] The eternal inheritance of grace and glory both here and hereafter is for those who "have been called"—for those who have already been designated "partakers of a heavenly calling"

111. "The redemption of the transgressions committed under the first covenant" could have direct relevance only to readers of Israelite birth or adoption, since these transgressions were breaches of the Mosaic law, which was an integral part of the "first covenant." This retrospective validity of the death of Christ is stated in more general terms, which cover Gentiles as well as Jews, in Rom. 3:25 ("whom God set forth as an atonement . . . to show his righteousness, because in his divine forbearance he had passed over former sins"); cf. Acts 17:30. With "redemption" (ἀπολύτρωσις) cf. the uncompounded λύτρωσις in v. 12 (p. 214, n. 84). E. Riggenbach (ZK, *ad loc.*) quotes Philo, *Special Laws* 1.215: "through the altar is given absolution (ἀπολύσεις) and complete forgiveness (ἀφέσεις) of all sins and transgressions."

112. To Mark's wording Matt. 26:28 adds "for the forgiveness of sins" (which is in any case implied in the shorter form). See p. 194 with n. 69. Paul's wording, probably preserving the tradition which he had received on becoming a Christian, appears in a document of A.D. 55 (some ten years earlier than Mark) and repeats what had been communicated orally to the Corinthian church five years before. Such variation in wording as is known today between one church tradition and another evidently existed in the first Christian generation.

113. This accounts for all the occurrences of αἰώνιος in the epistle with the exception of "eternal judgment" in 6:2 (see p. 143 with n. 33).

(3:1). The close connection between God's effectual calling of his people and the heritage which is theirs as his sons and heirs, joint-heirs with Christ, is set out more fully by Paul in Rom. 8:14-30.

16-17   But why was the Mediator's death necessary for the ratification of the covenant? It is not easy to follow the argument here in an English version, because we are almost bound to use two different English words[114] to represent two different aspects of the meaning of one Greek word, whereas our author's argument depends on his use of the same Greek word throughout. The Greek word is *diathēkē,* which has the comprehensive sense of "settlement."[115] As used elsewhere in the epistle, the particular kind of settlement which *diathēkē* denotes is a covenant graciously bestowed by God upon his people, by which he brings them into a special relationship with himself;[116] in other words, it is used, as it had been used by the Greek translators of the Old Testament, as the equivalent of the Hebrew *berîth.*[117] But in vv. 16 and 17 of our present chapter it is used of another kind of settlement, a last will and testament, in which property is bequeathed by the owner to various other persons on the understanding that they have no title to it until he dies.[118] There are, in fact, some scholars who have maintained that "testa-

---

114. This difficulty is eased in the NEB by the rendering of the opening words of v. 15: "And therefore he is the mediator of a new covenant, or testament, under which. . . ." Moffatt's version makes similar use of two words at the beginning of v. 18; after using "covenant" twice in v. 15, and "will" in vv. 16f., it continues: "Hence even the first covenant of God's will was not inaugurated apart from blood."

115. See F. O. Norton, *A Lexicographical and Historical Study of ΔΙΑΘΗΚΗ* (Chicago, 1908); consult also MM; BAGD; J. Behm and G. Quell in *TDNT,* II, pp. 106-34 (*s.v.* διαθήκη); J. Guhrt and O. Becker, *NIDNTT,* I, pp. 365-76 (*s.v.* "Covenant," etc.); they supply further documentation.

116. "The covenant is a sovereign dispensation of God's grace. It is grace bestowed and a relation established" (J. Murray, *The Covenant of Grace* [London, 1954], p. 19).

117. Heb. *berîth,* of course, is used in the OT of covenants between human beings as well as of covenants between God and human beings; but even "when all the instances of merely human covenants are examined, it would definitely appear that the notion of sworn fidelity is thrust into prominence in these covenants rather than that of mutual contract" (J. Murray, *Covenant of Grace,* p. 10). See also (in addition to works mentioned on p. 193, n. 62) W. Eichrodt, *Theology of the Old Testament,* E.T., I (London, 1961), pp. 36-511; M. G. Kline, *By Oath Consigned* (Grand Rapids, 1968); L. Perlitt, *Bundestheologie im Alten Testament,* WMANT 36 (Neukirchen-Vluyn, 1969); G. W. Buchanan, *The Consequences of the Covenant,* NovTSup 20 (Leiden, 1970); B. Baltzer, *The Covenant Formulary,* E.T. (Oxford, 1971); D. J. McCarthy, *Old Testament Covenant* (Oxford, 1972); K. M. Campbell, *God's Covenant* (Nutley, NJ, 1974); O. P. Robertson, *The Christ of the Covenants* (Grand Rapids, 1980); W. J. Dumbrell, *Covenant and Creation* (Exeter, 1984); T. E. McComiskey, *The Covenants of Promise* (Grand Rapids, 1985); E. W. Nicholson, *God and His People: Covenant and Theology in the Old Testament* (Oxford, 1986); R. T. Beckwith, "The Unity and Diversity of God's Covenants," *TynB* 38 (1987), pp. 93-118. Cf. p. 224, n. 132.

118. We may compare (and contrast) the use of the testamentary analogy made in the Valentinian *Gospel of Truth* (Jung Codex 20:15ff.), in a passage immediately following that quoted on p. 88, n. 86: "As the property of a deceased householder remains concealed so long

ment" is the sense of *diathēkē* throughout this epistle,[119] if not indeed throughout the Greek Bible.[120] "Testament" is certainly the predominant sense of the word in Hellenistic Greek;[121] but in the Greek Bible it usually takes its meaning from the Old Testament Hebrew word *berîth*, which does not have the sense of "testament."[122] On the other hand, there have been exegetes who have endeavored to retain the meaning "covenant" even in Heb. 9:16f.; among these B. F. Westcott is outstanding.[123] But it simply is not true that "where a *covenant* is, there must of necessity be the death of him that made it"—nor of necessity the death of anyone else. Westcott takes "him that made it" to point to the covenant victim,[124] with whom the maker of the covenant is representatively identified. But not only is this a straining of the natural force of the words here used; it is not always true that the maker of

---

as his testament has not been opened, so the All remained concealed so long as the Father of the All . . . remained invisible. Therefore Jesus appeared and revealed this book; he was nailed to a tree; he affixed the testamentary disposition from the Father to the cross."

119. So E. Riggenbach, "Der Begriff der ΔΙΑΘΗΚΗ im Hebräerbrief," in *Theologische Studien Theodor Zahn zum 10. Oktober 1908 dargebracht* (Leipzig, 1908), pp. 289ff.; cf. A. Deissmann, *Paul,* E.T. (London, 1926), p. 175 with n. 3; G. D. Kilpatrick, "Διαθήκη in Hebrews," *ZNW* 68 (1977), pp. 263-65.

120. Cf. J. B. Payne, *The Theology of the Older Testament* (Grand Rapids, 1962), pp. 71ff., where "testament" is preferred as the translation of Heb. $b^e rît$ as well as of Gk. διαθήκη.

121. Occasionally it may have the sense of "contract" or "compact," a sense more naturally expressed by classical συνθήκη (a word not found in the NT and but rarely in the LXX). Aristophanes (*Birds* 439f.) provides a classical instance of διαθήκη used in more or less this sense.

122. Another NT passage where a similar question arises regarding the precise sense of διαθήκη is Gal. 3:15, 17, where the principle that a person's διαθήκη, when once it has been validated, cannot be annulled or have a codicil added to it by anyone else, is invoked to prove that God's covenant with Abraham could not be affected by the law, which came four centuries later. Although the question of death does not enter into the immediate argument here, it may be that Gal. 3:15 means that "the will (διαθήκη) of a human being is irrevocable when once duly executed" (W. M. Ramsay, *Historical Commentary on Galatians* [London, 1899], p. 349; Ramsay has an extended discussion of the meaning of διαθήκη both here and elsewhere in the Pauline letters, pp. 349-70). In that case there is the same oscillation between general and particular senses of διαθήκη as we have here in Hebrews. Cf. H. N. Ridderbos, *Galatians,* NICNT (Grand Rapids, 1953), pp. 130-36; F. F. Bruce, *Galatians,* NIGTC (Exeter/Grand Rapids, 1982), pp. 168-74; R. Y. K. Fung, *Galatians,* NICNT (Grand Rapids, 1988), pp. 153-57.

123. B. F. Westcott, *The Epistle to the Hebrews* (London, 1903), pp. 300-304; see the critique of his arguments by G. Vos, "Hebrews, the Epistle of the Diatheke," *PTR* 13 (1915), pp. 614ff. (cf. p. 171, n. 69). The rendering of "covenant" throughout the passage has been upheld also by E. Hatch, *Essays in Biblical Greek* (Oxford, 1889), p. 48; G. Milligan, *The Theology of the Epistle to the Hebrews* (Edinburgh, 1899), pp. 152f., 166-70 (Milligan later modified his position); A. Nairne, *The Epistle of Priesthood* (Edinburgh, 1913), pp. 140, 364f. See K. M. Campbell, "Covenant or Testament? Heb. 9:16, 17 Reconsidered," *EQ* 44 (1972), pp. 106-11.

124. The part played by the covenant victim may be responsible for the idiom for covenant-making, found in various languages, which literally means to "cut" or "strike" a covenant—Heb. *kāraṯ $b^e rît$* (cf. p. 186, n. 40), Gk. ὅρκια τέμνειν, Lat. *foedus ferire.* But the subject of these verbs (the διαθέμενος) is, in the nature of the case, never the covenant victim.

the covenant is identified with the covenant victim so that "in the death of the victim his death is presented symbolically."[125] In the covenant made with Abraham in Gen. 15:1-18, and in that made with Israel at the foot of Mount Sinai in Ex. 24:3-8, covenant victims were slaughtered, but there is no suggestion that God, the covenant maker on both occasions, was represented by them; neither did they represent Abraham and Israel, the respective recipients of those divine covenants. "The death of him that made it" is, as the AV/KJV and the NEB simply and rightly put it, "the death of the testator";[126] a testament is the only kind of *diathēkē* which depends for its ratification on the death of the person who makes it.

"J. H. Moulton,[127] after embracing Westcott's conclusion, felt himself obliged to 'capitulate,' as he phrases it, to the dual version of the Authorized Version and Revised Version,[128] inconsistent as he deems it to be. But is that the case? If we revert to the teaching of the old theology (Turrettin, Witsius, Hodge), the covenant of redemption, viewed as the undertaking of the Son, will rank as the prior phase of the covenant of grace. By fulfilling that divine counsel of peace the heavenly Covenanter has met all the claims of outraged righteousness. His 'obedience unto death' fills up the breach with heaven as nothing else could do; and the covenant of grace in his hands at this stage assumes the aspect of a bequest accruing to His brethren through the death of the Testator, who in this unique transaction lives again to be the Administrator of His own mediatorial work" (E. K. Simpson).[129]

It is quite likely that the testamentary idea suggested itself to our author's mind because of his reference to the "eternal inheritance" at the end of v. 15. Nairne finds a difficulty in that "the mediator of a will would hardly be the testator, but what would now be called the executor, and his death would not come into the matter."[130] But all analogies from ordinary life must be defective when they are applied to him who rose from the dead and is thus able personally to secure for his people the benefits which he died to procure

---

125. Westcott, *Hebrews,* p. 267.

126. Gk. διαθέμενος. "Thus ὁ διαθέμενος (Heb. 9:17) signifies *the testator,* ἀδιάθετος became the technical term for *intestate,* and ἐπιδιαθήκη stands in Josephus for a codicil" (E. K. Simpson, "The Vocabulary of the Epistle to the Hebrews," *EQ* 18 [1946], p. 189). Cf. the present and aorist indicative of διατίθεσθαι (the verb of which διαθέμενος is the aorist participle) in Luke 22:29, "I settle (διατίθεμαι) on you a kingdom, as my Father settled (διέθετο) on me."

127. Cf. J. H. Moulton and G. Milligan, "Lexical Notes from the Papyri," *Exp.* VIII.vi (1908), p. 563: "We may suppose the author of Heb. using the obsolete, Biblical word, and then dropping into the modern use of it for purposes of illustration."

128. The AV/KJV renders διαθήκη by "testament" throughout Heb. 9:15-20 (as in 7:22), and by "covenant" elsewhere in the epistle; the ERV/ARV and the RSV have "covenant" throughout the epistle except in vv. 16 and 17 of this chapter.

129. "Vocabulary of Hebrews," p. 189.

130. *The Epistle of Priesthood,* p. 365.

for them. He is testator and executor in one, surety and mediator alike. "There is no more possibility or feasibility of interference with the effective application of the blessings of the covenant than there is of interfering with a testamentary disponement once the testator has died. This use of the testamentary provision of Roman law to illustrate the inviolable security accruing from the sacrificial death of Christ serves to underline the unilateral character of the new covenant" (J. Murray).[131] Christ, says our author, is the Mediator of the new *diathēkē,* and there is one kind of *diathēkē* which serves particularly well to illustrate this aspect of his ministry—namely, the testamentary *diathēkē* which does not come into effect before the death of the person who makes it.[132] It is well known that this kind of settlement cannot be ratified as long as its author lives. And so it is with the new *diathēkē;* its validity depends upon the fact that its author has died.[133]

18 For the matter of that, he goes on, the earlier *diathēkē* also required death for its ratification—not, in that case, the death of the one who made it, but death nonetheless. And he recalls the incident of Ex. 24:3-8, the inauguration of the covenant of Moses' day at the foot of Mount Sinai.

19-20 According to Ex. 24:3-8, "Moses came and told the people all the words of Yahweh and all the ordinances: and all the people answered with one voice, and said, 'All the words which Yahweh has spoken we will do.' And Moses wrote all the words of Yahweh. And he rose early in the morning, and built an altar at the foot of the mountain, and twelve pillars, according to the twelve tribes of Israel. And he sent young men of the people of Israel, who offered burnt offerings and sacrificed peace offerings of oxen to Yahweh. And Moses took half of the blood and put it in basins, and half of the blood he threw against the altar. Then he took the book of the covenant, and read it in the hearing of the people; and they said, 'All that Yahweh has spoken we will do, and we will be obedient.' And Moses took the blood and

---

131. *The Covenant of Grace,* p. 30.

132. M. G. Kline (*Treaty of the Great King,* p. 41), referring to Heb. 9:16f., suggests that if "one might assume that the author's parenthetical allusion in these verses is to the dynastic-testamentary aspect of ancient suzerainty covenants and especially of the Old Covenant as exemplified by Deuteronomy, the way would be open to a satisfactory solution," since one of the recurrent themes of the epistle is "dynastic appointment and perpetuity (*cf.* 1:2ff., 8; 5:6ff.; 6:20ff.), the precise area of covenantal administration for which the merging of the covenantal and the testamentary is attested." In that case Jesus is presented here as "both dying Moses and succeeding Joshua." While the ancient Near Eastern principle of the dynastic covenant is of prime relevance to the Old Testament covenant, and not least to that of Deuteronomy, it is improbable that it would have readily occurred as an analogy to our author's mind in the first century A.D.

133. Cf. J. S. Candlish, "The Notion of Divine Covenants in the Bible," *ExT* 4 (1892-93), pp. 19-23, 65-68, especially the paragraph on p. 21 dealing with διαθήκη in the Epistle to the Hebrews. "The death of Christ fulfilled the condition necessary for the bestowal of the forgiveness and renewal promised by God, and so made His disposition of grace effectual and unchangeable."

threw it upon the people, and said, 'Behold the blood of the covenant which Yahweh has made with you in accordance with all these words.'"

Verses 19 and 20 of Heb. 9 present what is for the most part a summary of these words from Exodus, but the summary includes certain features which do not appear in the Exodus narrative. The reference to goats in v. 19 is probably a later addition to the text of Hebrews;[134] in that case, this passage agrees with the Septuagint of Ex. 24:5 in specifying calves as the sacrificial animals used on this occasion.[135] But whereas in the Exodus narrative Moses sprinkles part of the sacrificial blood on the altar (as representing God, the Author of the covenant) and part on the people (who are thus brought into God's covenant), here he sprinkles it on the *book* and on the people.[136] The book indeed, containing the divine commandments which constituted the basis of the covenant, might represent God in this act as fittingly as would the altar. Again, whereas the Exodus narrative describes Moses as sprinkling nothing but blood, here the blood is accompanied by water, scarlet wool, and hyssop. We have no evidence for the origin of these variations on the Exodus narrative; for them as for some of the details of the tabernacle furniture in v. 4 (the position of the incense-altar and the contents of the ark) our author may well have drawn upon some source which is no longer extant.[137]

The hyssop, or marjoram, is probably envisaged as the means by which the blood was sprinkled on this occasion, just as hyssop was used to sprinkle the blood of the paschal lamb around the doorway of each Israelite house in Egypt (Ex. 12:22), to sprinkle blood (and water) on the cured leper or on the house which had been cleared of a "leprous" infection (Lev. 14:4-7, 49-53), and (most significantly) to sprinkle *mê niddāh* on persons or objects which had become ceremonially defiled by contact with the dead (Num. 19:18).[138]

---

134. See p. 219, n. 108. Those commentators who take the reference to goats here as original commonly regard "bulls and goats" as a locution of our author's meaning "sacrificial animals" (as in 9:12f.; 10:4). Philo (*Questions and Answers on Exodus* 2.32) emphasizes the fact that calves, and not lambs or kids, were sacrificed on this occasion, "for these animals are weaker than calves, whereas he seems to make the sacrifice from more powerful animals."

135. The LXX has μοσχάρια ("young calves") for MT *pārîm* ("oxen"). The word used by our author here is μόσχοι ("calves").

136. It is an undue straining of the language to take αὐτό τε τὸ βιβλίον as dependent on λαβών ("having taken") and coordinate with τὸ αἷμα ("the blood"); the participle τε links it with καὶ πάντα τὸν λαόν ("and all the people") as part of the object of ἐρράντισεν ("sprinkled").

137. Possibly a halakhic and haggadic midrash such as G. Allon postulates as underlying the account of the red heifer in *Ep. Barn.* 7–8 (see p. 216, n. 88). Scarlet wool, which is mentioned here in connection with the ratification of the covenant and in Num. 19:6 in connection with the red heifer, was bound on the head of the scapegoat, according to Mishnah *Yoma* 4.2; 6.6; Tertullian, *Against Marcion* 3.7; *Against the Jews* 14. See p. 207, n. 56.

138. The language of Ps. 51:7, "Purify me with hyssop, and I shall be clean," represents a figurative use of this last ritual—figurative, because no literal sprinkling of *mê niddāh* with hyssop could have cleansed the penitent from blood-guiltiness (Ps. 51:14).

The water and scarlet wool which our author mentions along with the sacrificial blood are also reminiscent of the ritual of the red heifer in Num. 19; it looks as if features of that ritual are here associated with the ratification of the ancient covenant. The two passages are linked by their common interest in ritual aspersion. A further link has been suggested in terms of the triennial synagogue lectionary, in which Ex. 24 and Num. 19 would have been read around the same season of the year in the second and third years respectively.[139]

21 Nor was the ratification of the covenant the only occasion on which similar purification by the sprinkling of blood was carried out under the old order. The tabernacle itself and the vessels of divine service were similarly sprinkled. In the Pentateuchal prescriptions the horns of the altar of burnt offering were to be smeared with the blood of the bullock which was sacrificed as a sin offering at the consecration of Aaron and his sons for their priestly service (Ex. 29:12; cf. Lev. 8:15); and on the Day of Atonement the mercy-seat and the horns of the altar of burnt offering were to be sprinkled with the blood of the bullock presented as a sin offering for Aaron and his house and of the goat which was killed as a sin offering for the people. Thus atonement was made for the "holy place," that is, the inner sanctuary (Lev. 16:14-19). That all the vessels of divine service were thus purified by the sprinkling of blood is not expressly stated in the Pentateuch; what is so stated is that the tabernacle and all its furnishings, inside and outside, were hallowed by being anointed with oil (Ex. 40:9-11; Lev. 8:10f.; Num. 7:1). But as Aaron and his sons were hallowed with the blood of the ram of consecration as well as with the oil of anointing when they were installed in their sacred office (Lev. 8:23f., 30), it might be inferred that the tabernacle and its furnishings, which were hallowed at the same time, were sprinkled with the blood in addition to being anointed with the oil. Josephus, to the same effect, says that Moses spent seven days[140] purifying the priests and their vestments, "as also the tabernacle and its vessels, both with oil . . . and with the blood of bulls and rams."[141]

22 Indeed, our author goes on, "almost everything" which requires to be ceremonially cleansed under the Old Testament law must be cleansed by means of blood. "Almost everything" but not absolutely everything; there are certain exceptions. For example, an impoverished Israelite might bring a tenth of an ephah (four pints) of fine flour to the priest as his sin offering instead of a lamb or even instead of two turtledoves or young pigeons (Lev. 5:11). In Num. 16:46 atonement was made for the congregation of Israel, after the de-

---

139. See p. 26, with nn. 111-12.

140. For the seven days cf. Ex. 29:35f.; Lev. 8:33, 35.

141. *Ant.* 3.206. Philo (*Life of Moses* 2.146-52) also associates the consecration of the priests closely with the consecration of the tabernacle and its furniture, but restricts the application of blood to the priests.

struction of Korah and his company, by means of incense; in Num. 31:22f. metal objects captured in war were to be purified by fire and *mê niddāh;*[142] in Num. 31:50 the Israelite commanders in the fighting against Midian brought the gold objects which they had captured "to make atonement for ourselves before Yahweh." But such exceptions were rare; the general rule was that ceremonial cleansing or atonement had to be effected by means of blood: "apart from the shedding of blood[143] there is no forgiveness."[144]

G. THE PERFECT SACRIFICE (9:23-28)

23 *If, then, the copies of the heavenly realities are cleansed by these means, the heavenly realities themselves are necessarily cleansed by better sacrifices than these.*

24 *For it is not into a holy place made with hands, a copy of the true one, that Christ has entered, but into heaven itself, to appear for us now in the presence of God.*

25 *Nor has he entered there in order to offer himself repeatedly, as the high priest enters annually into the holy place[145] with blood not his own,*

26 *for in that case he would have had to suffer[146] repeatedly since the world's foundation. But as it is, he has been manifested once for all at the consummation of the ages to do away with sin[147] by his own sacrifice.*

27 *Moreover, since it is laid up in store for human beings to die once (after which comes judgment),*

142. Cf. p. 215.

143. Gk. αἱματεκχυσία, possibly a coinage of our author's. T. C. G. Thornton ("The Meaning of αἱματεκχυσία in Heb. ix.22," *JTS* n.s. 15 [1964], pp. 63-65) and W. G. Johnsson ("The Cultus of Hebrews in Twentieth-Century Scholarship," *ExT* 89 [1977-78], pp. 104-8) argue that the word as used here involves not only the shedding but also the application or sprinkling of the blood. See, however, N. H. Young, "Αἱματεκχυσία: A Comment," *ExT* 90 (1978-79), p. 180. Cf. p. 314, n. 207.

144. This may have been a proverbial expression, to judge by instances in the rabbinical writings; cf. "Does not atonement come through the blood?" (TB *Yoma* 5a, twice); "Surely atonement can be made only with the blood" (TB *Zebaḥim* 6a). These aphorisms are regularly confirmed by the following quotation of Lev. 17:11 ("it is the blood that makes atonement, by reason of the life").

145. Gk. τὰ ἅγια, to which a few minuscules (including 69 and 1912), with the Armenian and Sahidic Coptic versions, add τῶν ἁγίων (yielding the rendering "holy of holies" for "holy place"). See p. 208.

146. Gk. παθεῖν, for which a few minuscules (including 241 and 1908) with the Sahidic version read ἀποθανεῖν ("have died"). Cf. p. 380, n. 77.

147. Gk. εἰς ἀθέτησιν τῆς ἁμαρτίας (cf. p. 231, nn. 164, 165); τῆς is omitted by 𝔓46 C and the Byzantine text (perhaps rightly, since our author has no objection to the use of ἁμαρτία without the article); D* (but not *d*) has the anarthrous plural ἁμαρτιῶν.

28 *so also Christ was offered once for all to bear the sins of many; and to those who are looking for him he will appear a second time, sin having been done away with, to bring them salvation.*[148]

23 With the blood of sacrificial animals, then, the material sanctuary and its accessories were cleansed from defilement and hallowed for the worship of God. Our author does not deny that such ritual cleansing was real and effective as far as it went. What he does deny is that cleansing of this kind could be of any use for the removal of inward and spiritual defilement. The various installations which were cleansed and fitted for the worship of God by the blood of animal sacrifices were but copies[149] of the spiritual realities; where the spiritual realities themselves are concerned, a superior sacrifice[150] and more effective cleansing must be forthcoming. It has frequently been asked in what sense "the heavenly realities"[151] needed to be cleansed; but our author has provided the answer in the context. What needed to be cleansed was the defiled conscience of men and women; this is a cleansing which belongs to the spiritual sphere. The argument of v. 23 might be paraphrased by saying that while ritual purification is adequate for the material order, which is but an earthly copy of the spiritual order, a better kind of sacrifice is necessary to effect purification in the spiritual order. If we envisage the heavenly dwelling-place of God in something like material terms (and, surrounded as we are by the material universe, it is difficult to avoid doing so), we shall find ourselves trying to explain the necessity for its cleansing in ways which are far from our author's intention.[152] But we have already had reason to emphasize

148. A few authorities add the gloss διὰ πίστεως ("through faith") either before εἰς σωτηρίαν (e.g., 69) or after it (e.g., A P). Cf. 1 Pet. 1:15.

149. Gk. ὑπόδειγμα, as in 8:5 (cf. p. 183, n. 25).

150. Why the plural, "better sacrifices"? Our author probably uses the generic plural in stating the principle (purification in the heavenly order must be effected by better sacrifices than those required to effect purification in the earthly order); but when he comes to show how this principle was put into practice, he makes it plain that in fact only one such superior sacrifice was ever offered.

151. Gk. τὰ ἐπουράνια, as in 8:5 (the same phrase is repeatedly rendered "the heavenly places" in Ephesians). H. Windisch (*Der Hebräerbrief*, HNT [Tübingen, ²1931], p. 85) assumes that by the law of correspondence (8:5) the heavenly sanctuary was also defiled by the people's sins; H. Strathmann, however, thinks (*Hebräerbrief*, NTD [Göttingen, ⁶1953], p. 113) that the point of comparison is simply the general thought of the dedication of the sanctuary by means of a sacrifice (cf. F. Hauck, *TDNT*, III, p. 426, n. 80, *s.v.* καθαρός). "The superior new regime requires a likewise superior sacrifice to establish it—the sacrifice of Christ" (N. H. Young, "The Gospel according to Hebrews 9," p. 210).

152. Thus it has been suggested that the cleansing was made necessary by the presence of Satan (Luke 10:18; Rev. 12:3-9) or of other "spiritual hosts of wickedness" (Eph. 6:12; Col. 1:20) in the heavenly sphere (cf., e.g., O. Michel, *Der Brief an die Hebräer*, MK [Göttingen, 1949], pp. 213f. [following F. Bleek, *ad loc.*]; G. H. Lang, *The Epistle to the Hebrews* [London, 1951], pp. 153f.). This, however, imports into our author's argument something which is alien

that the people of God are the house of God, that his dwelling-place is in their midst.[153] It is they who need inward cleansing, not only that their approach to God may be free from defilement, but that they may be a fit habitation for him. Just as the tabernacle in the wilderness, together with its furniture, had to be anointed and sanctified so that God might manifest his presence there among his people and they might serve him there, so the people of God themselves need to be cleansed and hallowed in order to become "a dwelling place of God in the Spirit" (Eph. 2:22). The same essential teaching recurs in 1 Pet. 2:5, where believers in Christ are described as being "built up a spiritual house, to be a holy priesthood, to offer up spiritual sacrifices, acceptable to God through Jesus Christ." But in order to be a spiritual house of this kind they must have experienced regeneration and cleansing by "sprinkling of the blood of Jesus Christ" (1 Pet. 1:2, 9, 22f.).

If more than this is felt to be involved in our author's language here, it may be supplied by the words of William Manson: "if we conceive our author to be writing to Jewish Christians who perhaps missed in the spiritual worship of Christianity the *many* holy sanctions and consecratory rites of the old religion, we shall not think it strange that he should, in effect, say to them that Christianity has its own sublime, though invisible, sanctions imparted by a greater Sacrifice. Following out this conception, we can well imagine him saying that the book of the New Covenant (the eternal gospel written in heaven . . .), the Christian sanctuary (the heavenly Zion, cf. 12:18-24), and the New Israel (the Christian Church, including the company of the redeemed in heaven) have all been consecrated by the blood of Christ. The stamp of the Cross is on all of them. After all, the things in heaven represent realities which have a present existence for Christians through Christ."[154]

24 It is not into any material sanctuary that Christ has gone as his people's high priest, but into the presence of God in heaven. One who is personally "holy, free from guile and defilement" (7:26) is at home and acceptable in the presence of God. But he appears now in the presence of God not only on his own behalf but on behalf of others, and those others are sinners.

---

to it, whereas he states repeatedly what it is that actually has been cleansed by the sacrifice of Christ. By the removal of the defilement of sin from the hearts and consciences of the worshipers, the heavenly sphere in which they approach God to worship him is itself cleansed from this defilement. The analogical use of language proper to the earthly sanctuary might give the impression that the heavenly sanctuary itself is envisaged as a locality; but we need not suppose that our author thought of it absolutely in local terms.

153. See the exposition of v. 11 (pp. 212f.), and cf. 12:22f. (pp. 355-60). In 4QFlorilegium, col. 1, l. 6, God replaces the material sanctuary after its destruction by a "sanctuary of men" *(miqdaš 'ādām)* who "will offer the works of the law like the smoke of incense" (cf. p. 384 with n. 91). In 1QS 8.5f. the council of the Qumran community *is* the holy of holies, as the community itself is the holy place (cf. p. 94, n. 18).

154. W. Manson, *The Epistle to the Hebrews* (London, 1951), pp. 140f.

If sinners are to appear before God, even by proxy, through the representation of a sinless high priest, they must be cleansed from sin, or else the very presence of God would be polluted. And this cleansing Christ has effected, so that he can minister on his people's behalf in "the true tabernacle" which no human hands have erected.[155] The earthly sanctuary and the priestly ministry associated with it were but faint foreshadowings[156] of the spiritual and heavenly order in which Christ exercises his perpetual priesthood as his people's representative with God.

25 Moreover, when Christ entered into the heavenly sanctuary, he entered once for all. His entrance into the presence of God on his people's behalf, by virtue of his own blood, is set in sharp contrast to the entrance of Israel's high priest into the material holy of holies on the Day of Atonement. Having entered in to present the sacrificial blood ("blood not his own"), Israel's high priest had to come out again immediately, to enter in and repeat the same ceremony the following year, and the year after that, and so on indefinitely. But the sacrifice of Christ, being a real sacrifice and not a token one, is perpetually effective and therefore calls for no repetition.

26 If his sacrifice did call for repetition, then he would have to endure suffering and death times without number throughout the ages of world history.[157] But that involves a patent absurdity: "it is appointed for human beings to die once," and the Son of Man, who became "like his brothers" in all things, cannot and must not die more than once. To talk about his sacrifice as "the eternal sacrifice" can therefore be misleading. If it means that his sacrifice is the historical expression of the eternal mercy of God, or that its efficacy is eternal, no exception can be taken to the term; but if it means (as it does for many who use it) that he is eternally offering himself in heaven (with the corollary that in the Eucharist his sacrifice is repeatedly reenacted on earth), then it is in plain contradiction to the emphatic teaching of this epistle. He appears eternally in heaven for his people on the basis of "his own sacrifice," presented and accepted once for all.

---

155. As in 8:2 (see p. 182, n. 17) the heavenly tabernacle is ἀληθινός. With "made with hands" (χειροποίητος) cf. "not made with hands" (οὐ χειροποίητος) in v. 11 (p. 212 with nn. 76-78). See also p. 182, n. 16.

156. The earthly sanctuary and its fittings are here described as ἀντίτυπα of the true heavenly sanctuary; ἀντίτυπος here has thus much the same meaning as τύπος ("pattern") in 8:5, and might be rendered "counter-pattern" or "corresponding pattern"; in other words, the earthly corresponds to the heavenly as a copy or symbol corresponds to the reality which is copied or symbolized. The only other occurrence of ἀντίτυπος in the NT is in 1 Pet. 3:21, where it refers to baptism as the Christian "counterpart" to Noah's salvation in the ark. Whereas in Hebrews it is the OT symbol that is called the "antitype," in 1 Peter it is the NT reality. The usage in Hebrews is in line with Philo's use of the word (cf. C. Spicq, *L'Épître aux Hébreux*, I [Paris, 1952], p. 75).

157. For "since the foundation of the world" (ἀπὸ καταβολῆς κόσμου) cf. 4:3 (p. 104, n. 8).

As it is,[158] Christ has been manifested on earth "once for all"[159] at the time of fulfilment, in order to deal conclusively with sin. The phrase "the end of the ages" or "the consummation of the ages"[160] (as the ARV mg. has it) is not found in this precise form elsewhere in the New Testament, although it closely resembles the Matthaean "consummation of the age,"[161] the Pauline "ends of the ages,"[162] and the Petrine "end of the times,"[163] being practically synonymous with the last two. It is not that Christ happened to come at the time of fulfilment but that his coming made that time the time of fulfilment. The purpose of his coming is stated to be the removal or cancellation of sin; the same substantive[164] is used here as in Heb. 7:18, where we are told that the announcement of the Melchizedek priesthood in Ps. 110:4 constitutes the "disannulling" or abrogation of the earlier law which set up the Aaronic priesthood. In the present context the word, says E. K. Simpson, "seems to imply *effacement*."[165] The statement of the purpose of the coming of Christ has a close parallel in 1 John 3:5: "you know that he was manifested to take away[166] sins." "His own sacrifice," like "his own blood" in v. 12, is emphatic, marking once more the contrast between his priestly action and that of Aaron and his successors, who made expiation with the blood of others, namely of sacrificial animals. In what "his own sacrifice" consisted is shortly to be explained.[167]

27-28 Men and women die once, by divine appointment, and in their case death is followed by judgment.[168] Christ died once, by divine appoint-

---

158. Gk. νυνὶ δέ, ARV "but now," where "now" (as in 8:6) is to be taken in a logical, not a temporal, sense.

159. Here the simple adverb ἅπαξ is used, but it has much the same emphatic force as the compound ἐφάπαξ in v. 12.

160. Gk. ἐπὶ συντελείᾳ τῶν αἰώνων. See H. Sasse, *TDNT*, I, p. 203 (*s.v.* αἰών).

161. Cf. Matt. 13:39f., 49; 24:3; 28:20 for (ἡ) συντέλεια (τοῦ) αἰῶνος.

162. 1 Cor. 10:11 (τὰ τέλη τῶν αἰώνων); cf. also Gal. 4:4 (τὸ πλήρωμα τοῦ χρόνου).

163. 1 Pet. 1:20, where Christ, "foreknown before the foundation of the world" (πρὸ καταβολῆς κόσμου), was manifested ἐπ' ἐσχάτου τῶν χρόνων. The Matthaean references are to the future; the present reference, like the Pauline and Petrine, is to the present order inaugurated by the advent and redemptive work of Christ. Cf. Heb. 1:2 ("at the end of these days"). The plural "ages" here and in 1 Cor. 10:11 may point to the intersection of the two ages when Christ appeared, or it may denote, more generally, "the climax of history" (W. Manson, *Hebrews*, p. 140). The phrase τῇ συντελείᾳ τῶν αἰώνων (*v.l.* τοῦ αἰῶνος) appears in *Test. Levi* 10:2.

164. Gk. ἀθέτησις (see p. 168, n. 56).

165. "Vocabulary of Hebrews," p. 190. "On the whole, then," he says, "the expression εἰς ἀθέτησιν ἁμαρτίας appears to be equivalent to Diodati's Italian version of it, *per annullare il peccato*, expressive of the *cancelling* or *elimination* of sin, a little more specific, that is to say, than our version, 'putting away.'"

166. Gk. αἴρειν (see p. 232, n. 169).

167. In 10:5ff. (see pp. 239-43).

168. Cf. 10:27, 30; 12:23. According to Sophocles, fragment 64, "life, my child, is the sweetest guerdon of all, for it is not possible for the same people to die twice."

ment, and his death is followed by salvation for all his people. This is so because in his death he bore[169] "the sins of many," offering up his life to God as an atonement on their behalf. The language here is a plain echo of the fourth Servant Song—more especially of Isa. 53:12, "he bore the sin of many," but also of vv. 10, "he makes himself an offering for sin,"[170] and 11, "by his knowledge shall the righteous one, my servant, make many to be accounted righteous, and he shall bear[171] their iniquities."[172] His bearing of sin implies the removing of sin from others, and the consequent liberation of those who enter into the benefits of his self-oblation.

The Israelites who watched their high priest enter the sanctuary for them waited expectantly for his reappearance; that was a welcome sign that he and the sacrifice which he presented had been accepted by God. His reappearance from the holy of holies on the Day of Atonement was an especially welcome sight. Ben Sira celebrates the joy with which the people saw the high priest Simon the Just emerge from the "house of the veil" after completing this sacred ministry:

> How glorious he was when the people gathered round him
>   as he came out of the inner sanctuary!
> Like the morning star among the clouds,
>   like the moon when it is full;
> like the sun shining upon the temple of the Most High,
>   and like the rainbow gleaming in glorious clouds;
> like roses in the days of the first fruits,
>   like lilies by a spring of water,
>   like a green shoot on Lebanon on a summer day;
> like fire and incense in the censer,
>   like a vessel of hammered gold
>   adorned with all kinds of precious stones;
> like an olive tree putting forth its fruit,
>   and like a cypress towering in the clouds. (Sir. 50:5-10)

---

169. Gk. ἀνενεγκεῖν, aorist infinitive of ἀναφέρειν (which is used in the sense of "offering up" sacrifices in 7:27; 13:15); the same verb is used of Christ's sin-bearing in 1 Pet. 2:24, and in both places may be influenced by the LXX rendering of Isa. 53:12 (ἁμαρτίας πολλῶν ἀνήνεγκεν). The Hebrew verb there used is nāśā', which may mean not only "bear" but also "take away"; the latter sense is conveyed in the NT in relation to Christ's redemptive work by Gk. αἴρειν, as in John 1:29; 1 John 3:5 (see p. 231, n. 166). On ἀνενεγκεῖν here as meaning "take upon oneself" see BAGD, s.v. ἀναφέρω (3).

170. Heb. 'āšām, "a guilt offering," LXX περὶ ἁμαρτίας, for which cf. 10:6, 18; 13:11. See p. 178, n. 93.

171. The Hebrew verb in v. 11 is not nāśā' (as in v. 12) but sābal, but both are rendered in the LXX by the same Greek verb (see n. 169 above).

172. The influence of the fourth Servant Song on our author's thought and language about the sacrifice of Christ is difficult to ignore: he "read the story of Jesus in the light of Isa. liii" (V. Taylor, *Jesus and His Sacrifice* [London, 1937], p. 47). See p. 178, n. 93.

So our author thinks of Jesus as going into the heavenly holy of holies, to re-appear one day in order to confirm finally to his people the salvation[173] which his perfect offering has procured for them. Meanwhile they wait expectantly for his parousia. This presentation of the return of Christ in terms of the high priest's emergence from the sanctuary was in Frances Ridley Havergal's mind when she wrote:

> Coming! In the opening east
>   Herald brightness slowly swells;
> Coming! O my glorious Priest,
>   Hear we not Thy golden bells?[174]

But when he appears the second time to those who expect him, it will not be to deal with sin once more. Sin was dealt with decisively at his first appearing. All the blessings which he won for his people at his first appearing will be theirs to enjoy in perpetual fulness at his second appearing. Therefore, let them not grow faint and weary but persevere in patience and faith.

173. For this future and final phase of salvation cf. 1:14 and other scriptures mentioned in the exposition *ad loc.*

174. Although on the Day of Atonement the high priest wore the "holy linen coat" (Lev. 16:4) and not the blue "robe of the ephod" (Ex. 28:31-35) to which the bells and pomegranates were attached.

HEBREWS 10

H. THE OLD ORDER A SHADOW OF THE REALITY (10:1-4)

1 *The law had a shadow of the good things which were to come, but not the exact image[1] of those things. Therefore, with the same sacrifices[2] which they offer without end year by year the law can[3] never bring to perfection[4] those who approach God.*

2 *Otherwise[5] they would have ceased to be offered, would they not? If the worshipers had been cleansed once for all, they would no longer have any conscience of sins.*

3 *But in those sacrifices there is an annual reminder of sins.*

4 *It is impossible, in fact, for the blood of bulls and goats[6] to take away sins.*

1 Both Paul and our author speak of the law as "a shadow"; but whereas Paul in Col. 2:17 has in mind the legal restrictions of Old Testament times (food-laws and regulations about special days),[7] our author is thinking more

---

1. 𝔓⁴⁶ has the interesting reading καὶ τὴν εἰκόνα ("and the image") for οὐκ αὐτὴν τὴν εἰκόνα ("not the very image"). This implies for εἰκών here the sense of a *mere* copy, something no better than a σκιά. But εἰκών normally has a more substantial meaning than this, and the construction of the sentence indicates that here it is contrasted with σκιά, not practically synonymous with it. Cf. G. Zuntz, *The Text of the Epistles* (London, 1953), pp. 20-23, where conclusive arguments are given against accepting the reading of 𝔓⁴⁶.

2. א P read "their same sacrifices" (ταῖς αὐταῖς θυσίαις αὐτῶν).

3. Gk. δύναται (𝔓⁴⁶ D*,² H K L), for which א A C D¹ 33 with the Harclean Syriac and other authorities have the plural δύνανται, whence ERV "they can. . . ." The plural reading makes our author guilty of a hanging nominative at the beginning of the sentence, whereas he is usually careful to observe grammatical accuracy.

4. For τελειῶσαι ("make perfect") D reads καθαρίσαι ("cleanse"), probably under the influence of v. 2. True inward cleansing is, of course, part of the perfecting (cf. v. 14).

5. Gk. ἐπεί, in the *koinē* sense "for if it were otherwise" (German *da sonst*); the clause thus introduced is to be read as a question. Failure to recognize this led to early emendations: H* 1739 and some other authorities omit οὐκ ("not"), producing the unexceptionable statement "they would have ceased to be offered"; 𝔓⁴⁶ 1518 improve the solecistic ἐπεὶ ἄν which results from the omission of οὐκ by the elegant emendation ἐπεὶ κἄν.

6. The order is reversed to τράγων καὶ ταύρων in 𝔓⁴⁶ א 69 and a few other authorities, in conformity with 9:13.

7. Cf. *Colossians–Philemon–Ephesians*, NICNT (Grand Rapids, 1984), pp. 116f.

especially of the law prescribing matters of priesthood and sacrifice in relation to the wilderness tabernacle and the Jerusalem temple. In both places,
however, "shadow" is used not so much in the Platonic sense of a copy of
the heavenly and eternal "idea" as in the sense of foreshadowing. For Paul,
the legal restrictions to which he refers are "a shadow of the things to come";
for our author, the sacrificial law of Israel provides "a shadow of the good
things to come"; both writers think of Christ and his new order as the perfect
reality to which the earlier ordinances pointed forward.

The "good things which were to come" have now come (9:11); they
embrace the unrepeatable sacrifice of Christ and his present high-priestly
ministry, which carry with them eternal redemption and uninhibited access
to worship the living God. They are the only absolutely "good" things, because they comprise the "perfection" which the old order was incapable of
supplying.

What now is the distinction which our author draws between "shadow"
and "image"—unless we are to adopt the improbable reading of our oldest
manuscript which equates the two and says that the law had only the "shadow
and image" of the coming reality?[8] The shadow is but a shadow; the "image"
(eikōn)—especially "the very image"—is an exact replica, "not an imperfect, partial reproduction, but a manifestation adequate to the reality itself."[9]
The "image" is thus something superior to the "copies" or "patterns" of 9:23f.
Platonic and Philonic antecedents for this use of eikōn can be readily adduced;[10] but within the New Testament itself we have Paul's repeated description of Christ as the eikōn of God (2 Cor. 4:4; Col. 1:15) and his statement of the divine purpose that believers should be conformed to the eikōn
of the Son of God (Rom. 8:29; cf. 2 Cor. 3:18; Col. 3:10).

In any case, the old order could never bring those who worshiped under
it to a state of perfection; this was plain enough from the fact that, as circling
time moved round and year succeeded year, the same sacrifices had to be re-

---

8. See p. 234, n. 1.

9. A. E. Garvie, *ExT* 28 (1916-17), p. 398 (in an article "Shadow and Substance").
C. Spicq (*L'Épître aux Hébreux*, I [Paris, 1952], p. 75) makes the point that an artist draws an
outline (σκιά) before he produces the finished portrait (εἰκών), and that a similar relation exists
in our author's mind between the Levitical ceremonial as the preliminary sketch and the high-
priestly work of Christ as the completed masterpiece.

10. J. Moffatt (ICC, *ad loc.*) quotes from Plato, *Cratylus* 306E, almost the same expression as our author uses here (εἰκόνα τῶν πραγμάτων). According to Philo (*Life of Moses* 2.51),
Moses regarded his laws as "an image most truly corresponding to the constitution of the world"
(ἐμφερεστάτην εἰκόνα τῆς τοῦ κόσμου πολιτείας). Cf. Spicq, *Hébreux*, I, p. 75; H. Willms,
EIKΩN: Eine begriffsgeschichtliche Untersuchung zum Platonismus, I: *Philon von Alexandria*
(Münster, 1935). G. Zuntz (*Text*, p. 22) compares the contrast between εἴδωλον (a synonym of
εἰκών) and σκιά in Iamblichus, who advocates a "turning from the shadows to the images (εἴδωλα)
and the light" (*On the General Mathematical Science* 6).

peated over and over again. The sacrifice which is uppermost in our author's mind is still the annual sacrifice on the Day of Atonement.

2 If the old order had been able to bring "perfection"—access to God without the constant necessity of removing the barrier of freshly accumulated sin—then surely the sacrifices which belonged to it would have come to an end. The natural implication of the question "Otherwise would they not have ceased to be offered?" is that the sacrificial ritual was still practiced in the temple at Jerusalem.[11] It might be argued that our author, writing after A.D. 70, means that if perfection were attainable under the Levitical economy, its sacrificial system would have come to an end long before it did—even within the Old Testament period. But that is a much less natural interpretation of his words; it is simplest to regard them as an incidental pointer to the dating of the epistle before A.D. 70.[12]

If the old sacrificial order had possessed true cleansing efficacy—that is to say, if it had been able to cleanse the *conscience*—then the worshipers would have enjoyed unrestricted communion with God. It is the presence of sin in the conscience that hinders such communion; "if I had cherished iniquity in my heart," said the psalmist, "the Lord would not have listened" (Ps. 66:18). The implication of our author's argument is that the true inward cleansing is permanently effective and therefore unrepeatable. When he speaks of the worshipers as having been "cleansed once for all," he emphasizes this by his use of the perfect tense. The sense is much the same as that of our Lord's words to Peter in John 13:10: "He that is bathed does not need to wash, except for his feet, but he is clean all over."[13] This cleansing marks the beginning of the Christian life: Peter referred to it when he reminded the Council of Jerusalem how God, in giving the Holy Spirit to the Gentile believers just as he had done to the Jewish disciples, "made no distinction between us and them, but cleansed their hearts by faith" (Acts 15:9).[14] But such a cleansing as this, which means that those who receive it are thenceforward "clean" without requiring any repetition of the cleansing, was unknown to the Levitical law.

3 As it is, the annually recurring ritual of the Day of Atonement in-

---

11. The similar ritual of the Jewish temple at Leontopolis in Egypt (founded by Onias IV *c.* 160 B.C.), which survived that at Jerusalem by a year or two (cf. Josephus, *War* 7.420-36), hardly comes into the picture (see p. 12, n. 49); whatever the Alexandrine affinities of this epistle may be, we may doubt whether the Leontopolis temple had much religious significance for the Alexandrine Jews (Philo, e.g., speaks of going on pilgrimage "to our ancestral temple" [εἰς τὸ πατρῷον ἱερόν] in Jerusalem [*On Providence* 64]).

12. Had he been writing after A.D. 70 and had he worded his argument precisely in these terms, it could have been said: "Well, they *have* ceased to be offered"—a superficial objection, no doubt, but even so one to which such a skillful disputant is not likely to have laid himself open.

13. Or, in the shorter reading reproduced in the text of the NEB: "A man who has bathed needs no further washing; he is altogether clean."

14. Cf. 1 Cor. 6:11, "you were washed (Gk. ἀπελούσασθε). . . ."

volved a "reminder"[15] of sins year by year. This reminder (as regularly in biblical usage) is more than a calling to mind; it involves some appropriate form of action. The remembrance of sins may involve repentance for them,[16] or it may involve persistence in them.[17] But the remembrance of sins *in the sight of God* involves appropriate action on *his* part, either pardon or retribution.[18] A pardon which has to be bestowed repeatedly—as far at least as its ceremonial expression is concerned—cannot convey the same peace of conscience as a pardon bestowed once for all. And there is a manifest contrast, to our author's mind, between the old order in which "there is an annual reminder of sins"[19] and the new covenant which embodies God's promise to his people: "I will remember their sins no more" (8:12).

It would not have occurred to an observant Jew under the Mosaic covenant to say that the Day of Atonement involved an annual "reminder" of sins; he would have said, rather, that there was an annual *removal* of sins. Our author might have replied, truly enough, that the ritual designed to effect the removal of sins necessarily involves their remembrance; but he is influenced chiefly by the promise that under the new covenant God will remember his people's sins no more. Since the new covenant is contrasted with the old, the implication is that there was no such absolute wiping out of sins from the divine record under the sacrificial law.

It has been suggested that even in some forms of Christian liturgy a "remembrance" is made repeatedly of sins to a point where the Christian's sense of being constantly welcome in the presence of God for Christ's sake is seriously threatened.[20] There is a difference between the humble and contrite confession of sins to God and a morbid dwelling on sins already

---

15. Gk. ἀνάμνησις. Cf. Num. 5:15, where the ordeal of jealousy involves "a cereal offering of iniquity, bringing iniquity to remembrance" (and Jub. 34:19, where the Day of Atonement is the anniversary of the day on which Joseph was sold by his brothers, and "has been ordained that they should grieve thereon for all their sins, and for all their errors, so that they might cleanse themselves on that day once a year"). On the biblical force of remembrance cf. pp. 191-95 (on Heb. 8:12).

16. Cf. Deut. 9:7.

17. Cf. Ezek. 23:19.

18. But mainly retribution (cf. 1 Kings 17:18; Rev. 16:19); pardon is regularly viewed in terms of God's *ceasing* to remember sins (cf. Ps. 25:7).

19. Philo (*Life of Moses* 2.107) says that the sacrifices of the wicked "effect not a remission (λύσις) but a remembrance (ὑπόμνησις) of sins" (cf. *Planting* 108, where the sacrifices of the wicked "do but put God in remembrance of the sins, inadvertent and otherwise, of the various offerers"). Therefore let me eschew wickedness, "for it would be foolish to have the sacrifices effecting remembrance (ὑπόμνησις) rather than forgetting of sins" (*Special Laws* 1.215). But those who offer from a pure heart both seek (*Life of Moses* 2.24) and obtain (*Special Laws* 1.242) ἀμνηστία of their sins on God's part. Our author, however, says that these sin offerings involve a remembrance of sins irrespective of the character of the offerers.

20. Cf. H. A. Williams, "Unchristian Liturgy," *Theology* 61 (1958), pp. 401-4.

confessed and forgiven which might well call forth the Pauline reminder that "the Spirit you have received is not a spirit of slavery leading you back into a life of fear, but a Spirit that makes us sons, enabling us to cry 'Abba! Father!'" (Rom. 8:15, NEB).

4 But this condition of spiritual imperfection was inevitable as long as people's ideas of God and forgiveness were bound up with a sacrificial cultus like that of early Israel. "It is impossible for the blood of bulls and goats to take away sins." This impossibility has only to be stated plainly like this for its truth to be obvious. Moral defilement cannot be removed by material means. Such spiritual value as the sacrificial ritual might have lay in its being a material foreshadowing or object-lesson of a moral and spiritual reality. The writer to the Hebrews was not the first man to appreciate this; the truth had been grasped centuries earlier, as by the penitent psalmist who prayed:

> Create in me a clean heart, O God;
>   and put a new and right spirit within me.
> For thou hast no delight in sacrifice;
>   were I to give a burnt offering, thou wouldst not be pleased.
> The sacrifice acceptable to God is a broken spirit;
>   a broken and contrite heart, O God,
>   thou wilt not despise.[21]

And he was only one among other psalmists and prophets who made substantially the same affirmation. In the closing years of the Second Temple, there were many pious Jews who, while paying lip-service to the sacrificial cultus and indeed participating in it according to the law, yet realized that this was not the means by which sin could be removed.[22] The members of the Qumran community believed that when their strict interpretation of the divine commandments was carried out perfectly, "then the oblation of the lips according to right judgment shall be as a sweet savor of righteousness, and the perfectness of one's ways as an acceptable freewill offering."[23] A Pharisee might have criticized the uncompromising manner in which our author here dismisses animal sacrifice, "but there is no reason for thinking that he would have rejected a more guarded statement of the truth. The relatively easy adaptation of the Palestinian synagogue to the new conditions after the destruction of the Temple in 70 A.D. shows that the principle of the insufficiency of animal sacrifice had been widely grasped."[24] Yet the Pharisees took part in the sacrificial cultus as long as it endured, and when it

21. Ps. 51:10, 16f. (LXX 50:12, 18f.); cf. 1 Sam. 15:22; Ps. 50:8ff. (LXX 49:8ff.); Isa. 1:11ff.; 66:1ff.; Jer. 7:21ff.; Hos. 6:6; 14:2; Amos 5:21ff.; Mic. 6:6ff.
22. Cf. R. A. Stewart, *Rabbinical Theology* (Edinburgh, 1961), pp. 120-23.
23. 1QS 9.4f. There is an echo of Hos. 14:2 here; cf. Heb. 13:15 (p. 384 with n. 91).
24. H. L. Ellison, *The Centrality of the Messianic Idea for the Old Testament* (London, 1953), p. 19.

disappeared they had to give serious thought to the question how sin was now to be expiated.[25] The seriousness of this question must be appreciated by all who understand the "exceeding sinfulness" of sin. Our author understood it well enough; but he could bid farewell to the sacrificial cultus the more cheerfully because he knew of a sacrifice, presented on quite another plane, which effectively dealt with sin as the old cultus could not.

I. THE NEW ORDER THE REALITY (10:5-10)

5 *That is why Christ says at his coming into the world,*
   "Sacrifice and offering you did not desire,
   but you have fashioned a body for me.

6   *You had no pleasure in whole burnt offerings[26] and sin offerings.*
   Then I said, 'See, I have come
   (as it is written[27] of me in the scroll of the book)
   to do your will, O God.' "[28]

8 *Saying first, "You had no desire for sacrifices, offerings, whole burnt offerings, or sin offerings; you had no pleasure in them" (all of which are offered according to the law),[29]*

9 *then he has said, "See, I have come to do your will."[30] He does away with the first order so as to establish the second.*

10 *And by his "will" we have been sanctified once for all through the offering of the body[31] of Jesus Christ.*

5-7 For a biblical statement of the sacrifice which *could* take away sins our author goes back to the Psalter, and in Ps. 40:6-8 he finds a prophetic utterance which he recognizes as appropriate to the Son of God at the time of his incarnation. The title of this psalm marks it as Davidic (in Masoretic and Septuagint texts alike); he may have argued (as Peter did with regard to Ps. 16 on the Day of Pentecost)[32] that the words of the psalm could not refer to David *in propria persona* (since David did offer sacrifices), and that therefore they should be understood as referring to "great David's greater Son."

---

25. Cf. A. Büchler, *Studies in Sin and Atonement in the Rabbinic Literature of the First Century* (Oxford, 1928).

26. Gk. ὁλοκαυτώματα (for which 𝔭[46] and D read the singular ὁλοκαύτωμα).

27. 𝔭[46] and D* (but not d) add γάρ ("for").

28. Quoted from Ps. 40:6-8 (MT 40:7-9; LXX 39:6-8).

29. Gk. κατὰ νόμον (D P and some other MSS, with the TR, read κατὰ τὸν νόμον).

30. ℵ[c] L 1739 and the TR, with the Latin and Syriac Peshitta, add "O God" (ὁ θεός) from v. 7.

31. For σώματος ("body") D* reads αἵματος ("blood"), in conformity with v. 29.

32. Acts 2:29-31. Cf. *Acts,* NICNT (Grand Rapids, [2]1988), pp. 65f.

However that may be, the appropriateness of his application of them is undeniable. He quotes them in the Septuagint version,[33] in which the Masoretic reading "ears hast thou digged for me" is replaced by the clause "you have fashioned a body for me." The Greek version cannot well be explained as representing a variant or corrupted Hebrew reading;[34] it is rather an interpretative paraphrase of the Hebrew text. The Greek translator evidently regarded the Hebrew wording as an instance of *pars pro toto;* the "digging" or hollowing out of the ears is part of the total work of fashioning a human body.[35] Accordingly he rendered it in terms which express *totum pro parte.* The body which was "fashioned" for the speaker by God is given back to God as a "living sacrifice," to be employed in obedient service to him.

But if our author had preferred the Hebrew wording, it would have served his purpose almost as well, for in addition to reminding him and his readers of the psalm from which it was taken, it might have reminded them also of the Isaianic Servant's language in the third Servant Song: "The Lord Yahweh . . . wakens my ear to hear as those who are taught. The Lord Yahweh has opened my ear, and I was not rebellious, I turned not backward" (Isa. 50:4f.).

Wholehearted obedience is the sacrifice which God really desires, the sacrifice which he received in perfection from his Servant-Son when he came into the world. As for the other kinds of sacrifice enumerated in the psalm, they had religious worth only insofar as they were the tangible expression of a devoted and obedient heart; the great prophets never tired of insisting that God did not desire them for their own sake.[36]

It is probable that the four terms which the psalmist uses for sacrifice are intended to cover all the main types of offering prescribed in the Leviti-

---

33. In a form approaching, as usual, the A text, except that he reads εὐδόκησας ("thou hadst . . . pleasure") for ἐξήτησας (perhaps under the influence of Ps. 51:16 [LXX 50:18]), places the vocative ὁ θεός before τὸ θέλημά σου instead of after it (the LXX has ὁ θεός μου, following the MT, "O my God"), and omits ἠβουλήθην ("I have resolved") at the end of his quotation, thus making the infinitive clause τοῦ ποιῆσαι ("to do") a clause of purpose dependent on ἥκω ("I have come").

34. As though MT *'oznayim*, "ears," were a corruption of *'āz gāwāh*, "then a body" (B. Kennicott). Neither can σῶμα be satisfactorily explained as due to a corruption in the transmission of the LXX, as though it replaced an earlier ὠτία ("ears"), as has been suggested, e.g., by F. Bleek, G. Lünemann, and A. Kuyper. J. Moffatt says: "Whether ὠτία was corrupted into σῶμα, or whether the latter was an independent translation, is of no moment" (ICC, *ad loc.*); true enough, but that it is a corruption is, as F. Delitzsch rightly says *(ad loc.),* "highly improbable." (Aquila, Theodotion, and Symmachus, with Origen's Quinta and Sexta, and some late LXX editions, read ὠτία, by way of conformity to the MT.)

35. There is no ground for relating Ps. 40:6 to the boring of the servant's ear in Ex. 21:6; Deut. 15:17.

36. Cf. H. H. Rowley, "The Meaning of Sacrifice in the Old Testament," in *From Moses to Qumran* (London, 1963), pp. 67-107.

cal ritual.[37] "Sacrifice" (Heb. *zebaḥ*), while capable of referring to any kind of animal sacrifice, is used in the Old Testament with more special reference to the peace offering;[38] "offering" (Heb. *minḥāh*), while used in a general sense,[39] is restricted in the Levitical terminology to the "cereal offering";[40] while the burnt offering (Heb. *'ôlāh*)[41] and sin offering (Heb. *ḥăṭā'āh*)[42] are specifically provided for by name in the Levitical legislation. The spiritual principles which underlay these various types of sacrifice are fulfilled and transcended in the perfect self-offering of Christ. Our author's contrast is not between sacrifice and obedience, but between the involuntary sacrifice of dumb animals and "sacrifice into which obedience enters, the sacrifice of a rational and spiritual being, which is not passive in death, but in dying makes the will of God its own."[43]

The Septuagint reading, "you have fashioned a body for me," suggests to our author the incarnation of the Son of God, and the whole passage from

---

37. "Every species of sacrifice had its own primary idea. The fundamental idea of the *'ōlāh* (burnt-offering) was *oblatio*, or the offering of worship; that of the *shelāmīm* (peace-offerings), *conciliatio*, or the knitting of fellowship; that of the *minḥāh* (meal-offering), *donatio*, or sanctifying consecration; that of the *ḥaṭṭā'th* (sin-offering), *expiatio*, or atonement; that of the *'āshām* (guilt-offering), *mulcta (satisfactio)*, or a compensatory payment. The self-sacrifice of the Servant of Jehovah may be presented under all these points of view. It is the complete antitype, the truth, the object, and the end of all the sacrifices" (F. Delitzsch, *The Prophecies of Isaiah*, E.T., II [Edinburgh, 1867], pp. 333f., on *'āšām* in Isa. 53:10). (Cf. n. 42 below.) In Ps. 40:6f. "sin offering" may include the idea of "guilt offering." Cf. also W. O. E. Oesterley, *The Psalms* (London, 1953), pp. 234f.; he suggests that the thank offering *(tôdāh)* is not mentioned because it was included under the *zebaḥ* ("sacrifice"), which comes first of the four. See further R. J. Thompson, *Penitence and Sacrifice in Early Israel outside the Levitical Law* (Leiden, 1963); R. de Vaux, *Studies in Old Testament Sacrifice* (Cardiff, 1964).

38. Heb. *šᵉlāmîm*. In the Levitical legislation *zebaḥ* (like its cognate verb *zābaḥ*, "to slaughter in sacrifice") is regularly restricted to peace offerings (under which thank offerings are subsumed).

39. E.g., in its earliest biblical occurrence it is used of Cain's vegetable sacrifice and Abel's animal sacrifice alike (Gen. 4:3ff.). Cf. pp. 281-84 (on 11:4).

40. Lev. 2:1ff.

41. In the LXX ὁλοκαύτωμα (the word used here), "whole burnt offering," "holocaust," is the commonest equivalent for Heb. *'ôlāh*.

42. Heb. *ḥăṭā'āh* is a variant of the more common *ḥaṭṭā'ṯ.* When this word is used in the sense of "sin offering," its regular LXX equivalent is the phrase περὶ ἁμαρτίας (so here). This phrase (for which cf. vv. 8, 18; 13:11; Rom. 8:3), according to E. K. Simpson, "should be read as a single vocable, indeclinable, if you will, for a *sin-offering*. That is manifest from the LXX usage (Lev. 4:33; 14:19; Num. 8:8, and the ὁλοκαύτωμα καὶ περιαμαρτίας of Ps. 40:7). We even find the verb περιαμαρτίζειν in Aquila and Symmachus, and the latter employs the noun περιαμαρτισμός of Zechariah's fountain opened for uncleanness" (*Words Worth Weighing in the Greek New Testament* [London, 1946], p. 29). In Isa. 53:10, where the Servant gives his life as an *'āšām*, the LXX rendering is περὶ ἁμαρτίας (cf. p. 178, n. 93; n. 37 above).

43. J. Denney, *The Death of Christ* (London, ⁶1907), p. 232. See also C. F. D. Moule, *The Sacrifice of Christ* (London, 1956); F. M. Young, *Sacrifice and the Death of Christ* (London, 1975); M. Hengel, *The Atonement*, E.T. (London, 1981).

Ps. 40 is understood as spoken by him "at his coming into the world." His incarnation itself is viewed as an act of submission to God's will and, as such, an anticipation of his supreme submission to that will in death. The psalmist's words, "I have come to do your will, O God," sum up the whole tenor of our Lord's life and ministry, and express the essence of that true sacrifice which God desires. But what of the parenthetic clause: "as it is written of me in the scroll of the book"?[44] Its meaning is clarified by the clause which immediately follows the clauses which are quoted here: "Your law is within my heart."[45] The "scroll of the book" is the written *tôrāh* of God;[46] what was written there the speaker recognized to be written concerning *him*, to be God's prescription for *him*. His life would accordingly be the active counterpart of the written law; the will of God, which was set down in the "scroll of the book," would be equally manifested in his obedience. It may be that for our author, as he applies these words to Jesus, the "scroll of the book" was enlarged to include all that God had said in earlier days "to the fathers by the prophets"; we recall how our Lord was led off to trial and death with the words on his lips: "Let the scriptures be fulfilled" (Mark 14:49). Yet it was not simply that he found his duty set down plainly in the written record and set himself to carry it out: it was at the same time the dearest desire of his heart to fulfil that special service which was his Father's will for him. While it was indeed his Father's will, it was also his own spontaneous choice. And therefore his undertaking and fulfilling it constituted a sacrifice utterly acceptable to God.

8-9 In these words of Ps. 40, then, interpreted as our Lord's declaration at his entry into the world, our author sees the abrogation of the old sacrificial cultus announced. The sacrifices in which God is said to take no pleasure are the sacrifices prescribed by the ancient cultic law of Israel; now that cultic law is to be superseded by a new order, inaugurated by Christ's perfect obedience to the will of God. The declaration falls into two parts: in the first part (which is said "above")[47] the old order is abolished; in the second the new is estab-

---

44. Heb. *bimᵉgillat sēper* (*mᵉgillāh* is a "roll" or "scroll"); but LXX ἐν κεφαλίδι βιβλίου (so here) refers strictly to the κεφαλίς, the knob at the top of the stick around which the scroll was rolled, used here by metonymy for the scroll itself. The genitive βιβλίου may be regarded as genitive of definition, "the book in scroll-form" or "the scroll of writing." It would be going too far to press the etymological sense of βιβλίον and so render the phrase "the scroll of papyrus."

45. Cf. Jer. 31:33, quoted in Heb. 8:10.

46. The suggestion that a heavenly book (cf. Ps. 139:16; Dan. 10:21, etc.) is meant here is unlikely (cf. W. E. Barnes, *The Psalms*, I [London, 1931], p. 204: "The Psalmist's commission is written down in heaven in the book of God, which is pictured as a roll"). Perhaps we should regard the scroll "as an expression of Yahweh's will without specifying its exact nature" (A. A. Anderson, *Psalms*, NCBC [London, 1972], p. 318).

47. Gk. ἀνώτερον, "higher up" in the passage quoted.

lished.[48] The terms of the new covenant include the provision that God's law will henceforth be engraved in his people's hearts; and it was supremely fitting that this should be preeminently true of him through whose obedience and blood the new covenant has been ratified. "I have come to do your will" is written over the whole record of our Lord's life; this was his attitude from first to last.

10   And it is by his fulfilling the will of God[49] to the uttermost that he has "sanctified" his people and provided the "perfection" which was unattainable on the basis of the ancient sacrifices. His fulfilment of God's will to the uttermost involved the "offering" once for all of his body—that body prepared for him at his incarnation. "It is the Atonement which explains the Incarnation: the Incarnation takes place in order that the sin of the world may be put away by the offering of the body of Jesus Christ."[50] The offering of his body is simply the offering of himself; if here sanctification and access to God are made available through his body, in vv. 19 and 29 they are made available through his blood.[51] Whether our author speaks of his body or his blood, it is his incarnate life that is meant, yielded to God in an obedience which was maintained even to death. So perfect a sacrifice was our Lord's presentation of his life to God that no repetition of it is either necessary or possible: it was offered "once for all."[52] The sanctification which his people receive in consequence is their inward cleansing from sin and their being made fit for the presence of God, so that henceforth they can offer him acceptable worship. It is a sanctification which has taken place once for all;[53] in this sense it is as unrepeatable as the sacrifice which effects it.

48. The Gk. perfect εἴρηκεν at the beginning of v. 9 expresses completed action: what the speaker said stands henceforth on permanent record (cf. the use of γέγραπται or εἴρηται, "it is written" or "it is said," to introduce a quotation of Scripture, as, e.g., in Luke 4:4, 8, 12). The ordinal numerals "first" (πρῶτον) and "second" (δεύτερον) are neuter here; no particular substantive is understood with them. "The first" is the old sacrificial system; "the second" is our Lord's perfect self-dedication to do the will of God.

49. Gk. ἐν ᾧ θελήματι, "by which will," means "by the will of God thus fulfilled b Christ." "Christ's act of obedience is as inclusive [here] as Paul shows it to be when he says in Rom. 5[:19] that a single act of obedience meant a putting right of all mankind, or when he says in II Cor. 5[:14] that if one died for all, then all were dead" (C. F. D. Moule, *The Phenomenon of the New Testament*, SBT 2.1 [London, 1967], p. 33).

50. J. Denney, *Death of Christ*, p. 234.

51. Cf. our Lord's words about his "flesh" and his "blood" in John 6:51-58; to "eat the flesh of the Son of man and drink his blood" are two expressions which equally denote his people's appropriation of, and participation in, himself. Similarly in the Eucharist the "body" and the "blood" of Christ are not two complementary parts of his being; in the bread as in the cup it is his whole self that Christ communicates to his people.

52. Gk. ἐφάπαξ, as in 7:27; 9:12 (see p. 175, n. 82); it receives special weight here from its emphatic position at the end of the sentence.

53. It is expressed here in the perfect tense (ἡγιασμένοι ἐσμέν). Cf. the present ἁγιαζομένους in v. 14 (n. 58); perhaps we should contrast the use of the aorist in the case of the apostate in v. 29 (p. 260, n. 129).

J. THE ENTHRONED HIGH PRIEST (10:11-18)

11 *Every priest[54] stands ministering day by day and repeatedly[55] offering the same sacrifices, which can never remove sins;[56]*

12 *but this high priest offered one sacrifice for sins, one effective for evermore,[57] and then took his seat at God's right hand,*

13 *waiting thenceforward for his enemies to be placed as a footstool for his feet.*

14 *For by one offering he has brought those who are sanctified[58] to perfection for evermore.*

15 *The Holy Spirit also assures us of this: after saying,*

16   *"This[59] is the covenant I will make[60] with them in days to come, says the Lord:*
    I will put my laws in their heart,
    and write them on their mind,"[61] [then he says,][62]

17   *"And I will no more remember their sins and iniquities."[63]*

18 *Now where these are forgiven,[64] there is no sin offering any longer.*

11-12 The unrepeatable character of the sacrifice of Christ, by contrast with the sacrifices of the old order, is underlined by an appeal to the language of Ps. 110. The introductory oracle of this psalm, in which the Mes-

---

54. Some authorities (including A C P 69 104 *al* syr$^{\text{pesh hcl}}$** cop^{sa}) read "high priest" (ἀρχιερεύς).

55. πολλάκις ("often") is omitted in the fragmentary seventh-century 𝔭^{79} (= *P. Berl.* 6774), which exhibits Heb. 10:10-12, 28-30. See *New Docs.*, II (1977), § 91 (p. 139).

56. 𝔭^{13} and the Coptic versions have the singular "sin" (ἁμαρτίαν).

57. Gk. εἰς τὸ διηνεκές (as in vv. 1, 14; 7:3; cf. p. 156, n. 7). Here a question of punctuation arises: should the phrase be constructed with the words that precede ("when he had offered . . .") or with those that follow ("sat down . . .")? It is equally appropriate with both. In favor of the former alternative it may be said that the phrase would then receive emphasis by coming at the end of a clause, like ἐφάπαξ in v. 10 (cf. n. 53 above); in favor of the latter we may recall the use of this phrase εἰς τὸ διηνεκές in 7:3 as a variant of εἰς τὸν αἰῶνα in Ps. 110 (LXX 109):4. The latter is preferred, e.g., by J. N. Darby (*New Translation, ad loc.*) and J. Moffatt (*New Translation, ad loc.*; cf. his note in ICC, p. 140); B. F. Westcott, however, rightly points out that the latter construction "is contrary to the usage of the Epistle; it obscures the idea of the perpetual efficacy of Christ's one sacrifice; it weakens the contrast with ἕστηκεν; and it imports a foreign idea into the image of the assumption (ἐκάθισεν) of royal dignity by Christ" (*ad loc.*).

58. Gk. ἁγιαζομένους (as in 2:11), for which 𝔭^{46} has the curious variant ἀνασωζομένους, "(those who are) being saved again"—probably due to the misreading of an indistinct exemplar.

59. Gk. αὕτη (𝔭^{13} D* and Vg. read αὕτη δέ, "But this").

60. Gk. διαθήσομαι, "I will covenant" (see p. 186, n. 40).

61. Jer. 31:33a. The whole context is quoted in Heb. 8:8-12 (see pp. 186f.).

62. These words, which in the authentic text are left to be understood, are supplied by several later manuscripts and versions, in the form ὕστερον λέγει (69 1739 etc., with the Harclean Syriac, Armenian, and Sahidic Coptic), or in the form τότε εἴρηκεν (1611).

63. Jer. 31:34b, in a telescoped form (cf. 8:12).

64. Gk. ἄφεσις, as in 9:22.

siah is invited by God to sit at his right hand, has already been quoted by our author (Heb. 1:13) and has influenced his phraseology in 1:3; 8:1; but only now does he draw out its full significance.[65] The Aaronic priests never sat down in the sanctuary; they remained standing throughout the whole performance of their sacred duties. In this our author sees a token of the fact that their sacred duties were never done, that their sacrifices had always to be repeated. In v. 1 the repetition of the ritual of the Day of Atonement "year by year" was mentioned; here, as in 7:27, the reference is to those sacrifices which were offered "day by day."[66] But whether the repetition was annual or daily, the main point is that repetition was necessary; not one of these sacrifices could remove sin or cleanse the conscience with permanent effect. The completion of one sacrifice meant only that a similar one would have to be offered in due course, and so on indefinitely; it was in keeping with this that the priests of the old order never sat down in the presence of God when a sacrifice had been presented to him.

But it was equally in keeping with the perfection of Christ's sacrifice of himself that, when he had presented it to God, he sat down. No further sacrificial service can be required of the priest who appeared on earth in the fulness of time to put away sin and sanctify his people once for all. A seated priest is the guarantee of a finished work and an accepted sacrifice. The heavenly high priest has indeed a continual ministry to discharge on his people's behalf at the Father's right hand; but that is the ministry of intercession on the basis of the sacrifice presented and accepted once for all; it is not the constant or repeated offering of his sacrifice. This last misconception has no doubt been fostered in the Western Church by a defective Vulgate rendering which springs from a well-known inadequacy of the Latin verb.[67]

Translations and commentaries differ on the construction of the phrase "for evermore" in v. 12; syntactically it might refer either to the preceding clause "this high priest offered one sacrifice for sins" or to the following words "took his seat . . ."; and as far as the sense is concerned, it would be

---

65. See pp. 49f., 63f.

66. See p. 177.

67. The Greek aorist participle προσενέγκας ("having offered") in v. 12 is in sharp contrast to the present participle προσφέρων ("offering") in v. 11. But since Latin has no perfect participle active (except in deponent verbs), the Latin version uses the present participle *offerens* as the rendering of both these forms. The context here really rules out the implication of the Latin present participle; it is a contradiction in terms to say (as R. A. Knox's translation of the Vulgate puts it): "he sits for ever at the right hand of God, offering for our sins a sacrifice that is never repeated" (a footnote in Knox's version points out that the Greek means: "he has taken his seat at the right hand of God after offering a sacrifice"). (The Latin replacement of the Greek aorist indicative ἐκάθισεν by the present *sedet* does not materially affect the sense.) For a similar difficulty arising from the absence of a perfect participle active in the Latin verb cf. 1:3 (p. 49, n. 31).

equally appropriate either way. On the whole, however, it seems that the familiar English versions are right in taking it with the preceding clause.[68]

Christ, then, has taken his seat in token that his sacrificial work is finished; but more, the worth of his sacrifice and the dignity of his person are further indicated in that he has taken his seat not merely in the presence of God but at "God's right hand."[69] From the shame of the cross he has been exalted to the place of highest glory. With the more confidence, therefore, may his people avail themselves of his high-priestly aid, assured that in him they have access to all the grace and power of God. To all who are uncertain of their acceptance with God comes the voice which brought encouragement to the soul of John Bunyan: "Sinner, thou thinkest that because of thy sins and infirmities I cannot save thy soul, but behold my Son is by me, and upon him I look, and not on thee, and will deal with thee according as I am pleased with him."[70]

13 Our author continues to give the substance of Ps. 110:1 by adding the words: "waiting thenceforward for his enemies to be placed as a footstool for his feet." He offers no exegesis of these words, but if he had attached no significance to them in the present context he could easily have omitted them altogether, as he does in every other place (apart from the direct quotation of Ps. 110:1 in Heb. 1:13) where he speaks of Christ as enthroned at God's right hand. In the light of the solemn admonition which follows in vv. 26-31, there may be an implied warning here to his readers not to let themselves be numbered among the enemies of the exalted Christ, but rather to be reckoned as his friends and companions by preserving their fidelity to the end (cf. 3:14). Paul has more to say about the eventual subjection of all the enemies of Christ ("principalities and powers") beneath his feet in 1 Cor. 15:24-28, where he gives a combined exegesis of Ps. 110:1 and Ps. 8:6.[71] But Paul has in mind here not the high-priestly ministry of Christ but his enthronement as mediatorial king: as such "he is destined to reign until God has put all enemies under his feet; and the last enemy to be abolished is death" (1 Cor. 15:25f., NEB).

14 Christ, then, by his self-oblation has accomplished once for all what generations of Levitical sacrifices had never done. After hundreds of years those sacrifices were no nearer the attainment of their aim than they had been at the beginning. Nor can this contrast between them and the death of Christ be dismissed as an apt conceit of our author's, elaborated here for

---

68. See p. 244, n. 57.
69. This is the only place in the epistle where this expression appears without periphrasis (cf. its amplifications in 1:3; 8:1; 12:2).
70. *Grace Abounding*, para. 258.
71. Cf. 2:6ff. (pp. 72-75).

apologetic purposes. Its force was tacitly acknowledged in Christian practice. Many, probably most, of the early converts to Christianity had been accustomed to a form of worship in which animal sacrifices played a part; this was so whether they had previously been Jews or Gentiles. That their new form of worship had no place for such sacrifices was in itself a recognition that they had been rendered forever obsolete by the death of Christ. "Those who looked upon this death as a sacrifice soon ceased to offer God any blood-sacrifice at all."[72] They might not all have used the language of the Epistle to the Hebrews, but the logic of its argument was implicit in their most elementary understanding of the gospel. The sacrifice of Christ has purified his people from the moral defilement of sin, and assured them of permanent maintenance in a right relation with God. "For by one offering he has perfected for all time those who are thus consecrated" (NEB).

In v. 10 the statement that "we have been sanctified" is made in the perfect tense; here, as in 2:11, the present passive participle is used. In v. 10 the emphasis lay on the unrepeatable nature of the death of Christ as the sacrifice by which his people have been set apart for the worship and service of God; here their character as the people thus set apart is simply indicated in timeless[73] terms, because emphasis is being laid on the fact that by that same sacrifice those who have been cleansed and "perfected" are now eternally constituted God's holy people. Three outstanding effects are thus ascribed to the sacrifice of Christ: by it his people have had their conscience cleansed from guilt; by it they have been fitted to approach God as accepted worshipers; and by it they have experienced the fulfilment of what was promised in earlier days, being brought into the perfect relation to God which is involved in the new covenant.[74]

15-18   That the "perfection" of which our author speaks is bound up with the new covenant is made plain by his repetition of the words of Jer. 31:33f. and his application of them to the effect of the sacrifice of Christ. These words, spoken by the prophet under inspiration, are naturally quoted as the words of the Holy Spirit,[75] and they are viewed as the Holy Spirit's confirmation of the conclusion to which our author's argument has just led him. The new covenant, according to Jeremiah's prophecy, not only involved

---

72. A. Harnack, *What is Christianity?* E.T. (London, 1904), p. 159.

73. As A. B. Davidson says of the present participles ἁγιάζων and ἁγιαζόμενοι in 2:11, "the words are timeless designations of the two parties, taken from the part characteristic of each" (*The Epistle to the Hebrews* [Edinburgh, 1882], p. 66). "He has perfected" (v. 14) is perfect tense.

74. See D. Peterson, *Hebrews and Perfection*, SNTSM 47 (Cambridge, 1982), pp. 149-53. Cf. also A. B. Davidson, *Hebrews*, pp. 203-9 ("Note on the Words Purge, Sanctify, Make Perfect").

75. Cf. "he says" in 8:8 (p. 187).

the implanting of God's laws, together with the will and power to carry them out, in the hearts of his people; it also conveyed the assurance that their past sins and iniquities would be eternally blotted out from God's record, never to be brought up in evidence against them. Here is something far beyond what the sacrificial law of Old Testament times could provide: in that law there was an annual "reminder of sins" (cf. v. 3), whereas in the new covenant there is no more remembrance of them. Repeated remembrance of sins and repeated sin offerings went inevitably together; therefore, the irrevocable erasing of sins from the divine record implies that no further sin offering is called for. The finality of the sacrifice of Christ is thus confirmed.[76]

In Heb. 8 the oracle of Jer. 31:31-34 was quoted in order to prove the obsolescence of the old economy; now it is quoted again in order to establish the permanence of the era of "perfection" inaugurated under the new covenant. "God has spoken in his Son"; and he has no word to speak beyond him.

VI. CALL TO WORSHIP, FAITH, AND PERSEVERANCE (10:19–12:29)

A. ACCESS TO GOD THROUGH THE SACRIFICE OF CHRIST (10:19-25)

19 *So, my brothers, we have freedom of access into the holy place by Jesus' blood,*
20 *along the new[77] and living way which he has dedicated for us through the curtain, that is to say, his flesh;*
21 *and we have a great priest over God's house.*
22 *Let us therefore approach God[78] with a true heart, in faith's full assurance, since our hearts have been sprinkled clean from an evil conscience[79] and our bodies have been washed with pure water.*

---

76. See A. Vanhoye, "L'oblation sacerdotale du Christ dans l'épître aux Hébreux," *Didaskalia* 14 (1984), pp. 27f.

77. Gk. πρόσφατος, etymologically meaning "freshly killed"; the second element in the compound became otiose at an early stage, and the word simply means "new," "fresh," "recent" (cf. such LXX occurrences as Eccl. 1:9; Ps. 80:9 [Eng. 81:9]; and the adverb προσφάτως ["lately"] in Acts 18:2).

78. Gk. προσερχώμεθα, for which 𝔭[46]* D K P and many other manuscripts have the indicative προσερχόμεθα ("we draw near"). In this hortatory context the subjunctive is required.

79. The ARV, following the punctuation of the TR, puts a heavy stop after "evil conscience," so that the participial construction "having had our hearts sprinkled clean (ῥεραντισμένοι) . . ." is attached to what precedes; it should be construed closely with the λελουσμένοι clause which follows, both clauses being subordinate to "let us approach" (so the AV/KJV, the ERV, the RSV, and the NEB). The participles are in the middle voice, as is appropriate for initiatory cleansing; cf. βάπτισαι . . . ἀπόλουσαι in Acts 22:16 and ἀπελούσασθε in 1 Cor. 6:11.

23 *Let us maintain without wavering the confession of our*[80] *hope, for he who has given us his promises is trustworthy.*

24 *Let us at the same time cultivate mutual consideration, stimulating one another*[81] *to love and good works.*

25 *Let us not abandon our meeting together, as some are in the habit of doing; let us rather encourage one another, and all the more so, as you see the Day approaching.*

The practical implications of the foregoing argument are now summed up in this sustained exhortation (one sentence in Greek), which might well have formed the conclusion of the homily, had not our author judged it wise to expand and apply in greater detail the points made here, for the further encouragement and strengthening of his readers. In view of all that has been accomplished for us by Christ, he says, let us confidently approach God in worship, let us maintain our Christian confession and hope, let us help one another by meeting together regularly for mutual encouragement, because the day which we await will soon be here.

19 The "boldness" which believers in Christ have to enter the heavenly sanctuary through him is set in contrast with the restrictions which hedged about the privilege of symbolic entry into the presence of God in Israel's earthly sanctuary. In it not all the people could exercise this privilege, but the high priest only, as their representative; and even he could not exercise the privilege any time he chose, but at fixed times and under fixed conditions. But those who have been cleansed within, consecrated and made perfect by the sacrifice of Christ, have received a free right of access into the holy presence; and our author urges his readers to avail themselves fully of this free right. As regularly in the New Testament, the *parrhēsia* enjoyed by Christians is "based on the revelation of God in Jesus Christ who restored the relation betweeen God and man."[82] The invitation to "approach the throne of grace with confidence" has already been issued in this epistle (4:16); on that occasion the invitation was based on the assurance that the high priest who has passed through the heavens is one whose own experiences of temptation enable him to sympathize with his people in their trials. Now a further assurance is given: the way by which this high priest has entered into the presence of God is a way which remains open for his people to follow him there.

---

80. "Our" (ἡμῶν) is supplied in a few authorities (ℵ* with the Latin Vulgate and Syriac Peshiṭta); in the others it is left to be understood.

81. Gk. εἰς παροξυσμόν, lit. "for provocation"; 𝔭⁴⁶ has ἐκ παροξυσμοῦ, which might be rendered "by way of provocation."

82. W. C. van Unnik, "The Christian's Freedom of Speech in the New Testament," *BJRL* 44 (1961-62), p. 487. Cf. p. 94, n. 20; p. 271, n. 188.

The AV/KJV describes this free right of access as "boldness to enter into the holiest[83] by the blood of Jesus." The Greek text, indeed, does not use the superlative expression here which distinguishes the holy of holies from the holy place; but in 9:8 we have already seen the more general term "the holy place" used with reference to the earthly sanctuary where the inner compartment was actually meant. So here, as is indicated by the words "through the curtain," it is to the very throne of God that believers in Christ have free entry—not to the material symbol of his throne where, as in the preexilic holy of holies, his invisible presence was upborne by the cherubim; but to his true and spiritual dwelling. Believers have no need to ask "Who shall ascend into heaven?" when it is a question of their approaching God; here upon earth they may enter his heavenly abode and know direct communion with him "by Jesus' blood."[84] He who, "by virtue of his own blood, entered the holy place once for all" (9:12) has procured for his people equal right of entry there by means of that same blood—that is, on the ground of his accepted sacrifice.

20 The way by which they enter the presence of God is a new way, which did not exist until he opened it up[85] and entered thereby himself. It is thus a new way; it is also a "living way." For in effect the ever-living Christ himself, as his people's sacrifice and priest, is the way to God; the present passage is our author's counterpart to the affirmation of John 14:6: "I am the way, and the truth, and the life; no one comes to the Father, but by me."[86] It is a way which (to continue the symbolism of the tabernacle and temple) leads "through the curtain" into the holy of holies.

It can scarcely be doubted that the "curtain" or "veil" of which our author is thinking is the inner veil which separated the holy place from the holy of holies, the "second curtain" of 9:3,[87] through the heavenly archetype

83. Gk. παρρησίαν εἰς τὴν εἴσοδον τῶν ἁγίων (with the expression cf. 9:8, τὴν τῶν ἁγίων ὁδόν).

84. Gk. ἐν τῷ αἵματι 'Ιησοῦ, the instrumental use of ἐν (as in 13:20) being practically indistinguishable from that of διά in the similar phrase in 9:12.

85. Gk. ἐνεκαίνισεν, "he consecrated *or* dedicated." See J. Behm, *TDNT*, III, p. 454 (*s.v.* ἐγκαινίζω); also W. Michaelis, *TDNT*, V, pp. 75-78 (*s.v.* ὁδός). "The death of Christ is seen as the new Encaenia or Dedication," says J. A. T. Robinson, adding that two ideas appear to be combined here, the Cross marking the dedication both of the new covenant—for "even the first covenant has not been dedicated (ἐνκεκαίνισται) without blood" (9:18)—and of the new temple (cf. the technical term ἐνκαίνια in John 10:22); "the whole argument of chapters 9 and 10 leads to the climax that Jesus has now 'opened' the new sanctuary in the temple of his body" (*Twelve New Testament Studies* [London, 1962], p. 172). See also O. Hofius, "Inkarnation und Opfertod Jesu nach Hebr 10, 19f.," in *Der Ruf Jesu und die Antwort der Gemeinde* (J. Jeremias *FS*), ed. E. Lohse (Göttingen, 1970), pp. 132-41.

86. Cf. Eph. 2:18; also Rom. 5:2; Eph. 3:12; 1 Pet. 2:4f.; 3:18. See N. A. Dahl, "'A New and Living Way'—the Approach to God according to Hebrews 10:19-25," *Interpretation* 5 (1951), pp. 401-12.

87. With διὰ τοῦ καταπετάσματος here cf. τὸ δεύτερον καταπέτασμα in 9:3 (and the earlier

of which Jesus has already passed as his people's forerunner (6:19f.). Here it is natural to ask whether these words contain an implicit allusion to the rending of the temple veil from top to bottom at the moment of Jesus' death (Mark 15:38; cf. Matt. 27:51; Luke 23:45). For the veil which was then rent in two was also probably the inner veil,[88] and its rending is recorded not as a natural portent[89] but as an event of theological significance: in the death of Jesus, we are to understand, God himself is unveiled to us and the way of access to him is thrown wide open. The teaching of the Synoptic passion narratives is thus to the same effect as that of our epistle; in both instances the teaching is given a cultic form, which is expressed realistically in the Gospels and symbolically by our author.[90] If our author knew about the rent veil, its significance was patent to him. But even if he did not know about it, his language here drives home the same lesson as the rending of the veil did.

A still more important question is raised by the following clause, "that is to say, his flesh."[91] Do these words qualify "the curtain" or the "new and living way"?[92] The Greek affords no more help in answering this question than the English does. The ERV/ARV render the passage in such a way as to preserve the ambiguity; the AV/KJV probably, and the RSV certainly ("through the curtain, that is, through his flesh"), identify "his flesh" with "the veil" ("the curtain"); the NEB comes down unambiguously on the side of the other alternative—"the new, living way which he has opened for us

---

instance of καταπέτασμα in the same sense in 6:19). In the LXX καταπέτασμα is sometimes used for the outer screen (Ex. 26:37; 38:18; Num. 3:26), but regularly for the inner curtain or *parōket*— "the inmost curtain" (τὸ ἐσωτάτω καταπέτασμα), as Philo calls it (*Giants* 53). See p. 199, n. 14.

88. This is the majority view; however, it has been identified with the outer veil by Jerome and Thomas Aquinas and also by G. Dalman, E. Klostermann, A. H. McNeile, B. T. D. Smith, E. Lohmeyer, etc. (see the list in V. Taylor, *The Gospel according to St. Mark* [London, 1952], p. 596).

89. Other portents associated with the temple are recorded for A.D. 30 and other occasions in the forty years preceding its destruction in A.D. 70 in Josephus (*War* 6.288-309), Tacitus (*Hist.* 5.13), *The Gospel according to the Hebrews* (quoted by Jerome, *Epistle* 120.8.1) and the Jerusalem Talmud (*Yoma* 6.5.3); it does not appear that the rending of the veil can be identified with any of these. But see H. W. Montefiore, "Josephus and the New Testament," *NovT* 4 (1960), pp. 139-60, 307-18 (esp. pp. 148-54). The rending of the veil has nothing to do with the legend that the veil bled when Titus slashed it with his sword (TB *Gittin* 56b).

90. Cf. C. H. Dodd, *The Apostolic Preaching and its Developments* (London, 1944), p. 51; G. Lindeskog, *Coniectanea Neotestamentica* 11 (1947), pp. 132ff.; R. H. Lightfoot, *The Gospel Message of St. Mark* (Oxford, 1950), pp. 55f.

91. Unless, with K. Holsten, we treat this clause as a gloss added later, but for such a conjecture there is no textual evidence.

92. If they qualify "the veil," the genitive τῆς σαρκός in τοῦτ᾽ ἔστιν τῆς σαρκός αὐτοῦ may be taken either as genitive in apposition with τοῦ καταπετάσματος ("the veil, that is, his flesh") or as genitive in dependence on τοῦ καταπετάσματος ("the veil, that is, [the veil] of his flesh"). If they qualify "new and living way," τῆς σαρκός can only be taken as genitive in dependence on ὁδόν ("new and living way, that is, [the way] of his flesh").

251

through the curtain, the way of his flesh" (the variant rendering, "through the curtain of his flesh," is relegated to a footnote).

In favor of taking "that is to say, his flesh" as epexegetic of "the veil" is, first, the word order; it is rather awkward to relate the clause closely to the words "new and living way" in view of the intervention of the phrase "through the veil." Nor is there any difficulty in supposing that our author could explain the veil as being our Lord's "flesh"; like "the body of Jesus Christ" in v. 10 and "the blood of Jesus" in v. 19, "his flesh" here could mean his human life, offered up in sacrifice to God. It is by his sacrifice that the way of approach to God has been opened up.[93] The veil which, from one point of view, kept God and mankind apart, can be thought of, from another point of view, as bringing them together; for it was one and the same veil which on one side was in contact with the glory of God and on the other side with the need of men and women. So in our Lord Godhead and manhood were brought together; he is the true "daysman" or umpire who can lay his hand upon both because he shares the nature of both. And by his death, it could be added, the "veil" of his flesh was rent asunder and the new way consecrated through it by which human beings may come to God. "This beautiful allegorizing of the veil cannot, of course, be made part of a consistent and complete typology. It is not meant for this. But as the veil stood locally before the holiest in the Mosaic Tabernacle, the way into which lay through it, so Christ's life in the flesh stood between Him and His entrance before God, and His flesh had to be rent ere He could enter. This is the fact and the history which suggest the figure. But under this fact lie principles in the mind of God, and in the public law of the universe, and in the heart and mind of man, the object to be awakened and touched, which give to *through* a deeper sense, and in this sense for us also the way lies through His flesh" (A. B. Davidson).[94]

The protagonist for the interpretation "the way of his flesh" is B. F. Westcott. He found the equation of "veil" with "flesh" unsatisfactory because one would not expect to find the "flesh" of Christ "treated in any way as a veil, an obstacle, to the vision of God in a place where stress is laid on His humanity" and because one would expect a complete parallelism to be pre-

---

93. So J. Moffatt (ICC, *ad loc.*): "He allegorizes the veil here as the flesh of Christ; this had to be rent before the blood could be shed, which enabled him to enter and open God's presence for the people." Similarly N. H. Young, "Τοῦτ᾽ ἔστιν τῆς σαρκὸς αὐτοῦ (Heb. x.20): Apposition, Dependent or Explicative?" *NTS* 20 (1973-74), pp. 100-104: "the grammatical grounds for taking τῆς σαρκὸς αὐτοῦ as an appositional explicative to καταπέτασμα are coercive"; if some balk at this conclusion, it is mainly because of the "daring, poetical touch" (J. Moffatt), but "provided one is sober in one's exegesis the 'poetic touch' makes a sublime addition."

94. *The Epistle to the Hebrews*, pp. 211f. Cf. also O. Michel and C. Spicq, *ad loc.*, and W. Manson, *The Epistle to the Hebrews* (London, 1951), p. 67.

served "between the description of the approach of Christ to God and the approach of the believer to God."[95] On the former score, it should suffice to remember, in J. Moffatt's words, that the expression here "is a daring, poetical touch, and the parallelism is not to be prosaically pressed into any suggestion that the human nature in Jesus hid God from men 'in the days of his flesh,' or that he ceased to be truly human when he sacrificed himself."[96] On the latter score, if our Lord's "flesh" and his "blood" alike denote his human life offered up in sacrifice, then he who entered into the heavenly sanctuary "by virtue of his own blood" (9:12) may equally well be thought of as entering there through his "flesh." Since Westcott's objections to the usual rendering and interpretation do not appear to carry as much weight as he assigned to them, it is better on the whole to take the line more naturally suggested by the word-order and conclude that our author looked upon the veil as symbolizing our Lord's human life, presented to God when he "suffered for sins once for all, the righteous for the unrighteous, that he might bring us to God" (1 Pet. 3:18).

21 Their confidence in entering the presence of God should be enhanced by the fact that there Jesus fulfils his ministry as "a great priest over God's house." The expression "great priest" is the literal rendering of the most common Hebrew title for the high priest; "great" has here comparative or superlative force, denoting "the priest that is great above [i.e., greater than] his brethren" (according to the more literal rendering of Lev. 21:10).[97] "God's house" over which he exercises his high priesthood is, of course, the community of God's people (cf. Heb. 3:6).[98]

22 "Let us draw near," our author repeats[99]—near to God, that is. No longer is the privilege of access to him carefully fenced about by conditions like those laid down for the high priest when he made his annual entrance

---

95. *The Epistle to the Hebrews*, p. 322. A. Nairne finds that Westcott's interpretation "does make the whole sentence consistent and is probably right" (*The Epistle of Priesthood* [Edinburgh, 1913], p. 381). Cf. also H. W. Montefiore, HNTC, *ad loc*. Westcott indicates that the construction favored by him is that followed by Tyndale ("by the newe and livynge waye, which he hath prepared for vs, through the vayle, that is to saye by his flesshe") and other earlier English versions (cf. Coverdale, Great Bible, Geneva Bible). But their use of "by" before "his flesh" may perhaps not be resumptive of "by" before "the new and living way" but intended rather to indicate that the preposition διά has a different sense in the phrase "through (*or* by) his flesh" from that which it has in "through the veil"; cf. A. B. Davidson's remark in the quotation above on the deepening of the meaning of "through."

96. ICC, *ad loc*.

97. RSV "the priest who is chief among his brethren"; LXX ὁ ἱερεὺς ὁ μέγας ἀπὸ τῶν ἀδελφῶν αὐτοῦ. In Num. 35:25, 28, we have the simple phrase *hakkōhēn haggādōl*, LXX ὁ ἱερεὺς ὁ μέγας, lit. "the great priest," ARV "the high priest," as also in Zech. 3:1, 9; 6:11, where Joshua (LXX Jesus) is so designated (cf. p. 109, n. 28; p. 116, n. 68).

98. See p. 94, n. 18.

99. From 4:16.

into the holy of holies on the Day of Atonement; the "better hope" of 7:19, "through which we draw near[100] to God," has now been realized. Naturally such an approach can be made only with sincerity of heart—it is the pure in heart who will see God—and the "full assurance"[101] which faith in God's word begets. It is of faith like this that our author speaks a little later when he says that "one who approaches God must believe that he exists, and that he is a rewarder of those who seek him out" (11:6). But those who have experienced the inward cleansing that Christ's self-offering has effected may well be marked by sincerity of heart and "faith's full assurance"; this is what our author means when he speaks of himself and his readers as "having had our hearts sprinkled clean from an evil conscience, and our bodies washed with pure water." The punctuation of the TR and the ARV, which makes a heavy stop between these two participial phrases, attaching the sprinkling of the heart closely to the preceding exhortation "let us approach" and the washing of the body closely to the following exhortation "let us maintain . . . ,"[102] may be due to the feeling that there is something incongruous in correlating the figurative sprinkling of the heart and the literal washing of the body. The same sense of incongruity has led some expositors to maintain that the washing of the body is as figurative as the sprinkling of the heart, and to deny that it refers to baptism.[103]

That the sprinkling of the heart denotes an inward and spiritual cleansing is obvious; it is equally obvious that our author has in mind the counterpart under the new order of the old ritual cleansing with the "water for impurity," the water prepared with the ashes of the red heifer.[104] He has made this plain by his rhetorical question in 9:13f.: ". . . the ashes of a heifer sprinkled on those who have been defiled have sanctifying power as far as bodily cleansing is concerned, how much more will the blood of Christ, who . . . offered himself to God as an unblemished sacrifice, cleanse our conscience from dead works so as to worship the living God?" Those who make bold to enter the heavenly sanctuary by the blood of Jesus are by that same blood purified and made fit for the divine presence; the cleansing of the conscience removes the barrier which prevented their free access. It is not so clear that the washing of the body with pure water is thought of as having a similar analogue in the Old Testament ceremonial, simply because our author

---

100. In 7:19 the verb is ἐγγίζω; here and elsewhere in the epistle προσέρχομαι is the verb used for approaching God.

101. So the AV/KJV, the RSV, and the NEB rightly render πληροφορία here (the πληροφορία of faith here differs but little, if at all, from the πληροφορία of hope in 6:11).

102. See p. 248, n. 79.

103. Cf. G. H. Lang, *The Epistle to the Hebrews* (London, 1951), p. 167.

104. Cf. also the "water of expiation" (Heb. *mê ḥaṭṭā'ṯ*) sprinkled on the Levites in Num. 8:7.

does not stress an analogue to this as he does stress the ritual of the red heifer. He may, however, have thought of the requirement that the priest on the Day of Atonement should "bathe his body in water" (Lev. 16:4) before putting on the linen vestments in which he was to approach God in the holy of holies.[105] But the present reality which he has in mind is most probably Christian baptism—consisting, of course, not merely in the outward application of water, but in the outward application of water as the visible sign of the inward and spiritual cleansing wrought by God in those who come to him through Christ. As we are told again in 1 Pet. 3:21, the baptismal water is not intended to remove bodily impurity but to express "a pledge to God proceeding from a clear conscience."[106]

There is no impossible incongruity here in the collocation of the cleansing which is inward and spiritual ("since our hearts have been sprinkled clean from an evil conscience") with its outward and visible sign ("since our bodies have been washed with pure water").[107] A similar collocation of the outward and inward cleansing may be recognized in the Qumran texts. The Qumran community attached great importance to ritual bathing, and there are recurring references in their literature to the "water for impurity."[108] But a merely external sprinkling or cleansing with water will do a person no good if he cherishes an impenitent and apostate heart. Such a person "cannot be purified by atonement or cleansed with water for impurity. He cannot be sanctified in seas or rivers, or cleansed with any lustral water. . . . It is through an upright and humble spirit that a man's sin will be expiated, and through his self-submission to all God's ordinances that his flesh will be cleansed, so that he may have water for impurity sprinkled on him and be sanctified by means of cleansing water."[109] Behind this passage from the Qumran *Rule of the Community,* as indeed behind the thought of the writer to the Hebrews and other New Testament writers, we may discern such an Old Testament prophecy as that of Ezek. 36:25f., where the

---

105. Cf. also Ex. 29:4 (cf. 40:12), where the priests at their hallowing are washed at the door of the tent of meeting; Num. 19:7f., where the priest who supervises the burning of the red heifer and the man who burns her must wash their bodies and their clothes. With the wording of this clause ("having had our bodies washed with pure water") A. Nairne (*Epistle of Priesthood,* p. 381) compares Aeschylus, fragment 32: καλοῖσι λουτροῖς ἐκλελουμένος δέμας / εἰς ὑψίκρημνον Ἱμέραν ἀφικόμην.

106. Cf. E. G. Selwyn, *The First Epistle of St. Peter* (London, 1946), pp. 204-6.

107. The purificatory "sprinkling" of the heart and conscience "is put first, though the body had also its place and part in the cleansing experience. The καρδία and the σῶμα are a full, plastic expression for the entire personality, as the ancients conceived it" (J. Moffatt, *ad loc.*). The sprinkling (by the blood of Christ, according to 9:14; cf. 12:24) and the washing are both denoted here by means of perfect participles; they are once-for-all and unrepeatable acts with abiding effects.

108. Cf. p. 215, n. 88.

109. 1QS 3.4-9.

terminology of the ancient ritual ablutions is used to describe God's inward cleansing of his people in the age of restoration: "I will sprinkle clean water upon you, and you shall be clean. . . . A new heart I will give you, and a new spirit I will put within you."[110] Those who have received this inward cleansing from God may well enjoy that spiritual nearness to him which is impossible for a polluted conscience.

23 The exhortation is threefold: "let us approach . . . let us maintain . . . let us cultivate mutual consideration." The importance of holding fast the Christian confession has already been emphasized: it is only "if we maintain our confidence and the hope in which we boast" that we are the house of God (3:6); it is only "if we maintain the beginning of our steadfastness firm to the end" that we are partakers or companions of Christ (3:14). The powerful incentive which the knowledge of Christ's high priesthood provides for firmly maintaining the confession of him has also been stressed (4:14);[111] here it is repeated together with the other incentives which are bound up with his high priesthood, including above all the faithfulness of God whose promises, embodied and fulfilled in Christ, are set forth in the gospel for the encouragement and support of his people. "Let us hold fast the confession of our hope," say ERV/ARV, "that it waver not"—doing justice to the Greek construction in which the adjective "unwavering" agrees with "confession";[112] but if the confession wavers it is because the confessors waver, and this is brought out by the RSV ("Let us hold fast the confession of our hope without wavering") and the NEB ("Let us be firm and unswerving in the confession of our hope"). Our hope is based on the unfailing promise of God; why should we not cherish it confidently and confess it boldly?

24 The readers will be the more apt to confess their hope courageously and unhesitatingly if they encourage one another. Christian faith and witness will flourish the more vigorously in an atmosphere of Christian fellowship. "We ought to see how each of us may best arouse others to love and active goodness" (NEB). The word "stimulate" (AV/KJV, ERV/ARV "provoke"; RSV "stir up"; NEB "arouse") is a strong one;[113] it appears in one other place in the New Testament, and there in a very different way, of the "sharp contention" that broke out between Paul and Barnabas when they could not agree on taking Mark with them on a second apostolic visit to Cyprus and South

---

110. In the LXX the "clean water" of Ezek. 36:25 is καθαρὸν ὕδωρ, as here. Cf. also John 3:5, where the new birth ἐξ ὕδατος καὶ πνεύματος probably alludes to the water of Ezek. 36:25 and the spirit (wind or breath) of Ezek. 36:26f.; 37:9f. In Mark 1:8 the two are divided: John the Baptist applies the water; the Coming One will baptize with the Holy Spirit.

111. In 4:14 κρατέω is the verb used for "holding fast" the confession (as also in 6:18 for laying hold on the Christian hope as an anchor of the soul); here (as in 3:6, 14) the verb is κατέχω.

112. Gk. κατέχωμεν τὴν ὁμολογίαν τῆς ἐλπίδος ἀκλινῆ.

113. Gk. παροξυσμός, from the verb παροξύνω.

Galatia (Acts 15:39). Perhaps this Greek word *paroxysmos,* like our English "provocation," is more commonly used in the unfavorable sense of irritation than in the more pleasant sense used here by our author. It is the former sense that Paul has in mind in 1 Cor. 13:5 when, using the cognate verb *paroxynō,* he says that love "is not provoked."[114] But here love *is* provoked in the sense of being stimulated in the lives of Christians by the considerateness and example of other members of their fellowship.

25 This will never happen, however, if they keep one another at a distance. Therefore, every opportunity of coming together and enjoying their fellowship in faith and hope must be welcomed and used for mutual encouragement. Our author exhorts his readers to continue meeting together the more earnestly because he knows of some who were withdrawing from the Christian fellowship. Paul had urged the Roman Christians to welcome one another for God's glory, as Christ had welcomed them (Rom. 15:7). But toward the end of the apostolic age we are made aware of a tendency in some quarters to withdraw from the Christian fellowship. "At first and indeed always," says Harnack, "there were naturally some people who imagined that one could secure the holy contents and blessings of Christianity as one did those of Isis and the Magna Mater, and then withdraw. Or, in cases where people were not so short-sighted, levity, laziness, or weariness were often enough to detach a person from the society. A vainglorious sense of superiority, and of being able to dispense with the spiritual aid of the society, was also the means of inducing many to withdraw from fellowship and from the common worship. Many, too, were actuated by fear of the authorities; they shunned attendance at public worship, to avoid being recognized as Christians."[115] What appears to have underlain the withdrawal which our author here describes as "the custom of some"?

We may find a clue in the word translated "meeting together." Basically this is the word which we know in its English form "synagogue," but

---

114. "Love . . . is not irritable" (RSV). There is one further NT instance of παροξύνω in Acts 17:16, where Paul's "spirit was provoked within him" (NEB "exasperated") at the spectacle of so many "idols" in Athens.

115. A. Harnack, *Mission and Expansion of Christianity,* E.T. (London, 1908), I, pp. 434f. On his last point he quotes in a footnote Tertullian, *On Flight in Persecution* 3; on the general necessity of Christians' coming together and seeking one another's society he refers to Clement of Rome, *Epistle* 48:1ff.; *Didachē* 4:2; Hermas, Similitude 9.20, 26; *Ep. Barn.* 4:10; Ignatius, *Ephesians* 13:1, *Polycarp* 4:2, *Magnesians* 4; Justin, *First Apology* 67. Cf. *Didascalia* 13: "When you teach, command and remind the people to be constant in the assembly of the church." M. Dibelius ("Der himmlische Kultus nach dem Hebräerbrief," *Theologische Blätter* 21 [1942], pp. 2f.) assigns the falling off in attendance at the church's meetings to a waning of early enthusiasm; similarly H. Köster, P. Vielhauer, and W. Marxsen, as cited by H. Feld, *Der Hebräerbrief* (Darmstadt, 1985), p. 9. In the NT the tendency to withdrawal is especially manifest on the part of those who embraced forms of teaching deviating from what had been taught from the beginning (cf. 1 John 2:19, 24). Cf. Heb. 3:13 (pp. 100f.).

here it carries the prefix *epi*, which in this place may conceivably have the force "in addition," as though the word were to be translated "episynagogue."[116] If this meaning were accepted, then we might think of a group of Jewish believers in Jesus who had not yet severed their connection with the synagogue in which they had been brought up, but who in addition to their synagogue services had special meetings of their own in a "Christian appendage to the Jewish synagogue," as William Manson puts it.[117] In that case, our author fears that the discontinuance of their special Christian meetings will mean their complete merging in the life of the larger Jewish community with the loss of their distinctive Christian faith and outlook. What he would really like to see would be their decisive separation from the synagogue—this is what he means by "let us go out" or "let us come out" in 13:13—but if they are not ready for that, let them, as they value their lives, maintain their common meetings as believers in Jesus and so encourage one another in their common hope.

It may be pointed out, however, that there is no evidence elsewhere for the use of "episynagogue" in a different sense from "synagogue" or "meeting";[118] and our author may simply be urging his readers not to give up attending the general meeting of the church, as some were doing.[119] Under the various pressures which were being brought to bear upon them, to withdraw from the society of their fellow-believers was to court spiritual defeat; only by remaining united could they preserve their faith and witness.

Instead of growing slack in the practice of their Christian fellowship, they are bidden to encourage one another—"and all the more so, as you see the Day approaching." It is plain from the closing verses of this chapter that the apparent postponement of the parousia was having its effect on their minds; at least the sense of tension created by the knowledge that they were living in the end-time was weakening.[120] Not only for them, but for their fellow-

116. Gk. ἐπισυναγωγή, appearing once elsewhere in the NT—"our gathering together to him" (2 Thess. 2:1), where, however, the prefix ἐπι- may have directive force, anticipating πρὸς αὐτόν.

117. *The Epistle to the Hebrews*, p. 69.

118. "Scarcely to be differentiated from συναγωγή" (BAGD, p. 301).

119. W. Manson suggests that the ERV reading of 4:2, "they were not united by faith with them that heard" (see p. 103, n. 4) implies that "the Christian group at Rome whom the author addresses was separating itself off in the matter of 'faith' from the true believing body of the Church" (*Hebrews*, p. 58). This reading of 4:2 might indeed be applicable to the people who are being addressed, but it would scarcely be applicable to Israel in the wilderness, of whom the words are explicitly spoken. Quite apart from that vexed textual crux, we could well visualize the community here addressed as members of a "house church" in Rome which tended to detach itself from the wider fellowship of the city church.

120. Cf. L. Goppelt, "The Existence of the Church in History according to Apostolic and Early Catholic Thought," *Current Issues in New Testament Interpretation: Essays in Honor of Otto A. Piper*, ed. W. Klassen and G. F. Snyder (New York, 1962), pp. 193-209.

Christians in many other places, the necessity of coming to terms with the church's continued existence in history as a community completely separated from Judaism involved an "agonizing reappraisal." The first generation of believers was passing away; a new generation was growing up. At this point in time other shocks were in store for them: the rather sudden hostility of the imperial power[121] (with which the church had henceforth to live for two and a half centuries) and the destruction of the city and temple of Jerusalem.

Before A.D. 70 those Christians who remembered and took seriously Jesus' prophecy of the destruction of the temple were scarcely in a position to keep it distinct in their minds from the final coming of the Son of Man and the ingathering of his elect, which he also foretold. Only after the events of A.D. 70 was it possible to appreciate clearly that two separate epochs were involved in the twofold question of the disciples in the form given to it in Matt. 24:3: "*(a)* When will this [the destruction of the temple] be? *(b)* and what will be the sign of your parousia, and of the consummation of the age?" It may be that our author, writing (as we think) before A.D. 70, had the impending fall of Jerusalem and dissolution of the old order in mind when he spoke of "the Day" as approaching.[122] The words "*you see* the Day approaching" suggest that signs of the impending catastrophe in Judaea were already visible to men and women of discernment; and the fulfilment of that phase of Jesus' prediction pointed on to the fulfilment of the final phase. Yet for our author, as for the other New Testament writers, "the Day" is primarily the final phase, the day of Christ's parousia. Whatever was implied by the church's adaptation in her thought and life to the conditions of a second and further generations of Christian existence in the world, her teachers continued, long after A.D. 70, to emphasize the certainty, and indeed the nearness, of the parousia. The period between the first advent of Christ and his parousia is the end-time, the "last days." Whatever the duration of the period may be, for faith "the time is near" (Rev. 1:3). Each successive Christian generation is called upon to live as the generation of the end-time, if it is to live as a *Christian* generation. This being so, "the question is: How can the tension between the eschatological and historical existence of faith be retained over a period of time?"[123] The most satisfactory answer is the Pauline answer which, while given in the first Christian generation, is equally ap-

---

121. How sudden the overt hostility of the imperial power was may be gathered from the language of 1 Peter: in 1 Pet. 3:13 "who is he that will harm you if you be zealous of that which is good?" implies that the situation of Rom. 13:3f., several years earlier, still continues; in 1 Pet. 3:14 suffering for righteousness' sake is a remote possibility, as the use of the optative mood shows ("even if you were to suffer . . ."); but in 1 Pet. 4:12-19 the fiery trial is imminent, and suffering as a Christian, enduring reproach for the name of Christ, is no longer a remote possibility but a matter of present and certain expectation.

122. Gk. ἐγγίζουσαν (cf. p. 254, n. 100).

123. L. Goppelt, "The Existence of the Church. . .," p. 199.

plicable to every Christian generation: "If we live by the Spirit, let us also walk by the Spirit" (Gal. 5:25)—for the Spirit is the pledge and the firstfruits of the heritage of glory to be entered by believers at the parousia of Christ (cf. Rom. 8:23; Eph. 1:13f.). In keeping with this answer, our author insists that since Christ appeared once for all, "at the end of the ages," to offer himself to God as the perfect sacrifice for his people's sin, those who acknowledge him as apostle and high priest have already experienced "mighty works of the coming age" and receive the "kingdom which is unshakable" (Heb. 6:5; 12:27f.). Thus they anticipate here and now the consummation for which they hope; let them hold this hope fast by unswerving loyalty to Christ.

B. FOURTH ADMONITION: THE WILFUL SIN OF APOSTASY (10:26-31)

26 *For if we sin deliberately after receiving the knowledge of the truth, no further sacrifice for sins*[124] *is left for us—*
27 *nothing but a fearful expectation of judgment and fiery indignation*[125] *which is about to consume God's adversaries.*
28 *Any one who has violated Moses' law dies without mercy*[126] *"on the testimony of two or three witnesses."*[127]
29 *How much more severe do you think will be the penalty deemed fit for one who has trampled the Son of God underfoot, treated as something common the covenant blood*[128] *with which he was sanctified,*[129] *and outraged the Spirit of grace?*
30 *We know the one who said,*
"Vengeance is mine; I will requite";[130]

124. Gk. περὶ ἁμαρτιῶν (cf. 5:1, 3), for which p46 D* 81 have περὶ ἁμαρτίας (cf. v. 6, p. 241, n. 42).

125. Gk. πυρὸς ζῆλος, lit. "zeal of fire"; the passage is an echo of Isa. 26:11 ("let them see your zeal for the people, . . . let *fire consume your adversaries*"; LXX "*zeal* shall take an uninstructed people, and *fire shall consume the adversaries*"). Isa. 26:11 occurs in a judgment context, from which a further quotation is taken in v. 37a (p. 273, n. 197). Cf. 12:29 (pp. 365f.).

126. D* and the Harclean Syriac (Western authorities) add "and tears" (καὶ δακρύων), perhaps an echo of 12:17.

127. Quotation from Deut. 17:6; 19:15 (cf. Matt. 18:16; 2 Cor. 13:1; 1 Tim. 5:19). Cf. H. van Vliet, *No Single Testimony* (Utrecht, 1958).

128. Cf. 9:20 (quotation from Ex. 24:8). The African Old Latin MS *r* adds "new" to "covenant."

129. Gk. ἐν ᾧ ἡγιάσθη, omitted in A and some MSS of Chrysostom. See p. 243, n. 53.

130. Cod. A and a few other authorities add from Rom. 12:19 "says the Lord" (so also the TR and the AV/KJV). The quotation from Deut. 32:35 here and in Rom. 12:19 takes a form different from that of the MT ("vengeance is mine, and recompense") and the LXX ("on the day of vengeance I will repay," which suggests that MT *lî*, "mine," was an abbreviation for *lᵉyôm*, "on the day"), but in agreement with that of the Targum of Onqelos (Aramaic: *qŏdāmay pōr'ānûṯâ wa'ānâ 'ăšallēm*), and of the Palestinian and Pseudo-Jonathan Targums. Evidently

and again,
"*The Lord will judge his people.*"[131]
31 *It is fearful to fall into the hands of the living God.*

26-29 This passage was destined to have repercussions in Christian history beyond what our author could have foreseen. By "sin deliberately" he means something like that sinning "with a high hand"[132] for which no pardon was provided by the Old Testament law of atonement. He has already emphasized that despising the saving message spoken by the Son of God must carry with it penalties even more severe than the sanctions attached to the law of Moses, "the word spoken through angels" (2:2); and he repeats the same argument here. The context suggests that something much more serious is in his mind than what Paul calls being "overtaken in any trespass"[133]—after all, he has pointed out more than once that in Jesus Christians have a high priest who can succor them when they are tempted, sympathize with them in their infirmities, and bear gently with them when they stray from the path through ignorance.[134] What he has in mind is rather that "deserting the living God" of which he spoke in 3:12, that renunciation of Christianity against which he warned his readers in 6:4-8. To have received the knowledge of the truth[135] and then reject it is to give up the only way of salvation. "No further sacrifice for sins is left" which can avail for those who have deliberately abandoned reliance on the perfect sacrifice of Christ. That outright apostasy is intended here seems plain from the language of v. 29; the man who has committed this wilful sin is described as having "spurned the Son of God, and profaned the blood of the covenant by which he was sanctified, and outraged the Spirit of grace" (RSV).

Our author is not given to wild exaggeration, and when he uses language like this, he chooses his words with his customary care. To spurn the Son of God, to trample him underfoot (as the word literally means), "denotes

---

our author (and Paul) derived this quotation, either directly or (more probably) by way of a collection of *testimonia*, from a Greek text-form varying from the LXX A and B types, related perhaps to the Theodotionic text (cf. O. Michel, MK, *ad loc.*, p. 237, n. 1).

131. Deut. 32:36 (cf. also Ps. 135:14, where, however, the LXX [134:14] shows οἰκτείρει, "pities," as a strong variant for κρίνει or κρινεῖ).

132. Num. 15:30 (cf. p. 67, n. 2). For the *a fortiori* argument see p. 68, n. 4.

133. Gal. 6:1.

134. Cf. 2:17f.; 4:15f.; 5:2.

135. "The knowledge of the truth" (ἐπίγνωσις (τῆς) ἀληθείας) is a recurring phrase in the Pastoral Epistles (1 Tim. 2:4; 2 Tim. 2:25; 3:7; Tit. 1:1; cf. 1 Tim. 4:3); similar language occurs in the Johannine writings (cf. John 8:32; 1 John 2:21; 2 John 1). A study of the expression in relation to the thought and vocabulary of Qumran is presented by H. Kosmala in *Hebräer-Essener-Christen* (Leiden, 1959), pp. 135-73; he is, however, certainly at fault in his view that "the knowledge of the truth" in Hebrews "does not yet include faith in Jesus Christ" (p. 137).

contempt of the most flagrant kind";[136] to treat the covenant blood of Christ, by which alone his people are sanctified, cleansed, and brought to God,[137] as no better than the most common[138] death is to repudiate decisively both his sacrifice and all the blessings which flow from it; to outrage the Spirit of grace[139] is, in the words of Jesus, to be "guilty of an eternal sin" (Mark 3:29).[140] Anyone who was convicted, on adequate testimony, of a deliberate breach of Israel's covenant law was liable to the death penalty: "your eye shall not pity him," so ran the inexorable sentence.[141] But that was the penalty of *physical* death; the spiritual death which lies in store for the apostate under the new order is a "much sorer punishment."

It was commonly inferred in the early church from this and other passages in the epistle that forgiveness for all kinds of postbaptismal sin, inadvertent as well as deliberate, was ruled out. The fact, however, that baptized Christians did sin was patent. Was there then no hope for them? If so, the disciples' question to their Master might well be echoed: "Then who can be saved?" (Luke 18:26). In the Roman church (where, thanks to our epistle, the issue may have been an especially live one) the question was taken up a generation or so later by Hermas in *The Shepherd*.[142]

136. J. Moffatt (ICC, p. 151); he recalls the Homeric phrase for oath-breaking (καταπατεῖν ὅρκια, lit. "to trample oaths underfoot") and more particularly the LXX of Zech. 12:3, where Jerusalem is described as "a stone trampled on (καταπατούμενον) by all the nations; every one who tramples on her (καταπατῶν αὐτήν) will utterly scorn her." But there is no indication that Zech. 12:3 was in our author's mind here, although he uses the same verb παταπατέω.

137. Cf. 9:14; 10:10, 14, 19ff. for all that, to our author's mind, is involved in being "sanctified" by the covenant blood of Christ. For his blood as "covenant blood" cf. p. 194 with n. 69; pp. 216-27 with nn. 91-144. The phrase αἷμα διαθήκης appears in a context of liberation in Zech. 9:11, which, however, is less likely to have influenced the wording of this and similar NT passages than Ex. 24:8 (quoted in Heb. 9:20).

138. Gk. κοινός, "common" and therefore "unholy" (cf. the use of the adjective in Acts 10:13f., 28, and the derivative verb κοινόω in the sense of "defile" in Heb. 9:13, as also in Mark 7:15, 18, 20, 23 and parallels; Acts 21:28).

139. Gk. τὸ πνεῦμα τῆς χάριτος ἐνυβρίσας. Cf. "the spirit of grace and of supplication" (πνεῦμα χάριτος καὶ οἰκτιρμοῦ) in Zech. 12:10; here, however, the Spirit is personal as in Heb. 6:4 (one might treat τῆς χάριτος as a Semitic adjectival genitive and render "the gracious Spirit"), and Eph. 4:30 suggests itself as a close parallel.

140. The sin which our Lord thus described was a deliberate closing of one's eyes to the light; in the immediate context that sin took the form of seeing the works of mercy and power which he wrought by the Holy Spirit and ascribing them to the activity of Beelzebul. Many have compared the "sin unto death" of 1 John 5:16 (which, however, may be a sin which has resulted in the sinner's bodily death, in which case his friends are not urged to pray for him). As appears from the quotation from the Qumran literature on p. 255 (n. 109), rebellious apostasy was regarded as an unforgivable sin in the Qumran community (cf. also 1QS 2.13f.: "his spirit, parched [for lack of truth] and watered [with falsehood] shall be destroyed without pardon").

141. Cf. Deut. 13:8; 19:13, etc.

142. It is going too far, however, to say with E. J. Goodspeed that it was the Epistle to the Hebrews that "had most definitely stirred him [Hermas] to write" (*The Apostolic Fathers* [London, 1962], p. 97).

We shall not properly understand the anxiety which this problem caused unless we realize that the kind of sin which in practice aroused greatest concern was sexual irregularity. It was precisely here that the ordinary canons of everyday behavior differed most between Christians and pagans. We may think today that equal attention ought to be paid to the other six deadly sins; the fact remains that this was the one which involved the greatest heart-searching in the Christian community. The writer to the Hebrews, indeed, did not dwell particularly on offenses of this character;[143] and perhaps it was not sufficiently considered that sexual irregularity often lacks that element of premeditated policy which he condemns most severely. But experience showed that it was in this realm that postbaptismal sin was most prone to occur. Hermas, knowing in his heart how liable human nature is to yield to this form of temptation, even if it be confined to the thought-life,[144] and having received the assurance of divine forgiveness himself, taught (on the basis of a revelation imparted to him) that a second repentance was possible, but no more. According to him, baptism in Christ's name wipes out all previous sins, and baptized persons who keep the law of Christ consistently need not fear the last judgment.[145] But anyone who sinned once after baptism could, after due repentance, receive forgiveness once more, and be assured of ultimate salvation if he did not fall again.[146] This curious concession shows that Hermas and those who thought like him had really failed to grasp the real principle at stake, although they must be given credit for treating sin in believers as a very serious matter. The logic of the argument, however, left something to be desired, for if forgiveness was available once for postbaptismal sin properly repented of, why might it not be available twice or more often still? A rigorist like Tertullian appreciated the logic of the situation, and condemned Hermas for a concession which, as he saw it, was the thin end of a very dangerous wedge.[147] Others, less rigorist than Tertullian, also appreciated the logic of the situation, and extended Hermas's concession indefinitely, making it an essential element of the institution of penance. According to this institution, every baptized person is required periodically to seek, by confession and penance, absolu-

---

143. He warns against them in 12:16; 13:4.

144. It might indeed be supposed that Hermas's thought, that he would be happy if he had a wife comparable to Rhoda for beauty and character (Vision 1.1.2), would not be regarded by any healthy mind as sinful at all, and Hermas himself did not think of it as sinful (perhaps an instance of the "adultery in the heart" mentioned in Matt. 5:28) until it was revealed to him that it was so (Vision 1.1.8; 1.2.4).

145. Hermas, *Shepherd*, Vision 3.5.1ff.; Mandate 4.3.1ff.; Similitude 5.5.3; 5.6.3.

146. Hermas, *Shepherd*, Vision 2.2.1ff.

147. See p. 148, with n. 55; the whole exposition there of 6:4-8 is relevant to the present discussion.

tion for sins committed to date.[148] The writer to the Hebrews might well have considered that this institution differed but little in principle from the Old Testament institution of the Day of Atonement, in which "there is an annual reminder of sins" (10:3). What he urges his readers to do is to avail themselves continuously of the intercessory offices of their enthroned high priest, who appears in God's presence on their behalf by virtue of his perfect self-offering presented and accepted once for all. He would probably have thought it preposterous that his stern words of warning should in due course give rise to a penitential procedure so similar to that which he dismisses as forever superseded.

30 He drives his warning home with two quotations from the Song of Moses in Deut. 32. The Song of Moses furnished the early Christians with a remarkable number of *testimonia*—largely, but not exclusively, on the subject of Jewish unbelief.[149] The later writers of anti-Judaic apologies regarded it as a strong point in support of their argument that in this Song Moses himself (or God through the mouth of Moses) testifies against Israel.[150] It is God through the mouth of Moses in this Song who says, "Vengeance is mine, I will repay"—so our author quotes Deut. 32:35 in a version, attested in the Targums, which is followed also by Paul in Rom. 12:19.[151] Our author's application of the words is not inconsistent with their original context: God's own people are not exempt from his law that men and women reap what they sow.[152] And this is confirmed in the next verse of the Song (Deut. 32:36):

148. According to L. Goppelt ("Existence of the Church," p. 201), "the reformation of Luther began at this point; it was Luther who first cracked the basis of the penitential system started by Hermas, namely, the presupposition that baptism is merely a closed historical act and repentance a subsequent act (*WA*, VI, 529)."

149. Cf. the use of the Song in Rom. 10:19 (quoting v. 21); 1 Cor. 10:20, 22 (echoing vv. 16f.). Other quotations or allusions may be traced in Rom. 15:10 (quoting v. 43); Phil. 2:15 (echoing v. 5); Heb. 1:6 (see p. 57 with nn. 74-76). The Song, with its denunciation of Israel's apostasy, also played an important part in the thinking of the Qumran community; cf. the quotation of v. 28 in CD 5.17.

150. Cf. Justin, *Dialogue with Trypho* 20, 119, 130. See J. R. Harris, "A Factor of Old Testament Influence in the New Testament," *ExT* 27 (1925-26), pp. 6-11; B. Lindars, *New Testament Apologetic* (London, 1961), pp. 244f., 258, 274.

151. Paul quotes the words to show that Christians should not avenge themselves, since that would be encroaching upon the province of God. Similarly in the Qumran literature (CD 9.5) the members of the community are instructed to leave vengeance to God, since he "takes vengeance on his adversaries, and he keeps wrath for his enemies" (Nah. 1:2).

152. In the immediate context of this part of the Song the vengeance is evidently directed against Israel's enemies:

"For Yahweh will vindicate his people
　and have compassion on his servants,
　when he sees that their power is gone,
　　and there is none remaining, bond or free." (Deut. 32:36)

But much of the Song is an indictment of Israel's unfaithfulness and a warning of God's ensuing

"Yahweh will judge his people." This certainly means that he will execute judgment on their behalf, vindicating their cause against their enemies, but it carries with it the corollary that, on the same principles of impartial righteousness, he will execute judgment against them when they forsake his covenant. The privileges which Israel enjoyed as God's covenant people meant that their responsibilities were the greater and that retribution would be the more severe in their case if they gave themselves up to unrighteousness: "You only have I known of all the families of the earth: therefore I will visit upon you all your iniquities" (Amos 3:2). What was true then remains true for God's dealings with his people now.

31 Our author has a deep conviction of the awesome holiness of the divine majesty. "It is fearful," he says, "to fall into the hands of the living God." These words have no doubt been used frequently as a warning to the ungodly of what lies in store for them unless they amend their ways; but their primary application is to the people of God. "It is a splendid, but it is an awful thing to say, 'We know that we are of God.'"[153] This is what Isaiah meant when he said, after God had acted so signally in his people's behalf by removing the Assyrian menace from Jerusalem: "Who among us can dwell with the devouring fire? who among us can dwell with everlasting burnings?"[154] (Isa. 33:14). The revelation of the consuming righteousness of God which they had just witnessed spoke more loudly to them than it did to Sennacherib's warriors who had fallen before it; in that hour of judgment Israel learned something new about the character of the God who dwelt constantly in her midst.[155] Yet, when the question must be faced, into whose hands would any one of the people of God more readily fall than into his? When King David was commanded to choose between three forms of judgment

---

judgment against her; if in the end he crushes her enemies, who were the instruments of his judgment on her, it is for his own name's sake:

"I would have said, 'I will scatter them [Israel] afar,
  I will make the remembrance of them cease from among men,'
had I not feared provocation by the enemy,
  lest their adversaries should judge amiss,
lest they should say, 'Our hand is triumphant,
  Yahweh has not wrought all this.'" (Deut. 32:26f.)

153. G. G. Findlay, *Exp.* V.ix (1899), p. 91, in reference to 1 John 5:19 (in the article "St. John's Creed," pp. 81-96).

154. Cf. pp. 365f. (on 12:29). With language like this we may compare the "fiery indignation" of v. 27 (cf. p. 260, n. 125). Cf. Deut. 5:26, where the title "the living God" occurs in a context of fiery symbolism: "who is there of all flesh, that has heard the voice of the living God speaking out of the midst of fire, as we have, and has still lived?" The same title recurs in the situation which forms the background of Isa. 33:14; Sennacherib's doom is sealed when he sends his minister "to mock the living God" (Isa. 37:4, 17). Cf. our author's other uses of the title in 3:12; 9:14; 12:22.

155. Cf. Isa. 31:9.

after his numbering of the people, his wise reply was the fruit of his previous experience of God: "let us fall into the hand of Yahweh; for his mercy is great" (2 Sam. 24:14). Perhaps this very passage was in our author's mind and suggested the form of words he chose: "to fall into the hands of the living God."[156] For "the living God" appears repeatedly in the Bible as a synonym of Yahweh.[157] And if our author were asked why it is so fearful to fall into *his* hands, he might well reply: "Because he is the *living* God."

"It is a fearful thing," said the translators of the AV/KJV in the peroration of their preface,[158] "to fall into the hands of the living God; but a blessed thing it is, and will bring us to everlasting blessedness in the end, when God speaketh unto us, to hearken; when he setteth his word before us, to read it; when he stretcheth out his hand and calleth, to answer, Here am I, here we are to do thy will, O God. The Lord work a care and conscience in us to know him and serve him that we may be acknowledged of him at the appearing of our Lord Jesus Christ, to whom with the Holy Ghost be all praise and thanksgiving. Amen."

C. CALL TO PERSEVERANCE (10:32-39)

32 *But remember your earlier days,*[159] *when after your enlightenment you endured a hard struggle with sufferings.*
33 *You were either exposed to public shame*[160] *with insults and persecutions, or else you became partners with those who were so treated.*
34 *Indeed, you manifested your sympathy with those who were impris-*

---

156. David's words are echoed in Sir. 2:18:

Let us fall into the hands of the Lord,
   but not into the hands of men;
for as his majesty is,
   so also is his mercy.

157. In addition to the passages mentioned on p. 265, n. 154, cf. Josh. 3:10; 1 Sam. 17:26; Pss. 42:2; 84:2.

158. *The Translators to the Reader,* compiled by one of their number, Miles Smith, Canon of Hereford (later to be Bishop of Gloucester).

159. Gk. τὰς πρότερον ἡμέρας. A few good minuscules (including 33 69 1739) and the Bohairic Coptic add ὑμῶν ("your former days"); ℵ* not only adds ὑμῶν but in place of ἡμέρας exhibits the odd reading ἁμαρτίας ("your former sins," perhaps through a vague reminiscence of 2 Pet. 1:9).

160. Gk. θεατριζόμενοι (cf. Paul's use of θέατρον, "spectacle," in 1 Cor. 4:9); D* and the Sahidic Coptic read ὀνειδιζόμενοι ("being reproached") under the influence of ὀνειδισμοῖς ("reproaches") in the same clause; cf. the collocation of the same substantive and verb in Rom. 15:3 (quoting Ps. 69:9). The verb θεατρίζω (here only in the Greek Bible) was not attested elsewhere earlier than Gregory of Nazianzus until it was discovered on a Gerasa inscription of Trajan's principate (A.D. 98-117); cf. A. H. M. Jones, "Inscriptions from Jerash," *JRS* 18 (1928), pp. 144-78, § 14.18.

oned,[161] *and you put up cheerfully with the plundering of your property, for you knew that you yourselves[162] had a better possession,[163] a permanent one.*

35 *So then, do not throw away your confidence, for it carries a great reward with it.*

36 *What you need is patience, so that, when you have done God's will, you may receive what he has promised.*

37   *For "yet a very little while,[164]*
     The Coming One will come; he will make no delay.

38   *But my righteous one will live by faith;[165]*
     and if one draws back, I have no pleasure in him."[166]

39 *We, however, are not in the ranks of those who draw back and perish; we belong to those who believe[167] and thus gain our lives.*

32-34 Like the warning of 6:4-8, so the warning of 10:26-31 is followed by words of reassurance and encouragement. Our author does not wish to discourage his readers, but to embolden them so that they will emerge victorious from the present growing test of their faith. This he does now in the first place by reminding them of how they stood a severe test in the earlier days of their life as Christians, not long after their "enlightenment"—an expression repeated from 6:4.[168]

The identification of this earlier test, even if any independent informa-

---

161. Gk. τοῖς δεσμίοις (so p[13] apparently, with A D 33 and other minuscules, the Latin and Syriac versions), for which p[46] Ψ 81 and Origen read τοῖς δεσμοῖς ("on the bonds"); attempts to make this latter reading intelligible are found in the Old Latin texts *d* and *e*, which read "on their bonds," and in ℵ with the majority of manuscripts and Clement of Alexandria (followed by the TR and the AV), which read τοῖς δεσμοῖς μου ("on my bonds")—a reading which evidently originated in Alexandria under the influence of the belief that the writer was Paul (cf. Col. 4:18b).

162. Gk. ἑαυτούς (p[13] p[46] ℵ A 1912 with the Latin versions, Clement, and Origen); the inferior reading ἑαυτοῖς (D K L and many other MSS) is followed by the ARV ("knowing that ye have for yourselves a better possession . . .").

163. A few authorities (including P 1739 and the Peshitta and Harclean Syriac, followed by the TR) add ἐν οὐρανοῖς (whence AV/KJV "ye have in heaven a better and an enduring substance").

164. This phrase, introducing the quotation which follows, echoes Isa. 26:20 (see p. 273, n. 197).

165. Gk. ὁ δὲ δίκαιός μου ἐκ πίστεως ζήσεται. "Here the writer transferred the pronoun μου from after πίστεως to after δίκαιος—a small alteration of great consequence" (G. Zuntz, *The Text of the Epistles*, p. 173). D* and a few other authorities with the Syriac versions and Eusebius restore the LXX B text by transposing μου to follow πίστεως, giving the sense "by my faith(fulness)"; p[13] with the majority of later MSS and the TR omit μου altogether (under the influence of Rom. 1:17; Gal. 3:11), whence AV/KJV "Now the just shall live by faith" (see p. 273, n. 196).

166. Hab. 2:3f. (see pp. 272-75).

167. Lit. "we are not of withdrawing (ὑποστολῆς) unto perdition, but of faith (πίστεως) unto the saving (περιποίησιν, 'gaining,' 'acquiring') of the soul." The two genitives are descriptive in effect; a class of people is denoted in either case.

168. Gk. φωτισθέντες (cf. p. 145, n. 39).

tion survives about it, must be precarious as long as we are uncertain of the place where the addressees of this epistle lived. The identification, however, is made a little easier if we link with the present passage the words of 12:4: "In your struggle against sin you have not yet resisted to the point of shedding your blood" (RSV/NEB).[169] It is a reasonable inference from these words that, while the people addressed had undergone persecution, none of them had thus far suffered martyrdom. This appears to rule out, for example, the church of Jerusalem. Members of that church had suffered death in the persecution which broke out immediately after Stephen's execution about A.D. 33,[170] as also in A.D. 43, under Herod Agrippa I, when James the son of Zebedee was beheaded,[171] and in A.D. 62, when James the Just was stoned at the instance of the high priest Annas II[172] (if indeed the last-named incident had taken place by the writing of this epistle). It might also be thought to rule out any of the communities established through the witness of Hellenistic refugees from Jerusalem in A.D. 33 and the following years, though this would be by no means a conclusive inference.

Again, others have compared the language of our author here with the descriptions by Tacitus and Clement of the indignities inflicted on the Christians of Rome under Nero in the aftermath of the great fire of A.D. 64. "Their death," says Tacitus, "was made a matter of sport: they were covered in wild beasts' skins and torn to pieces by dogs; or were fastened to crosses and set on fire in order to serve as torches by night when daylight failed."[173] Clement tells how Christian women had to "enact the parts of Dirce and the daughters of Danaus."[174] But in spite of the correspondence between these descriptions and our author's reminder that some of his readers had been "abused and tormented to make a public show" (NEB), it could never have been said to Roman Christians after A.D. 65 that "in their struggle against sin they had not yet resisted to the point of shedding their blood"; that is precisely what they had done, and right nobly. While those Roman Christians had literally been made "a public show," our author may use the term somewhat more figuratively, rather as Paul does in 1 Cor. 4:9 when he compares himself and his fellow-apostles to "men condemned to death in the arena, a spectacle to the whole universe" (NEB).[175]

---

169. See p. 342 with nn. 62-64.
170. Acts 8:1-3. That believers suffered death, as well as imprisonment and exile, in this persecution is suggested by Paul's words in Acts 26:10 ("when they were put to death" seems to be more than a generalizing plural, and to imply that Stephen was not the only martyr at this time).
171. Acts 12:2.
172. Josephus, *Ant.* 20.200.
173. Tacitus, *Annals* 15.44.6.
174. 1 Clem. 6:2.
175. See p. 21, nn. 90, 91; p. 266, n. 160.

If, however, our author is addressing a group of Roman Christians *before* A.D. 65, we may recall another occasion which could satisfy his terms. Shortly after Claudius became emperor in A.D. 41, he imposed certain restrictions on the Jewish colony in Rome.[176] These restrictions evidently did not accomplish the purpose for which they were imposed, so some eight years later he took the more drastic step of expelling them from the capital. According to the well-known account of Suetonius, he expelled them because "they were constantly indulging in riots at the instigation of Chrestus."[177] The common inference from Suetonius's account—that these riots resulted from the recent introduction of Christianity into the Jewish colony in Rome—is supported by the fact that two of the expelled Jews, Priscilla and Aquila (who settled in Corinth where Paul made their acquaintance in A.D. 50), were Christians at the time.[178] A large-scale eviction of this nature would inevitably have been attended by widespread looting by the city proletariat, together with many other kinds of insults and indignities. We have a vivid account in Philo of what happened in Alexandria in A.D. 38 when the Jews of that city were forced to leave their homes in four of its five wards and be herded together in one ward. "Their enemies overran the houses now left empty and began to loot them, dividing up the contents like spoils of war."[179] The looting was accompanied by other acts of public outrage and violence. While there is no reason to suppose that the Roman Jews in A.D. 49 suffered anything like the extremes of brutality suffered by the Alexandrian Jews eleven years earlier, their experiences would very probably have been such as to merit our author's description here.

That these words could reasonably be interpreted with reference to the circumstances attendant on Claudius's expulsion of the Jews of Rome does not, of course, exclude the possibility, and indeed the high probability, that from time to time Jewish communities in other cities (not excluding those members of such communities who were disciples of Jesus) had to endure persecution of much the same kind. After the outbreak of the Jewish revolt against Rome in A.D. 66 the Jewish communities of many cities throughout Syria and Palestine were the victims of riot and massacre,[180] and Jewish Christians would be in no way exempt from such assaults. But since most of these in-

---

176. Dio Cassius, *Hist.* 60.6: "He did not directly banish them, but forbade them to gather in accordance with their ancestral way of life." See E. M. Smallwood, *The Jews under Roman Rule* (Leiden, 1976), pp. 210-16.

177. Suetonius, *Claudius* 25.4.

178. See F. F. Bruce, *New Testament History* (London, 21971), pp. 279-82; *Acts*, NICNT, pp. 346-48 (on Acts 18:2). If this interpretation is right, the Christians of Rome, being in a minority, would inevitably come off worst in the riots of which Suetonius speaks. Those who were expelled probably began to make their way back on the death of Claudius in A.D. 54.

179. Philo, *Flaccus* 56.

180. Cf. Josephus, *War* 2.457-80.

volved wholesale slaughter, they are excluded from consideration here. Besides, the statement that the readers suffered these things in their early Christian days, after they were "enlightened," may suggest that they suffered them on account of their adherence to the gospel. This could be said, no doubt, of the Jewish believers of Rome in A.D. 49, who may even have had some persecution to endure at the hands of the synagogue authorities in addition to the hostile attentions of the pagan population; it would not be as applicable to those occasions on which Jewish communities were attacked simply because they were Jewish. This, for example, rules out the events in Alexandria in A.D. 38, because in them the Jews were attacked as Jews (it is nowhere implied that Christianity had anything to do with that trouble);[181] in addition, many of the Alexandrian Jews lost their lives in the pogroms of that year.[182]

In short, the events of A.D. 49 at Rome could be referred to here; it is perfectly conceivable that events at some other time or place could be referred to,[183] but on these we are even less well informed than we are about the events at Rome.

At any rate, the readers had at one time "endured a hard struggle with sufferings," as our author puts it, using an athletic metaphor.[184] They had met the challenge of those sufferings as good athletes of Christ, and stood firm. Those of them who had not been personally exposed to suffering showed their solidarity with those who were directly attacked, and so shared the public scorn. When some of their number were imprisoned, the others did not shrink from visiting them, although in this way they ran the risk of being imprisoned themselves. They thus secured a place for themselves among those to whom the Son of Man says: "I was in prison, and you came to me" (Matt. 25:36). Prisoners who had no means of their own were liable to starve unless their friends brought them food and whatever other form of help they required; throughout the whole age of imperial persecution of the church the visiting of their friends who were in prison was a regular, though dangerous, duty of Christian charity.[185]

181. Claudius's rescript to the Alexandrians of A.D. 41, preserved in *P. Lond.* 1912 (*editio princeps* in H. I. Bell, *Jews and Christians in Egypt* [London, 1924], pp. 1-37), with its reference to illegal Jewish immigration into Alexandria from Syria or other parts of Egypt, has sometimes been thought to refer to the coming of Christianity to that city; but this is a very precarious interpretation (cf. Bruce, *New Testament History*, pp. 277f.).

182. Philo, *Flaccus* 65ff.

183. If the reference is indeed to events at Rome, this might suggest that the author knew of them at first hand (e.g., Priscilla or Aquila) or at second hand (e.g., Apollos). Cf. p. 274, n. 199.

184. Cf. 12:1f.; such metaphors are a commonplace of ancient literature (for their Pauline use cf. 1 Cor. 9:24-27; 2 Tim. 4:7f.).

185. Cf. Lucian, *Death of Peregrinus* 12; Aristides, *Apology* 15; Tertullian, *To the Martyrs* 1f.; *Apology* 39; Eusebius, *Hist. Eccl.* 4.23.10, etc.; A. Harnack, *Mission and Expansion of Christianity*, I, pp. 162-65, II, p. 117. See p. 372.

They had accepted this persecution, too, in a spirit of Christian cheerfulness. "Blessed are you," their Master had said, "when men hate you, and when they exclude you and revile you, and cast out your name as evil, on account of the Son of man! Rejoice in that day, and leap for joy; for behold, your reward is great in heaven" (Luke 6:22f.). It was exactly in the sense of this exhortation that these Hebrew Christians took the plundering of their property not merely in a spirit of equanimity but joyfully; it was for such as they, as well as for himself, that Paul spoke when he said, "we rejoice in our sufferings" (Rom. 5:3).[186] The eternal inheritance laid up for them was so real in their eyes that they could lightheartedly bid farewell to material possessions, which were short-lived in any case. This attitude of mind is precisely that "faith" of which our author goes on to speak. They manifested it in those earlier days, and that is why he is so confident that they will continue to manifest it, although the trials which confront them now are different from those which they faced then, and more subtle in character.

35 You showed your courage in those days, he says; do not abandon it now.[187] The word he uses (Gk. *parrhēsia*) has appeared three times already in this letter. In 4:16; 10:19 it is used of the confidence with which Christians may approach the throne of God since Christ is there as their prevailing high priest; in 3:6 it is used more generally of the courageous confession which Christians should maintain without fail. It is in this last sense that it is used here, with special reference to steadfastness in adverse and disheartening circumstances: "it is, so to say, the content of the Christian attitude in the world, the security of God's salvation and the open confession amidst . . . opposition."[188] We may think of the "boldness" of Peter and John which made such an impression on the Sanhedrin (Acts 4:13); the forthrightness of their language evinced an inner confidence of heart and life. So it had been with these "Hebrews"; preserve that former confidence of yours, says our author, for it carries a great reward with it (using a word which is peculiar to him among biblical writers, and which is not known before his time).[189] This is the "reward" of which Jesus spoke in the words quoted above from Luke 6:23; it is the realization of the promise in the good of which people of faith already live.[190]

---

186. Cf. Acts 5:41; 1 Pet. 4:13.

187. With our author's μὴ ἀποβάλητε οὖν τὴν παρρησίαν ὑμῶν Moffatt (ICC, p. 155) compares Dio Chrysostom's very similar δέδοικα μὴ τελέως ἀποβάλητε τὴν παρρησίαν (*Oration* 34.39); but Dio uses παρρησία here of the Tarsian citizens' right of free speech.

188. W. C. van Unnik, "The Christian's Freedom of Speech in the New Testament," p. 485. Cf. p. 249, n. 82.

189. Gk. μισθαποδοσία (cf. 2:2; 11:26); cf. μισθαποδότης, 11:6.

190. Cf. Rabbi Tarphon in *Pirqe Aboth* 2.21: "It is not for you to finish the work, neither are you free to desist therefrom; if you have studied much Torah, much reward will be given you, and faithful is your Employer to pay you the reward of your labor; and know that the recompense of reward (Heb. *mattan śākār*) for the righteous is for the time to come."

36 What they need is patience.[191] God will certainly fulfil his promise; they will enter into the utmost enjoyment of it; but in the meantime they must remain loyal, and not give up doing God's will. Their Master came expressly to do the will of God, as they have been told already (10:7, 9f.), although the doing of that will involved suffering and death for him; his servants can expect no easier path as they in their turn do the will of God and await the promised bliss. Sometimes the promised bliss seemed close at hand, as they saw "the Day approaching";[192] but at other times it looked as though it would never come, and they had to be reassured, like people to whom another New Testament letter was sent, that "the Lord is not slow about his promise" (2 Pet. 3:9). Let their hearts take courage, as they wait for their Lord.

37-38 The exhortation to patience is supported by a quotation from Old Testament prophecy. The prophet Habakkuk, in the later part of the seventh century B.C., cried out to God because of the oppression which was rife on every hand, and wondered when divine righteousness would at last be vindicated on earth. God answered his complaint and bade him be patient: the oppressor would at last reap the judgment which his heaven-defying ways had incurred and God's purpose would be accomplished; meanwhile, the righteous man would preserve his life by his loyal trust in God.[193]

> "For still the vision awaits its time,
>   it hastens to the end—it will not lie.
> If it seems slow, wait for it;
>   it will surely come, it will not delay.
> Behold, he whose soul is not upright in him shall fail,
> but the righteous shall live by his faith." (Hab. 2:3f.)[194]

In the Septuagint version as quoted by our author some of these words are given a different emphasis:[195]

---

191. Gk. ὑπομονή, cognate with the verb ὑπεμείνατε ("you endured") in v. 32; but there is probably no deliberate harking back to ὑπεμείνατε. See p. 151, n. 67 (on 6:12).

192. See pp. 258f.

193. Cf. J. H. Eaton, *Obadiah, Nahum, Habakkuk, Zephaniah*, TC (London, 1962), pp. 82-84, 94-98.

194. The Targum of Jonathan renders the passage: "Behold, the prophecy will be for an appointed time, and its term is fixed; it will not be in vain. If there is a long period of waiting for the event, keep looking out for it; behold, it will come in its appointed time, and will not be late. Behold, the wicked say to themselves, 'None of these things is happening'; but the righteous will be established by their truth."

195. Not only is there a different emphasis in the LXX; there are some points of textual divergence from the MT. Heb. *'uppᵉlāh* ("is puffed up," with *napšô*, "his soul," as subject) is rendered ὑποστείληται ("draws back"), perhaps because the *Vorlage* had *'ullᵉpāh* ("faints"), which is actually read in some MSS, and is presupposed by RSV "shall fail" (quoted above). Possibly the verb *'āpal* was confused with its homophone meaning "be neglectful" (cf. Num. 14:44); this confusion may account for Aquila's rendering of the verb by νωχελεύομαι, "be slug-

"Because the vision is yet for an appointed time,
and it will appear at length and not in vain:
if he is late, wait for him;
because he will surely come, he will not delay.
If he draws back, my soul has no pleasure in him,
but my righteous one[196] will live by faith (faithfulness)."

Here it is not simply for the fulfilment of the vision that the prophet is told to wait, but for a person, presumably an expected deliverer. When this deliverer appears, he will vindicate the righteousness of God and put down the oppressor; if, however, he draws back, that will indicate that he is not God's chosen agent. But if he does not draw back, but shows himself to be indeed God's chosen agent, his "righteous one," then by his faithfulness he will win his life. The deliverer in question is not called "the Lord's anointed" in so many words, but the Septuagint interpretation of this passage is essentially messianic.

Our author, then, is but dotting the i's and crossing the t's of the Septuagint interpretation when he applies Hab. 2:3b to the second coming of Christ. The clause with which he introduces the quotation ("for yet a very little while")[197] is not taken from any otherwise attested text of Hab. 2:3, but it may be a reminiscence of the Septuagint version of Isa. 26:20 ("a little moment"). Then the identity of the expected deliverer is made clearer. In the Septuagint "he will surely come" is literally "coming he will come" (an imitation in Greek of a common Hebrew idiom).[198] Our author places the def-

---

gish." Heb. *napšô* ("his soul") is read as *napšî* ("my soul"), while the rendering εὐδοκεῖ ("takes pleasure in") presupposes some such word as *rāṣᵉṯāh* in place of *yāšᵉrāh* ("is upright"; cf. Aquila's rendering εὐθεῖα). The B text of the LXX presupposes *'ĕmûnāṯî*, "my faith(fulness)," for *'ĕmûnāṯô*, "his faith(fulness)." See n. 196 below.

196. The LXX witnesses differ in their placing of the possessive pronoun "my"; the B text reads ὁ δὲ δίκαιος ἐκ πίστεώς μου ζήσεται ("but the righteous one will live by my faithfulness"), while the A text and 'C' group of MSS attest the reading ὁ δὲ δίκαιός μου ἐκ πίστεως ζήσεται ("but my righteous one will live by faith[fulness]"). (Cod. A itself, indeed, has μου in both positions, but this is self-evidently a secondary reading.) Most editors prefer the B reading; it has even been suggested that the A reading has been influenced by the present text of Hebrews (cf. B. Lindars, *New Testament Apologetic* [London, 1961], p. 231; see also G. Zuntz, as quoted on p. 267, n. 165). The A reading is strongly defended by T. W. Manson in "The Argument from Prophecy" (*JTS* 46 [1945], pp. 129-36)—an article to which the exposition above is considerably indebted. "In view of the general sense of the passage as presented in the LXX version," he says (p. 134), "it is not difficult to decide between these alternatives"—the B alternative, "the solid foundation for all the hopes of the righteous man is the faithfulness of God," and the A alternative, "God's righteous one will live by faithfulness." "The leader who plays the coward," he goes on, "*eo ipso* shows that he is not God's chosen. The genuine choice of God, God's righteous one, will be faithful to his God, his people, and his task, and so he will win life." "My righteous one," that is to say, is the one who "will surely come and not delay." But in Heb. 10:37f. "my righteous one" is not equated with "the coming one."

197. Gk. ἔτι γὰρ μικρὸν ὅσον ὅσον. Isa. 26:20, LXX, has μικρὸν ὅσον ὅσον for Heb. *ki-mᵉ'aṭ regaʻ*. For another echo of Isa. 26 cf. v. 27 above (p. 260, n. 125).

198. Cf. the same construction in 6:14 (p. 153, n. 75).

inite article before the participle "coming" so as to yield the messianic title "The Coming One"—the title used, for example, by John the Baptist[199] when he sent his disciples to Jesus with the question: "Are you the Coming One, or are we to expect someone else?" (Matt. 11:3//Luke 7:19). "The Coming One will come; he will not delay."[200]

In his quotation of Hab. 2:4 our author inverts the two parts of the verse: "my righteous one shall live by faith" is applied to the Christian believer, tempted to wonder if Christ will ever return in accordance with his promise; and the warning about the divine displeasure which will rest upon anyone who draws back is applied to him who yields to the temptation to relapse from his Christian profession into his earlier way of life. The reason for the inversion is not hard to determine: by this means "my righteous one" becomes the subject of both parts of the verse.[201] If he perseveres in faith he will gain his life; if he shrinks back he will prove himself reprobate.

The clause "the righteous shall live by [his] faith" is twice quoted by Paul (Rom. 1:17; Gal. 3:11) in a context which suggests that he gave it the meaning: "it is the one who is righteous by faith that will live." Indeed, this clause might well be regarded as the "text" of the Epistle to the Romans, and along with Gen. 15:6 it forms a principal *testimonium* for the doctrine of justification by faith. There is no fundamental difference in this respect between Paul and the author of Hebrews;[202] but our author, reproducing this clause

199. "A fact which becomes the more interesting if, as I think is probable, the author of Hebrews is Apollos, who was a Johannite before he became a Christian" (T. W. Manson, "Argument from Prophecy," p. 134). Cf. p. 270, n. 183.

200. Cf. Article 18 of the Creed of Maimonides: "I believe with perfect faith in the coming of Messiah, and though he tarry, I will wait daily for his coming."

201. Cf. Matt. 24:45ff., where the possibility is envisaged that the same servant may turn out to be either "the faithful and wise servant" who is found doing his duty when his master comes, or "that evil servant" who misconducts himself because his master seems to be so long in coming.

202. Paul omits the possessive pronoun from the clause altogether. It is plain that our author does not take the quotation from Paul. C. H. Dodd suggests that the quotation was current as a *testimonium* to the coming of Christ in primitive Christian times, and that its use in this way is reflected independently both in Paul's writings and in Hebrews. That it was current as a *testimonium* even before Paul wrote Galatians is the more likely, he thinks, because Paul's argument is very much *ad hominem*, and would be all the more effective if it was already common ground between him and his opponents that when the Coming One came, the righteous would live by faith (*According to the Scriptures* [London, 1952], pp. 50f.). We may compare the exegesis of the same passage in the Qumran commentary on Habakkuk, where the statement "the righteous shall live by his faith" is applied to "all the doers of the law in the house of Judah, whom God will save from the place of judgment because of their toil and their faith in the Teacher of Righteousness" (1QpHab 8.1-3). It is plain that the Teacher of Righteousness "was not only a spiritual leader but a figure of eschatological significance. Acceptance of his teaching, loyally keeping to the path which he marked out for his followers—this was the way to eternal life" (F. F. Bruce, "The Dead Sea Habakkuk Scroll," *Annual of Leeds University Oriental Society* 1 [1958-59], p. 16; cf. *Biblical Exegesis in the Qumran Texts* [London, 1960], pp. 77, 82f.).

together with part of its context, emphasizes the forward-looking character of saving faith, and in fact includes in "faith" not only what Paul means by the word but also what Paul more often expresses by the companion word "hope."[203] If Paul speaks about being "saved through faith" (e.g., Eph. 2:8), he also speaks of the "hope" in which "we were saved" (Rom. 8:24).[204] And we remember our Lord's words to his disciples when he warned them of coming days which would test their faith severely: "By your endurance you will gain your lives" (Luke 21:19).[205] It is patient endurance of this kind that our author desires his readers to show, and he is persuaded, for all his solemn warnings, that they will indeed show it, and gain true life thereby.

39 For, says he, in a further affirmation of his essential confidence in them, and including himself among them, "we are not in the ranks of those who draw back and perish; we belong to those who believe and thus gain our lives."[206] They had begun their Christian career in that carefree spirit which accepts without questioning the assurance of Christ that "whoever would save his life will lose it; and whoever loses his life for my sake and the gospel's will save it" (Mark 8:35). Let them maintain that spirit of faith to the end, and they would certainly gain their souls and "take hold of the life which is life indeed."[207] That this will prove true with our author and his readers alike is his firm assurance.[208]

---

203. "Faith is indeed the primary Christian virtue; but it is so, to our writer, not merely because it enables the believer to make real in himself the righteousness freely offered to him in the grace of the Lord Jesus, a sense which the word has so conspicuously in the Pauline letters and with which there is no reason whatever for thinking that our writer would not be in entire agreement, but also because it sustains and gives substance to hope and demonstrates the reality of the invisible" (R. V. G. Tasker, *The Gospel in the Epistle to the Hebrews* [London, 1950], p. 60). Cf. 11:1, with the whole exposition of faith which follows.

204. Cf. F. F. Bruce, *Epistle to the Romans*, TNTC (Leicester, ²1985), pp. 159-65.

205. Gk. κτήσεσθε τὰς ψυχὰς ὑμῶν (cf. εἰς περιποίησιν ψυχῆς in Heb. 10:39).

206. The phrase εἰς περιποίησιν ψυχῆς here is a variant expression for ζήσεται in the Habakkuk quotation in v. 38.

207. 1 Tim. 6:19.

208. See E. Grässer, *Der Glaube im Hebräerbrief* (Marburg, 1965).

HEBREWS 11

D. THE FAITH OF THE PEOPLE OF OLD (11:1-40)

1. Prologue: The Nature of Faith (11:1-3)

1 *Now faith is the firm foundation[1] of what we hope for; it is a conviction regarding things which are not seen.*

2 *It is by faith that the men and women of old established their record.*

3 *It is by faith that we understand the universe[2] to have been fashioned by God's utterance, so that what is seen has not come into being from things which are visible.*

1 Our author might well have proceeded from 10:39 to the exhortation to "run with steadfast endurance the race for which we are entered" (12:1); but first he encourages his readers further by reminding them of examples of faith in earlier days. In Old Testament times, he points out, there were many men and women who had nothing but the promises of God to rest upon, without any visible evidence that these promises would ever be fulfilled; yet so much did these promises mean to them that they regulated the whole course of their lives in their light. The promises related to a state of affairs belonging to the future; but these people acted as if that state of affairs were already present, so convinced were they that God could and would fulfil what he had promised. In other words, they were men and women of faith. Their faith consisted simply in taking God at his word and directing their lives accordingly; things yet future as far as their experience went were thus present to faith, and things outwardly unseen were visible to the inward eye. It is in these terms that our author now describes the faith of which he has been speaking. It is, he says, the *hypostasis* of things that are hoped for.[3] This word *hypostasis* has appeared twice already in the epistle. In 1:3 the Son was stated to be the very image of God's

---

1. Gk. ὑπόστασις (ERV/ARV, RSV "assurance").
2. Gk. αἰῶνες (lit. "ages"), as in 1:2 (see p. 47, n. 17).
3. The form of the definition (ἔστιν δὲ πίστις . . .) is paralleled in Philo; cf. his definition of prayer: "Now prayer is (ἔστιν δὲ εὐχή) a request for good things from God" (*On the Unchangeableness of God* 87).

hypostasis; in 3:14 believers are said to be Christ's associates if they hold fast the beginning of their *hypostasis* firm to the end. In the former place it has the objective sense of "substance" or "real essence" (as opposed to what merely seems to be so).[4] In the latter place it has the subjective sense of "confidence" or "assurance."[5] Here it is natural to take it in the same subjective sense as it bears in 3:14, and so the ERV/ARV and the RSV render it "assurance."[6] There is, however, something to be said for the objective meaning, represented by the AV/KJV ("faith is the substance of things hoped for") and the NEB ("faith gives substance to our hopes").[7] That is to say, things which in themselves have no existence as yet become real and substantial by the exercise of faith. But on the whole the subjective meaning "assurance" is the more probable, especially as this meaning chimes in well with the companion word "conviction." From another use of the word attested in the Hellenistic papyri Moulton and Milligan "venture to suggest the translation 'Faith is the *title-deed* of things hoped for.'"[8] In the instances which they cite from the papyri this meaning is indicated by the context. It might no doubt be said that if we adopt this meaning here, we have something comparable to Paul's language about the Holy Spirit as the "firstfruits" or "earnest" of the coming inheritance of believers;[9] but one would require stronger evidence from the present context before adopting it here. Our author is making much the same point as Paul makes in Rom. 8:24f.: "hope that is seen is not hope; for who hopes for what he sees? But if we hope for what we do not see, we wait for it with patience."[10]

The word rendered "conviction" (Gk. *elenchos*) has the same twofold sense as the English word. In 2 Tim. 3:16 it occurs as a variant reading for the cognate *elegmos* to denote the "conviction" or "refutation" of error which Holy Scripture provides; here it means "conviction" in much the same sense as "assurance" in the preceding phrase. Physical eyesight produces conviction or evidence of visible things; faith is the organ which enables people (like Moses in v. 27) to see the invisible order.[11] Philo similarly links "faith towards God" with "apprehension of the unseen."[12]

---

4. See p. 48 with nn. 26, 27.

5. See p. 101, with n. 67 (and particularly the work by H. Dörrie cited there).

6. Tyndale, Coverdale, and the Great Bible render it "sure confidence."

7. Following Vg. *substantia.* Cf. the Geneva rendering: "Faith is that which causeth those things to appear in deed which are hoped for."

8. MM, pp. 659f.

9. Cf. Rom. 8:23; 2 Cor. 1:22; 5:5; Eph. 1:14.

10. Gk. ὑπομονή (cf. Heb. 10:36).

11. This "conviction of things not seen" (πραγμάτων ἔλεγχος οὐ βλεπομένων) embraces things which are invisible because they belong to the spiritual order and things which are invisible because they belong to the future, like the fulfilment of God's promises (cf. F. R. Tennant, "The Central Problems of Faith," *ExT* 32 [1920-21], pp. 561-65).

12. *On Dreams* 1.68; cf. *Planting* 20: the human body was made erect so that people could look up to heaven and "apprehend clearly by means of what was visible that which was not visible."

2 It was for faith of this kind that men and women of old[13] received the divine commendation, and this has been placed on permanent record as an example to their descendants. The record is surveyed in vv. 4-38. This catalogue of spiritual heroism belongs to the same literary category as "The Praise of the Elders" in Sir. 44:1–50:21, beginning: "Let us now praise famous men, and our fathers that begat us."[14] Ben Sira celebrates at length all the commendable qualities of the men of God whom he commemorates; our author, more concisely, confines himself to those features of his heroes' careers which illustrate their faith in God, for the encouragement of those who come after them. In some ways a better parallel is presented by the last words of Mattathias, father of Judas Maccabaeus and his brothers, in which he stimulates the zeal of his sons by reminding them of the faithfulness under testing of Abraham, Joseph, Phinehas, Joshua, Caleb, David, Elijah, the three Hebrews who were saved from Nebuchadnezzar's fiery furnace, and Daniel (1 Macc. 2:51-60).[15] Indeed, the literary genre is by no means confined to the Judaeo-Christian tradition; it shares many characteristics with the *diatribē* of Stoic-influenced rhetoric, which was given to the accumulation of historical or legendary examples of the particular quality under discussion.[16] Our author, however, does not only accumulate a series of examples; he sets them in historical sequence so as to provide an outline of the redemptive purpose of God, advancing through the age of promise until at last in Jesus, faith's "pioneer and perfecter,"[17] the age of fulfilment is inaugurated.

3 Before he proceeds to celebrate the faith of the elders, however, he illustrates in another way his statement that faith is a conviction or proof of things not seen. The visible universe, he says, was not made out of equally visible raw material; it was called into being by divine power. "By faith[18] we

13. Gk. οἱ πρεσβύτεροι (lit. "the elders"); cf. "the fathers" in 1:1.

14. Cf. also the illustrations of wisdom from early OT narratives in Wisdom 10:1ff., the list in CD 2.16ff. of those who went astray through "guilty inclination and lustful eyes," the lists in 1 Clement of those who suffered through envy and jealousy (4:1ff.), of those who were found faithful, obedient, and hospitable (9:1ff.), of those who sacrificed themselves for the good of others (55:1ff.).

15. So in 4 Macc. 16:20ff. the mother of the seven martyr-brothers encourages her sons to faithful endurance by reminding them of Abraham, Daniel, and the three Hebrews; in 4 Macc. 18:11ff. she adds Abel, Isaac, Joseph, and Phinehas as examples for them to follow.

16. Cf. O. Michel, *Der Brief an die Hebräer,* MK (Göttingen, 1949), pp. 244f.; H. Thyen, *Der Stil der jüdisch-hellenistischen Homilie* (Göttingen, 1955), pp. 40ff. A question-mark has been placed by H. D. Jocelyn against the whole concept of the Stoic (or "Stoic-Cynic") *diatribē* ("Horace, Epistles 1," *Liverpool Classical Monthly* 4.7 [July 1979], pp. 145f.): he suggests that it was invented *ex nihilo* by H. Usener in 1887.

17. 12:2 (pp. 337f.).

18. Here begins the succession of sentences commencing with πίστει which "provides

understand[19] that the worlds have been framed by the word of God"
(ERV/ARV). Here, as in 1:2, the "worlds" are the *aiōnes* (lit. "ages"); in both
places the universe of space and time is meant.[20] There God is said to have
made the universe by the agency of the Son; here he is said to have fashioned
it by his word. It is unlikely that "God's utterance" here is hypostatized as in
John 1:1-3, so as to be practically synonymous with "the Son of God"; for
one thing, the Greek substantive translated "utterance" here is not *logos* (as
in John 1:1-14) but *rhēma*, referring to the utterance by which God summoned into existence what had no existence before.[21] Our author is thinking
of the creative command "Let there be light" (Gen. 1:3), interpreting it and
the following commands after the fashion of the psalmist:

> By the word of Yahweh were the heavens made,
> and all their host by the breath of his mouth . . .
> For he spoke, and it came to be;
> he commanded, and it stood forth.[22]

Thus "the visible came forth from the invisible" (NEB). But how do we know
this? By faith, says our author. Greek speculation about the formation of the
ordered world out of formless matter had influenced Jewish thinkers like
Philo and the author of the book of Wisdom;[23] the writer to the Hebrews is
more biblical in his reasoning and affirms the doctrine of *creatio ex nihilo,*
a doctrine uncongenial to Greek thought. The faith by which he accepts it is
faith in the divine revelation; the first chapter of Genesis is probably upper-

---

the finest example of anaphora in the whole Bible and perhaps in all literature, secular as well"
(C. Spicq, *L'Épître aux Hébreux,* I [Paris, 1952], p. 362).

19. Gk. νοοῦμεν. So in Rom. 1:20 Paul speaks of "the invisible things" of God as "being
perceived (νοούμενα) through the things that are made, even his everlasting power and divin-
ity." Moffatt (ICC, p. 161) quotes A. T. Goodrick's note on Wisdom 13:4 (where this verb occurs) to the effect that "νοεῖν is in Hellenistic Greek the current word for the apprehension of
the divine in nature."

20. See p. 47 with nn. 17, 18.

21. Cf. ῥῆμα in 1:3 (pp. 48f.); note also the quotation from Philo, *On Flight and Finding*
137, on p. 146, n. 43.

22. Ps. 33:6, 9 (LXX 32:6, 9).

23. "Just as nothing comes into being out of that which has no existence, so nothing is
destroyed into that which has no existence" (Philo, *The Eternity of the World* 5, where Em-
pedocles and Euripides are quoted in this sense). Elsewhere Philo expresses himself more bib-
lically, as when he says that "God, the begetter of all things, not only brought them into sight,
but even made things which previously had no existence, being not merely an artificer but the
Creator himself" (*On Dreams* 1.76). Cf. Wisdom 11:17, where the "all-powerful hand" of God
"created the world out of formless matter (ἐξ ἀμόρφου ὕλης)." The author of Wisdom might have
appealed to *tōhû wā-bōhû* in Gen. 1:2 (see n. 24 for the LXX rendering); but the idea of impos-
ing form on preexistent matter is Greek rather than Hebrew in origin. See also R. A. Stewart,
"Creation and Matter in the Epistle to the Hebrews," *NTS* 12 (1965-66), pp. 284-93.

most in his mind,[24] since he is about to trace seven living examples of faith from the subsequent chapters of that book.

2. The Faith of the Antediluvians (11:4-7)

4 *By faith Abel offered to God[25] a better[26] sacrifice than Cain; by virtue of this sacrifice he was attested as a righteous man, for God bore witness to the gifts he brought,[27] and through it he continues to*

24. He may have thought of the LXX rendering of Gen. 1:2, "the earth was invisible (ἀόρατος) and unfurnished" (ἀκατασκεύαστος), although in the LXX this seems to refer to the condition of the earth after its creation. With his language we may further compare 2 Macc. 7:28, where the mother of the seven martyrs reminds her youngest son how God made the world "out of things that had no existence" (ἐξ οὐκ ὄντων); 2 Baruch 21:4, "O thou . . . that hast fixed the firmament by the word, . . . that hast called from the beginning of the world that which did not yet exist"; 2 Enoch 25:1-4, "I commanded . . . that visible things should come down from invisible." *Creatio ex nihilo* is an inference from Gen. 1:1–2:4a and not an unambiguous statement of those verses; neither Heb. *bārā'* nor Gk. κτίζω in itself bears this meaning. Indeed, even in the passage now under consideration our author does not in so many words assert *creatio ex nihilo,* but that is practically what is implied in his denial that the universe was created out of things phenomenal. Cf. A. Ehrhardt, "Creatio ex Nihilo," in *The Framework of the New Testament Stories* (Manchester, 1964), pp. 200-233 (on p. 216 he compares Jub. 12:4, "the God of heaven . . . makes everything on the earth, and created everything by his word"); also *The Beginning* (Manchester, 1968), pp. 162-68.

25. 𝔭[13] and possibly 𝔭[46] omit "to God" (τῷ θεῷ); the phrase is omitted also by Clement of Alexandria and the Armenian version of Ephrem's commentary (cf. G. Zuntz, *The Text of the Epistles* [London, 1953], p. 33, for an argument that the omission is original).

26. Gk. πλείονα θυσίαν. C. G. Cobet's "brilliant conjecture"—as Professor Zuntz calls it (*Text,* p. 16)—of ΗΔΕΙΟΝΑ for ΠΛΕΙΟΝΑ, i.e., ἡδίονα ("more pleasant") for πλείονα ("more abundant") was accepted by J. M. S. Baljon and F. Blass in their critical editions of the text. The point is, as Zuntz says, that Abel's offerings were "more agreeable" and not "more" in quantity. The corruption of ἥδιον into πλεῖον is established for Demosthenes, *Prooemium* 23 (as Moffatt points out, *ad loc.*); as for the sense, Justin says that God accepts the sacrifices of believing Gentiles more gratefully (ἥδιον) than those of the Jews (*Dialogue* 29), while Josephus uses the cognate verb ἥδεται when he describes God as being "more pleased" with Abel's sacrifice than with Cain's (*Ant.* 1.54). The received reading has been supported by an appeal to Matt. 6:25 with its parallel Luke 12:23, where life is said to be "more" (πλεῖον) than food (cf. R. V. G. Tasker, "The Text of the 'Corpus Paulinum,'" *NTS* 1 [1954-55], p. 183, on the "qualitative rather than quantitative significance" of πλεῖον here), and to Matt. 12:41f. with the parallel Luke 11:31f., where "something more" (πλεῖον) than Solomon or Jonah is said to be present—the "something more" being presumably the kingdom of God. See J. D. Maynard, "Justin Martyr and the Text of Hebrews xi,4," *Exp.* VII.vii (1909), pp. 164-71; G. Zuntz, *Text,* pp. 16, 285.

27. Gk. μαρτυροῦντος ἐπὶ τοῖς δώροις αὐτοῦ τοῦ θεοῦ, "God bearing witness by accepting his gifts" (RSV). This reading, which is that of our Byzantine witnesses, is confirmed by 𝔭[13*] 𝔭[46] with the Latin, Syriac, Coptic, and Armenian versions; it is so plainly the true reading that, if it had disappeared from the textual tradition completely, it would have been an obvious and certain conjectural emendation. The marginal note in the ERV/ARV, "The Greek text in this clause is somewhat uncertain," is due to the fact that the Byzantine reading has opposed to it the authority of ℵ* A D* and a few other witnesses, which exhibit τῷ θεῷ for τοῦ θεοῦ (either by "mechanical permutation," as Hort says, or under the influence of τῷ θεῷ earlier in the verse [cf. n. 25], as Zuntz suggests). Another variant, attested by a corrector of 𝔭[13] and Clement of Alex-

speak[28] *even after he has died.*
5 *By faith Enoch was translated so as not to experience death. He was not found, because God had translated him; for before his translation, as it has been attested of him, he had given pleasure to God.*[29]
6 *Now without faith it is impossible to give him pleasure, for one who approaches God must believe that he exists, and that he is a rewarder of those who seek him out.*[30]
7 *By faith Noah, divinely warned about things not yet seen, was moved by reverent submission and built an ark to save his household. By this means he put the world in the wrong and became an heir of the righteousness which is according to faith.*

4   The first example of faith that our author finds in the biblical record is Abel. According to the narrative of Gen. 4:3-5, Abel and his elder brother Cain brought their offerings to God at the appropriate season; Abel brought "of the firstlings of his flock and of their fat portions," since he was a shepherd, while Cain, the agriculturalist, brought "an offering of the fruit of the ground." In either case the material of the offering was suitable to the offerer's vocation; yet "Yahweh had regard for Abel and his offering, but for Cain and his offering he had no regard." Why was there this discrimination? Cain was dejected because his offering was disregarded, but God pointed out to him the way of acceptance: "If you do well, will you not be accepted? And if you do not do well, sin is couching at the door; its desire is for you, but you must master it" (Gen. 4:7). This rendering of the Masoretic text is quite in line with the later prophetic teaching about sacrifice; sacrifice is acceptable to God not for its material content, but insofar as it is the outward expression of a devoted and obedient heart.[31] Let Cain gain the mastery over the sin which threatens to be his undoing,[32] and his sacrifice will be accepted as readily as Abel's was.

---

andria, is αὐτῷ τοῦ θεοῦ for αὐτοῦ τοῦ θεοῦ—also due, in all probability, to "mechanical permutation," although Hort and Moffatt, rather oddly, give it their vote as the true reading. Cf. F. J. A. Hort in Westcott and Hort, *The New Testament in the Original Greek*, II (Cambridge and London, 1882), Appendix, p. 131; G. Zuntz, *Text*, pp. 33, 51; B. M. Metzger, *A Textual Commentary on the Greek New Testament* (London/New York, 1971), pp. 671f.

28. Gk. λαλεῖ, for which D with the majority of later manuscripts and the TR reads λαλεῖται. If this is intended to be middle voice, it does not alter the sense (cf. AV/KJV "speaketh") but would be a pointless change; probably it was intended to be taken as a passive ("is spoken of"), from an inability to understand how Abel could still be speaking.

29. Gen. 5:24, following the LXX text (see p. 286, n. 52).

30. Gk. τοῖς ἐκζητοῦσιν αὐτὸν μισθαποδότης γίνεται. The substantive μισθαποδότης (here only in the NT) is cognate with μισθαποδοσία of 2:2; 10:35; 11:26 (see p. 67, n. 2). For ἐκζητοῦσιν 𝔭[13] and P have the simple verb ζητοῦσιν. (Cf. the similar variant in v. 14, p. 297, n. 111.)

31. See p. 240 with n. 36.

32. In Gen. 4:7 the word which the ERV/ARV translates "coucheth" is Heb. *rōbēṣ*, which is cognate with Akk. *rabiṣu*, the name of a demon. Sin is depicted as a maleficent power lying in wait to pounce upon its prey, but it is powerless against a person of righteous life.

The Septuagint version, however, suggests that there was a ritual reason for the rejection of Cain's sacrifice; according to it, God says to Cain: "Have you not sinned if you offer it rightly without dividing it rightly?" (Gen. 4:7).[33] Other ancient interpretations explained its rejection, in contrast to the acceptance of Abel's sacrifice, in terms of the substance of the two offerings. So Philo: "Abel's offering was living, Cain's was lifeless. His was prior in age and quality, Cain's was inferior. His was superior in strength and fatness, Cain's was weaker."[34] Similarly Josephus: "The brothers having decided to sacrifice to God, Cain brought the fruits of the cultivated ground and of trees, while Abel brought milk and the firstlings of his flocks. This latter offering gave the greater pleasure to God, who is honored by those things which grow spontaneously and in accordance with nature, and not by those things which are forcibly produced by the ingenuity of covetous man"[35]—a farfetched distinction indeed, although Josephus was not the last commentator on this passage to suggest that the shepherd's life involves less expenditure of energy than that of the agriculturalist! "Cain brought of the fruits of the earth, that is to say, less valuable things," says the Midrash *Genesis Rabba*,[36] while the Palestinian Targum makes Abel say to Cain: "The fruits of my works were better than yours and took precedence over yours; so it was my sacrifice that was accepted as well-pleasing." A more recent variation on these accounts sees the distinction in that Abel's offering involved the shedding of blood, apart from which, as our author has said above, the law knows no forgiveness (Heb. 9:22).[37] But it is nowhere suggested in the Genesis narrative that

---

33. Gk. οὐϰ, ἐὰν ὀρθῶς προσενέγϰῃς, ὀρθῶς δὲ μὴ διέλῃς, ἥμαρτες; Theodotion's Greek version implies that the divine acceptance or nonacceptance of the offering was shown by the falling or withholding of fire (as in the sacrificial ordeal of 1 Kings 18:21-39), since it translates Heb. *šāʿāh* ("had regard") in Gen. 4:4f. by ἐνεπύρισεν ("set on fire"). Another view of the way in which the acceptance or nonacceptance was shown is suggested by S. H. Hooke: "At the time when such rituals were practised only one criterion of success or failure was recognized, namely the pragmatic test of increased fertility or the opposite. The shepherd's flocks increased and multiplied while the unfortunate tiller of the soil saw his crops wither as the heat of the year increased in strength towards the summer" (*The Siege Perilous* [London, 1956], p. 68).

34. *The Sacrifices of Abel and Cain* 88.

35. *Ant.* 1.54.

36. *Gen. Rabba* 22 (on Gen. 4:3).

37. So, e.g., the seventeenth-century Puritan scholar John Owen says that Abel's faith was "accompanied with a sense of sin and guilt, with his lost condition by the fall, and a trust in the way of redemption and recovery which God had provided. And this he testified in the kind of his sacrifice, which was by death and blood; in the one owning the death which himself by reason of sin was obnoxious unto; in the other the way of atonement, which was to be by blood, the blood of the promised Seed" (*Exposition of Hebrews* [1668-74], ed. W. H. Goold [Edinburgh, 1855], VII, pp. 24f.). Contrast Calvin's more disciplined exegesis: "Abel's sacrifice was preferred to his brother's for no other reason than that it was sanctified by faith; for surely the fat of brute animals did not smell so sweetly, that it could, by its odour, pacify God. The Scripture indeed shows plainly why God accepted his sacrifice, for Moses' words are these: 'God had

it was a sin offering which the two brothers brought; it was in either case the appropriate presentation of the firstfruits of their increase. The unvarnished Masoretic text makes the situation plain enough; since Cain was told that he would be accepted if he did well, it follows that Abel was accepted because he did well—because, in other words, he was righteous. And in fact the righteousness of Abel is emphasized elsewhere in the New Testament: our Lord refers to "the blood of Abel the righteous" (Matt. 23:35)[38] and John tells us that Cain killed his brother "because his own deeds were evil, and his brother's righteous" (1 John 3:12).[39] To the same effect our author says that Abel "was attested as a righteous man." How? Because "God bore this witness to the gifts he brought." This echoes the Septuagint rendering of Gen. 4:4, "God looked [i.e., with pleasure] on Abel and his gifts."[40] The abiding principle of Scripture in this regard is summed up in the words of Prov. 15:8, "The sacrifice of the wicked is an abomination to Yahweh; but the prayer of the upright is his delight."

But how could it be known that it was "by faith" that Abel brought God a more acceptable sacrifice than his brother? Probably the close association between righteousness and faith in 10:38, "my righteous one will live by faith," was ground sufficient in our author's eyes for his statement about Abel's faith; moreover, his affirmation in v. 6 below, while primarily applicable to Enoch, is equally applicable to Abel: "without faith it is impossible to give him [God] pleasure"—and since Abel manifestly pleased him, it follows that Abel lived and acted by faith.

Through his faith, too, Abel continues to speak, even in death. When God accused Cain of Abel's murder, he said: "The voice of your brother's blood is crying to me from the ground" (Gen. 4:10).[41] Our author's point appears to be that Abel is still appealing to God for vindication, until he obtains

---

respect to Abel and to his gifts.' It is hence obviously to be concluded that his sacrifice was accepted because he himself was graciously accepted. But how did he obtain his acceptance, save that his heart was purified by faith?" (*Commentary on Hebrews, ad loc.*).

38. The adjective (δίκαιος) is absent from the parallel in Luke 11:51.

39. So Josephus says that Abel "had a concern for righteousness" (δικαιοσύνης ἐπεμελεῖτο) while Cain "was very wicked and has an eye for nothing but gain" (*Ant.* 1.53). In Wisdom 10:3 Cain is "an unrighteous man" (ἄδικος) who "in anger revolted against wisdom and perished in his fratricidal fury." Tanḥuma (*Balak* 16) gives Abel second place in a list of "seven righteous men who built seven altars, from Adam to Moses." See B. Lindars, *New Testament Apologetic* (London, 1961), pp. 20f.

40. Gk. ἐπεῖδεν ὁ θεὸς ἐπὶ ᾿Αβὲλ καὶ ἐπὶ τοῖς δώροις αὐτοῦ.

41. Philo, continuing his allegorical interpretation of the story of Cain and Abel as a conflict between self-love and the love of God, paradoxically asserts that while, superficially speaking, Cain "slew him" (ἀπέκτεινεν αὐτόν), i.e., his brother, he really "slew himself" (ἀπέκτεινεν ἑαυτόν), and that Abel only seemed to die, since in fact "he is clearly found making use of his voice and crying out what things he has suffered at the hands of a wicked brother—for how could he speak if he no longer existed?" (*The Worse Attacks the Better* 47f.).

it in full in the judgment to come. The idea in that case is paralleled in Rev. 6:9-11, where the souls of the martyrs cry aloud for vindication, and are told that they must wait until the full tale of martyrs is complete. It has been held, on the other hand,[42] that our author simply means that Abel, by his faith, bears abiding witness to succeeding ages; but that more than this was in his mind is suggested by Heb. 12:24, where he says that the purifying blood of Christ "has something better to say than Abel's"—a clear reference to Gen. 4:10.

5 The second example of faith is Enoch. All the Hebrew Bible has to say of him is that he was born to Jared when the latter was 162 years old, and then, that "when Enoch had lived sixty-five years, he became the father of Methuselah.[43] Enoch walked with God after the birth of Methuselah three hundred years, and had other sons and daughters.[44] Thus all the days of Enoch were three hundred and sixty-five years. Enoch walked with God; and he was not, for God took him" (Gen. 5:18, 21-24). In the Septuagint the repeated clause "Enoch walked with God" is rendered "Enoch pleased God"[45]—from a desire, no doubt, to make the language less anthropomorphic—and the words "he was not; for God took him" are rendered "he was not found, because God translated him."[46] Our author follows the Septuagint here as elsewhere.

In one well-known strand of Jewish and Christian tradition Enoch appears as the recipient of special revelations about the spirit-world and the ages to come;[47] in this rôle he appears once in the New Testament, when Jude

---

42. Cf. Moffatt (ICC, p. 164). See further on 12:24 (p. 361).

43. Cf. 1 Chron. 1:3.

44. In the LXX Enoch is 165 years old at Methuselah's birth and the interval between that event and Enoch's "translation" is correspondingly reduced to 200 years.

45. Gk. εὐηρέστησεν . . . τῷ θεῷ, whence our author says μεμαρτύρηται εὐαρεστηκέναι τῷ θεῷ.

46. Gk. οὐχ ηὑρίσκετο, ὅτι μετέθηκεν αὐτὸν ὁ θεός, words which our author quotes verbatim. Moffatt (ICC, p. 165) quotes from Epictetus 3.5.5f. an instance of εὑρίσκεσθαι in the sense of "die" ("be found" by death), and suggests the rendering here: "did not die." Josephus (*Ant.* 1.85) paraphrases "God translated him" by saying that he "withdrew to the divine" (Gk. ἀνεχώρησε πρὸς τὸ θεῖον)—a phrase which he uses also to describe the mysterious passing of Moses (*Ant.* 4.326; cf. 3.96; also Philo, *Life of Moses* 2.288, where Moses' whole being is said to have been transformed "into mind, pure as sunlight," εἰς νοῦν ἡλιοειδέστατον). On Enoch cf. 1 Clem. 9:3.

47. Cf. in particular the compilation of Enoch-literature called the First Book of Enoch, extant *in toto* only in Ethiopic, for about one third of its compass in Greek, and fragmentarily in the original Aramaic. The Aramaic fragments form part of the manuscript discoveries at Qumran; among them all the sections of 1 Enoch are represented except chs. 37–71, the *Parables of Enoch*. This section, containing the "Son of Man" passages, may thus be later than the others (see p. 286, n. 50). The other sections narrate such things as Enoch's journey through other worlds and his dream-visions of world history from the creation to the author's day. Similar, but later compilations are 2 Enoch ("The Book of the Secrets of Enoch"), composed in Greek but extant only in a Slavonic version, and 3 Enoch, a Hebrew mystical treatise of the fifth or sixth century A.D. originally called (it appears) the "Book of Palaces." Translations of all three Enoch books are presented in J. H. Charlesworth (ed.), *The Old Testament Pseudepigrapha*, I (Garden City, NY, 1983), pp. 5-315.

(vv. 14f.) quotes the prophecy of "Enoch, the seventh from Adam," about the coming of the Lord with his holy myriads to execute judgment on the ungodly (1 Enoch 1:9). More generally he is said to have been "the first among men that are born on earth who learned writing and knowledge and wisdom" (Jub. 4:17). Of all this our author has nothing to say; he is more in line with the school of thought which regarded Enoch as the typically righteous man. Ben Sira, for example, says:

> Enoch was found perfect, and he walked with Yahweh, and was taken;
> a sign of knowledge to every generation. (Sir. 44:16)

His grandson, turning these words from Hebrew into Greek, conformed them to the sense of the Septuagint:

> Enoch pleased[48] the Lord, and was translated;
> he was an example of repentance to all generations.

In this last clause the reference to Enoch's translation appears to be interpreted of a *moral* change in his life—an interpretation which we find also in Philo.[49]

More striking still is the account of Enoch in Wisdom 4:10-15:

> There was one who pleased God and was loved by him,
> and while living among sinners he was translated.
>
> He was caught up lest evil change his understanding or guile
> deceive his soul.
> For the fascination of wickedness obscures what is good,
> and roving desire perverts the innocent mind.
> Being perfected in a short time, he fulfilled long years;
> for his soul was pleasing to the Lord,
> therefore he took him quickly from the midst of wickedness.
>
> Yet the peoples saw and did not understand,
> nor take such a thing to heart,
> that God's grace and mercy are with his elect,
> and he watches over his holy ones.

Here Enoch is brought forward as the *beau idéal* of righteousness, the type of the person who, according to his enemies, "professes to have knowledge

---

48. Gk. εὐηρέστησεν, as in Gen. 5:22, 24, LXX.

49. "Concerning him it is said that 'Enoch pleased God and was not found, for God translated (μετέθηκεν) him'; for 'translation' (μετάθεσις) denotes turning and changing, and that a changing for the better . . ." (*On Abraham* 17f.). On the same passage Philo elsewhere says: "By 'translation' is clearly signified the new home [granted to him 'who escaped the insurrections of the body and deserted to the side of the soul'], and by 'not found' the solitary life" (*On Rewards and Punishments* 17). See p. 287, n. 57; p. 288, n. 67.

of God, and calls himself a child of the Lord" (Wisdom 2:13). So, in Jub. 10:17, Enoch is perfect in righteousness, excelling even Noah in this respect, "for Enoch's office was ordained for a testimony to the generations of the world, so that he should recount all the deeds of generation unto generation, till the day of judgment" (here Enoch's righteousness is linked with his prophetic ministry). And in 1 Enoch 71:14, in the conclusion of the section commonly called the *Parables of Enoch,* Enoch is acclaimed by the interpreting angel as the ideal just man:

> "Thou art the Son of Man born unto righteousness;
> and righteousness abides upon thee;
> yea, the righteousness of the Head of Days forsakes thee not."[50]

It is, however, specifically as an example of *faith* that our author adduces Enoch here. Righteousness and faith, as we have seen already, are inseparably associated in his mind. If he is asked why Enoch should be regarded as a man of faith, his answer is that otherwise God would have had no pleasure in him.[51] But the record makes it plain that Enoch did please God;[52] the Septuagint paraphrase of the Hebrew idiom "walked with God"[53] is completely consistent with the teaching of the great prophets, according to which walking humbly with God, together with the practice of justice and lovingkindness, is God's fundamental requirement of human beings.[54]

6 Apart from faith neither Enoch nor anyone else could ever have been pleasing to God. The faith which our author has in mind embraces belief in the invisible spiritual order, and belief in the promises of God which have not yet been fulfilled. Belief in the invisible spiritual order involves, first and foremost, belief in him who is "King of ages, immortal, invisible, the only God" (1 Tim. 1:17); and belief in God carries with it necessarily belief in his word. It is not belief in the existence of *a* God that is meant, but belief in the

---

50. M. Black, "The Son of Man Problem in Recent Research and Debate," *BJRL* 45 (1962-63), pp. 305-18, suggests that while 1 Enoch 71 belongs to the section called the *Parables,* which is now commonly given a date in the Christian era (see p. 284, n. 47), this particular chapter may be earlier.

51. Cf. 10:38b.

52. A nice point of interpretation hangs on the question whether the adverbial phrase "before his translation" belongs with "he had given pleasure to God" (so the ARV and the NEB) or with "it has been attested of him" (so the AV/KJV, the ERV, and the RSV). The former construction fits the facts better; Gen. 5:24 (LXX) bears witness that he had pleased God before he was translated, but the witness itself (i.e., the witness of the biblical record) was borne to him *after* his translation.

53. Similarly of Noah (Gen. 6:9); so also the expression "walk before God" is rendered εὐαρεστεῖν ἐναντίον (ἐνώπιον) τοῦ θεοῦ (κυρίου, etc.), "to be well-pleasing before God," of Abraham (Gen. 17:1; 24:40), of Abraham and Isaac (Gen. 48:15); of the pious Israelite (Ps. 56:13 [LXX 55:13]; 116:9 [LXX 114:9]).

54. Mic. 6:8.

existence of *the* God who once declared his will to the fathers through the prophets and in these last days has spoken in his Son. Those who approach[55] him can do so in full confidence that he exists, that his word is true, and that he will never put off or disappoint the person who sincerely seeks him. For all that he has revealed of himself, whether through the prophets or in his Son, assures us that he is altogether worthy of his people's trust.

> The God who created the skies,
>> The strength and support of His saints,
> Who gives them all needful supplies,
>> And hearkens to all their complaints:

> This, this is the God we adore,
>> Our faithful, unchangeable Friend,
> Whose love is as large as His power,
>> And neither knows measure nor end.[56]

The reward desired by those who seek him is the joy of finding him; he himself proves to be their "exceeding joy" (Ps. 43:4).

No doubt our author states the basic principle, as revealed by the record of Enoch, for the benefit and encouragement of his readers. Of their desire to please God he has no doubt; he insists, however, that they cannot please him apart from faith—the faith which not only believes that he exists but waits patiently and confidently for the reward promised to those who seek him.

7 The next example of faith illustrates this willingness to believe that what God has promised he will certainly perform. Noah was a righteous man, like Abel; he walked with God, as did Enoch;[57] but what is emphasized here is that when God announced that he would do something unprecedented in the experience of Noah and his contemporaries, Noah took him at his word, and showed that he did so by making practical preparations against the day when that word would come true. Noah received a divine communication[58] that a deluge would sweep over the earth. Such a catastrophe had never been known before, but Noah's faith supplied the proof of "things not seen."[59] The building of an ark far inland must have seemed an absurd procedure to his

---

55. Gk. προσέρχεσθαι, as used already in 4:16; 7:25; 10:22.

56. Joseph Hart (1712-68).

57. Gen. 6:9 (see p. 286, n. 53). Philo, having mentioned Enoch as the ideal example of repentance (see p. 285, n. 49), goes on to mention Noah as the ideal lover of God (or man loved by God) and lover of virtue (θεοφιλῆ καὶ φιλάρετον); later he praises Noah as a victorious athlete, who won the citation "that he had pleased God" (*On Abraham* 27, 35). In Jewish lore Noah, like Enoch, was the recipient of divine revelations apocalyptic in character (Jub. 7:20-25); these were embodied in a now lost "Book of Noah," fragments of which have been incorporated in 1 Enoch. Two accounts of his birth describe him as a wonder-child (1Q *Genesis Apocryphon* 2.1ff.; 1 Enoch 106:2-18).

58. Gk. χρηματισθείς (cf. 8:5; 12:25), regularly of a divine oracle.

59. With περὶ τῶν μηδέπω βλεπομένων here cf. πραγμάτων . . . οὐ βλεπομένων in v. 1.

neighbors; but in the event his faith was vindicated and their unbelief was condemned: "through his faith he put the whole world in the wrong" (NEB). He paid careful heed[60] to the divine admonition and got ready the means by which he and his household would be kept safe when the deluge broke; thus he became a living witness to the truth of the scripture already cited: "my righteous one will live by faith" (10:38). Thus, says our author, he "became an heir of the righteousness which is according to faith"; if the Genesis narrative represents God as saying to him, "I have seen that you are righteous before me in this generation" (Gen. 7:1), it was because of his ready acceptance of what God had said. Of him as of Enoch the statement is true: "without faith it is impossible to please God."[61]

The Jewish wisdom writers not unnaturally found in Noah an outstanding example of true wisdom. "When the earth was flooded," says the author of the book of Wisdom, "wisdom saved it again, steering the righteous man in a cheap structure of wood" (Wisdom 10:4). Ben Sira speaks at greater length:

Noah was found perfect[62] and righteous;
    in the time of wrath he was taken in exchange;
therefore a remnant was left to the earth
    when the flood came.
Everlasting covenants were made with him
    that all flesh should not be blotted out by a flood.[63]

In other places in the New Testament the flood of Noah's day is an illustration of sudden judgment, a foreshadowing of the advent of the Son of Man;[64] his safe passage through the waters which overwhelmed others is a figure of Christian baptism;[65] he himself is described as a preacher of righteousness.[66] But here it is his faith that is set in relief, and it cannot be said that our author had to look far to discover faith in the Old Testament story of Noah. The great gospel terms righteousness and grace appear first in relation to him, as far as the canonical order of Scripture goes;[67] and the quality of his faith was proved by his prompt obedience: "Noah . . . did all that God commanded him" (Gen. 6:22).

60. Gk. εὐλαβηθείς, "*out of reverent regard* (for God's command)" (BAGD, *s.v.* εὐλαβέομαι). Cf. the cognate substantive εὐλάβεια in 5:7; 12:28. See p. 129, n. 61.

61. Cf. Gen. 6:9 (LXX), τῷ θεῷ εὐηρέστησεν Νῶε (cf. p. 286, n. 53).

62. Cf. Gen. 6:9, "Noah was . . . perfect in his generations" (with 1 Clem. 7:6; 9:4, Νῶε πιστὸς εὑρέθη).

63. Sir. 44:17f. Cf. Gen. 9:8-17 for the covenant with Noah.

64. Cf. Matt. 24:37-39; Luke 17:26f.

65. Cf. 1 Pet. 3:20f.

66. Cf. 2 Pet. 2:5; Josephus, *Ant.* 1.74; *Sibylline Oracles* 1.125-282. *Genesis Rabba* 30.7 (on Gen. 6:9) says of Noah, "God had a herald *[kārôz]* in the generation of the flood."

67. "Noah was a righteous (Heb. ṣaddîq, Gk. δίκαιος) man" (Gen. 6:9); "Noah found grace (Heb. *hēn*, Gk. χάρις) in the eyes of Yahweh" (Gen. 6:8). Philo points out that Noah is "the first man recorded as righteous in the sacred scriptures" (*Preliminary Studies* 90); indeed, he gives

3. The Faith of Abraham and Sarah (11:8-12)

8 *By faith Abraham, in obedience to the call of God,*[68] *went forth into a place which he was to receive as his inheritance: he went forth, not knowing where he was going.*

9 *By faith he took up residence in the land which he had been promised, as though it belonged to others; he became a tent-dweller, as did Isaac and Jacob, fellow-heirs of the same promise.*

10 *For he looked forward to the city which has the (true) foundations, the city of which God is the architect and builder.*

11 *By faith—Sarah herself being barren*[69]*—he received power to beget a child*[70] *even after the natural season of life,*[71] *because he reckoned the one who gave the promise to be trustworthy.*

12 *Therefore from one man, one who was as good as dead, there sprang*[72] *offspring as numerous as the stars in the sky, as unnumbered as the sand on the seashore.*[73]

8 Of Abraham's title to be included in this catalog there can be no ques-

---

"righteous" alongside "rest" as the etymology of his name (*On Abraham* 27). He explains the name Enoch as meaning "recipient of the grace of God" (κεχαρισμένος), linking this with his presentation of Enoch as the ideal repentant man (*On Abraham* 17). (See p. 285, n. 49; p. 287, n. 57.)

68. Gk. καλούμενος, to which 𝔓⁴⁶ A D* 33 1739 and a few other authorities preface the definite article ὁ, yielding the sense "he who was called" (instead of "when he was called")— the reference would then be to the divine changing of his name from Abram to Abraham (Gen. 17:5). But the reference is certainly not to God's renaming him, but to his first calling him to leave his home and seek the promised land.

69. Gk. καὶ αὐτὴ Σάρρα στεῖρα (a circumstantial clause). The construction of αὐτὴ Σάρρα as though Sarah were the subject of this sentence and not Abraham (see pp. 295f., nn. 96-103), has given rise to a number of early glosses, *Schlimmbesserungen* ("false improvements"), as G. Zuntz calls them (*Text*, p. 170). Thus, he says, 𝔓⁴⁶ D* Ψ with the Latin and Syriac versions add here στεῖρα, "barren" (which, however, may well be part of the original text), 69 1739 and the Coptic versions read ἡ στεῖρα ("she who was barren"), P 1912 and some other authorities read στεῖρα οὖσα ("being barren").

70. Gk. δύναμιν εἰς καταβολὴν σπέρματος ἔλαβεν (for the proper sense see pp. 295f. with n. 99). A further *Schlimmbesserung* is the insertion here of εἰς τὸ τεκνῶσαι ("so as to give birth") in D* P 69 and a number of other manuscripts with Vg. Cod. L and the Harclean Syriac (τεκνόω occurs nowhere else in the NT).

71. Gk. καὶ παρὰ καιρὸν ἡλικίας, "even beyond the season of life." (In a letter of September 15, 1969, commenting on the first edition of this commentary, B. F. C. Atkinson pointed out the parallelism in sense between καὶ παρὰ καιρὸν ἡλικίας, if referring to Sarah, and what is said of her in Gen. 18:11.) K L P and the bulk of Byzantine witnesses (followed by the TR), construing καί as the conjunction "and," added ἔτεκεν after ἡλικίας (so AV/KJV, "and was delivered of a child when she was past age").

72. Gk. ἐγενήθησαν, for which ℵ 1739, with the bulk of later manuscripts and the TR, read ἐγεννήθησαν ("were begotten").

73. Gen. 15:5; 22:17; 32:12. 𝔓⁴⁶ D* Ψ with the Ethiopic version omit ἡ παρὰ τὸ χεῖλος ("which is by the shore"), leaving the shorter phrase ὡς ἡ ἄμμος τῆς θαλάσσης ("as the sand of the sea").

tion. The faith of Abel, Enoch, and Noah might have to be inferred from what is recorded of them (although for all three of them it is a certain inference); but Abraham's faith is explicitly attested in the Genesis narrative: "he believed Yahweh; and he reckoned it to him as righteousness" (Gen. 15:6). Our author has already referred to Abraham's faith in the promise of God and his patient waiting for its fulfilment;[74] here he enlarges on the same theme. Repeatedly throughout his career Abraham acted as a man who walked by faith and not by sight, and made good his claim to be recognized by all subsequent ages as the father of the faithful. The Levites' prayer of confession in the days of Nehemiah and Ezra recalled God's dealings with him in these terms: "Thou . . . didst choose Abram and bring him forth out of Ur of the Chaldaeans and give him the name Abraham; and thou didst find his heart faithful before thee, and didst make with him the covenant to give to his descendants the land of the Canaanite, . . . and thou hast fulfilled thy promise, for thou art righteous" (Neh. 9:7f.). Ben Sira includes this panegyric on Abraham in his "Praise of the Elders":

> Abraham was the great father of a multitude of nations,
>   and no one has been found like him in glory;
> he kept the law of the Most High,
>   and was taken into covenant with him;
> he established the covenant in his flesh,
>   and when he was tested he was found faithful.
> Therefore the Lord assured him by an oath
>   that the nations would be blessed through his posterity;
> that he would multiply him like the dust of the earth,
>   and exalt his posterity like the stars,
> and cause them to inherit from sea to sea
>   and from the River to the ends of the earth. (Sir. 44:19-21)

The author of the book of Wisdom refers to Abraham when he says that "Wisdom . . . recognized the righteous man and preserved him blameless before God" (Wisdom 10:5). Paul invokes the example of Abraham in support of his claim that the gospel way of righteousness by faith is "attested by the law and the prophets" (Rom. 3:21); if people are justified by their works, then Abraham of all men has something of his own to glory in, but the testimony of Holy Scripture is clear that it was his faith in God that was reckoned to him for righteousness (Rom. 4:3-5; Gal. 3:6-9). Stephen begins his defense before the Sanhedrin by reminding them how "the God of glory appeared to our father Abraham, when he was in Mesopotamia, before he lived in Haran, and said to him, 'Depart from your land and from your kindred and go into the land which I will show you.' Then he departed from the land of the Chal-

---

74. 6:13ff. See pp. 151-55.

daeans, and lived in Haran. And after his father died, God removed him from there into this land, in which you are now living; yet he gave him no inheritance in it, not even a foot's length, but promised to give it to him in possession, and to his posterity after him, though he had no child" (Acts 7:2-5).[75] Stephen's point is that, even in the promised land, Abraham lived a pilgrim life; and our author makes precisely this point in the exposition which follows.

Abraham's faith was manifested first of all by the readiness with which he left his home at the call of God, for the promise of a new home which he had never seen before and which, even after he entered it, he never possessed in person. "By faith Abraham, in obedience . . ."; faith and obedience are inseparable in one's relation to God. If the patriarchal narrative says in one place that Abraham was justified because he *believed* God, in another place God confirms to Isaac the promise made to Abraham "because Abraham *obeyed* my voice and kept my charge, my commandments, my statutes, and my laws" (Gen. 26:5). He would not have obeyed the divine call had he not taken God at his word; his obedience was the outward evidence of his inward faith. So Philo: "impelled by an oracle calling him to leave his native land and family and paternal home, and move to another country, he made eager haste to do so, considering that speed in giving effect to the command was as good as its full accomplishment; in fact, it looked as though he were returning to his homeland from foreign parts and not leaving his homeland for foreign parts."[76] Philo, after his fashion, interprets the story of Abraham's call and migration in a thoroughgoing allegorical manner, to denote the experiences "of a virtue-loving soul in its quest for the true God."[77] But he gives all due prominence to the part of faith in Abraham's response to God; pointing out that in Gen. 12:1 God speaks to Abraham in the future tense of "the land that I *will show* you," he says: "This is a testimony to the faith which the soul placed in God, manifesting its gratitude not on the basis of accomplished facts but on the basis of expectation of things to come. For the soul, utterly dependent on good hope and considering those things which are not present to be indubitably present already because of the trustworthiness of him who has promised, has won as its guerdon that perfect blessing, faith; as it is said farther on: 'Abraham believed God' [Gen. 15:6]."[78]

Our author points out that Abraham did not receive the promise of the inheritance at the time of his first call; the land to which he was directed to go was the "place which he was to receive as his inheritance"; the promise of the

---

75. Cf. *Acts*, NICNT (Grand Rapids, ²1988), pp. 133-35.

76. *On Abraham* 62.

77. *On Abraham* 68.

78. *Migration of Abraham* 43f. He emphasizes that God said to Abraham, δείξω, "I will show," and not δείχνυμι, "I am showing."

inheritance was not given until he had returned from Egypt and Lot had chosen the well-watered circuit of Jordan to settle in (Gen. 13:14-17); it was reaffirmed to him along with the promise of an heir (Gen. 15:18-21), and again after the bestowal of the covenant of circumcision (Gen. 17:8). The divine bidding was sufficient for him at his first call,[79] and "he went forth, not knowing where he was going." The promise of the inheritance was not in the first instance an incentive to obedience; it was the reward of his obedience.

9 Even when he received the promise of the inheritance, it was the promise that he received, not the visible possession of the land; but to Abraham the promise of God was as substantial as its realization. He lived thereafter in the good of that promise. Year after year he pitched his moving tent amid the settled inhabitants of Palestine,[80] "in them but not of them," commanding their respect as "a prince of God,"[81] but owning not a square foot of the country until he bought the field of Machpelah near Hebron from Ephron the Hittite as a family burial-ground. Yet, living like a resident alien[82] in the land which had been promised to him and his descendants, he did not grow impatient. Some visible tokens of the word of God he did indeed receive, in Isaac the promised child of his old age, and even in Isaac's son Jacob, through whom the line of promise was to run.[83] But Isaac and Jacob in their turn did not live to see the fulfilment of the promise that the land would be theirs;[84] they remained nomads like Abraham himself.

10 What was the secret of Abraham's patience? This, says our author: the commonwealth on which his hopes were fixed was no transient common-

---

79. So Philo: "he removed the moment he was bidden" (ἅμα τῷ κελευσθῆναι μετανίστατο)—although he immediately shows his allegorical understanding of the passage by saying that "his migration was one of soul rather than of body, for heavenly love (ἔρως οὐράνιος) tamed his desire for mortal things" (*On Abraham* 66).

80. "Abram the Hebrew" (Gen. 14:13) is rendered in the LXX Ἀβρὰμ ὁ περάτης ("Abram the migrant"). Cf. H. Braun, "Der Fahrende," *ZTK* 48 (1951), pp. 32-38. See also p. 4, n. 9.

81. Gen. 23:6.

82. Gk. παρῴκησεν, "he lived as a πάροικος (sojourner)," or, to give full force to the following preposition εἰς, "he migrated to" (not κατῴκησεν, "he settled down"). The verb occurs in one other place in the NT, Luke 24:18, where the two disciples on the Emmaus road ask the unrecognized Jesus: "Are you the only visitor (παροικεῖς) to Jerusalem who does not know the things that have happened there in these days?" (Cf. p. 298, n. 114). For πάροικος cf. Ex. 2:22, where Moses says πάροικος εἰμι ἐν γῇ ἀλλοτρίᾳ (compare ὡς ἀλλοτρίαν here); also Acts 7:6, 29; Eph. 2:19; 1 Pet. 2:11; for παροικία cf. Acts 13:17; 1 Pet. 1:17. So much did the early Christians pattern themselves on the patriarchs in this respect that the terminology of pilgrimage became part of their habitual language and survived long after its original force had disappeared; it is from Gk. παροικία, e.g., that we get the word "parish." Cf. p. 299, n. 123.

83. According to the chronology of the received text of Genesis, Abraham's grandsons Esau and Jacob were fifteen years old when he died (cf. Gen. 21:5; 25:7, 26), although Abraham's death is recorded before the birth of Esau and Jacob. For συγκληρονόμοι ("fellow-heirs") see *New Docs.*, I (1976), § 85; II (1977), § 75.

84. Cf. v. 13, where Isaac and Jacob are included with Abraham.

wealth of this temporal order. He was looking for a city of a different kind: the city with the eternal foundations,[85] planned and built by God.[86] Just as the true rest of God is not the earthly Canaan into which the first Joshua led the people of Israel (Heb. 4:8), so Abraham kept his eyes fixed on the well-established city of God which was to be revealed in the time of fulfilment.

Here certainly our author may be said to allegorize—to discern in the promise to Abraham that the earthly Canaan would be his and his descendants' an underlying promise of a richer and eternal inheritance. With his statement that Abraham looked for "the city with firm foundations" (NEB) we may compare Philo's description of the land which God promised to give Abraham as "a city good and wide and very prosperous, for the gifts of God are very great."[87] To Philo this city is the abode of the individual soul which spends its time in the contemplation of the universe and cultivation of the knowledge of God; it is the natural habitat of the true philosopher.[88] To our

85. Gk. ἐξεδέχετο γὰρ τὴν τοὺς θεμελίους ἔχουσαν πόλιν (translated literally in ERV/ARV, "he looked for the city which hath the foundations," i.e., the only city with enduring foundations). C. F. D. Moule suggests that our author has in mind Ps. 87 (LXX 86):1, "His foundation (LXX θεμέλιοι) is in the holy mountains"; he refers to C. Gore's point (in *The Reconstruction of Belief* [London, 1926], p. 770) that in Gal. 4:26 ("the Jerusalem that is above. . . , which is our mother") Paul is echoing v. 5 of the same psalm (μήτηρ Σιών), and compares also Phil. 3:20 (*The Birth of the New Testament* [London, ³1981], p. 60, n. 2).

86. Gk. ἧς τεχνίτης καὶ δημιουργὸς ὁ θεός. Elsewhere in the NT (Acts 19:24, 38; Rev. 18:22) τεχνίτης means "craftsman" or "artificer"; here it is used of God in much the same sense as the verb κατασκευάζω in Heb. 3:4, "the one who built all things is God." In Wisdom 13:1 idolaters are condemned (much as in Rom. 1:19ff.) for failing to "recognize the Artificer (τεχνίτης) while paying heed to his works." As for the other word δημιουργός (lit. "public workman," "constructor"), this is its only NT occurrence. It (or one of its derivatives) is used repeatedly in Philo along with τεχνίτης (or τεχνιτεύω) in reference to God as Creator. For example: "Through this power the Father who is Begetter and Artificer (τεχνιτεύσας) appointed the universe, so that 'I am God' is tantamount to 'I am Maker and Constructor' (δημιουργός)" (*On Change of Names* 29); "It is said, 'Let us make man in our image,' in order that, if the wax receives . . . a noble impress, it should appear to be the construction (δημιούργημα) of him who is the Artificer (τεχνίτης) of noble and good things alone" (*ibid.*, 31); "The Artificer (τεχνίτης) . . . constructed (ἐδημιούργει) the world" (*Who Is the Heir?* 133). Other Philonic references are given by C. Spicq, *L'Épître aux Hébreux*, I, p. 44. The *Epistle to Diognetus* (7:2), perhaps echoing the present passage in Hebrews, describes Jesus as "the very artificer and constructor (τεχνίτης καὶ δημιουργός) of the universe, by whom God created the heavens." In gnostic thought δημιουργός was used of the divine power who created the material universe, envisaged as an inferior deity to the Supreme God. See G. W. H. Lampe (ed.), *A Patristic Greek Lexicon* (Oxford, 1961-68), p. 342 (*s.v.* δημιουργός).

87. *Leg. Alleg.* 3.83.

88. Cf. Philo on Jacob's dream at Bethel (Gen. 28:15); God's promise to bring Jacob back to the promised land may "hint at the doctrine of the immortality of the soul, which, leaving its heavenly abode. . . , entered the body as if it were a foreign land; but the Father who gave it being says that he will not allow it to remain imprisoned for ever, but will take pity on it and loose its chains and conduct it in freedom and security to its mother-city (μητρόπολις)" (*On Dreams* 1.181).

293

author it is the heavenly Jerusalem,[89] the commonwealth of God in the spiritual and eternal order, now effectively made accessible by the completion of Christ's high-priestly work, so that all the men and women of faith come to be enrolled there as free citizens. In Philo's treatment not only the promised land but Abraham himself is allegorized; our author is content to treat Abraham and all the others listed in this catalogue as real historical characters from whose experience later generations can learn. Nor was his insight at fault in discerning in the promise to Abraham something more abiding than the fairest earthly possession. To those who place their trust in him God gives possessions of real and incorruptible value. Since, in our Lord's words, Abraham, Isaac, and Jacob "live to him" (Luke 20:38), their true heritage must be based in the being of God; if the New Testament writers are not misguided in portraying them as the ancestors of the family of faith, their essential blessings must be of the same order as the blessings enjoyed by their spiritual children under the new covenant.[90] "The Old Testament is not contrary to the New: for both in the Old and New Testament everlasting life is offered to Mankind by Christ, who is the only Mediator between God and Man, being both God and Man. Wherefore they are not to be heard, which feign that the old Fathers did look only for transitory promises. . . ."[91]

11 According to the transmitted text, as commonly translated, we now have a statement about the faith of Sarah. There are difficulties in the way of the traditional interpretation, some of them less weighty and some of them more so.

(i) Sarah, it is said, is not a good example of faith.[92] According to Gen. 18:12 she laughed when she overheard the divine promise that she would give birth to a son, and the comment of God on her laughter (Gen. 18:13f.) makes it plain that it was the laughter of incredulity. Chrysostom indeed, in dealing with this difficulty, suggests that her subsequent denial of her laughter was "by faith";[93] but of course it was nothing of the kind: "Sarah denied, saying, I laughed not; *for she was afraid*" (Gen. 18:15). Yet according to promise she gave birth to Isaac nevertheless.[94] No doubt when Isaac

---

89. Cf. 12:22 (pp. 356f. with nn. 146-51). *New Docs.*, II (1977), § 95, quotes ὁ δημιουργήσας τὰ πάντα of God from *P. Berl.* 16389 (a 7th-cent. hymn).

90. "There is *an instinct of immortality* in saintship. He who lives to God *knows* that he must live for ever. . . . Canaan *could* not be the *goal* of one who walked with God" (C. J. Vaughan, *The Epistle to the Hebrews* [London, 1890], p. 221).

91. The Thirty-Nine Articles: Article VII ("Of the Old Testament").

92. "The mention of Sarah with Abraham is an astonishment to the expositor," says J. R. Harris, who finds her inclusion a possible token of feminine authorship of the epistle (*Side-lights on New Testament Research* [London, 1908], pp. 154f.). But see 1 Pet. 3:6.

93. *Homilies on Hebrews* 23.

94. One might ask what the character of Abraham's laughter was when he received the promise of God that Sarah would bear a son (Gen. 17:17); even in the Genesis narrative, however,

was born she laughed in a manner that betokened no incredulity but exulting wonder: "God has made laughter for me; every one who hears will laugh over me" (Gen. 21:6).[95] But our author speaks of an act of faith that preceded her conception of Isaac. Still, this is not an insuperable objection. Our author elsewhere in this chapter can see faith where most people would not, and there may be something in R. V. G. Tasker's comment:[96] "It is surely just the paradoxical character of the illustration which is a sign of its genuineness; and *kai autē* ['even herself'] so far from making a poor connexion, as Zuntz asserts,[97] may well give us the insight we need into the author's thought about Gen. xviii. *Even* Sarah's acceptance of a promise which at first she seemed to hear with indifference is to the mind of the *auctor ad Hebraeos* a venture into the unseen world which faith makes real."[98]

(ii)   In v. 12 it is still Abraham's faith that is the subject, so that v. 11, if it refers to Sarah, is a digression. Even so, it would not be an irrelevant digression; Sarah was very much involved in the fulfilment of the promise that Abraham would have a son.

(iii)   The Genesis narrative lays stress on the quality of Abraham's faith in accepting God's promise that he would have descendants when he was still childless. It is in this particular context that Abraham "believed Yahweh; and he reckoned it to him as righteousness" (Gen. 15:6). Paul, following the Genesis narrative, emphasizes that "no distrust made him waver concerning the promise of God, but he grew strong in his faith as he gave glory to God, fully convinced that God was able to do what he had promised" (Rom. 4:20f.). But on the usual reading of our present passage the author of Hebrews has nothing to say about this signal demonstration of Abraham's faith. If the language of v. 11 were unambiguous, we should simply have to accept this situation; but in fact the language of v. 11 points in another direction.

(iv)   The one firm argument against taking v. 11 as a statement of Sarah's faith lies in the fact that the phrase traditionally rendered "to conceive seed" just does not mean that; it refers to the father's part in the genera-

---

he is not blamed for laughing, and we may be intended to infer that this laughter was due to his appreciation of the divine absurdity of the situation.

95. Philo, commenting on Sarah's laughter at Isaac's birth, allegorizes the incident in terms of Virtue's giving birth to Happiness (*Leg. Alleg.* 2.82; cf. *Preliminary Studies* 1-7).

96. "The Text of the 'Corpus Paulinum,'" pp. 182f.

97. "καὶ αὐτή makes a poor connexion (it is typical of 'Scholiasten Griechisch'): 'likewise' is the only admissible translation. This makes nonsense of the context: who else had been said to have received, through faith, δύναμιν εἰς καταβολὴν σπέρματος?" (Zuntz, *Text*, p. 16, n. 4).

98. On this last point reference is made to A. Nairne, *The Epistle of Priesthood* (Edinburgh, 1913), p. 395. But the quality of Sarah's faith is not in question: she participated fully in Abraham's departure by faith for an unknown destination and in his sojourning by faith in Canaan (vv. 8, 9; cf. Isa. 51:1f.).

tive process, not the mother's. A literal translation would be, "for the deposition of seed";[99] it does not denote the receiving or conception of seed. This is a straightforward matter of the natural sense of a Greek word, and had it not been for the apparent presence of "Sarah" as subject of the sentence no one would ever have thought of finding a reference to conception here.[100] Tasker describes this objection to the traditional interpretation as a "notorious difficulty"; but adds: "do we know enough about Greek usage at the time to say definitely that an active noun of this kind could not also carry a passive sense?"[101] All that we know of the usage of *this* Greek noun at the time renders it in the highest degree improbable that it would be employed in the sense of "conception," especially by one so sensitive to Greek usage as our author is. But Tasker is certainly right in saying that the solution proposed by Zuntz and others "seems a too drastic cutting of the knot." They suggest that the words "Sarah herself" should be rejected as a very early addition to the text; the verse would then be rendered: "By faith he [Abraham] also received power to beget a child even after the natural season of life. . . ."[102] But it is not necessary to cut out "Sarah herself" from the text. If the adjective "barren" belongs to the original text, "Sarah herself being barren" is best taken as a circumstantial clause[103] and "Abraham" remains the subject of "received power." If "barren" is regarded as a later addition to the text, then "Sarah herself" may be construed in the dative case instead of the nominative,[104] and the verse then runs: "By faith he [Abraham] also, together with Sarah, received power to beget a child even after the natural season of life, because he reckoned the one who gave the promise to be trustworthy." In either case, v. 12 then follows on naturally.

12 Thus from this one man Abraham, when he was already "as good as dead" as far as the hope of founding a family was concerned, there sprang a host of descendants, in fulfilment of the divine promises that his offspring

---

99. Gk. εἰς καταβολὴν σπέρματος. The expression "for the conception of seed" would be εἰς σύλληψιν σπέρματος.

100. Of course the Byzantine addition of ἔτεκεν (see p. 289, n. 71) would compel us to take καταβολή in the sense of "conception"; but it is so clearly a later insertion that there is no question of such compulsion.

101. He mentions Moulton and Milligan's reference to the first-century papyrus attestation of καταβολαῖος in the sense of "store-place"; but καταβολαῖος (*sc.* τόπος) used thus is "a place where one deposits (καταβάλλει) things."

102. Zuntz, *Text*, pp. 16, 170; F. Field, *Notes on the Translation of the New Testament* (Cambridge, 1899), p. 232; H. Windisch, *Der Hebräerbrief,* HNT (Tübingen, 1931), p. 101.

103. The words are printed as a parenthesis in *GNT*³. See M. Black, *An Aramaic Approach to the Gospels and Acts* (Oxford, ³1967), pp. 83-89; B. M. Metzger, *A Textual Commentary on the Greek New Testament,* pp. 672f.

104. Reading αὐτῇ Σάρρα, not αὐτὴ Σάρρα, with E. Riggenbach, *Der Brief an die Hebräer,* ZK (Leipzig, 1913), pp. 356ff.; O. Michel, *Der Brief an die Hebräer,* p. 262; A. Snell, *A New and Living Way* (London, 1959), pp. 138f. The dative is "dative of accompaniment."

would be as numerous as the stars in the sky (Gen. 15:5; 22:17) and "as the sand which is upon the seashore" (Gen. 22:17).[105] The word rendered "as good as dead" is the same perfect passive participle as Paul uses in reference to the same subject when he says that Abraham, on receiving the promise of God, weighed up all the adverse circumstances and "did not weaken in faith when he considered his own body now *as good as dead*[106] (he being about a hundred years old), or the deadness of Sarah's womb" (Rom. 4:19), but concluded that the certainty of God's word far outweighed them all.[107] "That is why," adds Paul, "it was reckoned to him as righteousness" (Rom. 4:22);[108] and our author is in full agreement. The point of v. 12, however, is all the more clearly made if Abraham is the subject of v. 11.

4. The City of God the Homeland of the Faithful (11:13-16)

13 *All these died in faith: they had not received[109] the promises, but they saw[110] and greeted them from afar, acknowledging themselves to be aliens and pilgrims on earth.*

14 *For those who say such things show clearly that they are seeking[111] a homeland.*

15 *If indeed the homeland they referred to[112] was the one they had left, they would have had an opportunity to go back there.*

16 *But as it is, it is a better homeland that they long for—that is, a heavenly one. That is why God is not ashamed to be called their God, for he has prepared a city for them.*

105. This pair of similes appears in classical literature; cf. Plato, *Euthydemus* 294b; Catullus 7.3-12, 61.206-10.

106. Gk. νενεκρωμένος. The only other NT occurrence of νεκρόω is in Col. 3:5, in the sense "put to death" (RSV) or rather "reckon as dead."

107. "In a hopeless situation Abraham hoped in God" (C. K. Barrett, *From First Adam to Last* [London, 1962], p. 37).

108. Echoing Gen. 15:6, which comes immediately after God's promise that Abraham's offspring would be as numerous as the stars. (Abraham's obedience, faith, and hospitality are celebrated also in 1 Clem. 10:1-7; 31:2.)

109. There is a curious variation in the Greek word rendered "having received": 𝔭46 D 1739 with the majority of later MSS and the TR read λαβόντες, ℵ I P 326 and others read κομισάμενοι, while A reads προσδεξάμενοι. The original reading is probably λαβόντες (cf. 9:15); the reading κομισάμενοι may have been influenced by 10:36; 11:39, and προσδεξάμενοι possibly by v. 35. Cf. G. Zuntz, *Text*, pp. 52f.; F. W. Beare, "The Text of the Epistle to the Hebrews in 𝔭46," *JBL* 63 (1944), p. 394.

110. 1518 with a few MSS and the TR add καὶ πεισθέντες (whence AV "and were persuaded of them").

111. 𝔭46 D* and a few other MSS have the simple verb ζητοῦσιν; the majority reading is the compound ἐπιζητοῦσιν (for a similar variation in v. 6 see p. 281, n. 30).

112. 𝔭46 ℵ* D* 1739 and a few other authorities read the present μνημονεύουσιν, 33 and a few others read the aorist ἐμνημόνευσαν, A and the remaining witnesses read the imperfect ἐμνημόνευον. The present tense, as the more difficult reading, is probably to be preferred (cf. Zuntz, *Text*, p. 119; see also p. 299, n. 120).

13 "These all"—more particularly, those mentioned in the five preceding verses, Abraham (with Sarah), Isaac, and Jacob—"died in faith,"[113] as they had lived in faith. Their lives were regulated by the firm conviction that God would fulfil the promises he had given them, and in death they continued to look forward to the fulfilment of those promises, as is evident from the words in which Isaac and Jacob bestowed their final blessings on their sons or grandsons, as vv. 20 and 21 indicate. But more generally it is true of all the men and women of God in Old Testament days that they "died in faith: they had not received the promises, but they saw and greeted them from afar," as indeed our author affirms in v. 39, at the end of his honors list. It was Abraham, Isaac, and Jacob, however, who lived preeminently as "aliens and pilgrims[114] on earth" in a sense which is inapplicable to those Israelites of later generations after the settlement in Canaan. To Abraham, Isaac, and Jacob Canaan remained a "promised" land to the end of their days; their descendants saw the fulfilment of what was a promise to the patriarchs. But to the patriarchs that promise was sure because it was God's promise; and they staked everything on its certainty. In one sense, as our author has said earlier, Abraham, "having shown steadfastness, obtained the promise" (6:15)[115]—he obtained the promised son, not only by his birth but also by his restoration from death "as a type," as v. 19 puts it—but the full realization of the promises had to await the day of Christ. "I am a stranger and a sojourner[116] among you," said Abraham to the sons of Heth (Gen. 23:4); he recognized and accepted his status as a pilgrim. So too Jacob, in old age, speaks of the long course of his life as "the days of the years of my pilgrimage"[117] (Gen. 47:9).

14 When the patriarchs used language like this, says our author, they made it plain[118] that the place of their sojourning was not their home.[119] Their "pilgrim's progress" through this world had as its goal a home elsewhere.

---

113. Here the author departs from his anaphoric use of πίστει and says κατὰ πίστιν, simply by way of literary variation. We have had κατὰ πίστιν already in v. 7, but in the attributive position (τῆς κατὰ πίστιν δικαιοσύνης).

114. Gk. ξένοι καὶ παρεπίδημοι. Cf. Gen. 23:4, LXX, where Abraham describes himself as πάροικος καὶ παρεπίδημος (MT gēr wᵉṭôšāḇ); Ps. 39:12 (LXX 38:13), where the psalmist says πάροικος (MT gēr) ἐγώ εἰμι ἐν τῇ γῇ καὶ παρεπίδημος (MT ṭôšāḇ); it is probably from this passage that our author derives his ἐπὶ τῆς γῆς, "in the land" or "on the earth" (cf. Ps. 119 [LXX 118]:19). See p. 292, n. 82; p. 299, n. 123.

115. See p. 153 with n. 76. Cf. the description of Abraham in v. 17 as "the one who had received (ἀναδεξάμενος) the promises" (where the promises themselves, not their fulfilment, should be understood).

116. See n. 114 above.

117. LXX ἃς παροικῶ (MT mᵉgûrai). Cf. p. 292, n. 82.

118. Gk. ἐμφανίζουσιν, "they make it manifest" (cf. the passive of the same verb, rendered "to appear" in 9:24).

119. What they seek is a πατρίς, their native land or hometown (cf. Luke 4:23f.); the fact that they still seek it is proof that they have not found it here.

Canaan was no more their home as they sought the country of their hearts' desire than the wilderness was the home of their descendants in Moses' day who journeyed from Egypt to Canaan.

15 It is equally plain that, although they spoke of themselves as pilgrims in a foreign land, they did not refer to[120] the land they had left as being their true home. In that case, they could easily have gone back there. But in fact they had no thought of doing so.[121] When Abraham's servant suggested to his master that Isaac might have to go to Mesopotamia in person to persuade his bride to come to Canaan, Abraham said: "See to it that you do not take my son back there" (Gen. 24:6). In the following generation Jacob had to flee to Mesopotamia from the anger of his brother Esau, but his vision at Bethel on the first night of his journey there made it impossible for him ever to think of Mesopotamia as his home; Canaan, to which his returning steps were directed twenty years later, was now the "land of his fathers" (Gen. 31:3), even if in it he had no settled abode.

16 The truth is, their true homeland was not on earth at all. The better country on which they had set their hearts was the heavenly country.[122] The earthly Canaan and the earthly Jerusalem were but temporary object-lessons pointing to the saints' everlasting rest, the well-founded city of God. Those who put their trust in God receive a full reward, and that reward must belong not to this transient world-order but to the enduring order which participates in the life of God. The example of the patriarchs is intended to guide the readers of the epistle to a true sense of values; like the elect sojourners of the Dispersion addressed in 1 Peter they are to live in this world as "aliens and exiles"[123] (1 Pet. 2:11), and like the Philippians to whom Paul wrote,

120. Gk. μνημονεύουσιν (see p. 297, n. 112). The verb is used in v. 22 below, where Joseph is said to have "made mention of" or "referred to" Israel's exodus from Egypt, and probably has much the same sense here. We might paraphrase: "In describing themselves as pilgrims and strangers in Canaan the patriarchs show that they are journeying to another country, their true homeland. It is equally clear that *they are not referring to* the former Mesopotamian home which they had left, for then they could have gone back there." See G. Zuntz, *Text*, p. 119: "Discussing the quotation in ver. 13, the writer argues: 'the reference is not to the country they had left: this interpretation is excluded by the fact that they did not turn about. Their longing in fact is for a better country,' &c."

121. "Who else [other than the 'proper' (ἀστεῖος) man] would not have felt it burdensome both to leave his own country and to be driven from every civilized community (πόλις) into pathless places most difficult for the traveller to penetrate? Who would not have turned right about and retraced his homeward way, paying but little heed to future hopes but making haste to escape the present difficulty, thinking it folly to choose acknowledged ills in hope of good things which he could not see?" (Philo, *On Abraham* 86).

122. According to Philo (*Confusion of Tongues* 78-82), the heavenly country is the patriarchs' domicile of origin, and therefore in seeking it they do aim at returning to the place from which they set out.

123. Gk. παροίκους καὶ παρεπιδήμους, as in Gen. 23:4, LXX (cf. p. 292, n. 82, p. 298, n. 114). In Eph. 2:19, "you are no more strangers and sojourners" (Gk. ξένοι καὶ πάροικοι), the

their "citizenship[124] is in heaven" (Phil. 3:20). This ideal has proved too high for many Christians throughout the centuries of our era; yet there has never failed a distinguished succession of men and women possessed of this pilgrim attitude who have sung with Henry Francis Lyte:

> It is not for me to be seeking my bliss
> And building my hopes in a region like this;
> I look for a city which hands have not piled,
> I pant for a country by sin undefiled.

Yet those who have shared most truly the otherworldliness of the patriarchs have not been unpractical people, too heavenly-minded to be of any earthly use. Abraham's neighbors were enriched by the presence of this wandering stranger in their midst; when the territory of some of them was devastated by an invading army on one occasion, it was "Abram the Hebrew"[125] who took immediate and effective action to deal with the situation.[126] There have indeed been many occasions when practical men of the world have been thankful to saints and mystics for timely help in an emergency beyond their own power to cope with.

"Those who honor me I will honor," says God (1 Sam. 2:30). The patriarchs honored God by putting their faith in him; he honored them by calling himself "the God of Abraham, the God of Isaac, and the God of Jacob" (Ex. 3:6).[127] What higher honor than this could be paid to any mortal? These three patriarchs were not faultless, but God is not ashamed to be called their God, because they took him at his word. It is noteworthy that, while Jacob is in many ways the least exemplary of the three, God is called the God of Jacob much more frequently in the Bible than he is called the God of Abraham or of Isaac. For all his shortcomings, Jacob had a true sense of spiritual values which sprang from his faith in God.[128] For these, then, and for all who tread the same path of faith, God has prepared his city, his commonwealth.[129] There

---

words are used in a different setting; there the point is that Gentile believers are no longer aliens but fellow-citizens with the people of God.

124. Gk. πολίτευμα.

125. See p. 4, n. 9; p. 292, n. 80.

126. Gen. 14:8-16; cf. pp. 156-62 above (on 7:1-4).

127. "God does not need us. Indeed, if He were not God, He would be ashamed of us. We, at any rate, cannot be ashamed of Him" (K. Barth, *The Epistle to the Romans*, E.T. [Oxford, 1933], p. 35). On the identification (and self-identification) of Yahweh as "God of the fathers" see A. Alt, "The God of the Fathers" (1929), in *Essays on Old Testament History and Religion*, E.T. (Oxford, 1966), pp. 1-77; B. Gemser, *Vragen rondom de Patriarchenreligie* (Groningen, 1958); F. M. Cross, Jr., "Yahweh and the God of the Patriarchs," *HTR* 55 (1962), pp. 225-59; R. de Vaux, "El et Baal, le Dieu des Pères et Yahweh," *Ugaritica* 6 (1969), pp. 501-17.

128. See the note on Esau, described *per contra* as a "profane person" (12:16f.), on p. 351.

129. It is probably on a passage like this or v. 10 or 13:14 (see p. 382) that Hermas depends when he tells how the angel said to him: "You know that you, the servants of God, live

is, of course, no difference between the heavenly country[130] and the city of God. Words could hardly make it clearer that the patriarchs and the other men and women of God who lived before Christ have a share in the same inheritance of glory as is promised to believers in Christ of New Testament times.[131]

5. More about the Faith of the Patriarchs (11:17-22)

17 *By faith Abraham offered up Isaac[132] when he was put to the test: Yes, the one who had received[133] the promises was on the point of offering up[134] his only son,[135]*

---

in a foreign land, for your city is far from this city. If then you know your city, in which you are going to dwell, why do you prepare here fields and costly establishments and buildings and dwellings which are to no purpose? He who prepares these things for this city cannot go back home to his own city" (*Shepherd*, Similitude 1.1).

130. With the "heavenly" (ἐπουράνιος) homeland prepared by God for the patriarchs Moffatt (ICC, p. 176) compares 2 Macc. 3:39, where God is described as the one whose dwelling is "heavenly" (ἐπουράνιος). It is to God's own dwelling, indeed, that men and women of faith are admitted as free burgesses, just as it has been emphasized earlier (3:11-19; 4:3-11) that it is God's own "rest" that may be attained by faith and forfeited by unbelief.

131. Cf. B. W. Newton's retort to those who pressed an unscriptural distinction between the people of God in OT days and those of the present age: "Are we to say that Abraham hath 'THE promises,' and yet that the chiefest results of those promises he hath *not?* Are we to say that Abraham belongs to that heavenly city whose maker and builder is God, . . . and yet that he hath not the blessings which pertain to that city?" (*The Old Testament Saints not to be Excluded from the Church in Glory* [London, 1887], p. 14).

132. Gk. πίστει προσενήνοχεν ᾽Αβραάμ τὸν ᾽Ισαὰκ πειραζόμενος. p[46] with a few later authorities omits ᾽Αβραάμ. The perfect tense προσενήνοχεν may denote the completeness of the sacrifice as far as Abraham's resolution was concerned; cf. n. 134 below. The participle πειραζόμενος echoes ἐπείραζεν of Gen. 22:1 (LXX); cf. also Sir. 44:20, ἐν πειρασμῷ εὑρέθη πιστός (p. 290).

133. Gk. ἀναδεξάμενος. The only other occurrence of ἀναδέχομαι in the NT is Acts 28:7, where Publius, chief man of Malta, "received" Paul, Luke, and their companions.

134. Here, by contrast with the preceding clause (cf. n. 132 above) the imperfect tense προσέφερεν is used, indicating that, as far as outward action was concerned, the sacrifice of Isaac was not completed, since in the event his life was not taken; one might render the verb here: "was on the point of offering up."

135. Gk. τὸν μονογενῆ, corresponding to Heb. *yāḥîd* in Gen. 22:2 (so Aquila's version and Josephus, *Ant.* 1.222). The LXX renders *yāḥîd* here by ἀγαπητός, "beloved," while Symmachus renders by μόνος, "only." The Hebrew adjective combines the two ideas (adding to its proper force "only" that of *yādîd*, "beloved"); hence Philo speaks of Isaac (in his allegorizing way) as "the beloved and only (ἀγαπητὸν καὶ μόνον) trueborn offspring of the soul" (*On the Unchangeableness of God* 4). There are three instances of μονογενῆς in reference to an only child in Luke (7:12; 8:42; 9:38); its best-known NT usage, however, is its application to Christ, the Son of God, in the Johannine writings (John 1:14, 18; 3:16, 18; 1 John 4:9), where it is practically synonymous with ἀγαπητός in Mark 1:11; 9:7 (and parallels) and ἐκλελεγμένος in Luke 9:35. Cf. also the Parable of the Vineyard, where the proprietor "had still one other, a beloved son" (Mark 12:6), and Paul's echo of Gen. 22:12 in Rom. 8:32, "He who did not spare his own Son" (where Gk. ἴδιος represents Heb. *yāḥîd*, as also, probably, in Acts 20:28, where God purchased the church "with the blood of his own," i.e., "of his only-begotten").

18 *the son concerning whom it had been said, "In Isaac your offspring will be called."*[136]

19 *He reckoned that God was able to raise people up*[137] *even from the dead, and it was from the dead that he received Isaac back as a type.*

20 *By faith Isaac blessed Jacob and Esau, even*[138] *in respect of things to come.*

21 *By faith Jacob on his deathbed blessed each of the sons of Joseph, and he worshiped, (leaning) on the top of his staff.*[139]

22 *By faith Joseph, when his end was near, mentioned the departure*[140] *of the people of Israel and gave directions with regard to his bones.*

17-18 The "Binding of Isaac,"[141] as the story of Gen. 22 has traditionally been called among the Jews, is treated in Jewish interpretation as the classic example of the redemptive efficacy of martyrdom.[142] Its influence is probably to be traced in several New Testament passages,[143] but only in two places is the story expressly referred to—here and in Jas. 2:21-23—and in both of these places it is set forth as an example of faith, faith manifested in action. "Was not Abraham our father justified by works," asks James, "when he offered his son Isaac on the altar? You see that faith was active along with

---

136. Gen. 21:12.

137. Gk. ἐγείρειν, for which a few authorities (A P etc.) have ἐγεῖραι, the aorist infinitive, as though the reference was to Abraham's faith that God could raise *Isaac;* the present infinitive implies Abraham's faith that God could raise *the dead.*

138. Gk. καί, omitted by ℵ K L P etc., followed by the TR (cf. the AV/KJV); omitted also by the Syriac and Coptic versions.

139. Gen. 47:31 (LXX); cf. p. 306.

140. Gk. ἔξοδος.

141. Heb. *'ăqēdaṯ yiṣḥāq,* from Gen. 22:9.

142. In the Additional Service for the Jewish New Year these words occur: "Remember unto us, O Lord our God, the covenant and the loving-kindness and the oath which thou swarest unto Abraham our father on Mount Moriah; and may the binding with which Abraham our father bound his son Isaac on the altar appear before thee, how he overbore his compassion in order to perform thy will with a perfect heart." Cf. also the prayer in *Leviticus Rabba* 29.8: "If the sons of Isaac walk in rebellion and wicked works, remember the binding of their father Isaac, and leave the throne of judgment and sit on the throne of mercy" (this example is selected by C. K. Barrett, *From First Adam to Last,* pp. 27f., from the collection of relevant passages in N. Johansson, *Parakletoi* [Lund, 1940], pp. 168ff.); cf. also H. Riesenfeld, *Jésus transfiguré* (Uppsala, 1947), pp. 87ff.; H.-J. Schoeps, *Aus frühchristlicher Zeit* (Tübingen, 1950), pp. 229-38; I. Maybaum, *The Sacrifice of Isaac* (London, 1959); L. Morris, *The Apostolic Preaching of the Cross* (London, 1965), pp. 139f.; *The Cross in the New Testament* (Exeter, 1965), p. 39, n. 62, p. 138, n. 67; N. A. Dahl, "The Atonement—An Adequate Reward for the Akedah (Ro 8:32)?" in *Neotestamentica et Semitica: Studies in honour of M. Black* (Edinburgh, 1969), pp. 15-29; and especially J. Swetnam, *Jesus and Isaac: A Study of the Epistle to the Hebrews in the Light of the Aqedah,* AnBib 94 (Rome, 1981).

143. Rom. 8:32 (ὅς γε τοῦ ἰδίου υἱοῦ οὐκ ἐφείσατο) echoes Gen. 22:16 (LXX, οὐκ ἐφείσω τοῦ υἱοῦ σου τοῦ ἀγαπητοῦ). H.-J. Schoeps, not too convincingly, finds other traces of the Binding of Isaac in Pauline soteriology (*Paul,* E.T. [London, 1961], pp. 141-49). John 8:56 possibly alludes to a phase of the story (cf. p. 305 with n. 152).

his works, and faith was completed by works, and the scripture was fulfilled which says, 'Abraham believed God, and it was reckoned to him as righteousness';[144] and he was called the friend of God."[145] James's emphasis is in line with his general argument in that context; but he is in essential agreement with our author: Abraham's offering up of Isaac was a signal demonstration of his faith. Not only so, but this interpretation is consistent with the original narrative, in which God's command to Abraham to offer up Isaac was intended to "test" him (Gen. 22:1),[146] and Abraham's ready obedience attested the unreserved quality of his allegiance to God. "When he was tested he was found faithful," says Ben Sira, plainly in reference to this incident (Sir. 44:20), while the author of Wisdom says that it was wisdom that "kept him strong in the face of his compassion for his child" (Wisdom 10:5).[147] In 4 Maccabees the mother of the seven martyrs appeals to this example when pleading with her sons to preserve their faithfulness to God in face of deadly threats; it was for God's sake, she says, that "our father Abraham hastened to sacrifice his son Isaac, the ancestor of our nation, and was not overcome by fear at the sight of his own paternal hand descending on him with the knife" (16:20; cf. also 18:11).

What our author emphasizes, however, is Abraham's indomitable faith in the promises of God. God promised Abraham, long after the hope of progeny had receded for himself and Sarah, that he would have a numerous posterity, and at last the long-awaited son was born—the son on whose survival the fulfilment of God's promises to Abraham depended. In this regard Ishmael and any other sons of Abraham did not count, for the word of God was quite specific: "Through the line of Isaac your posterity shall be traced" (NEB). Isaac was unique and irreplaceable—this is the point of the epithet rendered "only begotten"; he was, in God's own words to Abraham, "your only son, whom you love, even Isaac" (Gen. 22:2).[148] And it was *Isaac* who

144. Gen. 15:6 (quoted also by Paul in Gal. 3:6; Rom. 4:3). The counting of Abraham's faith to him for righteousness preceded the sacrifice of Isaac by many years, but his sacrifice of Isaac showed how implicit was his faith in God's promise (of Gen. 15:5) and in God's power to fulfil his promise, come what might.

145. A reference to Isa. 41:8, "Abraham my friend"; cf. 2 Chron. 20:7, "Abraham thy friend."

146. "With ten trials our father Abraham was tried, and he stood firm in them all, to make known how great was our father Abraham's love" (*Pirqê Aboth* 5:4). The ten are enumerated one by one in *Pirqê de-Rabbi Eliezer* 26-30 and in the Jewish morning service for the second day of the New Year; the Binding of Isaac is the tenth and greatest of them. In Jub. 17:16–18:16 God's command to Abraham to sacrifice Isaac is the result of a challenge presented to him by Mastema, the prince of evil, just as the trials of Job were the result of a challenge presented to him by Satan.

147. This point is made also by Philo in his account of the incident (*On Abraham* 167-77): "mastered by his love for God, he mightily overcame all the names and loving tokens of kinship" (170).

148. See p. 301, n. 135.

had to be sacrificed! The ethical problem which the story presents to twentieth-century readers[149] is not the problem on which our author concentrates. The problem to which he invites his readers' attention is this: The fulfilment of God's promises depended on Isaac's survival; if Isaac was to die, how could these promises be fulfilled? And yet Abraham had no doubt that the one who had given the promises required the sacrifice of Isaac. What was he to do? It was Abraham's problem; apart from the dictates of natural affection, how could the promise of God and the command of God be reconciled? Later writers, reflecting on the incident, make much of the turmoil in Abraham's heart, although the biblical narrative has little enough to say on this score. Indeed, the impression which we get from the biblical narrative is that Abraham treated it as God's problem; it was for God, and not for Abraham, to reconcile his promise and his command. So, when the command was given, Abraham promptly set about obeying it; his own duty was clear, and God could safely be trusted to discharge *his* responsibility in the matter.

19 Our author's statement that Abraham believed in God's ability to raise the dead[150] is not a gratuitous reading into the narrative of something which is not there. When Abraham left his servants behind while he and Isaac went to the place of sacrifice, he said to them: "The boy and I will go on there and worship, and we will come back to you" (Gen. 22:5). The plain meaning of the text is that Abraham expected to come back with Isaac. But how could he come back with Isaac if Isaac was to be offered up as a burnt offering? Only if Isaac was to be raised from the dead after being sacrificed. Abraham reckoned, says our author, that since the fulfilment of the promises depended on Isaac's survival, God was bound (as he certainly was able) to restore Isaac's life if his life had to be taken. And in fact, as far as Abraham's resolution was concerned, Isaac was as good as dead, and it was practically from the dead that he received him back when his hand was arrested in mid-air and the heavenly voice forbade him to proceed further. He received him back from the dead, says our author, "as a type"[151]—meaning, probably, in a manner which prefigured the resurrection of Christ. Is it this incident which

---

149. Cf. S. Kierkegaard, *Fear and Trembling,* E.T. (Oxford, 1939); E. Wellisch, *Isaac and Oedipus* (London, 1954).

150. Cf. Philo, *On Abraham* 175, where Abraham's reply to Isaac in Gen. 22:8 is expanded by the words: "but know that to God all things are possible, including those that are impossible and impracticable for human beings."

151. Gk. ἐν παραβολῇ. The sacrifice of Isaac was early treated by Christians as a detailed parable of the sacrifice of Christ. "Our Lord . . . was himself going to offer the vessel of the spirit as a sacrifice for our sins, for the fulfilment of the type established in Isaac, who was offered upon the altar" (*Ep. Barn.* 7:3). According to Irenaeus (*Heresies* 4.5.4) and many later writers, Isaac carrying the wood is a type of Christ carrying the cross. More generally, *Genesis Rabba* 56.4 (on Gen. 22:6) compares Isaac's carrying the wood to "one carrying the cross on his shoulder."

is referred to in the words of Christ in John 8:56: "Your father Abraham rejoiced that he was to see my day; he saw it, and was glad"?[152]

20   In some strands of Jewish interpretation the attitude of Isaac himself, in submitting to being bound by his father with a view to his sacrifice, is commended as an example of obedience, not only to his father but to God.[153] On this our author says nothing; the one incident from Isaac's career which he mentions as a token of his faith is his blessing of Jacob and Esau[154]—their names are given in this order and not in the order of seniority, perhaps because this was the order in which they received their father's blessing. Nothing is said about the deception practiced on Isaac, in consequence of which the blessing which he had intended for Esau was bestowed on Jacob. The line of promise ran through Isaac, and as Isaac himself had received from God a reaffirmation of the promised blessings after Abraham's death,[155] so he determined to transmit those blessings to the following generation. When he learned that Jacob had received the blessing intended for Esau, he made no attempt to revoke it; rather he confirmed it: "yes, and he shall be blessed" (Gen. 27:33). Yet he did reserve a blessing for Esau, and although it was not the blessing bound up with the promise, yet it was a blessing concerning "things to come," as truly as Jacob's blessing was. Isaac, like his father, believed God, and his faith too was an "assurance of things hoped for, a proof of things not seen."

21   Jacob in his turn demonstrated similar faith. Isaac was misled by the plotting of his wife and younger son into giving the younger son the blessing which he had designed for the elder; but when Jacob on his deathbed blessed the two sons of Joseph he deliberately bestowed the greater blessing on Ephraim, the younger son.[156] But he blessed both of them concerning "things to come," as he himself had been blessed by Isaac; and thus, while

152. Alternatively, these words may refer to Abraham's reply to Isaac: "God will provide himself the lamb for a burnt-offering" (Gen. 22:8). Since this is the only statement which Abraham is recorded in canonical Scripture as having made to Isaac (apart from "Here am I, my son" in the preceding verse), this is presumably the statement referred to in the *Testament of Levi* (18:6), where it is said of the priest of the new age: "The heavens shall be opened, and from the temple of glory shall come upon him sanctification, with the Father's voice as from Abraham to Isaac." Cf. M. Black, "The Messiah in the Testament of Levi XVIII," *ExT* 60 (1948-49), pp. 321f.

153. Cf. 4 Macc. 13:12 ("Isaac endured to be slain for the sake of piety"). Josephus, after the long and tasteless speech which he puts into Abraham's mouth at this moment, tells how Isaac made answer in terms of exemplary duty, and "rushed to the altar to be slain" (*Ant.* 1.232). Similarly Clement of Rome: "Isaac, knowing with confidence what was about to be, was gladly brought as a sacrifice" (1 Clem. 31:3). Several writers underline the reality of Isaac's cooperation by emphasizing that he was a grown man at the time—23 years old, according to Jubilees (cf. 16:12 with 17:15); 25, according to Josephus (*Ant.* 1.227); 37, according to *Seder 'Olam*. His age is not recorded in Genesis, but the impression is given that he was but a boy.

154. Cf. Gen. 27:27-29, 39f.; cf. p. 351 (on 12:17).

155. Gen. 26:2ff.

156. Gen. 48:14, 19.

his earlier career had been marked by anything but faith, as he endeavored repeatedly by his own scheming to gain advantages for himself, yet at the end of his days he recognized the futility of all his scheming, and relied on the faithfulness of the "Mighty One of Jacob."

The statement that he "worshiped, leaning on the top of his staff," is based on the Septuagint version of Gen. 47:31.[157] The Masoretic text says that "Israel bowed himself on the bed's head";[158] but the Septuagint translators read Hebrew *miṭṭāh,* "bed," as though it were *maṭṭeh,* "staff."[159] The picture of the patriarch sitting on his bed and leaning on his staff is convincing enough; the same cannot be said for the mistranslation in the Latin New Testament, which makes him worship the top of his staff—a form of words from which some curious inferences have been drawn.[160]

22   Joseph also, at the end of his days, showed the same firm faith in the fulfilment of God's promises. Joseph's career certainly presents instances of faith in abundance, such as his steadfastness under temptation and his patience under unjust treatment:

> Joseph was sold as a slave:
> his feet were hurt with fetters,
> his neck was put in a collar of iron;
> until what he had said came to pass
> the word of Yahweh tested him.[161]

He endured his trials nobly and triumphed over them, for (as Stephen puts it) "God was with him, and rescued him out of all his afflictions, and gave him favor and wisdom before Pharaoh king of Egypt; and he made him governor over Egypt and over all his house" (Acts 7:9f.). Other writers enlarge on his righteousness, his fortitude, and his wisdom;[162] but the one incident singled

---

157. Gk. καὶ προσεκύνησεν Ἰσραὴλ ἐπὶ τὸ ἄκρον τῆς ῥάβδου αὐτοῦ.

158. Cf. 1 Kings (LXX 3 Kms.) 1:47, where King David "bowed himself upon the bed" *(miškāḇ);* here the LXX renders ἐπὶ τὴν κοίτην αὐτοῦ.

159. In Gen. 48:2; 49:13, where the context makes the meaning unambiguous, the LXX renders *miṭṭāh* by κλίνη ("bed"). Gen. 47:31 is the first occurrence of *miṭṭāh* in the MT (*maṭṭeh* has been used in Gen. 38:18, 25). See J. Barr, "St. Jerome and the Sounds of Hebrew," *JSS* 12 (1967), pp. 31f.

160. Vg. *adorauit fastigium uirgae eius;* whence Rheims-Challoner, "adored the top of his rod." In Gen. 47:31 Jerome translates from the Hebrew: *adorauit Israel Deum, conuersus ad lectuli caput.* He was probably not responsible for the Vulgate translation of Hebrews. R. A. Knox renders the present clause "made reverence to the top of Joseph's staff" (Joseph's staff, not Jacob's; in classical Latin *eius,* "his," refers to someone other than the subject of the sentence). Knox explains in a footnote that the staff or sceptre was a symbol of the tribe (Heb. *maṭṭeh,* like *šēḇeṭ,* doing duty for both "staff" and "tribe").

161. Ps. 105:17-19; cf. Wisdom 10:13f.; 1 Macc. 2:53; 4 Macc. 18:11.

162. E.g., Philo, *On Joseph;* Josephus, *Ant.* 2.9ff.; and such pseudepigrapha as the *Testament of Joseph* and *Joseph and Aseneth* (also *Qur'ān,* Sura 12). Indeed, we might carry the bibliography down to our own day to include Thomas Mann's cycle of *Joseph* books.

out by our author to illustrate his faith belongs to the end of his life, because, above everything else recorded of him, it expresses his conviction regarding "things to come." "I am about to die," he said to his kinsmen, "but God will visit you, and bring you up out of this land to the land which he swore to Abraham, to Isaac, and to Jacob . . . and you shall carry up my bones from here" (Gen. 50:24f.). Joseph had spent the whole of his long life, apart from the first seventeen years, in Egypt; but Egypt was not his home. Even when the rest of his family came down to Egypt at his invitation, he knew that their residence there would be but temporary. Just as his father Jacob had insisted on being carried back to the promised land for burial, so Joseph made his relatives swear that they would perform the like service for him. He "mentioned the departure [lit. the exodus] of the people of Israel," says our author, "and gave directions with regard to his bones." And in due course the coffin which contained his embalmed body was carried from Egypt when the Israelites left that land under the guidance of Moses, and was buried at Shechem after the settlement in Canaan.163 After a study of the motif of the bones of Joseph in Jewish literature M. Wilcox concludes that our author's reference to it "fits at once with the picture found elsewhere in Jewish exegesis of the piety and faithfulness of Joseph, and of the view that the visitation of which he spoke referred not only to Moses and the exodus but also to the final liberation of Israel at the hand of the Second Redeemer."164

6. The Faith of Moses (11:23-28)

23 By faith Moses, at his birth, was hidden by his parents for three months, because they saw that he was a beautiful child; they were not deterred by the king's decree.165

24 By faith Moses, when he grew up, refused to be called the son of Pharaoh's daughter:

25 he chose the endurance of hardship with the people of God in preference to the temporary enjoyment of sin.

26 He reckoned the stigma attaching to the Messiah to be greater wealth than the treasures of Egypt, for he kept his eyes fixed on the reward.

27 By faith he abandoned Egypt, and not because he was afraid of the king's anger, for he persevered because he saw the Invisible One.

163. Ex. 13:19; Josh. 24:32.

164. M. Wilcox, "The Bones of Joseph: Hebrews 11:22," in *Scripture: Meaning and Method. Essays presented to A. T. Hanson*, ed. B. P. Thompson (Hull, 1987), pp. 114-30 (p. 126).

165. Gk. διάταγμα (here only in the NT), for which A and a few other MSS have the synonymous δόγμα. This verse is followed in D* 1827 and many Latin MSS by the insertion: "By faith Moses, when he was grown up, slew (ἀνεῖλεν) the Egyptian when he saw the oppression (κατανοῶν τὴν ταπείνωσιν) of his brethren." This incident is recorded in Ex. 2:11f., and is referred to by Stephen in Acts 7:23-25 (cf. *Acts*, NICNT, pp. 139f.). The insertion here is quite without authority.

28 *By faith he has instituted*[166] *the Passover, with the sprinkling of the blood, to prevent the destroyer of the firstborn from touching them.*[167]

23 The next example of faith is Moses, whose whole life is marked by awareness of the presence and power of the unseen God, and believing obedience to his word. In Jewish legend the achievements of Moses were magnified far beyond the biblical account.[168] A more sober summary of his career is given in Stephen's speech (Acts 7:20-44). Stephen mentions that "Moses was instructed in all the wisdom of the Egyptians, and he was mighty in his words and deeds" (Acts 7:22); but he lays chief emphasis on the fact that Moses was God's appointed messenger and redeemer to the people of Israel, the man who "led them out, having performed wonders and signs[169] in Egypt and at the Red Sea, and in the wilderness for forty years" (Acts 7:36). Our author's assessment of Moses is closely akin to Stephen's. He has already spoken of his faithfulness as a servant in God's house (Heb. 3:2, 5); here he singles out those features from the history of Moses which best illustrate his present theme of faith in God.

The faith which was shown at Moses' birth was, of course, not his own but his parents'.[170] He was born in Egypt, soon after the reigning Pharaoh, to restrict the rapidly increasing numbers of Israelites in his realm, had issued a decree ordering that all male childrn born to them should be put to death at birth. But, according to the Exodus narrative, when Moses'

166. Gk. πεποίηκεν, ERV/ARV mg. "he instituted"; NEB "he celebrated." A. Nairne explains the perfect tense as meaning: "he has left us the institution of the Passover" (*The Epistle of Priesthood*, p. 400).

167. A non-Vulgate Latin insertion at this point reads: "By faith they spoiled the Egyptians at their departure" (so the 9th-cent. *Codex Harleianus*) or "By faith they spoiled the Egyptians because they believed they would not return to Egypt" (so the 8th- or 9th-cent. commentator Sedulius Scotus).

168. Josephus (*Ant.* 2.230f.) enlarges on Moses' outstanding wisdom and exceptional beauty of stature, and (*Ant.* 2.238ff.) describes a victorious expedition which he led against the Ethiopians as Egyptian commander-in-chief. Philo (*Life of Moses* 1.20ff.) credits him with proficiency in arithmetic, geometry, poetry, music, philosophy, astrology, and all branches of education. Eupolemus, a Hellenistic Jewish writer, makes him the inventor of the alphabet, which the Phoenicians acquired from him, and the Greeks from them; Artabanus, another Hellenistic Jew, says that Egypt owed her civilization to him; others of the same school put Homer and Plato in his debt for whatever of truth and goodness their writings contain. See Justin, *First Apology* 59f.; Eusebius, *Preparation* 7.14; 9.26f.; 13.12. See also I. Abrahams, M. Greenberg, and others, *Encyclopaedia Judaica*, XII (Jerusalem, 1971), cols. 371-411 (*s.v.* "Moses"). For his reputation in the non-Jewish world see J. G. Gager, *Moses in Greco-Roman Paganism*, SBLMS 16 (Nashville/New York, 1972).

169. Cf. Wisdom 10:16, where Wisdom is said to have inspired him: "she entered the soul of a servant (θεράπων, as in Heb. 3:5) of the Lord, and withstood dread kings with wonders and signs." (For "wonders and signs" see p. 69 with n. 6.) See also the encomium of Moses in Ben Sira's "Praise of the Elders" (Sir. 45:1-5).

170. Gk. πατέρες (lit. "fathers").

mother "saw that he was a goodly child, she hid him three months" (Ex. 2:2), and after that she placed him in a basket of bulrushes on the brink of the Nile, where he was found by Pharaoh's daughter. While the Hebrew text makes his mother the active party in thus circumventing the royal decree, the Septuagint says that both his parents hid him for three months,[171] and it is the Septuagint account that is followed by our author, as also by Philo[172] and Josephus.[173] Nature itself might suggest that his mother took the initiative, with the acquiescence of his father. Had their defiance of the law been discovered, the penalty would have been severe; but "they were not deterred by the king's decree."

Wherein precisely did their "faith" lie? Probably the statement that Moses was a "goodly"[174] child means more than that he was a beautiful baby. We are perhaps intended to infer that there was something about the appearance of the child which indicated that he was no ordinary child,[175] but one destined under God to accomplish great things for his people. Our author does not repeat the story of the divine revelation to this effect which, according to Josephus,[176] was given in a night vision to Moses' father Amram; but some appreciation of the divine purpose to be fulfilled through Moses is implied in his ascription of faith to Amram and Jochebed.

24 When Pharaoh's daughter found the infant Moses by the Nile, she adopted him and brought him up as her own son. But "when Moses had grown up,[177] ... he went out to his people, and looked on their burdens" (Ex. 2:11). Stephen makes him "about forty years old" at the time, thus dividing his life of 120 years into three clearly demarcated periods of forty years each. According to Stephen, Moses presented himself to his fellow-Israelites as their

---

171. In Ex. 2:2b, LXX, the verbs are plural: ἰδόντες δὲ αὐτὸ ἀστεῖον, ἐσκέπασαν αὐτὸ μῆνας τρεῖς.

172. Philo, *Life of Moses* 1.9. Philo says that their nerve failed after three months and they wished that they had exposed the child at birth.

173. *Ant.* 2.218.

174. Gk. ἀστεῖος, from Ex. 2:2, LXX (Heb. *ṭôb*, "good"). Stephen (Acts 7:20) says the child was ἀστεῖος τῷ θεῷ ("exceedingly beautiful," lit. "beautiful to God"); Philo, using the same adjective, describes him (*Life of Moses* 1.9) as of a "more beautiful appearance than ordinary (ὄψιν ... ἀστειοτέραν ἢ κατ' ἰδιώτην)."

175. Calvin (*ad loc.*) says that it was not the external beauty of the child that moved them, since faith, like God himself, does not look on the outward appearance but on the heart (cf. 1 Sam. 16:7); rather "there was some mark, as it were, of future excellency imprinted on the child, which gave promise of something out of the ordinary." We may compare the descriptions of Noah's beauty at his birth (cf. p. 287, n. 57).

176. *Ant.* 2.210-16; cf. also *Mekhilta*, tractate *Shirata* 2, where the revelation is given to Amram not in a dream but by his daughter Miriam in her rôle as a prophetess (cf. Ex. 15:20).

177. Gk. μέγας γενόμενος, LXX, as also here. An anticipation of Moses' adult renunciation of royal status in Egypt appears in Josephus's tale of the infant Moses throwing Pharaoh's crown to the ground and standing on it (*Ant.* 2.233f.; cf. *Mekhilta* and *Tanḥuma* for variants of the tale).

champion, supposing that they "understood that God was giving them deliverance by his hand, but they did not understand" (Acts 7:25). Our author reads the Exodus narrative as Stephen did, and concludes that, by thus identifying himself with the downtrodden Israelites, Moses renounced the status which he enjoyed in Egypt as a member of the royal household. He could not identify himself both with the Israelites and with the Egyptians; he had to choose the one or the other. To choose the side of a slave-nation, with all the contempt and privation which that entailed, in preference to the substantial advantages and prospects which were his as "the son of Pharaoh's daughter,"[178] must have seemed an act of folly by all worldly standards. It is, however, an act which has been repeatedly reproduced in our day by outstanding members of subject nations who have stood well with the imperial power, but have preferred to cast in their lot with their own people even if this involved them in loss, discomfort, and imprisonment.

25 It was "by faith" that Moses made his great refusal, with all that it cost him in material terms. His people were being ill-treated, but he chose to share their ill-treatment[179] "rather than enjoy the transient pleasures of sin"[180] (NEB). The privileges and advantages which are attached to high rank and political power are not sinful in themselves; they can indeed be used very effectively to promote the well-being of others and to help the underprivileged. Moses might have argued to himself that he could do much more for the Israelites by remaining in Pharaoh's court and using his influence there on their behalf than by renouncing his Egyptian citizenship and becoming a member of a depressed group with no political rights. But for *Moses* to do this, when once he had seen the path of duty clear before him, would have been *sin*—the crowning sin of apostasy, against which the recipients of this letter

178. We have no means of identifying this princess. One tradition, found in Jub. 47:5 and Josephus (*Ant.* 2.224f.), calls her Tharmuth or Thermuthis (a daughter of Rameses II, *c.* 1290-1224 B.C.); another, attested by Artabanus (Eusebius, *Preparation* 9.27), calls her Merris (cf. Meri, a daughter of Rameses II by his Hittite wife, who was, however, in all probability younger than Moses himself). Some writers of more recent times have toyed with the improbable idea that she might have been Hatshepsut (*c.* 1500 B.C.), princess and queen-regnant of the Eighteenth Dynasty, daughter of Tuthmosis I (so J. Feather, "The Princess who rescued Moses: who was she?" *ExT* 43 [1931-32], pp. 423-25). That her father was an early king of the Nineteenth Dynasty (*c.* 1300 B.C.) is probable; more than that cannot be said.

179. Gk. συνκακουχεῖσθαι, a hapax legomenon. For the simple verb see v. 37.

180. Gk. πρόσκαιρον ἔχειν ἁμαρτίας ἀπόλαυσιν (lit. "have a temporary enjoyment of sin"). For ἀπόλαυσις cf. 1 Tim. 6:17; for its use here cf. the verb ἀπολαύειν in 4 Macc. 5:8, where a pious Jew is upbraided for refusing "to enjoy what is pleasant without being disgraceful" (by Gentile standards, that is). The adjective πρόσκαιρος is used in Matt. 13:21 par. Mark 4:17 of converts who give up their confession as soon as persecution arises; in 2 Cor. 4:18 it is used of the transience of the visible world by contrast with the eternity of the invisible. Josephus (*Ant.* 2.51) makes Joseph, when tempted by Potiphar's wife, disparage "the transient (πρόσκαιρος) pleasure of lust." A scholiast on Aristophanes (*Clouds* 360) says that "the exertions involved in the practice of virtue are preferable to the transient (πρόσκαιρος) pleasures of wickedness."

needed so insistently to be warned. Even if (as some have imagined) the crown of Egypt was within Moses' reach had he remained where he was,[181] and his name had been perpetuated in history as the greatest and wisest of the rulers of that land, he would never have attained such a reputation as he did by making the great refusal. But when Moses made that refusal he did not foresee the reputation which he was going to establish for himself; he had nothing to look forward to but privation, danger, scorn, and suffering—with Israel's liberation, please God. To have remained at Pharaoh's court would have been lasting dishonor, and that dishonor would be a price too high to pay for material advantages which at best would be but short-lived.

26 Moses weighed the issues in his mind, and decided that the temporal wealth of Egypt was far less valuable than "the stigma that rests on God's Anointed"[182] (NEB). What others would have considered as something to be shunned at all costs he esteemed as a prize to be eagerly sought. Like Paul after him, whatever gain he had, he counted as loss for Christ's sake.[183] The identification of Christ with his people is noteworthy. The words which the God of Israel put in Moses' mouth when he went to Pharaoh to demand his people's release, "Israel is my son, my firstborn" (Ex. 4:22), are as applicable to Jesus personally as they are to Israel corporately. The Messiah is one with the messianic people, bone of their bone and flesh of their flesh.[184] "In all their affliction he was afflicted" (Isa. 63:9), and in the fulness of time he too, like his people before him, was called out of Egypt[185] and had his Exodus to accomplish.[186] The "stigma" and disrepute which the people of God bore were borne in concentrated form by the Lord's Anointed; to him the New Testament applies the psalmist's cry to God: "the insults of those who insulted thee have fallen on me" (Ps. 69:9).[187] The national his-

---

181. Philo says that Pharaoh's daughter was her father's only child who, though now married for a long time, was childless herself; Moses was thus heir to the throne (*Life of Moses* 1.13). To this idea neither the biblical narrative nor Egyptian history gives any color.

182. Gk. τὸν ὀνειδισμὸν τοῦ Χριστοῦ. Cf. Ps. 89:51 (LXX 88:51f.): "Remember, O Lord, the insult (ὀνειδισμός) of thy servants . . . wherewith thy enemies have insulted (ὠνείδισαν), O Lord, wherewith they have insulted thy Anointed by way of recompense" (lit. "have insulted the recompense of thy Anointed, ὠνείδισαν τὸ ἀντάλλαγμα τοῦ χριστοῦ σου").

183. Cf. Phil. 3:7.

184. It is doubtful whether there is a veiled reference here to the belief that Jesus, so long before his incarnation, accompanied the Israelites through the wilderness (cf. p. 97 with n. 46). On the present passage see A. T. Hanson, *Jesus Christ in the Old Testament* (London, 1965), pp. 72-75.

185. Cf. the quotation of Hos. 11:1 in Matt. 2:15, where the implication is that the Messiah recapitulates in his own experience the experiences of his people. (But see on this J. Barr, *Holy Scripture* [Oxford, 1983], p. 98.)

186. Cf. Luke 9:31, where Jesus' "departure, which he was about to accomplish at Jerusalem," is, in the Greek, his ἔξοδος.

187. Quoted in Rom. 15:3 (οἱ ὀνειδισμοὶ τῶν ὀνειδιζόντων σε ἐπέπεσαν ἐπ' ἐμέ). On the significance of this quotation see C. H. Dodd, *According to the Scriptures* (London, 1952), pp. 57-59.

tory of Israel, which began under Moses' leadership, led on to Christ; by his obedience to the heavenly vision Moses, like Abraham at an earlier date, looked forward to the day of Christ.

To readers whose perseverance was in danger of faltering because of the stigma attached to the name of Christ[188] the example of Moses was calculated to be a challenge and encouragement. It would help them to fix their eyes on the reward[189] held out to faith if they remembered how Moses weighed the issues of time in the balances of eternity: "his eyes were fixed[190] upon the coming day of recompense" (NEB). To have such a secure place in the history of redemption might have been reckoned reward enough; but to our author's mind Moses, as truly as the patriarchs, looked for his perfect recompense in the well-founded city of God.

27 With this forward-looking faith Moses abandoned[191] Egypt. His heart-renunciation of Egypt, with all that Egypt had to offer him, was the essential act of faith; but our author probably thinks of the occasion when he left Egypt to live in the wilderness of Midian,[192] a stranger in a strange land.[193] A difficulty may be felt here, since the Exodus narrative tells how Moses was afraid when he realized that his killing of the Egyptian whom he saw ill-treating a Hebrew was public knowledge. "Moses was afraid, and thought, 'Surely the thing is known.' When Pharaoh heard of it, he sought to kill Moses. But Moses fled from Pharaoh, and stayed in the land of Midian" (Ex. 2:14f.).[194] Our author, who follows the biblical record so closely, cer-

---

188. Cf. 13:13, where they are urged to bear the "stigma" (ὀνειδισμός) attaching to him.

189. Gk. μισθαποδοσία, here as in 10:35 (see p. 271); it is the reward that comes from God, the great μισθαποδότης (cf. v. 6).

190. Gk. ἀπέβλεπεν, used of keeping one's attention fixed on something, as an artist keeps his fixed on the object or model which he is reproducing in painting or sculpture; cf. ἀφοράω, 12:2 (p. 337 with n. 33). See MM and BAGD, s.vv. ἀποβλέπω, ἀφοράω.

191. Gk. κατέλιπεν, a verb which may denote physical departure (cf. n. 197 below), but also heart-renunciation, as when Levi (Matthew) the tax-collector "forsook all" (καταλιπὼν πάντα) to follow Jesus (Luke 5:28). So Philo (*Life of Moses* 1.149) says that Moses "abandoned the government of Egypt" (τὴν Αἰγύπτου κατέλιπεν ἡγεμονίαν).

192. Ex. 2:15.

193. Cf. Ex. 2:22, where he gives his firstborn son the name Gershom ("a stranger there") in acknowledgment of his impermanent status as a sojourner in a foreign land (cf. Acts 7:29; see also p. 292, n. 82; p. 298, n. 114).

194. Perhaps a variant tradition read "Moses saw" *(wayyîrā')* instead of "Moses was afraid *(wayyîrā')*. Philo emphasizes that Ex. 2:15 (LXX) says that Moses "withdrew" (ἀνεχώρησεν) from the face of Pharaoh (although the Hebrew text says quite plainly *wayyibrah*, "and he fled"). "Moses does not flee (φεύγει) from Pharaoh, for then he would have run away (ἀπεδίδρασκεν) without returning, but 'withdraws' (ἀναχωρεῖ), like an athlete taking an interval to regain his breath" (*Leg. Alleg.* 3.14). He contrasts him with "any other who was running away (ἀποδιδράσκων) from a king's relentless wrath" (*Life of Moses* 1.49). Josephus (*Ant.* 2.254-56) says nothing about Moses' killing of the Egyptian, but describes him as escaping from Egypt because of an envious plot against his life: "he left the land taking no supply of food, proudly confident of his power of endurance (καρτερία)."

tainly does not intend to contradict it, but rather to interpret it. "The fear of Moses is not immediately connected with his flight in the Hebrew story, so that the author may have felt warranted by this in denying that the flight was due to fear."[195] He was afraid, admittedly, but that was not why he left Egypt; his leaving Egypt was an act of faith. "By faith he left Egypt, and not because he feared the king's anger" (NEB). By his impulsive act of violence he had burned his boats as far as the court of Egypt was concerned; but he might have raised a slaves' revolt there and then. By faith, however, he did nothing of the kind; "he had the insight to see that God's hour had not yet struck, and therefore he resolutely turned his back on the course he had begun to tread, and retraced his steps till he entered on the harder way. For it was harder to live for his people than it was to die for them."[196]

Some commentators, however, have preferred to see here a reference to Moses' departure from Egypt at the time of the Exodus.[197] One argument in favor of this view is the statement that "he persevered because he saw the Invisible One," which might be understood as an allusion to his experience at the burning bush.[198] Against it, however, is the consideration that a reference to the Exodus here, before the institution of the Passover in v. 28, would be out of its natural order, as well as the consideration that fear of the king's wrath[199] would be irrelevant to this later departure from Egypt, since the king and his people alike then urged Moses and the Israelites to get out as quickly as they could.[200] As for Moses' endurance, "seeing the Invisible One,"[201] this

---

195. A. S. Peake, *The Heroes and Martyrs of Faith* (London, 1910), p. 118.

196. Peake, *Heroes*, pp. 120f.

197. So Calvin *(ad loc.)*, although he agrees that the reference could be to Moses' earlier departure, the mention of his fear in Ex. 2:14 notwithstanding; Westcott also *(ad loc.)* concedes the possibility that his earlier departure is meant, but concludes that "it is however more likely that the words refer to the Exodus." He compares the use of καταλείπω in Josephus, *Ant.* 2.318, in reference to the Exodus: "they left (κατέλιπον) Egypt in the month Xanthicus ..." (but see n. 191 above). He also suggests that the perfect πεποίηκεν in v. 28 (see p. 308, n. 166) "helps to explain the historical transposition."

198. Ex. 3:1-6; cf. Acts 7:30-34.

199. The king at the time of the Exodus was not the Pharaoh from whom Moses fled earlier; that Pharaoh died while Moses was in Midian (Ex. 2:23).

200. Ex. 12:31ff. Several other attempts at reconciling our present passage with Ex. 2:14f. have been made. A. B. Davidson *(ad loc.)* says: "So far as his life was concerned he feared, but in a higher region he had no fear; he took steps to save his life in faith of a time when God in accordance with His promises would interpose to redeem His people, just as in this faith he had already acted in opposition to the king." C. J. Vaughan *(ad loc.)* explains that "the two fears are different: the one is the fear arising from the discovery of his slaying the Egyptian, the other is the fear of Pharaoh's anger on discovering his flight." C. Spicq *(ad loc.)* follows H. von Soden in seeing a reference to the whole series of interviews and disputes with Pharaoh from Moses' return from Midian to the Exodus (Ex. 5:1–15:21).

201. Gk. τὸν γὰρ ἀόρατον ὡς ὁρῶν ἐκαρτέρησεν. G. H. Whitaker ("Hebrews xi. 27," *ExT* 27 [1915-16], p. 186) quotes examples from Plutarch where καρτερέω, in association with a verb of seeing, means "to behold without wavering."

need not be taken as a specific allusion to the burning bush, but to the fact that Moses paid more attention to the invisible King of kings than to the king of Egypt. If faith is "a conviction regarding things not seen," it is first and foremost a conviction regarding the unseen God, as has been emphasized already in the affirmation that he who comes to God must believe that he is (v. 6). Our author probably means that Moses' lifelong vision of God was the secret of his faith and perseverance.[202] Philo describes Moses as the "beholder of that world of nature which cannot be seen,"[203] by contrast with Pharaoh, who "did not acknowledge any deity that could be discerned by the mind alone, or any apart from those that could be seen."[204] Here again there is a suggestion to the readers of the epistle that the invisible order is the real and permanent one, and not such a visible but transient establishment as Judaism enjoyed in the temple order up to A.D. 70.

28 It was by faith, too, that Moses instituted the Passover in accordance with the divine command. The Passover became a perpetual memorial[205] for Israel of the last night that their forefathers spent in Egypt, when the angel of death[206] passed through the land destroying the firstborn in every home, apart from those whose doorways were marked by the blood of the paschal lamb, for at the threshold of those dwellings the God of Israel himself stood guard and prevented the destroyer from entering.[207] Elsewhere in the New Testament Jesus is presented as the antitype of the paschal lamb;[208] if our author does not press this correspondence, it may be that he did not

202. For Moses' perseverance cf. Josephus's use of καρτερία in *Ant.* 2.256, quoted at the end of n. 194 (p. 312); although our author means something more than the ability to go without food!

203. *Change of Names* 7: "Moses' entry into the darkness (Ex. 20:21) is explained as denoting that essence which is invisible (ἀόρατος) and incorporeal." Elsewhere Philo, in reference to Moses' prayer that he might see the divine glory (Ex. 33:13), speaks of that purified and initiated mind which, "lifting its eyes above and beyond creation, receives a clear vision of the Uncreated" (*Leg. Alleg.* 3.100f.; cf. *Life of Moses* 1.158).

204. *Life of Moses* 1.88.

205. This is probably the force of the perfect tense πεποίηκεν (cf. p. 308, n. 166).

206. Called here "the destroyer" (ὁ ὀλοθρεύων), after Ex. 12:23, LXX. In Wisdom 18:15 the agent of destruction is the "all-powerful word" (λόγος) of God, leaping down from his throne into the doomed land, "a stern warrior carrying the sharp sword of thy authentic command" (cf. p. 112). In the Exodus narrative the agent of the destruction is for the most part left out and the work is ascribed directly to Yahweh, as is also the protection of the Israelites.

207. The word translated "sprinkling" here is not the usual ῥαντισμός (cf. 12:24), but πρόσχυσις (here only in the NT), which means "pouring on." The prefix προσ- gives this word the sense of "application" which, despite the arguments of some scholars, is absent from αἱματεκχυσία (9:22; see p. 227, n. 143). The divine promise, "When I see the blood, I will pass over you" (Ex. 12:13, 23), means "I will cross over your threshold" (from the Hebrew verb *pāsaḥ* used in this clause is derived the name *pesaḥ* given to the feast, taken over into Greek as the loanword πάσχα, "Passover," as here).

208. 1 Cor. 5:7; the same thought underlies John's passion narrative (cf., e.g., John 19:36, quoting Ex. 12:46).

wish to detract from the correspondence between the death of Jesus and the annual sacrifice on the Day of Atonement.

7. Faith at the Exodus and Settlement (11:29-31)

29 *By faith they crossed over the Red Sea as though it were dry land, but when the Egyptians tried to do the same[209] they were swallowed up.[210]*
30 *By faith the walls of Jericho fell down, after the people had marched around them for seven days.*
31 *By faith Rahab the harlot[211] did not perish with those who were disobedient,[212] because she received the spies hospitably.[213]*

29 The crossing of the Red Sea—the "Sea of Reeds,"[214] as the Hebrew has it—was the immediate sequel to the keeping of the Passover. It might well have been cited as a further instance of Moses' faith, but here "all those who came out of Egypt under Moses' leadership" (3:16) are associated with him in this act of faith. Nevertheless it was Moses' faith that inspired them to move forward into the sea; they were full of fear and complaint as they saw the water before them and the pursuing Egyptian army overtaking them from the rear, until at Moses' command they advanced and saw "the salvation of Yahweh" (Ex. 14:13). For the Sea of Reeds receded in front of them by reason of the strong east wind which blew all that night,[215] and they were able to walk across as on dry land.[216] But the pursuing Egyptians were but halfway across when the sea returned to its usual place and overwhelmed them. This great victory which Yah-

209. Gk. ἧς πεῖραν λαβόντες οἱ Αἰγύπτιοι, lit. "of which [i.e., of the sea] the Egyptians making trial." They ventured upon the sea without faith and were drowned. See p. 327, n. 278 (on v. 36).

210. Gk. κατεπόθησαν (as in Ex. 15:4, LXX), "were swallowed up" (aorist passive of καταπίνω). A few minuscules, including 104 and 1912, have κατεποντίσθησαν, "were plunged or drowned in the sea."

211. Gk. ἡ πόρνη, for which ℵ* reads ἡ ἐπιλεγομένη πόρνη, "she who was called the harlot" or "the so-called harlot," as though to tone down the uncompromising wording of the text. Cf. 1 Clem. 12:1. See p. 318, n. 228.

212. Gk. τοῖς ἀπειθήσασιν, for which 𝔓⁴⁶ reads τοῖς ἀπιστήσασιν (cf. 3:18 for the same variant).

213. That is, in a friendly manner. "Peace" may refer to the customary greeting *Shālōm* ("Peace be upon you" or "Peace be upon this house"), which was honored in action as well as in word (cf. Luke 10:5f.).

214. Heb. *yam sûp* (Ex. 13:18, etc.), used of the Gulfs of Suez and Aqaba, in this instance of a northern extension of the Gulf of Suez. The LXX renders it ἡ ἐρυθρὰ θάλασσα ("the Red Sea").

215. Ex. 14:21.

216. Philo exaggerates the miracle by telling how the seabed between the two walls of water "dried up and became a broad highway capable of carrying a host of people" (*Life of Moses* 1.177).

weh won for his people was celebrated in the "Song of the Sea" preserved in Ex. 15:1ff., and commemorated elsewhere in terms of the primeval cosmic triumph of the Creator over the forces of chaos.[217] It supplied a pictorial form of language for describing later deliverances, like the release from the Babylonian exile;[218] and it is used in the New Testament as a type of Christian baptism.[219] But our author is concerned with it for its bearing on the theme of faith. Why did the sea recede before the Israelites so that they passed over dry-shod? At one level it was an act of God;[220] at another level it could be ascribed to the east wind; but our author ascribes it to the Israelites' faith. It was nonetheless an act of God, who used the east wind to accomplish his saving purpose, but it was by faith that they appropriated the deliverance thus procured for them. And why were the Egyptians drowned when they tried in their turn to cross the sea? At one level this also was an act of God;[221] at another level it could be ascribed to the abating of the east wind, coupled with the sinking of their chariots in the mud;[222] but our author implies that they came to grief because they had no faith.

The Israelites' faith on this occasion consisted in their willingness to go forward at God's word,[223] although it seemed impossible to get across the sea. Moses assured them that their God would act on their behalf, and although they could not see how he would do so, they obeyed. But no further act of faith is recorded here throughout the wilderness wanderings. These forty years have already been described in the epistle as a period of unbelief, throughout which God was displeased with that generation.[224] Reference might have been made to Caleb and Joshua's encouraging minority report when they came back from surveying the promised land (Num. 13:30; 14:38); but our author is not attempting to exhaust the biblical examples of faith. Even of Moses' patience throughout those years nothing is said, although indeed the words "he persevered because he saw the Invisible One" (v. 27) belong to this final phase of his life at least as much as to the earlier phases.[225] But the closing obituary testimony of the Pentateuch, "there has not arisen a

217. Cf. Isa. 51:9-11.
218. Cf. Isa. 35:6b, 7; 40:3-5; 44:27; Jer. 23:7f.
219. 1 Cor. 10:1f.
220. Cf. Ex. 14:14: "Yahweh will fight for you, and you have only to be still."
221. Cf. Ex. 15:1: "The horse and his rider he has thrown into the sea."
222. Cf. Ex. 14:25.
223. Cf. Ex. 14:15: "Tell the people of Israel to go forward."
224. Cf. 3:7-11 (pp. 95-99).
225. According to the original text of the now incompletely preserved *Assumption of Moses* (early 1st cent. A.D.), the final reward of Moses' fidelity was that his body was taken to heaven after his death (there is an allusion to this in Jude 9; cf. Clement of Alexandria, *Comments on Jude;* also *Strom.* 6.15.132; Origen, *First Principles* 3.2.1).

prophet since in Israel like Moses, whom Yahweh knew face to face" (Deut. 34:10), would have been regarded by our author as no longer valid, now that a greater than Moses had come and established a better covenant than that of Moses' day.

30 The record of faith, then, is suspended for forty years and resumed with the entry into Canaan. By whose faith did the walls of Jericho fall down? Primarily by Joshua's; he believed and obeyed the divine instructions given him when he saw the angel "commander of Yahweh's army" (Josh. 5:14). But the people's faith was involved as well, for they carried out faithfully the instructions which Joshua communicated to them, until the city fell. But they could not see how it would fall; on the face of it, nothing could seem more foolish than for grown men to march around a strong fortress for seven days on end, led by seven priests blowing rams' horns. Who ever heard of a fortress being captured that way?[226] Nevertheless, when they marched around the city seven times on the seventh day and heard the last blast on the rams' horns, they "raised a great shout, and the wall fell down flat, so that the people went up into the city, every man straight before him, and they took the city" (Josh. 6:20).

Archaeology can throw much light on the collapse of ancient cities—although in the case of Late Bronze Age Jericho it has thrown much less light than might have been hoped, less indeed than was at one time believed.[227] But the forces which operate in the unseen realm, such as the power of faith, cannot be dug up by the excavator's spade. We may now never discover in material terms what made the walls of Jericho fall, whether earthquake or subsidence or something else, but our author ascribes their fall to the power of that faith which found expression in Joshua's submissive reply to the divine messenger: "What does my lord bid his servant?" (Josh. 5:14). It is by this same faith that other Jerichoes, both large and small, can still be overthrown. "The weapons we wield," says Paul, "are not merely human, but divinely potent to demolish strongholds; we demolish sophistries and all that rears its proud head against the knowledge of God; we compel every human thought to surrender in obedience to Christ" (2 Cor. 10:4f., NEB).

---

226. The Egyptian of Acts 21:38 promised his followers that the walls of Jerusalem would fall before them at his word (Josephus, *Ant.* 20.169-71; cf. *War* 2.261-63).

227. The excavations made under the direction of J. Garstang from 1929 onward, which were once thought to relate to Joshua's Jericho (cf. J. Garstang, *The Story of Jericho* [London, 1940]), relate rather to earlier settlements on the site. The destruction of Late Bronze Age Jericho is very difficult to date archaeologically, owing to the considerable erosion of the site during the four centuries which elapsed before the foundation of Iron Age Jericho (1 Kings 16:34); but it cannot be fixed before the second half of the fourteenth century B.C. Cf. K. M. Kenyon, *Digging Up Jericho* (London, 1957); K. M. Kenyon and others in *Encyclopaedia of Archaeological Excavations in the Holy Land*, ed. M. Avi-Yonah, II (London, 1976), pp. 550-75 (*s.v.* "Jericho").

31 The next example of faith is the most surprising that we have met thus far—Rahab, the harlot[228] of Jericho. Yet this is not the only place in the New Testament where she receives honorable mention for her faith: in Jas. 2:25 her kindly treatment of Joshua's spies is one of two arguments for the thesis that faith without works is dead, the other argument being Abraham's offering up of Isaac. In fact Rahab, despite her antecedents, enjoys a place of esteem in Jewish and Christian records. The two scouts whom Joshua sent to spy out Jericho found a night's lodging in Rahab's house, and when the authorities discovered where they were, she concealed them and then helped them to escape, stipulating only that her life should be saved when Jericho fell into their hands. For, as she told them, the news of the Exodus and of Israel's victories in Transjordan had already reached Jericho and caused great alarm and despondency there; "for Yahweh your God is he who is God in heaven above and on earth beneath" (Josh. 2:11). Jericho's fall was therefore a foregone conclusion. They promised to protect her, and so, when Jericho was taken, she and the members of her household were saved from the massacre when the city was "devoted" to Israel's God, and incorporated in the commonwealth of Israel (Josh. 6:25). It was self-evidently her faith in the God of Israel that moved her to behave as she did, and led to her preservation. Indeed, she is probably mentioned in yet another place in the New Testament, for (in spite of a difference of spelling)[229] there can be little doubt that she is the Rahab who appears in Matt. 1:5 as the wife of Salmon, prince of Judah, the mother of Boaz, the ancestress of King David and therefore also of our Lord.[230] The earliest Christian writer outside the New Testament canon, Clement of Rome, recounts the story of Rahab to illustrate the virtues of faith and hospitality, and makes her a prophetess to boot, since the scarlet rope by which she let the spies down from her window on the city wall,[231] and by which her house was identified at the capture of the city, foreshowed "that through the blood

228. Heb. *zônāh* (Josh. 2:1), i.e., a secular harlot, not a temple prostitute *(qᵉdēšāh)*. Attempts were made in antiquity to give her a more respectable calling (cf. p. 315, n. 211); thus Josephus *(Ant.* 5.7ff.) makes her the keeper of an inn (καταγώγιον), as does also the Targum of Jonathan at Josh. 2:1 (Aram. *pundᵉqîṯā* a loanword from Gk. πανδοκεύτρια, "innkeeper"). Rashi in his commentary makes her a seller of food. Cf. D. J. Wiseman, "Rahab of Jericho," *Tyndale House Bulletin* 14 (Cambridge, June 1964), pp. 8-11.

229. ʽΡαχάβ in Matt. 1:5 as against ʽΡαάβ here and in Jas. 2:25, but the χ of ʽΡαχάβ represents more accurately the *h* of Heb. *rāhāb*.

230. According to TB *Megillah* 14b she married into another illustrious house, becoming the wife of Joshua and the ancestress of eight priests who were also prophets, including Jeremiah and Huldah. (How descendants of the Ephraimite Joshua and the Canaanite Rahab could be priests in Israel is quite a problem.)

231. Her house was on the city wall (Josh. 2:15), so their egress from Jericho was comparable to Paul's from Damascus (Acts 9:25; 2 Cor. 11:33).

of the Lord all who trust and hope in God shall have redemption" (1 Clem. 12:7).[232]

8. Further Examples of Faith (11:32-38)

32 And what shall I say further? Time will fail me if I tell[233] about Gideon, Barak, Samson, Jephthah, David, and Samuel and the[234] prophets.

33 Through faith they conquered kingdoms,[235] established justice, obtained promises, shut the mouths of lions,

34 quenched the force of fire, escaped the edge of the sword, had their weakness turned to strength,[236] proved mighty in war, put foreign armies to flight.

35 Women[237] received their dead children back by resurrection. Others were tortured to death,[238] refusing to accept deliverance, in order to attain a better resurrection.

36 Others had to experience mocking and scourging, and chains and imprisonment too.

37 They were stoned, sawn in two,[239] killed by the sword; they went about in sheepskins and goatskins; they were destitute, afflicted, ill-treated.

38 The world was not worthy of such people, as they wandered in[240] deserts and on mountains, and in caves and holes in the ground.

32 The comparative detail in which examples of faith have been adduced from the earlier period of Old Testament history now gives place to a more

232. So also Justin, *Dialogue with Trypho* 111; Irenaeus, *Heresies* 4.20.12, and many another since their day.

233. Gk. ἐπιλείψει με γὰρ διηγούμενον ὁ χρόνος. For the bearing of the masculine participle διηγούμενον on the authorship of the epistle see p. 18, n. 77.

234. Before "prophets" (προφητῶν) a few minuscules (e.g., 69, 1288) with the Peshitta and Harclean Syriac and several other eastern versions add "other" (ἄλλων).

235. Gk. βασιλείας, for which 𝔭⁴⁶ reads βασιλεῖς ("kings").

236. Gk. ἐδυναμώθησαν, for which אᶜ with many later witnesses and the TR have the compound ἐνεδυναμώθησαν (cf. Rom. 4:20). Cf. p. 324, n. 262.

237. Gk. γυναῖκες (nom.), which is certainly the required form here (so א² D² Ψ byz TR against 𝔭¹³ א* A D* 33 1912 *pc*, which exhibit the accusative γυναῖκας, impossible in this context).

238. Gk. ἐτυμπανίσθησαν, for which D* has the classical compound ἀπετυμπανίσθησαν. The martyrs here referred to were stretched on a frame, as skin is stretched on a drum (τύμπανον), and beaten to death (see p. 325).

239. Gk. ἐπρίσθησαν (so 𝔭⁴⁶ 1241 1984 syrᵖᵉˢʰ *al*). 𝔭¹³ A 1739 and many other Greek witnesses with the Latin and Armenian versions and the TR read ἐπρίσθησαν ἐπειράσθησαν ("they were sawn in two, they were tempted"); א L P 048 33 81 326 2495 *al* read ἐπ(ε)ιράσθησαν ἐπρίσθησαν. These latter readings probably represent a false dittography and the original reading is ἐπρίσθησαν alone (cf. Calvin, *ad loc.*; G. Zuntz, *Text*, pp. 47f.). A variant spelling of ἐπρίσθησαν, the itacistic ἐπρήσθησαν, appears in the minuscule 1923 and is implied in the Bohairic rendering ("they were burned"), as though it were aorist passive of πίμπρημι and not of πρίζω (cf. p. 328, n. 290). See B. M. Metzger, *Textual Commentary on the Greek New Testament*, pp. 674f.

240. Gk. ἐν, for which several ancient witnesses have ἐπί (𝔭¹³, ⁴⁶ א A P 33 etc.); the two prepositions were easily confused in uncial writing.

summary account covering the later period. With a rhetorical transition[241] our author goes on, first of all, to mention six men by name spanning the interval between the settlement in Canaan and the early monarchy. The six names are not given in strict chronological order (or the order in which they appear in the biblical narrative); in fact, if we arrange them in three pairs, the two men in each pair are named here in the reverse order to that of their Old Testament appearance, for in the Old Testament Barak appears before Gideon, Jephthah before Samson, and Samuel before David. The reversal of the order of Samuel and David may be intended to bring Samuel into closer contact with "the prophets" who are mentioned immediately after, Samuel being the first in the continuous "prophetic succession" of the age of the Hebrew monarchy.[242] The four figures from the book of Judges who here precede "David and Samuel" remind us of the four who are listed in 1 Sam. 12:11, where Samuel, in a speech to the people after they have chosen Saul to be their king, recalls how in their earlier times of distress "Yahweh sent Jerubbaal and Bedan, and Jephthah and Samuel, and delivered you out of the hand of your enemies on every side." Jerubbaal is another name for Gideon, and if Bedan is a corruption of Barak (as the Septuagint and Peshitta versions indicate), then Gideon and Barak appear in the same order as here. (The inclusion of Samuel in this way alongside the others may seem strange, since Samuel is the speaker; but it is not unparalleled: in the twentieth century General de Gaulle referred to himself in the third person when speaking historically. It is interesting, however, that for "Samuel" in 1 Sam. 12:11 the Syriac Peshitta reads "Samson.")[243] On three out of these four—Gideon (Judg. 6:34), Jephthah (Judg. 11:29), and Samson (Judg. 13:25, etc.)—the Spirit of Yahweh is said to have come, and this could be taken as conclusive evidence of their faith.

Gideon was Israel's champion against the bedouin Midianites; his small force of three hundred men, equipped with torches in earthenware jars, and trumpets, threw the host of Midian into panic and won a signal victory.[244] Barak was commander of the army of the tribes of Israel who united against Sisera, commander of the confederate Canaanite chariot-force, and defeated him and his followers "at Taanach by the waters of Megiddo" (Judg. 5:19). It

---

241. Gk. καὶ τί ἔτι λέγω; (cf. τί δεῖ πλείω λέγειν; Josephus, *Ant.* 20.257). The following turn of phrase, "for the time will fail me if I tell . . ." (ἐπιλείψει με γὰρ διηγούμενον ὁ χρόνος), has no lack of parallels in the classical orators and in Philo (cf. Spicq, *ad loc.*).

242. David was a prophet (Acts 2:30; cf. 2 Sam. 23:2), but he was not reckoned in the prophetic "succession," still less was he a member of any prophetic guild.

243. The Peshitta of 1 Sam. 12:11 replaces "Jerubbaal" by his more familiar name "Gideon"; hence it lists the four as Gideon, Barak, Jephthah, and Samson. But its insertion of Deborah between Gideon and Barak shows that we are dealing with a targum of the original and not with the kind of translation which could be used for textual criticism.

244. Judg. 7:19-25.

is surprising to find Barak mentioned here as an example of faith rather than the prophetess Deborah, not to mention Jael, "the wife of Heber the Kenite, blessed . . . above women in the tent" (Judg. 5:24). For Barak refused to take the field against Sisera when Deborah commanded him, in Yahweh's name, to do so, unless she went with him.[245] Yet his very refusal may have been, in its way, a token of faith; his insistence on having Deborah with him was perhaps an expression of his faith in the God whose servant and spokeswoman Deborah was. And when he was told by her that the expedition which he was undertaking would not be for his own honor, he led it nonetheless; it was not his own honor, but the triumph of Yahweh and his people, that he sought.

Samson, who championed Israel's cause against the Philistines in his own single-handed way, may strike one as an odd choice among illustrations of faith; yet the narrative of Judges portrays him as one who was deeply conscious of the invisible God, and of his own call to be an instrument in God's hand against the enemy.[246] And what of Jephthah, commander of the Transjordanian tribes against the Ammonites? Posterity remembers him chiefly for his rash vow; yet, rash as it was, it was a token of his sincere though uninstructed devotion to the God of Israel. The message which he sent to the king of Ammon (Judg. 11:14-27), with its historical retrospect reaching back to the Exodus and wilderness wanderings, expresses his appreciation of Yahweh's guidance of his people in those early days and his confidence that Yahweh will judge their cause today.

David is the only king to be mentioned by name; his record displays faults enough, but it also displays a humble readiness to repent and seek pardon from God, and a conviction of God's providence and faithfulness.[247] He made an earnest endeavor to put into practice the ideal of kingship portrayed in the poem which has come down to us with the title "The last words of David":

> "When one rules justly over men,
>   ruling in the fear of God,
> he dawns on them like the morning light,
>   like the sun shining forth upon a cloudless morning,
>   like rain that makes grass to sprout from the earth.
> Yea, does not my house stand so with God?
>   For he has made with me an everlasting covenant,
>   ordered in all things and secure." (2 Sam. 23:3-5)

Like Abraham and others before him, he too received promises from God, promises regarding his house "for a great while to come" (2 Sam. 7:19), "the

245. Judg. 4:8.
246. Cf. esp. Judg. 14:4.
247. Cf. 2 Sam. 12:13; 24:10-14.

sure mercies of David" which found their fruition, as did the promises to Abraham, with the coming of Christ.[248]

None can question Samuel's fitness for inclusion here.

> Samuel, beloved by his Lord,
>> a prophet of the Lord, established the kingdom
>> and anointed rulers over his people.
> By the law of the Lord he judged the congregation,
>> and the Lord watched over Jacob.
> By his faithfulness he was proved to be a prophet,
>> and by his words he became known as a trustworthy seer. (Sir. 46:13-15)

Samuel's name is well worthy to stand alongside those of Moses, Joshua, and David in the annals of Israel. He manifested the prophetic gift in his youth, and when the central sanctuary at Shiloh was destroyed by the Philistines, and the ark of the covenant, the palladium of Israel's nationhood, taken into captivity, it was he who proved equal to the task of rallying the shattered morale of his people. He showed them that God was still in their midst, even if the ark was in the hands of the Philistines; and indeed, when the ark was restored, he left it in an obscure place, lest the people's faith should once more be reposed in it instead of God. He went annually in circuit as judge in Israel, and undertook priestly duties as the nation's representative with widespread acceptance. The central sanctuary was no more, but one man, under God, served as the focus of national life. He recalled Israel to its covenant loyalty, and thanks to his inspiring leadership they defeated the Philistines on the very field of their earlier disaster.[249] Not without cause has Samuel been described as "God's emergency man."[250]

It is in the time of Samuel that we first meet prophetic guilds,[251] and from then on to postexilic days the Old Testament narrative presents us with a sequence of prophets who not only spoke but acted for God—Elijah and Elisha, Amos and Hosea, Isaiah and Jeremiah, and others who, not expressly named by our author, were certainly in his mind as he penned these words.

33 The exploits of these warriors and messengers of God are listed in general terms. The subduing of kingdoms, beginning with the overthrow of Sihon and Og in Transjordan, goes on through the period of Joshua and the judges, and reaches its climax in the reign of David, whose empire

---

248. In Isa. 55:3f. "the sure mercies of David" are bound up with the sending of "a witness to the peoples, a leader and commander to the peoples," who must be identified both with the Davidic king of Isa. 11:1-10 and with the Servant of Yahweh of Isa. 42:1-4 (cf. Acts 13:34).

249. 1 Sam. 7:3-16.

250. In the title of a book by W. W. Fereday, *Samuel: God's Emergency Man* (Kilmarnock, 1945).

251. Cf. 1 Sam. 10:5, 10f.; 19:20.

stretched from the Egyptian frontier to the Euphrates.[252] Those rulers of Israel also established righteousness within the areas they controlled, in the spirit of that ancient "coronation oath" preserved to us as Ps. 101. This they did through faith[253] in God, whose own throne is founded on "righteousness and justice" (Ps. 97:2). They "obtained promises"[254] that God would be with them as they served his cause in faith, and obtained the fulfilment of his promises in the event; the promises made to David, as we have seen, had regard not only to his personal fortune but to the destiny awaiting his house. It was of these latter promises that Paul spoke in the synagogue at Pisidian Antioch when, after telling how God raised up David to be Israel's king, he continued: "Of this man's posterity God has brought to Israel a Saviour, Jesus, as he promised" (Acts 13:23).

As for stopping the mouths of lions, we recognize immediately the reference to Daniel, thrown into the lions' den for his fidelity to God, but protected from their attacks "because" (in his own words) "I was found blameless before him" (Dan. 6:22).[255]

34 Those who "quenched the force of fire" were Shadrach, Meshach, and Abednego, who refused to fall down and worship Nebuchadnezzar's great golden image. They knew that their God was able to deliver them from the furnace, but they had no means of knowing whether he would in fact deliver them or not—"but if not," said they, "be it known to you, O king, that we will not serve your gods, or worship the golden image which you have set up" (Dan. 3:18).[256] Had they received a special revelation that their lives would be preserved, it would have called for considerable faith to act upon it in face of the burning fiery furnace; but to behave as they did without any revelation of the kind called for much greater faith. The people to whom this epistle was sent might well have a fiery ordeal[257] to face in the near future, but whether life or death was their portion they could be sure of divine companionship in the midst of it such as the three Hebrews enjoyed.

252. The verb καταγωνίζομαι, "subdue," is used by Josephus of David's subduing the Philistines, καταγωνισαμένῳ Παλαιστίνους (*Ant.* 7.53).

253. In vv. 33, 39 διὰ πίστεως is a variation on the recurrent πίστει of this chapter (cf. κατὰ πίστιν in vv. 7, 13).

254. Gk. ἐπέτυχον ἐπαγγελιῶν, as in 6:15 (see p. 153 with n. 76). Whether the verb is ἐπιτυγχάνω, as here, or λαμβάνω, as in v. 13 (see p. 297, n. 109), or ἀναδέχομαι, as in v. 17, or κομίζομαι, as in v. 39, it is the context that must determine whether the receiving of the promise itself is meant, or the experiencing of its fulfilment, or both.

255. Cf. the references to this incident in 1 Macc. 2:60 (where Mattathias on his deathbed reminds his sons how "Daniel because of his innocence was delivered from the mouth of the lions"); 4 Macc. 16:3, 21; 18:13 (in the martyrology of the seven brothers and their mother).

256. Cf. 1 Macc. 2:59; 4 Macc. 13:9; 16:3; 18:12. In 4 Macc. 16:21f. the mother reminds her seven sons how Daniel and his three companions "endured (ὑπέμειναν) for God's sake" and exhorts them: "You also, then, having the same faith toward God, be not embittered."

257. Cf. the πύρωσις of 1 Pet. 4:12.

We can think of several prophets and others who "escaped the edge of the sword": Elijah was delivered from Jezebel,[258] Elisha from her son Jehoram,[259] Jeremiah from Jehoiakim.[260] (But not all were delivered, as v. 37 reminds us.)

It could be said of many of the judges and prophets that they "won strength out of weakness" (RSV). Gideon was least in his father's house, by his own account, and his family was the poorest in Manasseh;[261] yet Gideon and his three hundred were used by God to accomplish a great deliverance. The earliest comment on these words is provided by Clement of Rome. Clement was well acquainted with the Epistle to the Hebrews; in particular, he had studied this chapter and attempted to identify some of the heroes of faith who are here referred to anonymously. On the words "had their weakness turned to strength" he comments: "Many women have been made strong[262] through the grace of God and have accomplished many deeds of valor" (1 Clem. 55:3). He goes on to instance Judith and Esther.[263] What he says of Judith suggests that he thought of her as one in whom the remaining words of this verse came true: "became mighty in war, and put foreign armies to flight" (RSV).[264] "The blessed Judith," he says, "when her city was besieged, asked the elders to let her go out into the camp of the aliens.[265] So, exposing herself to danger, she went out for love of her country and people when they were being besieged, and the Lord delivered Holofernes into the hand of a woman" (1 Clem. 55:4f.). But what was true of Judith in literature was equally true of many Israelites in history, from the days of Joshua and the judges down to the war of independence led by Judas Maccabaeus and his brothers; they and their followers had their "weakness . . . turned to strength, they grew powerful in war, they put foreign armies to rout" (NEB). They knew, in the words of Jonathan, that "nothing can hinder Yahweh from saving by many or by few" (1 Sam. 14:6); they believed that the battle was not theirs but God's,[266] and therefore one of them chased a thousand, and two put ten thousand to flight.[267]

258. 1 Kings 19:2-18.
259. 2 Kings 6:31–7:2.
260. Jer. 36:19, 26.
261. Judg. 6:15.
262. Gk. ἐνδυναμωθεῖσαι, the same verb as here (ἐδυναμώθησαν) with the prefix ἐν (both forms are found elsewhere in the NT). See p. 319, n. 236.
263. He describes Esther as exposing herself to danger on her people's behalf because she was "perfect in faith" (ἡ τελεία κατὰ πίστιν).
264. Gk. ἐγενήθησαν ἰσχυροὶ ἐν πολέμῳ, παρεμβολὰς ἔκλιναν ἀλλοτρίων. (The Gentile foes are repeatedly called ἀλλότριοι in 1 Maccabees.)
265. Gk. εἰς τὴν παρεμβολὴν τῶν ἀλλοφύλων, using παρεμβολή in the sense of "camp" (cf. Heb. 13:11, 13), whereas here our author uses it in the sense of "army," a sense which it bears very frequently in 1 Maccabees.
266. Cf. 2 Chron. 20:15.
267. Cf. Josh. 23:10; Deut. 32:30; also Lev. 26:8.

35   The women who "received their dead children back by resurrection" were the poor widow of Zarephath and the wealthy woman of Shunem; the son of the former was restored to her by Elijah, the son of the latter by Elisha.[268] In the former instance the faith was Elijah's rather than the woman's; when her son died, she could only think that the prophet was a visitant of judgment to her house, bringing nemesis in this form for her sin. But Elijah's prayer of faith, "O Yahweh my God, let this child's soul come into him again" (1 Kings 17:21), was heard and the boy was restored to his mother. The woman of Shunem was an Israelite (not a foreigner, like the widow of Zarephath), and when her little son died, she showed what spirit she was of by hasting to Mount Carmel to lay her plaint before the man of God. Elisha matched her faith with his own, and by prayer and appropriate action he brought the child back to life. Both these incidents are described as resurrections;[269] nowadays we sometimes distinguish between the resuscitation of a body to mortal life and the resurrection of the dead to life immortal; but no such distinction is made in the biblical vocabulary. The distinction is nevertheless real, though not verbal; our author goes on to speak of some who sought a "better resurrection"[270] than that experienced by the two boys just mentioned, this "better resurrection" being a rising to the life of the age to come.

"Others were tortured to death," he says, "refusing to accept deliverance,[271] in order to attain a better resurrection." The particular form of torture indicated by the Greek verb is being stretched on a frame and beaten to death.[272] This was precisely the punishment meted out to Eleazar, one of the noble confessors of Maccabaean days, who willingly accepted death rather than forswear his loyalty to God.[273] In 2 Maccabees the story of his martyrdom is followed by the record of the mother and her seven sons who

268. 1 Kings 17:17-24; 2 Kings 4:17-37.
269. Gk. ἐξ ἀναστάσεως.
270. Gk. ἵνα κρείττονος ἀναστάσεως τύχωσιν. See T. E. Pollard, "Martyrdom and Resurrection in the New Testament," *BJRL* 55 (1972-73), pp. 240-51.
271. Gk. ἀπολύτρωσις (which normally means "redemption," as in 9:15). For the more general sense of "deliverance" cf. Dan. 4:32, LXX (4:36, EVV), where Nebuchadnezzar tells how, after his madness, "the time of my deliverance (ἀπολύτρωσις) came." "But even here the deliverance not accepted resolves itself into a ransom refused, the price of recantation, and in *Daniel*, as with Ahab [1 Kings 21:27-29], reformation is viewed as the price of the prolongation of Nebuchadnezzar's tenure of power" (E. K. Simpson, *Words Worth Weighing in the Greek New Testament* [London, 1946], p. 8, n. 1). Cf. p. 214, n. 84 (on the uncompounded λύτρωσις in Heb. 9:12).
272. Gk. τυμπανίζω (cf. p. 319, n. 238).
273. Cf. 2 Macc. 6:19, 28, where Eleazar goes willingly and unhesitatingly to the rack (τύμπανον) rather than taste unlawful food. In 4 Maccabees it is on the wheel (τροχός) that Eleazar and the seven young men are tortured, in a manner reminiscent of the medieval penalty of breaking on the wheel (4 Macc. 5:32; 8:13; 9:12, 17, 19, 20; 10:7; 11:10, 17; 15:22).

endured this and other forms of torture sooner than transgress the law of God.[274] In this story one brother after another declares his readiness to accept torture and death because of the hope of resurrection. One says to the king: "You accursed wretch, you dismiss us from this present life, but the King of the universe will raise us up to an everlasting renewal of life, because we have died for his laws" (2 Macc. 7:9). Another holds out his limbs to be mutilated, saying: "I got these from heaven, and because of his laws I disdain them, and from him I hope to get them back again" (2 Macc. 7:11). And yet another at the point of death says: "One cannot but choose to die at the hands of men and to cherish the hope that God gives of being raised again by him. But for you there will be no resurrection to life!" (2 Macc. 7:14). The resurrection to which they looked forward was "better" than that to which the boys of Zarephath and Shunem had been raised by Elijah and Elisha. Those boys were restored to mortal life, and in due course died; the resurrection for which the Maccabaean martyrs hoped was a resurrection to endless life. They could have avoided torture and death and accepted "deliverance" had they been prepared to compromise with the idolatrous requirements of Antiochus Epiphanes and his officers, but they knew that, if they did so, resurrection to life could never be theirs. They remained faithful unto death, and have been honored ever since by all who set loyalty to God above all else. In the Christian calendar the first day of August is marked as the festival of the "martyrdom of the holy Maccabees"; the Kontakion in the *Horologion* or office book of the Greek Church calls them the "greatest martyrs before the martyrs."[275]

The Old Testament has but little to say about the future life. Long life in the land which Yahweh their God had given them bulked more largely in the eyes of pious Israelites throughout most of the Old Testament period than the life of the world to come. Even at the beginning of the second century B.C. Ben Sira regards posterity's remembrance of a good man's virtues as the kind of immortality which ought chiefly to be desired.[276] But when the persecution broke out under Antiochus Epiphanes, the fear of the Lord was more likely to lead to an early and painful death than to length of days. The martyrs had the faith to perceive that death and the gloom of Sheol could not be

---

274. 2 Macc. 7:1-41; 4 Macc. 8:1–17:24.

275. Gk. πρὸ μαρτύρων μέγιστοι μάρτυρες. Gregory of Nazianzus defended their enrollment among Christian martyrs on the ground that "if they suffered so courageously before the coming of Christ, their achievement would have been so much greater still, if they had lived after him and had his death for their example" (*Oration* 15: *Panegyric on the Maccabees* 1). On the Christian commemoration and elaboration of their martyrdom see M. Simon, "Les saints d'Israël dans la dévotion de l'église ancienne," *RHPR* 34 (1954), pp. 98-127; B. M. Metzger, *An Introduction to the Apocrypha* (New York, 1957), pp. 147-50. See p. 334, n. 11.

276. This is the main point of the passage entitled "The Praise of the Elders" (Sir. 44:1–49:16). Cf. p. 278.

the final issue of their loyalty to God. The hope of resurrection blazed up and burned brightly before their eyes, giving them added courage to endure their torments. While the doctrine of resurrection was implicit in the biblical revelation at a much earlier date—Jesus pointed out that it is involved in God's designation of himself as the God of Abraham, Isaac, and Jacob in Ex. 3:6[277]—it did not receive general acceptance among the Jews until the age of persecution, but from then on it became a cardinal doctrine in Judaism (except among the Sadducees, whose party, however, did not survive the catastrophe of A.D. 70).

36 When the recipients of the letter read of some who experienced[278] "mocking and scourging, chains and imprisonment," they might well think of members of their own community who had suffered some of these things in earlier days, as our author had already reminded them. And if similar experiences awaited them again, it might help them to realize that they were not the first to tread this path. The martyrs referred to in v. 35 experienced mockery and scourging before they died;[279] and so did the pioneer and perfecter of faith himself. Since, however, the subject of this verse is "others,"[280] our author probably had in mind others than the martyrs alluded to in v. 35. And one Old Testament figure of whom he may very well have thought was Jeremiah, the prophet of the new covenant. On one occasion Jeremiah was beaten and put in the stocks,[281] and complained that he had been made a laughingstock and an object of mockery not only by the public at large but by members of his own family.[282] At a later date he was beaten again and put in prison,[283] from which he was taken out and thrown into the muddy cistern from which he was rescued by Ebed-melech the Ethiopian.[284]

37a Jeremiah may also have been in our author's mind when he speaks of those who were stoned; this was his fate, according to tradition, at the hands of the Jews in Egypt who could not abide his protest against their continuing idolatry.[285] Jerusalem itself had a reputation, our Lord himself

---

277. Mark 12:26f. and parallels.

278. Gk. πεῖραν ἔλαβον (cf. πεῖραν λαβόντες in v. 29, p. 315, n. 209).

279. The same word as is used here for "mocking" (ἐμπαιγμός) appears in 2 Macc. 7:7 ("they brought forward the second [brother] for their *sport*"); the cognate verb ἐμπαίζω is similarly used in 2 Macc. 7:10. The word used here for "scourging" (μάστιξ), with its derivative verb μαστιγόω, appears repeatedly in the martyrologies of Eleazar and the seven brothers in both 2 and 4 Maccabees.

280. Gk. ἕτεροι.

281. Jer. 20:2.

282. Jer. 20:7-10.

283. Jer. 37:15.

284. Jer. 38:6-13.

285. Tertullian, *Scorpion Antidote* 8; Jerome, *Against Jovinian* 2.37; cf. C. C. Torrey (ed.), *Lives of the Prophets* (Philadelphia, 1946), pp. 21, 35; H.-J. Schoeps, "Die jüdischen Prophetenmorde," *Aus frühchristlicher Zeit* (Tübingen, 1950), pp. 126-43.

being witness, for killing the prophets and stoning those who were sent to her;[286] and our author may have in mind (among others) the example actually mentioned by Jesus: the priest-prophet Zechariah, who was stoned to death at the instance of King Joash "in the court of Yahweh's house" (2 Chron. 24:21).[287]

As for being "sawn in two," this was the traditional fate of the prophet Isaiah during Manasseh's reign. The apocryphon called the *Ascension of Isaiah,* which records the prophet's death,[288] is a composite work, Christian in its completed form; but the record of Isaiah's martyrdom which it incorporates (especially parts of *Asc. Isa.* 1:1–3:12; 5:1b–14) is of Jewish origin and exhibits affinities with the Qumran literature.[289] It tells how Isaiah, to avoid the wickedness rampant in Jerusalem under Manasseh, left the capital for Bethlehem and then withdrew to the hill country. There he was seized and sawn in two with a wooden saw; before his death he commanded his disciples to escape the persecution by going to Phoenicia, "because," he said, "for me only has God mingled the cup" (*Asc. Isa.* 5:13).[290]

Some through faith, we have been told, "escaped the edge of the sword," but some through faith "were killed by the sword." Elijah escaped Jezebel's vengeance, but other prophets of the Lord were "slain . . . with the sword" at that time (1 Kings 19:10). If Jeremiah was delivered from Jehoiakim when that king sought his life, his fellow-prophet Uriah was not so fortunate; he foretold the doom of Judah and Jerusalem in similar terms to those of Jeremiah, and when he fled to Egypt he was extradited from there and brought before Jehoiakim, "who slew him with the sword, and cast his dead body into the burial place of the common people" (Jer. 26:23). By faith one

---

286. Matt. 23:37; Luke 11:49ff.; 13:33f.; cf. Acts 7:52.

287. Luke 11:51 (called in Matt. 23:35 "Zechariah son of Barachiah"; cf. Zech. 1:1; Josephus, *War* 4.335-43). In the *Protevangel of James* 23:1–24:4 he is confused with Zechariah the father of John the Baptist. Cf. p. 361, n. 178.

288. Cf. also TB *Yebamoth* 49b; *Sanhedrin* 103b; Justin, *Dialogue with Trypho* 120; Tertullian, *On Patience* 14; Torrey, *Lives,* pp. 20, 34.

289. Cf. D. Flusser, "The Apocryphal Book of *Ascensio Isaiae* and the Dead Sea Sect," *IEJ* 3 (1953), pp. 30-47. The work is introduced and translated in J. H. Charlesworth (ed.), *The Old Testament Pseudepigrapha,* II (Garden City, NY, 1985), pp. 143-76.

290. Our author's reference is scarcely to the solitary LXX instance of πρίζω in Amos 1:3. On the text here see p. 319, n. 239. If the itacistic spelling of ἐπρίσθησαν as ἐπρήσθησαν were taken as the aorist passive of πίμπρημι and rendered "they were burned," we might think of the incident in 2 Macc. 6:11, where some pious Jews who had gathered in caves to observe the sabbath day secretly were betrayed to the Seleucid authorities and "were all burned together (συνεφλογίσθησαν), because their piety kept them from defending themselves, in view of their regard for that most holy day" (conceivably a variant account of the incident of 1 Macc. 2:29-38, mentioned on p. 329). Even if this incident is not in our author's mind, it is nevertheless true that while some through faith "quenched the force of fire" (v. 34), others through faith endured death by fire.

lived, and by faith the other died. So too in the apostolic age Herod Agrippa I "killed James the brother of John with the sword" (Acts 12:2); but when he tried to do the same to Peter, Peter escaped his hands.

37b-38   The following words are echoed by Clement of Rome when he exhorts his readers to be "imitators of those who 'went about in sheepskins and goatskins,' announcing the advent of Christ"; he refers, he says, to the prophets Elijah and Elisha, and also Ezekiel (1 Clem. 17:1). Elijah, we know, wore "a garment of haircloth" (2 Kings 1:8);[291] and in the *Ascension of Isaiah* (2:10) those who accompanied Isaiah to his wilderness retreat "were all clothed in garments of hair." But the whole description of those who, roughly clad like this, endured destitution, affliction, and ill-treatment as they wandered in desolate places and sought the shelter of caves, reminds us especially of those godly Jews who fled from the persecution under Antiochus Epiphanes—the "wise among the people" who, in Daniel's vision, fell "by sword and flame, by captivity and plunder, for some days" (Dan. 11:33).[292] Such were the "many who were seeking righteousness and justice" who, in the narrative of 1 Macc. 2:29-38, "went down to the wilderness to dwell there" with their families, "because evils pressed heavily upon them." When they were besieged in their hiding places they refused to break the law by offering resistance or leaving their caves on the sabbath day, but died "in their innocence" to the number of a thousand persons. *"C'était magnifique, mais ce n'était pas la guerre";* these were indeed men and women "of whom the world was not worthy." They were outlawed as people who were unfit for civilized society; the truth was that civilized society was unfit for them.[293] They might well take on their lips the psalmist's cry to God:

> For thy sake we are slain all the day long;
>   and accounted as sheep for the slaughter.[294]

Faith in God carries with it no guarantee of comfort in this world: this was no doubt one of the lessons which our author wished his readers to learn. But it does carry with it great reward in the only world that ultimately matters.

---

291. This may have been the "mantle" which Elisha inherited (2 Kings 2:13f.). Gregory of Nazianzus speaks of it as "Elisha's fair inheritance, the sheepskin mantle, accompanied by the spirit of Elijah" (*Panegyric on Basil* 74). A "hairy mantle" appears to have been the recognized uniform of the prophets (Zech. 12:4); we may compare John the Baptist's garment of camel's hair (Mark 1:6). But such raiment was voluntarily worn by the prophets; our author here is describing instances of privation and harsh necessity.

292. Cf. 1 Macc. 2:28; 2 Macc. 5:27; 6:11; 10:6 ("they had been wandering in the mountains and caves like wild animals").

293. But, in the words of Wisdom 3:5, "God tested them and found them worthy of himself."

294. Ps. 44:22 (LXX 43:23); cf. Rom. 8:36.

9. Epilogue: Faith's Vindication Comes with Christ (11:39-40)

39 All these[295] were well attested for their faith, yet they did not receive what they had been promised,[296]

40 for God had provided something better with us in view, so that they could not attain their perfection apart from us.

39 From righteous Abel to those whose faith was so nobly manifested on the very eve of the coming of Christ, they all "won their record for faith"[297] (Moffatt). Some of them, as we were told in v. 33, "obtained promises," but none of them received *the* promise in the sense of witnessing its fulfilment. They lived and died in prospect of a fulfilment which none of them experienced on earth; yet so real was that fulfilment to them that it gave them power to press upstream, against the current of the environment, and to live on earth as citizens of that commonwealth whose foundations are firmly laid in the unseen and eternal order. Their record is on high, and on earth as well, for the instruction and encouragement of men and women of later days.

40 But now the promise has been fulfilled; the age of the new covenant has dawned; the Christ to whose day they looked forward has come and by his self-offering and his high-priestly ministry in the presence of God he has procured perfection for them—and for us. "With us in mind, God had made a better plan,[298] that only in company with us should they reach their perfection" (NEB). They and we together now enjoy unrestricted access to God through Christ, as fellow-citizens of the heavenly Jerusalem. The "better plan" which God had made embraces the better hope, the better promises, the better covenant, the better sacrifices, the better and abiding possession, and the better resurrection[299] which is their heritage, and ours.

---

295. Gk. καὶ οὗτοι πάντες (cf. οὗτοι πάντες in v. 13). 𝔭[46] 1739 with the Sahidic Coptic omit οὗτοι (so Clement of Alexandria and Augustine). G. Zuntz expresses the view that while οὗτοι is necessary in v. 13 after ἀπέθανον, it is intolerable in v. 39 after καί. He adds that a full stop before the present clause "ruins the context"; the clause continues straight on from the preceding ones: "and although they all had won their record because of their faith ..." (*Text*, p. 34).

296. Gk. οὐκ ἐκομίσαντο τὴν ἐπαγγελίαν. A I with a few minuscules and the Sahidic Coptic read the plural τὰς ἐπαγγελίας (after v. 13).

297. Gk. μαρτυρηθέντες, "having had their names entered on the record" (cf. NEB: "These also, one and all, are commemorated for their faith").

298. Gk. τοῦ θεοῦ . . . τι προβλεψαμένου. As used thus, προβλέπω is best translated "provide" ("God had made some better provision with us in view"). MM compare its use in the active voice in a sepulchral inscription where a man, knowing how prone one's heirs are to forgetfulness, provides (προβλέπων) a tomb for himself and his family (G. Kaibel, *Epigrammata Graeca ex lapidibus conlecta* [Berlin, 1878], 326). Cf. J. Moffatt (ICC, *ad loc.*): "God in his good providence reserved the messianic τελείωσις of Jesus Christ until we could share it."

299. 7:19, 22; 8:6; 9:23; 10:34; 11:35. In all these (and other) passages the comparative adjective used is κρείττων, as here.

E'en now by faith we join our hands
  With those that went before,
And greet the blood-besprinkled bands
  On the eternal shore.[300]

300. C. Wesley (1707-88).

HEBREWS 12

E. JESUS, THE PIONEER AND PERFECTER OF FAITH (12:1-3)

1 *We for our part, then,[1] surrounded as we are by so great a cloud of witnesses, must get rid of every weight, and of sin which so readily ensnares[2] us, so as to run with steadfast endurance the race for which we are entered,*

2 *keeping our eyes fixed on Jesus, the pioneer of faith and the one who has finished the course. For the sake of the joy set before him, he bore the cross,[3] despising the disgrace, and has taken his seat at the right hand of the throne of God.*

3 *Yes, consider him, how he has borne[4] such hostility of sinners against himself;[5] this will keep you from growing weary in soul and losing heart.[6]*

1. Gk. τοιγαροῦν. Although none of the three component elements of this word can stand at the head of a Greek sentence, this compound itself does so stand in classical Greek, as also in both its NT occurrences (cf. 1 Thess. 4:8).

2. Gk. εὐπερίστατος (see p. 336 with nn. 28, 29). Against this, the reading of all other authorities, 𝔭⁴⁶ has εὐπερίσπαστος, to be understood here in its transitive sense "easily distracting" (cf. BAGD; F. W. Beare, "The Text of the Epistle to the Hebrews in 𝔭⁴⁶," *JBL* 63 [1944], pp. 390f.), which, says G. Zuntz, "suits the context of Hebrews supremely, or even uniquely, well: as ὄγκος is liable to hamper the Christian athlete, thus sin is liable to divert him from his goal. The meanings which can be attached to the rival reading are so far inferior to this as to make it justifiable, nay necessary, to regard the reading of 𝔭⁴⁶ as original" (*The Text of the Epistles* [London, 1953], p. 28). Cf. NEB mg., "the sin which all too readily distracts us."

3. Or "endured a cross"; the majority of witnesses have anarthrous σταυρόν here (τόν is prefixed, however, by 𝔭¹³ 𝔭⁴⁶ D* with the Sahidic Coptic and Armenian versions).

4. Gk. τὸν . . . ὑπομεμενηκότα (𝔭¹³ 𝔭⁴⁶ D* omit τόν, the sense then being "one who has endured"). Paul never uses ὑπομένω of Jesus' endurance.

5. Gk. εἰς ἑαυτόν (αὑτόν, αὐτόν): so A P Dᶜ K L with the bulk of later MSS and the TR. The ARV mg. renders "against themselves" [cf. ἑαυτοῖς in 6:6], which the ERV places in the text; this reading, Gk. εἰς ἑαυτούς (αὑτούς, αὐτούς), has ancient and weighty attestation, being exhibited by 𝔭¹³ 𝔭⁴⁶ ℵ D* 256 1288 1319 1739 2127 and several early versions. (The aberrant *in uobis* found in *d* can be ignored.) "The singular is the only imaginable reading that fits the context, yet there is no ancient evidence for it. It looks like a correct conjecture. The plural is established as being the oldest recoverable reading by the consensus of all the ancient witnesses and of most versions. The attempts at making sense of it only prove its absurdity. It would, then, have to be put down as one more instance of that 'primitive corruption' which Westcott and Hort recognized in this

1 In surveying the men and women whose faith was exhibited so signally in pre-Christian ages, our author has said repeatedly that they were well attested by virtue of their faith; to them all, as to Abel, God himself bore witness. But now they in turn are called witnesses. A "cloud" of witnesses is a good classical locution for a "host" of witnesses.[7] But in what sense are they "witnesses"? Not, probably, in the sense of spectators,[8] watching their successors as they in their turn run the race for which they have entered; but rather in the sense that by their loyalty and endurance they have borne witness to the possibilities of the life of faith. It is not so much they who look at us as we who look to them—for encouragement. They have borne witness to the faithfulness of God; they were, in a manner of speaking, witnesses to Christ before his incarnation, for they lived in the good of that promise which has been realized in him. "The divinely inspired prophets," said Ignatius, "lived according to Jesus Christ. That is precisely why they were persecuted, being inspired by his grace, so as to convince the disobedient that there is one God, who has manifested himself through Jesus Christ his Son . . ." (*Magnesians* 8:2).[9]

This is one of the early examples of the beginning of the semantic change by which the ordinary Greek word for "witness" acquired its distinctive Christian sense of "martyr"—a change which we find so thoroughly established by the time we come to Origen's *Exhortation to Martyrdom* (c. A.D. 235) that he uses the word, without feeling himself under any necessity to

---

epistle" (G. Zuntz, *Text*, p. 120). Westcott found in the phrase "sinners against themselves" an echo of Num. 16:38 (17:3 in the MT and the LXX); but the LXX rendering of the phrase, τῶν ἁμαρτωλῶν τούτων ἐν ταῖς ψυχαῖς αὐτῶν, would scarcely have suggested to our author the locution τῶν ἁμαρτωλῶν εἰς ἑαυτούς. Besides, the phrase εἰς ἑαυτούς or εἰς ἑαυτόν is placed here in the attributive position and therefore is to be taken closely with ἀντιλογίαν. That being so, εἰς ἑαυτόν yields the only tolerable sense in the context, as is recognized by the RSV and (presumably, though not expressly) by the NEB. Riggenbach does not exaggerate when he describes the plural reading as "very strongly attested, but absolutely meaningless" (*ad loc.*, ZK, p. 391). See B. M. Metzger, *Textual Commentary on the Greek New Testament* (London/New York, 1971), p. 675.

6. Gk. ἐκλυόμενοι (present middle or passive participle), for which 𝔭[13] 𝔭[46] D* 1739 read the perfect participle ἐκλελυμένοι, which F. W. Beare ("Hebrews in 𝔭[46]," p. 395) and G. Zuntz (*Text*, p. 118) incline to prefer.

7. Gk. νέφος, as in Herodotus 8.109, νέφος τοσοῦτο ἀνθρώπων ("so great a host of men").

8. The word (Gk. μάρτυς) is capable of this sense, which it probably bears, e.g., in 1 Tim. 6:12, "thou . . . didst confess the good confession in the sight of many witnesses" (ἐνώπιον πολλῶν μαρτύρων). In Heb. 10:28 (cf. p. 260, n. 127) both senses of "witness" are implied: the "two or three witnesses" testify to what they have personally seen or heard. In 4 Macc. 17:11-16, where the sufferings of the martyrs under Antiochus are described in agonistic terms, the verb used of the spectators is θεωρέω, not μαρτυρέω (in 16:16 the διαμαρτυρία is borne by the martyrs themselves).

9. Cf. Irenaeus, *Heresies* 4.35.10: "For since they [the prophets] themselves were members of Christ, it was as such that each of them delivered his prophecy. Many as they were, they all prefigured One; their message referred to One."

explain why he so uses it, of "one who of his own free choice chooses to die for the sake of religion" rather than save his life by renouncing it.[10] Other New Testament occurrences of the word which could have encouraged this semantic change are found in Acts 22:20, where Paul in prayer speaks of "the blood of Stephen thy witness," and in Rev. 2:13, where the glorified Christ, addressing the Pergamene church, mentions "Antipas my witness, my faithful one, who was killed among you." T. W. Manson, in an important article on this subject,[11] points out that the association between faithful witness and martyrdom goes back well before New Testament days; he illustrates his point with a reference to Neh. 9:26, where the Levites, in their prayer of confession to God, recall how the people of Israel "killed thy prophets who had warned[12] them in order to turn them back to thee." And certainly the testimony and sufferings of the prophets play a prominent part in our author's survey of men and women of faith toward the end of Heb. 11.

There they are, then, and with their record to encourage us let us in our turn cultivate endurance like theirs as we run "the race for which we are entered" (NEB).[13] Even those who have greeted the promise to which Old Testament saints looked forward, who live in the age of fulfilment and have experienced "the mighty works of the coming age" (6:5), continue to need patience (10:36).[14] Christ has appeared on earth, in fulfilment of the promise of God, and has done "away with sin by his own sacrifice" (9:26); but now he is no longer present on earth in visible form, for he is exalted above the heavens. His people therefore, while they wait for his second appearing to bring them final salvation (9:28), must still endure, like Moses, as seeing "the Invisible One" (11:27). True, they have greater incentive and fuller encourage-

---

10. Origen, *Exhortation to Martyrdom* 5, 22. Cf. *Protevangel of James* 23:3 (see p. 328, n. 287), where Zechariah, father of John the Baptist, says, "I am a martyr for God" (μάρτυς εἰμὶ τοῦ θεοῦ).

11. "Martyrs and Martyrdom," *BJRL* 39 (1956-57), pp. 463-84. He traces the introduction of the idea of suffering into the meaning of μάρτυς and its cognates back to the Jewish traditions about the persecution of the prophets, who were "witnesses" in the twofold sense that they testified to what they saw and heard when they "stood in the council of Yahweh" (Jer. 23:18, 22). Cf. C. C. Torrey (ed.), *Lives of the Prophets* (Philadelphia, 1946); H.-J. Schoeps, *Aus frühchristlicher Zeit* (Tübingen, 1950), pp. 126-43. The glorification of martyrs is first found in Hellenistic Judaism, according to A. Schlatter, *Der Märtyrer in den Anfängen der Kirche* (Gütersloh, 1915), pp. 13ff. A. Ehrhardt, "Judaeo-Christians in Egypt," *SE* 3 = *TU* 88 (1964), pp. 360-82, finds a close connection between μαρτυρέω and πάσχω in early Christian and Hellenistic thought. See also N. Brox, *Zeuge und Märtyrer* (Munich, 1961); W. H. C. Frend, *Martyrdom and Persecution in the Early Church* (Oxford, 1965); W. Horbury and B. McNeil (eds.), *Suffering and Martyrdom in the New Testament* (Cambridge, 1981).

12. Heb. *hē'îdû*, LXX διεμαρτύραντο.

13. Gk. τὸν προκείμενον ἡμῖν ἀγῶνα. Cf. Herodotus 9.60 (ἀγῶνος μεγίστου προκειμένου); Plato, *Laches* 182a (ὁ ἀγὼν πρόκειται); 4 Macc. 15:2 (δυοῖν προκειμένων); Philo, *Agriculture* 112 (προτεθέντα ἀγῶνα); Epictetus 3.25 (ὁ ἀγὼν πρόκειται), *Testament of 40 Martyrs* 1, etc.

14. The word there and here is ὑπομονή. See n. 21 below.

ment than any of their predecessors who lived before Christ came, but they too have their contest to engage in, their race to run. The description of the good life in terms of an athletic engagement is readily paralleled both within the New Testament[15] and outside it.[16] It may have suggested itself the more readily to our author's mind at this point because of the athletic or agonistic terminology in which the sufferings of the martyrs under Antiochus Epiphanes are repeatedly portrayed in 4 Maccabees—an Alexandrine treatise of which there are several echoes in the present context of our epistle. The martyrs contend[17] in a contest[18] in which the pagan king is their antagonist;[19] and true religion[20] wins the victory by their endurance;[21] the universe and the whole race of mankind are the spectators,[22] while Virtue occupies the president's box. The prize with which the martyrs are crowned is eternal life.[23]

So in the Christian contest the prize is assured to all who compete lawfully[24] and run with patient endurance. "So run," said Paul to the Corinthians, "that you may obtain" the prize (1 Cor. 9:24); and our author's advice to his readers is to the same effect.

The athlete must discipline himself;[25] he must divest himself of all superfluous weight,[26] not only of heavy objects carried about the body but of excess bodily weight. There are many things which may be perfectly all right

---

15. Cf. Luke 13:24 (ἀγωνίζεσθε); but especially the Pauline instances of this language (1 Cor. 9:24-27; Gal. 2:2; Eph. 6:10-17; Phil. 1:30; 2:16; 3:14; 4:3; Col. 1:29; 2:1; 4:12; 1 Thess. 2:2; 1 Tim. 6:12; 2 Tim. 2:3ff.; 4:7; cf. Acts 20:24). While our author here uses ἀγών in the sense of "race" (as the context indicates), Paul uses it in the more general sense of "contest"; when he means "race," he says δρόμος (2 Tim. 4:7; cf. Acts 13:25; 20:24) or στάδιον (1 Cor. 9:24).

16. Cf. the examples quoted in n. 13 above and others in Moffatt and Spicq, ad loc. Such language is common in Christian martyrology; cf. 1 Clem. 5:2ff. (of Peter and Paul and other victims of the Neronian persecution); Eusebius, Hist. Eccl. 5, praef. 4; 50.19 (of Blandina and other victims of the persecution in the Rhone valley in A.D. 177); see further G. W. H. Lampe (ed.), A Patristic Greek Lexicon (Oxford, 1961-68), s.vv. ἀγών and derivatives, ἀθλέω and derivatives.

17. ἀγωνίζομαι (4 Macc. 17:13); Eleazar προηγωνίζετο.

18. ἀγών (11:20; 13:15; 15:29; 16:16; 17:11).

19. ἀντηγωνίζετο (17:14); cf. Heb. 12:4.

20. θεοσέβεια, which "crowned her own athletes" (17:15).

21. ὑπομονή (17:12), a word which occurs 11 times in 4 Maccabees, while the verb ὑπομένω in a similar context occurs 15 times.

22. ὁ δὲ κόσμος καὶ ὁ τῶν ἀνθρώπων βίος ἐθεώρει (17:14).

23. ἠθλέτει γὰρ τότε ἡ ἀρετή . . . δοκιμάζουσα τὸ νῖκος ἐν ἀφθαρσίᾳ, ἐν ζωῇ πολυχρονίῳ (17:12).

24. 2 Tim. 2:5.

25. Cf. 1 Cor. 9:25.

26. The word here used is ὄγκος, which does not otherwise appear in the Greek Bible. It was used in Greek metaphorically in the sense of "pride," in addition to its literal sense; and in that sense the Sahidic Coptic version renders it here, but wrongly; the athletic terminology demands the sense "weight" or "impediment." The compound ὑπέρογκος in 2 Pet. 2:18 and Jude 16, perhaps echoing Dan. 11:36 (Theod.), means "overweening."

in their own way, but which hinder a competitor in the race of faith; they are "weights" which must be laid aside. It may well be that what is a hindrance to one entrant in this spiritual contest is not a hindrance to another; each must learn for himself what in his case is a weight or impediment. But there are other things which are not perfectly all right in their own way but are essentially wrong; there is "sin which so readily ensnares us." Our author is not referring so much to some specific sin, but to sin itself, as something which will inevitably encumber the runner's feet and trip him up before he has taken more than a step or two.[27] This appears to be the sense of the common reading here, the adjective *euperistatos*. "Some have indeed fancifully rendered it 'the sin which men admire,' inasmuch as *peristatos* may convey the sense of being gaped at.[28] But that supposition is utterly foreign to the context. The surest clue to the expression presents itself in the twofold meaning of *peristasis* and its cognate verb, which has been explicitly noticed both by Epictetus (ii.6) and Marcus Aurelius (ix.13). It can either indicate the *circumstantia* or surroundings of a person or event, or else be used in a pejorative acceptation of a state of beleaguerment, of exigencies and straits, in like fashion with *thlipsis,* 'a squeeze,' or the Latin *angustiae.* This latter sense dominates our *euperistatos.*" So writes E. K. Simpson,[29] adding that a constricting environment "may work for good or ill." "The difference in effect," he says, "is akin to that of a girdle or a shackle respectively. The girdle braces its wearer, the shackle impedes him. *Euperistatos* presents the latter spectacle by way of warning, the picture of *besetting* sin that has become a household word and a salutary admonition to the Christian athlete. The sin *so prone to hamper* or *trammel* would be our version," he concludes.

The alternative reading *euperispastos,* attested by our oldest extant witness for the text of the epistle, would bear the sense "easily distracting" in this context.[30] Anything that distracts an athlete from the contest in which he is competing will quickly put him out of the running.

27. RSV "sin which clings so closely"; NEB (less accurately) "every sin to which we cling."

28. From the use of the verb περιίσταμαι in the sense of standing around and gaping at: "περίστατος is, from classical times onwards, a synonym for περίβλεπτος ('noted,' 'famous'). Consequently εὐπερίστατος (ov) is he, or that, which is 'surrounded by many,' primarily in admiration. This in fact is the only notion of our adjective for which evidence independent of Hebrews can be adduced" (G. Zuntz, *Text,* pp. 25f.).

29. *Words Worth Weighing in the Greek New Testament* (London, 1946), pp. 26f. He further instances Polybius, θλιβόμενος ὑπὸ τῆς περιστάσεως (2.48), where "he appears to be envisaging this image of a clogging encumbrance," and ἀπερίστατοι ῥαστῶναι (6.44), for which the rendering "unshackled *laissez-faire*" is suggested; Epictetus (4.1.159), who describes Diogenes as ἀπερίστατος ("unencumbered"); Diodorus Siculus, who "represents a throttling or stifling environment as συμπνιγὴς περίστασις" (3.51).

30. See p. 332, n. 2. Cf. ἀπερισπάστως in 1 Cor. 7:35 with the passive sense "undistractedly."

2 Everything that would encumber him or divert his attention must therefore be put away, and the athlete must keep his eye fixed on the goal toward which he is pressing. In 4 Macc. 17:9f. the unknown Alexandrine writer suggests as an epitaph for the Maccabaean martyrs the following words: "Here an aged priest and an aged woman and seven sons lie buried through the violence of a tyrant who wished to destroy the Hebrews' polity. They verily vindicated our nation, keeping their eyes fixed on God[31] and enduring torments even unto death."[32] In language reminiscent of this our author now exhorts his readers to keep their "eyes fixed on Jesus,[33] on whom faith depends from start to finish" (NEB). The earlier witnesses supply incentive in abundance; but in Jesus we have one who is *par excellence* "the faithful witness" (Rev. 1:5).[34] He is faith's "pioneer and perfecter" (RSV). In Greek the definite article stands before "faith"; in the AV/KJV, the ERV/ARV, and the RSV this is represented by the possessive pronoun "our." But more probably we should recognize here the regular Greek usage of the article before an abstract noun,[35] where English as regularly omits it. Jesus, that is to say, is presented as the one who has blazed the trail of faith and as the one who himself ran the race of faith to its triumphant finish. But in what sense is he the trail-blazer or pathfinder of faith? We can understand how he is called the pioneer of salvation in Heb. 2:10;[36] apart from him there is no Savior. We can understand, too, how for his people in the Christian age he provides a better example and incentive in running the race of faith than all who went before him. But when we consider that they did go before him, how can he be called the *pioneer* of faith? Our author's answer might well be that they did not really go before him; *he* went before *them* as truly as he has gone before us. "Jesus, who saved a people out of the land of Egypt" (as Jude most probably says),[37] who accompanied and nourished that same people in the wilderness (as Paul quite explicitly says),[38] is perhaps envisaged here as having led all the people of God, from earliest times, along the path of faith, although, since his incarnation and passion, his personal example makes his leadership available to his people in a way that was impossible before. Moreover, since our author

---

31. Gk. εἰς θεὸν ἀφορῶντες.

32. Gk. μέχρι θανάτου. Cf. μέχρις αἵματος in v. 4 below (p. 342 with nn. 62-64).

33. Gk. ἀφορῶντες εἰς 'Ἰησοῦν. Cf. 11:26, ἀποβλέπω (p. 312, n. 190).

34. Cf. Rev. 3:14, where Jesus speaks in the rôle of "the Amen, the faithful and true witness."

35. Especially where, as here, the substantives which govern "faith" in the genitive case themselves have the article: τὸν τῆς πίστεως ἀπχηγὸν καὶ τελειωτήν.

36. For ἀρχηγός see p. 77, n. 50; p. 80, n. 60. In *Acts of Thomas* 39 Jesus is the "true and undefeated athlete (ἀθλητής)."

37. Jude 5 (see p. 97 with n. 46).

38. 1 Cor. 10:3f. (see p. 97).

clearly regards Jesus as the one to whom all the prophets and martyrs bore witness, from Abel who, "though dead, still speaks," right on to those who won their record through faith on the very eve of the Incarnation, Jesus could well be considered as having provided them in some degree with the incentive and encouragement they needed in running their race with patience, as he has provided his people ever since with similar incentive and encouragement in the fullest degree.

Not only is Jesus the pioneer of faith; in him faith has reached its perfection. "He trusts in God,"[39] they said as they stood by his cross; the implication was: "Much good his trust in God is doing him now!" The words, though not their implication, were truer than they knew. The whole life of Jesus was characterized by unbroken and unquestioning faith in his heavenly Father, and never more so than when in Gethsemane he committed himself to his Father's hands for the ordeal of the cross with the words: "not what I will, but what thou wilt" (Mark 14:36). It was sheer faith in God, unsupported by any visible or tangible evidence, that carried him through the taunting, the scourging, the crucifying, and the more bitter agony of rejection, desertion, and dereliction. "Come down from the cross, and we will believe," they said.[40] Had he come down, by some gesture of supernatural power, he would never have been hailed as the "perfecter of faith" nor would he have left any practical example for others to follow.

No; he "bore the cross, despising the disgrace."[41] To die by crucifixion was to plumb the lowest depths of disgrace; it was a punishment reserved for those who were deemed most unfit to live, a punishment for those who were subhuman. From so degrading a death Roman citizens were exempt by ancient statute; the dignity of the Roman name would be besmirched by being brought into association with anything as vile as the cross.[42] For slaves, and criminals of low degree, it was regarded as a suitable means of execution, and a grim deterrent to others. But this disgrace Jesus disregarded, as something not worthy to be taken into account when it was a question of his obedience to the will of God. So he brought faith to perfection by his endurance of the cross—and now the place of highest exaltation is his. The pioneer of

---

39. Matt. 27:43, echoing Ps. 22:8.

40. Mark 15:30, 32.

41. Gk. ὑπέμεινεν σταυρὸν αἰσχύνης καταφρονήσας. Christ is thus the supreme example of ὑπομονή as well as of πίστις. The martyrs under Antiochus are repeatedly said to have "despised" their sufferings for the sake of the law of God: thus "the seven brothers despised their pains even unto death" (τῶν μέχρι θανάτου πόνων ὑπερεφρόνησαν, 4 Macc. 13:1; cf. 6:9; 8:28; 14:1, 11; 16:2). Cf. p. 337, n. 32; p. 342, n. 63.

42. Cf. Cicero, *Pro Rabirio* 5: "Let the very mention of the cross be far removed not only from a Roman citizen's body, but from his mind, his eyes, his ears." Cf. Origen, *Commentary on Matthew* 27:22ff., L.T., *mors turpissima crucis* ("the utterly vile death of the cross"). See M. Hengel, *Crucifixion*, E.T. (London, 1977).

salvation has been made perfect through sufferings,[43] and has therefore taken his seat "at the right hand of the throne of God."[44] His exaltation there, with all that it means for his people's well-being and for the triumph of God's purpose in the universe, is "the joy set before him," for the sake of which[45] he submitted to shame and death.

It is not difficult to trace an affinity between the joy of which our author speaks here and the joy to which Jesus himself makes repeated reference in the upper room discourses of the Fourth Gospel. He tells his disciples there of his desire that his joy may be in them, so that their joy may be complete (John 15:11; cf. 16:20, 21, 22, 24); and in his high-priestly prayer he asks the Father "that they may have my joy fulfilled in themselves" (John 17:13). So here, "the joy set before him" is not something for himself alone, but something to be shared with those for whom he died as sacrifice and lives as high priest.[46] The throne of God, to which he has been exalted, is the place to which he has gone as his people's forerunner.[47] That is the goal of the pathway of faith; the Pioneer has reached it first, but others who triumph in the same contest will share it with him.[48] Our author would have found himself in perfect sympathy with the terms of the promise given to the Laodicean church in Rev. 3:21: "He who conquers, I will grant him to sit with me on my throne, as I also conquered and sat down with my Father on his throne."[49]

> Captain of Israel's host, and guide
>   Of all who seek the land above,
> Beneath Thy shadow we abide,
>   The cloud of Thy protecting love;
> Our strength, Thy grace; our rule, Thy word;
> Our end, the glory of the Lord.

---

43. Cf. 2:10; 5:8f.

44. Cf. 1:3; 8:1 (p. 180 with n. 2); 10:12. Here the tense is perfect (κεκάθικεν), indicating that he is still there; in the three other references it is aorist (ἐκάθισεν).

45. The preposition ἀντί has here the same force as in v. 16 below, where Esau sold his birthright for (ἀντί) a single helping of food. The interpretation according to which Christ accepted suffering and death *instead of* the joy which might otherwise have been his, whether a continuation of his preincarnate joy or joy without suffering in his incarnate life, is much less suitable in the context. It was in order to secure the joy set before him (τῆς προκειμένης αὐτῷ χαρᾶς) that he ran the race set before him (τὸν προκείμενον . . . ἀγῶνα). The "joy" here corresponds to the "glories" in 1 Pet. 1:11 ("the sufferings of Christ, and the glories that should follow them"; cf. Luke 24:26).

46. Cf. John 17:24: "Father, I desire that they also, whom thou hast given me, may be with me where I am, to behold my glory. . . ."

47. Cf. 6:20 (p. 155).

48. In 4 Macc. 17:18 the martyrs under Antiochus "now stand beside the divine throne and lead a blessed life" (cf. Rev. 7:9, 15).

49. Cf. Luke 22:29f.

By Thine unerring Spirit led,
   We shall not in the desert stray;
We shall not full direction need,
   Nor miss our providential way;
As far from danger as from fear,
While love, almighty love, is near.

We've no abiding city here,
   But seek a city out of sight;
Thither our steady course we steer,
   Aspiring to the plains of light,
Jerusalem, the saints' abode,
Whose founder is the living God.

Patient the appointed race to run,
   This weary world we cast behind;
From strength to strength we travel on
   The new Jerusalem to find;
Our labour this, our only aim,
To find the new Jerusalem.

Through Thee, who all our sins hast borne,
   Freely and graciously forgiven,
With songs to Zion we return,
   Contending for our native heaven;
That palace of our glorious King,
We find it nearer while we sing.

Raised by the breath of love divine,
   We urge our way with strength renewed;
The Church of the first-born to join
   We travel to the mount of God,
With joy upon our heads to rise,
And meet our Captain in the skies.[50]

3 Christ has thus become his people's supreme inspirer of faith. When they become weary on the way, and grow faint at heart because there seems no end to the trials they have to endure, let them consider[51] him. He suffered uncomplainingly the hostility and malevolence of sinful people; the recipients of this epistle had not been called upon to endure anything like their Master's sufferings.

The variant reading, which described our Lord's opponents as "sinners

---

50. C. Wesley. See W. G. Johnsson, "The Pilgrimage Motif in the Book of Hebrews," *JBL* 97 (1978), pp. 239-51.

51. Gk. ἀναλογίσασθε (the only NT instance of this verb); it conveys the idea of comparison as well as considering, and thus goes beyond πατανοήσατε of 3:1.

against themselves,"[52] for all the strength of its attestation does not seem to have much point in this context. Attempts to give it point—such as the observation that "He, whom we so often 'contradict,' is our true self"[53]—do not commend themselves as successful or convincing.

F. DISCIPLINE IS FOR SONS (12:4-11)

4 *In your struggle against[54] sin you have not yet[55] resisted to the point of shedding your blood.*
5 *You have forgotten the word of encouragement which addresses you as sons:[56]*

"*My son,[57] do not despise the Lord's discipline,*
and do not lose heart when you are reproved by him;
6 *for the Lord disciplines the one whom he loves, and chastises every son whom he receives.*"
7 *It is for discipline that you endure what you do.[58] God deals with you as sons. What son is there whom his father does not discipline?*
8 *But if you have no part in the discipline which is shared by all, then you are bastards and not trueborn sons.*
9 *Again, we had our natural fathers who disciplined us, and we paid them respect; shall we not much more[59] be submissive to the Father of our spirits[60] and so gain life?*
10 *Those fathers disciplined us for a few days as they thought fit, but our*

---

52. See p. 332, n. 5.

53. W. R. Inge, *Things New and Old* (London, 1933), p. 14.

54. Gk. ἀνταγωνιζόμενοι, for which p¹³ p⁴⁶ with 69 and a few other authorities have the simple verb ἀγωνιζόμενοι. The agonistic language is continued, although it is warfare with sin rather than a race to be run that is now envisaged.

55. Gk. οὔπω. D* L and a few minuscules, with the Armenian and Coptic versions, add γάρ ("for").

56. The following words are quoted from Prov. 3:11f., LXX (A-text).

57. Gk. υἱέ μου. D* 69 81 and some other minuscules with Clement, Augustine, and the Latin version of Origen omit μου, in harmony with the LXX.

58. Gk. εἰς παιδείαν ὑπομένετε, where (as far as the form is concerned) the verb may be either present indicative or present imperative. D reads the aorist imperative ὑπομείνατε (which is unambiguous) and makes it the first word in the sentence, for it attaches the phrase εἰς παιδείαν to the preceding quotation (so as to yield the sense: "and chastises every son whom he receives for discipline"). For εἰς, 35 241 and the majority of later minuscules, with the TR, read εἰ ("if"), whence AV/KJV "If ye endure chastening, God dealeth with you as sons." (This reading is probably influenced by the following conditional sentence in v. 8.)

59. Gk. οὐ πολὺ μᾶλλον. . . . After πολύ p¹³ p⁴⁶ D* 1739 add δέ, probably to balance the preceding μέν. "Proto-Alexandrian" reading though it is, this δέ is unacceptable (cf. G. Zuntz, *Text*, p. 189).

60. For πνευμάτων ("of spirits") the minuscule 440 reads πνευματικῶν ("of spiritual beings"), while 88 and a few others read πατέρων (as though the sense were "the Father of [our] fathers").

341

spiritual Father disciplines us for our advantage, so that we may receive a share in his holiness.

11 *No discipline*[61] *for the time being appears pleasant—indeed, it is painful. Later, however, it yields a peaceful harvest of righteousness for those who have been trained by it.*

4 In his endurance of the hostility of sinners Christ suffered death.[62] So too did many of the heroes of faith celebrated in ch. 11. Some of them are described as having "resisted even to the torments of death for the sake of the law."[63] The recipients of this epistle had in earlier days endured severe persecution for their faith, but they had not yet been called upon to seal their testimony with their blood.[64] (This, as we have seen, may give us some limited help in deciding who they were and at what time they could be addressed in these terms.)[65] They might yet have to meet fiercer trials than had come their way thus far; but this was no time to be discouraged, when they thought of others who remained steadfast amid sufferings much worse than theirs. They ought rather to realize that their present hardships were a token of their heavenly Father's love for them, and the means by which he was training them to be more truly his sons.

5-8 Let them recall the words of wisdom in Prov. 3:11f., and they would be able to view their troubles in their proper perspective. These words remind those who would be truly wise that when hardship is their lot they should accept it as God's method of training and disciplining them, and as a token that they are really his beloved sons and daughters.[66] A father would

---

61. Gk. πᾶσα δὲ παιδεία . . . οὐ δοκεῖ χαρᾶς εἶναι. . . . For δέ (*om* D* 048 104 *pc*) ℵ* P 33 1739 1881 *pc* read μέν, probably in anticipation of μέν in the following phrase πρὸς μὲν τὸ παρόν ("for the time being"). Cf. Zuntz, *Text*, p. 190.

62. Cf. Phil. 2:8, where he is said to have maintained his obedience to God μέχρι θανάτου ("unto death"); cf. other instances of this phrase listed in n. 63 below alongside μέχρις αἵματος here; also ἄχρι θανάτου, Rev. 2:10; 12:11.

63. Spoken of Eleazar in 4 Macc. 6:30, μέχρι τῶν τοῦ θανάτου βασάνων ἀντέστη . . . διὰ τὸν νόμον (with which cf. ἀντικατέστητε, "you have . . . resisted," here; cf. also 4 Macc. 17:14, p. 335 with n. 19, for ἀνταγωνιζόμενοι, "striving against," here). Cf. μέχρι θανάτου in 4 Macc. 13:1 (quoted p. 338, n. 41); 17:10 (quoted p. 337 with n. 32); similarly 4 Macc. 5:37; 6:21; 7:8, 16; 13:27; 15:10; 16:1; 17:7; also 2 Macc. 13:14, γενναίως ἀγωνίσασθαι μέχρι θανάτου περὶ νόμων . . . ("to contend nobly unto death for the laws . . .").

64. The phrase μέχρις αἵματος is used of mortal combat in Heliodorus, *Aethiopica* 8.8. Some commentators take the phrase in Heb. 12:4 as referring not to the yielding up of life in martyrdom but to engaging in a conflict which involves the risk of wounds (cf. J. Behm in *TDNT*, I, p. 173, *s.v.* αἷμα). In the light of 11:35-38 actual martyrdom seems much more probable. See also Riggenbach, *ad loc.* (ZK, p. 393).

65. See pp. 21, 268.

66. In the second half of Prov. 3:12 the LXX deviates from the MT, which reads: "Even as a father the son in whom he delights." The deviation is very slight: it consists in reading *ûkeʾāb* ("even as a father") as *weyakʾib* ("and inflicts pain on") or the like. The LXX may well repre-

spend much care and patience on the upbringing of a trueborn son whom he hoped to make a worthy heir; and at the time such a son might have to undergo much more irksome discipline than an illegitimate child for whom no future of honor and responsibility was envisaged, and who therefore might be left more or less to please himself.[67]

Philo quotes this passage from Proverbs to much the same effect as our author does. "So profitable a thing is some sort of hardship," he says, "that even its most humiliating form, servitude, is reckoned a great blessing."[68] Then he argues that Esau's servitude to his brother Jacob, foretold in their father Isaac's blessing, was intended for Esau's good, and continues: "For this reason, it seems to me, did one of Moses' disciples, a man whose name means 'peaceable,'[69] who is called Solomon in our ancestral tongue, say:

'Son, do not despise the Lord's discipline,
Nor faint when he reproves you;
For whom the Lord loves he disciplines,
And chastises every son whom he receives.'

So, then, reproof and admonition are counted such a good thing, that by their means confession of God becomes kinship with him; for what relationship is closer than that of a father to his son, or a son's to his father?"[70]

All sons have to be disciplined,[71] our author says; he has already said that even Christ, Son though he was, "learned obedience by what he suffered" (Heb. 5:8).[72]

9-10   Our earthly fathers, he continues, disciplined us[73] for the limited period of years which preceded our coming of age, and received proper respect from us. We accepted the discipline because it was their province to impose it and our duty to submit to it; they knew, or thought they knew, what

---

sent the original sense (cf. *Midrash Tehillim* on Ps. 94, in a reference to Prov. 3:12). On the general idea cf. R. Bultmann, *TDNT*, III, p. 647 with n. 13 (*s.v.* καυχάομαι).

67. A classical parallel to "you are bastards, and not sons" (ἄρα νόθοι καὶ οὐχ υἱοί ἐστε) is supplied by Aristophanes, *Birds* 1650-52, νόθος γὰρ εἶ κοὐ γνήσιος . . . ὤν γε ξένης γυναικός ("for you are illegitimate and no trueborn son, since your mother is a foreign woman"), where, however, the νόθος is the child of a mixed marriage which was not recognized as legal in Athens of the fifth century B.C.

68. Philo, *Preliminary Studies* 175.

69. Gk. εἰρηνικός (see p. 346 with n. 86, on v. 11). Solomon (Heb. *šᵉlōmōh*) is from the same root as *šālôm*, "peace" (see p. 159, n. 16); but it is unlikely that our author intends any allusion here to the etymology of Solomon's name.

70. Philo, *Preliminary Studies* 177.

71. Gk. παιδείας, ἧς μέτοχοι γεγόνασιν πάντες (v. 8), echoing πάντα υἱόν in the quotation from Proverbs in v. 6.

72. See pp. 130f. with nn. 65-69.

73. Lit. "we had the fathers of our flesh as our discipliners *or* correctors (παιδευτάς)"; παιδευτής occurs in one other place in the NT, in Rom. 2:20: "a corrector of the foolish."

was best for us and subjected us to the discipline which commended itself to them.[74] If our heavenly Father also imposes discipline on us, shall we not accept it willingly from him? Our earthly fathers may sometimes have been mistaken in their estimate of the discipline we needed; our heavenly Father, in the perfection of his wisdom and love, can be relied upon never to impose any discipline on us which is not for our good.[75] The supreme good he has in view for his children is this, that they should share his holiness.[76]

Here positive holiness of life is meant; the emphasis is rather different from that found earlier in the epistle where the sanctification procured for believers by the sacrifice of Christ is that cleansing of conscience which fits them to approach God in worship.[77] That was the initial gift of holiness; the holiness mentioned here is rather the goal for which God is preparing his people[78]—that entire sanctification which is consummated in their manifestation with Christ in glory.[79] But this consummation is not attained "sudden, in a minute"; as Paul and Barnabas told the young churches of South Galatia, "through many tribulations we must enter the kingdom of God" (Acts 14:22).

The designation of God as "the Father of our spirits"[80] is unique. We may compare it with the phrase "the God of the spirits of all flesh" in Num. 16:22; 27:16, and with the frequent designation of God as "the Lord of spirits" in the *Parables of Enoch* (1 Enoch 37:2, etc.).[81] But in the present context its force is plain: as "the fathers of our flesh" are our physical (or earthly) fathers, so "the Father of our spirits" is our spiritual (or heavenly) Father. To try to trace metaphysical implications in the phrase is unwarranted.

11 "Discipline, no doubt, is never pleasant; at the time it seems painful, but in the end it yields for those who have been trained by it the peaceful harvest of an honest life" (NEB). The pedagogical value of suffering finds classical expression in Elihu's interposition in the debate between Job and his friends (Job 32:2–37:24). Elihu does not speak the last or greatest word on suffering in the Old Testament, but he represents a marked advance on

74. Gk. κατὰ τὸ δοκοῦν αὐτοῖς (v. 10); NEB "according to their lights." The argument from earthly fathers to the heavenly Father appears repeatedly in the teaching of Jesus (cf. Matt. 7:9-11; Luke 11:11-13); in this connection G. K. Chesterton speaks of his "furious use of *a fortiori* argument" (quoted by H. J. Cadbury, *The Peril of Modernizing Jesus* [London, 1962], p. 58). Cf. p. 45, n. 6; p. 68, n. 4.

75. Cf. 1 Cor. 10:13; with the testing is given the power to endure it.

76. Gk. ἁγιότης (in the NT also at 2 Cor. 1:12); commoner NT words for this concept are ἁγιασμός (cf. v. 14) and ἁγιωσύνη.

77. Cf. 9:13; 10:10, 14, 29.

78. Cf. v. 14 (pp. 348f.).

79. Cf. 1 Thess. 5:23; Rom. 8:18, 21, 30; Col. 3:4.

80. Gk. τῷ πατρὶ τῶν πνευμάτων. The margin of the ERV/ARV rightly translates τῶν as "our."

81. Cf. also 2 Macc. 3:24, "the Sovereign of spirits and of all authority" (ὁ τῶν πνευμάτων καὶ πάσης ἐξουσίας δυνάστης).

the traditional position taken up by Job's three friends. If a man does not heed the admonition of God given in night-visions and the like then:

> "Man is also chastened with pain upon his bed,
>   and with continual strife in his bones;
> so that his life loathes bread,
>   and his appetite dainty food.
> His flesh is so wasted away that it cannot be seen;
>   and his bones which were not seen stick out.
> His soul draws near the Pit,
>   and his life to those who bring death.
> If there be for him an angel,
>   a mediator, one of the thousand,
>   to declare to man what is right for him;
> and he is gracious to him, and says,
>   'Deliver him from going down into the Pit,
>   I have found a ransom;
> let his flesh become fresh with youth;
>   let him return to the days of his youthful vigor';
> then man prays to God, and he accepts him,
>   he comes into his presence with joy.
> He recounts to men his salvation,
>   and he sings before men, and says:
> 'I sinned, and perverted what was right,
>   and it was not requited to me.
> He has redeemed my soul from going down into the Pit,
>   and my life shall see the light.'" (Job 33:19-28)

Similarly one of the psalmists could say:

> Before I was afflicted I went astray;
>   But now I keep thy word. . . .
> It is good for me that I was afflicted;
>   That I might learn thy statutes. (Ps. 119:67, 71)[82]

Our Lord bade his disciples rejoice when they were persecuted for righteousness' sake, because the kingdom of heaven was theirs (Matt. 5:10-12 par. Luke 6:22f.). The Christians of Thessalonica are similarly told that the persecutions endured by them, while they are a token of God's righteous judgment on their persecutors, are the means by which they themselves are fitted for the kingdom of God (2 Thess. 1:4-7).[83] So too, when four rabbis visited Rabbi Eliezer as he lay sick in bed, three of them praised him for his piety, but

---

82. Cf. also Lam. 3:19-39. Several further parallels, biblical and extrabiblical, are mentioned by Moffatt, ICC, *ad loc.*
83. Cf. 2 Pet. 2:9a.

Rabbi Aqiba comforted him with the assurance that "chastisements are precious"—and supported his statement by an argument which included a reference to the Proverbs of Solomon.[84] A twentieth-century restatement of much the same argument was made by C. S. Lewis in *The Problem of Pain.*[85]

It may be that our author's description of the "harvest of righteousness" as "peaceable" represents nothing more than a coincidence with Philo's explanation of Solomon's name as meaning "peaceable," in the quotation given above.[86] Even so, it is an interesting coincidence in view of our author's quotation of Prov. 3:11f. The person who accepts discipline at the hand of God as something designed by his heavenly Father for his good will cease to feel resentful and rebellious; he has "calmed and quieted" his soul,[87] which thus provides fertile soil for the cultivation of a righteous life, responsive to the will of God.

G. LET US THEN BE UP AND DOING (12:12-17)

12 *Therefore, strengthen your drooping arms and your paralyzed knees,*[88]

13 *and make*[89] *straight paths for your feet,*[90] *so that lame joints may not be dislocated but rather be healed.*

14 *Pursue peace*[91] *with everybody, and the sanctification apart from which no one will see the Lord.*

15 *See to it that no one falls short of the grace of God, and that no root*

---

84. TB *Sanhedrin* 101a. Aqiba argued from Prov. 25:1 that Hezekiah must have taught his young son Manasseh the proverbs of Solomon, but added that it was not this instruction which brought him to repentance but his affliction recorded in 2 Chron. 33:11ff. A different emphasis from Aqiba's is found in the words of the righteous martyr in *Leviticus Rabba* 32 (on Lev. 24:10) and *Mekhilta* on Ex. 20:6, "These wounds have endeared me to my Father in heaven" (based on a misinterpretation of Zech. 13:6).

85. "God whispers to us in our pleasure, speaks in our conscience, but shouts in our pains: it is His megaphone to rouse a deaf world" (C. S. Lewis, *The Problem of Pain* [London, 1940], p. 81). A harrowing personal experience later forced Lewis to recognize the inadequacy of this argument, as he acknowledged in *A Grief Observed* (London, 1961).

86. Cf. p. 343; εἰρηνικός is used in both places.

87. Cf. Ps. 131:2.

88. Cf. Isa. 35:3.

89. The weight of early Greek witnesses ($\mathfrak{p}^{46}$ ℵ* P 33 etc.) favors the present imperative ποιεῖτε, for which A D with the majority of later MSS and the TR have the aorist ποιήσατε. Prov. 4:26 (LXX) has the present imperative, but in the singular (ποίει). The aorist ποιήσατε may be due to assimilation with the tense of ἀνορθώσατε ("lift up") in v. 12; on the other hand, it could be argued that the aorist is stylistically better (cf. G. Zuntz, *Text*, p. 64).

90. Prov. 4:26, LXX. With the inferior reading ποιήσατε the clause makes a perfect hexameter: καὶ τροχιὰς ὀρθὰς ποιήσατε τοῖς ποσὶν ὑμῶν (in such a careful stylist as our author this might be regarded as an argument *against* ποιήσατε).

91. Cf. Ps. 34:14 = LXX 33:15 (quoted in 1 Pet. 3:11).

which produces bitter fruit springs up and troubles[92] *you, through the infection which many*[93] *contract from it.*

16 *Make sure that there is no fornicator among you, or any irreligious person like Esau, who sold his birthright for one helping of food.*

17 *You know*[94] *that when he later wished to inherit the blessing he was rejected, finding no opportunity for a change of mind, though he begged for it with tears.*

12-13   Reverting to his athletic figure of speech, our author bids his readers brace their flagging limbs and press on to the goal. Some of their number were feeling especially discouraged and disinclined to make the necessary effort; the others should do everything possible to help them. The exhortation is couched in Old Testament language—drawn partly from words of encouragement addressed to exiled Jews who felt that the promised deliverance and restoration would never come and partly, like the exhortation of vv. 5 and 6, from the book of Proverbs. The aptness of the Isaiah quotation needs no emphasizing:

> Strengthen the weak hands,
>   and make firm the feeble knees.[95]
> Say to those who are of a fearful heart,
>   "Be strong, fear not!
> Behold, your God will come. . . .
> He will come and save you." (Isa. 35:3f.)

The context of the quotation, if not the words actually reproduced, repeats the assurance of 10:37 that in "a very little while, the Coming One will come; he will make no delay." The precise meaning of the Hebrew verb in Prov. 4:26a is uncertain,[96] but the Septuagint is here used (with the singular num-

---

92. Gk. μή τις ῥίζα πικρίας ἄνω φύουσα ἐνοχλῇ, the last word of which seems to have risen by metathesis from ἐν χολῇ ("in gall") in Deut. 29:18 (LXX), μή τις ἐστιν ἐν ὑμῖν ῥίζα (A F add πικρίας) ἄνω φύουσα ἐν χολῇ καὶ πικρίᾳ. 𝔭46 perhaps read ἐν χολῇ here for ἐνοχλῇ. For ἐνοχλέω cf. Luke 16:18. See pp. 349f. with nn. 105-8.

93. Gk. δι' αὐτῆς μιανθῶσιν πολλοί. For δι' αὐτῆς (𝔭46 A H K P 048 33 *al*), as in 11:4; 12:11, ℵ D Ψ byz read διὰ ταύτης. Before πολλοί ℵ A 048 *al* prefix οἱ. The anarthrous reading is found in 𝔭46 D H Ψ 1739 byz TR (whence AV/KJV "and thereby many be defiled"). See p. 349 with n. 104. G. Zuntz regards the anarthrous reading as preferable (*Text*, pp. 53f.).

94. Gk. ἴστε, a classical form (cf. Eph. 5:5; Jas. 1:19), for which the NT usually has the Hellenistic οἴδατε (cf. the use of the classical ἴσασιν and not the Hellenistic οἴδασιν in Acts 26:4).

95. The LXX reads ἰσχύσατε χεῖρες ἀνειμέναι καὶ γόνατα παραλελυμένα, "Be strong, ye relaxed hands and palsied knees"; the quotation here approximates more closely to the Hebrew construction. For the form παρειμένας used by our author in place of LXX ἀνειμέναι cf. Sir. 25:23, χεῖρες παρειμέναι καὶ γόνατα παραλελυμένα . . . ("Drooping hands and weak knees are caused by the wife who does not make her husband happy").

96. Heb. *pallēs* (AV/KJV "ponder"; ERV/ARV "make level"; RSV "take heed to").

ber replaced by the plural) to urge the smoothing of the way[97] for those who are weak and spiritually lame, and who might be prevented from continuing their course if they were tripped up and permanently disabled. The verb translated "be put out of joint" (RSV, NEB) is rendered "be turned out of the way"[98] in the AV/KJV and the ERV/ARV, but dislocation, not deviation, is suggested by the following words, "but rather be healed." Sprains and similar injuries must be bound up, so that the whole community may complete the course without loss.

14 The athletic metaphor is now abandoned, and the same teaching is expressed in straightforward ethical terms.[99] "Pursue peace with everybody." We recall our Lord's benediction on the peacemakers, "for they shall be called sons of God" (Matt. 5:9), and Paul's injunction to the Roman Christians: "If possible, so far as it depends upon you, live peaceably with all" (Rom. 12:18).[100] It might not be possible, for their persecutors might refuse to countenance "peaceful coexistence" with them; but they themselves must remain peaceable in attitude and conduct and never take the initiative in stirring up strife. If this was their duty with regard to mankind in general, how much more was it their duty to "be at peace with one another" (Mark 9:50).

"The sanctification[101] apart from which no one will see the Lord" is, as the words themselves make plain, no optional extra in the Christian life but something which belongs to its essence. It is the pure in heart, and none but they, who shall see God (Matt. 5:8). Here, as in v. 10, practical holiness of life is meant, the converse of those things against which a warning is uttered in the verses which follow. We are reminded of Paul's words to the Thessalonians: "This is the will of God, your sanctification, that you abstain from fornication . . ." (1 Thess. 4:3)—for the things which are *unholy* effectively debar those who practice them from inheriting the kingdom of God (1 Cor. 6:9f.). Our author is as far as Paul was from encouraging antinomianism in his readers. Those who are called to be partakers of God's holiness must be holy themselves; this is the recurring theme of the Pentateuchal law of holiness, echoed again in the New Testament: "You shall therefore be

97. The Greek word here used for "path" (τροχιά) is found nowhere else in the NT, and in the LXX is confined to Proverbs (and Ezek. 27:19 in a different sense). Etymologically it means "wheel-track"; but that is not its meaning in the Greek Bible.

98. Gk. ἐκτραπῇ, second aorist passive subjunctive of ἐκτρέπω, lit. "turn out" or "turn away." The sense of "dislocation" is attested in Hippocrates and other medical writers.

99. Moffatt (ICC, *ad loc.*) points out a similar train of thought in *Test. Simeon* 5:2f.: "Make your hearts good before the Lord, and your ways straight before men, and you will find grace before the Lord and men. Beware, therefore, of fornication, for fornication is mother of all evils, separating from God, and bringing near to Beliar."

100. See also p. 346, n. 91.

101. Gk. ἁγιασμός, here only in this epistle (other NT occurrences are Rom. 6:19, 22; 1 Cor. 1:30; 1 Thess. 4:3, 4, 7; 2 Thess. 2:13; 1 Tim. 2:15; 1 Pet. 1:2). See p. 344, n. 76.

holy, for I am holy" (Lev. 11:45, etc.; cf. 1 Pet. 1:15f.). To see the Lord is the highest and most glorious blessing mortals can enjoy, but the beatific vision is reserved for those who are holy in heart and life.[102]

15 If such holiness is to be pursued, then care must be taken to detect and nip in the bud any tendency that would be inimical to it. Let them see to it that none of them fails to attain[103] the grace of God. If it is the grace of God that sets people's feet at the entrance of the pathway of faith, it is equally the grace of God that enables them to continue and complete that pathway. Paul too found it necessary to beg some of his converts not to "receive the grace of God in vain" (2 Cor. 6:1) and to warn others who had begun to run well but had come up against an obstacle at an early stage that they had "fallen away from grace" (Gal. 5:4, 7). "Grace for timely help" (4:16) is constantly available to the people of Christ, and Peter urges his readers to have their hope securely fixed "on the grace that is coming to you at the revelation of Jesus Christ" (1 Pet. 1:13). If nevertheless some of them fall short of the grace of God, it is not because his grace was inaccessible, but because they would not avail themselves of it, and have therefore failed to reach the goal which is attainable only by his grace— the vision of God of which our author has just spoken.

If some incipient sin manifests itself in their midst, it must be eradicated at once; if it is tolerated, this is a sure way of falling short of God's grace, for many, if not the whole community,[104] will then be contaminated. Such a sin is called a "root of bitterness,"[105] in language borrowed from Deut. 29:18, where Moses warns the Israelites against any inclination to fall into the idolatrous practices of Canaan, "lest there be among you a root bearing poisonous and bitter fruit" (lit. "breeding gall and wormwood").[106] Deut. 29:18 with its context plays a similar admonitory rôle in the literature of the Qumran community; for example, in one of the *Hymns of Thanksgiving* it is said of the opponents of the community: "A root breeding gall and worm-

---

102. Cf. Rev. 22:4. Philo regards the vision of God as the goal of the contemplative life; thus, commenting on the change of Jacob's name to Israel (which he interprets as "he who sees God," as though its etymology were Heb. *'iš rō'eh 'Ēl*), he says: "The task of him who sees God is not to leave the holy contest uncrowned, but to carry off the prizes of victory. And what garland composed of fairer flowers or more suited to its purpose could be woven for the victorious soul than that which will enable him to behold the Existent One with clear vision? Glorious indeed is the prize held out to the athlete-soul, that it should be blessed with eyes to apprehend clearly the One who alone is worthy to behold or to be beheld" (*On the Change of Names* 81f.).

103. Gk. ὑστερῶν ("falling short of").

104. Gk. πολλοί or οἱ πολλοί (on the text see p. 347, n. 93). With οἱ πολλοί may be compared Heb. *hā-rabbîm*, "the many," used in the Qumran literature to denote the general membership of the community; but no closer contact can be inferred from such a comparison. Cf. also τὸ πλῆθος in Acts 4:32, etc., and οἱ πλείονες in 2 Cor. 2:6.

105. NEB "no bitter, noxious weed."

106. Cf. Lam. 3:19, LXX, πικρία καὶ χολή μου μνησθήσεται ("my wormwood and gall will be remembered"); Acts 8:23, εἰς χολὴν πικρίας ("in the gall of bitterness").

wood is in their thoughts; and in the stubbornness of their hearts they go astray, and inquire of thee amid their idols."[107] But perhaps the best commentary on our author's words here is his earlier warning in Heb. 3:12: "See to it, brothers, that there is not in any of you an evil heart of unbelief, deserting the living God."[108]

16 In telling them to make sure that they have no fornicator among them, he may conceivably be following Old Testament usage in employing this terminology to denote idolatry or apostasy;[109] but most probably he has in mind the literal sense of the word. It may be that Esau is mentioned only as an example of an "irreligious person,"[110] since in the Old Testament record Esau is not charged with fornication—unless the meaning of the term be stretched to cover his marriage with two daughters of Heth, who made life bitter for his parents (Gen. 26:34f.).[111] Postbiblical tradition, however, makes Esau a vicious character. Philo interprets the statement that "Esau was a skillful hunter, a man of the field" (Gen. 25:27) to mean that "vice, which hunts after the passions, is unfit by nature to dwell in the city of virtue, but pursues a boorish and undisciplined life in complete senselessness."[112] Elsewhere he says, with reference to the description of Esau in Gen. 27:11, that "the 'hairy man' is the unrestrained, lecherous, impure and unholy man."[113] The Palestinian Targum on Gen. 25:29 enlarges on Esau's coming home exhausted on the day he sold Jacob his birthright by saying that "in that day he had committed five transgressions," one of which consisted in adultery with a betrothed maiden. Similar accusations against him are recorded in other places in rabbinical literature.[114] Whether our author had Esau in mind as a fornicator is not at all certain;[115] it is certain, however, that he judged it nec-

107. 1QH 4.14. The words of Deut. 29:19, "I shall be safe, though I walk in the stubbornness of my heart," are quoted in 1QS 2.13f. with reference to the violator of the Qumran covenant; cf. p. 188 with n. 48.

108. Cf. p. 99, with n. 60 (the "evil root" of 4 Ezra mentioned there is relevant to the present context too).

109. Judg. 2:17, etc.

110. Gk. βέβηλος ("profane"), applied in the LXX to Zedekiah because of his breach of oath to the king of Babylon (Ezek. 21:25).

111. In Jub. 25:1 Rebekah complains that all the deeds of Esau's two Canaanite wives "are fornication and lust"; in v. 8 Jacob tells her that Esau has often urged him to marry a sister of his Canaanite wives, but that he has always refused, "for with regard to lust and fornication Abraham my father gave me many commandments" (v. 7).

112. *Leg. Alleg.* 3.2.

113. *Questions and Answers on Genesis* 4.201.

114. Cf. *Genesis Rabba* 70d, 72a; *Exodus Rabba* 116a.

115. Delitzsch *(ad loc.)* says that if our author had meant to designate Esau as βέβηλος only, and not πόρνος, he would have written μή τις πόρνος ἢ ἢ βέβηλος. But since he leaves the subjunctive of the verb "to be" to be understood, we cannot be sure where he would have placed it if he had expressed it. Westcott *(ad loc.)* is more probably right in referring βέβηλος only of the two words to Esau; cf. E. Elliot, "Esau," *ExT* 29 (1917-18), pp. 44f.

essary to warn his readers against harboring any such person, for he reverts to the subject again in Heb. 13:4: "God will judge fornicators and adulterers."

The incident which he does recall from Esau's career illustrates not fornication but "profaneness" or "irreligion," that is to say, the lack of any sense of spiritual values. Nothing is related of him in Genesis which is positively to his discredit; he is the "hunting, shooting, fishing" type of man whose chief concerns are the material interests of the moment. When Jacob by deceit received the blessing intended for Esau, Esau fell into a towering rage, and threatened his brother's life; but he soon forgot his resentment, together (possibly) with the cause of it. Compared with such a sportsman, Jacob in some respects cuts a poor figure. Yet, even in his most disreputable moments, Jacob showed an appreciation of the heritage promised by God to his family and a determination not to miss that heritage; and at the end, as we have seen, he won his record for faith.[116] On the other hand, so little did Esau value the birthright with which that heritage was bound up that in a moment of hunger he sold it "for a mess of pottage."[117] "Thus Esau despised his birthright" is the summing up of that incident in the Old Testament record (Gen. 25:34).

17 He did, indeed, regret his hasty action later. Our author sees a close link between his despising of his birthright in Gen. 25:29-34 and his losing the blessing due to the firstborn in Gen. 27:1-40. It may be implied in the Genesis narrative itself that if Esau had not sold his birthright Jacob would not have found it so easy to steal the blessing from him. But when he came in from the field to receive the blessing, he found himself "rejected,"[118] and though he wept loudly and bitterly[119] there was no way of retrieving the situation. His father could not and would not call back the blessing pronounced on Jacob: "yes, and he shall be blessed" (Gen. 27:33). The ARV ("he found no place for a change of mind *in his father*") interprets the "repentance" for which Esau found no opportunity as a change of mind on Isaac's part, but this is not the natural construction of the words. "He found no way open for second thoughts" (NEB). The pronoun "it"[120] in the clause "though he begged for it with tears" most probably refers to the blessing.

---

116. 11:20f. (p. 305).

117. This proverbial phrase occurs in the *Pilgrimage of Perfection* (1526), in the headings to Gen. 25 in the Bibles of 1537, 1539, and 1560, and in the last paragraph of the AV/KJV translators' address to the reader. The termination -ετο in the aorist ἀπέδετο, "sold" (classical ἀπέδοτο), illustrates the Hellenistic tendency for the ω-conjugation to encroach on the μι-conjugation.

118. Gk. ἀπεδοκιμάσθη.

119. Although Esau's weeping (Gen. 27:38b, MT) is omitted from the best authenticated LXX text, his "exceedingly great and bitter cry" (v. 34) would give adequate ground for our author's statement about his tears.

120. Gk. αὐτήν, which might refer to μετανοίας ("repentance"), as the NEB takes it ("he found no way open for second thoughts, although he strove, to the point of tears, to find one"),

The application is plain; it is a reinforcement of the warning given at an earlier stage in the argument, that after apostasy no second repentance is possible. "Let us therefore fear lest, when the promise of entering into his rest has been left open, any of you should turn out to have fallen short of it" (4:1).[121]

H. THE EARTHLY SINAI AND THE HEAVENLY ZION (12:18-24)

18 *The mountain*[122] *to which you have come is not one which can be touched,*[123] *a mountain burning with fire, amid darkness, gloom, and storm,*[124]

---

but more probably to εὐλογίαν ("blessing"), in the light of Gen. 27:34, 38. Cf. R. T. Watkins, "The New English Bible and the Translation of Hebrews xii. 17," *ExT* 73 (1961-62), pp. 29f.; he suggests a slight modification of the NEB wording: "you know that although he wanted afterwards [μετέπειτα, here only in the NT] to claim the blessing, he was rejected; though he begged for it to the point of tears, he found no way open for second thoughts." The ARV mg. and the ERV indicate that what Esau sought was the blessing by printing the clause "for he found no place of repentance" as a parenthesis.

121. One commentator on Hebrews, G. H. Lang, was led by this mention of the Esau incident to his distinctive interpretation that the "rest" which may be forfeited in 3:11–4:11, like the "blessing" or "grace of God" of which some may fall short here, is the millennial reign of the resurrected saints with Christ (cf. his *Firstborn Sons: their Rights and Risks* [London, 1936], p. 217 et passim). See p. 107 with n. 21.

122. There is no word corresponding to "mountain" in the best-attested Greek text at this point (ὄρει appears here in D Ψ byz vg^cl syr^hcl), but it is to be understood here from v. 22 (Σιὼν ὄρει). As far as the construction goes, the absence of ὄρει makes possible the rendering of the ARV mg., "a palpable and kindled fire" (ψηλαφωμένῳ καὶ κεκαυμένῳ πυρί), which is preferred by Westcott; but the idea of a fire which could be "handled" is strange; the contrast is between the material mountain of Sinai which could indeed be touched (since the people were forbidden to touch it) and the spiritual and heavenly hill of Zion.

123. Gk. ψηλαφωμένῳ. The verb ψηλαφάω is not used in the LXX to render Heb. *nāga'* ("touch") in Ex. 19:12 (where the LXX uses ἅπτομαι and θιγγάνω); its verbal adjective ψηλαφητός is used, however, in Ex. 10:21, of the "darkness which may be felt." In our author's mind the darkness of the ninth plague of Egypt may have been associated with the "thick darkness" of Sinai. E. C. Selwyn ("On ψηλαφωμένῳ in Heb. 12:18," *JTS* 12 [1911], pp. 133f.) offers the conjectural emendation πεφεψαλωμένῳ, "calcined" (cf. Aeschylus, *Prometheus Vinctus* 363); he refers to A. P. Stanley's description of "the vast heaps, as of calcined mountains," of "what seemed to be the ruins, the cinders, of mountains calcined to ashes" (*Sinai and Palestine* [London, 1887], pp. 21, 71), and suggests that the author of Hebrews may have visited the site of Sinai. This emendation is quite unnecessary (and indeed improbable), as is also that offered by E. N. Bennett ("Hebrews XII.18," *Classical Review* 6 [1892], p. 263) of ὕψει νενεφωμένῳ ("a beclouded height") in place of ψηλαφωμένῳ—an emendation which, he says, "would fit in exactly with the Old Testament accounts, which represent the summit as burnt with fire, while lower down it was enveloped in a dense cloud." On ψηλαφάω here see E. Norden, *Agnostos Theos* (Leipzig, 1912), p. 15.

124. Gk. γνόφῳ καὶ ζόφῳ καὶ θυέλλῃ. In Deut. 4:11 the LXX uses the three words σκότος γνόφος θύελλα for the dark storm-cloud in which God was enshrouded on Sinai (cf. Ex. 10:22;

19 *with trumpet blast*[125] *and the sound of words, which caused the hearers to beg that nothing further might be said.*[126]

20 *They could not bear the command: "Even if a beast touches the mountain, it is to be stoned."*[127]

21 *Indeed, so fearful was the sight that Moses said, "I am filled with fear*[128] *and trembling."*[129]

22 *No: the mountain to which you have come is Mount Zion; you have come to the city of the living God, the heavenly Jerusalem, to myriads of angels*[130] *in festal array,*[131]

23 *to the assembly of firstborn ones who are enrolled in heaven,*[132] *to God the judge of all, to the spirits*[133] *of the righteous who have attained perfection,*[134]

24 *and to Jesus, the mediator of a new covenant, and to the sprinkled blood which has something better*[135] *to say than Abel's.*[136]

18-19 Our author reverts to the contrast already pointed in 2:2-4 between

---

20:21). It may be under the influence of this passage that several authorities here read σκότει (𝔭⁴⁶ Ψ) or σκότῳ (ℵ² D² 4 1739 byz) for ζόφῳ (ℵ* A C D* P *al*). (Only here in the NT does γνόφος or θύελλα occur; for ζόφος cf. Jude 6, 13; 2 Pet. 2:4, 17.)

125. Gk. ἤχῳ. The LXX (Ex. 19:16, 19; 20:18) has φωνή (or φωναί) τῆς σάλπιγγος, but the verb ἠχέω appears in Ex. 19:16, "the voice of the trumpet sounded (ἤχει) loud." The substantive ἦχος is probably used here by our author rather than φωνή since φωνή is used in the following phrase for the voice of God on Sinai (as in the LXX of Ex. 19:5, 13, 16, etc.).

126. Gk. παρῃτήσαντο μὴ προστεθῆναι αὐτοῖς λόγον. The negative particle μή is idiomatic, but not essential to the sense; it is lacking in ℵ* P and a few other MSS.

127. Ex. 19:13. A few MSS, followed by the TR, complete the quotation by adding ἢ βολίδι κατατοξευθήσεται ("or thrust through with a dart," AV/KJV).

128. Deut. 9:19. See p. 354, n. 140.

129. Gk. ἔντρομος (ℵ D* ἔκτρομος).

130. Gk. μυριάσιν ἀγγέλων ("myriads of angels"), for which D* reads μυρίων ἁγίων ἀγγέλων ("ten thousand holy angels"); cf. Deut. 33:2; Jude 14.

131. Gk. πανηγύρει, which should probably be taken closely with the preceding phrase as a circumstantial dative ("myriads of angels in festal array"). This construction is favored by those MSS which indicate punctuation, and by the Latin and Syriac versions. Moffatt deduces from citations in Ambrose, Augustine, Rufinus's Latin translation of Origen, and from the Bohairic Coptic version, that there was a variant reading πανηγυριζόντων (so F. Blass). See H. Seesemann, *TDNT*, V, p. 772 (*s.v.* πανήγυρις).

132. Gk. ἀπογεγραμμένων ἐν οὐρανοῖς. The Byzantine text has the order ἐν οὐρανοῖς ἀπογεγραμμένων, which is shown by 0228 to go back to the end of the fourth century (G. Zuntz, *Text*, p. 160).

133. Gk. πνεύμασι, for which D* and the Sixtine Vulgate read the singular πνεύματι.

134. Gk. τετελειωμένων, for which D* and Hilary read the curious variant τεθεμελιωμένων ("founded").

135. Gk. κρεῖττον, for which 𝔭⁴⁶ 33 and a few other MSS, followed by the TR, read κρείττονα ("better things," AV/KJV).

136. Gk. παρὰ τὸν Ἄβελ, "in comparison with Abel," a compendious construction for "in comparison with Abel's." But 𝔭⁴⁶ L and some other MSS read παρὰ τὸ Ἄβελ, "in comparison with that of Abel," a reading preferred by C.-H. Hunzinger, *TDNT*, VI, pp. 981f. (*s.vv.* ῥαντίζω, ῥαντισμός).

the giving of the law and the reception of the gospel. Awesome as were the circumstances of the giving of the law in Moses' day, more awesome by far are the privileges associated with the gospel, if they are despised or refused. Those who wholeheartedly believe the gospel and gladly embrace its privileges need have no fear; they are urged to enter the heavenly sanctuary with full confidence through the blood of Jesus.[137] The stern note of warning is for those who, having begun to make an approach, fall back. They are reminded that the consequences of despising the gospel are even more dreadful than were the consequences of despising the law.

The description of the terrors of Sinai is based on the account in Ex. 19:16-19; 20:18-21, with Moses' recollection of the scene forty years later in Deut. 4:11f. The mountain was so charged with the holiness of the God who manifested himself there that for man or beast to touch it meant certain death. "Mount Sinai was wrapped in smoke, because the LORD descended upon it in fire; and the smoke of it went up like the smoke of a kiln, and the whole mountain quaked greatly. And as the sound of the trumpet grew louder and louder, Moses spoke, and God answered him in thunder" (Ex. 19:18f.).[138] Then, "when all the people perceived the thunderings and the lightnings and the sound of the trumpet and the mountain smoking, the people were afraid and trembled; and they stood afar off, and said to Moses, 'You speak to us, and we will hear; but let not God speak to us, lest we die'" (Ex. 20:18f.).

20 If even a beast accidentally touched or trespassed on the hill of God, it contracted so much holiness from it that it too became highly dangerous to touch; it must be killed from a safe distance—stoned, or (as the AV/KJV adds, reproducing a later text amplified on the basis of the Exodus narrative) "thrust through with a dart."[139]

21 And not only were the people terrified; even Moses, privileged as he was to press up into the thick darkness where God was, was filled with numinous awe at the *mysterium tremendum et fascinans*. His words, "I am filled with fear and trembling,"[140] are not recorded in the Pentateuchal descriptions of the Sinai theophany; the closest Old Testament parallel is in Deut. 9:19, where he reminds the people of his supplication for them after the incident of the golden calf: "For I was afraid of the anger and hot displeasure, which Yahweh bore against you, so that he was ready to destroy

---

137. 10:19-22.

138. On the theophany at Sinai see B. S. Childs, *Exodus*, OTL (London, 1974), pp. 340-84.

139. A. H. McNeile explains the injunction to kill the trespassing beast from a distance in that to touch it would involve transgressing the barrier (*The Book of Exodus*, WC [London, 1931], p. 112).

140. Gk. ἔκφοβός εἰμι καὶ ἔντρομος. Cf. 1 Macc. 13:2, "the people were trembling and fearful" (ἔντρομος καὶ ἔμφοβος).

you." Another parallel appears in Stephen's speech, where in face of the theophany at the burning bush "Moses trembled, and did not dare to look" (Acts 7:32). Our author may have been acquainted with a haggadic account of the Sinai theophany which made explicit mention of Moses' fear and trembling on this occasion too.

22 The events of the Exodus and the wilderness wanderings, as we have seen before, are treated in the apostolic age as parables of Christian experience.[141] But Christians have come to no sacred mountain which can be touched physically but to the heavenly dwelling-place of God, the true and eternal Mount Zion. "You have come" may denote their conversion to Christianity; the Greek verb is that from which "proselyte" is derived,[142] and while it is such a common verb that normally no such implication could be read into it, the particular form used in this particular context carries with it overtones of conversion. Philo uses this same perfect tense of the verb in question when, in a meditation on Moses' vision of God in Ex. 33:13-23, he says that all kindred souls to Moses who refuse fables and embrace truth obtain the approval of God, whether this has been their attitude from the beginning or they have been converted to it subsequently.[143] These last, he goes on, Moses "calls 'proselytes' because they 'have come to' a new and God-loving commonwealth."[144] So, by virtue of their accepting the gospel, the readers of this epistle had come to that spiritual realm some of whose realities are detailed in the following clauses.

Mount Zion was the site of the Jebusite stronghold which David captured and made his royal residence in the seventh year of his reign.[145] He made it the religious center of his kingdom by installing there "the ark of God, which is called by the name of Yahweh of hosts, who sits enthroned on the cherubim" (2 Sam. 6:2). Thus Zion became the earthly dwelling-place of God, "the city which Yahweh had chosen out of all the tribes of Israel, to put his name there" (1 Kings 14:21). For (in the words of an Asaphite psalm):

> He chose the tribe of Judah,
>   Mount Zion, which he loves.
> He built his sanctuary like the high heavens,
>   like the earth, which he has founded for ever. (Ps. 78:68f.)

When later Solomon built his temple on the hill to the north of Zion, and in-

---

141. See pp. 96ff.

142. Gk. προσεληλύθατε, προσήλυτος.

143. *Special Laws* 1.51.

144. Gk. τούτους δὲ καλεῖ προσηλύτους ἀπὸ τοῦ προσεληλυθέναι κτλ. The perfect tense here as in our Hebrews passage is significant, denoting a permanent status resulting from the conversion event.

145. 2 Sam. 5:6-9.

stalled the sacred ark there, the name Zion was extended to include this further area, and became in practice synonymous with Jerusalem—

Jerusalem, built as a city
  which is bound firmly together,
to which the tribes go up,
  the tribes of Yahweh,
as was decreed for Israel,
  to give thanks to the name of Yahweh. (Ps. 122:3f.)

As the earthly Zion was the meeting point for the tribes of the old Israel, so the heavenly Zion is the meeting point for the new Israel.[146] Their heritage, the place of their solemnities, is "the city of the living God, the heavenly Jerusalem." If the movable tabernacle in the wilderness was constructed according to the pattern of the sanctuary on high, so the temple and city of Jerusalem were material copies of eternal archetypes.[147] Both in Jewish and in Christian thought the heavenly counterpart of the earthly Jerusalem is familiar—the rabbis inferred the existence of the heavenly archetype from the words of Ps. 122:3 (quoted above), which they rendered: "Jerusalem, which is built like the city that is its fellow"[148]—the oldest approximately datable reference to it being Paul's words in Gal. 4:26, "the Jerusalem above is free, and she is our mother."[149] In the Syriac *Apocalypse of Baruch*, which is to be dated soon after A.D. 70, Baruch is told on the eve of the destruction of the First Temple that this is not the true city of God; the true city was revealed by God to Adam before his fall, to Abraham when God made a covenant with him, and to Moses at the same time as he was shown the pattern in the mount.[150] In Rev. 21:2f. "the holy city, new Jerusalem," which has existed eternally in heaven, is seen coming down to earth, so that henceforth "the

---

146. Cf. Rev. 14:1, where "Mount Zion" on which the Lamb stands with the hundred and forty-four thousand is the heavenly Zion, since they sing their new song "before the throne and before the four living creatures and before the elders" (v. 3). But G. W. Buchanan infers that it was to the neighborhood of the earthly Zion that the people addressed in Hebrews had come: it is here called "the heavenly Jerusalem" as an affirmation of "its divine origin" (*To the Hebrews*, AB [Garden City, NY, 1972], p. 222).

147. Cf. 1 Chron. 28:11-19, where the plan of the temple given by David to Solomon is made clear "by the writing from the hand of Yahweh concerning it."

148. Heb. k^e'îr šeḥubb^{e}rāh lāh, vocalized as k^e'îr šaḥāḇērāh lāh. Cf. Targum and *Midrash Tehillim* on Ps. 122:3.

149. The manner in which Paul introduces the figure suggests that it was no novelty to him, nor yet, perhaps, to his readers. Cf. p. 293, n. 85.

150. 2 Baruch 4:2-6 (cf. 32:2-4). According to TB *Hagigah* 12b, Rabbi Meir (*c.* A.D. 150) said that of the seven heavens, the fourth is called z^eḇûl, "in which are Jerusalem and the temple, and an altar is built, at which Michael the great prince stands and offers sacrifice, as it is said: 'I have surely built thee a house of habitation, a place for thee to dwell in for ever' [1 Kings 8:13]. And how do we know that it [z^eḇûl] is called heaven? Because it is written: 'Look down from heaven, and behold from the habitation of thy holiness and of thy glory' [Isa. 63:15]."

dwelling of God is with men, and he will dwell with them" as their covenant-God.[151] This is not our author's perspective: the new Jerusalem has not yet come down to mankind, but in the spiritual realm they already have access to it. They have become fellow-citizens with Abraham of that well-founded city for which he looked; it is the city or commonwealth which comprises the whole family of faith, God's true dwelling-place.[152] Even now this city has not been manifested in its fulness; it is still in one sense "the city which is to come" (13:14), but the privileges of its citizenship are already enjoyed by faith. The people of God are still a pilgrim people, treading the "highways to Zion," but by virtue of his sure promise they have already arrived there in spirit. Our author may retain the symbolism of "up there" when he speaks of God, but he makes it clear that his people need not climb the heavenly steeps to seek him, for he is immediately accessible to each believing heart, making his dwelling in the fellowship of the faithful.[153]

You have come, he continues, "to myriads of angels in festal array."[154] The myriads of angels remind us of the "ten thousands of holy ones" who attended God at the giving of the law on Sinai (Deut. 33:2), or of the "thousand thousands" whom Daniel saw serving God, and "ten thousand times ten

---

151. Cf. Rev. 3:12; 4 Ezra 7:26; 8:52 (quoted above, p. 110); 13:36; 1 Enoch 90:29; *Test. Dan* 5:12, for the New Jerusalem of the future. The Qumran texts include several fragments of a New Jerusalem apocalypse—an Aramaic work based mainly on Ezek. 40–48. The fragments from Caves 1, 2, and 5 have been published (1Q 32, 2Q 24, and 5Q 15); see *DJD,* I (Oxford, 1955), pp. 134f.; III, Texte (Oxford, 1962), pp. 84-89, 184-93. Just how the Qumran community envisaged the New Jerusalem cannot be satisfactorily determined until the fragments from Caves 4 and 11 are published. The Cave 2 fragments at least seem to describe a literal city with material temple and animal sacrifices (like the purified city and temple of 1QM 2); but all this may have been given a spiritual meaning. Cf. M. Baillet, *DJD,* III, Texte, p. 85: "It must moreover be remembered that for the sect the temple is susceptible of identification with the community (cf. 1QS viii. 5-9; ix. 5-6) and that it is a replica of heaven: see *Revue Biblique* lxiii, 1956, p. 394." For the new temple cf. Tob. 13:16-18 (perhaps based on Isa. 54:11f.). See J. Strugnell, "The angelic liturgy at Qumran," *VT Supplement* 7 (Leiden, 1960), p. 320; B. Gärtner, *The Temple and the Community in Qumran and the New Testament,* SNTSM 1 (Cambridge, 1965).

152. See p. 293, n. 85 (on 11:10).

153. Cf. 3:6 (pp. 93f.). Since in the OT God dwells in Zion (Ps. 87:1; Isa. 18:7; 31:9; Amos 1:2; Mic. 4:7f.) and "with him also that is of a contrite and humble spirit" (Isa. 57:15; cf. 66:1f.), the identification of the spiritual abode of God with the community of his people is not farfetched. See further E. Lohse, *TDNT,* VII, pp. 282-87 (*s.v.* Σινά); G. Fohrer and E. Lohse, *TDNT,* VII, pp. 292-338 (*s.v.* Σιών); Ps.-Cyprian, *De montibus Sina et Sion;* Strack-Billerbeck, *Kommentar zum Neuen Testament,* III (Munich, 1926), p. 796; K. L. Schmidt, "Jerusalem als Urbild und Abbild," *Eranos Jahrbuch* 18 (1950), pp. 207-48; J. C. De Young, *Jerusalem in the New Testament* (Kampen, 1960); T. C. Vriezen, *Jahwe en zijn Stad* (Amsterdam, 1962); J. Schreiner, *Sion-Jerusalem: Jahwes Königssitz* (Munich, 1963); N. W. Porteous, "Jerusalem-Zion: The Growth of a Symbol," in *Living the Mystery* (Oxford, 1967), pp. 93-111; S. Talmon, "The Biblical Concept of Jerusalem," *Journal of Ecumenical Studies* 8 (1971), pp. 300-316; B. C. Ollenburger, *Zion, the City of the Great King: A Theological Symbol of the Jerusalem Cult* (Sheffield, 1987).

154. For the construction and punctuation see p. 353, n. 131.

thousand" who stood before him (Dan. 7:10).[155] In the Qumran *Hymn of the Initiants* a person who knows himself justified by God proclaims that God has caused him and his fellow-believers "to inherit the portion of the Holy Ones; he has joined their assembly to the sons of heaven, to be a council of the community, a foundation of the holy building, an eternal planting in all time to come."[156] Our author goes farther than this. He knows that the attendant angels are sent to minister to the heirs of salvation;[157] how exalted the status of the heirs of salvation is may be gauged from the fact that the Son of God passed by angels in order to partake of flesh and blood with mankind.[158] When, therefore, believers come to the myriads of angels it is not to worship *them*, but to worship the God whose servants they are.[159]

23 How then are we to understand the "assembly of firstborn ones who are enrolled in heaven"? One interpretation is that this is another way of designating the elect angels, called "firstborn" because they were created before human beings.[160] So, when Hermas asked about the six young men whom he saw building the tower, the ancient lady told him that they were "the holy angels of God who were first created"—the myriads of other men whom he saw bringing up stones for the building being also "holy angels of God," but inferior in rank to the six.[161] But against this interpretation is the description of these "firstborn" ones as "enrolled in heaven." The idea of enrollment in the heavenly book is regularly associated with human beings.[162] "Rejoice that your names are written in heaven," said Jesus to his disciples (Luke 10:20); and in the Apocalypse repeated reference is made to those whose names are inscribed in "the Lamb's book of life" (Rev. 21:27, etc.).[163] If, then, believers in Christ are said to have come to "the assembly of firstborn ones" in this sense, the reference may be to those men and women who lived and "died in faith" before Christ came, but who "apart from us" could not attain perfection.[164] If

155. Cf. 1 Enoch 40:1; Rev. 5:11 (see also Heb. 2:2, p. 67 with n. 3).

156. 1QS 11.8f. Cf. 1QSa 2.8f.; 1QM 7.6; also J. Strugnell, "The angelic liturgy at Qumran," pp. 318-45. Important NT parallels are 1 Cor. 11:10; Eph. 3:10.

157. 1:14 (pp. 64f.).

158. 2:16 (p. 87).

159. Cf. Rev. 19:10; 22:9, where the interpreting angel refuses homage from John because he is his fellow-servant.

160. So Spicq, *ad loc.;* he compares Ps. 89:7 (LXX 88:6), where the angels are the βουλὴ ἁγίων (Heb. *sôḏ qᵉḏôšîm*), and Clement's *Extracts of Theodotus* 27:3f., where the highest angels are called πρωτόκτιστοι, "first-created" (quoted by E. Käsemann, *The Wandering People of God*, E.T. [Minneapolis, 1984], p. 50, n. 89).

161. Hermas, *Shepherd*, Vision 3.4.1.

162. Cf. Westcott, *ad loc.;* Windisch, *ad loc.*

163. Cf. Acts 13:48 (*Acts*, NICNT [Grand Rapids, ²1988], p. 267, n. 111); Phil. 4:3.

164. Cf. Calvin, *ad loc.:* "The description *firstborn* is not given here to the children of God indiscriminately, as Scripture sometimes does, but he gives this distinction to honour particularly the patriarchs and the other prominent men of the old Church" (W. B. Johnston's translation).

so, the phrase is synonymous with "the spirits of the righteous" at the end of this verse. But more probably the reference is to the whole communion of saints, including those who, while "militant here on earth," are enrolled as citizens of heaven.[165] To this community believers have come—not merely into its presence (as they have come into the presence of angels innumerable), but into its membership. All the people of Christ are the "firstborn" children of God, through their union with him who is the Firstborn *par excellence;*[166] their birthright is not to be bartered away, as was Esau's.[167]

Further, the readers have come to "God the judge of all"—or, as the phrase is more precisely rendered in the RSV, to "a judge who is God of all."[168] The designation of God as "the Judge of all the earth" goes back to early biblical times (Gen. 18:25). The mention of God as judge in this context is calculated to emphasize the solemnity of the Christian's responsibility; it echoes an earlier reference to the one "to whom our account must be rendered," before whom our inmost being lies open to view (Heb. 4:13), and the warning of 10:30f. that, since the judgment of his people is God's prerogative, it is "a fearful thing" to fall into his hands.[169] If we recognize a continuance of proselyte terminology here, we may recall Boaz's words of blessing on Ruth: "a full reward be given you by Yahweh, the God of Israel, under whose wings *you have come* to take refuge"[170] (Ruth 2:12). The living God to whom believers have come is indeed the refuge and strength of his people, but the intimacy of their covenant-union with him is not unmixed with awe before his pure holiness.

As for "the spirits of the righteous who have attained perfection,"[171]

165. Cf. Westcott, *ad loc.*: "Christian believers in Christ, alike living and dead, are united in the Body of Christ." So in the eschatological conflict envisaged by the Qumran community "not only will the angels fight side by side with the earthly 'holy people' ([1QM] xii, 7-8), but also the 'elect of the holy people,' i.e. former earth-dwellers now in heaven, will fight side by side with the angels" (Y. Yadin, *The Scroll of the War of the Sons of Light against the Sons of Darkness* [Oxford, 1962], pp. 241f.).

166. Cf. 1:6, where Jesus is the πρωτότοκος (as against the plural πρωτότοκοι here); 2:13ff.; Rom. 8:29; Col. 1:15, 18; Rev. 1:5.

167. The birthright in v. 16 is πρωτοτόκια, lit. "right of the firstborn."

168. Gk. κριτῇ θεῷ πάντων, but the word order may have only stylistic significance.

169. The suggestion that God is here designated as the "vindicator" or "avenger" of his people against their enemies (so Delitzsch, Riggenbach, *ad loc.*) may be admitted, if we also bear in mind the recurrent emphasis throughout this epistle that even his people (or indeed, *especially* his people) will incur his judgment if they rebel against him or despise his saving message. See also Moffatt, Spicq, *ad loc.*, and cf. 9:27; 13:4.

170. Gk. ἦλθες. Ruth did not merely live in Israel as a resident alien but as a religious proselyte, as witness her words to Naomi: "your God [shall be] my God" (Ruth 1:16; the Targum makes Naomi tell her in detail all that becoming a proselyte involves).

171. In 1 Enoch 22:9 (cf. 41:8) a place of refreshment in the realm of the dead is reserved for "the spirits of the righteous" (τὰ πνεύματα τῶν δικαίων). Cf. also Hermas, *Shepherd,* Mandate 11.1.15, for the phrase πνεύματα δικαίων, where, however, living people of God in a Christian congregation are meant.

they are most probably believers of pre-Christian days, like those mentioned in 11:40, who could not attain perfection until Christ came in the fulness of time and "by one offering . . . brought those who are sanctified to perfection" (10:14; 11:40). If it was the divine plan that "apart from us they could not attain their perfection," it is equally true that apart from them we could not be made perfect; by coming to God we have also come to those who in earlier times came to him believing "that he exists, and that he is a rewarder[172] of those who seek him out" (11:6). They fulfilled the promise of 10:38, "my righteous one will live by faith"; and the words of Wisdom 3:1 have come true for them: "the souls of the righteous are in the hand of God."[173] No distinction in meaning can be pressed between "spirits" here and "souls" there. Our author's lack of reference to the coming resurrection does not mean that it found no place in his creed (we recall his words in Heb. 11:35 about a "better resurrection"); but it is plain that, for him, the souls of believers do not need to wait until the resurrection to be perfected. They are perfected already in the sense that they are with God in the heavenly Jerusalem.[174]

24 They have come to God; they have come to "the spirits of the righteous"; and they have come to him who is the mediator between God and mankind, "Jesus, the mediator of a new covenant." Their ancestors in Moses' day had been borne on eagles' wings and brought to God himself[175] in terms of the old covenant; that old covenant, as we have already learned, has now been antiquated by the new one, of which Jesus is mediator. A different word for "new" is used here from that employed in the similar phrase in 9:15, but the different word is to be accounted for in terms of rhythm and not because of any distinction in meaning.[176] Since Jesus' sacrifice of himself, those who come to God must "approach God through him" (7:25).

To "approach God through him" means "to have freedom of access into the holy place by Jesus' blood" (10:19); accordingly, believers are further said to have come to "the blood of sprinkling." This may remind us of "the sprinkling of the blood" at the time of the first Passover (11:28);[177]

---

172. Gk. μισθαποδότης, with which Spicq correlates κριτής in this verse.

173. Gk. δικαίων δὲ ψυχαὶ ἐν χειρὶ θεοῦ.

174. Cf. the *Westminster Shorter Catechism,* Answer to Question 37: "The souls of believers are at their death made perfect in holiness, and do immediately pass into glory; and their bodies, being still united to Christ, do rest in their graves, till the resurrection."

175. Cf. Ex. 19:4.

176. Here διαθήκης νέας as against διαθήκης καινῆς in 9:15. The conventional distinction between καινός ("new in character") and νέος ("new in respect of time") cannot be universally pressed; cf. the καινὸς ἄνθρωπος of Eph. 4:24 as against the νέος ἄνθρωπος of Col. 3:10 (Moffatt points out that the new Jerusalem of *Test. Dan* 5:12 is νέα, whereas elsewhere it is καινή).

177. On the two different words for "sprinkling" used here and in 11:28 see p. 314, n. 207.

but more probably our author is thinking of the covenant-blood of Christ as the antitype of the blood sprinkled at the inauguration of the old covenant. By the blood of the new covenant, symbolically applied, believers' hearts are "sprinkled clean from an evil conscience" (10:22). The removal of an evil conscience does away with the barrier between them and God; the sacrifice of Christ thus "has better things to tell than the blood of Abel" (NEB). Abel's blood cried out to God from the ground, protesting against his murder and appealing for vindication;[178] but the blood of Christ brings a message of cleansing, forgiveness, and peace with God to all who place their faith in him. (The idea that "the blood of Abel" here means the blood of Abel's sacrifice is totally inapposite.)

I. PAY HEED TO THE VOICE OF GOD! (12:25-29)

25 *See to it[179] that you do not refuse to hear the one who speaks. If there was no escape for those[180] who refused to hear him when he addressed them on earth,[181] still less will there be any escape for us if we refuse to hear him when he speaks from heaven.*

26 *At that time his voice shook the earth, but now he has promised: "Yet once more, I will shake[182] not only earth but heaven also."[183]*

27 *This phrase,[184] "Yet once more," portends the removal of the things*

"Was the author of Hebrews, when writing these words, aware of the Jewish tradition that the offering of Cain and Abel took place on the *14th of Nisan, i.e.* on the same day on which the blood of Jesus was shed (Targum Jonathan on Gen. 4:3)?" (E. Nestle, "Hebrews xii.24," *ExT* 17 [1905-6], p. 566).

178. Cf. 11:4 (pp. 283f.). In 1 Enoch 22:6f. Enoch asks Raphael whose spirit it is "whose voice goes forth and makes suit to heaven"; Raphael answers: "This is the spirit which went forth from Abel, whom his brother Cain slew; he makes his suit against him till his seed is destroyed from the face of the earth, and annihilated from among the seed of men." So, in TB *Sanhedrin* 96b, the blood of Zechariah the son of Jehoiada (2 Chron. 24:21; cf. p. 328) cried from the ground for vengeance and would not be appeased until the blood of many Jews was shed by Nebuzaradan, thus atoning for his murder.

179. Gk. βλέπετε, as in 3:12.

180. Gk. εἰ γὰρ ἐκεῖνοι οὐκ ἐξέφυγον, with οὐκ instead of μή since emphasis is laid on the fact that they did not escape. For ἐξέφυγον (cf. 2:3, ἐκφευξόμεθα) a few authorities (ℵᶜ D K L M Ψ etc.) have the uncompounded ἔφυγον.

181. Gk. ἐπὶ γῆς παραιτησάμενοι τὸν χρηματίζοντα, where ἐπὶ γῆς, while it modifies χρηματίζοντα, is thrown back to the beginning of the phrase for emphasis in contrast with the following ἀπ᾽ οὐρανῶν. The manuscript tradition shows variations in the word order.

182. Gk. σείσω (LXX συσσείσω, "I will shake together"), for which a few authorities (D K L P etc.) read the present σείω (probably under the influence of the similar oracle in Hag. 2:21).

183. Hag. 2:6, LXX.

184. Gk. τὸ δέ, introducing a quoted phrase, as in Eph. 4:9.

which are shaken,[185] *as belonging to the created order, so that the things which cannot be shaken may endure.*

28 *The kingdom which we receive is unshakable; therefore, let us give*[186] *thanks*[187] *and bring God acceptable*[188] *worship,*[189] *with humble reverence and awe,*[190]

29 *for indeed our God is a consuming fire.*[191]

25 It is not suggested in the Exodus narrative that there was anything culpable in the people's request to Moses that God should not speak to them directly, but through an intermediary. In Deut. 5:28 they are indeed commended for the request, which sprang from their terror at the awe-inspiring circumstances of the theophany. When our author warns his readers not to "refuse to hear the one who speaks," he uses the same verb for refusing as he did in v. 19,[192] where the people "begged that nothing further might be said"—or, as it might be rendered, "refused to have any further word spoken to them." But, whatever was the people's attitude when God spoke at Sinai, the Pentateuchal record makes it plain that time and again throughout their wilderness wanderings they failed to pay heed to the commandments of God, and suffered for their disobedience. This has formed the basis of a solemn warning in the earlier part of the epistle (3:7-15), and the warning is

185. Gk. τὴν τῶν σαλευομένων μετάθεσιν (ℵ* A C 33 and a few authorities); τήν is omitted by 𝔭⁴⁶ D* 1739, whose reading is preferred by G. Zuntz (*Text*, pp. 117f.). L P and the bulk of later manuscripts read τῶν σαλευομένων τὴν μετάθεσιν.

186. Gk. ἔχωμεν (𝔭⁴⁶ᶜ A D etc., with the Syriac Peshiṭta and Coptic versions, 3 Vg. MSS, and the TR), for which 𝔭⁴⁶* ℵ P 33 69 and the bulk of later MSS, with the Latin and Harclean Syriac versions, read ἔχομεν, "we have." This variation between the indicative and subjunctive is a common textual phenomenon, the pronunciation of the two forms being practically identical, and a decision must be reached mainly on the ground of context, which here unquestionably demands ἔχωμεν. There is a well-known instance of the same variation in Rom. 5:1.

187. Gk. ἔχωμεν χάριν (RSV "let us be grateful"; NEB "let us therefore give thanks to God"). This is the regular force of Gk. χάριν ἔχω (like Lat. *gratiam habeo*).

188. Either aorist subjunctive λατρεύσωμεν with 𝔭⁴⁶ or, more probably, present subjunctive λατρεύωμεν with A D L 33, the Latin versions, and the TR (the present indicative λατρεύομεν, in ℵ Ψ and the bulk of later MSS, is a further example of the common phenomenon mentioned in n. 186 above).

189. Gk. εὐαρέστως, "acceptably," here only in the NT.

190. Gk. μετὰ εὐλαβείας καὶ δέους, with 𝔭⁴⁶ ℵ A D* and a few other MSS, and the Syriac Peshiṭta and Armenian versions. Variant readings are μετὰ εὐλαβείας καὶ αἰδοῦς (M P 1739 etc., with the Latin and, apparently, Harclean Syriac versions) and μετὰ αἰδοῦς καὶ εὐλαβείας (K L with the majority of later MSS and the TR, whence AV/KJV "with reverence and godly fear"). For εὐλάβεια cf. 5:7 (p. 129 with n. 61). This is the only NT instance of δέος, "fear."

191. Gk. καὶ γὰρ ὁ θεὸς ἡμῶν πῦρ καταναλίσκον, from Deut. 4:24, LXX: ὅτι κύριος ὁ θεός σου πῦρ καταναλίσκον ἐστίν ("for the Lord your God is a consuming fire").

192. Gk. παραιτέομαι, not used in the Greek version of the Exodus narrative here referred to. Windisch (HNT, p. 113) thinks our author does represent the Israelites' παραίτησις as wicked. For παραιτέομαι cf. *New Docs.*, III (1978), § 54.

repeated here. The Israelites in the wilderness did not escape judgment when they disregarded the voice—the voice of God, surely[193]—that thundered from Sinai. But if it was from an earthly hill that God proclaimed the statutes which formed the basis of the old covenant, it is from the heavenly Zion, from his unseen throne, that he speaks in the gospel. The "how much more" argument of 2:2f. and 10:29 is pressed home again: to disobey the gospel incurs judgment more certain and terrible even than that incurred by disobedience to the law.

26 When God spoke from Sinai, "the whole mountain quaked greatly" (Ex. 19:18). This earthquake remained deeply rooted in the national memory, and is celebrated in the Psalter and other Old Testament poems.

O *God,* when thou didst go forth before thy people,
  when thou didst march through the wilderness,
the earth quaked, the heavens poured down rain,
  at the presence of *God,* the God of Sinai,[194]
  at the presence of *God,* the God of Israel. (Ps. 68:7f.)[195]

In the Old Testament an earthquake is also expected to mark the coming day of the Lord, "when he rises to terrify the earth" (Isa. 2:19, 21); and not only an earthquake, but the shaking of heaven too: "I will make the heavens to tremble, and the earth shall be shaken out of its place, in the wrath of Yahweh of hosts, and in the day of his fierce anger" (Isa. 13:13). In similar language the prophet Haggai conveys an oracle of assurance to Zerubbabel the governor and Joshua the high priest[196] at the dedication of the Second Temple (516 B.C.): "Once again, in a little while, I will shake the heavens and the earth and the sea and the dry land; and I will shake all nations, so that the treasures of all nations shall come in, and I will fill this house with glory, says Yahweh of hosts" (Hag. 2:6f.). In their context these words declare God's purpose, in the

193. Gk. τὸν χρηματίζοντα (cf. the passive uses of the same verb in 8:5; 11:7, where God is the speaker). Moffatt (ICC, *ad loc.*) argues that the one "that warned them on earth" is Moses, since in the Pentateuchal narrative God is repeatedly said to have spoken to Israel from heaven (Ex. 20:22; Deut. 4:36); he translates τὸν χρηματίζοντα as "their instructor" (comparing Acts 7:38, where Moses "received living oracles to give unto us"). But while the Sinaitic revelation was given from heaven, it was an earthly revelation in comparison with the revelation given in the gospel.

194. Heb. *zeh sînai* (cf. Judg. 5:5), perhaps a divine title: "He of Sinai." See A. R. Johnson, *Sacral Kingship in Ancient Israel* (Cardiff, 1955), p. 71 with n. 1; A. Weiser, *Die Psalmen,* ATD (Göttingen, ²1955), p. 326; A. A. Anderson, *Psalms,* NCBC (London, 1972), p. 487. As a comparison with the parallel in Judg. 5:4f. suggests, the three italicized occurrences of *God* reflect an earlier Yahweh—a regular feature of the "Elohistic Psalter" (Pss. 42–83).

195. Cf. also Judg. 5:4f.; Pss. 77:18; 114:4, 7. It may have been on one of these poetical passages that our author depended here, since the LXX of Ex. 19:18 speaks not of the quaking of the earth but of the terror of the people.

196. Cf. p. 109, n. 28.

day when he rises in vindication of his cause, to put down Gentile dominion, to exalt the throne of David, and to make Jerusalem and its temple the center of worship and allegiance for all nations.[197] Our author interprets them of the end of the present world-order; the picture is similar to that in the Apocalypse, where earth and heaven flee away from the face of the Judge on the great throne, to be replaced by a new heaven and a new earth (Rev. 20:11; 21:1).[198]

27-29 When, in accordance with the divine promise, this cosmic convulsion takes place—when (in Dryden's words)

> the last and dreadful hour
> This crumbling pageant shall devour—

the whole material universe will be shaken to pieces, and the only things to survive will be those that are unshakable. To this unshakable order, however, belongs the kingdom which believers in Christ share with him—a kingdom, because their great high priest is a *royal* priest.[199]

In the current debate whether the created world[200] was eternal or not our author stands right within the Hebrew tradition. He has already[201] quoted with approval the passage in Ps. 102:25ff. which emphasizes the transitoriness of all created things:

> They shall pass away, but thou endurest;
> Like clothes they shall all grow old;

---

197. Cf. the similar oracle in Hag. 2:21f. In A. T. Hanson's view "the most satisfactory interpretation of Hebrews 12.22-7 is to assume that Christ is thought of as the speaker all through" (*Jesus Christ in the Old Testament* [London, 1965], p. 80; he discusses the whole context on pp. 75-82).

198. Cf. Rev. 6:12ff.; 16:18ff.; 2 Pet. 3:10; 1 Enoch 60:1; 2 Baruch 32:1; 59:3. There is no need to suppose that this language was suggested to our author by some recent earthquake, like that at Antioch in A.D. 115 (so W. L. Dulière, "Les chérubins du troisième Temple à Antioche," *Zeitschrift für Religions- und Geistesgeschichte* 13 [1961], pp. 201-19).

199. The term "kingdom" may have been suggested to our author because in the oracle of Hag. 2:21f., a companion to that quoted in v. 26, God promises to "overthrow the throne of kingdoms" and "destroy the strength of the kingdoms of the nations"—although in both clauses the LXX says "kings" (βασιλέων) and not "kingdoms" (βασιλειῶν). The phrase βασιλείαν παραλαμβάνω is a common one for receiving (or succeeding to) a kingdom (cf. Dan. 5:31, LXX and Theod.); in Dan. 7:18 (LXX and Theod.) it is used of the receiving of the kingdom by the saints of the Most High (and for the sense we may compare Luke 12:32; 22:29, although different verbs are used with βασιλεία there). As in Dan. 7:27 the kingdom which the saints receive is "an everlasting kingdom," so here it is unshakable, ἀσάλευτος, an adjective used by Philo to describe the laws of Moses (*Life of Moses* 2.14). Our author thus shows himself conversant with the primitive gospel vocabulary, although for the most part he communicates the saving truth in a new idiom. The present participle παραλαμβάνοντες suggests that the people of Christ have not finally entered into their royal heritage with him, although it is already theirs by promise.

200. "The shaking of these created things (ὡς πεποιημένων) means their removal " (NEB). On the force of μετάθεσις here see A. Ehrhardt, *The Beginning* (Manchester, 1968), pp. 9f.

201. 1:10-12 (pp. 61-63).

Thou shalt fold them up like a cloak;
Yes, they shall be changed like any garment. (NEB)

Philo tries, rather awkwardly, to mediate between the biblical doctrine and the Platonic doctrine of the eternity of the world;[202] but our author is quite forthright. Earlier he has emphasized the transitoriness of the world in order to set in contrast the eternity of the Son of God; now he emphasizes it again in order to set in contrast the eternity of that new order into which the Son of God has brought his people.

"Let us be thankful," he says, "that the kingdom which we receive is unshakable; and in that spirit of thankfulness let us offer acceptable worship to God." To the grace of God the proper response is a grateful heart, and the words and actions which flow from a grateful heart are the sacrifices in which God takes delight.[203]

At the same time, such sacrificial worship must be offered with a due sense of the majesty and holiness of the God with whom we have to do: not only thankfulness, but humble reverence and awe must mark his people's approach to him; "for our God is a consuming fire."[204] He who descended on Mount Sinai in fire and spoke to his people from the midst of that fire still consumes in the white heat of his purity everything that is unworthy of himself.[205] On Isa. 33:14 George Adam Smith wrote:

> To Isaiah life was so penetrated by the active justice of God, that he described it as bathed in fire, as blown through with fire. Righteousness was no mere doctrine to this prophet: it was the most real thing in history; it was the presence which pervaded and explained all phenomena. We shall understand the difference between Isaiah and his people if we have ever for our eyes' sake looked at a great conflagration through a coloured glass which allowed us to see the solid materials—stone, wood, and iron—but prevented us from seeing the flames and shimmering heat. To look thus is to see pillars, lintels, and cross-beams, twist and fall, crumble and fade; but how inexplicable the process seems! Take away the glass, and everything is clear. The fiery element is filling all the interstices that were blank to us before, and beating upon the solid material. The heat becomes visible, shimmering even where there is no flame. Just so had it been with the sinners in Judah

---

202. The world, according to Philo, is indestructible, not per se, but by the will of its Creator. "The world has come to be, and its coming to be is the beginning of its dissolution, even if by the providence of its Maker it is rendered immortal; and there was once a time when it was not" (*Decalogue* 58). The authenticity of *On the Eternity of the World,* a treatise ascribed to Philo in which the world appears to be treated as uncreated and inherently indestructible, is suspect.

203. Cf. 13:15f. (pp. 383f.).

204. See p. 362, n. 191. Cf. 10:27, 31 (p. 260, n. 125; p. 265, n. 154).

205. Cf. 1 Cor. 3:13-15.

these forty years. . . . Isaiah alone faced life with open vision, which filled up for him the interstices of experience and gave terrible explanation to fate. It was a vision that nearly scorched the eyes out of him. Life as he saw it was steeped in flame—the glowing righteousness of God. Jerusalem was full *of the spirit of justice, the spirit of burning. The light of Israel is for a fire, and his Holy One for a flame.*[206] . . . So Isaiah saw life, and flashed it on his countrymen. At last the glass fell from their eyes also, and they cried aloud, *Who among us shall dwell with the devouring fire? Who among us shall dwell with everlasting burnings?*[207]

It is an aspect of the character of God as revealed in the Bible that plays little part in much present-day thinking about him; but if we are to be completely "honest to God," we dare not ignore it. Reverence and awe before his holiness are not incompatible with grateful trust and love in response to his mercy.

> Who can behold the blazing light?
>   Who can approach consuming flame?
> None but Thy wisdom knows Thy might;
>   None but Thy word can speak Thy name.[208]

---

206. Isa. 4:4; 10:17; cf. also Isa. 30:33.
207. G. A. Smith, *The Book of Isaiah*, I (London, ²1927), pp. 350f.
208. I. Watts (1674-1748).

HEBREWS 13

VII. CONCLUDING EXHORTATION AND PRAYER (13:1-21)

Our author's argument has now been rounded off, and if his work had been a written homily and nothing more, there would have been no need for anything further. What follows in ch. 13 resembles the usual assortment of ethical and practical admonition and personal information with which New Testament epistles tend to close. Why this document should end like an epistle although it does not begin like one is a general problem of introduction.[1] Most probably ch. 13 is an integral part of the text of the document, and there is no good reason in either internal or external evidence why it should be regarded as in some way a separate composition. Other views have been advanced from time to time, suggesting, for example, that ch. 13 or part of it was written in deliberate imitation of Paul's epistolary style in order to secure acceptance for the whole work as a Pauline epistle,[2] or that it was written by Paul himself as a "letter of commendation" to validate the author's thesis,[3] or that it was a

1. See pp. 3, 25.
2. Cf. W. Wrede, *Das literarische Rätsel des Hebräerbriefs* (Göttingen, 1906). Such arguments have been based, *inter alia,* on the presence of several Pauline words in Heb. 13 which do not appear in Heb. 1–12. C. R. Williams ("A Word-Study of Hebrews XIII," *JBL* 30 [1911], pp. 129-36) counts 25 such words, but points out that the chapter also contains several words which are not Pauline, or are used in a different sense from that which Paul gives them. G. W. Buchanan argues that ch. 13 is no part of the homiletical midrash of chs. 1–12: it was composed for a different constituency and by a different author—perhaps "to give a homily the appearance of a letter to allow its admission into the canon" (*To the Hebrews,* AB [Garden City, N.Y., 1972], p. 268). A. Q. Morton has concluded, on the basis of literary statistics, that "the last chapter of Hebrews is Pauline" (*British Weekly,* March 18, 1965). Cf. also C. Spicq, "L'authenticité du chapitre xiii de l'Épître aux Hébreux," *Coniectanea Neotestamentica* 11 (1948), pp. 226-36.
3. Cf. G. A. Simcox, "Heb. xiii; 2 Tim. iv," *ExT* 10 (1898-99), pp. 430ff. F. J. Badcock suggested that vv. 23-25 were Paul's postscript to a letter which was substantially the work of Barnabas (*The Pauline Epistles and the Epistle to the Hebrews in their Historical Setting* [London, 1939], pp. 199f.); cf. p. 16, n. 63. The Pauline authorship of vv. 22-25 was favored also by G. Estius (1631) and others cited by A. Vanhoye, *TRE* 14 (Berlin, 1985), p. 496 (*s.v.* "Hebräerbrief"). G. W. Buchanan describes vv. 22-25 as "a 'Pauline' postscript"—imitatively rather than authentically Pauline (*To the Hebrews,* pp. 242, 267).

fragment of a Pauline letter accidentally and mistakenly tacked on to a work with which it really had nothing to do.[4] These theories can be given no higher status than that of curiosities of literary criticism. The reversion in vv. 10-16 to the main theme of the epistle is sufficient evidence, if evidence were required, of the integrity of ch. 13 with the foregoing chapters.

A. ETHICAL INJUNCTIONS (13:1-6)

1 *Let brotherly love endure.*
2 *Do not forget to practice hospitality: by practicing hospitality some people have entertained angels without realizing it.[5]*
3 *Remember those who are imprisoned, as though you shared their imprisonment; remember those who are ill-treated because you yourselves are also in the body.*
4 *Let marriage be honorably esteemed among all; let the marriage bed be kept unpolluted,[6] for God will judge fornicators and adulterers.*
5 *Let your way of life be free from the love of money. Be content[7] with*

---

4. E. D. Jones ("The Authorship of Hebrews xiii," *ExT* 46 [1934-35], pp. 562-67) argues that this chapter was the end of Paul's "severe letter" to Corinth. He points out that a Corinthian destination and Pauline authorship for Heb. 13:23-25 were defended by T. W. L. Davies (*Pauline Readjustments* [London, 1927]), who, however, went on to argue that, since this section is integral to the whole epistle, the whole epistle was written by Paul to the Corinthians, and is, in fact, the "previous letter" referred to in 1 Cor. 5:9! A reply to E. D. Jones's argument by R. V. G. Tasker ("The Integrity of the Epistle to the Hebrews," *ExT* 47 [1935-36], pp. 136-38) is a good defense of the integrity of ch. 13 with the rest of the epistle.

5. Gk. ἔλαθόν τινες ξενίσαντες ἀγγέλους, an excellent classical idiom.

6. Since the verb is left to be understood (cf. the literal Rheims rendering, "Marriage honourable in all, and the bed undefiled"), it may be understood as indicative (so AV/KJV "Marriage is honourable in all, and the bed undefiled"), in which case we should have a defense of holy matrimony as against an insistence on the superiority of celibacy; or as imperative (as in the RSV, etc.), in which case we have an admonition to safeguard the sanctity of marriage against adulterous encroachments and the like. The latter is the more probable construction, both because of the following clause ("for God will judge fornicators and adulterers") and because the parallel construction at the beginning of v. 5 (ἀφιλάργυρος ὁ τρόπος) implies the imperative mood, "Let your way of life be free from the love of money" (the indicative, "Your way of life is free from the love of money," would be inappropriate). For this sense of τρόπος see *New Docs.*, III (1978), § 101.

7. Gk. ἀρκούμενοι τοῖς παροῦσιν, probably an imperatival use of the participle, common in such lists of ethical admonitions (cf. *Colossians–Philemon–Ephesians*, NICNT [Grand Rapids, 1984], p. 155, n. 134, on Col. 3:13; and see D. Daube, "Appended Note: Participle and Imperative in I Peter," in E. G. Selwyn, *The First Epistle of St. Peter* [London, 1946], pp. 467-88; N. Turner, MHT, III [Edinburgh, 1963], p. 343, with bibliography in n. 1). For the plural ἀρκούμενοι, p46 0121b 1739 read the singular ἀρκούμενος (a reading present also in manuscripts used by Augustine)—probably by mechanical conformity to τρόπος (the plural is an elegant "sense construction"). See G. Zuntz, *The Text of the Epistles* (London, 1953), p. 42. E. K. Simpson ("Vettius Valens and the New Testament," *EQ* 2 [1930], p. 392) points out an example of the phrase in Vettius Valens, *Anthologiarum Libri* (ed. W. Kroll), 220.25: ἀρκοῦνται τοῖς

the things which are available, for God himself has said, "I will never abandon you; I will never forsake you."[8]

6 *So we in turn may have courage and say,*[9]
   "The Lord is my helper; I will not be afraid;
   what can man do to me?"[10]

Like Paul and the other writers of New Testament epistles, our author is alive to the ethical implications of Christian doctrine. He does not systematize his ethical injunctions as some of them do[11] (his readers had probably been well grounded already in the early catechesis of Christian *didachē*), but he urges upon them certain Christian virtues which he presumably knew it was desirable to emphasize in their present situation—brotherly love, hospitality, help to those in need, chastity, and contentment.

1 Brotherly love was a virtue highly esteemed in antiquity. The Byzantine anthologist Stobaeus gathers together a number of quotations from ancient authors under the caption: "That brotherly love and a proper disposition towards one's kinsfolk is an excellent thing, and that it is necessary." In

---

παροῦσιν, and suggests that the construction in our present passage, which he regards as anacoluthic, is due to the fact that the expression was proverbial (which is confirmed by its occurrences elsewhere).

8. With the words introducing the quotation, αὐτὸς γὰρ εἴρηκεν ("he himself has said") cf. Acts 20:35, αὐτὸς εἶπεν (Lat. *ipse dixit*). The quotation is from Josh. 1:5, where there is an echo of Deut. 31:6, 8. The Greek (οὐ μή σε ἀνῶ οὐδ' οὐ μή σε ἐγκαταλίπω) does not correspond exactly to any surviving LXX text, but precisely the same form of the quotation appears in Philo (*Confusion of Tongues* 166). P. Katz, referring also to Philo, *On Dreams*, 1.3, 179-81, concludes that Philo and our author quote a variant LXX reading of Gen. 28:15, expanded from Deut. 31:6, 8 ("Οὐ μή σε ἀνῶ οὐδ' οὐ μή σε ἐγκαταλίπω [Hebr 13,5]: The Biblical Source of the Quotation," *Biblica* 33 [1952], pp. 523-25; cf. his "The Quotations from Deuteronomy in Hebrews," *ZNW* 49 [1958], pp. 221-23).

9. Gk. ὥστε θαρροῦντας ἡμᾶς λέγειν. 𝔓[46] Ψ 1739 omit ἡμᾶς ("this is hardly more than a scribal slip," says Zuntz, *Text*, p. 42).

10. Ps. 118 [LXX 117]:6. Before "I will not fear" (οὐ φοβηθήσομαι) 𝔓[46] A D with the majority of later MSS and the TR insert "and" (καί); so the AV/KJV, which also subordinates the following clause to "I will not fear." The construction of "What can man do to me?" as an independent question (RSV, NEB, etc.) is much preferable.

11. Cf. *Colossians–Philemon–Ephesians*, NICNT, pp. 137-75. O. Michel, however, sees evidence of topical arrangements in the injunctions of vv. 1-6; he discerns four pairs: (i) brotherly love and hospitality (vv. 1, 2); (ii) care for prisoners and others in trouble (v. 3); (iii) honor of wedlock and avoidance of unchastity (v. 4); (iv) avoidance of covetousness and cultivation of contentment (vv. 5, 6), and concludes that this chapter is no mere postscript but a section which has its distinctive contribution to make to the structure of the complete epistle. Future commentators on Hebrews, he suggests, should pay more attention to the artistic form of the epistle than has generally been paid in the past (*Der Brief an die Hebräer*, MK [Göttingen, 1949], pp. 328f.). A. Vanhoye ("La question littéraire de Hébreux xiii.1-6," *NTS* 23 [1976-77], pp. 121-39) similarly treats this paragraph as a well-composed unit; he argues further that it is the middle unit of three in 12:14–13:21, a subdivision placed between two more important ones (12:14-29 and 13:7-21).

the biblical area the classic passage is Ps. 133:1, "Behold, how good and pleasant it is when brothers dwell in unity!" The word used here *(philadelphia)* appears in the Pauline writings and in both the Petrine epistles; and the grace of brotherly love itself, whatever terms be used, is inculcated throughout the New Testament. "Concerning love of the brothers,"[12] writes Paul to the Thessalonians, "you have no need to have any one write to you: for you yourselves are taught by God to love one another; and indeed you do it . . ." (1 Thess. 4:9f.). Such brotherly love is no mere sentiment; it can be a very costly thing, as John emphasizes: "By this we know love, that he laid down his life for us: and we ought to lay down our lives for our brothers. But if any one has the world's goods and sees his brother in need, yet closes his heart against him, how does God's love abide in him?" (1 John 3:16f.). If a weakening of faith and resolution among the recipients of this epistle led to a weakening of the bonds which united them to their fellow-Christians, this would add urgency to the plea that brotherly love should *continue* among them. Some specific forms of brotherly love are enjoined in the following verses.

2 Strangers, and especially strangers belonging to the Christian brotherhood, must be shown hospitality. Among Jews and Gentiles alike hospitality to strangers ranked high as a virtue; it was, indeed, a religious obligation. Among the Greeks, strangers were under the special protection of Zeus, in his rôle as Zeus Xenios, "Zeus the patron of strangers." On occasion, indeed, Zeus or one of the other gods was believed to have assumed the disguise of a wayfarer and brought great blessing to those who treated him hospitably, not realizing whom they were entertaining.[13] Among the Jews Abraham was regarded as outstanding for his hospitality as for his other virtues;[14] a true son of Abraham must be hospitable too. In the New Testament hospitality is incumbent on all Christians,[15] and Christian leaders in particular are required to be hospitable (1 Tim. 3:2; Tit. 1:8). Christians traveling from one place to another on business would be especially appreciative of hospitality from fellow-Christians. Inns throughout the Roman Empire were places of doubtful repute, and indeed of positive danger, as the reader of Petronius and Apuleius is well aware, and would provide very uncongenial company for Christians.

---

12. Gk. φιλαδελφία, as here.

13. As in the story of Philemon and Baucis (cf. *Acts,* NICNT, p. 274).

14. According to Resh Laqish (TB *Sota* 10a) it was to refresh weary travelers that Abraham planted a tamarisk tree at Beer-sheba (Gen. 21:33). Some rabbis elaborated the story by saying that he planted a whole orchard, others that he erected an inn. He called there on the name of "Yahweh, the Everlasting God" *('Ēl 'Ôlām),* it was added, in order that all who passed that way might name his name.

15. Cf. Matt. 25:35f.; Rom. 12:13; 1 Pet. 4:9, etc.

The opportunity of free board and lodging might tempt some unscrupulous characters to masquerade as Christians. Proteus Peregrinus in Lucian's satire comes to mind;[16] and the necessity of some rough-and-ready rule of thumb for detecting impostors is implied in the *Didachē:* "Let every apostle who comes to you be received as the Lord, but he must not stay more than one day, or two if it is absolutely necessary; if he stays three days, he is a false prophet. And when an apostle leaves you, let him take nothing but a loaf, until he reaches further lodging for the night; if he asks for money, he is a false prophet."[17] Some Christians who had been deceived by such impostors might be chary of offering hospitality too readily next time they were asked for it, but here they are encouraged with the remark that some who have given hospitality to passing strangers found that they were entertaining "angels unawares." Those who are given to hospitality find that such happy experiences far outweigh the unhappy ones.

The reference is no doubt primarily to Abraham's experience when he entertained "three men" so hospitably by the terebinth of Mamre,[18] and found that one of them was no other than Yahweh,[19] who promised Abraham and Sarah that they would have a son the following year. When Yahweh stayed to speak with Abraham, his two angelic companions went on to Sodom and were entertained there in the house of Lot, to whom they brought deliverance from the catastrophe which overwhelmed the city the next day.[20] The incidents of Gideon[21] and Manoah,[22] and Tobit[23] at a later date, may also have been in our author's mind. He is not necessarily encouraging his readers to expect that those whom they entertain will turn out to be supernatural beings traveling incognito; he is assuring them that some of their visitors will prove to be true messengers of God to them, bringing a greater blessing than they receive.

3   The community addressed in this epistle had already, in earlier days, shown practical sympathy with their imprisoned friends.[24] Here they

16. Lucian, *The Death of Peregrinus* 11-13.

17. *Didache* 11:4-6.

18. Gen. 18:1-8. At the wedding of the son of Rabban Gamaliel II, the bridegroom's father poured wine for the guests, some of whom thought it unfitting that they should be waited upon thus by so distinguished a scholar. They remembered, however, that Abraham, a greater man than Gamaliel, had waited upon others. "Ah!" said someone, "but these were ministering angels." "Yes," was the reply, "but Abraham did not know that; to him they looked like Arabs" (TB *Qiddushin* 32b). Cf. Josephus, *Ant.* 1.196 ("he thought they were strangers"); Philo, *Abraham* 107-13.

19. To be understood, no doubt, as the "angel of the LORD" *(mal'ak Yahweh),* the executive agent or personification of God's relation of grace to his people.

20. Gen. 19:1-22.

21. Judg. 6:11-21.

22. Judg. 13:3-20.

23. Tob. 3:17; 5:4-16.

24. Cf. 10:32-34 (p. 270).

are urged to go on remembering this Christian duty. Lucian no doubt gives a fairly accurate account of Christian practice in this regard when he describes how Proteus Peregrinus, during his period of association with the Christians, was imprisoned: the Christians "left no stone unturned in their endeavor to procure his release. When this proved impossible, they looked after his wants in all other matters with untiring solicitude and devotion. From earliest dawn old women ('widows,' they are called[25]) and orphan children might be seen waiting about the prison-doors; while the officers of the church, by bribing the jailors, were able to spend the night inside with him. Meals were brought in, and they went through their sacred formulas."[26] This picture, satirical as it is in intention, can be duplicated many times over from other records of the concern which Christians showed for those who were in prison or otherwise suffering for their faith, ignoring the personal risks involved.[27]

In saying, "Remember those who are imprisoned, as though you shared their imprisonment," our author need not imply that his readers have themselves suffered imprisonment (this might be true of some, but not of all); we need see no more in his words than a specific application of the Pauline principle that if "one member suffers, all suffer together" (1 Cor. 12:26).[28] A capacity for putting oneself in another's place and exercising imaginative sympathy is part of true charity. This same imaginative sympathy should be extended to all who are ill-treated;[29] those who are themselves "in the body" are in a position to imagine how they would feel if the same ill-treatment were meted out to them. The phrase "in the body" should not be interpreted to mean "in the body of Christ (as fellow-members)."[30]

4 The injunction to honor the marriage union and abstain from sexual sin may also be brought under the general heading of brotherly love; chastity is not opposed to charity, but is part of it. Here is no exaltation of celibacy as something inherently superior to marriage;[31] the marriage union is divinely ordained, and its sacred precincts must not be polluted by the in-

---

25. Cf. 1 Tim. 5:3-16.

26. *The Death of Peregrinus* 12. Lucian possibly models his account on the behavior of Christians at various places where Ignatius broke his journey (*c.* A.D. 115) on the way from Syrian Antioch to the amphitheater in Rome (although that was some years before Lucian's birth).

27. See p. 270 with n. 185.

28. The *Epistle to Diognetus* (6:7) speaks of Christians as "confined in the world as in a prison" as the soul is imprisoned in the body, but that is hardly the thought here; the prefix συν- in συνδεδεμένοι implies some form of sharing in the lot of those who were actually in prison.

29. Gk. κακουχούμενοι, as in 11:37. Cf. also p. 310, n. 179.

30. This "interpretation . . .—beautiful as the thought is—is inadmissible" (B. F. Westcott, *ad loc.*).

31. One of G. W. Buchanan's arguments against ascribing ch. 13 to the author of Hebrews is that, whereas ch. 13 approves of marriage, the homily of chs. 1–12 was addressed (as he believes) to celibates (*To the Hebrews*, pp. 231, 267).

trusion of a third party, of either sex. Fornication and adultery are not synonymous in the New Testament: adultery[32] implies unfaithfulness by either party to the marriage vow, while the word translated "fornication"[33] covers a wide range of sexual irregularities, including unions within bounds prohibited by law.[34] Our author agrees with other New Testament writers that those who are guilty of such practices incur the judgment of God. "Let no one deceive you with empty words," says Paul; "for it is because of these things that the wrath of God comes upon the children of disobedience"[35] (Eph. 5:6; cf. Col. 3:5f.).

5-6 When Paul speaks like this, he includes among "these things" unchastity and covetousness. Covetousness, indeed, in its New Testament connotation can refer to illicit sexual desire as well as to love of money.[36] It was therefore a natural transition of thought for our author to pass from his injunction about chastity to his plea to his readers not to live for money. Here too he is in line with the pervasive teaching of the New Testament. Our Lord warned his hearers that they could not serve God and Mammon,[37] and that "a man's life does not consist in the abundance of his possessions" (Luke 12:15). We forget this warning every time we ask how much a person is worth, when we really mean how much he owns. The adjective which our author uses here, meaning "free from the love of money,"[38] occurs in one other place in the New Testament, where it is laid down that a "bishop" or leader in a Christian church must be "no lover of money" (1 Tim. 3:3); "for

---

32. Gk. μοιχεία.

33. Gk. πορνεία (cf. 12:16, pp. 350f.). On the whole question see D. S. Bailey, *Sexual Relation in Christian Thought* (New York, 1959); O. A. Piper, *The Biblical View of Sex and Marriage* (New York, 1960).

34. Cf. *Acts*, NICNT, p. 299 with n. 78.

35. Cf. Col. 3:5f.; 1 Cor. 6:9f.; 1 Thess. 4:3-6.

36. Cf. 1 Thess. 4:6, "that no man . . . wrong (πλεονεκτεῖν) his brother in the matter"— referring no doubt to conceiving a sinful desire and committing a trespass against another man's family circle, by illicit relations with one of his womenfolk.

37. Matt. 6:24; Luke 16:13. Cf. Dante, *Purgatorio* 19.73, where the avaricious (including Pope Adrian V) cry out, "My soul cleaves to the dust," *adhaesit pauimento anima mea* (Ps. 119 [LXX, Vg. 118]:25), like Bunyan's man with the muck-rake. Cf. also Milton (*Paradise Lost* 1.679-84):

> Mammon, the least erected spirit that fell
> From heaven; for e'en in heaven his looks and thoughts
> Were always downward bent, admiring more
> The riches of heaven's pavement, trodden gold,
> Than aught divine or holy else enjoyed
> In vision beatific.

(Milton's reference to heaven's "pavement" may have been suggested by Lat. *pauimentum* in Ps. 119 [Vg. 118]:25.)

38. Gk ἀφιλάργυρος.

the love of money[39] is a root of all evils; it is through this craving that some have wandered away from the faith and pierced their hearts with many pangs" (1 Tim. 6:10).

The chief pang which pierces the heart of the lover of money is gnawing anxiety. The greedy person can never be happy, but the opposite of covetousness is contentment. Here too there is a close affinity between this passage and 1 Timothy: "There is great gain in godliness with contentment;[40] for we brought nothing into the world, and we cannot take anything out of the world; but if we have food and clothing, with these we shall be content" (1 Tim. 6:6-8). Behind both documents lies our Lord's teaching: "Do not be anxious, saying, 'What shall we eat?' or 'What shall we drink?' or 'What shall we wear?' For the Gentiles seek all these things; and your heavenly Father knows that you need them all. But seek first his kingdom and his righteousness, and all these things shall be yours as well" (Matt. 6:31-33). "Be content with what you have," says our author. But the carefree contentment of which he speaks is not an irresponsible improvidence; it springs from an intelligent trust in God and acceptance of his promises. If to each one of his people God gives the assurance, "I will never leave you or desert you" (NEB), their reasonable response may well be made in the words of the psalmist: "With Yahweh on my side I do not fear: what can man do to me?" (Ps. 118:6).

B. EXAMPLES TO FOLLOW (13:7-8)

7 *Remember your guides, those who declared the word of God to you. Consider the outcome of their manner of life, and imitate their faith.*
8 *Jesus Christ is the same yesterday, and today, yes, and for ever.*

7 Three times in this chapter mention is made of their guides or leaders.[41] In v. 17 they are told to obey them; in v. 24 they are asked to convey the writer's greetings to them; here they are exhorted to remember them. In vv. 17 and 24 the reference plainly is to leaders who are still alive and active; here the reference seems rather to be to those who led them in earlier days but have now completed their service; the whole course of their lives, from start to finish, now lies before their disciples and followers for review and imitation. By precept and example they showed the right path to tread; being dead they yet speak, and the record of their faith is still alive in the memory of those who knew them. In ch. 11 the faith of men and women of earlier generations is pre-

---

39. Gk. φιλαργυρία.
40. Gk. αὐτάρκεια. Cf. Phil. 4:11, "I have learned, in whatever state I am, to be content (αὐτάρκης)."
41. Gk. οἱ ἡγούμενοι. Here the present participle may have imperfect force.

sented for emulation, but there is something in the vivid recollection of a life
that we have seen which cannot be conveyed by a record that has come to us
only by reading or hearing. Those who planted this community of Christians
and fostered it by the ministry of the word of God[42] and the example of faith
had run the race unwavering to the end; what they had done their followers
could also do. It is not necessary to suppose that they had suffered martyrdom;[43] but like the heroes of ch. 11 they "died in faith."

8   Yet they died; they lived on in the memory of those who had known
them, but they were no longer available for consultation and wise guidance
as they had once been. Jesus Christ, by contrast, was always available, unchanging from year to year, "the same yesterday and today and for ever." In
1:12 the words of Ps. 102:27 (LXX 101:28) were applied to him: "thou art
the same, and thy years have no end." These words, we saw, in their original context were addressed to the God of Israel; but this is not the only instance in which we find such a spontaneous transition of reference from the
Father to the Son. "I am He," says God to his people in Isa. 48:12; "I am the
first and I am the last"[44]—language which in the New Testament is taken
over and applied to Jesus without any sense of incongruity.[45] *Yesterday* Jesus
"offered up entreaties and supplications, with loud cries and tears, to the one
who was able to save him from death" (Heb. 5:7); *today* he represents his
people in the presence of God, a high priest who has a fellow-feeling with
them in their weakness, because he "endured trial in all respects like" themselves, "while remaining free from sin" (4:15); *for ever* he lives, this same
Jesus, "to intercede for them" (7:25). His help, his grace, his power, his
guidance are permanently at his people's disposal; why then should they lose
heart? Others serve their generation by the will of God and pass on; "but this
one, because he continues 'for ever,' has a priesthood which is untransferable" (7:24). He never needs to be replaced, and nothing can be added to his
perfect work.

---

42. The same persons are probably referred to in 2:3, where the gospel "was delivered
to us with assurance by those who heard him." "Does not . . . the aorist ἐλάλησαν ["spoke"] in
v. 7 refer to the *original* proclamation of the word of God to the hearers?" (R. V. G. Tasker, "Integrity," p. 138).

43. So Tasker, *loc. cit.* ("whose leaders have already suffered martyrdom"); Moffatt, *ad
loc.* ("They had laid down their lives as martyrs"). Moffatt compares "the issue (ἔκβασις) of their
life" with Wisdom 2:17, where the wicked say of the righteous person, whom they propose to
persecute and kill, "let us test what will happen at the end of his life (τὰ ἐν ἐκβάσει αὐτοῦ)."

44. Cf. Isa. 41:4; 44:6.

45. Cf. Rev. 1:17 (also 2:8; 22:13), where the glorified Christ says, "I am the first and
the last." A purely verbal near-coincidence appears in the Egyptian *Book of the Dead,* ed.
E. A. W. Budge (London, 1913), I, p. 177, where the deceased who has been assimilated to Osiris
says, "I am yesterday, today and tomorrow" (*'nk sf dw' bk'*). For an exposition of the theme see
F. V. Filson, *Yesterday: A Study of Hebrews in the Light of Chapter 13,* SBT 2.4 (London, 1967).

C. THE TRUE CHRISTIAN SACRIFICES (13:9-16)

9 *Do not be carried away[46] by all sorts of strange teaching. It is good for the heart to be strengthened by grace, not by food regulations, which have never brought any advantage to those who follow them.[47]*

10 *The altar we have is one from which those who carry out the worship in the tent have no right to eat.[48]*

11 *Those animals whose blood is carried into the holy place by the high priest as a sin offering[49] have their bodies burned outside the camp.*

12 *Therefore Jesus for his part suffered outside the gate[50] in order to sanctify the people by means of his own blood.*

13 *Let us then go out to him, outside the camp,[51] bearing the stigma which attaches to him.*

14 *We have no permanent city here; we look for the city which is to come.*

15 *Through Jesus, then,[52] let us offer up a sacrifice of praise to God continually, that is, the fruit of lips[53] which acknowledge his name.*

16 *But do not forget to do deeds of kindness or to share what you have with others; it is sacrifices like these that give pleasure to God.*

9 The reminder that "Jesus Christ is the same" links what precedes it with what follows it. Because "Jesus Christ is the same," says our author, "do not be swept off your course by all sorts of outlandish teachings;[54] it is good that our souls should gain their strength from the grace of God, and not from scruples about what we eat, which have never done any good to those who were governed by them" (NEB). The language here suggests something more than a relapsing into orthodox Judaism; it reminds us of Paul's appeal to the

---

46. Gk. μὴ παραφέρεσθε. For παραφέρεσθε ("be carried along") K L etc. with the Coptic versions and the TR read περιφέρεσθε ("be carried about," AV/KJV), perhaps under the influence of Eph. 4:14 ("carried about with every wind of doctrine").

47. Lit. "those who walk [in them]"—Gk. οἱ περιπατοῦντες (𝔭[46] ℵ* A D*), for which ℵ[c] K L with the majority of MSS and the TR read οἱ περιπατήσαντες.

48. Gk. ἐξ οὗ φαγεῖν οὐκ ἔχουσιν ἐξουσίαν. D* 0121b (and John of Damascus) omit ἐξουσίαν. The omission is a scribal slip, but as it happens the remaining words give reasonably good sense: "whereof they cannot eat" (for ἔχω with infinitive cf. 6:13). See G. Zuntz, *Text*, p. 140, n. 3.

49. Gk. περὶ ἁμαρτίας (cf. p. 241, n. 42, on 10:6).

50. Gk. ἔξω τῆς πύλης. For πύλης 𝔭[46] P read παρεμβολῆς ("camp"), under the influence of v. 13; 436 and the Syriac Peshitta read πόλεως, "city" (a reading possibly implied by Tertullian, *Reply to the Jews* 14: "One of the goats, begirt with scarlet, amid cursing and universal spitting, and tearing and piercing, was ejected by the people into perdition outside the city *[extra ciuitatem]*").

51. Gk. ἔξω τῆς παρεμβολῆς, from Lev. 16:27, LXX. (Cf. Acts 28:16, *v.l.*).

52. Gk. οὖν, omitted (by haplography, according to Zuntz, *Text*, p. 192) by 𝔭[46] ℵ* D* P Ψ and the Peshitta.

53. From Hos. 14:2, LXX; cf. p. 383, n. 90.

54. Gk. διδαχαῖς ποικίλαις καὶ ξέναις.

Colossian Christians not to let anyone sit in judgment on them in respect of food or drink, because things like these disappeared in the very act of being used; regulations and prohibitions regarding such evanescent things provided no spiritual support or defense.[55] "Food will not commend us to God," says Paul elsewhere. "We are no worse off if we do not eat, and no better off if we do" (1 Cor. 8:8). Our author makes the same point. It is by divine grace,[56] and not by rules about food, that the heart—that is to say, the spiritual life—is nourished; rules about food, imposed by external authority, have never helped people to maintain a closer walk with God. (Voluntary fasting, in the spirit of our Lord's instruction in Matt. 6:16-18, is quite a different matter; but that is not the subject here.) The strange teaching which laid such insistence on food was probably some form of syncretistic gnosis, perhaps with Essene or quasi-Essene affinities.[57] This kind of thing was so widespread at the time that the vague allusion to it here (vague to modern readers, not to the original readers, who probably understood the allusion perfectly) provides no clue to the destination of the epistle. It was current in Asia Minor, we know; but even to the Roman Christians[58] Paul judged it necessary to point out that "the kingdom of God is not food and drink but righteousness and peace and joy in the Holy Spirit"[59] (Rom. 14:17). To put such indifferent matters in a place of central religious importance would diminish the sovereignty of Jesus Christ, the same yesterday and today and forever.

Since the word translated "food" is the same as that used in 9:10,[60] where "matters of food and drink and various ablutions" are listed among the "material ordinances imposed until the time of the new order," it is possible that a reference to sacrificial meals of some kind is included here. In any case, food regulations of all kinds, whether positive or negative, are catalogued by our author among those external ordinances which Christianity has rendered null and void.

---

55. Col. 2:16, 21-23; cf. *Colossians–Philemon–Ephesians*, NICNT, pp. 113f., 126-29.

56. Gk. χάρις. In view of the force of this word in 12:28, it may be permissible to include here the idea of gratitude—gratitude in response to the grace of God.

57. Cf. the outline of the Colossian "heresy" in *Colossians–Philemon–Ephesians*, NICNT, pp. 17-26. T. W. Manson, because of the similarity between that "heresy" and the "strange teachings" implied here, suggested tentatively that this epistle might have been addressed to Christians in the Lycus valley when the heresy was in a less developed state than it had attained by the time Paul wrote Colossians (*Studies in the Gospels and Epistles* [Manchester, 1962], pp. 242-58).

58. Cf. the evidence that Roman Judaism (the matrix of Roman Christianity) had nonconformist affinities (pp. 8, 141f.).

59. Cf. 1 Tim. 4:3-5.

60. Gk. βρώματα, plural in both places. Although these are the only two places where the word occurs in this epistle, it is used in the singular (βρῶμα) or plural (βρώματα) repeatedly in the NT in the most general sense of food(s); cf. Matt. 14:15; Mark 7:19; Luke 3:11; 9:13; John 4:34; Rom. 14:15, 20; 1 Cor. 3:2; 6:13; 8:8, 13; 10:3; 1 Tim. 4:3.

10-11 In fact, the whole principle of attaching religious value to material food was inconsonant with the essence of Christianity. The sacrifice of Christ was the antitype of the sacrifice offered on the great Day of Atonement, and the flesh of the animals slaughtered in the course of that ritual was not eaten; their bodies were "carried forth outside the camp" and there completely burned[61] (Lev. 16:27). There were other sin offerings in which this was not done; when the blood was not presented to God in the holy of holies, the flesh was eaten by the priests in the sanctuary.[62] But since the blood of the bullock which made atonement for Aaron and his family, and of the goat which made atonement for the people, was carried into the holy of holies on the Day of Atonement, their bodies were incinerated. In other words, "those who carry out the worship in the tent"[63] have no permission to eat from the altar which typically foreshadows the sacrifice of Christ. But the sacrifice of Christ is a better sacrifice, not only because the spiritual antitype is superior to the material type, but also because those who enter the heavenly sanctuary "by Jesus' blood" (10:19) know that the one who became their perfect sin offering is permanently available as the source of their spiritual nourishment and refreshment, as they feed on him in their hearts by faith.[64]

The word "altar" is used by metonymy for "sacrifice"—"as when, e.g., we say that a man keeps a good *table*, meaning thereby good *food*."[65] Our

---

61. So also with the sin offerings of Ex. 29:14; Lev. 4:12; 8:17; 9:11.

62. Cf. Lev. 10:16-20.

63. Not only the priests, but all who participate in the "tabernacle" worship. The σκηνή here is surely the tabernacle in the wilderness, or, by extension, every phase of the earthly sanctuary which that tabernacle constituted in wilderness days. Windisch and Moffatt *(ad loc.)* take οἱ τῇ σκηνῇ λατρεύοντες to mean the worshipers under the new order, in which case the σκηνή must be the heavenly tabernacle: "we *have* an altar," our author would then say, "but it is not one from which we can derive material food; it is a figurative altar in the heavenly sanctuary which is the locus of our worship." But the reference to the Levitical sin offering which follows immediately makes it almost certain that the σκηνή is the material tabernacle. J. M. Creed was disposed to follow Windisch and Moffatt here ("Hebrews xiii. 10," *ExT* 50 [1938-39], pp. 13-15); but see J. P. Wilson ("The Interpretation of Hebrews xiii. 10," *ibid.*, pp. 380f.).

64. "Our great sin-offering, consumed in one sense outside the gate, is given to us as our food. The Christian, therefore, who can partake of Christ, offered for his sins, is admitted to a privilege unknown under the old Covenant" (B. F. Westcott, *ad loc.*). "In reality the only food that matters is the spiritual food of the sacrifice offered upon that altar to which, while they remain in the Mosaic stage, they have no access" (C. F. D. Moule, *JTS* n.s. 1 [1950], p. 38, in the course of an article "Sanctuary and Sacrifice in the Church of the New Testament," pp. 29-41. See also C. F. D. Moule, "The Sacrifice of the People of God," in *Essays in New Testament Interpretation* (Cambridge, 1982), pp. 287-97.

65. R. Anderson, *The Buddha of Christendom* (London, 1899), p. 302. It is unlikely that our author refers to the heavenly mercy-seat—a view proposed by A. S. Peake (CentB, *ad loc.*) and approved by J. P. Wilson *(loc. cit.)*—for the mercy seat is never called a θυσιαστήριον. In the spiritual antitype certainly both altar and mercy seat can be used by metonymy for the sacrifice of Christ, but this is not the same as saying that the mercy seat is specifically intended here.

author, who insists throughout that Christians have something better than an earthly sanctuary and animal sacrifices, certainly does not suggest that they have a material altar. It has, indeed, been thought by some commentators that by "we" in "we have an altar" he means "we Hebrews" and not "we Christians."[66] In that case the reference would be simply to the Levitical sacrifice prescribed for the Day of Atonement, as though he wished to say: "There is a sacrifice prescribed in the Levitical ritual which those who minister in the tabernacle have no right to eat." But "we have" here must surely have the same force as "we have" in 8:1, "we have such a high priest" ("this is the kind of high priest we have").[67]

Christians had none of the visible apparatus which in those days was habitually associated with religion and worship—no sacred buildings, no altars, no sacrificing priest. Their pagan neighbors thought they had no God, and called them atheists; their Jewish neighbors, too, might criticize them for having no visible means of spiritual support. So Archbishop Laud, when he came to Scotland in attendance on King Charles I in 1633, found that its benighted inhabitants had "no religion at all that I could see—which grieved me much."[68] The way in which Irenaeus expounds the nature of true Christian sacrifices suggests that he knew of people who said: "You Christians have no real religion, for you have no sacrifices."[69] If there were people in the first century who said, "You Christians have no altar," our author replies: "We *have* an altar—and a better one than the Jews had under the Levitical order." The Christian altar was the sacrifice of Christ, the benefits of which were eternally accessible to them. Material food, even if it was called sacred, perished with the using;[70] in this new and spiritual order into which they had been introduced by faith, Christ was perpetually available, "the same yesterday, and today, yes, and for ever."

What connection is there between this passage and the Eucharist? No direct connection at all. It is remarkable how our author avoids mentioning the Eucharist when he has every opportunity to do so; for example, it would have been easy for him to derive some eucharistic significance from the bread and wine which Melchizedek brought to Abraham when he met him "returning from the slaughter of the kings" (7:1); but he does not even mention the

---

66. R. Anderson, *Buddha*, pp. 301-4; *The Hebrews Epistle* (London, 1911), pp. 119-25; W. H. Spencer, "Hebrews xiii. 10," *ExT* 50 (1938-39), p. 284. The latter appeals to A. C. Downer, *The Principle of Interpretation of the Epistle of the Hebrews* (London, 1928).

67. Cf. C. F. D. Moule, "Sanctuary and Sacrifice," p. 37. In this article Heb. 13:10 is interpreted as part of a Christian apologetic answering the charge that Christians had neither priesthood nor altar, neither sacrifice nor sanctuary.

68. Quoted by T. Carlyle, *Cromwell's Letters and Speeches*, introduction.

69. Irenaeus, *Heresies* 4.17f.

70. Cf. Col. 2:20-23, with *Colossians–Philemon–Ephesians*, NICNT, pp. 123-29.

bread and wine (cf. p. 157 with n. 10). His failure to mention them, let alone discern some Christian meaning in them, can scarcely be accidental. If we had any independent knowledge of the community addressed, it might give us some clue to the omission of eucharistic references from his argument. It has, indeed, been suspected that they treated the Eucharist as a sacred meal[71] rather after the Essene or Qumranic fashion,[72] and did not appreciate that "the Body of Christ is given, taken, and eaten, in the Supper, only after an heavenly and spiritual manner," and that "the means whereby the Body of Christ is received and eaten in the Supper is Faith."[73] But this suspicion can be nothing more than a tentative inference from the general tenor of the epistle.

The most that can be said is that our author may be pointing to the truth of Christian experience which is independently attested in the Eucharist— that Christ is both the sacrifice and the sustenance of his people, and that as sacrifice and as sustenance alike he is to be appropriated by faith.[74]

12 The fact that the bodies of the animals sacrificed on the Day of Atonement were burned outside the camp suggests a parallel to the fact that Jesus was crucified outside one of the city gates of Jerusalem.[75] The parallel may seem inexact, since the animals of the sin offering were actually slaughtered within the camp; our author may, however, have also in mind the fact that the red heifer, which was a kind of sin offering, was slaughtered outside the camp.[76] Jesus died[77] in order to "sanctify the people"—bring

71. Cf. O. Holtzmann, "Der Hebräerbrief und das Abendmahl," *ZNW* 10 (1909), pp. 251-60; J. Moffatt, ICC, *ad loc.*, for the view that our author is engaging in a polemic against a rising "sacramentarianism" which interpreted the Eucharist as an "eating" of the body of Christ. "When θυσιαστήριον is identified with the Lord's table, it becomes possible to hear . . . an early protest against the realistic sacramental view of the Lord's supper which sought to base its efficacy on conceptions of communion popular among the pagan mysteries" (J. Moffatt, *Introduction to the Literature of the New Testament* [Edinburgh, ³1918], pp. 454f.). But it is not until a much later date that we find the Lord's Table spoken of as an altar—once doubtfully in Irenaeus (*Heresies* 4.18.6), once or twice in Tertullian (*On Prayer* 19; *Exhortation to Chastity* 10), and then regularly from Cyprian onward. Cf. Westcott's "Additional Note . . . on the History of the Word θυσιαστήριον," in his *Hebrews*, pp. 455-63; J. B. Lightfoot, *Philippians* (London, ⁶1881), p. 265, n. 2.

72. Cf. K. G. Kuhn, "The Lord's Supper and the Communal Meal at Qumran," *The Scrolls and the New Testament*, ed. K. Stendahl (London, 1958), pp. 65-93; M. Black, *The Scrolls and Christian Origins* (London, 1961), pp. 102-15.

73. The Thirty-Nine Articles, Article XXVIII ("Of the Lord's Supper").

74. Cf. John 6:48-58, with the interpretative principle in vv. 63f. Apart from the records of the institution, it is noteworthy how infrequently the Eucharist is mentioned in the NT—much less frequently than baptism.

75. Cf. John 19:20, "the place where Jesus was crucified was near the city"—but therefore outside it.

76. Num. 19:3 (cf. pp. 215f. with n. 88).

77. Gk. ἔπαθεν, "suffered." Cf. for the absolute use of this verb in reference to the death of Christ Luke 22:15; 24:46; Acts 1:3; 17:3; 1 Pet. 2:21; also Heb. 9:26 above.

them to God as worshipers purified in conscience—by means of his blood, the willing sacrifice of his life.[78] And the practical implication of his dying "outside the gate" is made plain in the exhortation which follows.

13   "Let us then go to him outside the camp, bearing the stigma that he bore" (NEB). Jesus was led outside Jerusalem to be crucified, and this is regarded as a token of his rejection by all that Jerusalem represented. To have his messianic claims rejected by the leaders of the people was in itself a stigma; to be cast out and crucified added to that stigma. But, as Moses in his day "considered the stigma that rests on God's Anointed greater wealth than the treasures of Egypt" (11:26, NEB), so the call came now to the people of Christ to consider that same stigma greater wealth than anything they could hope to gain by declining to burn their boats and commit themselves unreservedly to him. Our author may have recalled an Old Testament occasion when, according to the Septuagint version he knew, God was rejected in the camp of Israel and manifested his presence outside. For, after the incident of the golden calf, "Moses took his tent and pitched it outside the camp, far off from the camp, and it was called 'The Tent of Testimony'; and so it was, that everyone who sought the Lord would go out to the tent which was outside the camp."[79] Now, in the person of Jesus, God had again been rejected in the camp; his presence was therefore to be enjoyed outside the camp, where Jesus was, and everyone who sought him must go out and approach him through Jesus. In this context the "camp" stands for the established fellowship and ordinances of Judaism. To abandon them, with all their sacred associations inherited from remote antiquity, was a hard thing, but it was a necessary thing. They had been accustomed to think of the "camp" and all that was inside it as sacred, while everything outside it was profane and unclean.[80] Were they to leave its sacred precincts and venture on to unhallowed ground?[81] Yes, because in Jesus the old values had been reversed. What was formerly sacred

---

78. Cf. 10:10, 14, and (especially) 29.

79. Ex. 33:7, LXX. Philo (*Giants* 53f.) characteristically interprets this to mean the abandonment "of all created things and of the inmost veil and wrapping of mere opinion" so as to come to God with the mind unimpeded; Moses, in other words, "set up his judgment where it could not be deflected," outside the whole array of physical things, and then only began to worship God aright.

80. The bodies of Nadab and Abihu were carried outside the camp after they were burned as a result of offering "unholy fire" (Lev. 10:4f.); the blasphemer was stoned to death outside the camp (Lev. 24:14, 23); Miriam had to spend the seven days of her leprosy "shut up outside the camp" (Num. 12:14f.). The scapegoat (although the precise phrase is not used in connection with it) was taken as far outside the camp as possible, laden with the sins of the people (Lev. 16:20-22; see p. 207).

81. This aspect of the exhortation is well brought out by H. Koester, "Outside the Camp: Hebrews 13:9-14," *HTR* 55 (1962), pp. 299-315. He points out, *inter alia,* that, whereas the man who burned the carcasses of the animals sacrificed on the Day of Atonement was permitted to

was now unhallowed, because Jesus had been expelled from it; what was formerly unhallowed was now sacred, because Jesus was there. "Let us then go outside the camp" might be a hard exhortation; "Let us then go to him" should not be hard for any Christian; to whom else should they go? True, to be associated with him meant bearing the stigma he bore; it meant taking up the cross and following him; it meant leaving the shelter of their *collegia licita*[82] for a fellowship which invited the hostile attention of imperial law; but if, like Moses, they "kept their eyes fixed on the reward," they would see that the stigma carried eternal glory with it.[83] There, "outside the camp," stood Jesus, calling them to follow him. Inside they felt secure; they knew where they were amid its familiar installations; they were psychologically insulated from the world outside. But Jesus claimed the world outside for himself. Other Jewish Christians, Hellenists like themselves, had taken the initiative in evangelizing the Gentile world. The future lay not with the "camp" but with the Gentile mission;[84] let them exchange the imagined security of their old associations for the new venture to which Jesus was leading his followers out. Time and again in the history of the people of God a similar call has come when a new advance must be made into the unknown and unfamiliar, to occupy fresh territory under the leadership of Jesus. There is nothing static about him or his cause; to stand still is to fall behind him.

> New occasions teach new duties;
>> Time makes ancient good uncouth:
> They must upward still and onward
>> Who would keep abreast of truth.[85]

14 Moreover, the old securities to which their hearts clung were themselves insecure; the old order was about to crash. By responding to the call to go out, they would be the gainers; they would be leaving a "city" which was doomed to pass away for "the city which has the (true) foundations, of which God is the architect and builder"[86] (11:10). At present, the heavenly city was yet to come; but by faith those who went forth to Christ were already enrolled in its register of burgesses. Every earthly institution belongs to "the things that are shaken" (12:27); in none of them can the human heart find permanent rest. "The city of God remaineth."

---

come back into the camp after the due washing of his body and clothes (Lev. 16:28), the recipients of the epistle are commanded to stay outside the camp.

82. See S. Applebaum, "The Legal Status of the Jewish Communities in the Diaspora," in *The Jewish People in the First Century,* ed. S. Safrai and M. Stern, I (Assen, 1974), p. 460.

83. Cf. 11:26 (p. 312 with n. 188).

84. Cf. W. Manson, *The Epistle to the Hebrews* (London, 1951), p. 151.

85. J. R. Lowell (1819-91).

86. Cf. p. 293, n. 85; pp. 356f., nn. 148-51.

15 Were they told that they had no sacrifices and no altar? But of course they still had sacrifices to offer, even if there remained no more sacrifice for sin. The sacrifice of thanksgiving had once been accompanied by an animal sacrifice in the temple—it was a form of peace offering, according to Lev. 7:12.[87] Animal sacrifices had been rendered forever obsolete by the sacrifice of Christ, but the sacrifice of thanksgiving might still be offered to God, and indeed should be offered to him by all who appreciated the perfect sacrifice of Christ.[88] No longer in association with animal sacrifices, but through Jesus, the sacrifice of praise was acceptable to God. The dissociation of this sacrifice from animal sacrifices had already been adumbrated in an Asaphite psalm:

If I were hungry, I would not tell you;
  for the world and all that is in it is mine.
Do I eat the flesh of bulls,
  or drink the blood of goats?
Offer to God a sacrifice of thanksgiving;
  and pay your vows to the Most High;
and call upon me in the day of trouble;
  I will deliver you, and you shall glorify me.[89]

The sacrifice of praise is further described as "the fruit of lips which acknowledge his name," in language borrowed from the Septuagint version of Hos. 14:2 (MT, LXX 14:3). In the Masoretic text of that passage the sacrifice of praise is a substitute for animal sacrifices; so the ERV/ARV translate it: "so will we render as bullocks the offering of our lips."[90] In this spirit the Qumran *Rule of the Community* declares that when the prescriptions of the community are carried out in Israel, "to obtain favor for the land apart from the flesh of burnt-offerings and the fat of sacrifice, then the oblation of the lips according to right judgment shall be as a sweet savor of righteousness,

---

87. With ἀναφέρωμεν θυσίαν αἰνέσεως here, cf. Lev. 7:2, LXX (MT, EVV 7:12): ἐὰν μὲν περὶ αἰνέσεως προσφέρῃ αὐτήν, καὶ προσοίσει ἐπὶ τῆς θυσίας τῆς αἰνέσεως ἄρτους ἐκ σεμιδάλεως . . . ("If he offers it [the peace offering] for praise, then he shall bring for the sacrifice of praise loaves of fine flour . . ."). Our author's argument practically amounts to saying that, for Christians, their sin offering is also their peace offering—something which was impossible under the old order.

88. Cf. 1 Pet. 2:9, where Christians, as "a royal priesthood" (cf. Ex. 19:6), "declare the wonderful deeds" of their Savior God (cf. Isa. 43:21).

89. Ps. 50:12-15 (LXX 49:12-15). Cf. Ps. 141:2 (LXX 140:2) for the sacrificial value of prayer and heart-worship.

90. MT *pārîm śᵉpātēnû;* LXX καρπὸν χειλέων ἡμῶν (whence our author derived καρπὸν χειλέων here) implies a different division of the Hebrew words, *pᵉrî miśśᵉpātēnû,* "fruit from our lips." It is a disputed question which interpretation should be regarded as representing the prophet's meaning; the RSV ("the fruit of our lips") follows the LXX, but MT "bullocks" is appropriate to the sacrificial context.

and the perfection of one's ways as an acceptable free will offering."[91] At Qumran, however, this did not involve a total repudiation of animal sacrifices on principle. Similarly, while Philo provides parallels to this insistence on the sacrificial value of thanksgiving and deeds of piety, and holds that sacrifice is acceptable only if it is the expression of true heart-devotion, he does not suggest that the sacrificial ritual itself can be dispensed with.[92] Our author's treatment of the sacrificial ritual as antiquated is due to his understanding of the finality and perpetual efficacy of the sacrifice of Christ.[93]

16 To the sacrifice of praise is added the sacrifice of kind and loving action.[94] "Never forget to show kindness and to share what you have with others; for such are the sacrifices which God approves" (NEB). Here we have the proper ritual of Christianity. James expresses the same thing when he says: "That kind of religion which is without stain or fault in the sight of God our Father is this: to go to the help of orphans and widows in their distress and keep oneself untarnished by the world"[95] (Jas. 1:27, NEB). To the same effect, too, is Peter's exhortation to those who come to Christ, the chief cornerstone, to be themselves as "living stones, . . . built into a spiritual house,[96] to be a holy priesthood, to offer spiritual sacrifices, acceptable to God through Jesus Christ" (1 Pet. 2:5), as is also Paul's plea to the Roman Christians to present their bodies "a living sacrifice, holy and acceptable to God, which is your spiritual worship" (Rom. 12:1). Christianity is sacrificial through and through; it is founded on the one self-offering of Christ, and the offering of his people's praise and property, of their service and their lives, is caught up into the perfection of his acceptable sacrifice, and is accepted in him.

91. 1QS 9.4f.; see also p. 193 and the reference to 4QFlorilegium 1.6, p. 229, n. 153. Cf. 1QH 1.28: "Thou hast determined the fruit of the lips before ever they were." Cf. M. Mansoor, "Thanksgiving Hymns and Massoretic Text," RQ 3 (1961-62), no. 11, pp. 391f.

92. Cf. Philo, Noah's Planting 126-35 (on the primacy of praise); Special Laws 1.267-72 (where he expounds the spiritual significance of the red heifer ceremony); Migration of Abraham 89-93 (where he criticizes the view that the literal observance of ceremonial laws may be abandoned if their spiritual lessons are learned and practiced). Cf. pp. 209f., n. 63.

93. On "the sacrifice of praise" A. Snell says: "If any one wants to find here a reference to our Eucharist, he may be right in doing so" (New and Living Way [London, 1959], p. 161). Contrariwise J. A. Bengel says here in his succinct way: Nil de missa, "This has nothing to do with the Mass" (Gnomon, ad loc.). The sacrifice of praise always accompanies the Eucharist, but is not restricted to it.

94. Gk. εὐποιΐα (here only in the NT; cf. εὖ ποιῆσαι, Mark 14:7); see New Docs., III (1978), § 38. Cf. Philo, On Flight and Finding 18f., for the sacrificial quality of "the virtues and the modes of action that are in accordance with them" (by way of a remarkable exegesis of Ex. 8:26, "we will sacrifice the abominations of Egypt to the Lord our God").

95. Cf. Hermas, Shepherd, Similitude 1.8-11, where the true wealth which believers are urged to acquire consists of "afflicted souls"—i.e., they should "go to the help of widows and orphans."

D. SUBMISSION TO GUIDES (13:17)

17 *Obey your guides*[97] *and submit*[98] *to them: they keep watch over your souls in the knowledge that they must render an account of their service.*[99] *Help them to do this with joy and not with sighing: that would not do you any good.*[100]

17   The guides referred to here are probably the successors of those whose memory they are exhorted to cherish in v. 7. Our author evidently has as much confidence in the present leaders as in their predecessors. Perhaps they were leaders in the wider city church from whose fellowship and jurisdiction the group addressed in the epistle was tempted to withdraw. At any rate, the leaders carried a weighty responsibility; they were accountable for the spiritual well-being of those placed in their care. No wonder they lost sleep[101] over this responsibility—for the "watching" could well involve this as well as general vigilance—if some of their flock were in danger of straying beyond their control. The readers are invited to cooperate with their leaders, to make their responsible task easier for them, so that they could discharge it joyfully and not with sorrow.[102] The idea is on the same lines as Paul's exhortation to the Philippian Christians to lead such lives in this world "that in the day of Christ I may be proud that I did not run in vain or labor in vain"[103] (Phil. 2:16).

There would always be a tendency throughout the churches for visitors who came purveying new and esoteric doctrines to be regarded as much more attractive and interesting personalities than the rather humdrum local leaders, who never taught anything new, but were content with the conservative line of apostolic tradition. Nevertheless it was those local leaders, and not the purveyors of strange teaching, who had a real concern for the welfare of the church and a sense of their accountability to God in this respect. If the

96. For this conception of a living house or household cf. Heb. 3:6 (pp. 93-95).

97. Your ἡγούμενοι, as in vv. 7, 24.

98. Gk. ὑπείκω, here only in the NT; in the LXX only in 4 Macc. 6:35.

99. Gk. ὡς λόγον ἀποδώσοντες. D* reads ὡς λόγον ἀποδώσονται περὶ ὑμῶν ("because they will render an account concerning you"). Cf. p. 114, n. 58.

100. Lit. "this would be unprofitable (ἀλυσιτελές) for you." Gk. ἀλυσιτελής is a classical word, not found elsewhere in the Greek Bible.

101. Gk. ἀγρυπνέω, "keep watch," has the etymological sense of chasing away sleep.

102. Gk. στενάζοντες, "groaning." Moffatt (ICC, *ad loc.*) quotes Sir Edward Denny's lines:

O give us hearts to love like Thee,
  Like Thee, O Lord, to grieve
Far more for others' sins than all
  The wrongs that we receive.

103. Cf. 1 Thess. 2:19f.

discharge of their responsibility and the ultimate rendering of their account were made a burden to them, the resultant disadvantage would fall on those who were led as well as on the leaders.

E. REQUEST FOR PRAYER (13:18-19)

18 *Pray[104] for us: we are convinced[105] that we have a clear conscience, as we desire to behave honorably in all things.*
19 *I beg you the more earnestly[106] to do this, so that I may be restored to you the more quickly.*

18 The terms of our author's request for prayer for himself[107] may suggest that he himself occupied, or had occupied, some position of responsibility in regard to his readers. But what this position might be we can only surmise. The good conscience[108] of which he speaks is probably the fruit of a sense of duty done, a responsibility well discharged. Like Paul he could say: "our conscience assures us that in our dealings with our fellow-men, and above all in our dealings with you, our conduct has been governed by a devout and godly sincerity, by the grace of God and not by worldly wisdom. . . . In order that our service may not be brought into discredit, we avoid giving offence in anything" (2 Cor. 2:12; 6:3, NEB).

19 He had hoped to renew his former personal association with them, but had not been able to do so thus far; however, he hopes that the way for a reunion will soon be opened up, and he invites them to redouble their prayers for him to this end. It is difficult to be sure how much should be read between the lines of this petition. Does he suspect a certain spirit of resentment against him for some reason or other—perhaps because he has been so long away? Is there an element of personal apologia in his request for prayer and his protestation of conscientious and honorable behavior? And what was the nature of the restraint which prevented him from coming to see them sooner? Some have thought of imprisonment; but in that case he might have said so explicitly. His reference to Timothy's release in v. 23

---

104. D and Chrysostom read an intrusive καί ("also"), as though to say, "Pray for them, and pray for us (me) too."

105. Gk. πειθόμεθα, changed to the singular πείθομαι ("I am persuaded") in a few minuscules (256, etc.) and to the perfect πεποίθαμεν in ℵᶜ Cᶜ D Ψ *et al.* For πείθομαι ὅτι cf. Rom. 8:38; 2 Tim. 1:5, 12 (where, however, the perfect πέπεισμαι is used in this way); see *New Docs.*, IV (1979), § 15 (where πείθομαι ὅτι is quoted from *P. Oxy. Helsinki* 47b).

106. Gk. περισσοτέρως, as in 2:1.

107. That the plural is purely literary (cf. 5:11; 6:9, 11) is suggested by the immediate transition to the singular in v. 19. But see p. 19 with n. 81.

108. Cf. p. 209, n. 62 (on 9:9).

has been thought to suggest that he himself is not in custody, but a contrary inference has also been drawn.

F. PRAYER AND DOXOLOGY (13:20-21)

20 *Now may the God of peace, who by the blood of the eternal covenant brought back from the dead our Lord Jesus,*[109] *the great shepherd of the sheep,*

21 *fit you to do his will in everything that is good,*[110] *as he brings to pass*[111] *in us*[112] *whatever gives him pleasure, through Jesus Christ; to whom be the glory for ever and ever.*[113] *Amen.*

20, 21 This prayer has the general structure of a collect[114] in the third person, consisting of *(a)* the invocation ("Now may the God of peace"), *(b)* an adjective clause setting forth the ground on which the following petition is based ("who . . . brought back from the dead our Lord Jesus . . ."), *(c)* the main petition ("fit you to do his will in everything that is good"), *(d)* a subsidiary petition ("as he brings to pass in us whatever gives him pleasure"), *(e)* a pleading of the mediatorial merit of Christ ("through Jesus Christ"), *(f)* a doxology ("to whom be the glory for ever and ever"), and *(g)* the "Amen."

That God is invoked as "the God of peace"[115] may suggest that the community was troubled by disunity, which needed to be healed if the pleasure of God was to be wrought out in their midst. It is true that in the Old Testament "peace" has the fuller sense of well-being and salvation, but the Greek sense of the word would come more readily to our author's mind than the Hebrew sense.

This is the only place in the epistle where the title "shepherd" is given to

---

109. D* Ψ 33 etc., with some Latin authorities and the Syriac Peshitta, add "Christ" (a characteristic Western expansion).

110. Gk. ἐν παντὶ ἀγαθῷ, to which C, with the majority of later MSS, the Syriac Peshitta, and the TR, adds ἔργῳ (cf. AV/KJV "in every good work"), while A adds ἔργῳ καὶ λόγῳ (probably under the influence of 2 Thess. 2:17, "in every good work and word").

111. Gk. ποιῶν, to which the unintelligible αὐτῷ is prefixed by א* A C 33 etc., αὐτό by 𝔭46, and αὐτός by 1912 (cf. d, *ipso faciente*). Hort argued that αὐτός was the original reading, αὐτῷ being a corruption of it; it is much more probable that we have to do with a dittography of the preceding αὐτοῦ (in τὸ θέλημα αὐτοῦ, "his will"). Cf. G. Zuntz, *Text*, p. 62.

112. Gk. ἐν ἡμῖν, attested by 𝔭46 א D K 0121b and the majority of MSS, with the Peshitta; A and some other MSS, with the Latin versions and the TR, read ἐν ὑμῖν ("in you").

113. Gk. εἰς τοὺς αἰῶνας τῶν αἰώνων. 𝔭46 D H and some other authorities omit τῶν αἰώνων, and this shorter reading may be original, since the tendency was always to expand such doxologies (cf. Zuntz, *Text*, pp. 120ff.).

114. A prayer-form characteristic of the Western Church, from Lat. *collecta oratio* ("a gathered-together prayer")

115. Cf. Rom. 15:33; 16:20; 1 Thess. 5:23.

Jesus; but it is a title which comprehends the other rôles which are here assigned to him. Indeed, Markus Barth goes so far as to say, in a study of our author's use of the Old Testament, that for him "exegesis is the endeavor to help people in need by telling them what the Bible says of their shepherd Jesus Christ."[116] The form of the title is derived from the Septuagint version of Isa. 63:11: "Where is he who brought up out of the sea the shepherd of the sheep?" The words in their original context refer to Moses—or, if the plural "shepherds" be read, to Moses and Aaron, in the sense of Ps. 77:20, "Thou didst lead thy people like a flock by the hand of Moses and Aaron." Here they are applied to Jesus as the second Moses, who was brought up not from the sea but from the realm of the dead.[117] (In the Exodus typology of the New Testament the "sea of reeds" which Israel crossed on the way out of Egypt is a token of the death and resurrection of Christ into which his people are baptized.)

This is the only reference to our Lord's resurrection in the epistle; elsewhere the emphasis is on his exaltation to the right hand of God, in keeping with the exegesis of Ps. 110:1, 4, and the exposition of Jesus' high priesthood.[118]

Jesus was brought up from death "by the blood of the eternal covenant" (AV/KJV, RSV, NEB); that is to say, his resurrection is the demonstration that his sacrifice of himself has been accepted by God and the new covenant established on the basis of that sacrifice. The phrase "the blood of the eternal covenant" echoes 9:20, where Moses speaks of "the blood of the covenant" confirmed by God with Israel on the basis of the law.[119] But now a better sacrifice has been offered, and the new covenant ratified thereby is superior to the older one in this respect among others, that it endures forever. (There may also be an echo here of Zech. 9:11, where God promises Zion that he will release her captives from the waterless pit "because of the blood of my covenant with you"; if so, it is but a verbal echo, but one may think of the rôle of the shepherd in the following chapters, Zech. 11:4-17; 13:7.)

116. "The Old Testament in Hebrews," in *Current Issues in New Testament Interpretation*, ed. W. Klassen and G. F. Snyder (New York, 1962), p. 58.

117. For other NT applications of ποιμήν to Jesus cf. Mark 14:27 (quotation of Zech. 13:7); John 10:11, 14, 16 (echoing Ezek. 34, where Yahweh speaks of "my servant David," i.e., the coming Messiah, as the true shepherd of his own people Israel); 1 Pet. 2:25; 5:4 (ἀρχιποίμην). The ideal of the shepherd-king goes back to the beginnings of Greek literature, and appears earlier still in the literature of other Near Eastern peoples. (See F. F. Bruce, *This Is That: The New Testament Development of Some Old Testament Themes* [Exeter/Grand Rapids, 1968], pp. 100-114.) Philo depicts God as the supreme Shepherd (cf. Ps. 23:1), who entrusts his flock, the universe, to the shepherd care of the Logos, his firstborn Son (*Agriculture* 51; *Change of Names* 115f.).

118. See pp. 33, 87f.

119. Cf. p. 219, n. 109. The preposition ἐν ("by") here is instrumental, used in much the same sense as διά in 9:12 (see pp. 213f.). The choice of ἐν in this place may be due to the influence of Zech. 9:11 (LXX), ἐν αἵματι διαθήκης ("by the blood of the covenant").

The prayer, then, is that the people addressed may be spiritually equipped[120] for every form of good work, and thus fulfil God's will as he operates in them "both to will and to work for his good pleasure," as Paul would put it (Phil. 2:13).

The adjective clause which concludes this prayer ("to whom be the glory for ever and ever") is probably to be taken as an ascription of glory to God, the subject of the sentence (as is suggested by the punctuation of the RSV), rather than as referring to "Jesus Christ" as its immediate antecedent. Our author has already made it plain in v. 15 that it is through Christ that glory is to be given to God.

VIII. POSTSCRIPT (13:22-25)

A. PERSONAL NOTES (13:22-23)

22 *Now, my brothers, please put up[121] with my word of exhortation; I am sending you this letter in few words.*
23 *You should know[122] that our[123] brother Timothy has been set free; I shall see you with him if he comes fairly soon.*

22 The "word of exhortation"[124] refers to the whole of the preceding epistle. In Acts 13:15, where the rulers of the synagogue at Pisidian Antioch send a message to Paul and Barnabas inviting them to pass on any "word of exhortation" which they may have for the assembled company, the phrase clearly denotes a homily; it is thus a very suitable description for this epistle, which is a homily in written form, with some personal remarks added at the end. But could a document of this length be appropriately spoken of as written "in few words"?[125] It might be a long letter, but not a long homily; it can be read aloud within one hour. At one point the writer has said "there is much that we have to say" (Heb. 5:11); but at another point he indicates that

---

120. Gk. καταρτίζω, "put into a proper condition" or "make complete."

121. Gk. ἀνέχεσθε (imperative), for which D* Ψ 33 and a few other authorities read ἀνέχεσθαι (infinitive, dependent on παρακαλῶ, "I exhort").

122. Gk. γινώσκετε, in form indicative or imperative; the imperative (represented above by "you should know") is required by the sense here.

123. Gk. ἡμῶν ("our") is omitted by ℵ² D² K P Ψ byz and the TR, but even so it is understood (cf. the italicized *"our"* in the AV/KJV); it is expressed in 𝔭⁴⁶ ℵ* A C D* I *al* and the early versions.

124. Gk. λόγος παρακλήσεως. See p. 25.

125. Gk. διὰ βραχέων ἐπέστειλα ὑμῖν, "I have sent you a letter [ἐπιστέλλω being the verb corresponding to the substantive ἐπιστολή, "epistle," "letter"] by means of a few (words)." The aorist is probably epistolary.

he could have said much more (9:5b). Even if we regard it as a letter, it is not as long as Romans and 1 Corinthians. There is no need to suppose that the "word of exhortation" might be confined to the concluding admonitions of 13:1-19; these are so brief that no writer would think it necessary to ask his readers to bear with them[126] (the added remark about "few words" makes it clear that it is the length of the exhortation, not its content, that our author thinks the readers might begin to find wearisome).

23 Timothy is almost certainly Paul's friend of that name. We have no other account of his imprisonment. (It is just possible to argue that "set free" means not "released from prison" but "sent away on some commission";[127] but it is very unlikely that the verb, used absolutely as it is here, has this latter meaning.) The place of his imprisonment was at some distance from the author's residence at the time, yet nearer to the author than to his readers, since he has news of Timothy's release before his readers are likely to know of it, and if Timothy joins him where he is they can travel together to visit them. Timothy was with Paul when Philippians, Colossians, and Philemon were written; that is to say (in the opinion of the present commentator), he was with him in Rome. In 2 Tim. 4:9-13 Paul seems to summon Timothy from Ephesus to Rome, but this is uncertain, as is the chronological setting of these verses.[128]

---

126. G. A. Simcox, however, distinguishes the "word of exhortation" (chs. 1–12) from the "few words" (13:1-19); see p. 367, n. 3. R. Anderson similarly takes the "few words" to refer to ch. 13, written as a covering letter to accompany the treatise (*The Hebrews Epistle*, p. 12). But the identity of the "word of exhortation" with the few "words" is implied by the structure of this sentence. "The writer surely means . . . that he has refrained from developing his great theme at undue length, as he was writing a 'word of exhortation' and not a merely academic treatise" (R. V. G. Tasker, "Integrity," p. 138).

127. The verb is ἀπολελυμένον (perfect passive participle of ἀπολύω). It is used, e.g., in Acts 13:3 of the action of the Antiochene church in "releasing" Paul and Barnabas for a more extended apostolic ministry. E. D. Jones ("Authorship," p. 566) argues that the meaning here is that Timothy has already set out from the place where the writer is to go to Corinth *via* Macedonia (in the light of his theory mentioned on p. 368, n. 4); but "it must be confessed that the more obvious meaning of the word is 'released', and that the sentence refers to some otherwise unknown imprisonment of Timothy" (R. V. G. Tasker, "Integrity," p. 138). J. D. Legg ("Our Brother Timothy," *EQ* 40 [1968], pp. 220-23) has suggested that Timothy was the author of Hebrews, but that since he had been under restraint for a time this reference to his recent release was added by a friend of his, equally well known to the recipients.

128. Various suggestions have been made by commentators in harmony with their general views on the provenience and destination of the epistle. Thus A. Nairne hazards "the guess that both the author and Timothy may have been brought to Italy by the peril of their master S. Paul—that S. Paul has perished in Nero's persecution, that Timothy has been imprisoned, and that the freedom of both Timothy and the author is now assured" (*The Epistle of Priesthood* [Edinburgh, 1913], p. 432). W. F. Howard similarly suggests that Timothy, having been summoned to Rome by Paul (2 Tim. 4:9-13), was compromised by his association with the apostle and imprisoned, but was now at liberty again. He then goes on to argue that the community addressed must have been one, outside Italy, where Timothy was well known, and where he "would be a useful helper in the struggle to win back the waverers to their Christian loyalty

B. FINAL GREETINGS AND BENEDICTION (13:24-25)

24 Greet all[129] your guides, and all (God's) holy people. Those who are
from Italy send you their greetings.
25 Grace be with you all.[130]

24 They have already been exhorted to obey their leaders; now they are
asked to convey the writer's greetings to them, and to all their fellow-believers—that is, we may take it, to members of other house churches than their
own in the city-wide fellowship to which they belonged.

"Those from Italy" who send their greetings are probably, as the RSV
puts it, "those who come from Italy."[131] In that case our author is writing outside Italy to a community in Italy, and sending greetings home from a group
of Italian friends who are with him at the time. But contemporary usage does
not exclude the possibility that people *in* Italy are referred to[132]—"those who
are in Italy and send their greetings with mine from Italy," as A. Nairne suggests.[133] As far as translation goes, it is best to render the ambiguous Greek
by an ambiguous English phrase; so the NEB says: "Greetings to you from
our Italian friends!"

25 The benediction is identical with that of Tit. 3:15.[134] The final
"Amen" is textually doubtful and therefore omitted from our translation.

---

before the fatal die was cast. Ephesus seems the most likely place" ("The Epistle to the Hebrews," *Interpretation* 5 [1951], pp. 80-91). Contrariwise, J. A. Robertson thought it most likely
that "the letter was written *from* Ephesus, since Timothy is mentioned as a colleague" (*The Hidden Romance of the New Testament* [London, 1920], p. 180). But all that we can infer from this
reference to an imprisonment of Timothy of which we have no other information is that probably the readers and certainly "the writer stood in some relationship to the Pauline world-mission
circle" (W. Manson, *The Epistle to the Hebrews*, p. 169).

129. 𝔭[46] omits "all" (πάντας).

130. For "with you all" (μετὰ πάντων ὑμῶν) D* reads "with all the saints" (μετὰ πάντων
τῶν ἁγίων). "Amen" is absent from 𝔭[46] ℵ* I 33 and the Sahidic and Armenian versions; it is
probably a liturgical addition. Various scribal subscriptions appear in later MSS: that in the AV
("Written to the Hebrews from Italy by Timothy"), an obvious inference from vv. 23f., is found
in K 460 etc. and the TR; H P et al. have "Written from Italy"; A has "Written from Rome";
1911 has "Written from Athens."

131. Gk. ἀσπάζονται ὑμᾶς οἱ ἀπὸ τῆς 'Ιταλίας, lit. "they from Italy greet you." G. W. Buchanan thinks that "the location may have been fabricated to give the letter the appearance of
originality" (*To the Hebrews*, p. 243)—why, it is difficult to see.

132. Moffatt (ICC, *ad loc.*) quotes from *Oxyrhynchus Papyri*, I (London, 1898), 81, ll.
5f., τῶν ἀπ' 'Οξυρύγχων in a context where it must mean "the inhabitants of Oxyrhynchus." Cf.
also A. Deissmann, "Die griechische Titelatur des Triumvirn Marcus Antonius," *Hermes* 33
(1898), p. 344; *Light from the Ancient East*, E.T. (London, 1927), pp. 173, 200f. J. A. T. Robinson's comments on the passage (*Redating the New Testament* [London, 1976], pp. 206f.) are
most satisfactory: when the Roman destination is assumed, "a good deal else falls into place."

133. *The Epistle of Priesthood*, p. 433.

134. In the NT epistles "grace" (χάρις), whether at the beginning or at the end of a let-

Christians are Christians by virtue of certain acts of God which took place at a definite time in the past, but these acts of God have released a dynamic force which will never allow Christians to stick fast at any point short of that divine rest which in this life is always a goal to be aimed at and never a stage which has been reached. The faith once for all delivered to the saints is not something which can be caught and tamed; it continually leads the saints forth to new ventures in the cause of Christ, as God calls afresh. It was Abraham's firm faith in the unchanging God that made him so ready to go forth at God's bidding, not knowing whither he might be led. To stay at the point to which some revered teacher of the past has brought us, out of a mistaken sense of loyalty to him; to continue to follow a certain pattern of religious activity or attitude just because it was good enough for our fathers and grandfathers—these and the like are temptations which make the message of Hebrews a necessary and salutary one for us to listen to. Every fresh movement of the Spirit of God tends to become stereotyped in the next generation, and what we have heard with our ears, what our fathers have told us, becomes a tenacious tradition encroaching on the allegiance which ought to be accorded only to the living and active word of God. As Christians survey the world today, they see very much land waiting to be possessed in the name of Christ; but to take possession of it calls for a generous measure of that forward-looking faith which is so earnestly urged upon the readers of this epistle. Those first readers were living at a time when the old, cherished order was breaking up. Attachment to venerable traditions could avail them nothing in this situation; only attachment to the unchanging and onward-moving Christ could carry them forward and enable them to face a new order with confidence and power. So, in a day when everything that can be shaken is being shaken before our eyes and even beneath our feet, let us in our turn give thanks for the unshakable kingdom which we have inherited, which endures forever when everything else to which men and women may pin their hopes disappears and leaves not a wrack behind.

---

ter, tends to replace the similarly-sounding Greek word for "rejoice," "hail," or "farewell" (χαῖρε, χαίρετε, χαίρειν), regularly used in such formulas. See E. Lohmeyer, "Probleme paulinischer Theologie, I. Briefliche Grussüberschriften," *ZNW* 26 (1927), pp. 158-73.

INDEXES

CHIEF SUBJECTS

393

69, 220, 248; Old Testament sense of, 169, 191-92, 209 n. 63, 220; and sacrificial cultus, 238

Fornication, 350-51, 368 n. 6, 373

Forty years, significance of, 22, 99, 196

Fulfilment, time of: and Aaronic priesthood, 165-66; and believers, 334, 360; and city of God, 293; inaugurated by Christ, 46, 68, 110, 231, 278, 330; and Word of God, 111

Galatia, churches of, 6 n. 13, 69, 257, 344

Gentiles, 194 n. 72, 220 n. 111, 236, 280 n. 26, 364, 374, 382

Gethsemane, 127-28

Gideon, 319-20, 324, 371

Gift, heavenly, 145-46

Glory, 47-49, 60, 75-76, 81, 111, 252

Gospel, 29-34, 66-69, 105 n. 17, 354-55, 375 n. 42

Grace: and Christ's high-priestly service, 173; and covenant, 220, 223; divine initiative of, 192; and law, 67; and spiritual life, 144, 349, 376-77, 386; throne of, 116-17, 204, 249

Guides, spiritual, 374-75, 385-86, 391

Hasmonaeans, 122 n. 19, 125, 160 n. 21, 198

Heavens, 62, 115, 356 n. 150, 364

Hebrews: argument, xix-xxii; canonicity, 16-17, 22-25; date, 20-22, 209, 236, 268-70; and Dead Sea Scrolls, 7; exegesis in, 20, 26-29, 52, 207 n. 56; and gospel, 29-34; Greek text, 12, 26, 240; language, 15, 17; literary form, 3, 25, 44 n. 1, 367, 369 n. 11, 390 n. 126; midrash, use of, 27; purpose, 29; readers addressed, 3-14, 198, 268-71, 342, 368 n. 4, 371-72, 390 n. 128, 391; style, 19 n. 83, 20, 25, 47, 367; title, 3-4

Hebrews, authorship, 14-20; candidates: Apollos, 16 n. 63, 17 n. 74, 18, 20 n. 87, 274; Aquila, 18; Aristion, 18 n. 76; Barnabas, 11 n. 38, 16; Clement of Rome, 11 n. 38, 17, 19 n. 83; Epaphras, 18; Jude, 18 n. 76; Luke, 11 n. 38, 15, 16 n. 63, 17, 19 n. 83; Paul, 11 n. 38, 12-17, 20, 23, 166-67, 367-68; Peter, 18 n. 38; Philip (evangelist), 18 n. 76; Priscilla, 18-19; Silas/ Silvanus, 18 n. 76; Timothy, 18 n. 76, 390 n. 127; 391 nn. 128, 130

Hebron, 157, 292

Hellenists, 4, 8-10, 20, 382

Hendiadys, 120, 199

Herod the Great, 122 n. 19, 198

Herod Agrippa I, 268, 329

Hippo, Synod of (393), 17, 24

Holiness, 88, 265, 344, 348-49, 354, 359, 365

Holy of holies: heavenly, 155, 212, 230, 233,

250; and Qumran, 229 n. 153; ritual in, 214, 226, 230, 254, 378; tabernacle, 197-203, 206-9, 232, 252; throne of God, 155

Holy place, 197-99, 201, 250

Hope, 154-55, 169, 254, 256, 275, 292, 330

Hospitality, 370-71

Household of God, 91-94, 213, 229

Hymnody, early Christian, 47, 49, 73, 145 n. 40, 175 n. 81

Hyssop (marjoram), 215, 219, 225

Idolatry, 120 n. 12, 349-50, 354, 381

Image of God, 48-49, 57, 60, 276

Incarnation: and preexistence, 78 n. 55, 161 n. 22, 333, 337-38; purpose, 77, 85-88; representative aspect, 81-84, 88; significance, 78 n. 55, 81, 173, 243, 338; suffering, 82-84, 87-88, 115, 338; and will of God, 241-43. *See also* Logos

Incense altar, 27 n. 115, 197-202, 203 n. 35, 206-7, 225

Inheritance: eternal, 132, 220, 223, 293-94; promised, 291-93, 301, 330, 351

Isaac: and Abraham, 152-53, 154 n. 80, 286, 292, 294, 299, 302-5; Binding of, 302-5; blessing, 305, 343; example, 278 n. 15, 305; God of, 143, 300, 327; obedience, 305; and promise of God, 291, 298, 305, 307; and resurrection, 304; sacrifice, 152-53, 301-5; and title, divine, 129 n. 60

Isaiah, 328-29

Italy, church in, 13, 390 n. 128, 391

Jacob: blessing by, 305; dream, 186, 293 n. 88, 299; and Esau, 343, 350-51; faith, 298, 305-6, 351; God of, 143, 294, 300, 306-7, 327; name-change, 349 n. 102; pilgrim life, 154 n. 80, 292, 298-99; star from, 165 n. 42; trouble, time of his, 189

James the Just, 168 n. 53, 268

James, son of Zebedee, 101 n. 68, 127, 268, 329

Jephthah, 319-21

Jeremiah, 187-95, 324, 327-28

Jericho, 317-18

Jerubbaal. *See* Gideon

Jerusalem: church in, 4 n. 8, 8, 10-11, 21, 151, 268; city, 62, 262 n. 136, 265, 299, 317 n. 226, 328, 355-56, 380-81; Council of, 236; and David, 124, 355; heavenly, 8, 125, 293 n. 85, 294, 330, 356-57, 360, 382; king of, 158 n. 15; name, 159 n. 16, 356. *See also* City of God; Temple

Jezebel, 59 n. 83, 324, 328

Job, 344-45

John, apostle, 30, 34, 101 n. 68, 127, 329, 358 n. 159

John the Baptist: and baptism, 131, 142 n. 22,

216 n. 88, 256 n. 110; imprisonment, 68; and Jesus, 131, 274; preaching, 8, 140, 152, 329 n. 291
Jonathan (son of Saul), 324
Jonathan Maccabaeus, 122 n. 19, 125
Joseph (OT), 278, 299, 305-7, 310 n. 180
Joshua (son of Nun), 99, 102 n. 72, 108-9, 113 n. 51, 191, 224 n. 132, 278, 316-18, 322, 324
Joshua (son of Jehozadak; high priest), 109 n. 28, 121, 125, 253 n. 97
Josiah, 188-89, 191
Joy, 61, 339, 385
Judah, 124, 160, 165 n. 40, 167-68, 189, 318, 328, 355
Judaism: Alexandrian, 119 n. 6; ceremonial, 218, 314; and Christians, 100, 258-59; doctrine, 139, 141-43, 327, 377 n. 58, 381; and Melchizedek, 134 n. 78; relapse into, 100, 376; Roman, 377
Judas of Galilee, 85
Judas Maccabaeus, 85, 278, 324
Judgment: on disobedience, 111, 363, 373; doctrine, 139, 143, 263, 345, 359; final, 263, 272
Judith, 324

Kadesh-barnea, 98, 100, 113 n. 54, 204
Kingdom of God, 144 n. 36, 147, 344-45, 348, 364-65, 374, 377
Kingship, 60-61, 74-76, 124-25, 212. See also Enthronement; David, house of; Melchizedek

Lamb of God, 58 n. 78, 96, 175, 217 n. 92, 314, 356 n. 146, 358
Lampstand, 197-98, 206
Laodicea, church at, 11 n. 38, 339
Last days, 46, 259
Laughter, 294-95
Law, 51, 66-69, 166-67, 189-91, 234-39, 261-62, 334, 354, 357
Laying-on of hands, 139, 142-43, 146-47
Lectionary, triennial, 26, 203, 226
Leontopolis, Jewish temple at, 12 n. 49, 236 n. 11
Levi, 124, 162-65, 167-69, 203
Light, divine, 48, 144 n. 36, 145-46
Logos: in Philo, 48, 50 n. 36, 91 n. 8, 111, 113 n. 53, 165 n. 42, 173, 176, 388 n. 117; and Word of God, 112, 279, 314 n. 206
Lot, 157-58, 292, 371
Luke, 11 n. 38, 15, 16 n. 63, 17, 19 n. 83
Lycus valley, churches in, 6 n. 13, 11 n. 38, 377 n. 57

Maccabaeans, 325-26, 337
Mamre, 157, 371

Manasseh, 324, 328, 346 n. 84
Manna, 97, 146 n. 43, 197, 203-4
Manoah, 59 n. 81, 371
Marriage, 368, 372-73
Martyrdom: of Christians, 21, 85, 268, 284, 342, 375; in Judaism, 302-3, 323 n. 255, 325-28, 334 n. 11, 335, 337-38, 339 n. 48, 346 n. 84
Mary (mother of Jesus), 53, 55
Massah, 98
Mattathias, 278, 323 n. 255
Mediator, 50, 171-73, 185-86, 218-27, 294, 360, 388
Melchizedek: Genesis narrative, 29, 124, 153, 156-64, 379; and lectionary, 26; name, 124, 158; order of, 6, 64, 124-26, 132-36, 138, 144, 154-64, 168-72, 179, 181, 231; in Philo, 28, 158; and Roman Mass, 14 n. 55; superiority of, 161-64, 168-70, 180 n. 1
Menorah. See Lampstand
Mercy-seat, 116-17, 197, 201-4, 207-8, 226
Messiah: of Aaron, 123-24, 165 n. 46; anointing, 61; coming, 179, 216 n. 89, 273-74, 311, 347; Davidic, 29, 53, 55, 60, 63-64, 123-26, 165, 388 n. 117; enthronement, 244-45; of Israel, 123, 170; lay, 123; preexistence, 85 n. 77; priestly, 123, 170; rejected, 381; sufferings, 54 n. 60; temptations, 88
Michael, 57, 71, 356 n. 150
Midian, 227, 312, 320
Money, 373-74
Moses: blessing by, 67, 124 n. 29; and covenant, 190, 192, 194, 317, 388; faith, 308-15, 382; as intercessor, 91-92, 121, 311, 354, 362; leadership, 102, 307, 308 n. 168, 312, 315-16, 349, 381, 388; as middleman, 185, 363 n. 193; patience, 120, 316, 334; and priesthood, 124, 170, 172; rejection of, 98-105; revelations to, 92, 185, 192, 356; song of, 56, 71, 264; steward of God's house, 92; and tabernacle, 33, 183-84, 203; and tablets, 203-4; and theophanies, 313-14, 353-55, 362
Muratorian Canon, 12, 16 n. 64

Nebuchadnezzar, 278, 323, 325 n. 271
Nehemiah, 162, 290
Nero, 21, 268, 335 n. 16, 390 n. 128
New Year, 26, 212, 302 n. 142
Noah, 94 n. 18, 129 n. 61, 132 n. 73, 230 n. 156, 286-88, 290, 309 n. 175

Oath, divine, 153-54, 170-71
Obedience: and covenant, 187, 190, 243; and faith, 106, 111, 153, 291, 303-4, 308; high priest, needed by, 81; Isaac, example of, 305; of Jesus, 51, 54, 116, 130-32, 176, 218,

INDEX OF AUTHORS

407

SCRIPTURE REFERENCES

411

51:7	225	110	26, 28-29, 32, 50,	8:3	84
51:10	238		63, 123, 125, 244	8:6ff.	46
51:14	225	110:1	29-30, 52, 64-65,	8:13	63
51:16	240		74, 85, 134, 162,	8:14	82
51:16-17	209, 238		246, 388	8:16	83
56:13	286	110:4	6, 27-29, 54, 64,	8:17	78, 82
66:18	236		87, 122-25, 133,	8:18	78, 83-84
68:7-8	363		154, 156, 162,	9:6	60
69:1-3	129		168-70, 172, 179,	9:6-7	55
69:9	266, 311		231, 244, 388	9:7	61
73:28	169	114:4	363	10:17	366
76:2	124	114:7	363	11:1	59
77:18	363	116	129	11:1-10	322
77:20	388	116:9	286	11:5	61
78:8	102	118:6	369, 374	12:2	78
78:17	102	119:19	298	13:13	363
78:68-69	355	119:25	373	18:7	357
80:17	73	119:67	345	19:24-25	194
81:9	248	119:71	345	22:15	92
81:12	188	122:3-4	356	25:8	85
82:1	72, 134	131:2	346	26	273
84:2	266	132:11-18	55	26:11	260
85:10	159	133:1	370	26:19	143
87:1	293, 357	135:14	261	26:20	267, 273
87:5	293	139:16	242	30:33	366
89:7	359	141:2	383	31:9	265
89:14	60	145:17	176	32:1	61
89:19-37	55	148:8	58	32:17	159
89:21	61	149:6	112	33:14	265, 365
89:27	56			33:22	143
89:51	311	**PROVERBS**		35:3	346
92 (title)	109	3:11-12	341-42, 346	35:3-4	347
94	343	3:12	342-43	35:6-7	316
95	97-98, 107-8	4:26	346-47	37:4	265
95:1-7	97-98	5:4	112	37:17	265
95:7	27, 95, 99, 108	8:22	47	40:3-5	316
95:7-8	104	8:22-31	47, 63	41:4	375
95:7-11	22, 27-29, 95, 97	15:8	283	41:8	303
95:8ff.	27	22:29	134	41:17-18	96
95:10	99	25:1	346	42:1	54, 217
95:11	99, 104, 106-8			42:1-4	322
97:2	323	**ECCLESIASTES**		42:6	194
97:7	56	1:9	248	42:9	96
99:6	122			43:16-21	96
100:4	126	**CANTICLES**		43:21	383
101	323	1:15	59-60	43:25	191
102	28, 63	4:1	59-60	44:6	375
102:23	62			44:22	191
102:25-27	27, 52, 61	**ISAIAH**		44:27	316
102:25ff.	364	1:11ff.	238	45:17	132
102:27	375	2:2	46	45:23	63
104	28	2:19	363	48:12	375
104:4	27, 51, 58-59, 64	2:21	363	49:2	112
105:17-19	306	4:4	366	49:6	194
105:26	122	5:1-7	149	49:8	194
105:28	102	6:12	134	50:4-5	240
106:16	120	7:3	84	50:4-9	131
107:11	102	7:9	141	50:5-6	131